# EnCase® Computer Forensics
# The Official EnCE:
## EnCase® Certified Examiner
## Study Guide

# EnCase® Computer Forensics
# The Official EnCE:
## EnCase® Certified Examiner
## Study Guide

Steve Bunting

William Wei

Wiley Publishing, Inc.

Acquisitions and Development Editor: Maureen Adams
Technical Editor: Jon Bair
Production Editors: Angela Smith, and Daria Meoli
Copy Editor: Liz Welch
Production Manager: Tim Tate
Vice President and Executive Group Publisher: Richard Swadley
Vice President and Executive Publisher: Joseph B. Wikert
Vice President and Publisher: Neil Edde
Media Development Specialist: Angela Denny
Book Designer: Judy Fung
Compositor: Jeff Wilson, Happenstance Type-O-Rama
Proofreader: Jennifer Larsen, Word One
Indexer: Nancy Guenther
Cover Designer: Richard Miller, Calyx Design
Cover Photo Illustration: Anthony DiBello, Guidance Software
Cover Image: Getty Images

**Sybex®**
An Imprint of
**WILEY**

To Our Valued Readers:

Thank you for looking to Sybex for your EnCase® Certified Examiner (EnCE) exam prep needs. The Sybex team is proud of its reputation for providing certification candidates with the practical knowledge and skills needed to succeed in the highly competitive IT marketplace. We are especially proud of the partnership we have formed with Guidance Software, the leading computer forensics software company, to produce this official EnCase Computer Forensics Study Guide. Just as Guidance Software is committed to establishing measurable standards for certifying individuals who perform forensic investigation and analysis with EnCase software, Sybex is committed to providing those individuals with the skills needed to meet those standards.

The authors and editors have worked hard to ensure that the book you hold in your hands is comprehensive, in-depth, and pedagogically sound. We're confident that this book will exceed the demanding standards of the certification marketplace and help you, the EnCE candidate, succeed in your endeavors.

As always, your feedback is important to us. If you believe you've identified an error in the book, please visit the Customer Support section of the Wiley website. And if you have general comments or suggestions, feel free to drop me a line directly at nedde@wiley.com. At Sybex we're continually striving to meet the needs of individuals preparing for certification exams. Good luck in pursuit of your EnCE!

Neil Edde
Vice President & Publisher
Wiley Publishing, Inc.

# Wiley Publishing Inc End-User License Agreement

*To Donna, my loving wife and partner for life, for your unwavering love, encouragement, and support.*
*—Steve*

*To my children, Elizabeth and Brendan, my most precious gifts from God.*
*—William*

# Acknowledgments

Any work of this magnitude requires the hard work of many dedicated people, all doing what they enjoy and what they do best. In addition, many others have contributed indirectly and, without their efforts and support, this book would not have come to fruition. That said, there are many people deserving of my gratitude, and my intent here is to acknowledge them all.

I would like to first thank Maureen Adams, Wiley's Acquisitions Editor, who brought me on board with this project, tutored me on the fine nuances of the publishing process, and who kept me on track and on schedule for the six months that it took to complete. I would like to thank Angela Smith and Liz Welch of the Wiley editing team. They allowed me to concentrate on content as they kept my grammar on track, made difficult passages flow, and transformed everything into the "Wiley style." With several hundred screen shots in this book to mold and shape, I know there is a graphics department at Wiley deserving of my thanks. To those folks, I say thank you.

A special thanks goes to Jon Bair of Guidance Software, Inc. In addition to being a friend and mentor of many years, Jon is the technical editor for this project. He worked diligently, making sure that the technical aspects of this book are as accurate and as complete as possible.

A special thanks also goes to William Wei, my fellow author on this project. Will created the questions at the end of the chapters and contributed many of the Real World Scenarios, thereby adding his experiences and expertise to the project.

Creating the DVD that goes with this book was a last-minute challenge and could not have been done without the assistance of Bill Siebert at Guidance Software. In addition to being a friend and colleague, Bill is the director of customer relations for Guidance. Bill took charge, cut through the red tape, and got the job done when time was short. Thanks, Bill!

The study of computer forensics can't exist within a vacuum. To that extent, any individual examiner is a reflection and product of their instructors, mentors, and colleagues. Through them you learn, share ideas, troubleshoot, conduct research, grow, and develop. Over my career, I've had the fortune of interacting with many computer forensics professionals and have learned much through those relationships. In no particular order, I would like to thank the following people for sharing their knowledge over the years: Keith Lockhart, Ben Lewis, Chris Stippich, Grant Wade, Ed Van Every, Raemarie Schmidt, Mark Johnson, Bob Weitershausen, John Colbert, Bruce Pixley, Lance Mueller, Howie Williamson, Lisa Highsmith, Dan Purcell, Ben Cotton, Patrick Paige, John D'Andrea, Mike Feldman, Joel Horne, Mark Stringer, Fred Cotton, Ross Mayfield, Bill Spernow, Arnie "A. J." Jackson, Ed Novreske, Warren Kruse, Bob Moses, Kevin Perna, Dan Willey, Scott Garland, and Steve Whalen.

Every effort has been made to present all material accurately and completely. To achieve this I verified as much information as possible with multiple sources. In a few instances, published or generally accepted information was in conflict or error. When this occurred, the information was researched and tested and the most accurate information available was published in this book. I would like to thank the authors of the following publications as I relied on their vast wealth of knowledge and expertise for research and information verification:

Carrier, Brian, *File System Forensic Analysis*, Boston, Addison-Wesley, 2005.

Carvey, Harlan, *Windows Forensics and Incident Recovery*, Boston, Addison-Wesley, 2005.

Hipson, Peter, *Mastering Windows XP Registry*, San Francisco, SYBEX, 2002.

Honeycutt, Jerry, *Microsoft Windows XP Registry Guide*, Redmond, WA, Microsoft Press, 2003.

Kruse, Warren G. II, and Jay G. Heiser, *Computer Forensics: Incident Response Essentials*, Boston, Addison-Wesley, 2002.

Mueller, Scott, *Upgrading and Repairing PCs*, 16th Edition, Indianapolis, IN, Que Publications, 2005.

The above books are valuable resources and should be in every examiner's library. In addition to these publications, I relied heavily on the wealth of information contained in the many training, product, and lab manuals produced by Guidance Software. To the many staff members of Guidance Software who have contributed over the years to these publications, I extend my most grateful appreciation.

Last, but by no means least, I would like to acknowledge the contributions by my parents and my loving wife. My parents instilled in me, at a very young age, an insatiable quest for knowledge that has persisted throughout my life, and I thank them for it along with a lifetime of love and support. My best friend and loving wife, Donna, encouraged and motivated me long ago to pursue computer forensics. While the pursuit of computer forensics never ends, without her support, sacrifices, motivation, sense of humor, and love, this book would never have been completed.

Thank you everyone…

—Steve

My part in this project would not have been possible without the help of others. I would like to thank God for giving me the courage and wisdom to accomplish this task. To my wife, Susan, and children, Elizabeth and Brendan, for giving me the inspiration. To Jon Bair, who gave me the opportunity. To Maureen Adams, for her guidance. To the Monmouth County Prosecutor's Office for recognizing the need for a Computer Crimes Unit and their understanding and support toward the unit's progress. To Guidance Software for a great product and terrific training. To NW3C for their invaluable training and resources offered to law enforcement. And to the computer forensic community for the shared of knowledge and camaraderie.

—William

# Foreword

Many people in the computer industry are familiar with Moore's law, which states that processing power doubles every 18 months; however, most folks are unaware that the capacity of data storage devices has increased at an even faster rate. For instance, the first personal computer that I used had two 160-kilobyte single-sided, single-density floppy drives for storage. Today I can buy a 2-terabyte external hard drive system that I can carry around, as it weighs a mere 11 pounds. In fact, since the introduction of the first disk drive in 1956, there has been a 50 million-fold increase in disk drive capacity. (See Kryder's Law in the July 2005 Scientific American magazine online at www.sciam.com/print_version.cfm?articleID=000B0C22-0805-12D8-BDFD83414B7F0000).

Along with the trend in disk capacity, there have been corresponding trends of increasing connectivity (local area networks to the Internet and now high-speed wireless broadband) and increasing complexity of operating systems and applications (MS-DOS 1.0 and WordStar 3.31 to Microsoft's Windows XP and Office 2003). These trends have combined to make the job of the computer forensics professional vastly more challenging than just a few years ago. Forensic examiners have to search more storage to find more potentially relevant artifacts than ever before. To keep pace, the forensic tools that examiners use have incorporated many more features, have a more robust functionality than ever before, and have even greater efficiency. To validate this trend, just look at the additional functionality and efficiency differences between EnCase version 1 and EnCase version 5.

Every good forensic examiner will have multiple tools at their disposal. Gone are the days when one tool was used just to create an image, a second tool was used just to search for data, a third tool was used just to create MD5 hashes of files, and yet a fourth tool was used just to gather together unallocated disk space, and so on. Until a tool is produced that fulfills the often requested feature of a "find all the evidence (and print the report too) button," it is clear that the level of training, experience, and certification, just like in other professions, will separate the good from the not-so-good forensic examiners.

Nothing can replace the experience gained by imaging and analyzing dozens of computers on different cases. This book does contain references to real-world situations that reinforce specific points you are likely to encounter when using EnCase in the field. Additionally, there is a wealth of detailed data on forensic artifacts that will be a welcome addition to your reference library.

Finally, certification can help establish your credentials, whether in a proposal, a job interview, or during the voir dire process when you are called on to testify as an expert. As the private employer (outside of Guidance Software) having the most EnCEs on staff, I encourage all the qualified staff at PricewaterhouseCoopers to take the journey to achieve their EnCE certification. This book will become recommended reading for those of our staff preparing for the EnCE certification process, and I highly recommend it to others who are undertaking that journey as well.

—Darrell B. Lane, EnCE, Director

Forensic Technology Solutions, PricewaterhouseCoopers LLP

# About the Authors

## Steve Bunting, Author

Steve Bunting is a Captain with the University of Delaware Police Department, where he is responsible for computer forensics, video forensics, and investigations involving computers. He has over 30 years' experience in law enforcement, and his background in computer forensics is extensive. He is a Certified Computer Forensics Technician (CCFT) and an EnCase Certified Examiner (EnCE). He was the recipient of the 2002 Guidance Software Certified Examiner Award of Excellence for receiving the highest test score on his certification examination. He holds a BS in Applied Professions/Business Management from Wilmington College and a Computer Applications Certificate in Network Environments from the University of Delaware. He has conducted computer forensic examinations for the University of Delaware and for numerous local, state, and federal agencies on an extreme variety of cases, including extortion, homicide, embezzlement, child exploitation, intellectual property theft, and unlawful intrusions into computer systems. He has testified in court on numerous occasions as a computer forensics expert. He has taught computer forensics for Guidance Software, makers of EnCase, and taught as a Lead Instructor at all course levels, including the Expert Series, with a particular emphasis on the "Internet and E-mail Examinations" course. He has been a presenter at several seminars and workshops, the author of numerous white papers, and maintains a website for cyber-crime and computer forensics issues: http://128.175.24.251/forensics/.

## William Wei, Coauthor

William Wei, a detective in the Monmouth County Prosecutor's Office, has been a police officer for over 15 years and is currently employed as a detective with the Monmouth County Prosecutor's Office Computer Crimes Unit. He holds a BA in economics and an EdM in Adult and Continuing Education from Rutgers, The State University of New Jersey. William is certified by Guidance Software as an EnCase Certified Examiner (EnCE) and by the International Association of Computer Investigative Specialists as a Certified Forensic Computer Examiner (CFCE).

William is a member of the International Association of Computer Investigative Specialists (IACIS) and High Tech Crime Investigation Association (HTCIA). William has conducted hundreds of computer-related investigations and has been qualified as an expert witness in computer forensics. He has taught computer forensics at the Computer and Enterprise Investigations Conference (CEIC) and HTCIA conferences and lectured on Internet safety throughout New Jersey.

## Jonathan Bair, Technical Editor and Director of Business Development for Guidance Software

Jon Bair directs business development activities as part of Guidance Software's product management group, with primary responsibility for electronic evidence discovery utilizing the EnCase Enterprise technology. Jon has been with Guidance Software since 2001. His previous positions include directing the Product Development Division of Guidance Software and served as a director of Professional Development and Training.

A former US Army CID Special Agent, Jon has worked in the fields of complex computer investigations and incident response since the late 1990s. He holds a BS from Roger Williams University in Bristol, Rhode Island, and received his Federal Law Enforcement Training Center credentials in Seized Computer and Evidence Recovery and Network Investigations. In 2001, Jon co-created Guidance Software's EnCase Certified Examiner program, and he is a Certified Computer Crime Investigator and a Certified Computer Forensic Technician. In 2006, Jon received his MBA from Pepperdine University in Malibu, California.

# Contents at a Glance

# Contents

# Introduction

This book was designed for several audiences. First and foremost, it was designed for anyone seeking the EnCase Certified Examiner (EnCE) credential. This certification is rapidly growing in popularity and demand in all areas of the computer forensics industry. More and more employers are recognizing the importance of this certification and are seeking this credential in potential job candidates. Equally important, courts are placing increasing emphasis on certifications that are specific to computer forensics. The EnCE certification meets or exceeds the needs of the computer forensics industry.

This book was also designed for computer forensics students working in both a structured educational setting or in a self-study program. The chapters include exercises and evidence files that work with the version of EnCase that ships with the DVD, making it an ideal learning tool for either setting.

Finally this book was written for those with knowledge of EnCase or forensics, but who simply want to learn more about either or both. Every topic goes well beyond that needed for certification with the specific intent of overpreparing the certification candidate. In some cases the material goes beyond that covered in many of the formal training classes you may have attended. In either case, that added depth of knowledge provides comprehensive learning opportunities for the intermediate or advanced user.

The EnCE certification program is geared toward those who have attended the EnCase Intermediate Computer Forensics training or its equivalent. To that extent, this book assumes the reader has a general knowledge of computer forensics and some basic knowledge of EnCase. For those who may need a refresher in either, you'll find plenty of resources. Many users may have used earlier versions of EnCase and have not yet transitioned to EnCase 5. Those users may benefit by starting with Chapter 6, which discusses the EnCase environment.

The chapters are organized into related concepts to facilitate the learning process, with basic concepts in the beginning and the advanced material at the end. At the end of each chapter you will find the Summary, Exam Essentials, and Review Questions sections. The Summary is a brief outline of the essential points contained in the chapter; the Exam Essentials explain the concepts you'll need to understand for the examination.

I strongly urge you to make full use of the Review Questions. A good way to use them is as a pretest before reading each chapter and then again as a posttest when you're done. While answering correctly is always important, it's more important to understand the concepts covered in the question. Make sure you are comfortable with all the material before moving to the next chapter. Just as knowledge is cumulative, lack thereof impedes that accumulation. As you prepare for your certification examinations (written and practical), take the time to thoroughly understand those items that you may have never understood. The journey along the road to certification is just as important as the destination.

## What Is the EnCE Certification?

Guidance Software, Inc. developed the EnCE in late 2001 to meet the needs of its customer base, who requested a solid certification program covering both the use of the EnCase software and computer forensics concepts in general. Since its inception, the EnCE certification has become one of the most recognized and coveted certifications in the computer forensics industry. You might ask why; the answer is simple. The process is demanding and challenging. You must have certain knowledge, skills, and abilities to be able to pass both a written and a practical examination. For certain, it is not a "give-away" program. You will work hard and you will earn your certification. When you are certified, you'll be proud of your accomplishment. What's more, you will have joined the ranks of the elite in the industry who have chosen to adhere to high standards and to excel in their field. Remember, in the field of computer forensics, excellence is not an option; it is an operational necessity.

## Why Become EnCE Certified?

The following benefits are associated with becoming EnCE certified:

- EnCE certification demonstrates professional achievement.
- EnCE certification increases your marketability and provides opportunity for advancement.
- EnCE certification enhances your professional credibility and standing when testifying before courts, hearing boards, and other fact-finding bodies.
- EnCE certification provides peer recognition.

EnCE certification is a rigorous process that documents and demonstrates your achievements and competency in the field of computer forensics. You must have experience as an investigator and examiner as well as have received training at the EnCase Intermediate Computer Forensics level or other equivalent classroom instruction before you can apply for the program. Next, you will have to pass both a written and a practical examination before receiving your certification. EnCE certification assures customers, employers, courts, your peers, and others that your computer forensics knowledge, skills, and abilities meet the highest professional standards.

## How to Become EnCE Certified

There are two different paths leading to EnCE certification. One path is for those who have completed Guidance Software's computer forensic or incident response training at the intermediate level or above. For those candidates, the following applies:

- Possess licensed EnCase software with an order number. The copy may be personally owned or purchased through a training site or business.
- 18 months total investigative experience with at least 6 months experience in computer forensic examinations—experience must be verified via signed application and endorsement from department head.
- All application and supporting documents verified by Guidance Software prior to authorization for exam.
- Complete Phase I and Phase II of the EnCE Examination. Phase I is a computer-based test administered by Prometric (`http://www.2test.com`). Candidates must obtain a grade of 80 percent or higher to pass. Phase II is a practical test requiring candidates to examine computer evidence that is sent to them via CD-ROM. Candidates must submit their findings report to the certification coordinator within 60 days and receive a grade of 85 percent or higher to pass.

The other certification path is for those candidates who have *not* attended Guidance Software's intermediate-level training course, but who have other computer forensics training and experience. For those candidates, the following applies:

- Possess licensed EnCase software with an order number. The copy may be personally owned or purchased through a training site or business.

- 80 hours of authorized classroom computer forensic training with 18 months total investigative experience including 6 months experience in computer forensic examinations; *or* 32 hours of authorized classroom computer forensic training with 2 years total investigative experience, including 1-year experience in computer forensic examinations—experience must be verified via signed application and endorsement from department head.

- Training must be verified with copies of training certificates, or verification of training records from the training organization, and the training must have been authorized by the owner or copyright holder of the training course.

- All application and supporting documents will be verified by Guidance Software prior to authorization for exam.

- Complete Phase I and Phase II of the EnCE Examination. Phase I is a computer-based test administered by Prometric (`http://www.2test.com`). Candidates must obtain a grade of 80 percent or higher to pass. Phase II is a practical test requiring candidates to examine computer evidence that is sent to them via CD-ROM. Candidates must submit their findings report to the certification coordinator within 60 days and receive a grade of 85 percent or higher to pass.

The above requirements are quoted directly from Guidance Software's website and are current as of the publication date of this book. You should check the website before you apply to make sure you are complying with the most current requirements. The requirements, the application form, as well as other important information relating to the EnCE certification program, may be found on their website: `http://guidancesoftware.com/training/ence/index.asp`.

## How to Use This Book and DVD

We've included several testing features, both in the book and on the companion DVD. Following this introduction is an assessment test that you can use to check your readiness for the actual exam. Take this test before you start reading the book. It will help you identify the areas you may need to brush up on. The answers to the assessment test appear after the last question of the test. Each answer includes an explanation and tells you in which chapter this material appears.

As mentioned, to test your knowledge as you progress through the book, there are review questions at the end of each chapter. As you finish each chapter, answer the review questions and then check to see if your answers are right—the correct answers appear on the pages following the last question. You can go back to reread the section that deals with each question you got wrong to ensure that you answer the question correctly the next time you are tested on the material. You'll also find 100-plus flashcard questions on the DVD for on-the-go review. Download them right onto your Palm device for quick and convenient reviewing.

In addition to the assessment test and the review questions, you'll find two bonus exams on the DVD. Take these practice exams just as if you were actually taking the exam (i.e., without any reference material). When you have finished the first exam, move on to the next exam to solidify your test-taking skills. If you get more than 85 percent of the answers correct, you're ready to go ahead and take the real exam.

Additionally, if you are going to travel but still need to study for the EnCE exam, and you have a laptop with a DVD-ROM drive, you can take this entire book with you just by taking the DVD. This book is in PDF (Adobe Acrobat) format so it can be easily read on any computer.

Also included on the DVD are:

- A demonstration version of the EnCase Forensic software
- Evidence files for use with the EnCase Forensic software
- Guidance Software's EnCase Legal Journal
- Information on the Guidance Software Forensic and Enterprise products

## EnCase Forensics Software and Evidence Files on the DVD

This book's companion DVD contains a demonstration version of EnCase Forensic 5 software that will run directly from the DVD. It is not required to be installed on a personal computer and will work with the evidence files included on the DVD. For the busy overworked computer forensic professional, it means you can take the exam preparation with you wherever you go.

In addition, there are two sets of evidence files on the DVD. The first set, created by the author and referred to in chapters, is instructional and familiarizes you with the software. The second set, called the "PSC Company" evidence files, are included by the Guidance Software training staff. The PSC Company PDF file provides you with an investigative scenario and describes the evidence that you are to look for. The PSC Company examination will assist you in honing your EnCase software skills and preparing you for the Phase II practical examination required for the EnCE certification.

You can drag and drop the required evidence files from Windows Explorer onto the opened EnCase software to start your analysis. We have provided with you the capability to save your searches and bookmarked investigative findings to a case file, so that you can return later to continue the analysis. To continue a previously started analysis, you can drag and drop your case file onto the opened EnCase software.

Fully functional versions of the EnCase Forensic software are available for purchase from Guidance Software. Highly discounted fully functional versions of the EnCase Forensic and EnCase Enterprise software are now available for purchase by accredited colleges and universities.

## Guidance Software's EnCase Legal Journal on the DVD

The most important aspect of any computer forensic examination is the legal admissibility of the evidence found. Guidance Software's full-time legal staff provides case law research and litigation support for its EnCase Forensic and EnCase Enterprise customers. As part of their support, they provide the EnCase Legal Journal.

The EnCase Legal Journal was updated in November 2005 with the most up-to-date case law, and it is provided on the DVD in a PDF file. Updates to the EnCase Legal Journal are available for download from the Legal Resources section of the Guidance Software website: www.guidancesoftware.com.

The EnCE Prometric exam includes six legal questions, whose answers are found in the EnCase Legal Journal. Individuals preparing for the EnCE exam are strongly encouraged to review this document.

Guidance Software's legal staff can be contacted by e-mail at customerservice@guidancesoftware.com.

## Tips for Taking the EnCE Exam

When taking the EnCE written test, here are a few tips that have proven helpful:

- Get a good night's rest before your test.

- Eat a healthy meal before your test, avoiding heavy fats and starches that can make you lethargic or drowsy.

- Arrive at the Prometric testing site early so that you won't feel rushed. Once there, stretch, relax, and put your mind at ease.

- Read each question carefully. Some questions ask for one correct answer while other questions ask you to select all answers that are correct. Make sure you understand what each question is asking, and don't rush to a quick answer.

- If you don't answer a question, it will be scored as a wrong answer. Given that, it's better to guess than leave an answer blank.

- When you aren't sure of an answer, eliminate the obviously incorrect answers. Consider the remaining choices in the context of the question. Sometimes a keyword can lead you to the correct answer.

- You'll be provided with scratch paper at your examination station. As soon as you sit down and you can start, write down formulas, memory aids, or other facts you may need before starting the exam. Once you do that, you can relax, knowing you have committed those memory items to paper, freeing your memory to work on the questions. You might think of it as being somewhat analogous to the process by which RAM frees up memory space by writing it to the swap file.

- Visit Prometric's website (www.2test.com) for site-specific information or tips they may provide.

# Assessment Test

1. You are a computer forensic examiner tasked with determining what evidence is on a seized computer. On what part of the computer system will you find data of evidentiary value?

   A. Microprocessor or CPU

   B. USB controller

   **C.** Hard drive

   D. PCI expansion slots

2. You are a computer forensic examiner explaining how computers store and access the data you recovered as evidence during your examination. The evidence was a log file and was recovered as an artifact of user activity on the _____, which was stored on the _____, contained within a _____ on the media.

   A. partition, operating system, file system

   **B.** operating system, file system, partition

   C. file system, operating system, hard drive

   D. operating system, partition, file system

3. You are a computer forensic examiner investigating a seized computer. You recovered a document containing potential evidence. EnCase reports the file system on the forensic image of the hard drive is FAT (File Allocation Table). What information about the document file can be found in the FAT on the media? (Choose all that apply.)

   A. Name of the file

   B. Date and time stamps of the file

   **C.** Starting cluster of the file

   **D.** Fragmentation of the file

   E. Ownership of the file

4. You are a computer forensic examiner investigating media on a seized computer. You recovered a document containing potential evidence. EnCase reports the file system on the forensic image of the hard drive is NTFS (New Technology File System). What information about the document file can be found in the NTFS master file table on the media? (Choose all that apply.)

   **A.** Name of the file

   **B.** Date and time stamps of the file

   **C.** Starting cluster of the file

   **D.** Fragmentation of the file

   **E.** Ownership of the file

**5.** You are preparing to lead a team to serve a search warrant on a business suspected of committing large-scale consumer fraud. Ideally, you would you assign which tasks to search team members? (Choose all that apply.)

**A.** Photographer

**B.** Search and seizure specialists

**C.** Recorder

**D.** Digital evidence search and seizure specialists

**6.** You are a computer forensic examiner at a scene and have determined you will seize a Linux server, which according to your source of information, contains the database records for the company under investigation for fraud. What is the best practice for "taking down" the server for collection?

**A.** Photograph the screen and note any running programs or messages, etc., and use the normal shutdown procedure.

**B.** Photograph the screen and note any running programs or messages, etc., and pull the plug from the wall.

**C.** Photograph the screen and note any running programs or messages, etc., and pull the plug from the rear of the computer.

**D.** Photograph the screen and note any running programs or messages, etc., and ask the user at the scene to shut down the server.

**7.** You are a computer forensic examiner at a scene and are authorized to only seize media that can be determined to have evidence related to the investigation. What options do you have to determine whether evidence is present before seizure and a full forensic examination? (Choose all that apply.)

**A.** Use a DOS boot floppy or CD to boot the machine and browse through the directory for evidence.

**B.** Use an EnCase boot floppy or CD to boot the machine into Linux and use LinEn to preview the hard drive through a crossover cable with EnCase for Windows.

**C.** Remove the subject hard drive from the machine and preview the hard drive in EnCase for Windows with a hardware write blocker like FastBloc.

**D.** Use an EnCase boot floppy or CD to boot the machine into DOS and use EnCase for DOS to preview the hard drive through a crossover cable with EnCase for Windows.

**8.** You are a computer forensic examiner at a scene and have determined you will need to image a hard drive in a workstation while onsite. What are your options for creating a forensically sound image of the hard drive? (Choose all that apply.)

**A.** Use a DOS boot floppy or CD to boot the machine and use EnCase for DOS to image the subject hard drive to a second hard drive attached to the machine.

**B.** Use an EnCase boot floppy or CD to boot the machine into DOS and use EnCase for DOS to image the subject hard drive to a second hard drive attached to the machine.

**C.** Remove the subject hard drive from the machine and image the hard drive in EnCase for Windows with a hardware write blocker like FastBloc.

**D.** Use an EnCase boot floppy or CD to boot the machine into DOS and use EnCase for DOS to image the hard drive through a crossover cable with EnCase for Windows.

**9.** You are a computer forensic examiner and have imaged a hard drive on site. Before you leave the scene, you want to ensure the image completely verifies as an exact forensic duplicate of the original. To verify the EnCase evidence file containing the image, you should:

**A.** Use a hex editor to compare a sample of sectors in the EnCase evidence file with that of the original.

**B.** Load the EnCase evidence files into EnCase for Windows, and after the verification is more than halfway completed, cancel the verification and spot-check the results for errors.

**C.** Load the EnCase evidence files into EnCase for DOS and verify the hash of those files.

**D.** Load the EnCase evidence files into EnCase for Windows, allow the verification process to finish, and then check the results for complete verification.

**10.** You are a computer forensic examiner and need to verify the integrity of an EnCase evidence file. To completely verify the file's integrity, which of the following must be true?

**A.** The MD5 hash value must verify.

**B.** The CRC values and the MD5 hash value both must verify.

**C.** Either the CRC or MD5 hash values must verify.

**D.** The CRC values must verify.

**11.** You are a computer forensic examiner and need to determine what files are contained within a folder called Business documents. What EnCase pane will you use to view the names of the files in the folder?

**A.** Tree pane

**B.** Table pane

**C.** View pane

**D.** Filter pane

**12.** You are a computer forensic examiner and need to view the contents of a file contained within a folder called Business documents. What EnCase pane will you use to view the contents of the file?

**A.** Tree pane

**B.** Table pane

**C.** View pane

**D.** Filter pane

**13.** You are a computer forensic examiner and are viewing a file in an EnCase evidence file. With your cursor, you have selected one character in the file. What binary term is used for the amount of data that represents a single character?

**A.** A bit

**B.** A nibble

**C.** A byte

**D.** A word

**14.** You are a computer forensic examiner and need to search for the name of a suspect in an EnCase evidence file. You enter the name of the suspect into the EnCase keyword interface as **John Doe**. What search hits will be found with this search term with the default settings? (Choose all that apply.)

**A.** John Doe

**B.** John D.

**C.** john doe

**D.** John.Doe

**15.** You are a computer forensic examiner and need to determine if any Microsoft Office documents have been renamed with image extensions to obscure their presence. What EnCase process would you use to find such files?

**A.** File signature analysis

**B.** Recover Folders feature

**C.** File content search

**D.** File hash analysis

**16.** You are a computer forensic examiner and want to reduce the number of files required for examination by identifying and filtering out known good or system files. What EnCase process would you use to identify such files?

**A.** File signature analysis

**B.** Recover Folders feature

**C.** File content search

**D.** File hash analysis

**17.** You are a computer forensic examiner and want to determine if a user has opened or double-clicked a file. What folder would you look in for an operating system artifact for this user activity?

A. Temp

B. Recent

C. Cookies

D. Desktop

**18.** You are a computer forensic examiner and want to determine when a user deleted a file contained in the Recycle Bin. In what file is the date and time information about the file deletion contained?

A. Index.dat

B. Link file

C. INFO2

D. Deleted.ini

**19.** You are a computer forensic examiner and want to determine how many times a program was executed. Where would you find information?

A. Temp folder

B. Registry

C. Recycle Bin

D. Program Files

**20.** You are a computer forensic examiner and want to examine any e-mail sent and received by the user of the computer system under investigation. What e-mail formats are supported by EnCase? (Choose all that apply.)

A. Outlook

B. Outlook Express

C. America Online

D. Hotmail

E. Yahoo!

F. Mozilla Thunderbird

# Answers to Assessment Test

1.  **C.** The hard drive is the main storage media for most computer systems, holding the boot files, operating system files, programs, and data, and will be the primary source of evidence during a forensic examination of a computer system. See Chapter 1 for more information.

2.  **B.** A file system is nothing more than system or method of storing and retrieving data on a computer system that allows for a hierarchy of directories, subdirectories, and files. It is contained within a partition on the media. File systems are the management tools for storing and retrieving data in a partition. Some operating systems require certain file systems for them to function. Windows needs a FAT or NTFS file system, depending on its "flavor" or version, and won't recognize or mount other systems with its own native operating system. See Chapter 1 for more information.

3.  **C, D.** A major component of the FAT file system is the File Allocation Table or FAT, which, among other functions, tracks the sequence of clusters used by a file when more than one cluster is allocated or used. In addition to tracking cluster runs or sequences, the FAT tracks the allocation status of clusters, assuring that the operating system stores data in clusters that are available and that those storing data assigned to files or directories aren't overwritten. FAT does not track file ownership. The other information about the file is stored in directory entries. See Chapter 2 for more information.

4.  **A, B, C, D, E.** A file system used by the Windows operating system, starting with Windows NT, is the NTFS file system. NTFS, compared to FAT file systems, is more robust, providing stronger security, greater recoverability, and better performance with regard to read, write, and searching capabilities. Among other features, it supports long file names, a highly granular system of file permissions, ownership and access control, and compression of individual files and directories. The master file table in NTFS contains, among other items, the name of a file, the date and time stamps of the file, the starting cluster of a file, the fragmentation of a file, and the ownership of a file. See Chapter 2 for more information.

5.  **A, B, C, D.** After the area is secure, the search term enters the area and begins their job. Before anything is touched or removed, the scene is recorded through a combination of field notes, sketches, video, or still images. Once the area has been recorded to show how things were initially found, the search team(s) begin their methodical search and seizure process. Search teams often consist of the following functions:

    - Recorder: Takes detailed notes of everything seized
    - Photographer: Photographs all items in place before seized
    - Search and seizure specialist: Searches and seizes, bags and tags traditional evidence (documents, pictures, drugs, weapons, etc.)
    - Digital evidence search and seizure specialist: Searches and seizes, bags and tags digital evidence of all types

    See Chapter 3 for more information.

**6.**  **A.**  For Linux and Unix servers, photograph the screen and note any running programs or messages, etc., and use the normal shutdown procedure.

In many cases, the user will need to be root to shut down the system. If it's a GUI, right-click the desktop and from the context menu, select Console or Terminal. At the resulting prompt, look for # at the right end. If it doesn't appear type **su root**. You will be prompted for a password. If you have it, type it in. If you don't have it, you'll probably have no choice but to pull the plug if the system administrator isn't available or can't be trusted. When at root, note the # at the end of the prompt. When at root, type **synch;synch;halt** and the system should halt. See Chapter 3 for more information.

**7.**  **B, C, D.**  The purpose of the forensic boot disk is to boot the computer and load an operating system but to do so in a forensically sound manner in which the evidentiary media is not changed. Using a DOS boot disk will change the evidence. EnCase provides many options for previewing subject hard drives before seizure. See Chapter 4 for more information.

**8.**  **B, C, D.**  The purpose of the forensic boot disk is to boot the computer and load an operating system but to do so in a forensically sound manner in which the evidentiary media is not changed. Using a DOS boot disk will change the evidence. EnCase provides many options for imaging subject hard drives. See Chapter 4 for more information.

**9.**  **D.**  The verification of EnCase evidence files is conducted in EnCase for Windows and starts automatically when an EnCase evidence file is added to EnCase. The verification must be allowed to complete to confirm the validity of the image. See Chapter 5 for more information.

**10.**  **B.**  When an EnCase evidence file containing an MD5 hash value is added to a case, EnCase verifies both the CRC and MD5 hash values. Both must verify to confirm the complete integrity of the EnCase evidence file. See Chapter 5 for more information.

**11.**  **B.**  In the EnCase environment, the Table pane contains a list of all objects (files) within a folder selected in the Tree pane. This pane has columns for the metadata of each file, including the name. See Chapter 6 for more information.

**12.**  **C.**  In the EnCase environment, the View pane allows you to view the contents of a file, both in the Text and Hex tabs. See Chapter 6 for more information.

**13.**  **C.**  A single character stored on digital media is composed of eight bits, each either 0 or 1. This set of 8 bits is known as a byte. See Chapter 7 for more information.

**14.**  **A, C.**  By default, EnCase will find both upper- and lowercase versions of a search term. The other terms could be found with a properly crafted GREP expression. See Chapter 7 for more information.

**15.**  **A.**  Until a file signature analysis is run, EnCase relies on a file's extension to determine its file type, which in turn determines the viewer used to display the data. A file signature analysis is initiated or run from the Search menu. Once a file signature is run, EnCase will view files based on file header information and not based on file extension. This is critical for viewing files whose extensions are missing or have been changed. See Chapter 8 for more information.

**16.** D.   File hashing and analysis, within EnCase, are based on the MD5 hashing algorithm. When a file is hashed using the MD5, the result is a 128-bit value. The odds of any two dissimilar files having the same MD5 hash is one in $2^{128}$, or approximately one in 340 billion billion billion billion. Using this method you can statistically infer that the file content will be the same for files that have identical hash values and that the file content will differ for files that do not have identical hash values. This can be used to identify known good or system files. See Chapter 8 for more information.

**17.** B.   Certain actions by the user create link files without their knowledge. As the user is creating virtual "tracks in the snow," such files are of particular forensic interest. Specifically, when a user opens a document, a link file is created in the Recent folder, which appears in the root of the user folder named after the user's logon name. The link files in this folder serve as a record of the documents opened by the user. See Chapter 9 for more information.

**18.** C.   The INFO2 file is a database file containing information about the files in the Recycle Bin. When you look at files in the Recycle Bin, you are really looking at the contents of the INFO2 file. Thus, when a file is sent to the Recycle Bin, the following information is placed there: the file's original file name and path (entered twice, once in ASCII and again in Unicode), the date and time of deletion, and the index number. See Chapter 9 for more information.

**19.** B.   The Windows Registry contains a great deal of information and artifacts about user activity on a computer system, including the number of times a particular program is executed. See Chapter 10 for more information.

**20.** A, B, C, D, E, F.   EnCase v5 supports all of the listed e-mail formats, including Outlook (PST); Outlook Express (DBX / MBX); AOL 6, 7, 8, 9; Hotmail; Yahoo!; Netscape webmail; and mbox (a common flat file format used by Thunderbird and other e-mail programs). See Chapter 10 for more information.

# Chapter
# 1

# Computer Hardware

---

## ENCE EXAM TOPICS COVERED IN THIS CHAPTER:

✓ Computer hardware components

✓ The boot process

✓ Partitions

✓ File systems

Computer forensics examiners deal most often with the media on which data is stored. This includes, but is not limited to, hard drives, CDs, DVDs, Flash memory devices, floppies, and tapes. While those devices might be the bane of the examiner's existence, media devices don't exist in a void, and knowledge of a computer's various components and functions is a must for the competent examiner.

As an examiner, you may be called upon to explain how a computer functions to a jury. To do so requires that you not only know a computer's function from a technical standpoint, but also be able to translate those technical concepts into real-world, easy-to-understand terms.

As an examiner, you may also be subjected to a *voir dire* examination by opposing counsel to challenge your competence to testify. Acronyms are hardly in short supply in the field of computing, some well known and meaningful, and others more obscure. Imagine being asked during such an examination to explain several of the common acronyms used with computers, such as RAM, CMOS, SCSI, BIOS, and POST. If you were to draw a blank on some obscure or even common acronym, picture its impact on your credibility.

---

TWAIN – "Technology **W**ithout **A**n **I**nteresting **N**ame"

---

You may encounter problems with a computer system under examination or with your own forensic platform. Troubleshooting and configuration require knowledge of the underlying fundamentals if you are to be successful.

Thus, the purpose of this chapter is to develop a solid understanding of the various components of a computer and see how a single spark of electricity brings those otherwise dead components to life through a process known as *booting* the computer. In addition, you'll learn about the drive partitions and file systems used by computer systems.

# Computer Hardware Components

Every profession has, at its core, a group of terms and knowledge that is shared and understood by its practitioners. Computer forensics is certainly no exception. In this section, I discuss the various terms used to describe a computer's components and systems.

**Case**   The case, or chassis, is usually metal, and it surrounds, contains, and supports the computer system components. It shields electrical interference (both directions) and provides protection from dust, moisture, and direct-impact damage to the internal components. It is sometimes erroneously called the central processing unit (CPU), which it is not.

**ROM (read-only memory)**   This is a form of memory that can hold data permanently, or nearly so, by virtue of its property of being impossible or difficult to change or write. Another important property of ROM is its nonvolatility, meaning that the data remains when the system is powered off. Having these properties (read-only and nonvolatile) makes ROM ideal for files containing startup configuration settings and code needed to boot the computer (ROM BIOS).

**RAM (random access memory)**   A computer's main memory is its temporary workspace for storing data, code, settings, and so forth. It has come to be called RAM as it exists as a bank of memory chips that can be randomly accessed. Before chips, tape was the primary media, and accessing tape was—and still is—a slow, linear or sequential process. With the advent of chips and media on drives (both floppy and hard drives), data could be accessed randomly and directly, and therefore with much greater speed. Hence, *random access memory* was the name initially given to this type of memory to differentiate from its tape predecessor. Today most memory can be accessed randomly, and the term's original functional meaning, differentiating it from tape, has been lost to history. What distinguishes RAM from ROM, among other properties, is the property known as *volatility*. RAM is usually volatile memory, meaning that upon losing power, the data stored in memory is lost. ROM, by contrast, is nonvolatile memory, meaning that the data remains when the power is off. It is important to note that there are nonvolatile forms of RAM memory known as NVRAM (nonvolatile random access memory), and thus you should not be quick to assume that all RAM is nonvolatile.

The computer forensic examiner more often than not encounters computers that have been shut down, seized, and delivered for examination. Important information in RAM (the computer's volatile memory) is lost when the plug is pulled. All is not lost, however, as this data is often written to the hard drive in a file called the *swap file*. This swap file can grow and shrink by default in most Microsoft Windows systems, which means this data can be in the swap file itself as well as in unallocated clusters and in file slack as the swap file is resized. Unallocated clusters and file slack are areas containing data that is no longer in an allocated file. We'll cover them in detail in a later chapter. What's more, if the computer was in the "hibernate" mode, the entire contents of RAM are written to a file named hiberfil.sys so that the contents of RAM can be restored from disk and the system restored in the time it takes to read the hiberfil.sys file into RAM. It should be no surprise to learn that the hiberfil.sys file size is the same size as the system's RAM memory size!

**Power supply**   The power supply transforms supply voltage (120VAC or 240VAC) to voltages and current flows required by the various system components. DC voltages of 3.3 volts, 5 volts, and 12 volts are provided on a power supply for an ATX form factor motherboard.

The standard molex power connector used frequently by examiners has four wires providing two different voltages (yellow = 12VDC+, black = ground, black = ground, red = 5VDC+).

**Motherboard or mainboard**   This component is the largest printed circuit card within the computer case. It is mounted on "stand-offs" to raise it above the case, providing a space for airflow and preventing contact or grounding of the printed circuits with the case. The motherboard typically contains the following: the CPU socket, BIOS, CMOS, CMOS battery, Real-Time Clock (RTC), RAM memory slots, Integrated Drive Electronics (IDE) controllers, Serial Advanced Technology Attachment (SATA) controllers, Universal Serial Bus (USB) controllers, floppy disk controllers, Accelerated Graphics Port (AGP) or Peripheral Component Interconnect (PCI) Express video slots, PCI or PCI Express expansion slots, and so forth. Many features that once required separate expansion cards are now offered as "on-board," such as Small Computer System Interface (SCSI) controllers, network interface (Gigabit Ethernet and wireless), video, sound, and FireWire (1394a and b).

**Microprocessor or CPU**   The brains of the unit, this is a massive array of transistors arranged in microscopic layers. The CPU performs data processing, or interprets and executes instructions. Accordingly, most of the computer's function and instructions are carried out in this unit. Modern processors generate enormous amounts of heat, and quickly and efficiently eliminating heat is essential to both function and survival.

**Heat sink and fan**   At the very least, a heat sink and fan will be attached to the CPU to keep it cool. The heat sink interfaces directly with the CPU (or other heat-generating chip), usually with a thermal compound sandwiched between. The heat sink is made of a high-thermal conductance material whose job it is to draw the heat from the chip and to dissipate that heat energy into the surrounding air (with the assistance of the fan, with an array of cooling fins). Some high-end platforms will have thermal solutions (heat sinks and fans) mounted to RAM memory, chipsets, hard drives, and video cards. Water-cooling systems are becoming more popular with gamers. Use caution working around these systems as water and electricity are usually at odds and damage to systems can occur.

**Hard drive**   This is the main storage media for most computer systems, holding the boot files, operating system files, programs, and data. It consists of a series of hard thin platters revolving at speeds ranging from 4,800 to 15,000 revolutions per minute (RPMs). These platters (which are magnetized) are accessed by heads moving across their surfaces as they spin at high speed. The heads can read or write, detecting or creating microscopic changes in polarity, with positive changes being 1s and negative changes being 0s—hence the binary system of "1s and 0s."

Hard drive platters have an addressing scheme so that the various locations where data is stored can be located for reads and writes. Originally this addressing scheme involved the CHS system (C = Cylinder, H = Head, and S = Sector). A *sector* is the smallest amount of space on a drive that can be written to at a time. A sector contains 512 bytes that can be used by the operating system. Each side of the platter is formatted with a series of concentric circles known as *tracks*.

Sectors are contained in the tracks, and originally each track contains the same number of sectors. A *cylinder* is a logical construct; it is a point on all the platters where the heads align along a vertical axis passing through the same sector number on all the platters. There are two *heads* for each platter, one for each side (side 0 and side 1). Depending on the number of platters present, the heads will be numbered. To determine the number of bytes present on a hard drive, a formula is used: $C \times H \times S \times 512$ = total storage bytes. The "C" is the total number of cylinders, the "H" is the total number of heads, the "S" is the number of sectors per track, and 512 is a constant that represents the number of bytes in a sector usable by the operating system (OS).

This formula holds true as long as the number of sectors per track remains the same for all tracks, which applies as well to older, lower-capacity hard drives. This system, however, has limitations for hard drive storage capacity. The limitations reflect how densely populated (sectors per track) the inner tracks are. The outer tracks, by contrast, can always hold more data than the inner tracks and contain wasted storage space. To overcome this limitation, Zoned-Bit Recording (ZBR) was developed; in ZBR, the number of sectors per track varies in zones, with the outer zones containing more sectors per track than the inner zones. This system has vastly improved data storage capacities.

The formula, however, is not valid for modern drives, because the number of sectors per track is no longer constant if ZBR is present. To address the larger-capacity hard drives, a new addressing scheme has been developed, called Logical Block Addressing (LBA). In this system, sectors are addressed simply by sector number, starting with sector zero, and the hard drive's electronics translate the sector number to a CHS value understood by the drive. To determine the storage capacity of hard drives using ZBR, you determine the total LBA sectors and multiply that number by 512 (bytes per sector). The product yields the total storage capacity of the drive in bytes (total LBA sectors × 512 = total storage capacity in bytes).

Hard drives can be ATA (now often called PATA to differentiate parallel from serial with the advent of SATA), SATA (Serial ATA), and SCSI, depending on their electrical interface or controller.

**SCSI (Small Computer Systems Interface)**   SCSI is an electronic interface that originated with Apple computer systems and migrated over to other systems. It is a high-speed, high-performance interface, used on devices requiring high input/output, such as scanners and hard drives. The SCSI BIOS is an intelligent BIOS that queues read/write requests in a manner that improves performance, making it the choice for high-end systems. SCSI drives do not use the master/slave pin configurations of the IDE counterparts. Rather, they are assigned ID numbers that are most often set by pinning jumpers.

**IDE (Integrated Drive Electronics) controller**   IDE is a generic term for any drive with its own integrated drive controller. Originally there were three types, but only one survived; it is known as ATA (Advanced Technology Attachment). Officially, the IDE interface today is called ATA, and the two names will often be used interchangeably. Two IDE connectors are found on the motherboard, one labeled *primary IDE* and the other *secondary IDE*. Each is capable of handling two IDE devices (hard drive, CD, DVD), for a maximum of four IDE devices. Of the two devices on same IDE ribbon cable, one is the "master" and the other is the "slave." One places jumpers on pins to designate the "master" or "slave" status. Typically the boot hard drive will be attached to the primary controller, and it is the master if two devices are present on that IDE channel. Alternatively, you could use the CS, or "cable select," method of pinning by which the assignment of master/slave is done "automatically," provided you use a cable that properly supports CSEL (another way of abbreviating Cable SELect) signaling. On an 80-conductor IDE/ATA cable using CS, the drive at the end of the cable will be assigned as master and the drive assigned to the middle connector will be the slave.

**SATA (Serial Advanced Technology Attachment) controller**    By the beginning of this century, IDE (ATA) hard drives had been around for a long time, but the electronic circuitry by which the data was sent had reached its upper limit (133MB/s). In August 2001 a new standard, known as SATA 1.0, was finalized and approved. SATA uses serial circuitry and data can be sent, initially, at 150MB/s, with 300 or more on the near horizon as SATA II standards (released in October 2002) find their way into the market. Unlike IDE drives, SATA drives require no "pinning." SATA ports can be found on most modern motherboards and often have RAID 0 available to them. IDE drives are starting to phase out and are being replaced by SATA drives. Even though IDE drives are being phased out forensic examiners can expect to see them around for a long time, as they were in use for over 10 years.

**RAID (Redundant Array of Inexpensive Disks)**    A RAID is an array of two or more disks combined in such a way as to increase performance or increase fault tolerance. In a RAID 0, data is striped over two or more disks, which increases performance by reducing read and write times. However, if any disk fails in a RAID 0, all data is lost. In a RAID 1, data is mirrored over the drives in the array. A RAID 1 does not increase performance, but it does create redundant data, thereby increasing fault tolerance. In a RAID 5 configuration, typically data is stored on three drives, although other configurations can be created. Data is striped over two drives, and a parity stripe is created on the third. Should any one drive fail, it can be "rebuilt" from the data of the other two. RAID 5 achieves fault tolerance and increased performance. RAID 0 + 1 is a relatively new type of RAID. It is typically configured with four drives; one pair is used for striping data and the other pair is a mirror of the striped pair. With this configuration, you again achieve high performance and fault tolerance.

**Floppy drive**    Floppy drives used to be primary storage devices. Currently they are used to store and move small amounts of data, since the capacity of the 3.5-inch floppy is only 1.44MB of data. They are often used by forensic examiners as boot drives to boot systems for DOS acquisitions, which is a method of acquiring data using a DOS boot disk. We'll cover this extensively in a later chapter. Floppy drives are being phased out in lieu of CD/DVD and USB thumb drives.

When going out into the field to image a system, always pack a spare internal 3.5-inch floppy drive. You may have to do a DOS acquisition, and the target system may not be equipped with a floppy, or the one present may be defective, and a CD boot may not be an option.

**CD-ROM (Compact Disc – Read-Only Memory) or CD-RW (Compact Disc – Read/Write) drive** CD drives use laser beams to read indentations and flat areas as 1s and 0s. The data is formatted into a continuous spiral emanating from the center to the outside, whereas, by comparison, hard drive data is formatted into concentric circles. The former CD-ROM is read-only technology whereas the latter, CD-RW, permits writing to CD media in addition to reading.

**DVD-ROM (Digital Versatile Disc – Read-Only Memory) or DVD-RW (Digital Versatile Disc – Read/Write)**    DVD drives use a technology similar to that of CDs. The laser beam used with DVDs is a shorter wavelength, creating smaller pits and lands, which are actually depressions and elevations in the physical surface. The result is a spiral track that is more densely populated with data. Couple this gain with layered spiral tracks, and the gain in data storage capacity is tremendous. Whereas a CD stores, at most, approximately 700MB of data, a DVD can hold 8 to 17GB of data, with higher densities on the horizon.

**USB controller**    Universal serial bus (USB) is a relatively new external peripheral bus standard capable of high-speed serial input/output (USB 1.1 = 1.5Mb/s and USB 2 = 480Mb/s). It was developed to facilitate Plug and Play for external devices without the need for expansion cards and configuration issues.

**USB port**    This is a rectangular-shaped port connected to the USB controller, with pins for four conductors (one cable power, two data negative, three data positive, four ground—all surrounded by shielding). These ports are used for USB connections, which can be external storage devices, cameras, license dongles, keyboards, mice, and so forth.

**IEEE 1394**    Also known as FireWire (the name licensed by Apple) or iLink (Sony), 1394 is yet another high-speed serial I/O standard. Its plug-and-play capabilities are on a parallel with USB. 1394 comes now in two flavors, or speeds. 1394a is the original version, moving data at 400Mb/s. 1394b is the latest version, moving data at 800 Mb/s, with gigabit speeds planned soon. 1394 allows "daisy chaining" of devices, with a maximum of 63 nodes.

**IEEE 1394a ports**    FireWire ports are similar to USB ports, except that one end is slightly rounded or pointed. There are six wires/pins in a 1394 connection, with two pairs of clock and data lines, plus two for power (one positive, one negative). FireWire ports are used primarily for external high-speed storage devices, cameras, multimedia systems, and so forth.

**Expansion slots (ISA, MCA, EISA, VL-Bus, PCI, AGP, PCI Express)**    Expansion slots are populated by "cards" whose purpose is to connect peripheral devices with the I/O bus on the motherboard so that these peripheral devices can communicate with the CPU. There are several types of peripheral devices, and they expand the capabilities of the PC. Expansion slots come in different flavors, or speeds, that have evolved over time. Rarely do you encounter the older types, such as the ISA (Industry Standard Architecture 8 bit and 16 bit in 1981 and 1984, respectively), MCA (IBM Micro Channel Architecture, 32 bit in 1986), or the EISA (Extended Industry Standard Architecture – Compaq and Generic, 32 bit in 1986). The VL-Bus (VESA Local Bus, named after the VESA Committee who developed it) was in use during 1992 to 1994, and appears as a legacy slot on some older PCI bus systems still in use. The VL-Bus slot uses the 16-bit ISA plus an extension to handle legacy 16-bit and newer 32-bit cards. The PCI (Peripheral Component Interconnect) bus was born in 1992 and is still in use today. It exists primarily as a 32-bit card, but some high-end systems provide a 64-bit PCI interface. After 10 years, in July 2002 the PCI design had reached its upper speed limit and was replaced with the PCI Express 1.0 specification, which is finding its way into the mainstream market. The former was based on parallel data communications whereas the latter was based on serial data communications, with serial facilitating faster data communications. Sandwiched between the PCI and the PCI Express was the AGP (Accelerated Graphics Port). AGP was based on PCI, with enhancements, but was connected separately from the PCI bus and joined via a direct pathway for exclusive video/graphics use by the system. PCI Express replaces AGP altogether for graphics. PCI Express coexists on most new boards with "legacy" PCI slots, with the latter slated for extinction as the market shifts to PCI Express (which is expected to be the dominant PC bus architecture for the next 10 to 15 years). In laptops, extension cards are called PC Cards (also called PCMCIA cards after the organization that created them, the Personal Computer Memory Card International Association). "PC Card" is the trademarked name assigned by the PCMCIA. These cards, which are about the size of a credit card, plug into an externally accessible slot, and serve the same purpose for laptops as do the other extension cards for PCs.

**Sound card**    A sound card is the circuitry for recording or reproducing multimedia sound. The circuitry can be found in the form of an extension card, a sound codec (Compression/Decompression Module) chip on the motherboard, or hardware integrated into the motherboard's main chipset. These hardware devices have interfaces for microphones, headphones, amplified speaker output, line-in, CD player input, and so forth. The sound card hardware requires a software counterpart in the form of a driver in order to function.

**Video card (PCI, AGP, PCI Express)**    In its most basic form, the video card is the circuitry or interface for transmitting signals that appear as images on the computer display or monitor. High-end cards can perform video capture as well. The circuitry can be found, as with the sound card, in the form of an extension card, as a dedicated chip on the motherboard, or integrated into the motherboard's main chipset. Current display adapters use the 15-pin video graphics array (VGA) analog connectors or the Digital Video Interface (DVI) analog/digital connector. Like the sound card, the video card requires a software counterpart in the form of a drive in order to function. Both sound and video have undergone extreme improvements over time. Sound used to be used only for troubleshooting and in the form of beeps. Video used to be monochrome for text-only displays. Both are now capable of combining to deliver rich sound and three-dimensional (3-D) graphics for movies and games.

**RTC (Real-Time Clock)**    RTC is the system clock for storing the system date and time, which is maintained by means of a battery when the system powers down. This battery is often called the CMOS battery, and the chip hosting the RTC is often called the CMOS chip (as the chip material itself is produced using the Complementary Metal-Oxide Semiconductor process). Officially, however, the CMOS chip is called the RTC/NVRAM. The RTC component has already been explained. NVRAM stands for nonvolatile RAM memory, meaning that the data remains when the system powers down and the data can be accessed randomly rather than in linearly. The NVRAM stores the basic configuration data that we have come to call CMOS data, which is the amount of installed memory, type of floppy and hard disk drives, and other startup configuration settings.

**CMOS**    The process by which the RTC/NVRAM chip is produced (Complementary Metal-Oxide Semiconductor). CMOS is often used in lieu of RTC/NVRAM (the official term) and may be used in the context of the "CMOS settings," which includes the system date/time (RTC) and the basic configuration data.

**CMOS battery**    To maintain critical configuration data when the system is turned off, the RTC/NVRAM chip is powered by a battery. These batteries have a long service life. They are usually mounted on the motherboard and appear as a dime-sized, silver disk. On some systems (Dallas Semiconductor or Benchmarq), the battery is built into the chip itself. The expectation is that they will last ten years, which is usually more than the service life of most systems. Some systems use no battery at all, instead using a capacitor to store a charge to be used when the system is off. Some systems use a combination of battery and capacitor, so that the capacitor can power the chip during battery changes so that the data is never lost.

One of the configuration settings retained by the RTC/NVRAM aka CMOS is the boot or BIOS access passwords. One of the methods for bypassing these passwords is to remove the CMOS battery and allow the chip to lose its settings when the power is removed, reverting to factory defaults.

**BIOS**    BIOS stands for Basic Input Output System, and is a combination of low-level software and drivers that function as the interface, intermediary, or layer between a computer's hardware and its operating system. They load into RAM from three possible sources: 1) from the motherboard ROM (ROM BIOS), 2) from the adapter card ROM (examples: video card, SCSI card), and 3) from disk in the form of device drivers. The terms BIOS and CMOS (RTC/NVRAM) are often confused and erroneously used interchangeably. They are separate systems, although closely interrelated and interdependent. The user interface for the settings that are stored in RTC/NVRAM memory are accessed through a setup program contained within the BIOS. The settings stored in RTC/NVRAM are read by the BIOS during boot to apply settings for your system configuration.

---

**Two Important Settings in RTC/NVRAM for Examiners**

Computer forensic examiners should be concerned with at least two important settings stored in RTC/NVRAM, which is accessed by the BIOS software most often called Setup. Setup is accessed during system boot using a special key or combination of keys, such as F1, F2, Esc, or Delete. Those two settings are:

- System date and time

- Boot order

The first setting is important to help establish a baseline for system time, and the second may have to be changed by the examiner if the drive must be imaged "in place" through the use of a boot floppy disk or CD.

**Mouse port**   This is the interface port in which the mouse is connected to the computer. Older systems use a serial port, and newer systems use a PS2 connection. Although most computers still provide the PS2 port option, the mouse you purchase today will probably ship with the USB interface with a PS2 adapter as the industry moves away from PS2 in favor of USB.

**Keyboard port**   This is the interface port into which the keyboard is connected to the computer. Old systems use a five-pin round port, and newer systems use the PS2 (mini-DIN type) connection. As with the mouse, most systems today ship with PS2 ports, but keyboards ship normally with USB connections with PS2 adapters as the industry moves toward USB.

**Network interface card (NIC card)**   The NIC card is an extension card used to connect the computer to a network. This functionality is now available via USB connection and is built into the motherboard on most workstation-grade motherboards currently manufactured. Ethernet is the most common type of network in use, but Token Ring is still found in some environments. The type of network deployed determines which type of network adapter, Ethernet or Token Ring, will be used. Each NIC has a unique hardware address or serial number coded into its memory. This address is called its MAC (Media Access Control) address. The Data Link Layer protocol uses this address to identify and communicate with other NICs on the same network. This address is 48 bits, or six sets of hexadecimal values, and consists of two parts. The first three hexadecimal values identify the manufacturer. The second set of three hexadecimal values is a unique serial number applied by the manufacturer. Most network cards today are rated at 10/100Mbps; however, Gigabit Ethernet (1,000Mbps) is becoming quite common and will soon be standard. Another type of network is the wireless network, whereby the network packets are sent via radio waves instead of over wires. Wireless NIC cards are typically PCI or USB, or are offered as "on-board" the motherboard. All three types require an antenna to receive the signal.

**Modem**   A modem, which stands for modulate/demodulate, is used to connect a computer to other computers using a telephone as the signal carrier. The modem takes your computer's digital signals and modulates, or transforms, them to analog signals for transmission over telephone lines. On the receiving end, the modem demodulates, or transforms, the analog signals from the telephone line back to digital signals that the receiving computer can understand.

First Responder Hint: Upon discovering that a target computer is connected to a network (telephone, wired, wireless), one of your first concerns should be the potential for destruction of data via remote connection. Disconnect the network connection or, if it's wireless, power down the machine immediately. Keep in mind, though, that a decision to "pull the plug" must be weighed against the loss of possible evidence by doing so. Running processes, network connections, and data in volatile RAM will be lost once you pull the plug. If your case depends on this volatile data, you may opt to provide a shield to block wireless transmissions while you capture the volatile data.

**Parallel port**   The parallel port is a relatively large port used primarily for legacy printer connections, although some other devices are known to use this connection. *Parallel* describes a method of transmitting data in which data is sent down parallel electrical paths at the same time. Parallel data transmission suffers limitations at high speeds with timing issues, cable length limitations, and other problems. It is being replaced by serial data transmission methods and technologies.

**Serial port**   The serial port is an I/O port used for connecting devices that use serial data transmission connections. The most common serial port you'll encounter is the RS-232 connection. Most workstations have two serial ports but can support four; however, only two at a time can be used because each pair uses the same hardware resources.

---

### Watch That Terminology!

The realm of computer forensics is still relatively new, and newer still with regard to law enforcement. Our job as computer forensic examiners is not limited to just conducting examinations. We find ourselves having to explain and educate those around us. This includes coworkers, supervisors, attorneys, judges, and, most important of all, the jury.

I have witnessed countless reports, search warrants, and testimonies in which improper terms were used to describe a computer. I have read police reports where officers have requested examinations on CPUs and computer cases. Better yet, I have observed one search warrant signed by a judge allowing the computer forensic examiner to conduct a search of a computer monitor. Apparently, the officer witnessed something of evidentiary value on the screen and wanted it examined!

If as an examiner you are confronted with inaccurate terminologies describing the device to be examined, you do not have the legal authority to actually examine the device just because the request has been approved. In such scenarios, the police reports have to be corrected and the search warrant amended before you perform any examinations.

---

## The Boot Process

At this point, we have discussed a vast array of computer system components and systems. Next we are going to look at the boot process. Computer system components are useless pieces of silicon, copper, gold, and tin until they are awakened by a spark of electricity, which follows a predetermined path, testing the various system components, establishing configuration settings, loading pieces of code—all of which culminates in the loading of a functional operating system, custom-configured to your particular hardware and software environment. The process by which this occurs is the *boot process*, named for the process of "pulling yourself up by the bootstraps." It is the process by which PC computer systems come to life, and the process that computer forensics examiners must understand and may be called upon to describe.

The boot process begins when the user presses the power switch and starts the system. When this occurs, the following steps take place regardless of the operating system:

1. When you press the power switch, the process initiates the Power On Self-Test (POST). Before the power leaves the power supply, the power supply conducts its own POST, making sure that voltages and current levels are acceptable. The electrical current from the power supply follows a predetermined path to the CPU. Any residual data in the CPU is erased. This signal also resets a CPU register called the program counter. In the case of ATs and later computers, this value is F000. The value describes the address of the next piece of code to be processed. In this case, the address of F000 corresponds to the beginning of a boot program in the ROM BIOS.

2. The boot program (sometimes called "bootstrap") in the ROM BIOS initiates a series of system checks. The first step in the process is to run a set of instructions or code intended to check the CPU and the POST process, matching it against a set of values stored in the BIOS chipset. The CPU and POST must first be checked before they can be relied on to check the rest of the system. As long as the values match and they "pass," the POST process continues to the next step.

3. Signals are sent from the CPU to the system bus (main electrical pathway) to ensure that the bus is properly functioning. If this test passes, POST continues to the next step.

4. The CPU next tests the RTC, or system clock. This clock keeps all system electrical signals in synchronization. If the RTC passes its POST check, POST continues to the next step.

5. POST next tests the system's video components. The video memory is tested, as are the signals sent by this device. The video's BIOS is added to the overall system BIOS, which is stored in RAM. It is only at this point in the boot process that the user will see anything on the screen.

6. In the next phase of POST, the system's main memory, RAM, is tested. Data is written to RAM. The data is read and compared to the original data sent. If it matches, it passes; if it doesn't match, it doesn't pass. Depending on the system settings, the user may see the "countdown" as the volume of RAM is tested. If all the RAM memory passes this test, POST continues with the next step.

7. The CPU next tests to see if a keyboard is properly attached and if any keys are pressed. If you've ever accidentally left a book or papers on a keyboard during boot, you'll no doubt recall the error beep and screen message from this test! Assuming a successful test, POST continues to the next step.

8. POST next sends signals over specific bus pathways to determine which drives (floppies, CDs, hard drives, etc.) are available to the system.

9. The results of the POST are compared to the expected system configuration settings that are stored in CMOS, which we have learned is properly called RTC/NVRAM. If the settings do not match, the user is given the opportunity to update the configuration through the Setup utility. If it passes, the next step in POST occurs.

10. If any other system component contains its own BIOS, it is loaded into the overall BIOS in RAM at this time. A typical example is a SCSI BIOS. Plug and Play runs next, configuring

any Plug and Play devices, configuring systems resources, and writing those settings to RAM. At this point, the system is ready to load a specific operating system.

11. The bootstrap code (boot program) has finished one of its two primary missions, that of conducting the POST. Its final task is that of searching the available drives for an operating system according to the order set forth in the boot sequence. Thus, the ROM BIOS boot code looks to the very first sector of the default boot hard drive (first on the list in the boot sequence) for the master boot record (MBR) and, finding it, reads it into memory and tests it for a valid signature. The "signature" is hex 55AA, located at the last two bytes of this sector. If this doesn't match, an error message is returned; otherwise the boot process continues. Figure 1.1 shows a hard drive with both an MBR and a VBR while Figure 1.2 shows a floppy disk that has only a VBR.

The MBR pertains to hard disk drives only. If the bootable media is removable media (floppy disk), there is no MBR. Rather, only a volume boot record (VBR) is located at the very first sector. Thus, when the boot is from a floppy, the VBR only is read and executed as there is no MBR on a floppy.

**FIGURE 1.1**    Hard disk drive with MBR and VBR

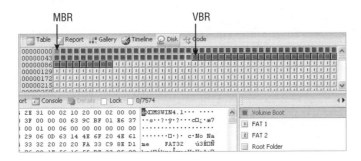

**FIGURE 1.2**    Floppy disk drive with VBR only

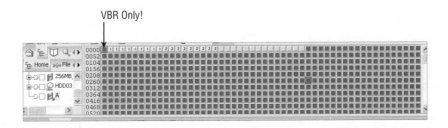

12. The MBR contains a 64-byte partition table located at byte offsets 446 to 509. Each of up to four partitions is described by 16 bytes in the 64-byte table. The MBR reads its own partition table for the "boot indicator byte" that marks one as the active partition. One must be active to boot, and there can't be more than one marked as active. The absence of the active partition or having more than one marked as active will result in an error message. The MBR reads the VBR of the partition marked as active, loads it into memory, and conducts the same "signature" test carried out with the MBR, looking for the last two bytes of the VBR to read as hex 55AA. If the signature test fails, an error message is returned. If it passes, the VBR code executes or runs. The VBR code or program searches for and runs the operating system on that volume. What happens next in the boot process depends on the operating system that is loaded on that active bootable partition.

Up through Step 12, the boot process is the same whether you're booting to DOS or to Windows. We will first boot to DOS, which will be described in steps 13 through 17. Next, we will boot to Windows. Steps 13 to 17 will be different for DOS and Windows.

**DOS boot:**

13. The code in the VBR locates and executes the initial or primary system file, which is IO.SYS (IBMBIO.COM for IBM systems). As part of execution, SYSINIT (a subroutine of IO.SYS) runs. This code copies itself into the highest region of contiguous DOS memory. The code next locates and reads MSDOS.SYS, copying it into low memory and overwriting that portion of IO.SYS in low memory that contains the initialization code (SYSINIT), as it is no longer needed there.

14. SYSINIT runs MSDOS.SYS (or IBMDOS.COM for IBM systems). MSDOS.SYS initializes basic device drivers and checks on the status of system equipment. It also resets the disk system, resets and initializes various devices that are attached to the system, and sets default system parameters. It works with the system BIOS to manage files, execute code, and respond to hardware signals.

15. With the DOS file system running and active, SYSINIT (contained within IO.SYS) resumes control of the boot process. SYSINIT reads the CONFIG.SYS file as many times as there are statements within it to process. The DEVICE statements are processed first in the order in which they appear, followed next by the INSTALL statements in the order of their appearance. Once they are done, if a SHELL statement is present, it is run. If none is present, the default shell with default parameters (COMMAND.COM) is run. SYSINIT is now complete, so COMMAND.COM is written into the section of memory previously occupied by SYSINIT.

16. If the file AUTOEXEC.BAT (.BAT is the extension for batch files) is present, COMMAND.COM will run it. Each command in the batch file is executed. If one of the batch commands calls for launching an application or shell, then the user is presented with that interface or prompt. Otherwise, when the batch commands have been executed, the user sees a blinking cursor at a DOS prompt.

17. If no AUTOEXEC.BAT file is present, COMMAND.COM runs the DATE and TIME commands and displays a copyright message, and then the user is shown a blinking cursor at a DOS Prompt. The entire process appears in Figure 1.3.

**FIGURE 1.3**    The boot process (DOS)

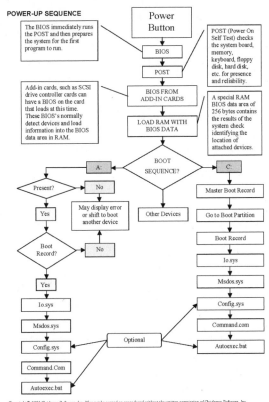

Windows NT/2000/XP boot:

13. The code in the VBR locates and runs the primary system file, which in the case of the various flavors of Windows NT is NTLDR (often called "NT Loader"). NTLDR places the processor in the "protected" mode, starts the file system, and reads the contents of the BOOT.INI file. Startup options and initial boot menu options are determined by the contents of the BOOT.INI file. If dual booting is configured, and the other OS is a non-NT type such as Linux, BOOTSEC.DOS runs. If SCSI drives are attached to the system, another file (NTBOOTDD.SYS) containing the SCSI drivers executes.

14. NTDETECT.COM executes and searches the system for installed hardware and passes configuration data to NTLDR. If more than one hardware profile exists, NTDETECT determines the correct profile for the current hardware and runs that profile.

**15.** The configuration data obtained in the previous step by NTDETECT is passed by NTLDR to NTOSKRNL.EXE. NTOSKRNL.EXE is the code that loads the kernel, the Hardware Abstraction Layer (HAL), and the system registry information.

**16.** The next step in the NT boot process is that of loading drivers and code for networking systems, typically TCP/IP. Simultaneously, services that are configured to run at startup load and run. One of the services is the logon service that provides the user with a logon prompt, unless configured otherwise. When the user successfully logs on, the current configuration status is considered "good" and is updated into the system registry as "Last Known Good Configuration."

**17.** As logon occurs, device detection takes place as a simultaneous process. If new devices are detected, Plug and Play assigns system resources, extracts drivers from the DRIVER.CAB file, and completes configuration and mounting of those devices. If drivers can't be found, the user is prompted to provide them. When done, the user has a graphical user interface (GUI) that allows them to interact with their system and its unique environment of software and hardware.

# Partitions

*Partitions* and *volumes* are terms that are often used interchangeably. Usually this doesn't cause a problem because typically they are the same thing. There are, however, some subtle differences, and defining the terms and understanding the differences is an important part of being a professional. A partition is a collection of consecutive sectors within a volume, and those sectors are addressable by a single file system specific to and contained within that partition. A volume, by subtle contrast, is a collection of addressable sectors that are used by an operating system or an application to store data. The addressable sectors in a volume do not have to be consecutive—and therein lies the difference. Rather, they need only give the appearance of being consecutive. When a volume consists of a single partition, they are functionally the same. When a volume spans more than one partition or drive, the difference becomes self-evident.

Volumes are logical storage units that are assigned drive letters by the operating systems. Theoretically, most operating systems can support up to 24 volumes, using the letters C through Z, and reserving A and B for floppy drives. If a single physical hard drive were installed in a system, that drive could, in theory, be partitioned into 24 volumes. Recall, however, from our earlier discussion that the partition table contained in the master boot record only permitted four 16-byte entries for four partitions. How then could such a system support 24 logical volumes?

The answer lies with the extended partition system. One of the four defined partitions in the MBR partition table must be an extended partition. The disk space assigned to the "extended partition" is further subdivided into logical volumes by the operating system. Each subpartition of the extended volume contains a partition table located in the first sector of that subpartition. That table defines its own subpartition and, optionally, points to another partition table in yet another subpartition. This "nesting" of subpartitions within the extended partition can extend as far as letter assignments permit, and each "nested" subpartition will have a partition table describing itself and pointing to the next level down until done. Seldom will you ever encounter more than few partitions, but in theory, you could encounter the upper limit of 24!

The partition types you can encounter are many and are usually specific to the operating system(s) on the host computer. The fifth byte within each 16-byte partition entry (byte offset 446–509 of the MBR) will determine the partition type/file system for each defined partition. The same holds true for partition tables within the extended partition and their subpartitions. The first byte of each of the four partition table entries determines which partition is "active" and therefore is the "boot" partition. Only one can be active. Hex 80 denotes the active partition. The other three partition entries, if defined, will have hex 00 for the first byte in their respective entries. Table 1.1 defines the partition table fields.

**TABLE  1.1**    Partition Table Fields Defined*

| Offset (Dec) | Name | Length | Description |
|---|---|---|---|
| 446 | Boot Byte | 1 byte | Boot status; hex 80 is active and bootable. Otherwise, it is hex 00. |
| 447 | Starting Head | 1 byte | For CHS mode, this is the start head or side of the partition. |
| 448 | Starting Cylinder & Sector | 2 bytes (16 bits) | For CHS mode, the starting cylinder is 10 bits and the starting sector is the next 6 bits, for a total of 16 bits. |
| 450 | Partition Type | 1 byte | This is the partition type/file system. |
| 451 | Ending Head | 1 byte | For CHS mode, this is the ending head or side of the partition. |
| 452 | Ending Cylinder & Sector | 2 bytes (16 bits) | For CHS mode, the ending cylinder is 10 bits and the ending sector is the next 6 bits, for a total of 16 bits. |
| 454 | Relative Sector | 4 bytes (32 bits or dword) | For LBA mode, this is the number of sectors before the partition, which is the starting sector of the partition. |
| 458 | Total Sectors | 4 bytes (32 bits or dword) | For LBA mode, this is the total number of sectors in the partition. |

* Fields repeat three more times, if partitions defined, starting at offsets 462, 478, and 494.

Typically FAT12, FAT16, FAT32, and NTFS partitions and file systems are used when running the various flavors of the Windows operating systems. These partitions can be created by utilities that ship with the Windows operating system, such as FDISK, DISKPART, or Disk Manager. Other partition types that are often encountered are Linux Native (EXT2/3 and Reiser) and Swap partitions, Solaris (UFS), and Mac OSX (HFS+), all of which are supported under EnCase Version 5. As with Windows operating systems, partitioning utilities ship with these operating systems. Third -party partitioning utilities are also available that you can use to create partitions of varied types, such as Symantec's PartitionMagic and V-Communications' Partition Commander.

Using Disk Manager (Windows 2000/XP), the formatting is done when you use the Create a New Partition wizard. If a partition is created with FDISK, the partition must be formatted with the high-level format command before it can be used. When you use the format command to format a FAT12/16/32 partition, the following occurs:

1.  The disk is scanned for errors and bad sectors are marked.

2.  Drive heads are placed at the first cylinder of the partition and a DOS VBR is written.

3.  FAT 1 is written to Head 1 Sector 2. Immediately following FAT 1, FAT 2 is written. The entries in the FAT are mostly null, except that bad clusters are marked.

4.  A blank root directory is written.

5.  If the /s parameter is selected, the system files are transferred.

6.  If the /v parameter is selected, the user is prompted for a volume label.

It is during the FDISK or disk partitioning process that the MBR is written, which contains the MBR booting code; the partition table entries are written; and the MBR signature is written. It is during the high-level formatting process (FORMAT) that the VBR is typically written, along with other file system features.

---

**EXERCISE 1.1**

### Examining the Partition Table

In this exercise, you will use EnCase to decode the information contained in the partition table.

1.  With EnCase open, and a case started, choose Add Device ➢ Local Drives. Select your own boot drive and select the physical device, not the logical device.

2.  In the left pane, select your drive. In the right pane, choose the Disk View tab.

3.  Go to the very first sector, which should appear in red in EnCase Version 5. Place your cursor on that sector. In the bottom pane, choose the Hex View. Locate and sweep (select by clicking and dragging) bytes 446–509. With these 64 bytes selected, right-click in the selected area and choose Bookmark Data. With the Bookmark dialog box open, under View Types, choose Windows/Partition Entry. The partition table is decoded and displayed.

---

Often FDISK is used to remove the partition, rendering the drive unreadable and causing the user to believe that the data is gone. All that really occurs is that the partition table entry is removed. As each defined and formatted partition contains a VBR, which is untouched by FDISK, the examiner can use EnCase to recover a deleted partition. Simply locate and select the VBR, right-click, and choose Add Partition from the context menu.

# File Systems

We have, thus far, made reference to *file systems* in our discussion of partitions and volumes, but we have not yet defined them or described their function and importance in data storage and retrieval. In this section, we'll discuss file systems in a generic sense. In the chapter that follows, we'll cover specific file systems in detail.

A file system is nothing more than a system or method of storing and retrieving data on a computer system that allows for a hierarchy of directories, subdirectories, and files. File systems must be consistent between systems using the same file system. If a library used the Dewey Decimal System to store books in one library, a user could go to another library using the same file system and locate a book in that library. Even though the book would be stored in different physical locations in both libraries, a common file system would enable the user to find the book using a common filing and locating system. Computer systems are no different in this regard.

A file system needs its own structural or organization files and data, and the other component is the user data. Because a file system is contained within a partition, there must be data or files that describe the layout and size of the file system, as well as how large the data storage units (clusters, blocks, etc.) will be. The data storage units, which are groups of sectors that hold content data, are referred to as allocation units, clusters, blocks, and similar names depending on the file system being used. A file system needs to have a method or convention for naming data and therefore a system of file names. File names are usually contained in directory entries or as an attribute or field in a database of file and directory names. File names have to be linked to actual data comprising that file name so that the operating system can locate the data. Thus, there must be an attribute or *metadata* (data within data describing data) to point to where the data starts. This is done, usually, via a directory entry (FAT systems) or an entry (field or attribute) in a file table such as the master file table (MFT) in NTFS systems.

Because the data may be larger than one allocation unit can hold, there must be a system that tracks the containing data storage units (clusters, blocks, etc.). In a FAT system, these clusters are linked together in the FAT table (file allocation table). In NTFS, the clusters containing the data are described by data runs in the MFT. The operating system must know the size of the data so it knows where the data ends in an allocation unit, and that data is typically stored in a directory entry or as an attribute or field in a database of file names, such as the MFT.

Finally, any file system must have a system that tracks allocation unit usage and availability. Without this function, data could be overwritten. In a FAT system, this is accomplished with the

FAT table. In NTFS and other systems, this is accomplished by the single-purpose volume bit map (VBM), which is an array of bits, with each representing an allocation unit. A 0 means it is available for use, and a 1 means it is allocated.

At a minimum, a file system needs to have the functions described thus far. Most file systems contain much more information about the files it stores and has metadata in the form of file attributes about the data. This information may take the form of dates and times for last written, file creation, and last modified. It may also take the form of file permissions or access control lists (ACLs).

In summary, when a partition is created, its boundaries and type are set forth in a partition table. The "type" is something akin to a zoning ordinance where a given piece of real estate is "supposed" to be used for a specific purpose. A piece of real estate could be zoned as "residential" while a partition type could, similarly, be declared as having a type of "Linux Swap." A real estate parcel is described in a deed by its meets and bounds as determined by a survey. A partition's "meets and bounds" are described, similarly, in a partition table by its starting point, ending point, and size, based on a survey conducted by the partitioning utility.

When a partition is formatted, among other things, the data structures needed for its specific file system are created. While these file system type structures are usually consistent with the file system type declared in the partition table, they do not have to be. One could have a FAT32 file system located in a partition type declared as a Linux Swap. This would be somewhat analogous to someone placing a business on real estate zoned for residential use. If you were using Linux for the operating system, Linux does not rely on the partition type; if instructed to mount the partition as FAT32, it would do so since the structure for FAT32 is present regardless of the declared type. Linux ignores the "zoning laws." Windows, however, strictly obeys "zoning laws" and would not permit an office in a residential zone. Windows relies on declared partition types for mounting partitions and file systems and would not mount a FAT32 partition declared as a Linux Swap partition or any other type not a FAT32. In this manner, partitions and file systems can be hidden from Windows.

File systems are the management tools for storing and retrieving data in a partition. Some operating systems require certain file systems for them to function. Windows needs a FAT or NTFS file system, depending on its "flavor," or version, and won't recognize or mount other systems with its own native operating system. Third-party software can enable mounting and reading (sometimes writing) other file systems from within the Windows environment. EnCase and VMWare are two examples. Many different file system schemes have been developed, and more will be forthcoming as computing evolves. In the next chapter, we examine the FAT file system in detail.

# Summary

This chapter explained the computer's components, its boot process, partitions, and file systems. We covered computer hardware components, including their acronyms, attributes, functions, and purpose. In addition, we examined the two major components of the boot process.

The first is the POST (Power On Self-Test), in which the major components are tested and initialized (added to the system). The second consists of the bootstrap code locating a bootable drive and loading the specified operating system.

We also defined and described partitions and volumes. A partition is a collection of consecutive sectors within a volume and is a container for a file system, with specific boundaries and properties. A volume is a collection of addressable sectors that are used by an operating system or an application to store data. A volume is assigned a drive letter by the OS; it may be limited to a single partition, or it may span partitions or physical hard drives. Finally, we discussed file systems and their purpose, function, and necessary generic components.

# Exam Essentials

**Know computer hardware components.**    Understand the proper terminology, acronyms, purpose, and function of the various computer hardware components.

**Be familiar with the boot process.**    Understand and be able to describe the POST process. Understand and be able to describe the process by which the system boots and loads an operating system.

**Understand partitions and volumes.**    Understand and be able to describe partitions and volumes, what the differences are, and how they are created. Understand the MBR and VBR, where they are found, their contents (boot code, partition table, signature), and how and when they are created. Understand a partition table, where it is located, its structure, length, and general properties.

**Understand file systems in general.**    Understand the purpose of a file system as a means to store and retrieve data. Be familiar with the functional components of any generic file system so as to be able to apply them to specific file systems.

# Review Questions

1. What is the definition of a CPU?

   **A.** The physical computer case that contains all its internal components

   **B.** The computer's internal hard drive

   **C.** A part of the computer whose function is to perform data processing

   **D.** A part of the computer that stores and manages memory

2. What is the BIOS?

   **A.** BIOS stands for Basic Input Output System, and is a combination of low-level software and drivers that function as the interface, intermediary, or layer between a computer's hardware and its operating system.

   **B.** BIOS stands for Bootstrap Initialization Operating System, and is a combination of low-level software and drivers that function as the interface, intermediary, or layer between a computer's hardware and its operating system.

   **C.** BIOS stands for Boot-level Input Output System and is a combination of low-level software and drivers that function as the interface, intermediary, or layer between a computer's hardware and its operating system.

   **D.** BIOS stands for Boot Initialization Operating System and is a combination of low-level software and drivers that function as the interface, intermediary, or layer between a computer's hardware and its operating system.

3. What is the definition of POST?

   **A.** A set of computer sequences the operating system executes upon a proper shutdown

   **B.** A diagnostic test of the computer's hardware and software for presence and operability during the boot sequence prior to running the operating system

   **C.** A diagnostic test of the computer's software for presence and operability during the boot sequence prior to running the operating system

   **D.** A diagnostic test of the computer's hardware for presence and operability during the boot sequence prior to running the operating system

4. Is the information stored on a computer's ROM chip lost during a proper shutdown?

   **A.** Yes

   **B.** No

5. Is the information contained on a computer's RAM chip accessible after a proper shutdown?

   **A.** Yes

   **B.** No

6. Can information stored in the BIOS ever change?

   **A.** Yes

   **B.** No

**7.** What is the purpose or function of a computer's ROM chip?

   **A.** Long-term or permanent storage of information and instructions

   **B.** Temporary storage area to run applications

   **C.** Permanent storage area for programs and files

   **D.** A portable storage device

**8.** Information contained in RAM memory (system's main memory), which is located on the motherboard, is _____.

   **A.** Volatile

   **B.** Nonvolatile

**9.** What is the maximum number of drive letters assigned to hard drive(s) partitions on a system?

   **A.** Four

   **B.** Sixteen

   **C.** Twenty-four

   **D.** Infinity

**10.** The smallest area on a drive that data can be written to is a _____ while the smallest area on a drive that a file can be written to is a _____.

   **A.** Bit and byte

   **B.** Sector and cluster

   **C.** Volume and drive

   **D.** Memory and disk

**11.** The size of a physical hard drive can be determined by which of the following?

   **A.** Multiplying the cylinder x head x sector

   **B.** Multiplying the cylinder x head x sector x 512 bytes

   **C.** Multiplying the total LBA sectors times 512 bytes

   **D.** Adding the total size of partitions

   **E.** Both B and C

**12.** Which is not considered an output device?

   **A.** Monitor

   **B.** Printer

   **C.** CD-RW drive

   **D.** Speaker

13. The electrical pathway used to transport data from one computer component to another is called?

    **A.** Bus

    **B.** RAM

    **C.** CMOS

    **D.** BIOS

14. What is the main component of a computer that essential internal devices such as CPU, memory chips, and other chipsets are attached to?

    **A.** BIOS

    **B.** Motherboard

    **C.** Expansion card

    **D.** Processor

15. IDE, SCSI, and SATA are different types of interfaces describing what device?

    **A.** RAM chips

    **B.** Flash memory

    **C.** CPUs

    **D.** Hard drives

16. What do the terms *Master*, *Slave*, and *Cable Select* refer to?

    **A.** External SCSI devices

    **B.** Cable types for external hardware

    **C.** Jumper settings for internal hardware such as IDE hard drives and CD drives

    **D.** Jumper settings for internal expansion cards

17. What can you assume about a hard drive that is pinned as CS?

    **A.** It's an IDE drive.

    **B.** It's a SATA drive.

    **C.** It's a SCSI drive.

    **D.** All of the above.

18. What is found at Cylinder 0, Head 0, Sector 1 on a hard drive?

    **A.** Master boot record

    **B.** Master file table

    **C.** Volume boot record

    **D.** Volume boot sector

**19.** What is the first sector on a volume called?

   **A.** File allocation table

   **B.** Volume boot record or sector

   **C.** Master boot record

   **D.** Volume boot device

**20.** Which of the following is incorrect?

   **A.** The MBR is typically written when the drive is partitioned with FDISK or DISKPART.

   **B.** A file system is a system or method of storing and retrieving data on a computer system that allows for a hierarchy of directories, subdirectories, and files.

   **C.** The VBR is typically written when the drive is high-level formatted with a utility such as FORMAT.

   **D.** The partition table is contained within the MBR and consists of a total of 16 bytes, which describes up to four partitions using 4 bytes each to do so.

# Answers to Review Questions

1. C. A CPU is the central processing unit, a microprocessor that performs data processing, or interprets and executes instructions.

2. A. BIOS stands for Basic Input Output System and consists of all the low-level software that is the interface between the system hardware and its operating system. It loads, typically, from three sources: the ROM/BIOS on the motherboard; the various BIOS ROMs on video cards, SCSI cards, and so forth; and finally, device drivers.

3. D. POST (Power On Self-Test) is a diagnostic test of the computer's hardware, such as the motherboard, memory, CD-ROM drive, and so forth. POST does not test the computer's software.

4. B. Information contained on a ROM chip, read-only memory, is not lost after the computer has been shut down.

5. B. Unlike a ROM chip, information contained on a computer's RAM chip is not readily accessible after a proper shutdown.

6. A. Although not very common, information stored in the BIOS can change, such as when the BIOS needs to be upgraded to support new hardware.

7. A. ROM (read-only memory) contains information about the computer, such as hardware configuration. Unlike RAM, the information is not lost once power is disconnected.

8. A. Information contained in RAM memory is considered volatile, which means that the data is lost after the computer has been disconnected.

9. C. The answer is 24 drive letters (C–Z), with drive letters A and B reserved for floppy drives.

10. B. Data is written to sectors, and files are written to clusters.

11. E. Multiplying C/H/S gives the total amount of sectors in older systems if the number of sectors per track is constant. When it's not, total LBA sectors give total sectors. Multiplying the total number of sectors from the appropriate method times 512 bytes per sector gives the total number of bytes for the physical drive. Adding up the total size of partitions does not include areas outside the partitions, such as Unused Disk Area.

12. C. A CD-RW (rewritable) drive is both an input and output device, as opposed to a CD drive, which only reads and inputs data to the computer system.

13. A. A Bus performs two functions: it transports data from one place to another and directs the information where to go.

14. B. The motherboard is the main circuit board used to attach internal hardware devices to its connectors.

15. D. IDE (Integrated Drive Electronics), SCSI (Small Computer System Interface), and SATA (Serial ATA, or Serial Advanced Technology Attachment) describe different hard drive interfaces.

**16.** C. Master, Slave, and Cable Select are settings for internal devices such as IDE hard drives and CD drives to identify and differentiate the devices on the same channel.

**17.** A. SATA and SCSI hard drives are not configurable as Master, Slave, or Cable Select. Only IDE drives are configured as Master, Slave, or Cable Select. Thus, any jumper setting denoting "CS" would apply only to an IDE drive.

**18.** A. The master boot record is always located at the first physical sector on a hard drive. This record stores key information about the drive itself, such as the master partition table and master boot code.

**19.** B. The first sector on a volume is called the volume boot record, or volume boot sector. This sector contains the disk parameter block and volume boot code.

**20.** D. All are true statements, except for a portion of D. The partition table is contained within the MBR and consists of a total of 64 bytes, not 16 bytes, which describes up to four partitions using 16 bytes each to do so, not 4 bytes each.

# Chapter

# 2

# File Systems

**ENCE EXAM TOPICS COVERED IN THIS CHAPTER:**

✓ FAT12 file system

✓ FAT16 file system

✓ FAT32 file system

✓ Other file systems (NTFS and CD file systems)

In the previous chapter, we made many references to file systems and discussed generally what a file system is and its functional purpose. We referenced some file system names, such as FAT, NTFS, and Linux. In this chapter, we thoroughly cover the file allocation table (FAT) file system's internal structures and function, and we touch on the New Technology File System (NTFS) and CD file systems.

The FAT file system has been around for nearly a quarter of a century, and will be with us for the foreseeable future. It is still used with floppy drives, Flash media, and USB thumb drives, and can still be used, optionally, with Windows XP. Windows 2000 defaults to a FAT file system, and XP defaults to NTFS. Thus, as a computer forensics examiner, you will encounter many cases involving FAT from both legacy and new systems.

In this chapter, you will learn about the data structures of the FAT file system, which consists of two major components: the file allocation table (FAT) and the directory entries. You will learn how the directory entries store file names and attributes (metadata) and how the FAT is used both to track the allocation status of the data storage area (organized as "clusters") and to link together the clusters used to store data. You will understand how the FAT system has been "tweaked" over the years to handle increasingly larger data storage devices. Finally, you will be exposed briefly to various CD file systems, and to the components of the NTFS file system. We'll also explain the similarities and differences among all these systems.

# FAT Basics

The first major component of the FAT file system is the directory entry. In all versions of the FAT file system (FAT12, FAT16, and FAT32), every file and directory is referenced and described in a separate directory entry. The directory entry is 32 bytes in length and contains the file's or directory's name, its size in bytes, its starting extent (or beginning cluster), and other file attributes or metadata (created, last accessed, and last written timestamps, etc.). None of the data content exists in the directory entry; rather, data content is stored in data allocation units called *clusters*. Clusters consist of one or more sectors, and a cluster is the smallest unit in which a file or directory can be stored. If a file's size exceeds the amount that can be contained in one cluster, it is assigned as many additional clusters as are needed to contain its data. The directory entry tracks only the starting cluster and does not track the other clusters used by a file.

The other major component of the FAT file system is the file allocation table, or FAT, which, among other functions, tracks the sequence of clusters used by a file when more than one cluster is allocated or used. In addition to tracking cluster runs or sequences, the FAT also tracks the allocation status of clusters, assuring that the operating system stores data in clusters that are available and that those storing data assigned to files or directories aren't overwritten. The FAT also tracks bad clusters, marking them as such so they won't be used.

The FAT file system comes in three versions that have evolved over time to accommodate the continual development of larger-capacity hard drives. The three versions of FAT are FAT12, FAT16, and FAT32. The number following the FAT describes the size of the entries in the FAT table.

In a FAT12 system, the table is an array of 12-bit entries, with each 12-bit sequence representing a cluster, starting at cluster 0 and ending with the last cluster in the volume. The theoretical maximum number of clusters for a 12-bit array is 4,096 ($2^{12}$), but certain values are reserved, making 4,084 clusters the largest number of clusters supported by a FAT12 system.

Similarly, a FAT16 system has 16-bit FAT entries and a FAT32 has 32-bit entries (although only 28 are used). Taking into account certain reserved values, a FAT16 system supports up to 65,524 clusters, and a FAT32 supports up to a theoretical maximum of 268,435,445 clusters (but with an MBR-imposed limit of 67,092,481 clusters, which makes it capable of supporting a partition size of 2 terabytes). There are some other differences between FAT12/16 and FAT32, but the major difference lies in the number of clusters they can support, as shown in Table 2.1.

**T A B L E   2 . 1**    Maximum Number of Sectors Supported by FAT Types

| FAT Type | Maximum Number of Clusters Supported |
| --- | --- |
| FAT12 | 4,084 |
| FAT16 | 65,524 |
| FAT32 | 67,092,481 |

## The Physical Layout of FAT

The FAT file system, as shown in Figure 2.1, has a distinctive physical layout consisting of three major components:

- Reserved area (volume boot sector)
- FAT (file allocation table) area
- Data storage area (directory entries and data content)

The reserved area consists of the volume boot sector, often abbreviated as simply *boot sector*. The size of this reserved area is defined within the boot sector data, but most often FAT12 and FAT16 systems use only one sector for this data. (See Figure 2.2.)

**FIGURE 2.1** Physical layout of FAT showing the three major components

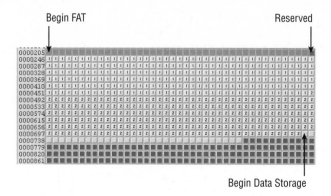

**FIGURE 2.2** Reserved area (boot sector) of the FAT16 file system using only one sector

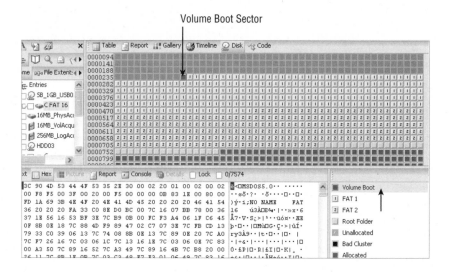

With FAT32 systems, the size of this area is likewise defined in the boot sector, but because it contains significantly more data, it will be several sectors in length (sectors 0, 1, and 2, with backups at sectors 6, 7, and 8), and the reserved area will usually be 32 sectors in length. The backup copy of the boot sector is unique to FAT32 and runs if volume sector 0, the boot sector, is corrupted. While its location is specified in the boot sector (as a sector number at byte offsets 50–51 in the boot sector), Microsoft standards call for it being located at volume sector 6. It only makes sense to have it located in a standard location. If its location were variable and that variable location relied on data in sector 0, a corrupted sector 0 could destroy the system's ability to find its backup boot sector. (See Figure 2.3.)

**FIGURE 2.3** Reserved area of a FAT32 file system using 32 sectors

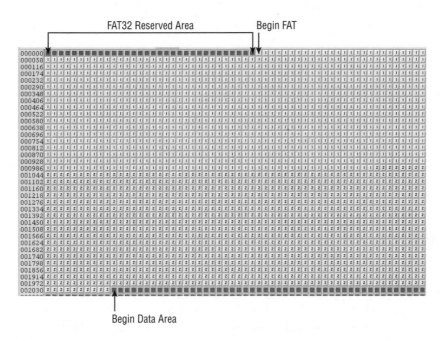

Begin Data Area

Also unique to FAT32 is a data structure known as File System Information, or FSINFO. Its location is specified as a sector number at byte offsets 48–49 in the boot sector, but it is typically found in sector 1, immediately following the boot sector and sandwiched between the boot sector (sector 0) and sector 2, which is a continuation of the FAT32 bootstrap code. Additionally, a backup copy of the FSINFO is maintained in the sector immediately following the backup boot sector, which is sector 7 (the backup boot sector is, by standard, located in sector 6). Its purpose is to provide information to the operating system about the number of free clusters available to the system and the location of the next free cluster. Interestingly, this data is only "suggested" information for the operating system and may or may not be used. Also, this data may or may not be updated or accurate; often the backup copy does not match the primary. Nevertheless, it is a feature unique to FAT32.

The volume boot sector, also called the volume boot record (VBR) and often abbreviated *boot sector*, is located at the first sector of the logical volume. It is the first sector of the reserved area; in FAT12/16, it is often the only sector in the reserved area. The boot sector contains four distinct segments:

1.  Jump instruction to the boot code (first 3 bytes).

2.  BIOS parameter block, or BPB (bytes 3–61 for FAT12/16 and bytes 3–89 for FAT32).

3.  Boot code and error messages (bytes 62–509 for FAT12/16 and bytes 90–509 for FAT32). Note: FAT32 boot bode continues at sector 2, bytes 0–509.

4.  Signature (bytes 510–511; should be 0x55AA).

**FIGURE 2.4**   Backup boot sector unique to the FAT32 file system

The jump instruction tells the machine where to find the beginning of the OS bootstrap code located in that sector. Bytes 3–35, as well as bytes 0–2, have the same structure and purpose for all three versions of FAT. Bytes 36–61 have a structure and purpose unique to FAT12/16, while bytes 36–89 have a structure and purpose unique to FAT32. The area beyond byte 61 for FAT12/16 and beyond byte 89 for FAT32, except for bytes 510–511 (the boot sector signature), is used for the bootstrap code, referenced in the first 3 bytes, as well as for error messages.

The BPB is nothing more than a database of sorts, with defined fields that set forth the parameters of the partition and the file system within. The boot sector can be demystified by breaking down the data into its components, as shown in Tables 2.2 and 2.3.

**FIGURE  2.5**    Default FAT configuration showing FAT1(selected) immediately followed by FAT2

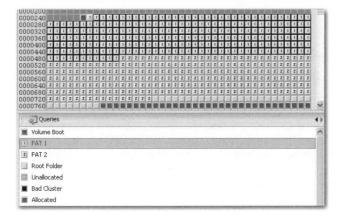

**TABLE  2.2**    Volume Boot Sector Format—FAT12/16 File System

| Byte Offset (Decimal) | Name or Description and Purpose |
|---|---|
| 0–2 | Assembly jump instruction to bootstrap code found in this sector, usually 0xEB3C90. |
| 3–10 | OEM ID in ASCII; indicates the OS that formatted the volume: Win95 = MSWIN4.0 Win98 = MSWIN4.1 Win2K/XP = MSDOS5.0 Linux  = mkdosfs (When Linux mkfs msdos command is used to create) |
| 11–12 | Bytes per sector; normally 512, but 1024, 2048 or 4096 may occur. |
| 13 | Sectors per cluster; value must be a power of 2 and greater than 0. Typical values are 1, 2, 4, 8, 16, 32 or 64. |
| 14–15 | Number of sectors in the reserved area. FAT12/16 is typically one. |
| 16 | Number of FAT tables; typically, this is 2, with FAT1 and FAT2 (FAT2 is a duplicate of FAT1 for redundancy). According to Microsoft, some small devices can have only one FAT! |
| 17–18 | Maximum number of 32-byte directory entries in the root directory. This is typically 512 for FAT12/16 and 0 for FAT32. |

**TABLE 2.2** Volume Boot Sector Format—FAT12/16 File System *(continued)*

| Byte Offset (Decimal) | Name or Description and Purpose |
| --- | --- |
| 19–20 | 16-bit integer describing the number of sectors in the partition. If 0, the number exceeds 65,536 and the byte offset 32–35 is a 32-bit integer describing the number of sectors in the partition. |
| 21 | Media descriptor; according to Microsoft, 0xF8 should be used on nonremovable media (hard disks) and 0xF0 should be used for removable media. This entry is duplicated in the first entry of the FAT where cluster 0 would be described, but since there is no addressable cluster 0 or 1, this value is used instead. |
| 22–23 | 16-bit integer that describes number of sectors used by each FAT in FAT12/16. For FAT32, expect a value here of 0. |
| 24–25 | Sectors per track value for interrupt 13h, typically 63 for hard disks. |
| 26–27 | Number of heads value for interrupt 13h, typically 255 for hard disks. |
| 28–31 | Number of hidden sectors before the start of the partition, typically 63 for the first volume on a hard disk. |
| 32–35 | 32-bit integer describing the number of sectors in the partition. If 0, the number does not exceed 65,536 and is described as a 16-integer in bytes 19–20. Only one of the two (19–20 or 32–35) and not both must be set to 0. |
| 36 | Interrupt 13h drive number, which is 0x00 for floppies or 0x80 for hard drives. |
| 37 | Not used except by Windows NT; should typically be 0. |
| 38 | Extended boot signature to determine the validity of the three fields that follow. If 0x29, the next three fields are present and valid. If otherwise, expect 0x00. |
| 39–42 | Volume serial number; used with the field that follows to track volumes on removable media. With some OSs this value is generated using a date/time seed value at time of creation. |
| 43–53 | Volume label in ASCII; the volume label is optionally given by the user at the time of creation. Its limit is 11 bytes, and it should match the value in the root directory of FAT12/16. If none is given by the user, "NO NAME" should appear here. |
| 54–61 | File system type at time of formatting. Shown in ASCII as FAT, FAT12, or FAT16. It is not used after formatting and could be altered. |
| 62–509 | Bootstrap program code and error messages. |
| 510–511 | Signature value; 2 bytes and should be 0x55AA. |

**TABLE 2.3**    Volume Boot Sector Format—FAT32 File System

| Byte Offset (Decimal) | Name or Description and Purpose |
| --- | --- |
| 0–2 | Assembly jump instruction to bootstrap code found in this sector, usually 0xEB3C90. |
| 3–10 | OEM ID in ASCII; indicates the OS that formatted the volume:<br>Win95 = MSWIN4.0<br>Win98 = MSWIN4.1<br>Win2K/XP = MSDOS5.0<br>Linux mkfs.msdos = mkdosfs |
| 11–12 | Bytes per sector; normally 512, but 1024, 2048, or 4096 may occur. |
| 13 | Sectors per cluster; value must be a power of 2 and greater than 0. Typical values are 1, 2, 4, 8, 16, 32, or 64. |
| 14–15 | Number of sectors in the reserved area. FAT12/16 is typically one. |
| 16 | Number of FAT tables; typically, this is 2, with FAT1 and FAT2 (FAT2 is a duplicate of FAT1 for redundancy). According to Microsoft, some small devices can have only one FAT! |
| 17–18 | Maximum number of 32-byte directory entries in the root directory. This is typically 512 for FAT12/16 and 0 for FAT32. |
| 19–20 | 16-bit integer describing the number of sectors in the partition. If 0, the number exceeds 65,536, and the byte offset 32–35 is a 32-bit integer describing the number of sectors in the partition. |
| 21 | Media descriptor; according to Microsoft, 0xF8 should be used on nonremovable media (hard disks) and 0xF0 should be used for removable media. This entry is duplicated in the first entry of the FAT where cluster 0 would be described, but since there is no addressable cluster 0 or 1, this value is used instead. |
| 22–23 | 16-bit integer that describes the number of sectors used by each FAT in FAT12/16. For FAT32, expect a value here of 0. |
| 24–25 | Sectors per track value for interrupt 13h, typically 63 for hard disks. |
| 26–27 | Number of heads value for interrupt 13h, typically 255 for hard disks. |
| 28–31 | Number of hidden sectors before the start of the partition, typically 63 for the first volume on a hard disk. |

**TABLE 2.3**     Volume Boot Sector Format—FAT32 File System *(continued)*

| Byte Offset (Decimal) | Name or Description and Purpose |
| --- | --- |
| 32–35 | 32-bit integer describing the number of sectors in the partition. If 0, the number does not exceed 65,536 and is described as a 16-integer in bytes 19–20. Only one of the two (19–20 or 32–35) and not both must be set to 0. When FAT32, this number cannot be 0. |
| 36–39 | 32-bit integer describing the number of sectors used by one FAT on FAT32 partition; bytes 22–23 must be set to 0 for FAT32. |
| 40–41 | A series of bit-field values used in FAT32 to describe how multiple FATS are written to. If bit 7 is off (value 0), then FAT is duplicated. If it is on (value 1), then duplication is disabled and only the FAT referenced in bits 0–3 is active. Bits 0–3 are only valid if bit 7 is "on" and duplication is not occurring. Bits 4–6 and 8–15 are reserved. Default is 0x0000, meaning that FAT1 and FAT2 are replicated. |
| 42–43 | The major and minor version numbers of the FAT32 volume, with the high byte being the major and the low byte being the minor. Expect values of 0x00 and 0x00. |
| 44–47 | Cluster number where the root directory begins, usually cluster 2. Remember that cluster 2 is the first addressable cluster and on a FAT32 starts immediately after FAT2 ends. Entries in FAT for clusters 0 and 1 are used for purposes other than addressing clusters. |
| 48–49 | Sector number for where FSINFO can be found, usually 1; a backup FSINFO follows sector 6 (location of backup boot sector), and is found at sector 7. |
| 50–51 | Sector number for location of backup boot sector, which defaults to sector 6. |
| 52–63 | Reserved and not currently used. |
| 64 | Interrupt 13h drive number, which is 0x00 for floppies or 0x80 for hard drives. |
| 65 | Not used except by Windows NT; should typically be 0. |
| 66 | Extended boot signature to determine the validity of the three fields that follow. If 0x29, the next three fields are present and valid. If otherwise, expect 0x00. |
| 67–70 | Volume serial number; used with the field that follows to track volumes on removable media. With some OSs this value is generated using a date/time seed value at time of creation. |
| 71–81 | Volume label in ASCII; volume label is optionally given by the user at the time of creation. Its limit is 11 bytes, and it should match the value in the root. If none is given by user, "NO NAME" should appear here. |

**TABLE 2.3**    Volume Boot Sector Format—FAT32 File System *(continued)*

| Byte Offset (Decimal) | Name or Description and Purpose |
| --- | --- |
| 82–89 | File system type at time of formatting. Shown in ASCII as FAT32. Not used after formatting and could be altered. |
| 90–509 | Bootstrap program code and error messages. Note: FAT32 boot program code continues at sector 2, bytes 0–509. |
| 510–511 | Signature value; 2 bytes and should be 0x55AA. |

The second major physical feature of the FAT file system is the file allocation table, which begins with the sector that follows the last sector of the reserved area. By default, there are usually two FATs (FAT1 and FAT2) in a FAT file system, as shown in Figure 2.5. The exact number, the size of a FAT, and the total size for all FATs are specified in the boot sector as described earlier.

The FAT, as previously mentioned, has two purposes. One is to account for the allocation status of a cluster, and the other is to find the clusters that follow the starting cluster (if any) for any given file or directory.

FAT1 starts immediately following the reserved sectors. FAT2, a duplicate of FAT1, is a default configuration and immediately follows FAT1. A second FAT (FAT2) is, however, not required, and a system could be configured to have only one FAT. FAT1 and FAT2 are equal in size and normally a duplicate image of each other.

Each cluster on the file system will be represented sequentially starting with cluster 0 in the table, with each entry or array of bits depending on which version of FAT is used. For FAT12, each entry is 12 bits; for FAT16, each entry is 16 bits; and for FAT32, each entry is 32 bits, with 28 used and 4 in reserve. Remember that cluster 2 is the first addressable cluster in all versions of FAT. With FAT12/16, cluster 2 starts immediately following the fixed-length root directory. With FAT32, cluster 2 starts immediately following the end of FAT.

**FIGURE 2.6**    FAT entry for nonaddressable cluster 0, which contains the value for the volume media type, in this case 0xF8

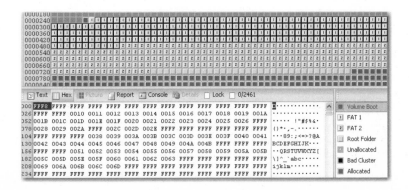

The first 16-bit FAT entry in a FAT16 file system is for nonaddressable cluster 0, which is used to store the value for the media type (see Figure 2.6). This value should match the value at byte 21 in the boot sector (0xF8 should be used on nonremovable media and 0xF0 should be used for removable media), as shown in Figure 2.7.

**FIGURE 2.7**   Byte offset 21 in the boot sector should and does match value in cluster entry 0, which in this case is 0xF8.

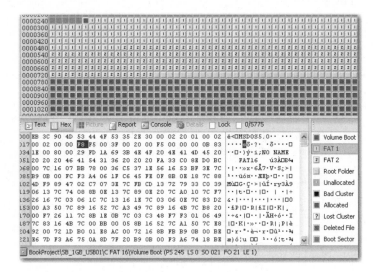

The FAT entry for nonaddressable cluster 1, shown in Figure 2.8, is used to store the value for the "dirty status" of the file system. If a file system was not properly "dismounted," usually from an improper system shutdown, this value is used to track that status, causing the OS to prompt the user to check the file system during a reboot. This value may or may not be accurate in this regard.

**FIGURE 2.8**   FAT entry for nonaddressable cluster 1, which contains the value for the "dirty status" of the file system

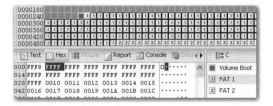

The third 16-bit entry in the FAT16 table represents cluster 2, which is the first addressable cluster in the FAT file system. For this entry and all others that follow in FAT1, certain values will be present:

1. Unallocated, represented by the value of 0, meaning that the cluster is available for use by the operating system to store a file or directory.

2. Allocated; its value will be represented by the next cluster used by the file, unless it is the last cluster used by the file (see item 3).

3. Allocated; the last cluster used by the file; will be populated by the end-of-file marker, which is a value greater than 0xFF8 for FAT12, greater than 0xFFF8 for FAT16, and greater than 0xFFFF FFF8 for FAT32.

4. Bad cluster; not available for use by the operating system. This value will be 0xFF7 for FAT12, 0xFFF7 for FAT16, and 0xFFFF FFF7 for FAT32.

The third major physical component of the FAT file system is the data area. The data area contains the clusters used to store directory entries and their data.

With FAT12/16, the root directory is the first part of the data area, which immediately follows at the end of the FAT area. The root directory is a fixed-length feature with FAT12/16 systems; a maximum of 32 sectors are allowed for it. Each directory entry is 32 bytes in length. We cover its structure in depth later in this chapter. Because a root directory in FAT12/16 systems has a maximum of 32 sectors, the number of bytes available to the root directory is 16,384 bytes (32 sectors × 512 bytes / sector). Since each directory entry is a fixed-length entry consisting of 32 bytes, the maximum number of directory entries in a FAT12/16 system is 512 entries (16,384 bytes / 32 bytes/entry). Cluster 2 immediately follows the root directory in a FAT12/16 system, followed by all the clusters contained within the defined partition.

As computing grew in the mid 1990s, the limitations of FAT12/16 file systems resulted in the development of the FAT32 file system. From our previous discussions, you already know that FAT32 allows for a greater number of clusters than its FAT12/16 predecessors. FAT32 also overcame the limitation of 512 entries in the root directory by making it "dynamic" in that its size is not fixed and it can appear anywhere in the data area. When you examine the data area of a FAT32 system, you will see a difference at the very beginning. With FAT12/16, cluster 2 started after the fixed-length root directory, as shown in Figure 2.9. With FAT32, cluster 2 starts immediately following the end of the FAT area, as shown in Figure 2.10. Interestingly, even though the root directory can occur anywhere in the data area of a FAT32 file system, it most always begins with cluster 2.

As previously mentioned, the data area contains the clusters that include the directory entries and the contents of the files and directories. FAT12/16 file systems keep the root directory outside and prior to the cluster structure, which fixes its size and imposes a limitation on the number of directory entries it can hold to 512 entries. FAT32 places the root directory inside the cluster area and thereby imposes no limit on its size.

**FIGURE 2.9** FAT12/16 physical layout, showing the fixed-length root directory immediately following the FAT

Root Directory, marked with green blocks, is 32 sectors long, its length is fixed, and it starts immediately following the FAT area. No cluster numbering is yet assigned.

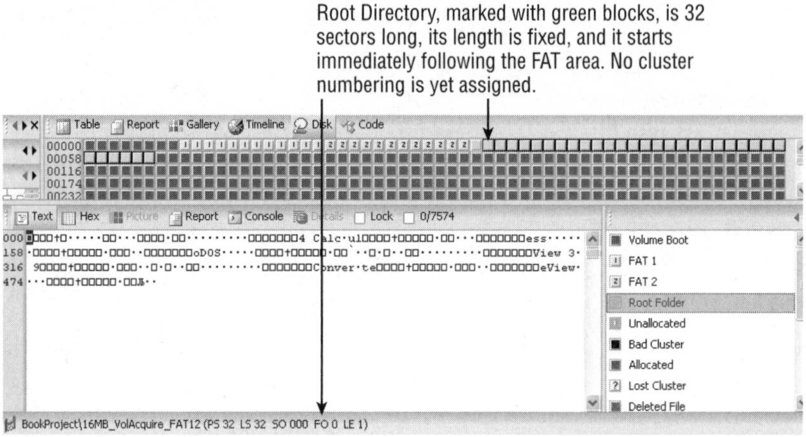

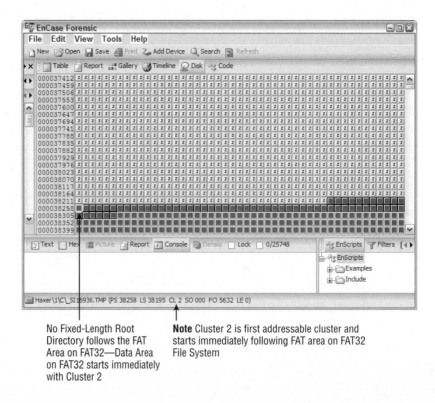

**FIGURE 2.10** FAT32 physical layout, showing cluster 2 starting immediately after the FAT

No Fixed-Length Root Directory follows the FAT Area on FAT32—Data Area on FAT32 starts immediately with Cluster 2

**Note** Cluster 2 is first addressable cluster and starts immediately following FAT area on FAT32 File System

Thus far, we have mentioned directory entries, but we haven't yet fully described their function, let alone their internal structures. The directory entry is a critical component of the FAT file system. For every file and directory within a partition, a directory entry exists. Regardless of which version of FAT is used, each directory entry is 32 bytes long. Within these 32 bytes, the name of the file or directory, its starting cluster, and its length are described, along with other metadata or attributes. These directory entries are found in the cluster(s) allocated to the file's parent directory.

In this and most systems, the parent directory keeps track of its children, be they files or subdirectories. If parent directory structures are deleted, children can become orphaned and thus we have lost files or folders, which are files and folders for which no parent directory structure can be found.

A 32-byte directory has sufficient space to name a file or folder (directory) using an "8 dot 3" DOS naming convention, with a maximum of eight characters for the file name and three characters for its extension. No "dot" or "period" actually exists in the directory entry. Should a long file name exist, an attribute set in the metadata is created and a series of 32-byte entries, sufficient to contain the long file name, will precede its main 32-byte entry. The data structure for the FAT directory structure is displayed in Table 2.4. Table 2.5 shows the bit-flag values for the various file or directory attributes.

**TABLE 2.4**    Data Structure for FAT Directory Entry

| Byte Offset (Decimal) | Description |
| --- | --- |
| 0 | First character of the file name or status byte |
| 1–7 | Characters 2–8 of the file name |
| 8–10 | Three characters of the file extension |
| 11 | Attributes (detailed in Table 2.5) |
| 12–13 | Reserved |
| 14–17 | Created time and date of file; stored as MS-DOS 32-bit date/time stamp. |
| 18–19 | Last accessed date; no time! |
| 20–21 | Two high bytes of FAT32 starting cluster; FAT12/16 will have zeros. |
| 22–25 | Last written time and date of file; stored as MS-DOS 32-bit date/time stamp. |
| 26–27 | Starting cluster for FAT12/16; two low bytes of the starting cluster for FAT32. |
| 28–31 | Size in bytes of file (32-bit integer). Note: will be 0 for directories! |

Determining the starting cluster for a FAT12/16 partition is a snap. You merely decode the 2 bytes at byte offsets 26–27 as a 16-bit little endian integer and you have the value. When the partition is FAT32, things get interesting. The data you need to make this determination is in two different locations and must be combined in the correct order to arrive at the correct value. To illustrate how this is done, consider the hex values below as constituting a FAT32 directory entry: 48 49 42 45 52 46 49 4C 53 59 53 26 18 02 C2 4C 25 30 26 30 **12 00** 6A 4A 26 30 **03 00** 00 80 F8 0F. The bolded values constitute the high bytes and low bytes, respectively, of this 32-bit value. To properly combine and calculate this value, you must enter the hex values into a scientific calculator in the following order: 00 12 00 03. This converts the stored values to little endian. The resulting decimal value for this starting cluster would be 1,179,651.

**TABLE  2.5**    Bit Flag Values for Attribute Field at Byte Offset 11

| Bit Flag Values (Binary) | Description |
| --- | --- |
| 0000 0001 | Read only |
| 0000 0010 | Hidden file |
| 0000 0100 | System file |
| 0000 1000 | Volume label |
| 0000 1111 | Long file name |
| 0001 0000 | Directory |
| 0010 0000 | Archive |

Attributes bit flag values can be combined, and the resultant hex value will reflect those combinations. If a file were a read-only hidden system file, it would have the following bit flags turned on: 0000 0111. The hex value representing such a combination would be 0x07.

When long file names are used, ones that exceed the length of the DOS 8 dot 3 limit, special entries are created in the directory entry to accommodate file names up to 255 characters in length (including the length of the path). When a long file name is created, an "8 dot 3 alias" is created as the file name in the 32-byte entry. It is done according to the following scheme (Windows 9x/Me):

1.  The first three characters of the extension (following the dot) are used as the extension of the 8 dot 3 alias.

2. The first six characters of the file name (spaces ignored) are rendered to uppercase and become the first six characters of the 8 dot 3 alias file name. Any "illegal" DOS 8 dot 3 characters are converted to underscores.

3. Two characters are added to the six characters. Character 7 is a tilde (~). Character 8 is the numeral *1*. If a file exists by the same alias name, the *1* sequences to *2* and so forth until a number is assigned for which there is no duplicate alias file name.

If you were to create a file named "SQL + Oracle Hacks.hash", the resultant 8 dot 3 alias file name would be "SQL_OR~1.HAS". The spaces are ignored, and the +, which is illegal, becomes an underscore (_). All characters become uppercase. After the "R" in Oracle, the six-character limit has been reached and the following two characters, ~1, are appended. The alias extension, HAS, is the first three characters of the long file name extension.

> Windows NT/2K/XP handles alias creation with a slightly different scheme. The first six legal DOS characters in the long file name are used as the alias; they are appended with *~1* if the first six characters are unique. If not, *~2*, and so forth, is used. For the extension, the first three legal characters of the LFN extension are used for the alias extension. As if that wasn't enough, yet another scheme is applied by NT/2K/XP whereby the first two characters of the LFN are taken for the first two characters of the alias. The LFN is hashed, and the next four characters are the hexadecimal values of that hash. Characters 7 and 8 are *~5*. The *~5* remains constant for all subsequent aliases, with only the hash values and, hence the hex values, changing.

The long file name itself is stored in a series of 32-byte entries that immediately precede the directory entry containing the 8 dot 3 alias. The long file name is stored in accordance with the convention described in Table 2.6.

**TABLE 2.6** Long File Name Storage Scheme

| Byte Offset | Description |
| --- | --- |
| 0 | Sequence number used to link together multiple LFN entries. 0xE5 if deleted or unallocated. Typically the first LNF entry above the alias 8 dot3 entry contains the beginning of the LFN, and they build on top of each other until the end is reached. |
| 1–10 | LFN characters 1–5 in Unicode |
| 11 | Attributes |
| 12 | Reserved |

**TABLE 2.6**   Long File Name Storage Scheme *(continued)*

| Byte Offset | Description |
| --- | --- |
| 13 | Checksum |
| 14–25 | LFN characters 6–11 in Unicode |
| 26–27 | Reserved |
| 28–31 | LFN characters 12–13 in Unicode |

Directory entry raw data can be viewed, analyzed, and bookmarked in EnCase. For any file of interest, determine its parent folder and place that parent folder in the right window, placing "focus" on it by highlighting it, as shown in Figure 2.11. In the bottom pane, you can choose either the text or hex view. FAT directory entries, shown in Figure 2.12, will appear in red when viewed in EnCase.

**FIGURE 2.11**   Parent folder for file of interest

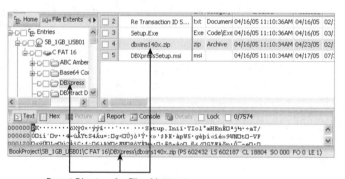

Parent Directory for File of Interest

The entries shown in Figure 2.12 are displaying with 32 bytes per line. Since each entry is 32 bytes in length, each directory entry sits on a line by itself, making the data easy to see and analyze. This view didn't magically appear; rather it was created using EnCase's Text Styles feature. The feature is accessed by selecting View ➢ Text Styles. In the right pane, right-click and choose New. This will present you with a dialog box for creating a new text style. Use the settings shown in Figure 2.13. On the Code Page tab, select Other and then select ISO 8859-1 Latin I for the code page. When done, click OK and select your newly created code page for viewing directory entries. When you use this custom view, all of your directory entries will appear on a separate line.

**FIGURE 2.12**     Directory entries in bottom pane shown in red of parent folder selected in right pane

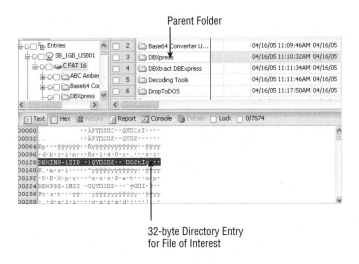

**FIGURE 2.13**     Creating a custom text view for viewing 32-byte directory entries

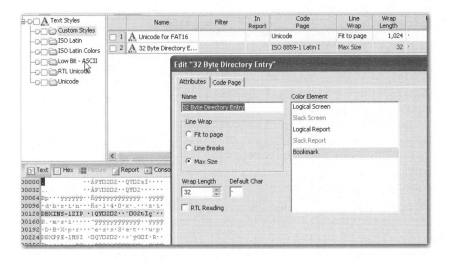

At this point, you could examine directory entries of interest for the selected parent folder. You could bookmark individual byte values within any directory entry using the byte offsets and descriptors in Table 2.3. While very precise and demonstrative of your forensic prowess, it is painstakingly slow and tedious work. Alternatively, if you were to "sweep" the 32 bytes making up the directory entry, bookmark it, and for a View Type choose DOS Directory Entry under the Windows folder, EnCase would decode the information for you and allow you to have the information in a bookmark, as shown in Figures 2.14 and 2.15.

**FIGURE 2.14** A 32-byte directory entry, selected, bookmarked, and viewed as a DOS directory entry—EnCase decodes the directory entry information and places it in a bookmark.

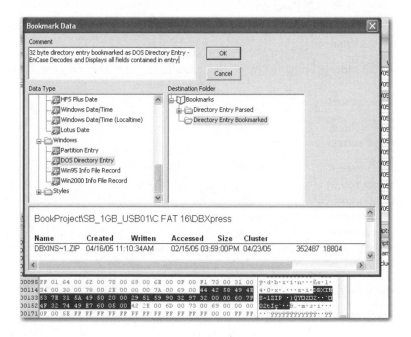

**FIGURE 2.15** EnCase Table view showing attributes from a directory entry that match information decoded in Figure 2.14

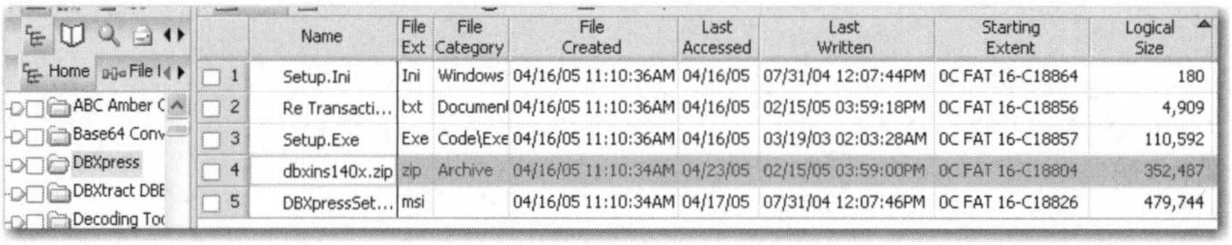

Another alternative for bookmarking directory entry information is to simply bookmark a file of interest and choose the various directory entry attributes to show in the resulting report, as shown in Figure 2.16.

## EXERCISE 2.1

### Viewing FAT Entries

In this exercise, we will show you how to locate and view FAT directory entries. All you need to follow along is any device formatted with FAT.

1. Preview a USB thumb drive (any FAT version) by turning on the write-protect switch and mounting it in Windows.

2. Launch EnCase (dongle required) and open a new case in EnCase, accepting the default values.

3. Click Add Device; in the screen that follows, locate your USB drive, place a blue check next to it, and click Next, then Finish. Your thumb drive should be visible in the left pane as a device. Make certain the file system is visible.

4. Find a file of interest in a folder somewhere. Note carefully this file's parent folder and path to that folder. You want to put the parent folder in the right pane. To do this, place the parent folder's parent in the left pane. If its parent is root, then place your focus on the root level in the left pane. When you see your file of interest's parent folder in the right pane, place your cursor on that parent folder in the right pane. The data for that parent folder is now in the bottom pane. In the bottom pane, select the Text View tab. The data for this parent folder should be in red.

5. We see our data in red, but it is not formatted into nice 32-byte wide entries. Let's fix that.

6. Under View choose Text Styles. In the left pane, right-click at the root level of the folders and select New Folder. Name the new folder "custom". Place your cursor on the Custom Folder, right-click, and choose New. You are given a pane to create a new text style. Use the settings in Figure 2.13. On the Code Page tab, select Other and select ISO 8859-1 Latin I for the code page. When done, click OK.

7. Go to any other text style and then come back to the one you just created. It acts to refresh.

8. Go back to the Cases➢Entries➢ Home tab and locate your parent folder in the right pane. Make sure you have the Text View in the bottom pane. You should see your entries in nice 32-byte rows.

9. With your cursor, select the data for the 32-byte entry for your file of interest, as shown in Figure 2.12. Right-click on the selected 32-byte entry and choose Bookmark Data. Under Data Type, choose Windows and then DOS Directory Entry. The directory information for your file is decoded and displayed.

10. Use this technique to bookmark directory information for a directory entry whose starting cluster is overwritten and in use by another file.

**FIGURE 2.16** Bookmark of file of interest with directory entry data showing in the report

```
File of Interest Bookmarked

Name    dbxins140x.zip
File Ext zip
File Category    Archive
File Created    04/16/05 11:10:34AM
Last Accessed  04/23/05
Last Written    02/15/05 03:59:00PM
Starting Extent  0C FAT 16-C18804
Logical Size    352,487
```

Bookmarking the file and showing its directory attributes in the report is the method most commonly used to report this information. However, you can't use this method when the file has been deleted and its starting cluster is in use by another file. EnCase is showing you the directory entry for such a file, but has no data to go with it as it is in use by another file. Any attempt to bookmark such a file will result in a bookmark of the file that has overwritten the data. When you encounter such a situation, having the knowledge and skills to bookmark the "raw data" is most useful!

# The Function of FAT

Thus far, we have thoroughly dissected the physical features of the FAT file systems and delineated its underlying structures. While examining these structures, some of the functions started to emerge. In this section, we describe how those structures function in detail as they interact with the operating system to read, write, and delete files.

From our previous discussions, we understand that the purpose of the FAT is twofold. One, whenever a file or directory's contents exceed one cluster, FAT tracks the sequence of clusters that constitute that file or directory. Two, FAT tracks which clusters are available to be used by the operating system, marking bad clusters so they won't be used and ensuring that clusters allocated and in use by files and directories aren't overwritten.

Also from our previous discussions, we understand that the purpose of the directory entry is to track every file and directory in a partition. It does so by storing its status, its name, its starting cluster, and its length in bytes, as well as other file metadata or attributes. Let's now examine how those functions interact with our operating system.

Our first task is discovering what takes place during the simple act of reading a small file that is contained within one cluster. When the operating system calls for a file to be read, it is called by file name and path. The path leads to the file name stored in the directory entry. It is the information stored in the directory entry that allows the operating system to begin to locate the data that constitutes this file. The file name for our example will be autorun.inf, which is located in a folder named New Report, which in turn is contained in the root directory of a FAT16 partition. The operating system looks in the parent folder and reads the directory information. Figure 2.17 shows the information contained in the directory entry.

**FIGURE 2.17**    Directory information for the file to be located and read in our example

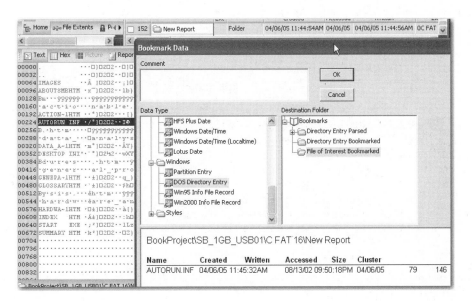

According to the directory entry, autorun.inf starts in cluster 146 and has a size of 79 bytes. The operating system goes to cluster 146 and starts to read the data, knowing its length is 79 bytes. After reading 79 bytes of data, it stops because the end of the data for the file has been reached. Any other data in the cluster is ignored since it is not part of the file. Seventy-nine bytes is the file's logical size. A file will also have a physical size, which is the size of the clusters it occupies. Since it occupies one cluster, its physical size is 16,383 bytes.

Figure 2.18 shows the FAT entry for cluster 146. Its value is 0xFFFF, which for a FAT16 partition means that cluster is marked as End of File (EOF) since it is greater than 0xFFF8. This particular FAT16 partition uses 32 sectors to constitute one cluster. One cluster will therefore hold 16,384 bytes of data before requiring an additional cluster, and thus 79 bytes fit easily in one cluster. Figure 2.19 shows cluster 146, which contains the file's data with 79 bytes selected.

In the previous example, the data was contained in one cluster. In our next example, the data will not fit in one cluster and will span several clusters. When this happens, the FAT is necessary to link together the clusters. Let's see how it actually works with real data.

Figure 2.20 shows the file agency.jpg having a starting cluster of 39 and a length of 53,745 bytes. We know that each cluster consists of 32 sectors on this particular partition, and therefore one cluster can hold 16,384 bytes. To find out how many clusters a file will occupy, we divide the file size by the number of bytes in a cluster or, in this case, 53,745 bytes divided by 16,384 bytes per cluster, which equals 3.28 clusters (and some change). Since partial clusters are not allowed, this file will require four clusters to hold its data. We will expect the file to completely occupy all of the first three clusters ($3 \times 16,384 = 49,152$ bytes) and the first 4,593 bytes of the fourth cluster (53,745 total bytes less 49,152 stored in first three clusters = 4,593 bytes). To check our reasoning and our math, EnCase Version 5 has a File Extents tab. By selecting our file of interest in the right pane and choosing the File Extents tab in the left pane, the right pane returns the File Extents information for our file, shown in Figure 2.21.

**FIGURE 2.18**    FAT entry for cluster 146, showing the cluster marked as EOF

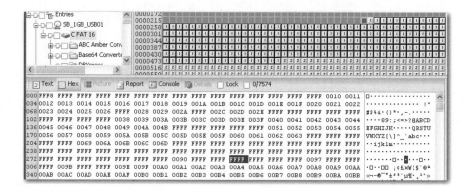

**FIGURE 2.19**    79 Bytes of data found in cluster 146 that constitute the file autorun.inf

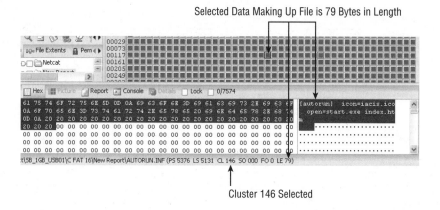

**FIGURE 2.20**    File agency.jpg has a starting cluster of 39 and a file length of 53,745 bytes.

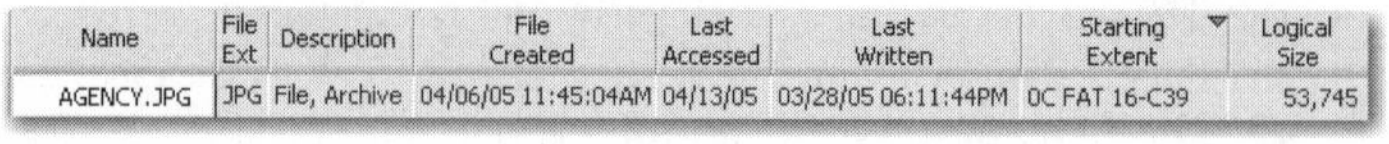

| Name | File Ext | Description | File Created | Last Accessed | Last Written | Starting Extent | Logical Size |
|---|---|---|---|---|---|---|---|
| AGENCY.JPG | JPG | File, Archive | 04/06/05 11:45:04AM | 04/13/05 | 03/28/05 06:11:44PM | 0C FAT 16-C39 | 53,745 |

**FIGURE 2.21**    The File Extents tab shows agency.jpg starts at cluster 39 and occupies four clusters and 128 sectors (4 × 32).

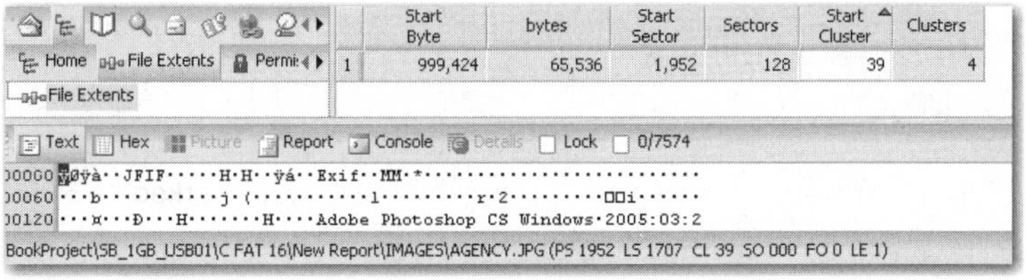

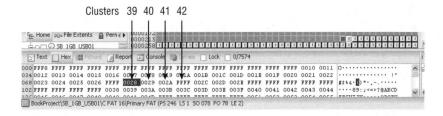

If we go to the FAT entry for cluster 39, since we know the file spans several clusters, we would expect cluster 39's entry to tell us where to find the next cluster for the file. Figure 2.22 shows the entry for cluster 39 as 0x0028, which is decimal value 40, meaning that cluster 40 is the next cluster in the chain. Looking at cluster 40, we see it has a value of 0x0029 (decimal 41), meaning that the next cluster in the chain is 41. Looking cluster 41, we find it has a value of 0x002A (decimal 42). Looking at cluster 42, we find it has a value of 0xFFFF, meaning it is the EOF. Since this is the fourth cluster in the chain, we expect the file to end there and to be marked as EOF. Table 2.7 reinforces and explains in chart form what we see in the raw data.

**FIGURE 2.22**    The FAT table shows cluster 39 (0x0028 and selected); the next three clusters (40, 41, and 42) constitute the remainder of the chain of clusters comprising the file agency.jpg.

**TABLE 2.7**    FAT Entries for File agency.jpg

| FAT Cluster # | Value Hex | Value Decimal | Meaning | Bytes of File Contained In Cluster |
|---|---|---|---|---|
| 39 | 0x0028 | 40 | Next cluster holding file's data is cluster 40 | 16,384 |

**TABLE 2.7**    FAT Entries for File agency.jpg *(continued)*

| FAT Cluster # | Value Hex | Value Decimal | Meaning | Bytes of File Contained In Cluster |
|---|---|---|---|---|
| 40 | 0x0028 | 41 | Next cluster holding file's data is cluster 41 | 16,384 |
| 41 | 0x002A | 42 | Next cluster holding file's data is cluster 42 | 16,384 |
| 42 | 0xFFFF | 65,535 | Greater than 0xFFF8 (65,528), meaning it is EOF | 4,593 |
| | | | | 53,745 Total Bytes |

Now that we understand how the directory entries work in conjunction with the FAT to read files and have analyzed this process using raw data in an actual FAT, writing a file is just an extension of what we already know. To get us started, we will use the values shown in Tables 2.8 and 2.9 as our hypothetical FAT and directory entries to write a file.

**TABLE 2.8**    File Allocation Table (FAT16: 1 Cluster = 8 Sectors = 4,096 bytes)

| 0 | 1 | 2 | 3 | 4 | 5 | 6 | 7 | 8 | 9 | 10 | 11 | 12 | 13 |
|---|---|---|---|---|---|---|---|---|---|---|---|---|---|
| ** | ** | E | 4 | E | E | 8 | E | E | 0 | B | 0 | 0 | 0 |

| 14 | 15 | 16 | 17 | 18 | 19 | 20 | 21 | 22 | 23 | 24 | 25 | 26 | 27 |
|---|---|---|---|---|---|---|---|---|---|---|---|---|---|
| 0 | 0 | 0 | 0 | 0 | 0 | 0 | B | 0 | 0 | 0 | 0 | 0 | 0 |

Bold numbers indicate cluster numbers (they don't exist in a real FAT!)
E = End of File  0 = Available  B = Bad Cluster
** Remember that the first addressable cluster is cluster 2, but the FAT array starts with entries for cluster 0 and cluster 1. The values for these two entries do not relate to cluster usage, but are used for other "housekeeping" chores as already described.

**TABLE 2.9**    Table of Directory Entries

| File Name | Extension | Created | Accessed | Written | Start Cluster | Length |
|-----------|-----------|---------|----------|---------|---------------|--------|
| file1234 | txt | 6/5/2005 1745 hrs | 6/5/2005 | 6/5/2005 1745 hrs | 2 | 4,095 |
| file5678 | txt | 6/5/2005 1756 hrs | 6/5/2005 | 6/5/2005 1756 hrs | 3 | 4,097 |
| Fileabcd | txt | 6/5/2005 1800 hrs | 6/5/2005 | 6/5/2005 1800 hrs | 5 | 4,096 |
| Filewxyz | txt | 6/5/2005 1815 hrs | 6/5/2005 | 6/5/2005 1921 hrs | 6 | 8,000 |
| file8765 | txt | 6/5/2005 1820 hrs | 6/5/2005 | 6/5/2005 1820 hrs | 7 | 286 |

To summarize the above FAT table and directory entries, the following are true:

1. File1234.txt is 4,095 bytes in length and starts with cluster 2. As it fits within a cluster (a cluster holds 4,096 bytes), only one cluster is needed and the entry in the FAT for cluster 2 is marked as EOF.

2. File5678.txt is 4,097 bytes in length and starts with cluster 3. As it exceeds one cluster by one byte, it requires a second cluster to hold its contents. The FAT entry for cluster 3 is "4", meaning that cluster 4 holds the one byte needed to hold the data. As the data ends in cluster 4, cluster 4 contains the EOF marker.

3. Fileabcd.txt is 4,096 bytes in length and starts in cluster 5. As its contents fit exactly in one cluster, no other clusters are needed and cluster 5 is marked as EOF.

4. Filewxyz.txt is 8,000 bytes in length and starts in cluster 6. Eight thousand bytes divided by 4,096 bytes (the bytes in one cluster) is 1.95, meaning this file will take two clusters to hold its data. We would expect the entry for cluster 6 to contain the value for the second and final cluster, which is cluster 8. The entry for cluster 8 is marked as EOF. This file is fragmented, meaning its data is not contained in contiguous clusters, since its data is contained in cluster 6 and 8. Cluster 7 holds data for another file.

5. File8765.txt is 286 bytes and starts in cluster 7. Its contents fit easily in one cluster, and cluster 7 is marked as EOF.

To write a file on this FAT16 file system, the file is given a name either by an application or the user. We'll create our first file and call it yourfile.txt. This file has a length of 7,580 bytes. We will write this file using Tables 2.7 and 2.8 and make the necessary writes or changes to Tables 2.9 and 2.10.

Our operating system first seeks an available cluster to which to write the data. Cluster 9 is available and will be the starting cluster for our data. As this file will require two clusters, the operating system seeks the next available cluster. As cluster 10 is marked Bad, cluster 11 is the next available. Thus the operating system stores the data in clusters 9 and 11, marking the FAT entry for cluster 9 with the value for cluster 11, and cluster 11 is marked as EOF. See these entries in Table 2.10. A directory entry is written in the appropriate parent directory indicating the file's name, starting cluster, length, and other metadata or attributes. See Table 2.11 for this entry. As our file is contained in two noncontiguous clusters (9 and 11), it is a fragmented file.

**TABLE 2.10**    File Allocation Table (FAT16: 1 Cluster = 8 Sectors = 4,096 bytes)

| 0 | 1 | 2 | 3 | 4 | 5 | 6 | 7 | 8 | 9 | 10 | 11 | 12 | 13 |
|---|---|---|---|---|---|---|---|---|---|----|----|----|----|
| ** | ** | E | 4 | E | E | 8 | E | E | 11 | B | E | 0 | 0 |

| 14 | 15 | 16 | 17 | 18 | 19 | 20 | 21 | 22 | 23 | 24 | 25 | 26 | 27 |
|----|----|----|----|----|----|----|----|----|----|----|----|----|----|
| 0 | 0 | 0 | 0 | 0 | 0 | 0 | B | 0 | 0 | 0 | 0 | 0 | 0 |

**TABLE 2.11**    Table of Directory Entries

| File Name | Extension | Created | Accessed | Written | Start Cluster | Length |
|-----------|-----------|---------|----------|---------|---------------|--------|
| file1234 | txt | 6/5/2005 1745 hrs | 6/5/2005 | 6/5/2005 1745 hrs | 2 | 4,095 |
| file5678 | txt | 6/5/2005 1756 hrs | 6/5/2005 | 6/5/2005 1756 hrs | 3 | 4,097 |
| fileabcd | txt | 6/5/2005 1800 hrs | 6/5/2005 | 6/5/2005 1800 hrs | 5 | 4,096 |
| filewxyz | txt | 6/5/2005 1815 hrs | 6/5/2005 | 6/5/2005 1921 hrs | 6 | 8,000 |
| file8765 | txt | 6/5/2005 1820 hrs | 6/5/2005 | 6/5/2005 1820 hrs | 7 | 286 |
| yourfile | txt | 9/5/2005 1712 hrs | 9/5/2005 | 9/5/2005 1712 hrs | 9 | 7,580 |

The first character of the file or directory name in a directory entry has a name and purpose. It is called the *status* byte. When in use by a file or directory, its purpose is somewhat obscured, because it is seen simply as part of the file or directory name. When a file or directory is deleted, its purpose becomes clear; the first character of the file or directory is changed to 0xE5 to signify to the operating system that the entry is deleted and to ignore and not display it to the user. Aside from making changes to the FAT to mark the clusters as unallocated, that is all there is to deleting a file. Let's delete a file in our FAT16 file system and see how it works.

Using Tables 2.12 and 2.13, we are going to delete file5678.txt. To do so, we simply change the first character of the file name in the directory entry to 0xE5. In our hypothetical table, the 0xE5 takes up four characters, but in a real system, 0xE5 is one byte as was the character it replaced. In a real directory entry, *f*, which is 0x66, is replaced by 0xE5. To complete the deletion, we go to FAT entry of the file's starting cluster, which is cluster 3. Cluster 3 contains a value of 4, which is noted by the OS. Cluster 3 is marked with a 0, making it available for allocation. Cluster 4 contains an EOF and the OS knows this is the end of the cluster sequence, so it marks it with a 0, making it available for allocation, and then stops. The file is deleted as far as the operating system is concerned. Aside from the first character of the directory, the remaining 31 bytes are untouched. The data in clusters 3 and 4 remains untouched. As clusters 3 and 4 are marked with zeros, they are available to hold the contents of another file and thus can be completely or partially overwritten. As they stand, however, they are easily and completely recoverable.

**TABLE 2.12**   File Allocation Table (FAT16: 1 Cluster = 8 Sectors = 4,096 bytes)

| 0 | 1 | 2 | 3 | 4 | 5 | 6 | 7 | 8 | 9 | 10 | 11 | 12 | 13 |
|---|---|---|---|---|---|---|---|---|---|----|----|----|----|
| ** | ** | E | 0 | 0 | E | 8 | E | E | 11 | B | E | 0 | 0 |

| 14 | 15 | 16 | 17 | 18 | 19 | 20 | 21 | 22 | 23 | 24 | 25 | 26 | 27 |
|----|----|----|----|----|----|----|----|----|----|----|----|----|----|
| 0 | 0 | 0 | 0 | 0 | 0 | 0 | B | 0 | 0 | 0 | 0 | 0 | 0 |

**TABLE 2.13**   Table of Directory Entries

| File Name | Extension | Created | Accessed | Written | Start Cluster | Length |
|-----------|-----------|---------|----------|---------|---------------|--------|
| file1234 | txt | 6/5/2005 1745 hrs | 6/5/2005 | 6/5/2005 1745 hrs | 2 | 4,095 |
| 0xE5ile5678 | txt | 6/5/2005 1756 hrs | 6/5/2005 | 6/5/2005 1756 hrs | 3 | 4,097 |

**TABLE 2.13** Table of Directory Entries *(continued)*

| File Name | Extension | Created | Accessed | Written | Start Cluster | Length |
|-----------|-----------|---------|----------|---------|---------------|--------|
| fileabcd | txt | 6/5/2005 1800 hrs | 6/5/2005 | 6/5/2005 1800 hrs | 5 | 4,096 |
| filewxyz | txt | 6/5/2005 1815 hrs | 6/5/2005 | 6/5/2005 1921 hrs | 6 | 8,000 |
| file8765 | txt | 6/5/2005 1820 hrs | 6/5/2005 | 6/5/2005 1820 hrs | 7 | 286 |
| yourfile | txt | 9/5/2005 1712 hrs | 9/5/2005 | 9/5/2005 1712 hrs | 9 | 7,580 |

To undelete or recover a file, you simply reverse the process by which it was deleted. In Tables 2.14 and 2.15, we will undelete this file. We start the process by going to the directory entry. We change the 0xE5 to the original character if known, a best guess if unknown, or use some standard character, such as an underscore. If the file has a long file name and its entries are intact, the original character can be derived from that source. In our example, we are going to change the first character to an underscore character (see Table 2.15).

The next step in the process is to go to the FAT entry for the starting cluster for this file, which from the directory entry we know to be 3. This file uses two clusters, so the value that must be entered for cluster 3's entry must be the next cluster in the chain. The next available cluster after cluster 3 is cluster 4. Thus a value of 4 is entered for cluster 3 and an EOF mark is made for cluster 4's entry. At this point, the file has been successfully recovered. This is the basic manner in which EnCase will recover files automatically for you.

**TABLE 2.14** File Allocation Table (FAT16: 1 Cluster = 8 Sectors = 4,096 bytes)

| 0 | 1 | 2 | 3 | 4 | 5 | 6 | 7 | 8 | 9 | 10 | 11 | 12 | 13 |
|---|---|---|---|---|---|---|---|---|---|----|----|----|----|
| ** | ** | E | 4 | E | E | 8 | E | E | 11 | B | E | 0 | 0 |

| 14 | 15 | 16 | 17 | 18 | 19 | 20 | 21 | 22 | 23 | 24 | 25 | 26 | 27 |
|----|----|----|----|----|----|----|----|----|----|----|----|----|----|
| 0 | 0 | 0 | 0 | 0 | 0 | 0 | B | 0 | 0 | 0 | 0 | 0 | 0 |

**TABLE 2.15**  Table of Directory Entries

| File Name | Extension | Created | Accessed | Written | Start Cluster | Length |
|-----------|-----------|---------|----------|---------|---------------|--------|
| file1234 | txt | 6/5/2005 1745 hrs | 6/5/2005 | 6/5/2005 1745 hrs | 2 | 4,095 |
| _ile5678 | txt | 6/5/2005 1756 hrs | 6/5/2005 | 6/5/2005 1756 hrs | 3 | 4,097 |
| fileabcd | txt | 6/5/2005 1800 hrs | 6/5/2005 | 6/5/2005 1800 hrs | 5 | 4,096 |
| filewxyz | txt | 6/5/2005 1815 hrs | 6/5/2005 | 6/5/2005 1921 hrs | 6 | 8,000 |
| file8765 | txt | 6/5/2005 1820 hrs | 6/5/2005 | 6/5/2005 1820 hrs | 7 | 286 |
| yourfile | txt | 9/5/2005 1712 hrs | 9/5/2005 | 9/5/2005 1712 hrs | 9 | 7,580 |

The undelete process is not perfect. The file filewxyz.txt is fragmented, occupying two noncontiguous clusters, which are clusters 6 and 8. This file has been deleted in Tables 2.16 and 2.17. The first character of the name in its directory entry has been changed to 0xE5, and the FAT entries for clusters 6 and 8 have been changed to 0, making them available for allocation by the system.

The file file8765.txt occupies a single cluster, which is cluster 7. This file has also been deleted. and that deletion is reflected in Tables 2.16 and 2.17. The first character of the name in its directory entry has been changed to 0xE5, and the FAT entry for cluster 7 has been changed to 0, marking it as available for allocation by the system.

**TABLE 2.16**  File Allocation Table (FAT16: 1 Cluster = 8 Sectors = 4,096 bytes)

| 0 | 1 | 2 | 3 | 4 | 5 | 6 | 7 | 8 | 9 | 10 | 11 | 12 | 13 |
|---|---|---|---|---|---|---|---|---|---|----|----|----|----|
| ** | ** | E | 4 | E | E | 0 | 0 | 0 | 11 | B | E | 0 | 0 |

| 14 | 15 | 16 | 17 | 18 | 19 | 20 | 21 | 22 | 23 | 24 | 25 | 26 | 27 |
|----|----|----|----|----|----|----|----|----|----|----|----|----|----|
| 0 | 0 | 0 | 0 | 0 | 0 | 0 | B | 0 | 0 | 0 | 0 | 0 | 0 |

**TABLE 2.17**   Table of Directory Entries

| File Name | Extension | Created | Accessed | Written | Start Cluster | Length |
|---|---|---|---|---|---|---|
| file1234 | txt | 6/5/2005 1745 hrs | 6/5/2005 | 6/5/2005 1745 hrs | 2 | 4,095 |
| _ile5678 | txt | 6/5/2005 1756 hrs | 6/5/2005 | 6/5/2005 1756 hrs | 3 | 4,097 |
| fileabcd | txt | 6/5/2005 1800 hrs | 6/5/2005 | 6/5/2005 1800 hrs | 5 | 4,096 |
| 0xE5ilewxyz | txt | 6/5/2005 1815 hrs | 6/5/2005 | 6/5/2005 1921 hrs | 6 | 8,000 |
| 0xE5ile8765 | txt | 6/5/2005 1820 hrs | 6/5/2005 | 6/5/2005 1820 hrs | 7 | 286 |
| yourfile | txt | 9/5/2005 1712 hrs | 9/5/2005 | 9/5/2005 1712 hrs | 9 | 7,580 |

Clusters 6, 7, and 8 are marked with zeros, with 6 and 8 holding the data for what used to be filewxyz.txt and cluster 7 holding the data for what used to be file8765.txt. Directory entries for these two files have had their status bytes changed to 0xE5, telling the operating system that these files are deleted and to ignore them. The files are both deleted as far as the operating system is concerned.

As with any busy operating system, data is constantly changing, with data being overwritten nearly every time a new file or directory entry is written. If the directory entry for what used to be file8765.txt were overwritten, recovering filewxyz.txt could be problematic. Let's see why by looking at Tables 2.18 and 2.19.

**TABLE 2.18**   File Allocation Table (FAT16: 1 Cluster = 8 Sectors = 4,096 bytes)

| 0 | 1 | 2 | 3 | 4 | 5 | 6 | 7 | 8 | 9 | 10 | 11 | 12 | 13 |
|---|---|---|---|---|---|---|---|---|---|---|---|---|---|
| ** | ** | E | 4 | E | E | 0 | 0 | 0 | 11 | B | E | 0 | 0 |

| 14 | 15 | 16 | 17 | 18 | 19 | 20 | 21 | 22 | 23 | 24 | 25 | 26 | 27 |
|---|---|---|---|---|---|---|---|---|---|---|---|---|---|
| 0 | 0 | 0 | 0 | 0 | 0 | 0 | B | 0 | 0 | E | 0 | 0 | 0 |

**TABLE 2.19**    Table of Directory Entries

| File Name | Extension | Created | Accessed | Written | Start Cluster | Length |
|---|---|---|---|---|---|---|
| file1234 | txt | 6/5/2005 1745 hrs | 6/5/2005 | 6/5/2005 1745 hrs | 2 | 4,095 |
| _ile5678 | txt | 6/5/2005 1756 hrs | 6/5/2005 | 6/5/2005 1756 hrs | 3 | 4,097 |
| fileabcd | txt | 6/5/2005 1800 hrs | 6/5/2005 | 6/5/2005 1800 hrs | 5 | 4,096 |
| 0xE5ilewxyz | txt | 6/5/2005 1815 hrs | 6/5/2005 | 6/5/2005 1921 hrs | 6 | 8,000 |
| coolfile | txt | 9/5/2005 1820 hrs | 9/5/2005 | 9/5/2005 1820 hrs | 24 | 286 |
| yourfile | txt | 9/5/2005 1712 hrs | 9/5/2005 | 9/5/2005 1712 hrs | 9 | 7,580 |

With the directory entry for file8765.txt overwritten, there's no way to tell that its former data was and still is in cluster 7. When it comes time to recover filewxyz.txt, we can restore the first character to an underscore and go to its starting cluster, which is cluster 6. We know it occupies two clusters, and without knowledge to the contrary, we make the assumption that the next available cluster is the next cluster in the series. Thus, when we recover the clusters, we are recovering clusters 6 and 7, not 6 and 8, which are the correct clusters. The data in cluster 6, the starting cluster, is correct, but the data in cluster 7 belongs to a different file. The entry, after recovery, for cluster 6, is 7 and cluster 7 contains the EOF marker. Tables 2.20 and 2.21 show this erroneous recovery.

**TABLE 2.20**    File Allocation Table (FAT16: 1 Cluster = 8 Sectors = 4,096 bytes)

| 0 | 1 | 2 | 3 | 4 | 5 | 6 | 7 | 8 | 9 | 10 | 11 | 12 | 13 |
|---|---|---|---|---|---|---|---|---|---|---|---|---|---|
| ** | ** | E | 4 | E | E | 7 | E | 0 | 11 | B | E | 0 | 0 |

| 14 | 15 | 16 | 17 | 18 | 19 | 20 | 21 | 22 | 23 | 24 | 25 | 26 | 27 |
|---|---|---|---|---|---|---|---|---|---|---|---|---|---|
| 0 | 0 | 0 | 0 | 0 | 0 | 0 | B | 0 | 0 | E | 0 | 0 | 0 |

**TABLE 2.21**     Table of Directory Entries

| File Name | Extension | Created | Accessed | Written | Start Cluster | Length |
|---|---|---|---|---|---|---|
| file1234 | txt | 6/5/2005 1745 hrs | 6/5/2005 | 6/5/2005 1745 hrs | 2 | 4,095 |
| _ile5678 | txt | 6/5/2005 1756 hrs | 6/5/2005 | 6/5/2005 1756 hrs | 3 | 4,097 |
| Fileabcd | txt | 6/5/2005 1800 hrs | 6/5/2005 | 6/5/2005 1800 hrs | 5 | 4,096 |
| _ilewxyz | txt | 6/5/2005 1815 hrs | 6/5/2005 | 6/5/2005 1921 hrs | 6 | 8,000 |
| Coolfile | txt | 9/5/2005 1820 hrs | 9/5/2005 | 9/5/2005 1820 hrs | 24 | 286 |
| Yourfile | txt | 9/5/2005 1712 hrs | 9/5/2005 | 9/5/2005 1712 hrs | 9 | 7,580 |

The method of recovery we just employed manually is the same logic and method used by EnCase and other data recovery software. The directory entry gives only the starting cluster. The second cluster in the chain is assumed be to be the next unallocated cluster after the starting cluster. The third is assumed to be the next unallocated cluster after that one, and so forth until the number of clusters holding the data is reached. We can see the error that occurred with a two-cluster file. With extremely large files that become fragmented on busy systems, the potential for errors in recovering files is significant.

Your best chances for successful recovery will be when fragmentation is minimal and the deletion was recent. When you have an erroneous recovery, the error will usually stand out. If it is an image, chances are you'll see a partial picture. If it is a web page, you'll see it begin as HTML code and suddenly change to something else, typically binary data. When this occurs, you'll understand what has happened and can explain why. Partial recovery is better than no recovery!

When EnCase recovers a deleted file, it will check to see if the deleted file's starting cluster is in use by another file. If not, it will recover the data by the above method. If the starting cluster is in use by another file, it will report this as an "overwritten file." In the right pane, you are looking at the information contained in the deleted file's directory entry. The bottom pane contains the data for the file that overwrote the deleted file's starting cluster. As previously mentioned, an attempt to bookmark an overwritten file will result in bookmarking the file and data that overwrote that file. It may be possible to manually recover some data in the second and subsequent clusters of an overwritten file.

When we were discussing logical file size and physical file size, we mentioned that the operating system ignored the data in the cluster after the logical file. Forensically, however, we don't want to ignore that data as it can contain valuable evidence. The data between the end of the logical file to the end of the cluster containing the data is called *slack space*. Slack space will usually contain data from files that used this space before, making it a rich depository of evidence.

Slack space is actually composed of data from two different sources. When data is written to media, it is written in blocks of 512 bytes or one sector. If only one byte is to be written, the system must write another 511 bytes such that it writes 512 bytes. Before Windows 95B, the "extra" data or filler was randomly taken from slack and caused many security concerns. With Windows 95B, that filler data became zeros. Because of its history, the portion of the slack space from the end of the logical file to the end of the sector (not the cluster) was called *RAM slack*. More recently, the term *sector slack* is also applied, and both refer to the same portion of the slack space. The remainder of the slack, from the end of the last sector containing the logical file until the end of the cluster, is called file slack. The entire slack space, comprising both RAM or sector slack and file slack, is shown in red when viewed in EnCase.

In Figure 2.23, you can see the data in the logical file in black. When the logical file ends, the characters are shown in red when seen in EnCase. At the beginning of the red characters, you can see that they are all 0x00 (RAM or sector sack) until the sector boundary is reached, at sector #511. After the sector boundary, what's left is data remaining from files that were deleted, which is called the file slack.

**FIGURE 2.23**    Slack space shown in red

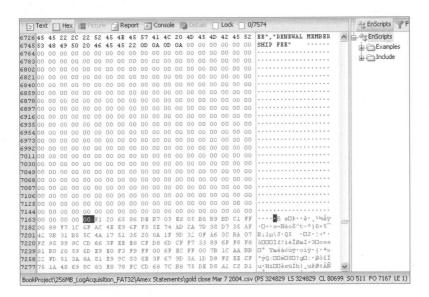

Before we conclude our discussion of FAT file systems, there's one more important point to cover. The directory entry status byte (the first byte of the 32-byte directory entry), as we have seen it used thus far, either has contained the first character of a valid file or directory name, or has contained 0xE5 to indicate a deleted file or directory. There are a few other values it can contain that have special meaning.

Believe it or not, if you wanted to have the first character of a file as hex E5, you'd need the value 0x05. Also, if the first byte contained the value of 0x00, that means the entry is not used and entries beyond this point are not searched. However, the most important value for the forensics examiner, of the ones not yet covered, is that of 0x2E or 0x2E2E. Most may recall it more affectionately as the "dot double dot" signature for a directory, as shown in Figure 2.24.

**FIGURE 2.24**    Classic "dot double dot" directory signature

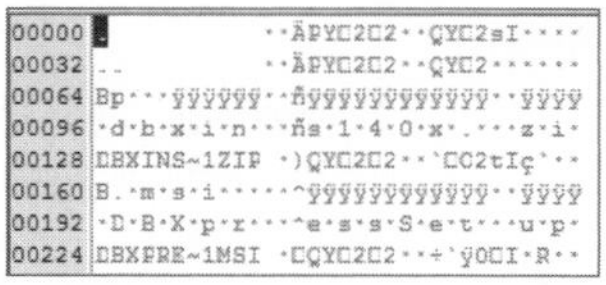

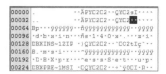

When the value of the first directory entry line begins with 0x2E, or "dot," it denotes that it is a directory entry and the "dot" points to itself. The second directory entry line that follows will begin with 0x2E2E, or "dot dot." This entry points to its parent directory. If you are at a command prompt and type in **cd..** you will change into the parent directory from where you were. In the "dot dot" line, the value contained in the "starting cluster" (byte offsets 26 and 27) will be that of the parent directory for the directory in which you presently are, as shown in Figure 2.25. If that value is 0x00, the parent directory is in the root directory, as shown in Figure 2.26.

**FIGURE 2.25**    Parent directory's starting cluster at byte offsets 26 and 27

**FIGURE 2.26**    Same value in hex as it is hex 00; the parent of this directory is in the root directory.

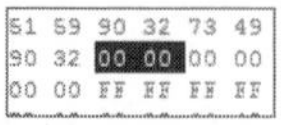

The importance of understanding the "dot double dot" directory signature is recognizing it when you see it, but also that of understanding its structure. Not all deleted directories are going to be shown initially by EnCase. You can instruct EnCase to "Recover Folders," at which time it will search for folders in the unallocated clusters of the partition looking for this signature and will then recover anything that is recoverable. If you are asked questions on the exam about how directories are structured or recovered, understanding these concepts is extremely important to establishing your credibility as a forensics examiner.

# NTFS (New Technology File System)

Another file system used by the Windows operating system, starting with Windows NT, is NTFS. NTFS, compared to FAT file systems, is more robust, providing stronger security, greater recoverability, and better performance with regard to read, write, and searching capabilities. Among other features it includes support for long file names, a highly granular system of file permissions and access control, and compression of individual files and directories. Accordingly, it is a far more complex file system. To cover it with the level of detail we have afforded the FAT system would not be feasible. Therefore, our purpose here is to provide a brief overview.

NTFS first rolled out in August 1993 with Windows NT. Windows 2000 and XP use a newer form of NTFS called NTFS5. NT must have Service Pack 4 or higher to use the NTFS5 partitions created by Windows 2K/XP.

Windows NT and 2000 provided NTFS5 as a formatting option, defaulting to FAT unless the user chose otherwise. Starting with Windows XP, the default format is NTFS5. Thus newer Windows systems will be mostly NTFS5, but FAT will still continue to coexist with NTFS (it is used on other forms of media, as discussed earlier).

From our previous analysis of file systems, we know that, regardless of their name, they must perform certain basic functions for the system:

- Track the name of the file (or directory)

- Track the point where the file starts

- Track the length of the file along with other file metadata, such as date and time stamps

- Track the clusters used by the file (cluster runs)

- Track which allocations units (clusters) are allocated and which are not

NTFS does all these things and more. An NTFS partition is identified as such, initially at least, by an entry in the partition table of the master boot record (MBR). From Chapter 1 we know that Windows requires the partition to be properly identified in the partition table in order for Windows to mount it. When the NTFS partition is formatted, the volume boot record (VBR) for NTFS is created and 16 sectors are reserved for its use, but typically only 8 are used for data. Bytes 3–6 of the first sector of the VBR will be "NTFS." Recall that FAT32 stored the backup of its volume boot record in the reserved area at the beginning of the volume. By contrast, NTFS stores its backup copy in the last sector of the partition.

In an NTFS partition, unlike FAT, all the important file system data is contained in actual files. NTFS uses many system files, but the very heart of the NTFS system is the $MFT (master file table) and the $Bitmap. The MFT is similar to the directory entry in FAT, and the $Bitmap is similar to the FAT1 and FAT2 in FAT.

The $Bitmap is a file that contains one bit for each cluster in the partition. It tracks allocation only and does not track cluster runs. If a cluster has a 0, that indicates it is available for use by the system. If a cluster has a 1, the cluster is allocated to a file. It is a very simple system.

The $MFT is a database with an entry for every file and directory in the partition, including an entry for itself. Each entry is fixed in length and is almost always 1,024 bytes. Each entry has a header (FILE0), which is followed by series of attributes. Everything about a file is an attribute, including the data itself. If a file is small, sometimes its data is stored within the $MFT and is called "resident data." Cookie files are an excellent example of files that are almost always resident data. Typically the average maximum length for resident files is around 480 bytes. This varies with the type and length of the attributes in the $MFT. If a file can't be stored in the $MFT, then it is stored in a cluster, and in place of the resident data, the cluster runs are stored.

When a file is deleted on an NTFS partition, a flag in the $MFT is set indicating it is not in use, and the allocated clusters are marked with 0s in the $Bitmap, which means they are unallocated. In addition, the index buffer entry for the logical folder is deleted. Because the $MFT record is otherwise untouched, an accurate record of cluster runs is usually intact, thus making recovery more reliable. The downside of recovering files in NTFS is that the MFT can grow but not shrink. As files are deleted, their $MFT records are efficiently and quickly overwritten, more so with XP.

Table 2.22 lists the major system files of the NTFS system along with a brief description of their function.

**TABLE 2.22**    NTFS System Files

| MFT Record # | File Name | Description |
|---|---|---|
| 0 | $MFT | Master file table; each MFT record is 1,024 bytes in length. |
| 1 | $MFTMirr | Contains a backup copy of the first four entries of the MFT. |
| 2 | $LogFile | Journal file that contains file metadata transactions used for system recovery and file integrity. |
| 3 | $Volume | NTFS version and volume label and identifier. |
| 4 | $AttrDef | Attribute information. |
| 5 | $. | Root directory of the file system. |
| 6 | $Bitmap | Tracks the allocation status of all clusters in the partition. |
| 7 | $Boot | Contains partition boot sector and boot code. |
| 8 | $BadClus | Bad clusters on partition are tracked with this file. |
| 9 | $Secure | Contains file permissions and access control settings for file security. |

**TABLE 2.22**　　NTFS System Files *(continued)*

| MFT Record # | File Name | Description |
|---|---|---|
| 10 | $UpCase | Converts lowercase characters in Unicode by storing an uppercase version of all Unicode characters in this file. |
| 11 | $Extend | A directory reserved for options extensions. |

## "You Won't Find Anything Because I Wiped the Hard Drive"

The superintendent of a local school district called to report that child pornography had been found on one of their computers. The school board had assigned a computer to the foreperson of a contractor hired to renovate their school. After the contractor was terminated and the computer returned to the school board, they discovered that the computer contained images of child pornography. Instead of notifying law enforcement, the superintendent turned the computer over to a school board member, who was employed as a computer system's administrator. According to the superintendent, the board member printed the images and provided them to the school board attorney. I quickly made arrangements to retrieve the printed images from the school board attorney and informed her of the possible ramifications of possessing images of child pornography.

I met with to the school board member (who still had possession of the computer) and advised him as well of the possible ramifications of his actions. When I asked for the computer, he said, "You won't find anything because I wiped the hard drive." He said his intentions were to remove any evidence of child pornography (since he had already preserved the photos in printed form) so the computer could be reused. When I asked what method he used to wipe the contents of the hard drive, he reminded me of his credentials and said he had used a wiping utility that he commonly uses at his job. Nonetheless, I received permission from the superintendent to examine the computer and took possession of it.

As I started the examination, I immediately observed that the hard drive did not contain a logical volume with a directory structure. However, I noticed actual data within the sectors, not just a repeat of some arbitrary hexadecimal value, which would indicate that the drive had indeed been wiped. I then pointed to physical sector 63 and observed the text "NTFS" in its complete context and in hexadecimal it was "EB 52 90 4E 54 46 53," which would indicate an NTFS partition. Why physical sector 63? At that time, I could not tell if it was ingrained in me to automatically go to physical sector 63 or that I actually knew that the first 63 sectors, physical sector 0–62, were reserved for the MBR and that the next sector contained information about the partition. Regardless, I pointed EnCase to physical sector 63, right-clicked, chose Add Partition, and selected the option to rebuild an NTFS partition. The Add Partition feature interprets the selected sector as the beginning of a VBR and rebuilds the previously removed partition based on the information contained within.

Upon a successful recovery of the partition, I was able to provide a detailed explanation of how and when the noted images were obtained.

# CD File Systems

When CDs first came out, as with many things standards were lacking—and history has shown that a lack of standards can limit the growth of an industry or product. Several representatives of the CD industry and Microsoft met at the High Sierra Hotel in Lake Tahoe. The standard they published in 1986 for CD standards was aptly named "High Sierra." Two years later in 1988 the International Organization for Standardization met and revised the High Sierra standard, calling it ISO 9660. ISO 9660 allowed for cross-platform capability for CDs between PCs, Unix, and the Macintosh. Such universality wasn't without a price, and ISO 9660 CDs had the following limitations at its Level 1 implementation:

- Only uppercase characters (A–Z), numbers (0–9), and the underscore were permitted in the file name.

- Names used the 8 dot 3 file-naming convention.

- Directory names could not exceed 8 characters and could not have extensions.

- Nesting of subdirectories was limited—no deeper than 8 levels.

- Files had to be contiguous.

Minor improvements to this standard were implemented. Level 3 interchange rules allowed (using the above rule set as a base) 30 characters in the file name. Level 3 implemented another improvement to the Level 2 rule set by not requiring files to be contiguous.

Microsoft developed the Joliet extension of ISO 9660 with the advent of Windows 95. Joliet offers significant improvements over its ISO 9660 predecessor. With Joliet, files or directories can be 64 characters long (Unicode support), directories can have extensions, the 8-levels-deep subdirectory barrier was removed and multiple session recording was supported.

When examining a CD that was created with Joliet, you will see an ISO 9660 directory and a Joliet directory, as shown in Figures 2.27 and 2.28. This won't be visible in Windows but only on software designed to analyze CDs. With two separate directory structures pointing to the same data, operating systems that support Joliet can use that directory system and its features. Those that don't support Joliet use the ISO 9660 with its limitations.

**FIGURE 2.27** CD with both ISO 9660 and Joliet directory structures. Note the Joliet directory names.

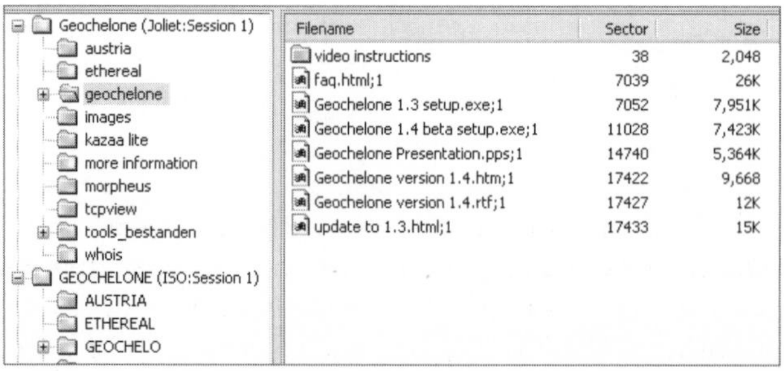

| Filename | Sector | Size |
|---|---|---|
| video instructions | 38 | 2,048 |
| faq.html;1 | 7039 | 26K |
| Geochelone 1.3 setup.exe;1 | 7052 | 7,951K |
| Geochelone 1.4 beta setup.exe;1 | 11028 | 7,423K |
| Geochelone Presentation.pps;1 | 14740 | 5,364K |
| Geochelone version 1.4.htm;1 | 17422 | 9,668 |
| Geochelone version 1.4.rtf;1 | 17427 | 12K |
| update to 1.3.html;1 | 17433 | 15K |

**FIGURE 2.28**   CD with both ISO 9660 and Joliet directory structures. Note the same directory names with ISO 9660 naming limitations.

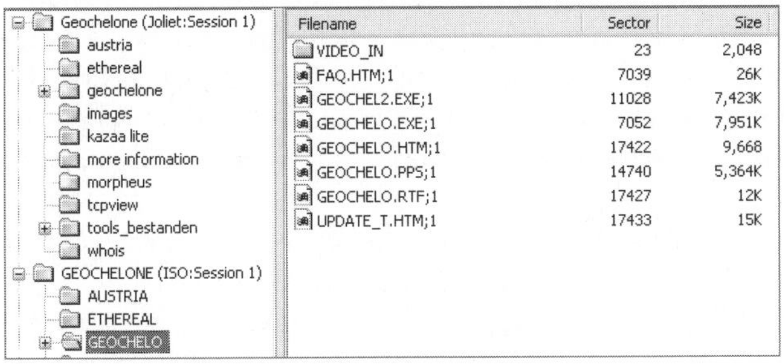

| Filename | Sector | Size |
|---|---|---|
| VIDEO_IN | 23 | 2,048 |
| FAQ.HTM;1 | 7039 | 26K |
| GEOCHEL2.EXE;1 | 11028 | 7,423K |
| GEOCHELO.EXE;1 | 7052 | 7,951K |
| GEOCHELO.HTM;1 | 17422 | 9,668 |
| GEOCHELO.PPS;1 | 14740 | 5,364K |
| GEOCHELO.RTF;1 | 17427 | 12K |
| UPDATE_T.HTM;1 | 17433 | 15K |

Tree structure:
- Geochelone (Joliet:Session 1)
  - austria
  - ethereal
  - geochelone
  - images
  - kazaa lite
  - more information
  - morpheus
  - tcpview
  - tools_bestanden
  - whois
- GEOCHELONE (ISO:Session 1)
  - AUSTRIA
  - ETHEREAL
  - GEOCHELO

Universal Disk Format (UDF) is a relative newcomer to the CD scene. UDF uses a technique called *packet wri*ting to write data in increments to CD-R/RW disks. UDF allows for 255 characters per file name, which is a significant improvement over Joliet. Roxio DirectCD is an example of packet-writing software that writes using the UDF format. Unless you have the driver installed, you can't read a CD written with UDF, which often causes problems for examiners. Roxio provides a free driver at its website, which enables you to read a CD created in the UDF format. Another, less preferred, option is to use DirectCD to close the session on a UDF CD. When this occurs, the file names are converted to Joliet and file names that had a 255-character limit are truncated to 64.

Macintosh uses a native HFS format on its media and can use it on CDs, but HFS CDs can't be read by PCs. The hybrid disc is often used to overcome this issue, creating both an HFS directory and a Joliet directory, both pointing to the same set of data, and readable by both the Macintosh and PCs.

Much like the Joliet extension, the Rock Ridge extension was created for Unix, which naturally supported Unix file system features. Rock Ridge can't be read by PCs, but the basic ISO 9660 feature is present and read, and thus the Rock Ridge extensions are ignored when read by a PC.

EnCase Version 5 supports CD images created by CD Inspector. You can use CD Inspector to examine CDs, including the "difficult" ones. CD Inspector provides an imaging utility that creates an image with a .zip extension. Those image files can be opened directly in EnCase. For this reason, many examiners prefer to use CD Inspector to examine and image problem CDs and rely on EnCase for analyzing the data.

# Summary

This chapter explained the file systems used on Windows operating systems. Because the FAT file system is the most prevalent and has a long history, we covered its structure and function in great detail. The FAT file system works primarily with the directory entries and the FAT to read and write data on its partition. The FAT tracks cluster allocation and cluster runs in use by a file. The directory entries track the names of files and directories, along with their starting clusters and lengths. Using these basic features, files are read, written, and deleted. By reversing the deletion process, we learned how to recover deleted files.

We also covered the NTFS file system. At the heart of the NTFS file system are the master file table (MFT) and the bitmap. The bitmap tracks only whether clusters are allocated or not. The MFT is similar to the directory entry in FAT, only much more robust. Everything about a file, including the data itself, is an attribute and stored in the MFT. If the data is small enough, it is stored as resident data in the MFT. If it is too large, it is stored in clusters and the data runs are stored in the MFT.

We examined the various CD file systems and their history and features. ISO 9660 is the universal format that can be read by all platforms, but it has limitations. The Joliet extension of ISO 9660 contains expanded features for Microsoft platforms. Packet-writing software creates a UDF format that greatly enhances the length of file names and allows for writing small amounts of data in increments. Its drawback is that it requires a driver to read on machines without the packet writing software. To create universality, CDs are often written with multiple directory structures pointing to the same set of data. In this manner, an operating system can use the best directory it can support.

# Exam Essentials

**Know the physical features of the FAT file system.**   Understand and locate the reserved area, the FAT, and the data area on FAT12/16/32 file systems. Understand how FAT12, FAT16, and FAT32 differ with regard to the physical features.

**Be familiar with the volume boot record (boot sector).**   Know how to locate the boot sector on FAT12/16 and FAT32 file systems. Understand the data contained therein and its importance, particularly in the event a partition must be restored.

**Understand the FAT and the directory entry.**   Be able to explain how files are read, written, and deleted using the FAT and directory entries. Know how files are recovered by reversing the process by which they were deleted and the limitations of that process.

**Define the basics of the NTFS file system.**   Explain how the bitmap is used only to track cluster allocation and how the MFT is used to store file attribute information, including file name, starting cluster, cluster runs, and data length, among other attributes.

**Know the common CD file systems.**   Know the various CD file systems commonly encountered on Windows operating systems, specifically the ISO 9660, Joliet, and UDF. Understand how placing multiple directory structures on CDs that point to the same data creates interoperability between OS platforms.

# Review Questions

1. FAT is defined as:

    **A.** A table consisting of master boot record and logical partitions

    **B.** A table created during the format that the operating system reads to locate data on a drive

    **C.** A table consisting of file names and file attributes

    **D.** A table consisting of file names, deleted file names, and their attributes

2. How does a corrupted sector located in the data area of a hard drive affect the corresponding cluster number on a FAT table?

    **A.** It does not affect the corresponding cluster number on a FAT table; therefore, the rest of the sectors associated with the assigned cluster can still be written to.

    **B.** It does not affect the corresponding cluster number on a FAT table; only the corrupted portion of the sector is prevented from being written to.

    **C.** It does affect the FAT table. The corresponding cluster number is marked as bad; however, only the corrupted sector within the cluster is prevented from being written to.

    **D.** It does affect the FAT table. The corresponding cluster number is marked as bad and the entire cluster is prevented from being written to.

3. Which of the following describes a partition table?

    **A.** It is located at cylinder 0, head 0, sector 1.

    **B.** Is located in the master boot record.

    **C.** It keeps track of the partitions on a hard drive.

    **D.** All of the above.

4. Which selection keeps track of a fragmented file in a FAT file system?

    **A.** File allocation table

    **B.** Directory structure

    **C.** Volume boot record

    **D.** Master file table

5. If the FAT table lists cluster number 2749 with a value of 0, what does this mean about this specific cluster?

    **A.** It is blank and contains no data.

    **B.** It is marked as bad and cannot be written to.

    **C.** It is allocated to a file.

    **D.** It is unallocated and is available to store data.

6. Which is the following is true abut a volume boot record?
   A. It is always located at the first sector of its logical partition.
   B. It immediately follows the master boot record.
   C. It contains BIOS parameter block and volume boot code.
   D. A and C.

7. The NTFS file system does which of the following?
   A. Supports long file names
   B. Compresses individual files and directories
   C. Supports large file sizes in excess of 4GB
   D. All of the above

8. How many clusters can a FAT32 file system manage?
   A. A.2 × 32 = 64 clusters
   B. B.$2^{32}$ = 4,294,967,296 clusters
   C. C.2 × 28 = 56 clusters
   D. D.$2^{28}$ = 268,435,456 clusters

9. The FAT tracks the _____ while the directory entry tracks the _____.
   A. File name and file size
   B. File's starting cluster and file's last cluster (EOF)
   C. File's last cluster (EOF) and file's starting cluster
   D. File size and file fragmentation

10. How many copies of the FAT does each FAT32 volume maintain in its default configuration?
    A. One
    B. Two
    C. Three
    D. Four

11. A file's logical size is displayed as?
    A. The number of sectors needed that the logical file contains
    B. The number of clusters that the logical file contains
    C. The number of bytes that the logical file contains
    D. The number of bits that the logical file contains

**12.** A file's physical size is?

   **A.** Always greater than the file's logical size

   **B.** The number of bytes in the logical file plus all slack space from the end of the logical file to the end of the last cluster

   **C.** Both A and B

   **D.** None of the above

**13.** A directory entry in a FAT file system has a logical size of:

   **A.** 0 bytes

   **B.** 8 bytes

   **C.** 16 bytes

   **D.** One sector

**14.** Each directory entry in a FAT file system is _____ bytes in length.

   **A.** 0

   **B.** 8

   **C.** 16

   **D.** 32

**15.** By default, what color does EnCase use to display directory entries within a directory structure?

   **A.** Black

   **B.** Red

   **C.** Gray

   **D.** Yellow

**16.** What is the area between the end of a file's logical size and the file's physical size called?

   **A.** Unused disk area

   **B.** Unallocated clusters

   **C.** Unallocated sectors

   **D.** Slack space

**17.** What three things occur when a file is created in a FAT32 file system?

   **A.** Directory entry for the file is created, the FAT assigns the necessary clusters to the file, and the file's data is filled in to the assigned clusters.

   **B.** The file name is entered in to the FAT, the directory structure assigns the number of clusters, and the file's data is filled in to the assigned clusters.

   **C.** The directory entry for the file is created, the number of clusters is assigned by the directory structure, and the file's data is filled in to the FAT.

   **D.** The directory structure maintains the amount of clusters needed, the file name is recorded in the FAT, and the file's data is filled in to the assigned clusters.

**18.** How does EnCase recover a deleted file?

   **A.** It reads the deleted file name in the FAT and searches for the file by its starting cluster number and logical size.

   **B.** It reads the deleted file name in the directory entry and searches for the corresponding file name in unallocated clusters.

   **C.** It obtains the deleted file's starting cluster number and size from the directory entry to obtain the data's starting location and number of clusters required.

   **D.** It obtains the deleted file's starting cluster number and size from the FAT to locate the starting location and amount of clusters needed.

**19.** What does EnCase do when a deleted file's starting cluster number is assigned to another file?

   **A.** EnCase reads the entire existing data as belonging to the deleted file.

   **B.** EnCase only reads the amount of data from the existing file that is associated with the deleted file.

   **C.** EnCase marks the deleted file as being overwritten.

   **D.** EnCase does not display a deleted file name when the data has been overwritten.

**20.** What information does a file's directory entry in a FAT file system store about itself?

   **A.** File name

   **B.** Date/time

   **C.** File extension

   **D.** Starting cluster (extent)

   **E.** All of the above

# Answers to Review Questions

1. B. The FAT (file allocation table) is created by the file system during format and contains pointers to clusters located on a drive.

2. D. When the FAT table marks a cluster as being bad, the entire cluster is prevented from being written to.

3. D. A partition table is located in the master boot record and is always located in the very first sector of a physical drive. The partition table keeps track of the partitions located on the physical drive.

4. A. The FAT table assigns numbers to each cluster entry pointing to the next cluster in the cluster run until the last cluster is reached, which is marked as EOF.

5. D. When the FAT table marks a cluster as 0, it is in unallocated blusters, which means it is freely available to store data.

6. D.

7. D.

8. D. A FAT32 file system allows up to $2^{28}$ = 268,435,456. The extra 4 bits are reserved by the file system; however, this is a theoretical maximum and there is an MBR-imposed limit of 67,092,481 clusters, which means it is capable of supporting a partition size of 2 terabytes.

9. C. The FAT tracks the location of the last cluster for a file (EOF), while the directory entry maintains the file's starting cluster number.

10. B. Each volume maintains two copies (one for backup): FAT1 and FAT2.

11. C. A file's logical size is displayed as the actual number of bytes that the file contains.

12. B. A file's physical size is the number of bytes to the end of the last cluster, and a file's logical size is the amount of bytes that the actual file contains. A file's physical size can be the same as its logical size.

13. A. A directory entry in a FAT file system has no logical size.

14. D. In a FAT file system each directory entry is 32 bytes in length.

15. B. Since directory entries are just names with no logical size and because they do not contain any actual data, EnCase displays the information in red.

16. D. The area between a file's logical size and its physical size is commonly referred to as slack space.

17. A. The directory structure records the file's information, the FAT tracks the number of clusters allocated to the file, and the file's data is filled in to the assigned clusters.

**18.** C. EnCase recovers deleted files by first obtaining the file's starting cluster number and its size from the directory entry. EnCase determines the number of clusters needed based on the file's size and then attempts to recover the data from the starting extent through the amount of clusters needed.

**19.** C. When EnCase determines that the starting cluster listed in the FAT has been reassigned to an existing file, it reports the previously deleted file as being overwritten.

**20.** E. A file's directory entry stores almost everything about the file with the exception of the actual data itself.

# Chapter

# 3

# First Response

## ENCE EXAM TOPICS COVERED IN THIS CHAPTER:

- ✓ Incident response planning and preparation
- ✓ Handling evidence at the scene

How we respond to an incident or crime involving computers is largely based on how well we plan and prepare for such a response. History has proven repeatedly that even a mediocre plan is better than no plan. That having been said, the importance of proper planning and preparation can't be emphasized enough.

Regardless of your response capacity, be it law enforcement officer, military personnel, civilian examiner, or a member of an enterprise incident-response team, you will have certain issues and concerns in common with other forensics examiners. You will always need a plan. Because every incident is different, you will have to tailor your plan to fit the incident.

Once at a scene or incident, the number and types of systems that you may encounter is vast and ever changing. It is important for you to be able to identify the various platforms and properly handle each type of evidence so as to secure the evidence and yet not damage critical systems in the process. How evidence is handled at the scene is often far more important than the laboratory analysis work that is done later. Data recovery and analysis and subsequent prosecution depend on proper seizure and handling of evidence at the scene.

Once the incident is over, an often-overlooked part of the process is that of debriefing. By critically analyzing what went well and what went wrong, you ensure that plans and procedures can be modified and improved so that future incidents are handled more effectively than the previous ones.

In this chapter, you will learn the basics of incident-response planning and preparation. We will discuss the various items and issues you should consider while making your plans and preparations. You will also learn the basic rules and procedures for handling computer evidence at the scene.

# Planning and Preparation

Incident response does not exist in a vacuum. Its successful implementation rests on policies and procedures, plans, drills, staff training and experience, and proper equipment. While this chapter will focus on the pragmatic aspects of planning and preparation, you should review and follow the policies and procedures unique to your organizational unit. Many organizations have well-developed incident-response plans and flowcharts that define various incident types as well as types of response. Furthermore, you should strive to continually build your knowledge and skills as well as to obtain and use the best hardware and software that your budget can support. Finally, even though we are all busy, we should take the time to test our plans and preparations by conducting practice drills. It is far better to make mistakes while practicing than to do so in the field. Practice drills provide the opportunity to build teamwork, improve techniques, and test your plan and your staff.

Responding to an incident or scene involving computers does require some specific considerations or protocols; however, in most respects they are like any other response. We need to know beforehand, as much as possible, the who, what, when, where, why, and how. Every scene holds its share of unknowns, but the goal is to minimize the unknowns as much as possible before responding. The more we know in advance, the better and safer our response will be.

## The Physical Location

Safety is the foremost consideration for all first responders, regardless of your response capacity. People who use computers to commit crimes can hurt you just as much and just as easily as people who don't use computers to commit crimes. When a person's livelihood is jeopardized (losing their job over computer misuse) or their freedom is at stake (going to jail for distributing child pornography with their computer), they can become unpredictable, desperate, or violent. This aspect of human behavior and its potential tragic consequences must be considered in every response plan.

When you're accessing a physical location, one of your first considerations must be its physical address, description, and what type of structure it is. It the location residential or business? Is it a single-family residence or an apartment building? Is it one-story, two-, or more? Is it a warehouse, laboratory, office building, strip mall, or office suite?

After determining the type of location, you must consider its size, scope, and other special characteristics. If it is a residence, what kind of neighborhood is it in; does it have an alarm system; is there a watchdog? Does your computer-assisted dispatch (CAD) show any calls for service at the location and, if so, what was their nature? Were weapons involved? If it is an apartment building, does the apartment complex management provide Internet access, and if so, where is the wiring closet, who is the administrator, and so forth? If it is in an office complex, does it cover one office on one floor, an entire floor, or multiple floors? Does it cover multiple buildings? Are some of the computers located with the suspected users while other involved computers, usually servers, are located elsewhere, perhaps thousands of miles away in another jurisdiction?

## Personnel

The personnel present at a scene affect safety and incident response plans. To the greatest extent possible, you should attempt to determine as much as possible about the persons expected to be present. Personnel records and criminal histories are possible sources, depending on your capacity.

If the location is a business, its hours of operation must be determined. In some cases it may be better to respond while employees are present. In this manner, a suspect can be placed physically at the computer, but it also poses the risk that the suspect may attempt to destroy data when first responders arrive. In other cases, an after-hours response may be preferred.

When accessing a business, determining the number and arrival pattern of employees is important, as well as how many employees are expected to be using computers when you arrive. When possible it is advisable to identify a friendly system administrator on the inside. This person is often very helpful and can save you countless steps. He or she can often point you to sources of information you would probably have overlooked, particularly when it comes to logs, old backups, and so forth. System administrators are also an excellent source of determining the network topography, usernames, and passwords.

If is it a business and the suspect is known, you should gather as much information as possible about the suspect(s):

- Determine if they work at a desk, on the road, in an office, in a lab, or in a warehouse.
- Determine if they are physically located so as to observe arriving first responders.
- Determine in advance their username and e-mail address.
- Determine their home address and phone number.
- Determine what kind of car they drive and its registration number and state.
- Determine their physical description or, better yet, obtain a photograph.
- Determine if they have a close friend in the office who may help them, tip them off, or be in collusion with them.
- Determine their "history" to the greatest extent possible, using the resources at your disposal, which vary according to your response capacity.

## Computer Systems

Although accessing the physical layout and personnel involved may be routine for most incident responses of any nature, it is the computer systems involved and the associated specialized pre-planning for them that makes computer incidents unique and challenging. The field of computer forensics is becoming increasingly specialized. There is simply too much out there for any one person to know it all. If you know you are going to be conducting a field acquisition of a live terabyte server, configured with RAID 5 and running Microsoft Exchange Server, you probably want to have someone on the team who is knowledgeable with those systems, and you want to have adequate resources to acquire an image from a live machine and store that image. Only by gathering information and planning can you be assured those resources will be available when needed.

Let's review a list of various questions or issues for you to consider that are specific to computer systems when they are subject to a first-response scenario. While not every question or issue will be present in every scenario, it is nevertheless a good checklist to use as a baseline:

What type of evidence is believed to be present? Are you searching for bootleg software on a company computer? Are you looking for child pornography? Are you looking for a set of "cooked books" in an embezzlement case?

What will be the limit or scope of your search? Are you only authorized to search certain computers? Are you only authorized to search for specific files?

How many computers will be at the location? Are those computers expected to be running, or does company policy dictate that they be turned off at night?

If it is a business or government facility, is there a computer-use policy? What are its provisions? Do the employees have any expectation of privacy on company machines? Have they consented to monitoring?

Will people who present special privacy concerns be there? Examples include publishers, attorneys, physicians, and clergy.

What kinds of computers are present? Are they all new with 80GB drives in each machine, or are they older machines with 20GB drives? What kind of operating system(s) are in use?

Is any form of encryption being used, such as Microsoft Encrypted File System (EFS), PGP-disk, Jetico's BestCrypt, or others?

Is a network present; if so, what kind? Is it an Ethernet or Token Ring network?

Where are the servers, and what operating systems are they running?

Is a map available showing the network topography?

Where are the server backups located (both on-site and off-site)?

Where are the proxy server, router, firewall, web server, and other critical system logs stored?

Is the network/IT function outsourced or in-house?

Is the network administrator a part of the problem or a part of the solution?

Who has the root or administrator passwords?

Will the network have to be shut down?

Is a wireless network present, and, if so, what is its type, scope, and other particulars?

Depending on the systems present and their use, will the computers be shut down if they are running? If so, at what point, how, and by whom?

Because some persons using computers may be innocent and others may be suspect, how will the incident- response team interact or direct persons using computers when they arrive? Will everyone be asked to step away from their computers, or only those who are suspects or targets?

Who are the suspects or targets? How many are present and where will they expected to be?

Does the suspect or target use a laptop or personal digital assistant (PDA)? If so, does the device belong to the company, and is it normally with the suspect when he or she is at work?

Will all computers be seized or all imaged in place? Will some be seized for lab imaging and some be imaged in place? What will be the criteria to determine if a machine is seized or imaged?

If you have a requirement for previewing and searching for keywords prior to seizure, what keywords can be used to distinguish computers containing evidence from those that do not?

Does the evidence sought involve images? What types of images are expected (stills or movies)? What is the expected image content?

If this is a civilian response, does the suspected activity rise to the level where law enforcement involvement is going to be necessary? Child pornography is one example. If so, who is going to coordinate this with the chief executive officer (CEO), corporate counsel, and law enforcement? Are suspects going to be brought in initially, or only if illegal activity is discovered during your incident response?

Are network connections, running processes, or other volatile data important to the investigation? If so, how is such going to be preserved and acquired?

Where is the nearest computer supply store? What's the address, phone number, store hours, and the manager's name? You may need something you don't have with you, and a local computer store might be much closer than your lab.

## Deciding What to Take with You Before You Leave

The best answer to this question is to pack everything imaginable and take at least two of everything! There is a basic rule in this business: Cables will never fail in the lab when you have a spare on the shelf; they will, however, invariably fail in the field when you are miles from the lab and it's after hours and the computer stores are closed. With that in mind, let's go over some basic items for your field kit.

Checklists are an absolute necessity for field work. Create them, customize them for various "jobs," and revise them as needed. Despite your best efforts, you will fail to include some much-needed item on your list. Make sure you update your lists as you find deficiencies.

Your goal in creating your list will be to replicate your lab function on a smaller scale for portability and field use. Here are some suggested items as a starting point for you to use to create your own lists:

Toolkits. A computer field technician service kit is a nice start. Include cable ties. Consider also a set of the star head attachments for the hard-to-open devices!

Portable lighting, flashlights, batteries, and a magnifying glass.

Latex gloves.

Small first aid kit.

PC reference guide.

Digital camera to capture live data on screens and the state of the scene. Include a ruler!

Extension cords, surge protectors, multistrip receptacles, and uninterrupted power supplies (UPSs). You take UPS power for granted in the lab, but when you must image in the field, the power will invariably fail near the end of the imaging job. Protect your data by packing a UPS or two.

Hub or switch and network cables for setting up a small network in the field. You may want to create a small gigabit network if you have a team and are acquiring several systems in the field. You could send all your images to one large storage device, keeping all your images in one place and sharing other resources as needed.

Network cross-over cables and spare network interface cards (NICs) for network cable acquisition or field intelligence module (FIM) acquisition.

Spare internal floppy drive—if direct DOS acquisition must be made from a suspect computer, it may or may not have a working floppy drive from which to boot.

EnCase network bootable floppies and CDs loaded with versions of EnCase to match versions on portable acquisition computer(s). Have images of the same and extra blank floppies and CDs to make more in the field as needed.

Storage hard drives on which to place images, wiped and formatted.

Guidance Software's FastBloc hardware write-blocking device. Include an IDE–SATA bridge for attaching SATA drives to FastBloc as well as a 2.5 notebook hard drive adapter.

Portable field imaging computer (laptop, custom briefcase model, small form factor unit, etc.). Include all adapter cards, cables, power supplies, peripherals, system disks, spare keyboard and mouse, and so forth needed for your unit. Have all necessary software loaded and an updated OS with patches, updated antivirus protection, and synch time with the time standard before going in the field. Don't rely on one field imaging computer. Carry a backup unit!

EnCase manuals on disk; keep a current set of manuals downloaded and loaded on your field units.

Cables, cables, and more cables! Pack power supply cables, IDE 80 wire cables, SCSI cables, SATA cables, molex power cables, floppy disk cable, and so forth. A good set of USB and FireWire cables with the "multiple personality" plugs for either end is a good thing to pack.

Adapters: IDE to SATA, USB to SATA, SCSI 50-pin to 68-pin, SCSI 68-pin to 80-pin, Toshiba Protégé 1.8 drive to 3.5-inch IDE (Apple iPods)…and the list goes on.

Tags, labels, bags, antistatic bags, evidence tape, and indelible ink markers.

Field logbook or notebook, pens, and pencils.

Anything special required for the upcoming job.

Pack your dongles! Need I say more?

You'll see references to various types of acquisition methods and devices, such as network cable acquisition, direct DOS or Linux acquisition, and FastBloc throughout this chapter. We'll be covering those methods and devices in more depth in the chapters that follow.

The more information you can acquire about the computer systems that you are about to search, the better you can pack for the job. The hardest jobs to pack for are the ones where you know next to nothing about what's there. When that occurs, you have to overprepare in all regards, including equipment and staffing.

Regardless, have a plan and work on that plan. Create your packing list, use it, and modify it, keeping it current at all times. When you have to go out in the field, many times the response will be unexpected and with a sense of urgency. You will have many things on your mind, and the stress level is often elevated. It's a great comfort to be able to pull out a list, pack, and mark off the items, knowing you probably will have most of what you need, consistently and reliably. If you do a significant amount of fieldwork, it is advisable to have most of what you need packed in field cases and ready to go. Even so, before venturing out, check what you have packed against your list. Preparation is the key to success when it comes to fieldwork.

## Search Authority

Regardless of your response capacity, your actions must be authorized by some process. In a law enforcement setting, the authorization could be a search warrant, consent to search, or a call from a victim whose computer system is in some way involved in their victimization, as in a network-intrusion case. In a non-law enforcement setting, the authorization to search for evidence may be a directive from corporate counsel, it may be authorized by policy pursuant to an incident-response activation, or it may be a court order to a special master for the court in a civil matter. Regardless, all responders are bound to certain limits imposed by your authorizing process.

In that regard, all first responders must be fully aware of the limits of that search authority as part of the preparation and planning phase. The limits may be specified computers, specified types of files, specified user files, or types of evidence. Each person conducting the search and seizure must limit the scope of their searches to stay within the boundaries of their authorized limits. Also, you need a plan in effect as to how to proceed if evidence is found in plain sight that exceeds the search authority. It happens often!

If, for example, you are investigating an embezzlement case, you would reasonably find yourself limited to searching for a set of "cooked books." If you find contraband images in the same folder as spreadsheets, with the latter being covered in your search authority, then the contraband images would be held to have been found in plain view while you were acting within the scope of your search authority or warrant and thus admissible as evidence. If you were to start searching for more contraband images, such an act would exceed the scope of your authority and subsequent images so found would generally be inadmissible. The proper course of action in such circumstances is to stop searching for contraband images and seek authorization in the form of an additional search warrant. Only then can you legally search for more contraband images. Your planning process should account for these possibilities so that you'll be prepared in the event they occur.

With regard to search warrants in general, the laws are much too variable to attempt any meaningful discussion as to form, substance, and specific procedures. As computer search warrants can get rather complex, I strongly advise you to review your warrant with your prosecutor as he or she will be the one ultimately carrying the burden of introducing it into evidence. When the prosecutor is involved early on in the process, things generally go better in court.

When you execute a search warrant, most jurisdictions require you to leave a copy of the warrant at the premises searched, but not the affidavit for probable cause. Also, you are usually required to leave behind a list of the items seized pursuant to the search warrant. I also strongly recommend that each member of the search team have a copy of the warrant in the preparation phase when possible. In this manner everyone involved knows their boundaries and misunderstandings are less likely to occur when you arrive on the scene.

 For additional legal information, please see the DVD that accompanies this book, which contains Guidance Software's *EnCase Legal Journal*.

# Handling Evidence at the Scene

In this section, we'll cover the various aspects of handling evidence at the scene. We'll begin with securing the scene. Once the scene is secured, you need to document everything in place. After documenting the scene, the next step is that of seizing various items, namely computers. Before computers can be seized they typically have to be shut down. We'll discuss the various issues associated with operating systems and system function as they relate to shutting down various systems. We'll end the discussion with the bagging and tagging process, transporting, and securing, all in support of the all-important chain of custody. Let's get started!

## Securing the Scene

When you arrive at the scene, safety is the number-one priority. Regardless of your response capacity, those assigned to search and seize digital evidence need to be able to do so safely. Typically, two basic functions or teams are designated.

One team is the entry or security team. Their job is to establish perimeter control, make the initial entry, secure the area for the search team, and provide ongoing security and perimeter control throughout the search-and-seizure operation. The second team conducts the actual search operation.

## Recording and Photographing the Scene

After the area is secure, the search term enters the area and begins their job. Before anything is touched or removed, the scene is recorded through a combination of field notes, sketches, video, or still images. Once the area has been recorded to show how things were initially found, the search team(s) begin their methodical search-and-seizure process. Search teams are often responsible for the following functions:

**Recorder**    Takes detailed notes of everything seized.

**Photographer**    Photographs all items in place before they are seized.

**Search-and-seizure specialist**    Searches and seizes, then bags and tags traditional evidence (documents, pictures, drugs, weapons, etc.).

**Digital evidence search-and-seizure specialist**    Searches and seizes, then bags and tags digital evidence of all types.

## Shutting Down Computers

Before a computer is shut down, many issues must be considered. However, before considering those issues, stick to the basics. One of the most fundamental rules is that you should employ measures that avoid contaminating any evidence. Computers may be subjected to computer forensic examinations, but they may also be subjected to other forms of analyses. Often fingerprints are lifted from computer components such as the mouse, CDs, or perhaps even a hard drive in some cases. It is best in these circumstances that the prints lifted be those of the suspect and not yours.

Also, computers may contain hairs, fibers, or body tissues, depending on the incident or circumstances. When other examinations are to be conducted, coordinate your activities with others who will be conducting such examinations. In all cases, you must avoid commingling your fingerprints, hairs, fibers, and body tissues with those already present. At a bare minimum, latex (or a nonallergenic substitute) gloves should be used as a standard practice when handling computer evidence. If you follow this guideline as a matter of practice, it minimizes the concern of whether you did wear them in one case and not in another. If the other examinations are going to include hairs, fibers, and body tissues, a Tyvek suit or equivalent is recommended while handling computer evidence, both at the scene and in the lab. Your goal is to protect the evidence from contamination, both digital evidence and more traditional forms of evidence.

Finally, some computer components are particularly unsanitary. Without going into great detail, suffice it to say that some computer components reflect the rather unsanitary habits and practices of their respective users. Gloves can serve as a barrier in these circumstances and help protect you from certain pathogens that can survive even when exposed to air. Because computers create an electrostatic field inside, they are magnets for dust, dirt, hair, fibers, and other airborne particles, aided by the fan that draws in outside air (and debris) for cooling. This collection of airborne debris has the potential to transmit disease, so many examiners opt to wear a breathing mask in addition to gloves when opening cases to remove hard drives.

---

### Those Computers Don't Work Anymore!

A large safe was stolen during a burglary and the case went cold. As luck would have it, the safe contained a wealth of credit card information and 6 months later one of the credit card holders reported unauthorized activity on their card. I'm sure most would be shocked to learn that some of the online purchases were pornography!

Once we got over our shock, which lasted less than a nanosecond, we traced the IP address, captured during the online purchase of pornography, to a residence in an adjoining state. The son of the owners of the residence used to work for the establishment from which the safe was stolen. Within 36 hours, we greeted those occupying the residence at dawn with a search warrant in hand.

We started in the living room of the main house and saw two computers sitting in the middle of the living room floor. They were a matching pair with the only apparent difference being the serial numbers. When questioned about the computers, the suspect's mother replied, "Those computers don't work anymore. They are pieces of junk (referring to them by brand name) and I was getting ready to throw them away." We seized them nevertheless, along with other computers in the main residence.

As we continued the search, we were very careful what we touched and where we stepped. There were young teens sleeping on every available bed or sofa, in varying stages of alertness from the previous night's activities. Pets roamed rather freely and relieved themselves where convenient. At best, the last time this house had been cleaned was most likely the day they moved in, and that was years ago.

Our suspect, however, was not to be found. As the occupants started to wake up, information started flowing, and to our surprise, we found that are suspect did not live in the residence. He was, however, supposed to be living in the equipment shed in the backyard. As we later discovered, our suspect was, in addition to being a burglar, an electrician. He had trenched in electricity, telephone, and cable (including high-speed Internet) from the house to the equipment shed, in which he had taken up residence.

When we looked at the shed, we were somewhat doubtful that anyone would be living inside. Nevertheless, when we hit the shed, our suspect was inside, asleep, and enjoying his air-conditioned abode. It was a two-room shed and both rooms were full of stolen goods, including computers, credit cards, checks, and the safe he had stolen. He had since peeled it open and removed its contents, but he could not dispose of it since he had wrecked the truck he originally used to steal and transport it. We needed a truck to remove all of the stolen goods. We also learned that in some areas, an equipment shed is also a residence.

Back in the lab, it was time to pull the hard drives from the computers. When I carefully opened the two that did not work and were about to be discarded, I was shocked when I saw the motherboards, CPUs, and cooling fans. The CPU cooling fans were jammed with hair (human, pet, and other) and other chunks of dust and debris. They looked more like nests or termite mounds on the motherboard than they did a CPU and cooling fan. They made weird noises and barely turned when powered on to get the system time. The motherboards and all electrical components were likewise coated with the same collection of materials that, when combined, would make a "Hazmat Cocktail" like no other!

Rather than risk cooking the components to get the system time, I subjected both systems to a thorough cleaning, using appropriate environmental and personal protection safeguards. Once cleaned, the systems worked flawlessly. As it turned out, these two systems were not stolen or involved in any of the criminal activity and were later returned to the mother. She was told she wouldn't have to discard them as they had been fixed. Since she opened the door asking what was wrong with them, the explanation involved a diplomatic lesson in cleanliness and housekeeping and how that might be more economical than discarding computers when they are less than a year old.

As an aside, one of my favorite findings in that case was from the laptop next to the suspect's bed and in the room that adjoined the "peeled safe." Two Google searches were found:

```
http://www.google.com/search?sourceid=navclient&ie=UTF-8&oe=UTF-
8&q=how+to+crack+a+vault
```

```
http://www.google.com/search?sourceid=navclient&ie=UTF-8&oe=UTF-
8&q=how+to+crack+a+safe
```

And, yes, you can find plenty of information on "how to crack a safe" using Google!

Now that we have protected the traditional evidence as well as the examiner, it is time to turn our attention to protecting and capturing the digital evidence. Therefore, as one of the first things on your list, you should photograph the screen to capture the "state" of the system as you found it. If there's an instant messenger dialog box open with a conversation recorded on the screen, this is likely your only chance to capture it because it is in RAM memory and gone upon shutdown (unless the user was logging their instant messenger traffic).

When photographing screens, a short desktop-style tripod is very useful for this task, coupled with a camera that affords macro-focusing for getting close-ups of screen details in sharp focus. If you are not going to take these photographs yourself, you want to make sure, as diplomatically as possible, that the person taking photographs of the screen has some experience doing so and knows what they are doing. I personally prefer doing this myself; you get what you want, you have the resultant images in your possession throughout, and you can easily include them in your report without having to seek them elsewhere. Regardless, you don't want a picture of the screen; you want pictures of the details shown on the screen!

As alluded to in the previous paragraph, data contained in volatile RAM memory is gone upon shutdown, as are running processes, network connections, and other important data. With increasingly frequency, investigations depend in varying degrees on the state of the system when it was live. For example, if it was a network-intrusion case in progress, the network connections, logged-in users, and running processes would be vital to the case. Shutting down a computer would effectively destroy some of your best evidence in the case.

Similarly, the live system state could be an issue in a child porn possession case if the defendant makes the claim that they were hacked and not responsible for the content of the computer. In other words, the "Trojan Defense" is raised by the accused. While an examiner could later restore an image to a drive and attempt to reconstruct the live state, you can only approximate it since the volatile RAM data disappeared the moment the system was shut down. In such circumstances, you use the best evidence you have available, which is the examination of the live restored system coupled with the forensic examination of the hard drive, along with antivirus and spyware scans.

Many cases, therefore, can benefit in various degrees by capturing live system state data before shutting down the computer. The nature of the case and your available resources (time, equipment, and staff) will determine whether you capture live system state data before shutting down the computer system. Although it is beyond the scope of this text to cover methods of capturing and analyzing system state data, it is worthwhile to note that the Enterprise and FIM versions of EnCase have the capability of capturing this data using the "snapshot" feature.

The same versions (Enterprise and FIM) can be used to image live systems via a network connection without shutting them down. This can be useful in a variety of circumstances. If you encounter an encrypted disk such as BestCrypt or PGPdisk and they are mounted (you can see the unencrypted data), they can be imaged while mounted, allowing the data to be captured in an unencrypted state in the resultant image. If, by contrast, the same computer was shut down and imaged, the resultant image would instead be a stream of encrypted data. If you are tasked with imaging a production server that cannot be shut down without harming a business operation, Enterprise or FIM will again be your tool of choice for the job.

The FIM version is available only to law enforcement or government entities. The Enterprise version has the same functionality and is available for corporate or civilian use. The differences between the two rest primarily with the "SAFE" configuration and licensing. SAFE stands for "Safe Authentication for EnCase."

If the Enterprise or FIM version is not available to you and the live system-state data is critical to your investigation, you have a decision to make: either forego the data or capture it by less-than-ideal means. If you must capture the data without Enterprise, FIM, or some third-party tool, you are left with carefully navigating to the areas where your data is located, capturing it, and meticulously documenting your rationale, process, and findings. Examples of areas of interest might be using the "netstat.exe" command to capture network connections, and porting the output to a floppy disk. Another might be capturing running processes using Task Manager or doing so using a command-line interface, again porting the output to a floppy disk. While not the best method to employ, if you can document the process and basis for doing so thoroughly, there's usually little difficulty resulting from this method.

At this point in our discussion, we are proceeding as though the decision has been made to shut down the computer and image it in the lab. The screen information has been photographed, and relevant information about its system state has been recorded to the greatest extent possible with the resources at hand. Before shutting down the computer, disconnect it from its network connection by removing the network cable. This prevents possible remote destruction of data.

The manner in which a computer is shut down is very much dependent on the operating system and function. Most Windows workstation models can simply be shut down by pulling the power cord. By contrast, some Windows servers running high-end business databases are not very fault tolerant, and a power loss (pulling the plug) can corrupt the database—and with it comes potential liability for you. To be safe, these systems require a normal system shutdown.

Since the decision of how to shut down a computer is operating system dependent, you must first determine what kind of operating system is running. Simplicity is often the best choice in this business, and in this case it means asking someone who likely knows. Usually the computer system owner or user knows what the operating system is. In an office, often the same operating system is deployed on all the workstations and someone in the office usually knows which operating system is in use. The system administrator is most helpful in making these determinations, especially when your work involves the server room. Often your preplanning information gathering will include what operating systems are at your target location. Table 3.1 shows the recommended shutdown procedures for various operating systems commonly encountered. Figure 3.1 shows a Linux prompt where the user is changed to "root" and the shutdown command has been entered. You will note that the "$" changes to a "#" when the user is changed to the "root" user.

**TABLE 3.1**   Best Shutdown Procedures Based on Operating System in Use

| Operating System | Characteristics | Shutdown Procedures |
| --- | --- | --- |
| DOS | Full-screen text on a solid background, usually black. Prompt includes drive letters, backslashes, and usually an >; for example, C:\DOS>. | Photograph the screen and note any running programs or messages, etc. Pull the plug from the rear of the computer. |
| Windows 3.1 | Program Manager instead of Windows Explorer. Colored tile bar. Standard menu. | Photograph the screen and note any running programs or messages, etc. Pull the plug from the rear of the computer. |
| Windows 95 | Start button with Windows symbol. | Photograph the screen and note any running programs or messages, etc. Pull the plug from the rear of the computer. |
| Windows NT Workstation | Start button with Windows symbol. | Photograph the screen and note any running programs or messages, etc. Pull the plug from the rear of the computer. |
| Windows NT Server | Start button with Windows symbol. | Photograph the screen and note any running programs or messages, etc. Use normal shutdown procedure. |
| Windows 98/Me | Start button with Windows symbol. | Photograph the screen and note any running programs or messages, etc. Pull the plug from the rear of the computer. |
| Windows 2000 | Start button with Windows symbol. | Photograph the screen and note any running programs or messages, etc. Pull the plug from the rear of the computer. |
| Windows 2000 Server | Start button with Windows symbol. | Photograph the screen and note any running programs or messages, etc. Use normal shutdown procedure. |
| Windows XP | Green Start button with Windows symbol. | Photograph the screen and note any running programs or messages, etc. Pull the plug from the rear of the computer. |
| Windows 2003 Server | Green Start button with Windows symbol. | Photograph the screen and note any running programs or messages, etc. Use normal shutdown procedure. |

**TABLE 3.1**    Best Shutdown Procedures Based on Operating System in Use *(continued)*

| Operating System | Characteristics | Shutdown Procedures |
|---|---|---|
| Linux/Unix | If GUI present, look to Start button with Unix/Linux version symbol or icon, such as a red hat or fedora. If in console (no GUI), look to prompt for something like: [root@localhost root]# [user@host dir]$. | Photograph the screen and note any running programs or messages, etc. Use normal shutdown procedure. In many cases, the user will need to be root to shut down the system. If GUI, right-click the desktop and from the context menu, select Console or Terminal. At the resulting prompt, look for # at the right end. If not, type **su root**. You will be prompted for a password. If you have it, type it in. If you don't you'll probably have no choice but to pull the power cord. When at root, note the # at the end of the prompt. When at root, type **synch;synch;halt** and the system should halt. |
| Macintosh | Apple symbol in top-left corner. Trash icon. | Photograph screen and note any running programs or messages, etc. Record time from the menu bar and simultaneously record the known standard time. Pull the plug from the rear of the computer. Note: If Mac is running OS X, BSD (a Linux variant) is running as a subsystem process. Also Macs can run as servers (web, database, e-mail, etc.). If any of these conditions apply, a normal Mac shutdown is the safer course of action. For OSX, click the "Apple" icon and choose "Shutdown" and you will be prompted to confirm. Legacy Macs, click Special and click Shutdown. When it is shut down, pull the power cord. |

**FIGURE 3.1**    A Linux prompt. Because you must typically be root to shut down most Linux/Unix systems, SU root switches the user to root and the password is then necessary. At the root prompt, the shutdown command sequence is entered.

```
[sbunting@host-244-226 sbunting]$ su root
Password:
[root@host-244-226 sbunting]# synch;synch;halt
```

The characteristics noted in Table 3.1 are general guidelines to follow when you are completely in the dark and have no other information. Alternatively, you can interact with the system to attempt to determine the operating system. If this becomes necessary, use caution and document, in detail, every step taken. Such cases are actually rare, and with experience, most examiners recognize most operating systems when they see them. What is tricky, however, is whether it is a server variety or needs to be treated as though it were a server. Sometimes a "workstation" flavor of an OS is used with a database server application. This rarely occurs in a home setting, but it is something to watch for in a business setting. When critical business applications are known to be running or you are in doubt, it pays to err on the side of a normal shutdown procedure.

If you are "pulling the plug" to shut down a system, you should pull the plug from the rear of the computer. If you get in the habit of pulling it from the wall, you may encounter a situation where a UPS might be in place, and pulling it from the wall under such conditions only triggers a power failure condition. If so configured, this information is recorded on the host computer, and sometimes e-mails or pages are sent, and the host may start into a normal shutdown. Instead of preserving data, your actions are now causing data to be written to the system, overwriting potential evidence in the process. Get into the habit of pulling the plug from the rear of the computer.

Similarly, if you are attempting to shut down a laptop and pull the power from either the wall or the rear of the computer, most often the battery still remains providing power to the laptop. You must remove the battery as well. Keep the battery and the power supply with the laptop when you seize them.

As a final note on shutting down computer systems, remember to document what procedure you used, when you did it, how you went about it in detail, and the rationale or reason why. For purposes of our discussion, assume that you must shut down and seize a Windows 2000 Professional system on which a large SQL-based business database application is running. While you would normally pull the plug on a Windows 2000 workstation, there is a more compelling need to protect the database from being corrupted from a sudden power outage caused by you pulling the plug. In this case a normal shutdown is advised so that the SQL database may go through a normal shutdown before the OS shuts down.

By documenting what you did and why, you will probably avoid questions regarding why you shut down normally when most of the documentation calls for pulling the plug for a Windows 2000 workstation. If the question is still asked, you can refer to your report, which is already in opposing counsel's hands, to answer that question.

## Bagging and Tagging

Once the computer is shut down, it is time—well, almost time—to treat it like most other forms of evidence, which involves subjecting it to the bagging and tagging process. Before bagging and tagging occurs, we need to make sure we label all the cables and photograph the rear of the computer with cables and tags in place. Since you should have already removed the network cable earlier, you should reconnect it for this process. If your photographer did not already photograph the rear of the computer, as they should have at the outset, have it done now before attaching labels so that the rear appears as you found it.

To label a cable and connection, attach a label to the cable near its terminal end and place one next to its corresponding port on the computer. For each cable and port pair, mark the labels with a unique letter, starting with "A" and sequencing through the alphabet until you have all labeled and marked. In this manner, cable "A" goes with port "A," cable "B" goes with port "B" and so forth. Photograph the rear from different angles. When done, remove the cables and you are ready for bagging and tagging. Using this method you can show how the computer was configured and connected when you found it and provide for a means to reconstruct that configuration if necessary.

Bagging and tagging has a purpose, and it is not to bolster the revenues of the makers of such products. Bagging protects against contamination and tampering. Tagging provides a means of associating the attached and bagged evidence with a particular location, date, time, case, event, and seizing agent. Tagging also provides for a means of creating the first link in the *chain of custody* of the evidence. Chain of custody is a concept in jurisprudence that applies to the process by which evidence is handled to assure its integrity as proof of a fact in court. Practically speaking, it refers to the "paper trail" that tracks seizure, custody, control, transfer, analysis, and disposition of all evidence. Tagging can also serve as an integrity seal for the bag, part of the chain of custody, depending on the type of tag used.

Because evidence, including computer evidence, comes in all shapes and sizes, bagging can be challenging. Computer evidence also presents another complication in that it is subject to potential damage from static discharges. This occurs when objects of dissimilar electrical potential make contact. Accordingly, you must avoid using plastic bagging materials that do not possess antistatic properties when bagging computer components. Large plastic antistatic bags can be purchased for this purpose; however, brown wrapping paper or paper bags are more economical alternatives.

When bagging smaller items such as hard drives, flash media, and the like, small antistatic bags are recommended as you can see the contents and have antistatic protection as well. These are often in surplus from component purchases and can be purchased quite inexpensively as well.

When completing information on the tag, don't skimp on details. If you get in a hurry and plan to do it "later," you may find that you forget to do it at all or complete it with the incorrect information since the details are no longer fresh. Be thorough and record the details at the time of the seizure event.

---

### Don't Forget to Look Up!

Once while investigating the criminal activities of a "rogue" system administrator, we interviewed one of his associates. Apparently our suspect admitted to his associate that, while working for his previous employer, he had installed a "hidden" NT server above the drop ceiling of the computer room while working the night shift. He told his associate that he made frequent use of this "hidden" resource for a long time.

I called the head of the IT department for this institution and advised them of my apparent discovery. Two hours later, the IT manager called back. Upon removing the ceiling panels, they had found an NT server hidden in the ceiling, discretely hardwired into their main system. He commented that for over a year he had system problems that defied resolution. Needless to say, another investigation commenced, with a clear suspect indicated.

When searching an area for computer evidence, look in unexpected or hidden areas. Especially nowadays, with ubiquitous wireless connectivity, it is easy to conceal a networked laptop almost anywhere.

When transporting computer evidence from the scene to the lab, pack it carefully so that a bump or sudden deceleration doesn't cause it to shift and become damaged. Also, you want to keep it away from strong magnets such as the type that are often found on the "Kojak lights" of unmarked police vehicles, which are the style that are temporarily attached to the roof via a strong magnet in the base.

Over the years much has been said about keeping magnetic media away from the radio frequency (RF) energy emitted by police radio transmitters located in police cars. Theoretically, this is to avoid data corruption from the radio frequency energy. As yet, no one I know has confirmed this in actual practice. Likewise, I have read accounts of persons deliberately attempting to induce such a loss by exposing magnetic media to RF energy and failing to corrupt the data. Regardless, it is hard to conceive of a burst of energy that would corrupt data in such a pattern as to create an image depicting child pornography where none previously existed! Nevertheless, it is probably still a good practice to keep the media as far away from such sources as possible to minimize such claims.

Once the evidence arrives at the lab, just like traditional evidence, it should be logged into the master evidence log or database and secured in an environment or space that assures its evidentiary integrity. In this manner, it is safeguarded against claims of tampering and the documentary trail secures the chain of custody for the evidence.

If at any point in the examination process the evidence is removed or the seal is broken, this should be recorded in the evidence log or database. Similarly when evidence is resealed and returned to storage, it should be dutifully recorded in the log.

## EXERCISE 3.1

### First Response to Computer Incident

The purpose of this exercise is to prepare you for part 2 of your EnCE examination, which is the practical. After passing your written examination, you'll be given a CD with a case to work. Part of that process will be to document your first response procedures for your report. To prepare for the phase, assume the following:

1.  You are responding with others to the scene of a computer incident. You are the one responsible for the computers at the scene. The target system (only one) is in a business. The screen is locked, with the operating system logo displayed as Windows 2000 server. The prompt explains that the computer is locked and that only the administrator can unlock it. The system administrator is available and is not the target of the investigation, and she is considered a person with high integrity who is willing to assist.

2.  Describe in detail how you would take down this machine and take it to the lab for imaging if the Enterprise or FIM version is not an option and your directive is to seize it and take it to the lab.

3.  Write your narrative as though it were going to be included in your report. Be sure to describe your shutdown methodology and reasoning. Include details sufficient to establish the complete chain of custody from the scene to the lab.

When all is said and done, the computer evidence has been preserved and secured in such as manner as to prevent contamination or tampering. Furthermore, its entire history of possession and processing has been documented in such a way as to maintain its chain of custody. While questions can always be raised, it is the answers to the questions that are important. If you consistently treat evidence in the manner we've described, you'll always be in a position to answer the questions in a way that ensures your evidence will be introduced in court to the finder of the facts.

# Summary

This chapter explained the fundamentals of the incident-response process. We discussed the importance of planning, with a focus on gathering information about the target of your incident response and on packing for the task at hand, thus ensuring that you have the staff and equipment resources you need on site.

Next, we discussed how to handle evidence at the scene, highlighting the importance of securing and then processing the scene. We explored the pros and cons of employing immediate shutdown versus first capturing the volatile system-state data. We examined the various shutdown methods based on the type of operating system in place and the function of the computer system. Finally, we discussed how to "bag and tag" computer evidence, as a means of protecting it from contamination and tampering, and thus assuring the chain of custody from the scene to the courtroom.

# Exam Essentials

**Know how to plan for an incident response.**   Understand the planning and preparation process. Know what information to seek about the target location, specifically the type of facility, the personnel present, the suspect or target, and the computer systems expected to be present. Know how to prepare a detailed packing list for field equipment needed for an incident response.

**Understand the importance of scene security and safety.**   Understand that the safety of all persons present is everyone's primary responsibility and, simply because it is a computer incident, this responsibility is in no way lessened or diminished. Understand how the scene is secured initially and throughout the process, most often by persons for whom scene safety and security is their primary function.

**Know what data is lost when you shut down a computer.**   Understand that volatile system-state data (network connections, running processes, logged-in users, etc.) is effectively gone when a system is shut down. Know your options for capturing this data if it is necessary to your investigation.

**Know when to shut down normally and when to pull the plug.**   Understand the risks involved when pulling the plug on certain computer systems. Know for which operating systems it is normally the best practice to pull the plug, and for which operating systems it is normally the best practice to go through a normal shutdown sequence. Be able to list what the exceptions are and why they exist.

**Understand the importance of "bagging and tagging."**    Understand the unique nature of computer evidence and how it must be carefully bagged so as to protect it from static discharges. Be able to explain how bagging and tagging protect the evidence from contamination and tampering, as well as preserve the chain of custody. Be able to explain the phrase *chain of custody*.

# Review Questions

1.  What is the very first consideration when responding to a scene?

    **A.** Your safety

    **B.** Safety of others

    **C.** Preservation of evidence

    **D.** Documentation

2.  What are some variables regarding a facility that you should consider prior to responding to a scene?

    **A.** What type of structure is it?

    **B.** How large is the structure?

    **C.** What are the hours of operation?

    **D.** Is there a helpful person present to aid in your task?

    **E.** All of the above.

3.  What are some variables regarding items to be seized that you should consider prior to responding to a scene?

    **A.** Location(s) of computers

    **B.** Type of operating system

    **C.** Workstations or mainframes

    **D.** System-critical or auxiliary machine

    **E.** All of the above

4.  Generally speaking, if you encounter a desktop computer running Windows XP, how should you take down the machine?

    **A.** Shut down using Windows XP.

    **B.** Shut down by pulling the power cord from the outlet.

    **C.** Shut down by pulling the plug from the computer box.

    **D.** All of the above.

5.  Generally speaking, if you encounter a computer running Windows Server 2000, how should you take down the machine?

    **A.** Shut down using its operating system.

    **B.** Shut down by pulling the power cord from the outlet.

    **C.** Shut down by pulling the plug from the computer box.

    **D.** All of the above.

6. Generally speaking, if you encounter a Unix/Linux machine, how should you take down the machine?

   **A.** Shut down using its operating system.

   **B.** Shut down by pulling the power cord from the outlet.

   **C.** Shut down by pulling the plug from the computer box.

   **D.** All of the above.

7. When unplugging a desktop computer, from where is it best to pull the plug?

   **A.** The back of the computer

   **B.** The wall outlet

   **C.** A or B

8. What is the best method to shut down a notebook computer?

   **A.** Unplug from the back of the computer.

   **B.** Unplug from the wall.

   **C.** Remove the battery.

   **D.** Both A and C.

9. Generally speaking, if you encounter an Apple Macintosh computer, how should you take down the machine?

   **A.** Shut down using the operating system.

   **B.** Shut down by pulling the power cord from the outlet.

   **C.** Shut down by pulling the plug from the computer box.

   **D.** All of the above.

10. Which selection displays the incorrect method for shutting down a computer?

    **A.** DOS: Pull the plug.

    **B.** Windows 2000: Pull the plug.

    **C.** Windows XP: Pull the plug.

    **D.** Linux: Pull the plug.

11. When shutting down a computer, what information is typically lost?

    **A.** Data in RAM memory

    **B.** Running processes

    **C.** Current network connections

    **D.** Current logged-in users

    **E.** All of the above

**12.** All of the below are acceptable for "bagging" a computer workstation except:

    **A.** Large paper bag

    **B.** Brown wrapping paper

    **C.** Plastic garbage bag

    **D.** Large antistatic plastic bag

    **E.** All of the above are acceptable for bagging a workstation

**13.** What are circumstances in which pulling the plug to shut down a computer system is considered the best practice?

    **A.** When the OS is Linux /Unix

    **B.** When the OS is Windows 2000 and known to be running a large business database application

    **C.** When the OS is Windows (NT/2K/2003) Server

    **D.** When Macintosh OS X Server is running as a web server

    **E.** None of the above

**14.** How is the chain of custody maintained?

    **A.** By bagging evidence and sealing it to protect it from contamination or tampering

    **B.** By documenting what, when, where, how, and by whom evidence was seized

    **C.** By documenting in a log the circumstances under which evidence was removed from the evidence control room

    **D.** By documenting the circumstances under which evidence was subjected to analysis

    **E.** All of the above

**15.** It is always safe to pull the plug on a Windows 2000 Professional operating system.

    **A.** True

    **B.** False

**16.** On a production Linux/Unix server, you must generally be which user to shut down the system?

    **A.** sysadmin

    **B.** administrator

    **C.** root

    **D.** system

**17.** When would it be acceptable to navigate through a live system?

    **A.** To observe the operating system to determine the proper shutdown process

    **B.** To document currently opened files (if Enterprise/FIM edition is not available)

    **C.** To observe an encryption program running

    **D.** To access virtual storage facility (if search warrant permits; some are very specific about physical location)

    **E.** All of the above

18. A console prompt that displayed backslashes (\) as part of its display would most likely be which of the following?

    **A.** Red Hat Linux operating system

    **B.** Unix operating system

    **C.** Linux or Unix operating system logged in as root

    **D.** MS-DOS

19. When called to large office complex with numerous networked machines, is it *always* a good idea to request the assistance of the network administrator.

    **A.** True

    **B.** False

20. Subsequent to a search warrant where evidence is seized, what items should be left behind?

    **A.** Copy of the affidavit

    **B.** Copy of the search warrant

    **C.** List of items seized

    **D.** A and B

    **E.** B and C

# Answers to Review Questions

1. A. Without consideration for your own personal safety, none of the other considerations can be accomplished.

2. E. When responding to a facility, your most helpful ally is prior knowledge of the location, its hours of activity, and the people who occupy it.

3. E. When responding to a facility, having prior knowledge of the types and functions of the computers and their locations will help reduce any unforeseen complications, thus easing the task.

4. C. Pulling the plug on a workstation, unlike doing so on a server, will not lose any critical information.

5. A. Unlike with a Windows desktop computer, certain information may not be recovered if a server is not properly shut down. It is best to properly shut down a Windows server and document your actions.

6. A. Unix/Linux machines can store critical information that may be lost if the machine is improperly shut down.

7. A. When unplugging a desktop computer, it is best to unplug a power cord from the back of the computer at the power supply. Unplugging a cord from the outlet connected to an uninterrupted power supply (UPS) will not shut down the computer.

8. D. Removing both the power cord (AC) and the battery (DC) will ensure that no electricity is being fed to the computer.

9. C. A Mac should generally be shut down by pulling the power plug from the back of the computer.

10. D. The proper way to shut down a Linux/Unix system is to perform a proper shutdown using the operating system.

11. E. When the system is shut down normally or the plug is pulled, all of the above live system-state data is lost.

12. C. A plastic garbage bag has properties that are conducive to static electricity discharge, which could damage sensitive computer components, including media.

13. E. In all circumstances described, the best course of action would be a normal shutdown, and thus pulling the plug would not be considered best practice for any of these.

14. E. The evidence steps described here are an important component in maintaining the chain of custody and hence the integrity of the evidence.

15. False. In a business setting, anything is possible. A large business database could be hosted on a Windows 2000 operating system, as could a number of other critical applications, which include access control systems, critical process control software, life-support systems, life-safety alarm monitoring, and so forth.

**16.** C. Generally, unless configured otherwise, you must be "root" to shut down a Linux/Unix system in a production environment. This prevents a typical user from stopping the system and halting mission-critical computing processes.

**17.** E. Certain information may not be retrievable after the system has been shut down. Given that, it is acceptable to access a system to retrieve information of evidentiary value as long as the actions are justified, documented, and explained.

**18.** D. Microsoft PC operating systems use backslashes for the directory path structure whereas Linux/Unix uses forward slashes (/) for the same purpose.

**19.** B. Although most of the time, the network administrator knows much more about the computers than the responding examiner and may be of great help, the idea of requesting that person's assistance may be detrimental to the investigation if the network administrator is the target of the investigation. As part of your preplanning, you must determine if the administrator is part of the problem or part of the solution before you make such an approach.

**20.** E. Upon leaving the scene of a search, a copy of the signed search warrant and a list of items seized should be left behind.

# Chapter

# 4

# Acquiring Digital Evidence

## ENCE EXAM TOPICS COVERED IN THIS CHAPTER:

- ✓ Creating EnCase DOS boot disks
- ✓ Booting computers using EnCase DOS boot disks
- ✓ Drive-to-drive acquisitions
- ✓ Network and parallel cable acquisitions
- ✓ FastBloc acquisitions
- ✓ LinEn acquisitions
- ✓ Enterprise and FIM acquisitions

Following best forensics practices, we typically conduct our examinations or analyses on copies of the original evidence. In this manner we preserve the original, protecting it from alteration or corruption. The *copy* of the original evidence is more commonly called an *image*. For this image to be a copy and the legal equivalent of the original, it must represent a duplicate image of the original. Thus, every one and zero on the original must be replicated on the copy or image. In this chapter, we discuss the various methods of acquiring the original evidence and rendering from it an image upon which we can conduct our forensic examinations.

In the previous chapter, we discussed first-response issues, from preparation to processing the scene. During that discussion, we made several references to different methods of acquiring digital evidence, both in the field and back at the lab. EnCase provides many different options for acquiring digital evidence, some of which are available in all models of EnCase and some that are available only in the Enterprise and FIM versions.

Each case is unique and presents its own set of challenges and obstacles. No doubt you will use one or two favorite acquisition methods for most of your casework. You should, however, be familiar with other options or methods to use when circumstances force you to use another method to get that image.

We begin with the basics: creating boot disks in either floppy or CD format. Using those boot disks, we boot a computer into a DOS mode that is forensically sound. From there we acquire media using drive-to-drive, network cable, and parallel cable methods.

EnCase 5 now offers Linux EnCase, or *LinEn*, which provides similar functionality to the DOS boot; however, LinEn runs under Linux, which means that instead of a 16-bit operating system, as with DOS, you are running under a full 32-bit operating system. Thus, you have all the features of the traditional EnCase for DOS with the added bonus of the Linux command-line features and much faster performance.

FastBloc is a hardware write-blocking device developed for use with EnCase. It has undergone an evolution that now encompasses three models. We discuss how it can be used to acquire hard drives in Window, DOS, and LinEn.

Finally, we discuss the feature set of the Enterprise and FIM versions, with their unique ability to acquire media over the network while maintaining an extremely secure environment known as SAFE (Secure Authentication for EnCase). As an added feature, these versions can capture volatile system state data, thus making them valuable tools when such data is critical to the investigation.

# Creating EnCase Forensic Boot Disks

The purpose of the forensic boot disk is to boot the computer and load an operating system, in a forensically sound manner in which the evidentiary media is not changed. A normal DOS boot disk will make calls to the C: drive primarily via COMMAND.COM, but also with IO.SYS, as shown in Figure 4.1. Also it will attempt to load DRVSPACE.BIN if present. An EnCase forensic boot disk will be modified so that any calls to the hard drive (C:) are redirected to the floppy (A:). To do so, EnCase will modify the COMMAND.COM and IO.SYS files when creating or converting to forensic boot disks, as shown in Figure 4.2. If DRVSPACE.BIN (disk compression software) is found, it will be deleted to prevent it from mounting the drive. In this manner, an EnCase forensic boot disk can boot a computer to a forensically sound, safe version of DOS.

**FIGURE 4.1**  Normal Windows startup disk with COMMAND.COM making call to C:

| □ 1 | COMMAND.COM | UTOEXE.BAT ÿ □v ÚA PATH= C:\WINDOWS\COMMAND PROMP |
|---|---|---|

**FIGURE 4.2**  Windows startup disk modified by EnCase with COMMAND.COM making same call to A:

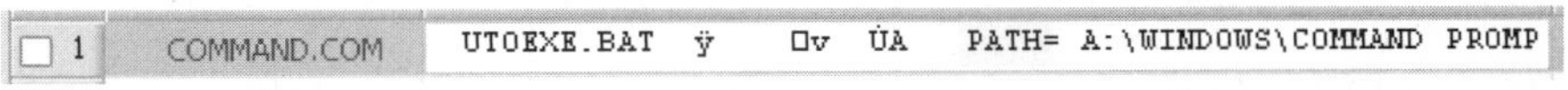

| □ 1 | COMMAND.COM | UTOEXE.BAT ÿ □v ÚA PATH= A:\WINDOWS\COMMAND PROMP |
|---|---|---|

EnCase can update an existing boot disk running on Windows 2K/XP/2003. EnCase can convert an existing startup disk to a forensic boot floppy (as shown in Figure 4.2) under those same versions of Windows. Under any version of Windows thus far referenced, it can create a boot disk from an evidence file or boot disk image. During this process, files such as the drivers or the updated version of EN.EXE can be added. Version 5 can create a bootable CD as well from an ISO image with the same ability to add files as it is rendered to CD.

All this functionality is available by choosing Tools ➢ Create Boot Disk, as shown in Figure 4.3. In the resulting window, you choose a Floppy (A) or an ISO Image (CD), as shown in Figure 4.4. If you select a floppy, the next choices will be Update Existing Boot Floppy, Overwrite Diskette with a Boot Floppy Base Image, or Change from a System Diskette to a Boot Floppy, as shown in Figure 4.5.

**FIGURE 4.3**  Creating a boot disk using the Tools menu

**FIGURE 4.4**   Choose a floppy or CD (ISO image)

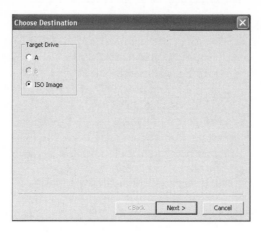

**FIGURE 4.5**   Forensic boot floppy formatting options

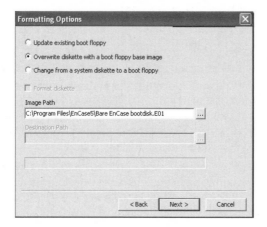

With the first option (Update Existing Boot Floppy), you are given the opportunity to add or replace files on an existing boot floppy, such as drivers or the latest version of EN.EXE. With the second option (Overwrite Diskette with a Boot Floppy Base Image), the floppy in your drive is overwritten with the boot floppy image of your choice. Many examiners keep custom boot floppy images on hand for a variety of specialized tasks. The third option (Change from a System Diskette to a Boot Floppy) allows the user to take a regular startup diskette (one that is not forensically sound) and convert it to a forensic boot disk. The files (COMMAND.COM, IO.SYS) are modified (DRVSPACE.BIN, if found, is deleted) as described earlier and as shown in Figures 4.1 and 4.2. All three options provide, as a final step, the option to add or replace files, such as those given as examples for the first option, as shown in Figure 4.6.

**FIGURE 4.6** All three formatting options provide the option to add or replace files; in this example, EN.EXE is updated and SCSI drivers are added.

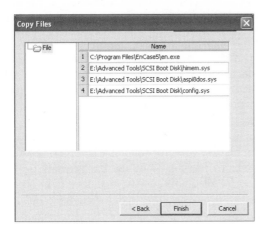

# Booting a Computer Using the EnCase Boot Disk

Despite advances in technologies that allow acquisitions to occur in the Windows environment using FastBloc or other write-blocking methods, there are still times when a DOS boot is needed and, worse yet, you have to use the suspect machine to host the boot. Some of these issues requiring this method occur when the geometry mismatches between the host BIOS (legacy) and your exam machine BIOS (the latest and greatest), the suspect hard drive is "married" to the host motherboard via a security scheme, or the hard drive is part of a hardware RAID, particularly when reconstructing the RAID from individual hard drives is not supported by EnCase.

You may also encounter a *Host Protected Area (HPA)* or a *Device Configuration Overlay (DCO)*. HPA was introduced with the ATA-4 standard. Its purpose is to create a place at the end of the drive for vendors to store information (recovery, security, registration, etc.) that will not be seen by the BIOS and hence protected from user access or erasure (format, etc.). DCO was introduced with ATA-6 and was initially intended as a means of limiting the apparent capacity of a drive. DCO space will also appear at the end of the drive and is also not seen by the BIOS.

As neither can be seen by the BIOS and both can contain hidden data, the way to access this data is via Direct ATA access instead of BIOS access. This method is available using EnCase for DOS on a forensic boot disk. Using the Direct ATA mode, EnCase communicates directly with the ATA controller and is able to access all sectors, including HPA and DCO sectors that weren't seen or accessed by the BIOS.

When trying to determine if you are seeing all the sectors in a drive, we often look to the sectors reported by the manufacturer, which can, in some cases, result in missing sectors. Recently while imaging a Western Digital WD800 80 GB drive, I noted that the manufacturer reported on the drive label that the drive contained 156,250,000 LBA sectors. While looking at the physical drive attached to FastBloc FE in Windows, EnCase was reporting all 156,250,000 sectors as seen by the BIOS, which matches the sectors reported by the manufacturer. Should we conclude that there is no HPA or DCO in place?

Your first clue that this is a problem is typically when you connect your target drive to Fast-Bloc in Windows and note that the total number of sectors on the drive, as reported by EnCase, is lower than the number of sectors known to be available on the drive (Total LBA Sectors). As best forensic practices call for accounting for all sectors on a drive, this should be standard practice with all drives. When EnCase is reporting fewer sectors than the manufacturer, you should suspect HPA or DCO and use Direct ATA access with EnCase for DOS to reconcile the difference and to obtain all the sectors on the drive.

LinEn, or EnCase running under Linux, is also an option in lieu of EnCase for DOS. We'll cover its feature set later in this chapter.

Sometimes, for other reasons (HPA, DCO, etc.), you may opt for a DOS boot when the storage drive is on your examination machine. Because this is a known, safe, forensic environment, it is a far better situation than using the suspect's computer. Even so, you still must control the boot process so that you boot from your forensic boot disk and not the target drive.

When booting with the suspect machine, there is always risk since it is an unknown environment. When you have no other good option, you must proceed carefully. If you make an error or omission along the way, the end result can be alteration of your evidence drive due to an accidental boot of that drive. Your goal is to control and test the boot process so that you can boot the machine with your known safe forensic boot disk and at the same time ensure that your target evidence drive is safe from calls and writes during the boot.

Chapter 1 gave you a solid understanding of the boot process, and Chapter 3 explained when and how we shut down a system. It is now time to put that knowledge to work. The following steps provide a framework for safe forensic booting of the suspect machine, but keep in mind that nothing is guaranteed. Even if you are DOS-booting from your examination machine, you should still follow the basic format: configure the boot process, test, confirm, and proceed carefully. Always be prepared for the unexpected by having your hand on the power cord, ready to pull it immediately if something goes wrong.

## Steps to Follow

1.  First and foremost, make certain that the target computer is powered off. Refer to your own policies and the guidelines in Chapter 3 with regard to appropriate shutdown procedures, which depend on the operating system, applications, function, and environment.

2. Disconnect the power cord from the back of the computer and open up the case. Inspect the interior for hard drives and connections, noting in particular anything unusual. It is common to find disconnected hard drives inside as well as additional connected hard drives mounted in any available space.

3. Disconnect both the power cable and data cable from any connected hard drive. If more than one hard drive exists, label the data connections before disconnecting them so they are reconnected properly when the time comes to do so.

4. Insert the forensic boot disk into the drive. If you are booting with a CD, use a paperclip to open the drive first. For those not familiar with this technique, there is a tiny hole in the face of most CD/DVD drives. Pressing a straightened paperclip into the hole opens the tray when the unit has no power.

5. With all hard drives disconnected and your boot disk inserted, reconnect the power cord and start up the computer. Immediately be prepared to enter the Setup routine, which occurs around the time that you first see something on the screen. Typically you will see something such as "To Enter Setup Press F2." Many times, the key you need to press to enter Setup is displayed, but in some systems this is hidden from the user. When this happens, you can refer to the system manual, if available, or you can try the more common keys, which are as follows:

   - F1 (for IBMs and many clones).
   - F2 or Delete (common with many Gateways, Dells, HP, and other clones).
   - F10 (common with Compaqs).
   - Ctrl+Alt+Esc or Ctrl+Alt+Enter (if the above keys don't work).
   - Sometimes removing all bootable media, including your forensic boot disk, will force a system to enter Setup or provide a prompt for doing so, which reveals the elusive key that accesses Setup.

6. Once inside Setup, locate the boot settings, more specifically the boot order. This is the process you seek to control! Before making changes, note the current order. Set the order so that your forensic boot disk device (floppy or CD) appears before the target hard drive.

7. Save your changes as you exit Setup. If you don't save the changes, the old settings will apply.

8. It is now time to test the boot environment to make certain that the settings you configured work and also that the forensic boot devices also work. At this point, your target hard drive(s) should still be disconnected. Start the computer and make certain your boot device works. If so, power down the computer and disconnect the power cord.

9. If you are going to be using a storage hard drive on the target machine to store the image, you should connect it and again test your boot environment to see if the system attempts to boot to the hard drive. If all is well and your system boots to the forensic boot disk, again power down your system and disconnect the power cord.

10. If all is safe at this stage, it is time to reconnect your target hard drive. Once the target hard drive is reconnected, double-check that your forensic boot disk is still inserted. Reconnect the power cord and keep your hand on it where it connects to the case so you can abort the process if it fails. Start the system and watch the boot process. If you followed the steps

carefully and thoroughly tested your boot environment, it should boot to the forensic boot disk. If, however, it does not, at the first sign of a problem immediately pull the power cord.

Before connecting this storage drive to your system, make sure you have formatted it with FAT (DOS doesn't recognize NTFS), that you've given it a unique volume label to identify it later, and that you have created a directory (use DOS naming conventions) for your image.

In this case, if we thought we were seeing all the sectors on this drive, we would be wrong. If you use EnCase for DOS or LinEn for Linux and use the direct access mode, you will see that an HPA starts as sector 156,250,000 and ends at sector 156,301,487 with 51,488 sectors (26,361,856 bytes) hidden from the BIOS.

If you trusted the label on the drive, you would miss almost 27 MB of data hidden in an HPA. Interestingly if you visit Western Digital's web site, they report 156,301,488 user sectors for this drive. So what information do you trust? Clearly you must trust your software, but you must check both BIOS and Direct modes to make sure there is no difference.

# Drive-to-Drive DOS Acquisition

A drive-to-drive DOS acquisition takes place entirely in DOS, and the target drive and the image storage drive are attached to the same motherboard, hence the name, *drive-to-drive*. It is a simple means of acquisition because you need only pack an EnCase boot disk and a storage hard drive. No dongle is needed. Many examiners, having started forensics years ago when this was the standard acquisition method, still prefer it.

Drive-to-drive is a relatively fast acquisition. The speed limitation is usually imposed by the slowest component in the ATA subsystem, be it the controller, cable, configuration, or the drive speed. The faster configuration will usually be master-to-master on different channels (primary and secondary), versus master-to-slave on the same channel. If you're providing your own cable for your storage drive, make sure it is an 80-conductor IDE cable; shorter is better. The closer you get to the 18-inch limit for these cables, the greater the possibility of communications errors during acquisition.

## Steps to Follow

When conducting a drive-to-drive DOS acquisition, you should follow these steps:

1. Make sure your system is configured, tested, and ready for a safe boot to a forensic boot disk as outlined in the previous section.

2. If you are booting using the suspect's computer, install the storage drive on that system. If you are booting to your examination machine, install the suspect's hard drive on that system. When doing so, keep in mind the following:

   - Configure your drives so they are each cabled and pinned as masters. Master-to-master data transfer will give you better performance.

- EnCase for DOS can only write to a FAT-formatted drive, so format FAT only.

- Use a volume label name on the storage drive that uniquely identifies it in the EnCase for DOS environment to avoid confusion and mistakes that could result in imaging your storage drive onto your evidence or target drive.

- The file directory path on the storage drive that will contain the image files must already exist. Create a directory after formatting and before having the evidence drive attached to the system. In this way, accidental writes to the evidence drive are avoided.

3. With the EnCase boot disk inserted, and the target and storage drives properly attached, start the computer and carefully monitor the boot; be in a position to pull the cord immediately if things go wrong.

4. When DOS boots and the A prompt appears, type **en** and press Enter. EnCase for DOS will start. On the left pane you will see physical devices and on the right pane you will see logical devices. The logical devices will be color-coded to correspond with the color coding on the physical devices on which they are installed.

5. If you have selected a DOS boot because all sectors were not accessible through FastBloc in Windows, now is the time to change from BIOS access (default) to Direct ATA access. Do this by pressing M or by tabbing to the Mode tab. If you started with a DOS boot for other reasons, you should check at this stage to make certain that the sectors reported by the BIOS access match those reported by the manufacturer. If they do, you can proceed with the next step. If they don't, as in Figure 4.7, you need to switch to the Direct ATA access using the Mode tab, as shown in Figures 4.8 and 4.9.

**FIGURE 4.7**    Two Western Digital 30 GB drives. Western Digital reports these drives as having 58,633,344 LBA sectors. XBIOS is only reporting 58,621,185 sectors (see arrow). 12,159 sectors (6,225,408 bytes) are not being seen by the BIOS!

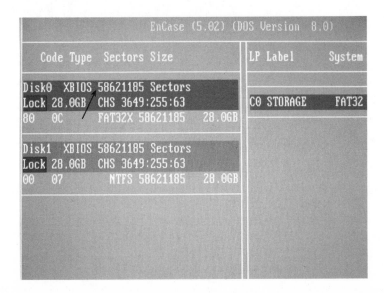

For a logical device to appear on the right pane, it must be a partition recognized by DOS, which limits it to showing only FAT partitions. NTFS partitions, even though they are Microsoft, do not show in the right pane! Similarly, don't expect to see Linux, Mac, or other non-DOS partitions here either.

**FIGURE 4.8**    Since 12,159 sectors aren't being seen by the BIOS, one should suspect an HPA and / or DCO and switch to Direct ATA access using the "Mode" tab as shown here.

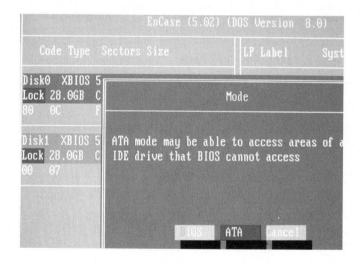

**FIGURE 4.9**    After having switched to the Direct ATA access mode, all 58,633,344 sectors are now seen (see arrow).

6. By default, EnCase for DOS implements a software write-block on all devices as indicated by the word "Lock" appearing in red next to each device. You will need to unlock your storage drive before EnCase can write to it. This is where it is important to have given a unique name to the volume so it can be unmistakably identified and unlocked. When you are certain you have identified your storage drive, unlock it by pressing L or tabbing to the Lock tab and pressing Enter. You will be given a choice of drive letters and numbers to unlock. Once you choose your storage drive, the word "Lock" in red will no longer be next to your drive. Check and double-check before proceeding.

7. When you have unlocked the storage drive, press A to acquire. You will be given a choice of drives to acquire, both by letter (logical) and number (physical). Normally you will want every sector on the drive and will choose the physical drive.

8. You will be prompted for the path on the storage drive on which to place the drive image. You must enter the path exactly as it exists on the storage drive along with the name of the file. As a safeguard, this path must already exist.

9. You are prompted for the case number; enter it and continue to the next step.

10. You are prompted for the examiner's name; enter your name.

11. You are prompted for an evidence number. Many naming conventions are possible. Use your lab protocol and enter the number.

12. You are next prompted for a brief description of the evidence; enter it and continue with the next step.

13. The system date and time appears next. If correct, press Enter. If not, enter the correct date and time. Entering the correct date and time doesn't change your system time, but does reflect in the acquisition information reported by EnCase as Reported Time and Actual Time.

14. The next prompt allows you to enter any notes you wish.

15. You are then given the option to compress the evidence or not. As compression saves you disk space (two to three times less space) but costs you more time to process the compression algorithm (up to five times as long), here is where you ask yourself whether you have more time or more disk space available to you. As time seems to be the scarcer of the two, I rarely use compression.

16. You are next asked whether you wish to generate an MD5 hash of the drive as it is acquired. It is by this process that the acquisition hash is generated that later allows you to verify that the copy you made is the same as the original. It is recommended that you always generate this value. At no time have I ever skipped this process, nor can I conceive of a situation where I would. Nevertheless, it is optional.

17. EnCase next prompts you to provide a password. Simply pressing Enter here negates applying a password—which I recommend you do unless you have a compelling need to include a password. Keep in mind that if you apply a password and then forget or lose it, the recovery is expensive. Passwords are useful in some applications. In special master situations, the evidence can be acquired by an examiner, but the special master applies the password. In this manner, the examiner can acquire and retain the image, but it can only be read and examined in the presence of or with the permission of the special master who holds the password. This is often done in cases in which the image contains privileged information and special protective measures must be used.

**18.** Your next option will be that of determining the file segment size (chunk size) of the image file. Rather than creating one massive file, the files are created in segments, or what we commonly call chunks. The smallest size is 1MB and the largest size is 2,000MB (2GB). The default of 640MB is recommended, as a file this size fits on a CD and seven fit nicely on a DVD (4.7GB).

**19.** Your next choice is the number of sectors to acquire. This will default to the number present on the device you are acquiring, which is almost always what you want. There are times, naturally, when you'll need a different number to acquire. Sometimes you have to acquire an image of a drive that has been restored onto another drive. As often happens, the drive receiving the restored image is larger than the drive image placed on it. When acquiring such a drive, you'll want to only acquire the number of sectors reported in the image restored and not the entire drive. If you restored a 20GB drive onto a 30GB drive, you'll want to only acquire the number of sectors comprising the 20GB drive.

**20.** The next option is new with EnCase 5: the ability to vary the granularity of the acquisition. In prior versions, if EnCase discovered a sector with an error, the entire block of 64 sectors (32K) was zeroed out. If only one sector was bad, 63 sectors of potentially valuable data was disregarded and counted as null. With Version 5, you can change the default of 64 sectors to one, in powers of two. Thus, settings can be 64, 32, 16, 8, 4, 2, or 1. If one sector is bad and the setting is 64, then all 64 sectors are zeroed out. If one sector is bad and the setting is 32, then 32 sectors are zeroed out. If one sector is bad and the setting is 1, only the bad sector is zeroed out, meaning no data is lost. It might seem that the best setting would be one, but such granularity results in a performance hit, slowing down acquisition. Typically you use the default setting of 64 and lower it only if you encounter a drive with errors.

**21.** At this point the acquisition will start. Depending on the system, the drive sizes, and the options selected, the process can take hours. A progress bar will appear giving you a lapsed time and an approximation of the time remaining. EnCase will create files using the name you designated earlier and with extensions starting with .E01, .E02, etc. until done. The files created will be in the chunk sizes you specified in the earlier setting, 640MB by default. With large drives and no compression, the number of files can be significant. If one hundred or more files are needed, after the .E99 extension is reached, the extension will change over to .EAA, .EAB, .EAC, etc. If the files needed to store the image exceed that on the current storage drive, you will be prompted for a location for additional storage. It is important to have adequate storage space formatted, ready, and mounted even if it is more than one storage drive so that it is available when EnCase needs it.

## Supplemental Information

We cover FastBloc in detail later in this chapter. In the meantime, you need to know that FastBloc LE (Lab Edition) can be used for drive-to-drive DOS acquisitions. FastBloc LE is permanently connected to the master of one of the IDE channels. The target or suspect hard drive can be connected to the FastBloc LE and uses hardware write-blocking features to protect it from accidental writes in the event that the wrong drive is unlocked using the software write-blocking feature of EnCase for DOS. Aside from the initial connection, all else is the same.

## Dead Hard Drives Are Not Always Dead!

After a domestic-violence incident and initiation of a divorce proceeding, the soon-to-be former spouse of a network administrator walked into the office of her soon-to-be ex-husband's supervisor. She told her husband's supervisor that he had "trojanized" the entire network, that he had captured passwords and was eavesdropping on his boss's e-mail account, from his home machine. Among other things, she placed a hard drive on the supervisor's desk, claiming that it had been in her husband's computer and that he had left it behind when he moved out.

The police were immediately notified and I was called in to examine the machines in that network. I isolated the infected network segment and began the task of acquiring images of each machine for later examination. This occurred several years ago and EnCase Enterprise or FIM as tools for capturing volatile data were not options at the time. The subsequent examination established that the various machines on that subnet either had Back Orifice currently installed or at one time. The "BO Server" had been "built" on the network administrator's workstation and had been deployed in a "dancing cat" program popular with the staff. A list of staff passwords was found, as was a similar list from the network administrator's previous place of employment. Old habits seem to die hard!

The suspect's home hard drive was dead. It would not spin up and it appeared that its only use was going to be as a "bithead" paperweight. The spouse indicated that her husband would experiment with hard drives, attempting to "kill" them by zapping them with high voltages. She thought he had zapped that one and that was probably the reason he had left it behind. She commented that is was a shame as she was certain that drive was in his machine when he was getting into all those e-mail accounts.

The drive sat around for a while until one day I decided to send it out to a clean room. Before I underwent that expense, I thought I would try replacing the circuit board on the drive. With a little bit of "googling" I located two identical model drives and had them shipped overnight. I took the circuit board from one and placed it on the "dead drive." When I connected it and powered it on, the drive spun up and the acquisition was a success.

Needless to say, the drive was loaded with e-mails intercepted from his boss's account. The date and time stamps coincided with modem connection logs from the server that were tied to his telephone number.

We spent two days in court successfully defending against a motion to suppress the recovered hard drive evidence. As it was marital property at the time, the spouse had a legal right to the hard drive and could turn it over to the police if she elected to do so. With that issue resolved, a guilty plea followed.

Just because hard drives may seem dead, there are ways of bringing them back to life!

Thus far, our discussions have dealt with PC-based systems. If you encounter Macintosh hard drives, you can't boot them with an EnCase boot disk in their host systems. Rather, you need to move the drive to your examination machine and acquire as another IDE drive. The same goes for Unix and BSD; those drives will have to be transferred to the examination computer for imaging. None of these partitions will show as logical partitions in the right pane because DOS does not recognize them. Nevertheless, their physical drives will populate the left pane and they can be acquired as physical drives. Later when the images are brought into EnCase for Windows, their file structures can be interpreted and mounted and processed as with any other partition.

So far we have discussed primarily IDE drives. If you encounter an SCSI drive, you can image it in its host computer in a drive-to-drive DOS acquisition as long as you load the SCSI drivers onto your EnCase boot disk. Figure 4.6 earlier in this chapter shows these being added within EnCase. You may image it in a like manner on your examination machine as long as you have an SCSI adapter expansion card or the same chipset "on-board."

Once you have acquired your drive, regardless of type, you need to power down, disconnect your target or suspect drive, and return it to secure storage, applying best practices throughout (documentation, antistatic bags, labeling, and so forth). At this point, make sure the image you acquired is a good one. To do so, boot to Windows, open EnCase, and open the image you just acquired. Make sure that EnCase can read the file structure and that you successfully completed the verification process before you consider the imaging job complete.

# Network and Parallel Cable Acquisitions

Another method of acquiring hard drives is via a network cable between a machine containing the target media, booted to EnCase for DOS, and a second machine running EnCase in the Windows environment. It often provides the best of both worlds, allowing some of the advantages of a DOS boot (Direct ATA access) combined with the enhanced functionality of EnCase in Windows.

If you encounter an HPA or DCO, you can place the drive in a safe lab machine and boot to EnCase for DOS while connected to your regular lab acquisition machine running EnCase in a Windows environment. Likewise a network cable acquisition is useful for booting from the suspect's machine when encountering geometry mismatches between a legacy BIOS (usually the suspect's machine) and a new BIOS (usually your lab machine) or when encountering RAID configurations. A RAID can be booted to DOS using its native hardware configuration to mount the logical physical device. EnCase will see this RAID as a mounted physical device, enabling acquisition and preview via the network cable connection to EnCase in Windows.

Sometimes removing a hard drive from a laptop is problematic due to physical access or other concerns, such as proprietary security schemes marrying the hard drive to the motherboard. If you are able to access the BIOS and control the boot process, a network cable acquisition is a viable option as long as you use a great degree of care and prudence.

A network cable acquisition is also very handy for "black bag" jobs where you have to quickly acquire a target hard drive when the owner or user of the target hard drive is not physically present. With little disturbance to the physical environment, you can connect your examination laptop to the target machine via a network cable, boot to EnCase for DOS, and preview or acquire if needed.

EnCase for DOS doesn't allow direct previewing of the data; however, when connected via network cable to EnCase for Windows, you can see the drive completely in the EnCase GUI environment. In circumstances where the presence of certain images or keywords must be present to warrant seizure, a network cable acquisition is very useful. Thus it is a great tool for a variety of field and lab situations.

Before starting a network acquisition, you must keep a few other considerations in mind. The first is the cable. We have been calling it simply a *network cable acquisition*, but the cable used is more specifically a *network crossover cable*. A "yellow" crossover cable is shipped with each version of EnCase.

Yellow does not necessarily denote a crossover cable in the field. Twisted-pair cable comes in a variety of colors, and those colors can be used to denote cable for a room, subnet, or any other differentiating purpose. Sometimes there is no purpose—someone needed to make a cable and used whatever color was available. Often a crossover cable has a tag or label to denote it, but don't depend on it!

A crossover cable is a network cable used for special purposes, one of which is to enable two computers to have network connectivity by connecting directly to each other via a single network cable. A regular network cable will not work for this purpose. On a crossover cable, on one end only, the positive and negative "receive" pair are switched with the positive and negative "transmit" pair, respectively with regard to the positive and negative to maintain polarity. In this manner, the machines can "talk" to each other over the network crossover cable.

When packing for the field, it is a good idea to pack an extra crossover cable. To avoid extra bulk, a nice alternative is to pack a crossover adapter, which allows you to use any network cable as a crossover cable. If you have to image several machines in a small area, using a crossover cable adapter allows you to situate your examination laptop in one spot and use a very long network cable to reach the various target machines. In a pinch, a network hub can serve as a crossover adapter, enabling you to use regular network cables!

Now that you understand the need for a crossover cable, you must ensure a couple of other things. First, make sure that the target machine is equipped with a network interface card (NIC). Second, make sure that you have an EnCase boot disk configured for network support, specifically a set of DOS packet drivers for the installed NIC card.

Not all NIC cards serve this purpose equally well. Some are otherwise great but lack DOS driver support. Some have great features and very reliable DOS driver support. Others fall in the middle of these two extremes.

You could experiment with different NIC cards and drivers, or you could use the ENBD (EnCase Network Boot Disk) or the ENBCD (EnCase Network Boot CD). The ENBD/ENBCD was developed and is continually updated by the Ontario Province Police (OPP), and through their generosity this resource is available to all EnCase users via the Guidance Software website.

The ENBD.EXE file is a self-extracting floppy disk image, as shown in Figure 4.10. Since a floppy disk is a limited resource (1.44MB), the amount of support you can pack on a floppy is limited, although ENBD currently provides 29 different drivers supporting over 190 device variants. The ENBD comes also in different flavors depending on the laptop PCMCIA NIC card it supports. These versions don't have the variety of support, but they occupy less floppy space, allowing room for other tools. The ENBD is ready to go after extraction to the floppy, but it does not include EN.EXE. Before you can use it, you must place the version of EN.EXE that is packaged with the version of EnCase you are currently running on the Windows machine. You can manually copy EN.EXE onto the floppy or use the EnCase Update Existing Boot Floppy feature.

**FIGURE 4.10**    ENBD self-extracting to a floppy; when done, place EN.EXE on the floppy before use.

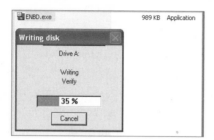

The ENBCD currently is a CD mirror of the ENBD in its full version. Because a CD provides much more file space, it ultimately has the potential to offer much more support than its floppy counterpart. The ENBCD is under constant development; the devices it supports are listed on the Guidance Software website. A major difference between the two is that the ENBCD already contains the most current version of EN.EXE and does not need updating. The caveat here is that problems can occur if the EN.EXE version does not match the version in use on the Windows platform. Therefore, make sure you use the correct version of the ENBCD. The extension of each ENBCD file indicates the EnCase version it contains.

The ENBCD is a self-extracting file that creates an ISO file and launches a quick set of instructions describing how to burn the CD image (ISO file) using either Nero or Roxio. You are given a choice as to where the ISO will be extracted. Take careful note of the location so you can later locate it. Easier yet, use the browse feature to locate the ISO to your desktop. With Roxio, you need only insert a blank CD and double-click on the ISO image on your desktop, and everything happens automatically, making it a very simple process and circumventing the steps provided in the instructions. Either way, creating the ENBCD is a simple process.

If your target machine contains an NIC and it is one supported by the ENBD or ENBCD, you are set to go. If your target machine does not have an NIC or has one that isn't supported, you'll need to install one in the target machine. You should choose one from the supported list of NIC cards and pack it, along with a spare, in your field kit.

The ideal configuration is to use a supported gigabit NIC in conjunction with a gigabit NIC in your examination machine. In that manner you'll get gigabit transfer speed between the two machines and the network connection will not be the limiting factor. If both the DOS and the Windows platforms are robust systems, you'll get extremely fast acquisitions.

Once you have a supported NIC in each machine connected via a crossover cable and you have created your EnCase network boot disk in either the floppy or CD version, you are ready to begin a network cable acquisition.

In lieu of ENBD/ENBCD, the machine containing the target drive can be booted with a forensically configured version of Linux. LinEn, which is EnCase for Linux, can be run in Linux in a manner akin to EnCase for DOS. A network cross-over cable acquisition can be carried out in the same manner after LinEn is started. The Linux distribution will determine the level of support for NIC, SCSI, and USB devices. The LinEn feature set will be covered later in this chapter.

# Steps to Follow

When conducting a network cable acquisition, you should follow these steps:

1.  With regard to the Windows machine, it is best to wait until the DOS machine is ready before starting EnCase in Windows. Simply run Windows with the crossover cable connected, don't start EnCase, and focus your attention first on the target machine.

2.  With regard to the target machine, as with the DOS drive-to-drive acquisition, you need to control and test the boot process so that the target machine boots from your ENBD/ENBCD before it attempts to boot from the target hard drive. The safest configuration is to enable a boot only from the floppy or CD and to disable the hard drive boot by removing it from the boot order altogether. Follow the same procedures outlined in the DOS drive-to-drive acquisition section to make certain the target hard drive is disconnected while you configure and test the boot order in the Setup utility.

3.  Once you are completely satisfied that the boot process is tested and under control, reconnect the target media drive, make certain the network crossover cable is connected between the two machines, make sure the ENBD/ENBCD is in the boot drive, and reconnect the power cable. Boot the target machine (suspect or lab machine) with your hand on the power cord at the rear of the machine. If the machine doesn't boot to the ENBD, disconnect the power at once.

4.  Once the ENBD starts, a menu will appear with the following choices:

    ▪ Network Support: A second menu will launch providing various driver support installation options for network support. For network cable acquisitions, choose this option.

    ▪ USB – Acquisition (no drive letter assigned): If you wish to acquire a USB device, this option loads the USB drivers to enable acquisition of a USB-connected device.

    ▪ USB – Destination (drive letter assigned): If you wish to store an EnCase evidence file or other data to a USB-connected device, this option will load the drivers to allow you to mount a USB-connected device with a drive letter so that DOS can write to that drive. Since DOS is the operating system, it must be a FAT partition. After the ASPI USB Manager loads and configures your USB device, EnCase for DOS launches automatically. You have to look in EnCase for your drive letter. This is useful for drive-to-drive acquisitions when your storage drive is a USB-connected storage device.

    ▪ Clean Boot: As with a bare-bones floppy boot, you are presented with a DOS prompt from which you can carry out DOS tasks or launch EnCase for DOS (EN.EXE) without any of the ENBD support features.

5.  You should choose #1 to load network support options. You are next given the choice of several options. If SCSI devices are present, you should first load the SCSI drivers before the NIC drivers. The SCSI driver menu will offer an "auto detect" or manual select options. "Auto detect" usually works and is the recommended first choice. Once your SCSI drivers are loaded, if they were needed, you next load your NIC drivers. The recommended method is again the "auto detect" method. Manual selection and loading is usually only necessary if you encounter difficulty with the automated detection and installation methods. Once your NIC is detected and the DOS packet drivers are installed, ENBD launches EnCase for DOS preconfigured to run in the server mode. Note that the default mode is BIOS.

6.  If you have chosen the ENBD due to HPA/DCO issues, you will have to press Esc and then click OK to temporarily shut down the server while you change the mode to Direct ATA access. Once that is done, press V or tab to Server to launch the Server panel. At this point you have a choice to make between a parallel port or a network connection. Choose Network and you will be back where you were when EnCase started, with the program preconfigured to launch to this mode. At this point, EnCase for DOS is in the Server mode with a network connection listening for EnCase for Windows to connect. It is time to turn your attention to the Windows machine.

Note that one of your choices when starting the server was to use a parallel cable. Before network connectivity became available in EnCase, the parallel cable was the method of connecting two machines and pulling data from the target machine to the Windows examination machine. It still works, but it is horribly slow when you consider the size of modern hard drives. If no other options are available, this is still a choice. Instead of connecting the machines via network cable, connect them via a parallel cable. Instead of choosing Network on both the DOS and Windows machines, choose Parallel Cable. Aside from the speed difference, all else is much the same.

7.  Before launching EnCase on the Windows machine, first consider firewall and other issues affecting connectivity. If you have your own firewall installed, you must configure it to allow EnCase to use a network connection. The number and types of firewalls prohibit a detailed explanation of how to do this. Suffice it to say that this approach won't work until you configure your firewall to allow the EnCase network connection to pass. The easiest solution is to turn off your firewall altogether for this operation, remembering to enable it again when done. If you are using Windows XP Service Pack 2 or later, a firewall was installed with SP2 whether or not you wanted it. If it is present and enabled, it will prevent this connection until you disable it, as shown in Figure 4.11, or until you add "Encase.exe" to the Exceptions tab. To access the Windows firewall options, click on Start ➤ Control Panel ➤ Windows Firewall.

**FIGURE 4.11** Windows Firewall Options - if configured to "OFF", do nothing. If "ON", turn it "OFF" or go to the "Exceptions" tab and add "Encase.exe" as a program.

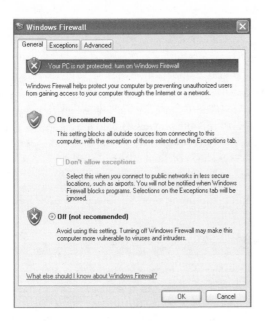

8. Usually, you do not have to change anything on the Network Settings tab as EnCase usually works well and allows a connection without you altering anything. I recommend only changing your network connections if you have a problem. If you have difficulty achieving the network connection described in the next step, come back and adjust your network settings. Remember that when you are done, you'll need to restore your previous settings if you want to connect to your network again! Therefore, note your settings before changing them. To modify your network settings, click Start ➤ Control Panel ➤ Network Connections. Next, right-click on Local Area Connection and choose Properties. Then, double-click on TCP/IP and the properties dialogue box will launch. Configure the settings as follows:

   - Change to a fixed IP, entering **10.0.0.50** in the IP address box.

   - For a subnet mask, enter **255.255.255.0**.

   - Remove any DNS or WINS settings; they can prevent the crossover cable connection from taking place.

9. Once you are satisfied that a firewall won't stop the connection, you are ready to launch EnCase in Windows. Open your case or start a new case. (If you aren't familiar with that process, we'll cover it in Chapter 6.) Click Add Device on the EnCase toolbar. In the resulting dialog box, place a blue check in the Network Crossover option in the right pane by simply clicking in the selection box. Click Next, and EnCase will poll the EnCase for DOS

server for a list of the available devices. Select the device you wish to examine, then click Next, and then Finish. EnCase for DOS will transmit the data to EnCase for Windows that allows you to view the file structure of the selected devices in the Windows version. This process may take a few minutes, depending on the network connection and the complexity of the device you selected. If you watch the EnCase for DOS server, the amount of data being transferred can be viewed in "real time."

10. In this manner, you can now preview the selected device in EnCase for Windows, as shown in Figure 4.12. There is no local image of the remote drive; therefore, the data is pulled over the wire as it is needed for the preview. There can be a lag time when viewing large files. You can create bookmarks and a report of your previewed data at this stage. You can also create a Logical Evidence File to preserve individual files or entire directories on the target drive—before, during, or after the acquisition of the entire physical disk.

**FIGURE 4.12**    A drive being previewed over a network cable. Note the lower right of the physical device icon has a little blue triangle, indicating that the device being viewed is a live device versus an image.

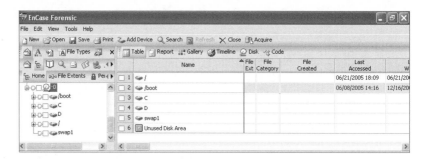

11. If your intent was to preview only, you are effectively done and may disconnect after you have finished with the report of your findings. If, however, your intent is to acquire an image of the selected device, you may do so at this time.

12. To acquire a device that you are previewing, in the left pane right-click on the device you wish to acquire, usually the physical device, so you can acquire all the data. From the resulting context menu, select Acquire, as shown in Figure 4.13.

13. You are presented with a dialog box that basically tells EnCase what to do with the image after the image is acquired, as shown in Figure 4.14. You may conduct a search, hash, and file signature analysis immediately following acquisition. If you are going to search, you must first have created and selected the keywords you intend to use. If you choose this option, you'll have the ability to run any or all of these tools against either the entire case or the newly acquired device, with the latter being the default. If you are imaging a floppy, you'll have the option to acquire another disk, and the next disk will sequence the number of the first disk by one to facilitate the imaging of a batch of floppies. With regard to the new image, you can choose whether or not to add it to the case. Another option is to replace the source drive that is already in the case with the image. When the image is done, the image will replace the live device and the little blue triangle will disappear. If you have

previewed the drive, conducted searches, or made bookmarks, when the image replaces the source drive, those search hits and bookmarks will be resolved from the live device to the image. A new option that became available with EnCase 5 is the ability to restart an acquisition in progress without starting over. For a host of reasons, an image can abort short of completion. With this option, you tell EnCase where the interrupted image file is located, and it picks up where it left off.

**FIGURE 4.13**    To acquire a device being previewed, in the left pane right-click on the device and choose Acquire.

**FIGURE 4.14**    In this dialog box you tell EnCase what to do with the image after it is acquired.

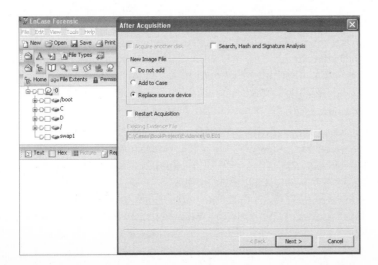

14. For our purposes, we are imaging a hard drive over a network cable and we want to replace the source drive with the image, so we select the Replace Source Drive option. Because we have no search defined, we leave that option unchecked. Since we aren't restarting an image, we leave that option deselected as well. At this point, we are ready for the next step. Click Next to see the wide range of acquisition options shown in Figure 4.15.

**FIGURE 4.15** Maximum "Error Granularity Setting" is determined by the "Block Size" setting. Here they are both set at their maximum value of 32,768 sectors.

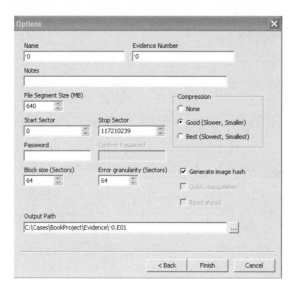

15. When we did our imaging in EnCase for DOS, we were presented with a linear series of questions and options. In EnCase for Windows, those options plus added features are all presented in one dialog box. When we type in the name of the evidence, EnCase automatically adds this name in the Evidence Number text box and appends the name to the path of the Output Path at the bottom of the dialog box. You can change either or both (Evidence Number or the file name in the Output Path text box) later if you wish, but normally the default is the better option. You may wish to double-check your output path to be certain it is going where you intend. Other options are as follows:

   ▪ Notes: As with EnCase for DOS, enter whatever brief notes you wish that can help link the evidence to the case.

   ▪ File Segment Size: As with EnCase for DOS, this is the "chunk size" option that determines the size of the EnCase evidence files. They can range from 1MB (to fit on a floppy) up to 2GB. Again, the default of 640MB fits nicely on a CD, and seven fit on a 4.7GB DVD. The default is the recommended setting.

   ▪ Compression: As with EnCase for DOS, you can choose to compress or not. As compression takes less disk space, but more time, you have to decide which is the scarcer resource when you have to acquire. EnCase for Windows gives you the added choice of a middle ground, where you can choose "good" compression instead of "best." It's a good compromise when both time and disk space are concerns. When doing a network acquisition, the compression occurs on the server side and can result in a faster acquisition if your network connection is slow or if you are using parallel cable because you have less data to pass through the connection.

- Start and Stop Sectors: As with EnCase for DOS, the defaults represent the beginning and end of the selected device. Recall from our previous discussion that you may need to change this setting if you are acquiring a device that was restored onto a larger device. You would only want to acquire the sectors associated with the original device, not the extra sectors at the end of the larger device.

- Password: There is no difference between a password applied within EnCase for DOS or Windows, which means everything from our discussion about this topic in EnCase for DOS applies. Just remember, if you apply a password, don't lose it!

- Block Size: This is a new setting in EnCase 5 and does not appear in EnCase for DOS. The block size refers to the size of the buffer used for acquiring data and computing the Cyclical Redundancy Check (CRC). DOS has an upper limit of 64 sectors, so this is not an option in DOS. With EnCase for Windows and LinEn, block sizes can range from 64 sectors to 32,768 sectors. We will discuss the EnCase evidence file in detail in Chapter 6, but for now you need to understand that EnCase normally writes a CRC for every 64 sectors of data. If you increase the block size, CRCs are written for larger blocks of data, thereby speeding up the acquisition process. If the block size is set to 256 sectors, for example, instead of writing a CRC for every 64 sectors, one will be written for every 256 sectors. You may be asking, why not make the setting 32,768 sectors every time and get the fastest possible acquisitions? As with many things in the computing world, performance gains often come with a trade-off. Every time that EnCase accesses data in the evidence file for processing, it first checks the integrity of that data by checking the CRC of the block in which the data resides. When accessing very small files, instead of checking the CRC of 64 sectors, EnCase must read and calculate the CRC of 32,768 sectors, which could slow down the program. Furthermore, if the evidence file contains a corrupted bit, EnCase knows only that the CRC for the block is bad and doesn't know which bit is corrupted. The larger the block size, the larger the amount of data affected by this error. Although such problems are rare, they can and do occur. The default block size of 64 sectors is a good compromise that we recommend. If you increase it, just understand its impact in other areas. There is also a relationship between this setting and the setting that follows, Error Granularity.

- Error Granularity: This is also new in EnCase 5 and is available in EnCase for Windows, DOS, and Linux. In prior versions of EnCase, if an error was found in one sector, the remaining sectors in that block were zeroed out to increase the speed of the acquisition, meaning data that could have been included was not. Numerically, this means that a block of data contains 64 sectors, or 32,768 bytes. If only one sector (512 bytes) was bad, 32,256 bytes of good data would have been zeroed out when brought into the evidence file. Needless to say, 32,236 bytes of data could contain valuable evidence of guilt or innocence. The data is still available through a network preview of the drive with errors, but this is a time-consuming manual process. The default setting for error granularity is 64, and if left unchanged, EnCase will handle errors as it always has, which is in the manner just described. You should leave this option set at 64 unless you encounter errors, because lowering it slows down the acquisition proportionally to the degree of granularity. If you encounter errors, you can acquire the image again with a lower error granularity setting. You can lower Error Granularity from 64 in powers of two, down to one (64, 32, 16, 8, 4, 2, 1). With a setting of 1, if one sector is bad no good data will be zeroed out. Thus far, we have discussed lowering the Error Granularity setting to capture more data if errors occur. If using a lower Error Granularity setting slows down the acquisition, increasing the setting speeds up the acquisition. If both the Block Size and the Error Granularity settings are left at their default value of 64 for each, nothing changes. If you increase the block size to 128, you can then adjust the error granularity up to 128. By increasing the block size you increase acquisition performance. By raising the granularity setting, you are increasing acquisition performance as well. Increasing both obviously yields even higher performance. The upper limit for the Error Granularity setting is the block size, which explains relationship between the two. Figure 4.16 shows a Block Size setting of 32,768 sectors. With this setting, a CRC is computed and written for every 32,768 sectors instead of every 64 sectors. It also increases the buffer size (memory) to hold this data. Both combine to give faster acquisitions. As the Block Size setting is 32,768, this becomes the upper limit for error granularity, and this setting is also set to 32,768 sectors. These settings would combine to give faster acquisitions, but are not very practical as one bad sector would result in the loss of over 16MB of good data. These settings are shown at their extreme to show their effect on performance and the relationship between the two values. Again, the defaults of 64 are recommended, and you can adjust in either direction based on preference or circumstance.

- Generate Image Hash: By default, this setting is enabled and an MD5 hash value is computed for the device being acquired; that value is stored in the evidence file as a means of verifying the authenticity of the original evidence stored in the evidence file. An MD5 hash is a 128-bit value that is calculated based on an algorithm developed by Rivest, Shamir, and Adleman (RSA). It is often called an electronic fingerprint because it uniquely identifies any stream of data or file. The odds of any two files having the same MD5 are one in $2^{128}$, which is, more graphically, one in 340,282,366,920,938,000,000,000,000,000,000,000,000. Needless to say, when two files have matching MD5 values, there is an extremely high confidence factor in stating that the contents of the two files are identical. The MD5 algorithm, which is publicly available, is the industry standard in the computer forensics field. However, it does take time to calculate, so turning it off would speed up an acquisition. This might be of some value if you were testing or working on some data that was not of evidentiary value and time was critical. It is recommended that you always leave this feature enabled and that you generate an MD5 hash of all evidentiary data in accordance with best forensic practices.

- Quick Reacquisition: This feature is new to EnCase 5. It is only an option when you are acquiring an image from an EnCase evidence file. It is not available when acquiring a device. After you have acquired a device and created an image of it in the form of an evidence file, you may have occasion to acquire it again. The purpose behind doing so is to change certain limited properties of the evidence file. By reacquiring an evidence file, you may change its compression (adding or removing), you may add or remove a password, or you may change its file segment size (chunk size). With EnCase 5, you may also adjust the block size or error granularity upon reaquisition. These are, however, the only things that you can change in an EnCase evidence file. Often you will acquire an image in the field and do not use any compression because that is the fastest way to acquire. You may also increase the Block Size and Error Granularity settings to further speed up the acquisition. When you get back in the lab and need to create your working copy of your evidence file, you can do so by reacquiring it with "best" compression. You may also change the Block Size and Error Granularity settings back to their defaults, increasing the integrity of the evidence file. You can then let the program run overnight, thus saving space on your lab drive, and store the uncompressed original separately when done. Reacquiring with or without compression does not in any way change the MD5 of the original data stream. Adding or removing compression or changing the block size or error granularity requires a full reacquisition process and can't be accomplished via the Quick Reacquisition option. The other two properties, changing a password or changing the file segment size, can be achieved quickly using the Quick Reacquisition option. Thus, if you need only add or remove a password or change the chunk size, use this option to save time on the reacquisition process. It is important to understand that reacquiring the image does not change the MD5 value of the original data stream acquired from the device if you change any or all of these five properties (compression, password, file segment size, block size, or error granularity). There is another setting that can be changed during reacquisition: the start and stop sectors, although this is rarely done. If you acquire a physical device and want to reacquire only a logical partition, you can do so with this feature. You enter the start sector at the first sector of the partition and the stop sector at the last sector of that partition. As you are changing the size of the original image, your new acquisition hash will be different from your original acquisition hash; they now represent different data streams. The new verification hash will match your new acquisition hash, however, during the verification process.

- Read Ahead: If you are using the Enterprise or FIM versions of EnCase 5, this option speeds up acquisitions through sector caching. If you are not using Enterprise or FIM, this box is grayed out.

- Output Path: As previously mentioned, this value defaults to the proper location and the file name is generated from the value you entered when you completed Name. If all is correct and to your liking, you need not change it. If you want to, simply browse to the desired location, also changing the file name if you prefer.

16. When all acquisition options are set, click the Finish button and EnCase will acquire the image according to the settings you entered.

**FIGURE 4.16**    Acquisition options for EnCase 5 in Windows

The speed of your acquisition will vary depending on the size of your target drive, the speed of your network connections, the overall performance of your two machines, and the acquisition settings you specified. As EnCase acquires the data, it calculates the amount of data imaged as a function of the time required to do so. Based on the amount of data remaining to be imaged, EnCase gives you an approximation of the time required to complete the job. This data is displayed in the progress bar in the lower right. As the imaging progresses, the figure usually becomes increasingly accurate.

If for any reason you need to stop the acquisition, you can do so by double-clicking on the progress bar. A window will appear asking you if you wish to stop. Click OK and the process will stop.

When the process has completed, an acquisition report window will appear that provides information about the acquisition. This information may be directed to the Console for use by EnScript, to a Note in your bookmarks, or to a Log Record, as depicted in Figure 4.17.

**FIGURE 4.17**   Acquisition completion report with options for directing the output to various locations

If you opted to have your image added to the case or to replace the source drive upon completion, a verification process starts immediately upon the image coming into the case. The verification process involves recalculating the CRC for each block in the data stream and recalculating the MD5 hash. All recalculations are compared with the original values, and all must match to successfully verify. The original hash value is called the Acquisition Hash, and the hash value calculated during verification is called the Verification Hash. To achieve a successful verification, all CRC acquisition values must match all CRC verification values, and the Acquisition Hash must match the Verification Hash.

Figure 4.18 shows the result of a successful verification where the verification process is reporting zero errors (all CRC values matched) and the Acquisition and Verification Hashes show identical MD5 values. The verification information is available on the Report tab for the selected device. Only when you have conducted a successful verification of your acquisition should you consider the job complete.

**FIGURE 4.18**   Verification shows zero errors (CRC values matched), and the Acquisition and Verification MD5 hashes are identical.

| File Integrity: | Completely Verified, 0 Errors |
| Acquisition Hash: | fa1a32b57675a4a6e5466f8db8337e1f |
| Verify Hash: | fa1a32b57675a4a6e5466f8db8337e1f |

# FastBloc Acquisitions

FastBloc is an IDE hardware write-blocking device developed by Guidance Software to work in conjunction with EnCase, but it does not require EnCase. FastBloc can function as a stand-alone write-blocking device in the Windows environment, allowing you to preview the data directly in the Windows Explorer interface. Additionally, third-party tools such as antivirus or spyware detection software can be run against the target drive with full write-block functionality.

FastBloc has undergone three model evolutions since its inception. All three models provide write-blocking on an IDE interface for the target drive. The original FastBloc is FastBloc Classic, which has a SCSI interface with the host computer. While still supported, it is no longer available for purchase. Currently available are the FastBloc LE (Lab Edition) and the FastBloc FE (Field Edition). The FastBloc LE has an IDE interface with the host computer and is better suited for semipermanent installation in the host computer. With its IDE host interface, it can be used equally as well in the DOS or Windows environment.

The latest model of FastBloc is the FastBloc FE. It is designed for field use and has a flexible interface, allowing USB-2 or 1394a (FireWire) host interfaces. Although both interfaces are present, you should not use both at the same time.

The 1394a protocol allows "daisy chaining" of FireWire devices, which means you can add FireWire devices to the second FireWire FastBloc port, provided you have connected to the host computer via the other FireWire port and have not connected via the USB port. As a caveat, the daisy-chained devices attached to FastBloc are turned on or off with the FastBloc power switch. Furthermore, write-blocking by FastBloc occurs only to the 40-pin and 44-pin IDE interfaces. Daisy-chained devices are not afforded write-block protection.

FastBloc is currently offered with an IDE interface for write-blocking. With the addition of an IDE-to-SATA bridge, FastBloc can be used with SATA drives as well, greatly adding to its functionality.

## Steps to Follow

To conduct a FastBloc acquisition, you should follow these steps:

1. Connect your FastBloc to your host computer via either a USB or a 1394a connection, but not both. The host computer can be running when you make this connection or you may make your connections while the computer is off and then boot the system.

2. Your target drive should be set for master or single. Adjust the jumper accordingly. Western Digital drives can be a little persnickety and often work better with no pins at all.

3. Connect the DC power from the FastBloc to the target hard drive. This applies only to 3.5-inch drives; 2.5-inch drives from laptops derive their power (5 volts only) directly through their 44-pin connection.

4. Connect the IDE cable from FastBloc to the target hard drive. Most 3.5-inch hard drives should be connected using the 80-conductor cable. Some older drives, designed to operate with the 40-conductor cable specification, should use that cable. Laptop drives should be connected to

the 44-pin connection. When connecting IDE connections, take care to attach the pin-one connection to its corresponding pin-one connection on the cable. Most connectors are "keyed" with a notch to prevent incorrect connections. Believe it or not, with a little force you can "bypass" this protection, thus forcing the protruding notch to fit where it isn't supposed to fit, totally reversing all the connections. The side wall of the connection flexes and bulges outward to facilitate the notch. As IDE connectors get "worn," this is even more likely to occur. Just because it "fits" doesn't make it right! Pay careful attention to what you are doing or you may see smoke where it shouldn't be. Also, take care if using longer IDE cables; the nearer you get to the 18-inch maximum, the more likely communications errors will occur.

Flat ribbon cables don't like being bent and twisted, especially repeatedly. They protest this treatment by failing when you least want them to! Invest in a few 6-inch and 12-inch-round shielded IDE cables with a single IDE 40-pin connection on each end. Use the 6-inch one when you have the hard drive detached, and use the 12-inch one when you have to "reach" a mounted hard drive in a case. The shielding in these cables guards against communications errors, facilitating fast, error-free acquisitions. The round cable design makes them very flexible and impervious to wear and tear from the repeated use that is typical of forensics work.

5.   Connect the power supply to FastBloc and power on FastBloc. If the host computer is already running, Plug and Play (PnP) should recognize FastBloc and mount the attached hard drive.

6.   If the host computer is not on, boot it up at this time. During startup, PnP should recognize FastBloc and mount the attached drive.

7.   You can confirm that FastBloc was detected and mounted by opening the Device Manager (right-click on My Computer and choose Properties; on the Hardware tab, choose Device Manager). Under Disk Drives, you should see FastBloc listed, as shown in Figure 4.19. If Windows can recognize and successfully mount any of the partitions on the target drive, it will do so when FastBloc is mounted. When this is the case, you can preview the partitions with Windows Explorer. There are times when partitions aren't mounted, but they are partitions that Windows should recognize and mount. Perhaps there is something about the partition that Windows finds problematic and won't mount. If the physical drive is mounted, EnCase will see the partitions when Windows refuses to do so.

**FIGURE 4.19**   When FastBloc is successfully detected and mounted by Windows PnP, FastBloc is listed under Disk Drives, as shown here in Windows XP Device Manager.

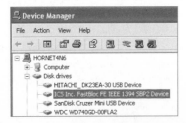

8. Run EnCase in Windows on the host examination computer to which FastBloc is attached. Open a case or start a new case. When a case (new or old) is open, click Add Device on the EnCase toolbar.

9. In the right pane of the Add Device dialog box, you'll have several options. As FastBloc is a mounted local device, click in the box (place a blue check) next to Local Drives and click Next, as shown in Figure 4.20.

**FIGURE 4.20** FastBloc is a mounted local device; therefore, click Local Drives to access FastBloc.

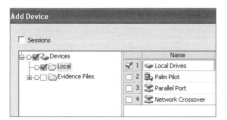

10. Under Choose Devices, you see a listing of all local devices, both logical and physical. Recall that the "blue triangle" at the lower right of the icon denoted a live device. FastBloc doesn't have a blue triangle; instead it has its own special icon, making it easy to identify the write-blocked target drive. The FastBloc icon is the device symbol with a blue square around it. Additionally, in the Write Blocked column you'll see an indicator in the column next to the FastBloc device. The indicator is a Boolean indicator for true, meaning the device is write-blocked. Sometimes this blue square can be missing along with the Boolean indicator for true in the Write Blocked column. The cause is typically a cable issue or an improperly jumpered drive. Even if the blue square and the Boolean indicator for true are missing, the device attached to FastBloc is still write-protected. With a blue check, select the physical device that is indicated with the FastBloc icon, as shown in Figure 4.21. Any mounted partitions on the device connected to FastBloc will also be displayed with a blue square. Selecting the physical device gives you all the sectors on the physical device, whereas selecting the logical device gives you only the sectors within that partition. Almost always you will seek all the sectors and will select the physical device.

The Boolean indicator for Show True is, by default, a dot. For Show False, the default indicator is nothing or null. Many examiners prefer to change this to Yes and No for added clarity. This can be done under Tools ➢ Options ➢ Global. The dot for Show True can be replaced with Yes and the null for Show False can be replaced with No. Figure 4.21 reflects this change.

**FIGURE 4.21** "Choose Devices" Window - FastBloc devices are denoted with a "Blue Square" icon indicating their "write-blocked" status.

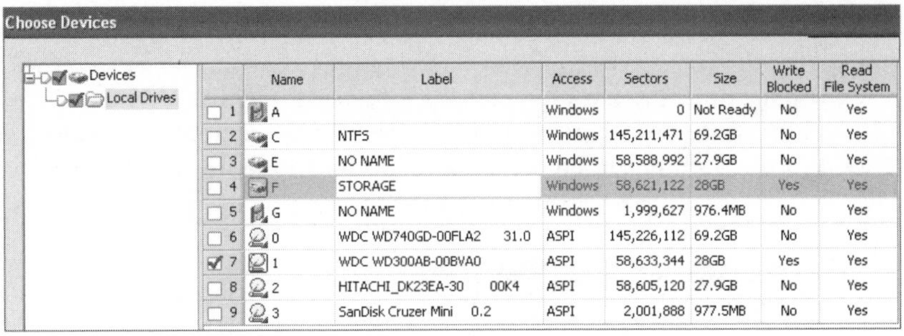

Choose Devices
Devices
Local Drives
Name
Label
Access
Sectors
Size
Write Blocked
Read File System
1 A Windows 0 Not Ready No Yes
2 C NTFS Windows 145,211,471 69.2GB No Yes
3 E NO NAME Windows 58,588,992 27.9GB No Yes
4 F STORAGE Windows 58,621,122 28GB Yes Yes
5 G NO NAME Windows 1,999,627 976.4MB No Yes
6 0 WDC WD740GD-00FLA2 31.0 ASPI 145,226,112 69.2GB No Yes
7 1 WDC WD300AB-00BVA0 ASPI 58,633,344 28GB Yes Yes
8 2 HITACHI_DK23EA-30 00K4 ASPI 58,605,120 27.9GB No Yes
9 3 SanDisk Cruzer Mini 0.2 ASPI 2,001,888 977.5MB No Yes

11. Before clicking Next to proceed, confirm that EnCase, through the BIOS interface in Windows, is able to see all the sectors on the drive as reported by the manufacturer. For the FastBloc physical device (not logical!), you see in the Sectors column that EnCase is reporting 58,633,344 sectors for this device. As this number matches the number of LBA sectors reported by Western Digital for this device, you know that you are accessing all the sectors on this drive and that it is acceptable to proceed and acquire this drive by this method. Once satisfied you can access all the sectors on your target drive, select the FastBloc physical device and click Next.
12. You are presented with yet another window, Preview Device. Most examiners simply click Finish at this stage; however, there are more features present in this window than meet the eye. If you highlight the device and right-click, you can choose Edit. With the Device Attributes menu open, you can give the device a name and include notes, as shown in Figure 4.22. Using this feature gives the device an identifiable name when it is brought into the EnCase device pane. If you have many devices in your case, this can be helpful. Otherwise, it will simply come into EnCase with a boring name, which is the physical device number or logical drive letter. When you later acquire the device, these names and notes carry forward into the Acquisitions Options dialog box. You can accept them or change them. When finished with the Preview Device dialog box, click Finish.

**FIGURE 4.22** Edit Option in the "Preview Device" window from which you can name your device and attach notes.

Preview Devices
Name
Label
Access
Sectors
Size
Write Blocked
Read File System
1 1 WDC WD300 ASPI 58,633,344 28GB Yes Yes
Device Attributes
Evidence Number
WD30GBFAT32HDD01
Evidence Name (unique within the case)
WD30GBFAT32HDD01
Notes
Western Digital 30 GB (28GB) FAT32 HD belonging to victim
Read File System
OK
Cancel

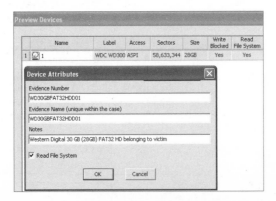

**13.** Your device will be read by EnCase, and the file structure will be mounted. In the previous Edit option, you could have opted to deselect Read File Structure. If you did not intend to preview and move immediately to acquire, deselecting this option can speed up the process of opening the device in EnCase, particularly with complex or multiple file structures. When this option is selected, you have a pure physical device with Unused Disk Area only and no file structure, as shown in Figure 4.23. If you leave the default (Read File Structure) or bypass Edit altogether, you will normally see the file structure of the device mounted in EnCase, as shown in Figure 4.24. Additionally, you will see the device in EnCase with the blue square denoting that the device is write-protected by FastBloc.

**FIGURE 4.23**    Physical device with "Unused Disk Area" and no file structure. In this case, this occurred when the "Read File Structure" was deselected in the "Edit" option in the "Preview Device."

**FIGURE 4.24**    Hard drive connected to FastBloc and mounted in EnCase. Note the device name provided in the "Edit" option appears with the device in EnCase and that the FastBloc "blue square" icon appears as well.

**14.** At this stage you can preview the drive, searching and bookmarking as is necessary. You can produce a report, printing it directly or saving it as a web document or as a Rich Text File (RTF)-formatted file, which is usable by most word processing software. If you create search hits, bookmarks, and so forth and acquire the device (selecting the Replace Source Drive option), those search hits and bookmarks will transfer and resolve to the image, keeping your work intact.

**15.** If you opt to acquire the FastBloc device, you may do so at this time. The acquisition will occur completely in the EnCase for Windows environment with full hardware write-block protection for the target drive. Right-click on the FastBloc device and choose Acquire, as shown in Figure 4.25. At this point, you will have the same set of EnCase in Windows options we discussed in the preceding section, "Network and Parallel Cable Acquisitions." You may go back to that section and review those options as needed. When your acquisition is done, in the Report tab for the imaged FastBloc device a notation appears that the acquisition was completed using FastBloc, which documents the write-protected acquisition method.

While other hardware write-blocking devices can be used in EnCase, only Fast-Bloc will currently show with a blue square icon and the Boolean true for write-blocked. Also, only FastBloc will show as FastBloc write-protected in the device-acquisition report.

**FIGURE 4.25**    Acquiring a FastBloc device by right-clicking on the FastBloc device and choosing Acquire.

Windows 98/Me are not recommended for forensic platforms. Windows 2000 Professional (or higher) should be used because it is more robust and stable. Another issue with Windows 98/Me involves disk caching. Although it is not recommended that you attempt disk writes to actual evidence media, you can attempt to write to a FastBloc-attached device through Windows Explorer. It will appear to have taken place, and this is occurring through disk caching. If you reboot and check again, you will see that nothing was written to the FastBloc-protected device. With Windows 98, if you attempt a logical acquisition before rebooting, the disk-cached information will be included in the resulting image. This does not occur with Windows 98 with a physical acquisition. It is best not to use Windows 98/Me for forensic use, and the platform is not supported with EnCase 5. If using Windows 98/Me, begin your acquisition immediately after booting the computer and don't do anything that would cause information to be disk cached and transferred to the logical image. When you're using Windows 2000/XP, disk caching information is not included in either the logical or physical acquisition.

**EXERCISE 4.1**

### Preview Your Own Hard Drive

Previewing your own hard drive using EnCase is an excellent technique for testing and research. You can also use it to study or familiarize yourself with various acquisition options. Here are the steps:

1. Launch EnCase (with dongle), start a new case, and simply accept the defaults.

2. Click Add Device.

3. Place a blue check on Local Drives and click Next.

4. Place a blue check next to your hard drive (the physical device) and click Next. Then click Finish on the next screen. EnCase should mount your local hard drive in the new case.

5. Your hard drive is now mounted along with its file system. You can preview it at this point if you'd like.

6. In the left pane, right-click on the physical device and choose Acquire.

7. In the After Acquisition options screen, simply click Next since you aren't going to make an actual acquisition.

8. You are now presented with the Options screen.

9. Under Name type in a name, such as **HDD01**. Note how EnCase automatically inserts this name in two other locations: the Evidence Name text box and the file name portion of the Output Path entry. You can change either or both of these if you like.

10. Note that the Block Size and Error Granularity settings are both set to 64 sectors. Attempt to raise the Error Granularity setting and you will find that it won't go higher than 64. Next raise the Block Size to a higher setting. Then increase the Error Granularity setting. You will find that you can raise it, but no higher than the Block Size setting. You may return them both to 64 or leave them be.

11. Click Cancel, and you are back to your case.

12. Close EnCase.

# LinEn Acquisitions

LinEn, or EnCase for Linux, is a brand-new feature with EnCase 5. It is similar to EnCase for DOS, but offers all the advantages of running under Linux. DOS is a legacy 16-bit operating system, whereas Linux, like Windows, is a 32-bit operating system. Thus, you get tremendous performance advantages using LinEn compared with EnCase for DOS.

Unlike DOS or Windows, Linux enables you to manually select whether you wish to mount a file system as read-only. In doing so, you are able to manually mount target evidence media in a write-protected manner, protected by the operating system instead of other methods or devices. To achieve this, however, you'll need to turn off the auto-mounting of file systems feature of Linux so that when it boots, file systems are not mounted. That enables you to do so manually, carefully controlling the process. To do this in SuSE and RedHat, do the following:

- For SuSE, run "Yast" (Yet Another System Tool), which is located in Main Menu ➤ System ➤ Configuration. Open the Runlevel Editor and disable the autofs feature.

- For Red Hat, run Services, which is located in Main Menu ➤ System Settings ➤ Server Settings. Disable the autofs feature.

Many people prefer to run LinEn from their favorite Linux distribution from a boot CD, such as Helix, Knoppix, SPADA, and so forth. Many of these security distributions of Linux already boot with auto-mounting of file systems disabled or mount them read-only, depending on how they have been configured or reconfigured in some cases. You should test your version to see how it mounts file systems when it boots. You could remaster the boot CD to include LinEn, but that necessitates doing so each time LinEn is updated. Instead, you place your updated copy of LinEn on your FAT32 storage volume or removable USB drive and run LinEn from that location. This keeps your Linux boot CD clean with no need for constant updating and places the updated copy of LinEn on the writable storage volume, making for an efficient working platform or methodology.

When running LinEn, you must be running as root because you must be in total control of the system. Although LinEn will run in the Linux GUI, the GUI uses system resources and limits the resources available to LinEn. For best performance, run LinEn in the console mode.

To configure Linux to boot in the console mode, you'll need to modify the boot runlevel, which is controlled by the file inittab located in the /etc folder. Edit the inittab file with your favorite text editor (vi is one such tool). Locate the line in the inittab file that reads: `id:5:initdefault:`. The 5 tells Linux to boot to the GUI. Change the 5 to a 3, which will cause Linux to boot to the console mode. Remember to save your changes! When Linux reboots, it will start in console mode. You should leave your forensic Linux system set up to boot this way. You can always run the GUI by typing **startx**.

Before mounting drives and starting LinEn, you need to get used to a different way of looking at devices from what you may be accustomed to viewing in Windows. Linux will list IDE devices as follows:

hda: Primary Master

hdb: Primary Slave

hdc: Secondary Master

hdd: Secondary Slave

For partitions on a hard drive, Linux will append a partition number to the hard drive designator. Examples include the following:

hdc1: Secondary Master First Partition

hda3: Primary Master Third Partition

If you are not sure what devices are on a system, at the console type **fdisk -l** and the devices will display. If you wish to see all the mounted devices, type **mount** at the console and press Enter. All mounted devices and their properties will display. To see more display options for either of these or any Linux command, type **man fdisk** at the console and press Enter. Replace **fdisk** with the command of your choice to see others. **man** means "manual," and you are asking to read the manual for any command that follows **man**.

Before you start, have a storage volume ready to accept your EnCase evidence file. When creating any storage volume, it is recommended that you employ best forensic practices and wipe the drive first. This avoids any claims of cross-contamination of evidence file data. Use a FAT32 volume with a unique volume label for this purpose. While Linux can read NTFS, with the appropriate distribution or module, writes to NTFS are not stable enough for evidentiary work, with few drivers available for this purpose (and they are in beta at best). An EXT2/3-formatted partition can be used for faster evidence file writing in Linux; however, the evidence file segments must be moved to a FAT or NTFS partition prior to examination with EnCase Windows. Given that, you should connect your storage volume to your Linux imaging platform.

At this point, you should be ready to begin. You should have done the following:

- Configured your Linux system so that the autofs (auto-mounting of file systems) is off and that file systems will not be mounted on boot.

- Configured your Linux system to boot into the console mode.

- Attached your target drive to the Linux imaging platform.

- Attached your storage drive (FAT32 with unique volume label) to the Linux imaging platform.

- Placed LinEn on either the Linux volume or on the storage drive. Either way, it should be in a known location so you may easily find and execute it.

## Steps to Follow

To conduct an acquisition using LinEn, you should follow these steps:

1. Boot your Linux machine to the console and log in at root

2. Check to see what file systems are mounted. Type **mount** and press Enter. Your target drive should not be mounted.

3. Check to see what devices are available. Type **fdisk -l** and press Enter. Locate your target drive and your storage drive. You should know how you connected them (primary master, etc.) and should be able to locate them using the Linux naming convention (hda for primary master, etc.).

4. Mount your storage drive. Create a directory by typing **mkdir /mnt/fat32**. Mount the storage volume on this mount point by typing **mount /dev/hda1 /mnt/fat32**. Remember that Linux is case sensitive and that *FAT* and *fat* are quite different in Linux. Remember also that *hda1* means the first partition on the primary master. If you storage volume is elsewhere, adjust accordingly.

5.  Check that your storage drive is mounted by again typing **mount** and pressing Enter. You should see your storage volume mounted.

6.  If you have not yet done so, create the folder on your storage volume to hold the EnCase evidence file. (This location must already exist and will not be created by LinEn.) Do so by typing **cd /mnt/fat32**. You will be in the root of your mounted storage volume. Using the mkdir command, you can create a suitable directory, such as /cases/casename/evidence. It is best to do this when you format it and when you don't have evidence drives mounted. With that methodology, mistakes are less likely to occur.

7.  Navigate to the location where LinEn is located. Assuming it is in /mnt/fat32/encase/linen, type **cd /mnt/fat32/encase** and press Enter. Then type **ls -al** and press Enter. You should see *LinEn*, but note that it is spelled as it appears by default, which is *linen*. As Linux is case sensitive, you must type it as it appears! If you prefer it as *LinEn*, as it is often dubbed, just rename it.

8.  Launch LinEn, spelled *linen* in Linux, by typing **./linen** and pressing Enter. Unless the path where LinEn is located appears in your defined PATH, you'll need to prefix the command with **./**, which tells Linux to look in the present directory for the command that follows. There is no space between **./** and the command that follows, which is **linen**. If you insert a space, you'll get an error. If you get a Permission Denied error, you'll need to change the permissions on the file. Type **chmod 777 linen** and it should work.

9.  LinEn should launch and you should see an interface that is very similar to EnCase for DOS. Note that the Lock tab is missing; Linux is handling that function. Linux communicates directly with the hardware, which means the Mode tab is also not needed. You are left with Acquire, Hash, Server, and Quit, as shown in Figure 4.26.

**FIGURE  4.26**    LinEn as shown at startup with options for Acquire, Hash, Server, and Quit

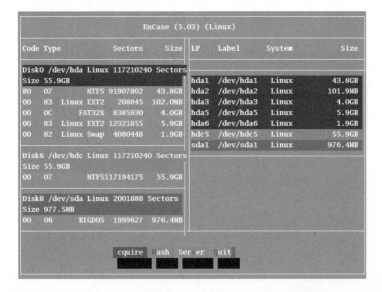

**10.** You may conduct an MD5 hash using the Hash tool. With this you may hash a physical drive or logical volume.

**11.** To acquire an image, press A to acquire or tab to Acquire and press Enter. What you see next is a choice of physical and logical devices available to image, as shown in Figure 4.27. However, they appear as Linux sees them. Therefore you'll need to know how you connected your device and its properties such as its size, volume name, and so forth, to identify it. If you are accustomed to Linux, it's a snap. If you are accustomed to Windows, it will require some learning on your part. Select your device and press Enter.

**12.** You are next prompted for the path for your evidence file. While this prompt is the same as EnCase for DOS, the path you type must satisfy the Linux path requirements and must be case sensitive as well. Recall that we created a directory on our storage drive (FAT32) and called it /cases/casename/evidence. To address that in Linux, we need to prefix it with the path to the mount path; it would appear as /mnt/winfat/cases/casename/evidence/ *USBTD001*, with *USBTD001* representing the name of the evidence file we wish to create.

**13.** From this point forward all screens are the same as you found in EnCase for DOS with one exception. In EnCase for DOS, the block size was fixed at 64 sectors due to DOS limitations, and changing the block size was not an option. In Linux, however, it is an option. After you enter your Maximum File Size or file chunk size option, you will have the opportunity to adjust the block size. The same pros and cons we previously discussed for block sizes apply; they apply equally to the Error Granularity setting, which immediately follows the Block Size option.

**FIGURE 4.27** Choose a drive to "Acquire" in LinEn, noting that devices use the Linux naming conventions.

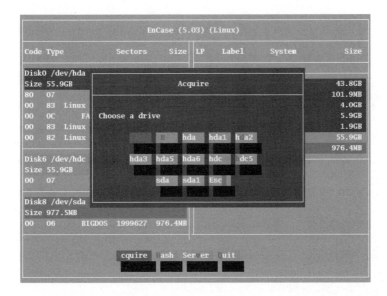

14. Once you've entered the Error Granularity setting, LinEn starts acquiring, providing you with the same acquisition status screen you saw in EnCase for DOS. When the image is complete, you get another window telling you it is done, the name and path of the file, and the time it took to acquire.

15. You have the option in LinEn to acquire via network cable. (Thankfully, there is no parallel cable option!) The physical setup is the same: you connect your Linux imaging machine (lab or suspect) to a Windows machine running EnCase, using a network crossover cable. At this point the process is the same. If you can't make a connection, exit LinEn. To make things work, you may have to assign an IP address to the Linux platform and different host IP on the same logical network for the Windows machine. We covered the method of changing the Windows IP and network settings earlier. Refer to that information and set the Windows machine to 10.0.0.50 and a subnet mask of 255.0.0.0. For the Linux machine, do the following:

- At the console command line, type **ifconfig eth0**.

- If no IP is assigned or one is assigned that doesn't fall in the 10.0.0.x network, you need to assign one. Type **ifconfig eth0 10.0.0.1 netmask 255.0.0.0** and press Enter.

- Type **ifconfig eth0** and check to make sure your settings are there (if you belong to the doubtful lot, like many of us do who like to check and double-check). It's like a carpenter who measures three times and cuts once!

- Restart LinEn and start the Server. Restart EnCase on Windows and follow the steps for making a network cable acquisition. When you have to choose devices in EnCase for Windows, the list of available devices will again be as Linux sees them and names them. All else is the same.

# Enterprise and FIM Acquisitions

EnCase Forensic allows you to preview and acquire over a network crossover cable, with the length of the crossover cable setting the limit as to how far apart the machines can be. With the EE (EnCase enterprise) and FIM (field intelligence module) editions of EnCase, the preview and acquisition occurs over the network and can occur over thousands of miles if need be. The only practical limit is the speed of the connection. This method of preview and acquisition cuts travel expenses drastically and enables incident-response time to be cut to near zero levels, if the systems are in place when the incident occurs.

Another distinction between the network cable preview and acquisition and one done with EE or FIM is that with EE and FIM, the target system is live and running its native operating system. As such, the target machine can be examined without the user's knowledge and the live system-state data (volatile data) can be previewed and captured. By capturing the volatile system-state data, examiners can analyze running processes, network connections, logged-in users, and much more. Such data is valuable when examining network intrusions, mounted encrypted volumes (if mounted they can be previewed and acquired intact), cases where malicious code is running, and cases where covert analysis is warranted. The live system-state data is accessed by an optional feature called the "Snapshot," which is a very sophisticated EnScript located, naturally, in the EnScript section.

This is not intended to be a tutorial on how to configure, administer, and use EE or FIM. That involves two weeks of training and is beyond the scope of this book. Rather, the intent here is to familiarize you with the function and features so that you can understand them well enough to intelligently decide on their applicability in any given situation should the need arise to deploy them.

The major differences between the EE version and the FIM version are in licensing and configuration. The FIM version can only be licensed to law enforcement and military customers. The EE version is, essentially, for everyone else needing EE/FIM features. Additionally, typically the FIM is licensed for only one simultaneous connection whereas EE starts at three connections and goes up depending on customer need and licensing agreements. The Snapshot feature that captures live system-state data is a separate license and is enabled for all connections when purchased.

To understand the configuration differences, you must first understand how EE is configured and functions. Only then can you appreciate how FIM differs from EE. There are three major components of an EE/FIM system. As shown in Figure 4.28, those components are the examination machine, the servlet node (target machine), and the SAFE.

**FIGURE 4.28**    Schematic of EnCase Enterprise. Note the three components: the examination machine, the servlet node (target machine), and the SAFE (Safe Authentication for EnCase).

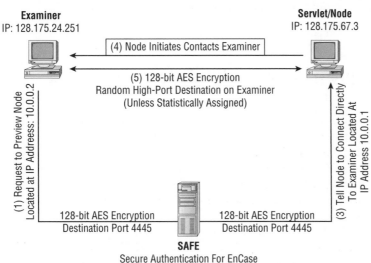

As the examiner, you have EE on your examination machine. Your target machine (servlet node), however many miles away, must have a servlet installed and running. A servlet is a small piece of code that places the target machine in a server mode listening on the network for a connection. The servlet is thus a server that will communicate with your examination machine, and it must also communicate with yet another machine called a SAFE. SAFE, as explained earlier, stands for Secure Authentication for EnCase. The SAFE is not technically necessary for a network forensic connection, but it is necessary to place a high level of security and supervisory control over the entire process.

The function of the examination machine and the servlet node (target machine) are self-evident, as they are analogous to the two machines in the network cable acquisition model. What is slightly different, however, is the installation of the servlet. The servlet serves as a secure network connection to the examination machine, after first authenticating through the SAFE. The servlet allows EE to have physical-level access to the target computer at a level below the operating system. When installed, the servlet listens on port 4445, but you can configure it to other ports when you create and install it.

The servlet can be preinstalled by a variety of methods, or it can be installed when needed. You can be physically present for the installation, or you can deploy the servlet remotely by using one of many remote administration tools or "push technologies," such as Active Directory. It can be done manually or automated with scripts. To install the servlet on Windows systems, you must have administrator rights and on Linux/Unix, you must have root-level privileges. Guidance Software has published a small manual that deals strictly with deploying servlets. This document is available on their web site.

The SAFE, the new piece in the model, is a stand-alone machine that stands between, initially, the examination machine and the servlet node. The SAFE is usually administered by, or at the direction of, a high-level person in the organization, typically at the level of the chief information officer or equivalent.

This SAFE administrator controls what servlet nodes the examiner can access and is dubbed the *keymaster*. The granularity of control is very coarse or very fine. The controls can determine days and times an examiner can access a given node. Further, the controls can determine the level of functions permitted to the examiner. For example, an examiner can be limited to previewing only and not permitted to acquire or copy files.

Each examiner must be added to the list of examiners for each SAFE and is assigned keys for authentication and encryption. Before a node can be accessed by an examiner, the keymaster must log on to the SAFE and add the servlet node to the list of nodes the examiner may access, along with any limitations on that access. Furthermore, all traffic between any devices in the EE system is encrypted using 128-bit AES encryption. Thus the SAFE provides supervisory oversight, serves as an authentication gateway, and facilitates the encryption of the network connection.

When an examiner wishes to connect to a target machine, the examiner communicates with the SAFE with a request to do so. If the requested connection and access is permitted by the established rules, the SAFE communicates with the target node. The SAFE tells the target node to communicate directly with the examination machine. The servlet node (target machine) then communicates directly with the examination machine, and the session takes place with whatever controls may be in place as directed by the SAFE. This connection is depicted in Figure 4.28.

Firewalls will have to be configured to enable this traffic to pass. Any host-based firewall on a servlet node will also have to be configured to allow the servlet connection to pass. As a fail-safe, if for any reason the servlet node can't connect directly to the examination machine, the connection may route to the examination machine through the SAFE. Although the connection will be somewhat slower, it will, nevertheless, occur.

The FIM is basically an EE system with one slight configuration modification. With the FIM, the SAFE is located directly on the examiner's machine, usually a laptop, and the examiner and the keymaster are the same person. As there is no third-party keymaster overseeing the connections, the FIM becomes a very powerful tool. It was developed for law enforcement and military applications.

Figure 4.29 shows the FIM configuration. If you look carefully, the major difference is where the SAFE is located. In the EE, the SAFE is located on the SAFE administrator's PC. In the FIM, the SAFE is located on the examination machine, removing the third party altogether. Otherwise, they function in the same manner.

**FIGURE 4.29**    FIM schematic with SAFE located on examiner's machine. Compare this to EE schematic in Figure 4.28, where SAFE is a separate machine controlled by the SAFE administrator (keymaster).

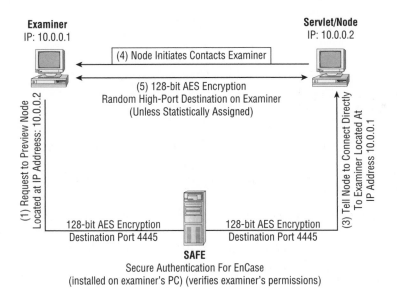

In law enforcement and military applications, the FIM is often connected to a target host (servlet node) directly with a crossover cable. Of course, this differs from the network cable acquisition since the target host is live and the servlet is installed directly by the examiner. Usually, with most home machines, the user has administrator rights and servlet deployment is a minor task. When the connection is made, the examiner has access to the storage media on the target host plus the live system-state data.

The FIM is not limited to a crossover cable connection and can also connect to any network machine on which the servlet is deployed. In law enforcement and military use, it is ideal for surreptitious remote previewing and acquisitions, with proper search authority having been secured.

Another extremely useful application of the FIM is when conducting previews or acquisitions on business servers that can't be shut down. It's a simple matter for the examiner to connect to the network on which the server resides. The examiner next deploys the servlet on the target server. With that done, the examiner logs in as keymaster and adds the IP address of the target server to the list of nodes the examiner can access. The examiner logs off as keymaster and then logs back into the SAFE as the examiner. At this point the examiner can connect to the target server and conduct a preview or acquisition as needed. All storage media is available, as is the live system-state data. The examiner completes the job at his or her leisure, the server stays up, and business goes on as usual.

EE and FIM are very powerful and flexible tools. As live forensics becomes more necessary and mainstream, their value will be increasingly accepted by the industry and the judiciary. As that evolves, instead of just being accepted, they will become expected in many cases where their value makes a significant evidentiary difference.

# Helpful Hints

As you encounter various devices, here are some suggested acquisition solutions:

- If you encounter a floppy, flip the write-protect notch to read-only and acquire in EnCase for Windows on a system where the floppy drive has been tested for its ability to write-protect. Alternatively, you could do a DOS acquisition, but there's usually no need.

- If you encounter a zip or Jaz disk, use an IDE zip or Jaz drive and acquire in EnCase for DOS. You will need the guest.exe file to mount the Iomega drivers. The easiest solution is to download the zip-booter boot disk image from the Guidance Software website, update it with the latest EN.EXE, and you are set.

- If you encounter a CD, you can safely image it in Windows. You may encounter difficulties with some CD file systems. An alternative in these cases is to use CD Inspector, create a zip image file, and bring the zip file into the EnCase environment. This functionality is new to EnCase 5.

- If you encounter USB flash media, you can usually image it in Windows by flipping the write-protect switch and doing so in combination with the Registry setting that makes USB devices read-only. This setting is only available in XP SP2 or higher. If neither of these write-protect features is an option, the ENBD/ENBCD has a feature to load DOS USB drivers. EnCase for DOS can then be used. Another option is to use LinEn on a version of Linux that has support for your USB devices, making sure you first disable auto-mounting of the file system as previously discussed.

# Summary

This chapter covered the many facets of acquiring digital evidence. We covered the process by which we control the boot process by modifying the boot order in Setup and modifying boot disks so that any calls made to the hard drive are redirected to the boot disk. We examined three methods of creating EnCase boot disks within EnCase.

After understanding the process and making EnCase boot disks, we discussed the reasons why EnCase boot disks are needed despite advances in write-blocking technology allowing acquisitions in Windows. For example, we may encounter geometry mismatches between legacy and modern BIOS code. We may encounter proprietary security schemes that marry hard drives to chips on the motherboard. We may also encounter HPA or DCO areas of the drive that can't be seen by the BIOS in Windows. Any of these conditions warrant booting with EnCase for DOS or LinEn in Linux to be able to access the drive directly through the ATA controller.

We detailed the process of booting a computer with EnCase boot disks using a carefully controlled sequence. Before connecting the target drive, you must configure the system to boot from the EnCase boot disk and make certain it works before reconnecting the target drive.

Drive-to-drive acquisitions occur when the storage media and the target media are mounted on the same machine. We detailed how to use EnCase for DOS for these acquisitions, based on the foundation we laid for creating EnCase boot disks and booting from them. We discussed the importance of preparing storage media formatted to FAT32, with a unique volume label, and with a preconfigured directory path for the EnCase evidence files. We showed how to account for all sectors on a drive and how to switch to the Direct ATA mode when encountering HPA or DCO areas, usually indicated when all sectors can't be seen by the BIOS.

Network cable acquisitions occur between two machines connected by a network crossover cable. One machine is running EnCase for Windows while the other machine is running EnCase for DOS or LinEn under Linux. The target host machine runs EnCase (DOS) or LinEn in a server mode first. Once that machine is waiting to connect, the EnCase for Windows machine is started. When choosing the devices to acquire, the network crossover option is selected, which then connects with the waiting server, and a network connection is established over which previewing or acquisition occurs.

Network cable acquisitions can be used to overcome HPA or DCO issues. They are relatively fast acquisition methods and even faster using gigabit NIC cards on both ends and LinEn as the tool. In lieu of a network cable, a parallel cable connection can be substituted. Parallel cable transmission rates are horribly slow, and network cable is much faster and preferred.

While discussing network cable acquisitions, we detailed the many acquisition options in EnCase for Windows. We examined the pros and cons of adjusting block sizes and error granularity, both of which are new in EnCase 5. You can increase block sizes and make error granularity less coarse and increase acquisition speeds. The downside is possible data loss when encountering errors during acquisition or later if data corrupts in the evidence file.

FastBloc is a hardware write-blocking device that blocks writes to IDE drives or SATA drives if connected via an IDE/SATA bridge. We examined how FastBloc integrates with EnCase or as a stand-alone device within Windows.

FastBloc comes in three models, which are the Classic, the LE, and the FE. The Classic has a SCSI interface with the host. The LE has an IDE interface with the host. The FE has a USB or 1394a interface with the host. FastBloc shows as a special icon with a blue square around the physical device. It also shows as "Write Blocked" with a Boolean indicator for true. FastBloc also is reported in the acquisition details listed in the report tab for the acquired image.

Windows 98/Me is not recommended for forensic use. If you must use Windows 98, be aware that disk-cached changes made in Windows are conveyed in a logical acquisition of the drive. If you must use Windows 98, boot, start EnCase, and start your acquisition immediately. Note the EnCase 5 will not run on Windows 98/Me.

LinEn is EnCase for Linux, which is new in EnCase 5. Linux affords many advantages over DOS as Linux is a 32-bit OS while DOS is a 16-bit OS. Linux controls how devices are mounted, and whether file systems are mounted; if file systems are mounted, they can be mounted as read-only. We detailed how to configure mainstream Linux to not auto-mount file systems and how to change the runlevel so that Linux starts in the console mode and not the GUI mode. Using the fdisk -l command we can see what devices are available; using the mount command we can see what file systems are mounted and how. Using the Linux naming conventions, hda2 is the second partition on the primary master while hdd1 is the first partition on the secondary slave. When running LinEn we can acquire, hash, or run in the server mode for network cable acquisition with nearly the same interface options as EnCase for DOS.

EE and FIM can preview and acquire target systems (servlet nodes) over a network connection with no limitations on distance. If the Internet can reach the target, you can reach it with EE or FIM. FIM is for law enforcement or military customers, and EE is for all others. The three components of the EE or FIM system are the examiner machine, the servlet node (target host), and the SAFE. The SAFE, which stands for "Safe Authentication for EnCase," authenticates the connection, acts to limit and supervise the process, and facilitates the encrypted connection. With EE the SAFE is on a separate PC administered by a SAFE administrator known as the *keymaster*. With FIM, the SAFE resides on the same PC as the examination machine, making the examiner and keymaster the same person. In addition to previewing and acquiring a live host, EE or FIM can capture live system-state data using the Snapshot feature.

# Exam Essentials

**Understand why and how an EnCase Boot Disk is made.**    Know what system files are changed or modified by EnCase when making a boot disk and why. Be able to explain the three methods of creating a boot disk within the EnCase environment.

**Understand how to boot a computer with an EnCase boot disk.**    Be able to explain the various conditions that would warrant booting a computer with an EnCase boot disk. Explain the process of preparing the target host computer for a safe boot using the EnCase boot disk. Know how to change the boot order in Setup and why this step is important. Describe each step in booting the computer using an EnCase boot disk and the importance of each step.

**Know how to do a disk-to-disk acquisition.**   Be able to explain the various conditions that would warrant a disk-to-disk acquisition. Be able to explain the difference between the BIOS and Direct ATA modes, how to switch between them, and why this would be necessary. Understand why an NTFS partition would not be seen in the right pane of EnCase for DOS. Explain why it is necessary to prepare the storage volume with a FAT32 partition and to create a directory path for the EnCase evidence files. Know how to adjust the Error Granularity setting and be able to explain the effects of raising or lowering the setting. Be able to explain the connections and steps necessary to conduct a disk-to-disk acquisition using EnCase for DOS. Understand that LinEn is also an option for drive-to-drive acquisitions.

**Know how to conduct a network cable acquisition.**   Be able to explain the various conditions that would warrant a disk-to-disk acquisition. Know what kind of cable is required for this acquisition and explain the difference between this cable and a regular network cable. Explain how to create and prepare both an ENBD and an ENBCD. Explain the importance of controlling the boot process on the target host. Explain the steps involved in booting the target host and making the connection to EnCase for Windows. Describe the various acquisition options. Understand how to adjust the block size and explain the pros and cons of increasing or decreasing it. Understand which evidence file properties you can change by reacquiring. Explain why the MD5 hash does not change when you reacquire and change any of these properties unless you change the number of sectors.

**Know how to conduct a FastBloc acquisition.**   Know the three different FastBloc models and explain how their host connections are different. Explain how to connect the FastBloc to the host and to the target drive. Describe the process by which FastBloc is powered on and its attached drive is mounted in Windows. Know what the FastBloc icon looks like and where and how its "write-block" status is reported or indicated in EnCase. Describe how FastBloc can be used as a stand-alone write blocking device by which to use third-party tools to examine the drive in Windows without EnCase. Understand the disk-caching problems associated with using FastBloc with Windows 98/Me.

**Know how use the LinEn for Linux tool.**   Be able to explain the various conditions that would warrant a LinEn acquisition. Explain the importance of modifying Linux to disable the automatic mounting of file system upon boot. Explain why it is important to boot Linux to the console mode and how to configure this change. Explain what acquisition options are available in LinEn. Understand how Linux names devices and partitions.

**Understand EE and FIM configuration and capabilities.**   Know the three components in EE or FIM systems and explain how they function. Understand under what circumstances an EE or FIM would be valuable to an investigation. Understand what types of data that EE or FIM can capture that other EnCase models can't. Explain volatile system-state data and its importance to an investigation. Explain how EE and FIM differ.

# Review Questions

1. When acquiring a hard drive in the DOS mode, what would be the cause of EnCase not detecting partition information?

   **A.** Drive has been FDisked and partition(s) removed.

   **B.** Partition(s) are not recognized by DOS.

   **C.** Both A and B.

   **D.** None of the above.

2. A standard DOS 6.22 boot disk does not make calls to the C:\ volume of a hard drive when the diskette is booted.

   **A.** True

   **B.** False

3. As a good forensic practice, why would it be a good idea to wipe a forensic drive before reusing it?

   **A.** Chain-of-custody

   **B.** Cross-contamination

   **C.** Different file and operating systems

   **D.** Chain of evidence

   **E.** No need to wipe

4. If the number of sectors reported by EnCase does not match the number reported by the manufacturer for the drive, what should you do?

   **A.** Suspect HPA

   **B.** Suspect DCO

   **C.** Boot with EnCase for DOS and switch to Direct ATA access

   **D.** Boot with LinEn in Linux

   **E.** All of the above

5. When acquiring digital evidence, why shouldn't the evidence be left unattended in an unsecured location?

   **A.** Cross-contamination

   **B.** Storage

   **C.** Chain-of-custody

   **D.** Not an issue

**6.** Which describes an HPA? (Choose all that are correct.)

 **A.** Stands for Host Protected Area

 **B.** Is not normally seen by the BIOS

 **C.** Is not normally seen through Direct ATA access

 **D.** Was introduced in the ATA-6 specification

**7.** Which describes a DCO?

 **A.** Was introduced in the ATA-6 specification

 **B.** Stands for Dynamic Configuration Overlay

 **C.** Is not normally seen by the BIOS

 **D.** It may contain hidden data, which can be seen by switching to the Direct ATA mode in EnCase for DOS

 **E.** All of the above

**8.** What system files are changed or in any way modified by EnCase when creating an EnCase boot disk?

 **A.** IO.SYS

 **B.** COMMAND.COM

 **C.** DRVSPACE.BIN

 **D.** All of the above

 **E.** None of the above

**9.** Reacquiring an image and adding compression will change the MD5 value of the acquisition hash.

 **A.** True

 **B.** False

**10.** When reacquiring an image, you can change the name of the evidence.

 **A.** True

 **B.** False

**11.** Which of the following should you do when creating a storage volume to hold an EnCase evidence file that will be created with EnCase for DOS or LinEn? (Choose all that are correct.)

 **A.** Format the volume with the FAT file system.

 **B.** Give the volume a unique label to identify it.

 **C.** Wipe the volume before formatting to conform to best practices and avoid claims of cross-contamination.

 **D.** Create a directory to contain the evidence file.

 **E.** Format the volume with the NTFS file system.

 **F.** All of the above.

**12.** In Linux, what describes hdb2? (Choose all that are correct.)

    **A.** Refers to the primary master

    **B.** Refers to the primary slave

    **C.** Refers to hard drive number 2

    **D.** Refers to the second partition

    **E.** Refers to the secondary master

**13.** In Linux, what describes sdb? (Choose all that are correct.)

    **A.** Refers to an IDE device

    **B.** Refers to a SCSI device

    **C.** Refers to a USB device

    **D.** Refers to a FireWire device

**14.** When acquiring USB flash memory, you should write-protect it by:

    **A.** Engaging the write-protect switch, if equipped

    **B.** Modifying the Registry in XP SP2 (or higher) to make USB read-only

    **C.** Using ENBD/ENBCD USB DOS drivers and having EnCase for DOS "Lock" the flash media

    **D.** Using LinEn in Linux with auto-mount of file system disabled

    **E.** All of the above

**15.** Which type or types of cables can be used in a network cable acquisition?

    **A.** Standard network patch cable

    **B.** CAT-6 network cable

    **C.** Network crossover cable

    **D.** Standard network patch cable used with a crossover adaptor

**16.** Should zip/Jaz disks be acquired with EnCase in DOS or Windows?

    **A.** DOS

    **B.** Windows

**17.** How can a floppy disk be acquired by EnCase?

    **A.** DOS mode

    **B.** Windows mode

    **C.** Both modes

**18.** How should CDs be acquired using EnCase?

    **A.** DOS

    **B.** Windows

**19.** Select all that are true about EE and FIM.

    **A.** They can acquire or preview a system live without shutting it down.

    **B.** They can capture live system-state volatile data using the Snapshot feature.

    **C.** With EE, the SAFE is on a separate PC, administered by the keymaster.

    **D.** With FIM, the SAFE is on the examiner's PC and the keymaster and the examiner are the same person.

    **E.** FIM can be licensed to private individuals.

**20.** How does an EnCase boot disk differ from a DOS 6.22 disk?

    **A.** EnCase boot disk adds the EnCase executable, EN.EXE.

    **B.** EnCase boot disk switches all calls from C:\ to A:\.

    **C.** Both A and B.

    **D.** None of the above.

# Answers to Review Questions

1. C. When partitions have been removed or if partitions are not recognized by DOS, EnCase still recognizes the physical drive and acquires it as such.

2. B. A standard DOS 6.22 boot disk accesses the C:\ volume of a hard drive, thus causing changes to date/time stamps to certain files.

3. B. Although EnCase only examines the contents within the evidence files, it is still good forensic practice to wipe/sterilize each hard drive prior to reusing it to eliminate the argument of possible cross-contamination.

4. E. You should suspect an HPA or a DCO. Booting with LinEn or booting with EnCase for DOS with Direct ATA access should enable you to see all sectors.

5. C. Digital evidence must be treated like any other evidence, whereas a chain of custody must be established to account for everyone who has access to the property.

6. A and B. HPA stands for Host Protected Area and is not normally seen by the BIOS. It was introduced in the ATA-4 specification, not ATA-6, and is seen when directly accessed via the Direct ATA mode.

7. E. All are correct statements with regard to DCO.

8. D. EnCase will modify IO.SYS and COMMAND.COM to redirect any calls from C: to A:. If DRVSPACE.BIN is present, it will be deleted.

9. False. When reacquiring an image, the MD5 of the original data stream remains the same despite the compression applied.

10. False. When reacquiring, you can change the compression, you can add or remove a password, you can change the file segment size, you can change the block and error granularity sizes, or you can change the start and stop sectors. Other properties can't be changed.

11. A, B, C, D. This is a case where you have to choose several correct answers, and there will be questions like this on the examination! All are correct except for E, therefore making F also incorrect. DOS can't read or write to NTFS. Linux can read NTFS, but can't reliably write to it.

12. A and D. Here, hdb2 refers to the second partition on the primary master.

13. B, C, and D. Linux will name an IDE device, normally, with *hda*, *hdb*, *hdc*, or *hdd*, to denote their position on the ATA controller (primary master, primary slave, secondary master, secondary slave, respectively). sdb is the second SCSI device, and since Linux calls USB or FireWire devices SCSI devices, any of the three (B, C, or D) could be represented by sdb.

14. E. All are methods of write-protecting USB devices, some arguably better than others, but methods nevertheless.

**15.** C and D. A and B are references to standard network cables with no crossover capability. To connect directly between two computers, a network crossover cable must be used, or you can use a regular cable with a crossover adapter, which achieves the same effect.

**16.** A. Zip and Jaz disks should be acquired by EnCase in the DOS mode using the guest.exe command.

**17.** C. Floppy disks can be acquired using both methods. Be sure to write-protect floppy disks before inserting them into the drive.

**18.** B. CDs can be safely acquired in the Windows environment.

**19.** A, B, C, D. A FIM can only be licensed to law enforcement or military customers. All other statements are correct.

**20.** C. An EnCase boot disk changes all calls to the C:\ volume to the A:\ volume and removes unnecessary files. It also adds the EN.EXE file so EnCase can run in the DOS version.

# Chapter

# 5

# EnCase Concepts

## ENCE EXAM TOPICS COVERED IN THIS CHAPTER:

- ✓ EnCase evidence file
- ✓ CRC and MD5
- ✓ EnCase evidence file format
- ✓ Evidence file verification
- ✓ Hashing disks and volumes
- ✓ EnCase case file
- ✓ EnCase backup file
- ✓ Configuration, or "ini," files

This book has made numerous references to the EnCase evidence file. We've talked about many of its properties, such as compression, file chunk size, protection via password, MD5 hash, and CRC frequency. In this chapter, we'll closely examine the evidence file. We'll describe its major components and its various properties in detail. The evidence file, as you'll see, is constructed to maintain the authenticity and integrity of the original evidence, both of which are crucial in maintaining the chain of custody.

It is important that you understand how EnCase works with the evidence file "under the hood" so that you explain or demonstrate why or how the evidence is preserved and unaltered in the EnCase environment. To that end, we'll even use evidence files included on the CD in an exercise that demonstrates what happens when the evidence file is corrupted or subjected to deliberate tampering. When you finish this chapter, you'll thoroughly understand the EnCase evidence file and have a high degree of confidence in the integrity of the data under examination.

Examples are included on the CD and in the exercise.

# EnCase Evidence File Format

The EnCase evidence file is often called the image file. This is a carryover from the original imaging methods that had their roots in the Unix dd command. In Linux or Unix, everything is a file. Thus a device, such as a hard drive, can be addressed as a file. Using the dd command, you can copy one hard drive onto another hard drive with the apparent ease of copying a file, although the process certainly takes longer. The copy produced can be a stream of data sent from the original drive to the copy drive, with the end result being two identical drives, assuming the copy drive contained the same number of sectors. Alternatively, you could direct the copy to an actual file instead of a device. The end result of this process is a large file whose contents are a bit-by-bit copy of the original device. This is often called an "image" file and is given the extension .img to denote it as such.

Regardless of its name, the primary purpose of an EnCase evidence file is to contain an exact bit-for-bit copy of the target media. Unlike a Linux dd image, which contains only a bit-for-bit copy of the target media, the EnCase evidence file contains the bit-for-bit copy plus other information that serves to "bag and tag" the evidence file to preserve the chain of custody. To achieve this same bag-and-tag effect in Linux would require several separate steps. Even then, the bag-and-tag items are still separate items and not integrated into the image. With EnCase, by contrast, this bag-and-tag information is created automatically and integrated into the evidence file as it is created. By doing so in one automated step, you ensure that the evidence is placed in a sealed, self-authenticating evidence container, thus preserving the integrity of the evidence.

# CRC and MD5

Throughout, we have made many references to the CRC and the MD5. During our discussion of acquisitions, we described the MD5 in detail. For purposes of understanding the file integrity component or function of the EnCase evidence file, we need to digress at this point and review and expand our understanding of the CRC and MD5. In this manner, we can better appreciate what these values mean and how they contribute to the file integrity measures employed by EnCase.

You may recall from our previous discussions that an MD5 (Message Digest 5) is an algorithm or calculation applied to streams of data (files, devices, etc.). The result of this calculation is a 128-bit hexadecimal value (32 characters with each character or byte containing 8 bits each). The number of possible values for this hexadecimal number is $2^{128}$. Thus the odds of any two files having the same MD5 value are one in $2^{128}$. In tangible terms, to the extent that such numbers are tangible, that is one in approximately 340 billion billion billion billion. As the odds are so remote of two files having the same hash value, one can statistically infer, with an extremely high degree of confidence, that two files having the same hash value have the same file contents. The reverse can also be inferred: if two files have different hash values, their contents are different. For this reason, the MD5 is an industry standard in the computer forensics field for verifying the integrity of files and data streams.

A CRC (Cyclical Redundancy Check) is similar in function and purpose to the MD5. The CRC algorithm results in a 32-bit hexadecimal value compared to the 128-bit value produced by the MD5. The number of possible values for a 32-bit hexadecimal value is $2^{32}$ and the odds of any two numbers having the same CRC is one in $2^{32}$. Translated, this means that the odds of any two files having the same CRC are one in 4,294,967,296 (4 billion and some change!). While the odds associated with a CRC hardly approach those offered by the MD5, one in 4 billion is still a statistically strong validation.

The MD5 requires more calculations than the CRC, and hence more time and system resources are required to generate an MD5. Because the CRC is faster to generate and uses less system resources, it has value in that regard and is used frequently for maintaining data integrity in a variety of applications. It is good compromise solution for providing data integrity checking when performance is an issue. As you'll come to appreciate, EnCase makes frequent use of the CRC during its program operations and uses both the CRC and the MD5 when validating the entire evidence file. Combined, the CRC and MD5 provide powerful data integrity tests throughout the entire acquisition and examination process.

# Evidence File Components and Function

An EnCase evidence file has three major components: the header, the file integrity component (CRC and MD5), and the data blocks. The header will appear on the front end of the evidence file, and the data blocks follow the header. The file integrity component exists throughout and functions to provide redundant levels of file integrity.

Each compartment has is own integrity *seal,* and the header is *sealed* with its own CRC. Each data block is verified with its own CRC. The entire data block section is subjected to an MD5 hash, called an *acquisition hash,* which is appended after the data blocks. The header and all CRCs are not included in this MD5 hash. It is important to understand that the MD5 hash is calculated only on the data.

Although the header and the data blocks are clearly separate data areas, the file integrity component is interwoven throughout. It can be viewed abstractly as a separate component, but when viewed in its physical form, it is ubiquitous throughout the evidence file, as you can see in Figure 5.1.

**FIGURE 5.1** Physical layout of the EnCase evidence file. The header appears at the front of the file, followed by the data blocks. Note that the file integrity components (CRCs and MD5) are interwoven throughout.

Now that you have an overall understanding of the construction of the evidence file, let's see how one is created, starting with the header. The header contains much of the case information that you entered at the Options screen during acquisition, along with other information. You may expect the following, among other data, to be contained within the header:

- Evidence name
- Evidence number
- Notes
- Date/time of acquisition
- Version of EnCase used for acquisition
- Operating system under which acquisition took place

Once the acquisition options (name, number, notes, etc.) have been entered and the system information has been gathered, this information is placed in the header. The header is subjected to a CRC and compressed. The header is always subjected to compression even when the data is not. Compressing it saves space and removes the ability to alter clear text data. In this manner, the documentary information concerning the evidence is sealed for integrity. This component, the header and its CRC, are placed on the front of the evidence file.

Immediately following the header are the blocks of data. Before EnCase 5, these data blocks were always 64 sectors (32K), except for the last data block, which was almost always less than 64 sectors. EnCase 5 in Windows and LinEn in Linux both allow the block sizes to be changed up to 32,768 sectors (16MB). The default size is still 64 sectors, but in the discussions that follow, you must understand that changing the block size when you acquire will affect the block sizes in the evidence file and, with that, changes in the frequency of the CRC values.

For now, let's assume that the block size is unchanged and remains the default size of 64 sectors. With this default setting, the buffer or memory size is set at 64 sectors. This means that data will be read into memory in blocks of 64 sectors. Once this data is in memory, a CRC is computed for this block of 64 sectors. Additionally, this block is computed into the cumulative MD5 hash that is being calculated over the entire block of data from the first sector to the last sector acquired. If you opted for No Compression, the data block and its CRC are appended to the evidence file. If you selected Compression, the block of data and its CRC are compressed and appended to the data file.

EnCase uses industry-standard compression algorithms when compressing its evidence files. The amount of compression you will achieve will vary, depending on the type of data on your drive. Drives with lots of zeros in the unallocated space compress very well. By contrast, if the unallocated space contains considerable data and is of the type that doesn't compress well, you'll obviously achieve less overall compression. On the average, using "best" compression, you'll see average compression rates approaching 50 percent. Compression comes with a cost, which is increased acquisition time. Therefore, you should expect best compression to achieve compression rates approaching 50 percent and with acquisition times approaching three times the amount that No Compression requires.

When the last block of data in the target device is reached, it will rarely be exactly 64 sectors— usually less than 64 sectors. That block of data is written to the evidence file along with its CRC. At this point, there is no more data to process and the acquisition hash (MD5 value) is complete and is written in the section, which is then appended to the end of the evidence file. In addition to the MD5 acquisition hash, you will find other data in this area. This data area is the last segment of the evidence file. It is approximately 3K in size and contains metadata that describes various properties of the evidence file, such as offsets for start and stop points for header, data area, and so forth. The MD5 is part of the metadata contained in this final segment.

If the target media will not fit in one evidence file, as defined in the file segment size (file chunk size) setting, it will span as many evidence files as are needed to contain it. The first evidence file created will contain the header at its beginning, followed by as many data blocks as will fit based on the file segment size and the degree of compression selected, if any. When more than one evidence file is required, the MD5 can't be completed and written until the last block of data is read. Therefore, no MD5 will be written to the first evidence file when multiple files are required.

Since the header is contained in the first evidence file, it is not necessary for it to be written again. This means that all subsequent evidence files will have no header section. The MD5 value can't be completely calculated and written until the last data block is processed, so only the last evidence file in the series will contain the MD5 value and metadata appended to the end.

Figure 5.2 shows how evidence files are constructed when multiple evidence files are required. Any evidence file that is neither the first nor the last will contain only data blocks and

CRC values for each block. In Figure 5.2, the diagram in the middle, between the first and last blocks, depicts how evidences files appear that are neither first nor last. In most cases, evidence file segments looks like the middle one in Figure 5.2 because most cases involve relatively large devices that result in a large number of evidence files when the image is acquired.

**FIGURE 5.2**   Evidence file format when multiple evidence files are required

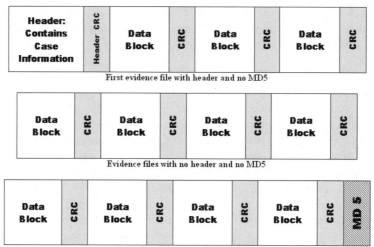

First evidence file with header and no MD5

Evidence files with no header and no MD5

Last evidence file with MD5 appended and no header

When the first evidence file is written, the file name is the one you designated when selecting the acquisition options. The extension for the first file is .e01; the extension for the second file is .e02, and so on until evidence file numbers reach 100. At evidence file 100, the extension is .eaa. The extension for evidence file 101 is .eab, which continues until evidence file numbers exceed 126 (.eaz). At evidence file 127, the file extension is .eba. The sequencing continues as needed until the last evidence file is created.

When selecting a source drive to hold your evidence file, you generally try to contain it on one drive, and thus the size of the source drive should be adequate to hold the target drive. If you are imaging an 80GB drive with no compression, logic might lead you to think you can contain the image on an 80GB drive. Assuming the two 80GB drives contain the same number of sectors, this will not be the case because an evidence file contains some data overhead in addition to the actual data. The header takes some space, the MD5 area takes some space, and the CRC values require 4 bytes per block of data. The overhead is small, but it is enough that you can't put the uncompressed image of a drive on a drive of equal size.

If you make this mistake, EnCase will warn you when your source drive is full and will prompt you for a path to continue the acquisition. In such a case, you could finish the acquisition by placing the small amount remaining on your system drive. It must, however, be placed on a drive that is currently mounted on your system. If you were forced to image a drive that was 100GB and you only had two 60GB drives, you could mount them both and start your acquisition. When the first one fills, EnCase will prompt you for a path to continue, at which point you would point EnCase to your second source drive.

If you span your acquisition over two or more drives, when you add your image to EnCase, it will eventually prompt you for the location of the rest of the evidence files as it loads the image. The capability to span drives when acquiring is a nice feature. There have been many times when this feature has saved my day.

When choosing a source drive size to contain the target image using compression, you may expect to achieve a nearly 50 percent compression factor using best compression. You can't, however, count on that factor; it is only an average and your actual results will depend on the type of data on the target drive. It is best to always have extra room for storage beyond what you expect. As a general rule, when using best compression, I prefer to have 75GB available on a source drive to image a 100GB device. Even then, you should still have some reserve space mounted and ready in the event your storage drive fills.

## Evidence File Verification

At this point, we know that when EnCase creates an evidence file, it calculates CRC values for its header and each block of data. Additionally, it calculates an MD5 value for the data only. No other data (header, CRC, metadata, etc.) is included in this MD5 hash. If you were to use a third-party tool to calculate an MD5 hash of the device imaged by EnCase, the MD5 hashes should match. If EnCase included data other than the target drive in the hash, those values would not match. Thus, it's important to understand that EnCase calculates the MD5 value from the data contained in the target device only.

After a device is imaged, its image file can be brought into EnCase automatically or manually later, depending on the options chosen during acquisition. Whenever an evidence file is added to an open case, a file verification process automatically occurs. When an evidence file is verifying, as shown in Figure 5.3, there is a progress bar indicator in the bottom-right corner of the EnCase window. If the evidence file is small, as in the case of a floppy disk, the verification occurs so quickly that the progress bar isn't seen.

**FIGURE 5.3**    File verification progress bar shown in lower-right corner of EnCase window

If for any reason you want to cancel the verification process, double-click on this progress bar and you will be provided with a prompt that lets you terminate the verification process.

If you look at the Report tab for a device that is currently verifying, such as the one shown in Figure 5.4, you'll note the absence of a verification hash, and the File Integrity field will indicate that the file is being verified. Figure 5.5 shows the same report after the verification process has completed. The verification hash value is included in the report and should match the acquisition hash. Additionally, the File Integrity field should report that the file verified with zero errors.

**FIGURE 5.4**   Report view for a device in which verification is under way. Note the absence of a verification hash.

```
Examiner Name:    Bunting
Drive Type:       Fixed
File Integrity:   Verifying
Acquisition Hash: fa1a32b57675a4a6e5466f8db8337e1f
GUID:             e8e266da44b41b43a8143895926bf2d3
EnCase Version:   5.02
System Version:   Windows XP
Fastbloced:       No
Is Physical:      Yes
Raid RHS:         No
Error Granularity: 64
```

**FIGURE 5.5**   Report view for a device after verification has completed. Note that the verification hash is present and matches the acquisition hash. Note also that the File Integrity field reports that the file verified with zero errors.

```
Examiner Name:    Bunting
Drive Type:       Fixed
File Integrity:   Completely Verified, 0 Errors
Acquisition Hash: fa1a32b57675a4a6e5466f8db8337e1f
Verify Hash:      fa1a32b57675a4a6e5466f8db8337e1f
GUID:             e8e266da44b41b43a8143895926bf2d3
EnCase Version:   5.02
System Version:   Windows XP
Fastbloced:       No
Is Physical:      Yes
Raid RHS:         No
Error Granularity: 64
```

The fact that our image file verified is reassuring; however, you should understand what happens "under the hood" when this process occurs. By understanding that process, you'll feel even better about the results. Furthermore, you'll be in a position to explain the process to a court or jury if the authenticity of the evidence is challenged. A solid explanation can thwart defense challenges regarding the authenticity of the evidence and bolster your image as a competent examiner.

The verification process is actually very simple. Each block of data in the evidence file is subjected to a verification CRC calculation. For a block of data to pass the test, its verification CRC must match the CRC value calculated when it was acquired and stored in the evidence file with the block of data. If a CRC for a block of data does not match its stored acquisition value, an error is reported for that block of data. This CRC recalculation and verification occurs for each block of data in the evidence file.

In addition to the CRC verifications, the blocks of data are subjected to a recalculation of the MD5 hash. The resultant value is called the verification hash value. The verification hash value and the acquisition hash value are compared and should match. To achieve successful file verification, the verification CRC values for all blocks of data must match their acquisition values, and the verification MD5 hash must match the acquisition MD5 hash. As you can see, the verification process is a redundant process, with one (CRC) cross-validating the other (MD5), thus providing an extremely strong mechanism for ensuring the integrity of the digital evidence within the EnCase environment.

The verification process occurs automatically whenever an evidence file is added to a case. There are times when you should reverify an evidence file. If you have copied the evidence file to another drive, you may want to check that the evidence file did not get corrupted in the process. Also, you may want to check it one more time before going to court. Whatever the reason, there is a mechanism for doing this.

As with most features in EnCase, you can access the reverification feature by right-clicking. In the left pane, select the device that you wish to manually verify (at its root level), right-click, and choose Verify File Integrity, as shown in Figure 5.6. You will be prompted to confirm that you want to do so. When you click Yes, you will see the verification progress bar in the lower-right corner. When the reverification is complete, you won't see a report of the results, regardless of the success or failure of the process. To view the results, you must view the bottom pane Report tab for the device you are verifying. You can force the device to the right pane by selecting the device view. Alternatively, in the left pane you can select the case, which forces the devices in the case into the right pane. Once your device is in the right pane, select it, and then choose the Report tab in the bottom pane.

**FIGURE 5.6**    To reverify an evidence file, right-click on the device in the left pane and select Verify File Integrity.

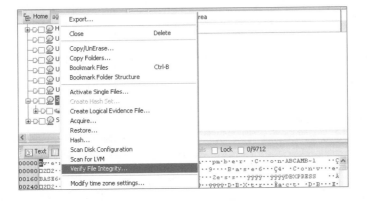

To demonstrate how a corrupted evidence file would appear upon reverification, a *4* in an evidence file was altered to a *5* with a hex editor. This effectively changes one bit in the evidence file (0000-0100 is changed to 0000-0101). After reverifying the evidence file, Figure 5.7 shows the results seen in the Report tab for the selected device.

The File Integrity field indicates that the verification completed and found one error, meaning the CRC for one block failed to match its stored acquisition value. The one block of data could have one or many errors. All that EnCase can determine is that the CRC values for one block do not match, which is reported as one error. If another block of data also contained one or many errors, then EnCase would report two errors.

**FIGURE 5.7**    Report view for device with corrupted data. Note that changing one bit from a 0 to a 1 produces a drastic change in the verification hash (MD5 value) when compared to the acquisition hash.

```
Examiner Name:    Bunting
Drive Type:       Removable
File Integrity:   Completely Verified, 1 Errors
Acquisition Hash: fe19a5da44bfd084e94ff52ad13a64f6
Verify Hash:      bc4a4f35424e7856b539cc3bded2c919
GUID:             d485083c4ada8b4aaa55db93bb529ed6
EnCase Version:   5.02
System Version:   Windows XP
Fastbloced:       No
Is Physical:      No
Raid RHS:         No
Error Granularity: 64
Acquisition Info: No
Sources:          No
Subjects:         No
Disk Elements:    No
CRC Errors:       1
Compression:      None
CRC Errors
    Start    Count
    448      64

Total Size:       1,474,560 bytes (1.4MB)
Total Sectors:    2,880


The integrity of the following sector groups could not be verified
448-511
```

Next we see that the verification hash does not match the acquisition hash and that the difference is drastic despite the fact that only one bit changed. If we look further down the report, we can see the details of the errors. The block of data containing the CRC error begins at sector 448. Since our block size is 64, the block covers sectors 448 through 511, which is a range of 64 sectors.

You might be wondering what would happen if you failed to review the Report tab and didn't notice the data errors detected by the verification process. Fortunately, the very function of EnCase is such that it protects the data integrity in many ways. Whenever EnCase is tasked with reading data from the evidence file for any reason (viewing, searching, etc.), each requested data block is subjected to a CRC calculation. This value is compared to the stored acquisition CRC before the data can be used for any purpose. If the CRC values match, EnCase proceeds with the task at hand. If, however, the CRC values don't match, EnCase will return an Invalid Block Checksum error message, as shown in Figure 5.8, and the user is blocked from accessing any data in the block containing the error. In this way, EnCase precludes access to erroneous data while still allowing you access to valid data.

**FIGURE 5.8** The Invalid Block Checksum error occurs when stepping from sector 447 (which contains valid data) to sector 448 (beginning of the 64-sector block containing a CRC error; see Figure 5.7). Accessing any sector from 448 to 511 will produce this error message. Note the physical sector numbers in "GPS" at lower left of screen.

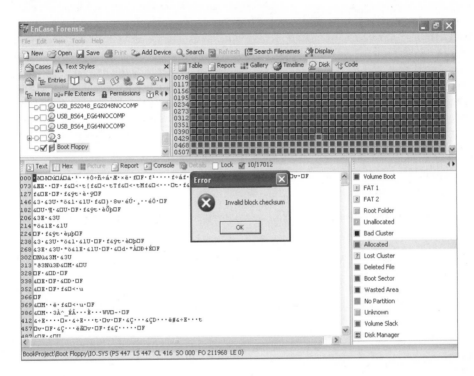

As you begin to grasp the inner workings of EnCase, you will appreciate the work that has gone into the program to ensure data integrity at every step of the process. Also, you will learn the importance of the relationship between acquisition block sizes and the corresponding frequency of the CRC values.

Increasing the block size can have an adverse effect if corruption later occurs in a block of data as the block of data protected by the CRC increases. If the block size is changed from the default size of 64 sectors to 128 sectors to speed up the acquisition, the downside is that a CRC value will be written for every 128 sectors instead of every 64 sectors. If the evidence file later developed a corrupted block, the affected block size would be 128 sectors instead of 64 sectors, and more data would be unavailable to the examiner. If you must increase the block size to speed up an acquisition, it is recommended that you reacquire it with a default setting of 64 sectors when time permits. In that way, you enjoy the faster acquisition when you need it. You can later restore your data integrity protection to a more acceptable level.

**EXERCISE 5.1**

### Understanding How EnCase Maintains Data Integrity

In this exercise, we will create a case and add to it an evidence file. That evidence file will verify correctly. We'll save our case and exit EnCase. We'll then substitute our verified evidence file with another one of the same name that is identical in all respects except for the fact that one bit has been changed. This change could simulate unintentional data corruption or it could simulate intentional alteration of evidence. Regardless of how or why the evidence file changed, EnCase cares not. We'll reopen the case with the altered evidence file and you'll see EnCase's file integrity protection features at work. When you are done, you'll be able to affirmatively assert and testify as to what happens if original evidence has been altered in the EnCase environment. You can also use these files to test versions of EnCase as they are released. Let's get started!

- Create a folder at the root of your drive and name it **Cases**. Create a subfolder under Cases and name it **DataIntegrityTest**.

- Under the folder DataIntegrityTest, create three subfolders named **Evidence**, **Export**, and **Temp**.

- On the CD is a folder named DataIntegrityTest. Under that folder are two subfolders: Normal and Corrupted. In each of these subfolders is one evidence file: MoneyTransferFloppyFD01.e01. From outward appearances, the files seem identical; however, their folder names are indicative of their true contents. Copy the evidence file from the Normal folder to the Evidence folder you just created.

- Create a new case in EnCase. Save it to the root of Cases\DataIntegrityTest\, naming it **DataIntegrityTest.case**.

- Click Add A Device. In the left pane, select Evidence Files, right-click, and select New from the context menu. In the resulting dialog box, browse to the folder Cases\DataIntegrityTest\Evidence and click OK. In the left pane, select the newly created evidence path. When you do, in the right pane you'll see the evidence file MoneyTransferFloppyFD01. Place a check next to this file, then click Next, Next, and Finish. The evidence file is now in your case.

- In the left pane, select the case level, which forces the device to the right pane. In the right pane, select the floppy device. In the bottom pane, choose the Report tab. Scroll down the report and note that the file verified successfully and that the verification and acquisition hashes match.

- In the left pane, place your cursor on the floppy device, and the root-level directory structure will appear in the right pane. Examine the contents of the only intact file in the root directory, which is a text file containing information about a money transfer. Note carefully the account numbers.

**EXERCISE 5.1** *(continued)*

- Save your case and exit EnCase.

- On the CD, locate the folder DataIntegrityTest\Corrupted\. Copy the evidence file in this folder into your Evidence folder. When asked if you wish to overwrite the existing evidence file by the same name, select Yes. You now have a file by the exact same name and attributes as your previously verified evidence file. The only difference between the files is that someone has altered your evidence file by one bit when they changed one digit in an account number.

- Start EnCase and open your previously saved case. EnCase thinks that it has already verified this evidence file and no file integrity check will occur. Check the contents of the text file in the root directory. When you attempt to do so, EnCase will read the data block containing the text file and run a CRC check on it. The CRC will not match and you will receive an error instead of seeing the data. Click OK as many times as are needed to exit the error. You still will not see the data.

- Right-click on the floppy device in the left pane and select Verify File Integrity. This process should take a matter of seconds as the evidence file is very small. When done, repeat the process for checking the results on the Report tab for the floppy device. You should see that the verification completed with an error. You should see that the hashes do not match, and you should be able to view the sectors containing the errors.

- Close EnCase without saving.

---

EnCase provides a tool that allows the examiner to verify individual evidence file segments. The need for this arises when evidence files are archived onto CDs and DVDs. You can access this feature by choosing Tools ➢ Verify Evidence Files. The MD5 hash can't be checked with this feature; however, EnCase verifies the CRC values for each block of data in a single evidence file.

## Hashing Disks and Volumes

At this stage we understand that when EnCase acquires data, it calculates and writes CRC values for each block of data and then computes an MD5 hash for the entire device or stream of data acquired. Whenever the resultant evidence file is added to a case, it is automatically verified. Every block of data is subjected to CRC reverification, and the entire device is subjected to a reverification of the MD5 hash. You can also reverify an evidence file manually at any time. As an added protection, whenever EnCase must access and read any data, any block of data containing the requested data is subjected to a CRC calculation that must match its stored CRC value before it can be used. Thus, EnCase was built with data integrity at its very core, and by understanding how it functions, you can better appreciate its built-in protections and be in a better position to explain them.

In addition to the protections and integrity checks thus far discussed, you can employ yet another integrity check by manually hashing a disk or volume that has been acquired. The hash feature will calculate an MD5 hash for the selected physical or logical device. You can compare this value to the acquisition hash. This feature is again available in the context menu you access by choosing the device to hash in the left pane and right-clicking, as shown in Figure 5.9. You are asked for the range of sectors to hash; normally you would select the defaults—which is the entire device, as shown in Figure 5.10.

**FIGURE 5.9** To hash a device, select it in the left pane, right-click, and choose Hash.

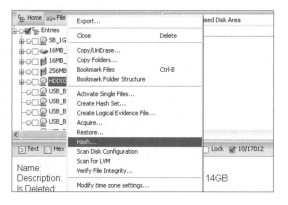

**FIGURE 5.10** Before hashing, you are given an option to choose a start and stop sector. Normally you choose the default, which is the entire device.

After the hash is done, you can compare this value to the acquisition hash and they should match. The nice part about this feature is that you will be presented with a report, as shown in Figure 5.11, which contains the date, time, evidence name, sectors hashed, and the hash value. This report can be included in your report as a "note bookmark" by checking the appropriate box. Since the Verify File Integrity function does not date/time-stamp its results, this hash report can be included to reinforce your report.

**FIGURE 5.11**    Results of hashing a physical device. All the details displayed can be bookmarked and included in a "note bookmark."

 The Verify File Integrity function can only be run at the level of the acquired device. If you acquired a physical device, you can use this feature at the physical level only and not at the volume level. If you acquired a physical device, you can hash it at either the physical level or the volume level. If you are using the hash feature to check the integrity of your acquired physical device, make sure you conduct your hash of the physical device. If you hash the volume instead, the results will differ as you are hashing a different set of sectors. In short, make sure you are comparing apples and apples, not apples and oranges!

## EnCase Case Files

A "case" file is created when you first save your case. It is at that time that you choose and name your storage path location. The recommended organizational structure for case folders and files appears in Figure 5.12. Note that the case file is in the root of the case name folder. In our example, in Figure 5.12, the case file name is "RobinsonCDs.Case" and it is located in the root of the case name folder "RobinsonCD".

**FIGURE 5.12**    Recommended folder structure for organizing an EnCase case. Note that the case file is in the root of the case name folder.

The case file is a plain text file, mostly in Unicode, that contains pointers to the evidence file and case-specific information. As the evidence file itself never changes, all search hits, bookmarks, notes, sorts, hash analysis, file verification information, and so forth must exist in the form of data in the case file with pointers to the evidence file. When you recover a partition, there is no partition inserted into the original evidence file. Rather, the partition is virtually reconstructed with data and pointers in the case file.

With time and analysis work, these case files can get quite large and can take some time to load. This file represents all your work in a case, so maintaining its integrity is important. You should frequently save your work by clicking Save as you complete a process or are about to start another step of the analysis. It only takes one unexpected crash and the loss of significant work to make this habit second nature.

Backing up the case file is also an important function. EnCase does a backup automatically, as we'll see in the next section, but it is important to back up the case file at various points in your case, preferably daily. If a case file develops a problem, the backup can also be corrupted. Keeping daily backups of your case file in appropriately named folders gives you the XP equivalent of "restore points." Figure 5.13 shows how you can organize such a daily case file backup system. It only takes a few seconds to copy your case file to a backup folder and, if faithfully carried out, this process can save you a full day of work at some future point.

**FIGURE 5.13** Folder naming and organizational structure to contain daily backups of your case file.

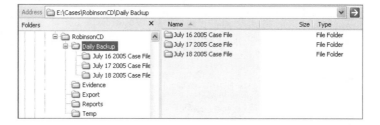

## EnCase Backup File (cbak)

As we mentioned earlier, EnCase creates an automatic backup of your case file. The name of this file is the same name as your case file, but it has a different extension: *.cbak*. In prior versions of EnCase, the backup file (.cbk in versions prior to 4) was stored in the same folder with the case file. While quite convenient, if something happened to the drive holding the case, the backup was gone as well. Starting with version 5, the backup file is located on the system drive under the EnCase5 folder in a subfolder appropriately named Backup, as shown in Figure 5.14. Most examiners follow good practices and keep their case files on a separate drive from their system drive, so the location of the backup on the system drive protects against data loss from a single point of failure on the case drive.

**FIGURE 5.14** Starting with EnCase 5, the case backup file (cbak) is now located on the system drive under \Program Files\EnCase5\Backup. Placing the backup on a separate drive from the case file helps eliminate data loss from a single point of failure.

You can modify the timing of the automatic backup by choosing Tools ➢ Options ➢ Global, which is shown in Figure 5.15. The range can be from zero minutes, which is no backup at all, up to 1440 minutes, which is every 24 hours. You need to think of this setting as a balance between performance—it takes time to back up a large case file—and how much work you care to repeat in the event of a system failure. The default setting is 10 minutes, but some examiners prefer 5 minutes. There are some facets of my life I wouldn't mind repeating, but generally work doesn't fit in that category, and I prefer backing up every 5 minutes. If you are running a long search and aren't doing other work in the meantime, you might consider backing up every 60 minutes or even less often to speed up your search. Just remember to readjust this setting when you are done.

**FIGURE 5.15** Global options menu from which you can change the time of the automatic backup as well as other EnCase environment options.

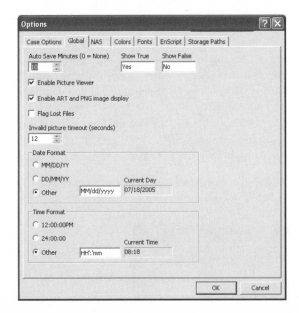

Sometimes we forget to click the Save button as often as we should. When we are neglectful, "Murphy" often looks over our shoulder and teaches us a lesson by crashing our system. When you look at your case file and you realize that you last saved it hours ago, you are not happy with the prospect of repeating several hours of work. This is when the backup file comes to the rescue. Instead of opening the case file, you open the backup file. To do so, select File ➤ Open as you normally would to open your case file. To open the backup file, you must change the Files of Type setting from Case File to Backup Case File in the Open dialog box. With EnCase5, you must navigate to the Program Files\EnCase5\Backup folder to specify the backup file, as shown in Figure 5.16. Select the proper one and open it.

**FIGURE 5.16**    Opening the backup case file (cbak) by changing the file type and navigating to the location of backup file

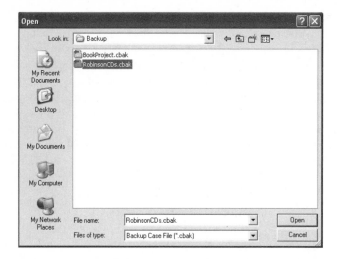

If you had your settings low, chances are you lost less than 10 minutes of your casework. You should save your case as soon as possible after opening your backup. When you attempt to save your case and you have opened your backup, as shown in Figure 5.17, you will be prompted to promote the backup to the case file, which involves overwriting the case file with the current open case, which is your backup file. Since your backup file is much more current than your case file, you would normally choose to do this. At that point you are back in business with minimal disruption. Also, you will probably start clicking the Save button much more often.

**FIGURE 5.17**    This prompt asks if you wish to promote your backup file to your case file, which is another way of asking if it is okay to overwrite your case file with your backup file.

If you need to, you can change the logical name of the evidence file. This does not change the contents of the evidence file, and the evidence file will still verify. For example, you can change SuspectFloppy01.e01 to SuspectFloppyFD01.e01. You may also move the evidence file to another path or drive. When EnCase opens a case and the evidence file is not where it last recorded it, it will prompt you for the new path. Changing the evidence file name or its location does not affect file integrity or the verification process at all. Changing the evidence file logical name on the examiner hard drive will not change the unique name of the evidence file displayed in the EnCase case file and report. That name is included in the header of the evidence file and is protected by a CRC. To change the unique name of an evidence file, the original evidence must be reimaged, thus creating a new evidence file with the new name.

# EnCase Configuration Files

EnCase stores its configuration settings in a series of INI (or initialization) files, which are stored in the Config folder under the EnCase5 program folder. In prior versions, the INI files were interspersed with the program files. With EnCase5, they are contained in their own folder. With each release of EnCase, the number of INI files has increased, as has the complexity and feature sets of EnCase. Some of the INI files are for system maintenance and integrity, such as the update.ini and local.ini files. Another INI file (AppDescriptors.ini) contains a database of application executables, their version numbers, and their hash values.

While all INI files are necessary for the function of EnCase some are of particular interest to the examiner. Figure 5.18 shows the "Storage Paths" tab under Tools ➢ Options. By default, the INI files are stored, as previously noted, in the Config folder under EnCase5. Often, in a multiuser lab setting, it makes sense to have one set of these INI files on a shared network resource path. In this manner, each EnCase user accesses the same set of INI files, as they are configured. All (or just some) of the INI files can be placed on a network share. Often the Keyword.ini file is shared because it allows all lab users access to the same set of global keywords. Either way, sharing one INI or many, it saves setup work and ensures all users are functioning in a standardized environment when it comes to EnCase settings.

Table 5.1 shows the INI files of primary interest to the examiner and a brief description of their function.

**TABLE 5.1**   Description of primary "ini" files

| File Name | Description |
| --- | --- |
| Keyword.ini | Stores global keywords; EnCase versions up through version 3 stored keywords exclusively in the case file. Version 4 stored them exclusively in the keyword.ini file. Version 5 stores case-level keywords in the case file and global-level keywords in the keyword.ini file. |
| TextStyles.ini | Stores the text styles contained under the Text Styles tab. Text styles allow you to create custom templates by which to view data. |

**TABLE 5.1**   Description of primary "ini" files *(continued)*

| File Name | Description |
| --- | --- |
| FileSignatures.ini | Stores the values for the file signature database used by EnCase. |
| FileTypes.ini | Stores the database of file extensions, their associated names, and the default viewer that EnCase will use when the file is double-clicked. |
| Viewers.ini | Stores the database of information regarding the viewers that EnCase can use when viewing data. Viewers installed in this database appear on the Send To: option usually found in the context menu. |
| SecurityIDs.ini | Stores the database of user ID numbers and usernames. For example, when a SID can't be resolved locally, as in a domain, the examiner can obtain the SID number and username from the domain controller and enter it manually in the Security IDs view. EnCase can resolve a SID to a username if it can't be locally resolved and the entry is in this table. |

**FIGURE 5.18**   Storage paths for INI files can be customized in the Storage Paths tab in the Options dialog box.

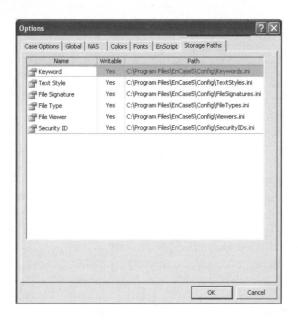

You should be aware that these files are not saved as data is added to them or they are modified. Likewise, they are not saved when a case is saved using the Save button. These files are saved when EnCase normally exits or when you click Save All. If you add or modify data that is associated with these files, be sure to click Save All when you are done to protect your work in the event of an unexpected system crash. There is nothing more frustrating than adding 15 or 20 complex global keywords, only to have them lost by a system crash. Click Save All often! Also, you should periodically back up the INI files and place them in a safe location to protect them in the event of data loss.

---

### Terminology is important!

It seems each time I attend a computer forensics course, I am told to rephrase the wording of how I acquire a forensic copy of digital evidence. Terms such as *mirror*, *bit-by-bit*, *bitstream*, and *image* have been used at one time or another to describe a forensic acquisition of digital evidence. With regard to acquiring evidence using EnCase, I use the phrase "an exact copy to an EnCase evidence file."

Defense attorneys have asserted that the EnCase evidence file is not an exact duplicate of the original evidence. Some savvy ones try to prove their point by mentioning that the MD5 hash value of the original evidence does not match that of an EnCase evidence file—and they are correct. Forensic examiners have commonly used the above terms to describe how they acquired evidence using EnCase because that is what they were taught. Now that you have a better understanding of the EnCase process, you can explain that an EnCase evidence file does contain an exact copy of the original evidence in the data blocks. The matching acquisition and verification hashes are derived from original evidence and the data blocks. In addition, an EnCase evidence file contains additional data such as case information, CRC checks, and MD5 hash values of the original evidence outside the data blocks.

So, when someone challenges an EnCase evidence file as not being an exact duplicate of the original evidence because of different MD5 hash values, you can argue that an EnCase evidence file does contain an exact duplicate of the original evidence along with additional information. As to whether or not an EnCase evidence file has the same MD5 hash value as the original evidence, of course it doesn't because of the additional information contained within the evidence file. However, EnCase will only verify and generate an MD5 hash value of the information contained within the data blocks of an evidence file, which is then compared to the MD5 hash value of the original evidence obtained during the acquisition.

# Summary

This chapter covered the EnCase evidence file. This file has three essential parts: the header, the data blocks, and the file integrity components.

The header contains the case information. It appears at the front of the evidence file and is subjected to its own CRC calculation to ensure its integrity. It is always compressed.

The data blocks contain, by default, 64 sectors (32K) of data. The block size can be adjusted upward with EnCase 5 to speed acquisitions. Each block of data contains its own CRC value, and each block is included in the overall MD5 calculation for the entire device being imaged. If compression is chosen, the block of data and its CRC are compressed.

The file integrity components are the CRC values and the MD5 hash. CRC values are calculated and stored for the header and all data blocks. The MD5 hash is calculated against the data only and does not include the header or any CRCs. The CRC values are stored with each block of data. The MD5 is stored at the end of the file in an appendix containing the MD5 along with other evidence file metadata.

Whenever an evidence file is added to a case in EnCase, it undergoes a file integrity check. The CRC for each block of data is recalculated and compared to the stored acquisition CRC value. The MD5 for the entire device is recalculated, resulting in a verification hash, which is then compared to the acquisition hash. For a file to be successfully verified, all CRC values must match and the verification and acquisition hashes must match. A reverification can be run at any time to reaffirm a file's integrity.

A CRC is an algorithm that results in a 32-bit value. The odds of any two files having the same CRC value are roughly one in 4 billion. An MD5 is an algorithm that results in a 128-bit value. The odds of any two files having the same MD5 value are roughly one in 340 billion billion billion billion.

EnCase has a feature that allows you to hash a physical device or volume. This feature generates an MD5 hash in a report that is date- and time-stamped. This can be included in your report to reinforce EnCase's file integrity features.

The EnCase case file stores information about the evidence file in the form of data and pointers to the evidence file. In this way, search hits, bookmarks, notes, file signature analyses, and so forth are contained in a file separate from the evidence file, yet "married" to it through metadata and pointers. The case file is saved when you exit EnCase or click the Save button. It is normally stored in the root of the case name folder.

The EnCase .cbak file is a file created automatically by EnCase. It is stored separately from the case file and is located in a folder named Backup located under Program Files\EnCase5. By default the .cbak file is saved every 10 minutes, but you can modify this setting by choosing Tools ➢ Options ➢ Global. A case can be opened using the backup file if the file type is changed and the path to the backup file is provided.

EnCase stores its configuration settings in INI files that are organized in a folder named Config under Program Files\EnCase5. With EnCase 5, keywords may be stored globally in a keywords.ini file or stored at the case level in the case file. The storage paths for the INI files may be changed and located on a network share so that examiners in a multiuser lab can share INI files and work under one "standardized" EnCase environment. When adding or modifying data stored in one of these INI files, the user should click Save All to save the changes to the INI file.

# Exam Essentials

**Understand the components and function of the EnCase evidence file.**   Be able to name and describe the three major components of an EnCase evidence file. Understand and be able to explain the mechanisms by which data integrity is maintained in the evidence file. Describe how an EnCase evidence file is created. Explain how changing the block size changes the frequency of CRC values.

**Know how the file verification process works.**   Know under what circumstances the verification process occurs. Understand and be able to explain what takes place during the file verification process and what must conditions must be met for a successful evidence file verification. Be able to conduct a manual file verification. Know where to find the results of the file verification process, and be able to describe the results and their meaning to the file integrity process.

**Know how to hash a physical device or a volume.**   Understand and be able to explain the MD5 hash. Describe how to hash a physical device or a volume and bookmark the results. Understand how to compare the results of these hash values with the acquisition and verification hashes. If hashing to verify an acquisition value, explain the importance of hashing the correct device (physical or logical).

**Understand the content and function of the EnCase "case file."**   Explain the purpose of the EnCase case file. Be able to explain in general terms the kind of information contained in the file. Explain when and how the file is named, its extension, when it is saved, and where it should normally be stored.

**Understand the content and function of the EnCase backup case file.**   Explain the purpose and contents of the EnCase backup case file. Be able to explain when and how the file is named, its extension, when it is saved, how to change the timing of when it is saved, and where it is stored. Be able to describe the process by which a case may be opened using the backup case file.

**Understand how and where EnCase stores its configuration settings.**   Know where the primary INI files are stored. Identify which INI files have a configurable storage location and explain how to change that location. Explain what kind of data is stored in each of the INI files that have a configurable storage location. Explain why you would store configuration files on a shared network resource. Understand when these files are saved and be able to explain the importance of frequently saving and creating backups of these files.

# Review Questions

1. The EnCase evidence file is best described as:

   **A.** A mirror image of the source device written to a hard drive

   **B.** A sector-by-sector image of the source device written to corresponding sectors of a secondary hard drive

   **C.** A bitstream image of a source device written to the corresponding sectors of a secondary hard drive

   **D.** A bitstream image of a source device written to a file or several file segments

2. How does EnCase verify the contents of an evidence file?

   **A.** EnCase writes an MD5 hash value for every 32 sectors copied.

   **B.** EnCase writes an MD5 value for every 64 sectors copied.

   **C.** EnCase writes a CRC value for every 32 sectors copied.

   **D.** EnCase writes a CRC value for every 64 sectors copied.

3. What is the smallest file size that an EnCase evidence file can be saved as?

   **A.** 64 sectors

   **B.** 512 sectors

   **C.** 1MB

   **D.** 2MB

   **E.** 640MB

4. What is the largest file segment size that an EnCase evidence file can be saved as?

   **A.** 640MB

   **B.** 1GB

   **C.** 2GB

   **D.** No maximum limit

5. How does EnCase verify that the evidence file contains an exact copy of the source device?

   **A.** By comparing the MD5 hash value of the source device to the MD5 hash value of the data stored in the evidence file

   **B.** By comparing the CRC value of the source device to the CRC of the data stored in the evidence file

   **C.** By comparing the MD5 hash value of the source device to the MD5 hash value of the entire evidence file

   **D.** By comparing the CRC value of the source device to the CRC value of the entire evidence file

**6.** How does EnCase verify that the case information—such as case number, evidence number, notes, etc.—in an evidence file has not been damaged or altered after the evidence file has been written?

    **A.** The case file writes a CRC value for the case information and verifies it when the case is opened.

    **B.** EnCase does not verify the case information because it can be changed at any time.

    **C.** EnCase writes a CRC value for the case information and verifies the CRC value when the evidence is added to a case.

    **D.** EnCase writes an MD5 value of the case information and verifies the MD5 value when the evidence is added to a case.

**7.** For an EnCase evidence file to successfully pass the file verification process, which of the following must be true?

    **A.** The MD5 hash value must verify.

    **B.** The CRC values and the MD5 hash value both must verify.

    **C.** Either the CRC or MD5 hash values must verify.

    **D.** The CRC values must verify.

**8.** The MD5 hash algorithm produces a _____ value.

    **A.** 32-bit

    **B.** 64-bit

    **C.** 128-bit

    **D.** 256-bit

**9.** The MD5 hash algorithm is ___ hexadecimal characters in length.

    **A.** 16

    **B.** 32

    **C.** 64

    **D.** 128

**10.** If an evidence file has been added to a case and completely verified, what happens if the data area within the evidence file is later altered?

    **A.** EnCase will detect the error when that area of the evidence file is accessed by the user.

    **B.** EnCase will detect the error if the evidence file is manually reverified.

    **C.** EnCase will allow the examiner to continue to access the rest of the evidence file that has not been changed.

    **D.** All of the above.

11. Which of the following aspects of the EnCase evidence file can be changed during a reacquire of the evidence file?

    **A.** Investigator's name

    **B.** Evidence number

    **C.** Notes

    **D.** Evidence file size

    **E.** All of the above

12. An evidence file was archived onto five CD-ROMs with the third file segment on disc number 3. Can the contents of the third file segment be verified by itself while still on the CD-ROM?

    **A.** No. All evidence file segments must be put back together.

    **B.** Yes. Any evidence file segment can be verified independently by comparing the CRC values.

13. Will EnCase allow a user to write data into an acquired evidence file?

    **A.** Yes, when adding notes or comments to bookmarks.

    **B.** Yes, when adding search results.

    **C.** A and B.

    **D.** No, data cannot be added to the evidence file after the acquisition is made.

14. All investigators using EnCase should run tests on the evidence file acquisition and verification process to:

    **A.** Further the investigator's understanding of the evidence file

    **B.** Give more weight to the investigator's testimony in court

    **C.** Verify that all hardware and software is functioning properly

    **D.** All of the above

15. When a noncompressed evidence file is reacquired with compression, the acquisition and verification hash values for the evidence file will remain the same for both files.

    **A.** True

    **B.** False

16. Search hit results and bookmarks are stored in the evidence file.

    **A.** True

    **B.** False

17. The EnCase evidence file's logical file name can be changed without affecting the verification of the acquired evidence.

    **A.** True

    **B.** False

**18.** An evidence file can be moved to another directory without changing the file verification.

   **A.** True

   **B.** False

**19.** What happens when EnCase attempts to reopen a case once the evidence file has been moved?

   **A.** EnCase reports that the file's integrity has been compromised and renders the file useless.

   **B.** EnCase reports a different hash value for the evidence file.

   **C.** EnCase prompts for the location of the evidence file.

   **D.** EnCase opens the case, excluding the moved evidence file.

**20.** During reacquisition, you may change which of the following? (Select all that are correct.)

   **A.** Block size and Error granularity

   **B.** Add or remove a password

   **C.** Investigator's name

   **D.** Compression

   **E.** File segment size

# Answers to Review Questions

1.  D. An EnCase evidence file is a bitstream image of a source device such as a hard drive, CD-ROM, or floppy disk written to a file (.E01) or several file segments (.E02, .E03, etc.).

2.  C. EnCase writes a CRC value for every 64 sectors copied, by default. If the block size has been increased, the CRC frequency will be adjusted accordingly.

3.  C. The smallest file size that an EnCase evidence file can be saved as is 1MB.

4.  C. The largest file size that an EnCase evidence file can be saved as is 2GB.

5.  A. EnCase compares the MD5 hash value of the source device to the MD5 hash value of just the data stored in the evidence file, not the entire contents of the evidence file, such as case information and CRC values of each data block.

6.  C. EnCase calculates a CRC value for the case information, which is verified when the evidence file is added to a case.

7.  B. When an evidence file containing an MD5 hash value is added to a case, EnCase verifies both the CRC and MD5 hash values.

8.  C. The MD5 hash algorithm produces a 128-bit value.

9.  B. The MD5 hash algorithm is 32 characters in length.

10. D. EnCase will detect the error and will still allow the examiner to access the unaffected areas of the evidence file.

11. D. The evidence file size can be changed during a reacquire.

12. B. EnCase can verify independent evidence file segments by comparing the CRC values of the data blocks.

13. D. EnCase does not write to the evidence file after the acquisition is complete.

14. D. As with any forensic tool, the investigator should test the tools to better understand how the tool performs and to verify that it is functioning properly.

15. A. Compressing an evidence file does not change its MD5 hash value.

16. B. Search hit results and bookmarks are stored in the case and cbak files.

17. A. An EnCase evidence file's logical file name can be renamed without affecting the verification of the acquired evidence.

18. B. EnCase evidence files can be moved without affecting the file verification.

19. C. When an evidence file has moved from the previous path, EnCase will prompt for the new location of the evidence file.

20. A, B, D, E. All may be changed during reacquisition with the exception of the investigator's name.

# Chapter 6

# EnCase Environment

## ENCE EXAM TOPICS COVERED IN THIS CHAPTER:

- ✓ EnCase layout
- ✓ Creating a case
- ✓ Tree pane Case Entries view
- ✓ Table pane Case Entries view
- ✓ View pane Case Entries view
- ✓ Adjusting panes
- ✓ Other case-level views
- ✓ Other global views
- ✓ EnCase options

In this chapter, we will explore the many views and features of EnCase. Each version of EnCase has introduced many more features than the previous version. When new features and functions are added, they often result in additional interfaces or views. Screen real estate is always a scarce resource and arrangement and placement of features will always be a programming challenge. EnCase 5 uses hierarchically arranged tabs for its user interface, which is slightly different from previous versions. Once you take the time to learn the new interface, you'll find that it is very logically arranged and easy to use. The best way to learn the new interface is to use it and, with that said, let's get started.

# EnCase Layout

EnCase divides its screen real estate into four windows that are named for their primary examination function: the Tree pane (formerly the Left pane), the Table pane (formerly the Right pane), the View pane (formerly the Bottom pane), and the Filter pane (new to EnCase Version 5), as shown in Figure 6.1. Granularity or detail increases as you move through the primary panes from the Tree pane, to the Table pane, and finally to the View pane. If you want details about an object (physical device, volume, or folder), place the cursor focus on it (in other words, highlight it) in the Tree pane, and the Table pane will display the details about that object. If you want more details about an object in the Table pane, highlight it in the Table pane and the details will appear in the View pane. Once you get down to the data level of granularity in the View pane, you can even view or interpret that data in different ways, effectively getting still more information or granularity from the View pane.

In addition to letting you work with a case in the Case Entries view, EnCase offers many other views or features that function in the same manner, providing more granularity as you move through the viewing panes. EnCase further organizes its views into global views, case-level views, and case-level view subtabs. This hierarchical view is controlled with three bars at the top of the Tree pane, populated with tabs representing the various views. The bars are arranged in a descending hierarchy, with the top bar representing global options, the second bar representing case-level options, and the third bar representing case-level view subtabs. As the tabs are highlighted (or brought to the front in a three-dimensional sense), their path becomes visible in the hierarchical tree. Once you take a few minutes to familiarize yourself with how it works, it is very intuitive and easy to find your way around.

**FIGURE 6.1**     EnCase divides its screen real estate into the Tree, Table, and View panes.

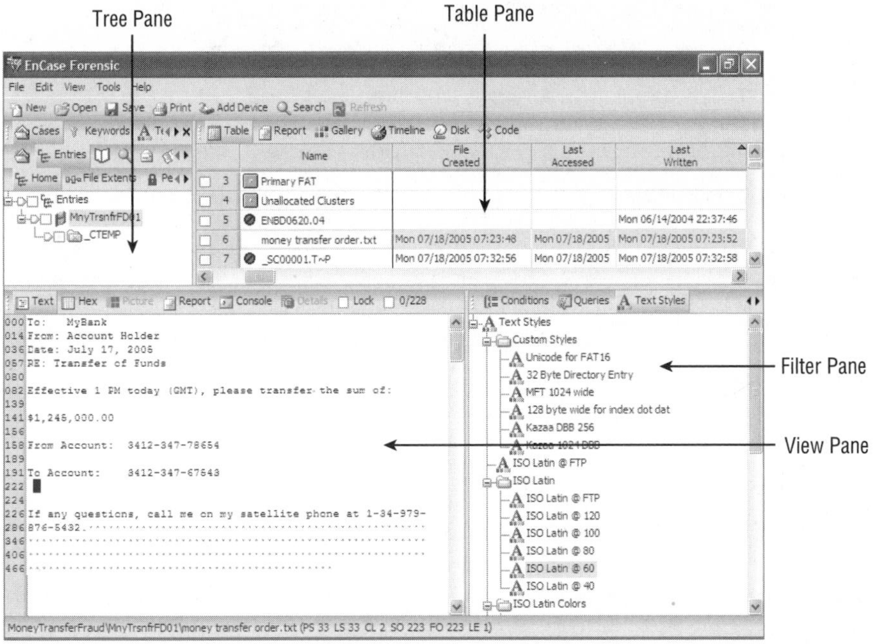

We cover many of these other views or features later in this section. For now, let's focus our attention on creating a case and working in the Case Entries view. The option to work with the case appears on the top bar (global level) and when clicked, the Case Entries view opens, which is also where you will be located by default when you launch EnCase. It is also where we will start our exploration of EnCase's environment and features.

# Creating a Case

The Tree pane is the starting point for the detail that follows in the other two panes. However, before we can work with the Tree pane, or any pane for that matter, we need to have a case open. And before we can have a case open, we need to create a case. When EnCase starts, it opens by default in the Case view. In the Case view, you create a case by clicking the New button on the toolbar. Alternatively, you could select File ➢ New. After you click the New button, you are presented with the dialog box shown in Figure 6.2.

**FIGURE 6.2**    The Case Options dialog box

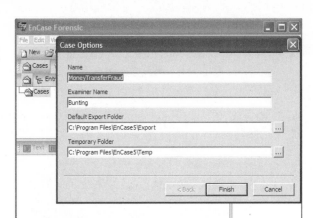

In the Case Options dialog box, enter the following:

**Name**    Enter a descriptive name for your case, which may include a case or complaint number. The text you enter here will show in the case folder under the Cases tab view. When you have many cases to manage, being very descriptive and detailed while still being brief is quite helpful.

**Examiner Name**    Enter the examiner's (your) name in this space. EnCase will not let you proceed if you don't make an entry, and it will remember your last entry for future cases in the local.ini file contained in the EnCase5\Config folder.

**Default Export Folder**    This folder will be the default location for files that are exported from within EnCase. Also, when you choose to "copy/unerase files, this will be the default location for that feature as well. Some EnScripts will use this location for output too.

**Temporary Folder**    The Temp folder is used to store files when EnCase is directed to send a file to an external viewer. Before the external viewer can see a file, it must first be copied out of EnCase and into the Windows environment. This folder holds those files for this purpose. When you exit EnCase, files in the Temp folder are removed. If a system crash occurs, this purging won't take place. For this reason, files can accumulate in the Temp folder, and if you have a system crash, you may wish to delete them as they can sometimes get quite large in number and size.

If you aren't careful, you can send data to an external viewer unintentionally. EnCase is a faithful servant and doesn't discriminate between smart requests and not-so-smart requests. If you send a search hit in the "unallocated clusters" to an external viewer, EnCase will do as you requested, copying out first the entire unallocated space to the Temp folder. When this occurs, you have two choices. You can let the task finish or you can abort EnCase completely. If the former, make sure you have the time and space for the task. If the latter, make sure your case is saved first and clear out the Temp folder manually after EnCase terminates. If you do this once, chances are very good that it will be the only time you do it!

If the paths to the Temp and Export folders don't exist, EnCase will create them if you provide the path name for the location where you want them to be located. To save time, create a folder structure for your cases on your desktop or another convenient location. Whenever you create a case, you can first copy this folder into the Cases folder onto your case drive and your complete folder structure will be created in seconds. All you need to do is rename the "template" to your case name. Figure 6.3 shows such a template on my desktop. It facilitates standardization and is a real timesaver. I detest repetitive tasks!

**FIGURE 6.3**    Create a case file template on your desktop. Whenever you need to create a case, copy this folder into the Cases folder of your case information drive. Rename the template folder to your case name, and you are done in seconds.

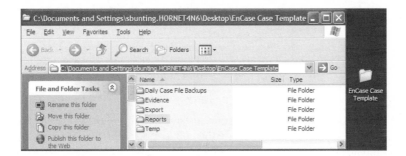

Case file organization and management are extremely important skills for an examiner to acquire. When computer forensics was in its infancy, best practices and technology at the time called for keeping one case image per drive to prevent comingling or cross-contamination of data. As case loads grew and technology evolved, best practices have been modified accordingly. As EnCase encapsulates a device image into an evidence file that has powerful and redundant internal integrity checks, cross-contamination of image files is not the issue it was in the past. In that regard and in many other areas, EnCase has changed the face of computer forensics and, with it, best practices.

Many labs have massive storage servers that store EnCase evidence and case files. Instead of segregating storage in separate physical devices as in the past, storage today is often networked and segregated by distinctive folder-naming conventions that are consistent with best practices for case management. In this manner, several examiners can access the same evidence files concurrently and work on different facets of the same case as a team.

EnCase also allows the examiner to open multiple cases at the same time and to conduct concurrent analyses on them. Sometimes cases are created separately and are found later to be related. In these instances, EnCase facilitates examining them as separate yet related cases. Or, if the cases are separate, the examiner can multitask, working manually on one case while another case is being subjected to simultaneous automated processing.

Regardless of how you use EnCase, file management and organization are critical components for keeping case evidence and information segregated. Guidance Software recommends case folder-naming conventions that follow along the lines of those shown in Figure 6.4. In this manner, all cases are contained under the folder Cases and yet are separated by distinct subfolder names. Under each separately named subfolder are a series of standardized folders

(Temp, Export, and Evidence) intended to separate and store various sets of data unique to that case. In Figure 6.4 you can also see that the "Template" folder was copied into the "Cases" folder and is about to be renamed and used to hold a case. This technique saves time and assures that a standard naming convention is used each time.

**FIGURE 6.4** Multiple cases stored in a single Cases folder.

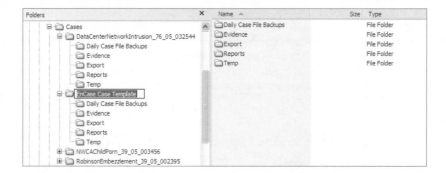

As soon as you have created your case, you should save it by clicking Save on the toolbar. Consistent with our file-naming and organization conventions, you want to save it in the root of the folder that names your unique case. The file name will default to the name of the case that you entered in the Name field of the Case Options dialog box shown earlier in Figure 6.2.

It is a good practice to have the case, the case file, and the case folder all named the same. It's also wise to incorporate the case file name as part of the evidence file name. When they are all named consistently, errors and confusion are less likely to occur. Table 6.1 shows an example of a good file- and folder-naming practice. If the files are misplaced, the naming convention alone can associate them with their lost relatives.

**TABLE 6.1** Examples of Good File and Folder Naming Conventions

| Description | Name |
| --- | --- |
| Case name entered in Case Options dialog box | ABCStockFraud_39_05_003487 |
| Case folder name under Cases folder | \Cases\ ABCStockFraud_39_05_003487 |
| Case file name | \Cases\ ABCStockFraud_39_05_003487\ ABCStockFraud_39_05_003487.case |

**TABLE  6.1**    Examples of Good File and Folder Naming Conventions  *(continued)*

| Description | Name |
| --- | --- |
| Hard drive evidence file | \Cases\ ABCStockFraud_39_05_003487\Evidence\ ABCStockFraud_39_05_003487_40GBWDHDD01 |
| USB thumb drive evidence file | \Cases\ ABCStockFraud_39_05_003487\Evidence\ ABCStockFraud_39_05_003487_1GBUSBTD01 |

Remember that with EnCase 5, the backup case file (.cbak) is now located under \Program Files\EnCase5\Backup\.

After you have created a case and saved it, it is time to add evidence to that case. To do so, click Add Device, which is located on the toolbar. Adding a device is not an option until you either create a case or open a case. At this stage, you can use the dialog box to add a live device for preview and possible acquisition, or you can add an evidence file to your case. If you are operating in the Enterprise or FIM environment, you can connect to a network device that is running the servlet. Once you have added a device to your case, save your case.

There is a saying that has its roots in Chicago during its earlier years: "Vote early and vote often." In forensics, you should apply similar logic by saving early and saving often. Get into the habit of clicking the Save button anytime you have completed significant work and when you are about to embark on a new task or process.

# Tree Pane Navigation

Let's navigate within the EnCase environment. We have created a case and have added a device (own local hard drive), which is an excellent place to explore and to conduct research. While in the Case Entries view, the Tree pane displays the devices in your case along with their hierarchical structure down to the folder level. Files contained at any level will be displayed in the Table pane along with any folders at that same level as the displayed files.

Figure 6.5 shows the EnCase Case Entries view with the local hard drive added to the case along with a floppy evidence file, a Mac OS X evidence file, a Linux evidence file, and three hardware RAID 5 evidence files configured and mounted as a logical RAID within EnCase. When you look at the Tree pane, you can see all the devices in the case along with their associated icons, which vary according to the device. EnCase uses a vast number of icons in its environment. A complete listing of them is found on the DVD.

**FIGURE 6.5**   EnCase supports many different file systems, which may be mounted in the same case and searched simultaneously.

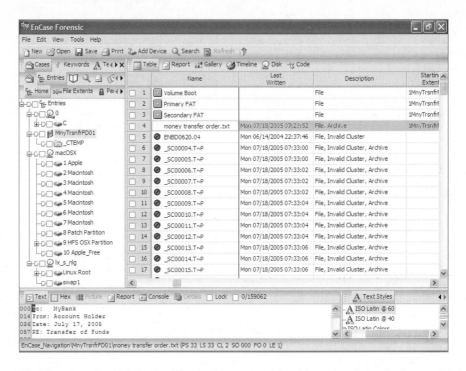

Figure 6.6 shows a physical device (live in this case, with a blue triangle in the lower right) and its associated volume. The physical device icon is a depiction of a hard drive with the arm and heads spanning the platter. It takes some imagination, but that's what it is. The volume icon is a gray 3-D box of some sort.

**FIGURE 6.6**   A "live" physical device and its associated volume. Note the "icon" for the physical device has a blue triangle in the lower right, indicating it is a live device.

Figure 6.7 shows a floppy disk and a folder. The floppy disk icon looks very much like a floppy, and the folder is clearly a folder. This particular folder has an "X" in it, meaning it is a deleted folder. One without an "X" is one that is not deleted, quite intuitively!

**FIGURE 6.7**   A floppy disk icon is shown with one folder, which has an "X" in it, indicating it is a "deleted" folder.

Figure 6.8 shows three devices that have no volumes as they are three physical devices imaged from a hardware RAID 5 system. As such, all you see are three physical device icons. Within EnCase, these devices have been manually configured to form a logical RAID 5 device, shown with the "gray box" with six red lines protruding from it (three at the top and three at the bottom). This logical physical RAID 5 device has a logical partition in it, labeled "RAID 5 Boot Vol C."

**FIGURE 6.8** Three physical devices from a hardware RAID 5 configured and mounted as a logical RAID 5 within EnCase. Note the "RAID" icon, which is a gray box with six protruding red lines.

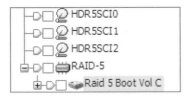

If you turn your attention back to the physical device and its volume in Figure 6.6, you will note that next to the volume icon is a plus sign. When you see a plus sign, it indicates that the object is collapsed and that there are more objects under it. You may view these additional items by clicking the plus sign and thus expanding the object to reveal its contents, as shown in Figure 6.9.

**FIGURE 6.9** Clicking a plus sign next to an object expands that object one level below the level of the object.

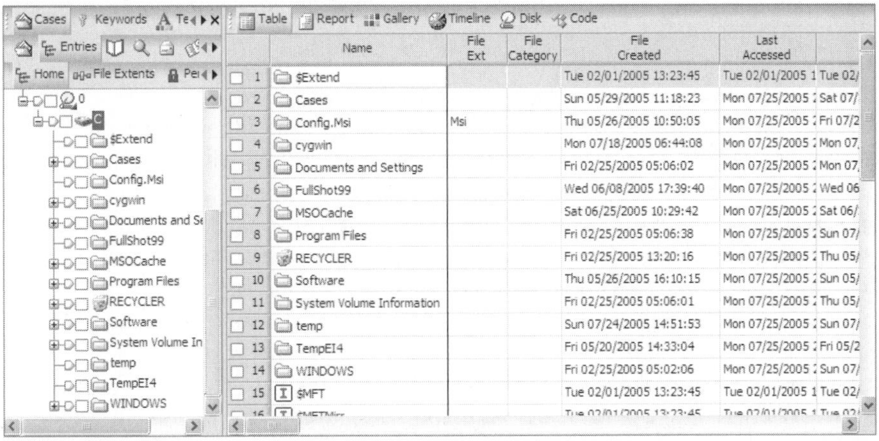

At times, you will drill down so deep into the hierarchical structure that you can't see the forest for the trees. You can right-click on any object and contract everything below it by selecting Contract All, as shown in Figure 6.10. By choosing this option at the level of the physical device, you can contract the device completely. Conversely, you may right-click and choose Expand All, at any level you choose.

**FIGURE 6.10**   You can "expand all" or "contract all" by right-clicking on an object in the Tree pane.

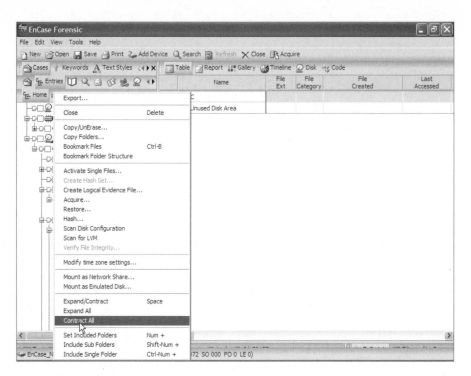

Between the plus or minus signs and the device icon are two other boxes. One is square, and the other is five-sided and shaped like home plate on a baseball playing field. The square box is for selecting objects for subsequent action or processing. When objects are selected, a blue check appears in the box next to the object. Selecting an object in the Tree pane selects that object and all child objects. Selecting an object in the Table pane selects only that object.

As objects are selected, a cumulative count of selected objects appears in the Dixon box, named after the examiner who suggested this feature. This box is located in the center of the bar that separates the bottom pane from the two panes above it, as shown in Figure 6.11. The count tells how many objects are selected out of the number of objects in the case. Before selecting an action based on selected files, it pays to check the Dixon box to make sure the count of selected files accurately reflects your intentions. If you really wanted to copy/unerase six files, but instead had accidentally selected 200,000-plus files, it's better to catch it before you click OK than after.

By clicking directly in the Dixon box, you can select or deselect all objects in the case with one click.

**FIGURE 6.11** The Dixon box shows the number of selected objects out of the number of objects in the case.

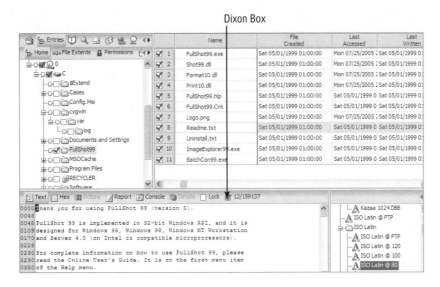

The five-sided "home plate" box has been called many things; it was unnamed when first introduced. It has been called the green box, the home plate, and the name that finally evolved into its official name, which is the "Set Included Folders" trigger or button. When this box is enabled, all files and objects at that level and below are shown in the Table pane. The "Set Included Folders" trigger remains at the level and location activated until you toggle it off or on at another location, as shown in Figure 6.12. Optionally, you can hold down the Ctrl key and selectively set included folders at different locations, as seen in Figure 6.13.

**FIGURE 6.12** The "Set Included Folders" trigger activated at the cygwin folder level, showing all child objects in Table pane

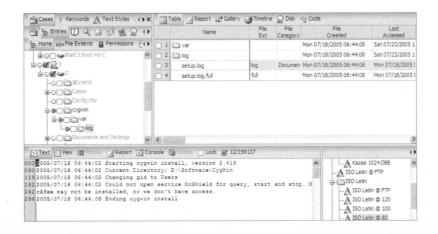

**FIGURE 6.13** In addition to having "Set Included Folders" activated at the cygwin folder, you can hold down the Ctrl key and activate it at multiple locations; in this case it is activated at the $Extend folder also.

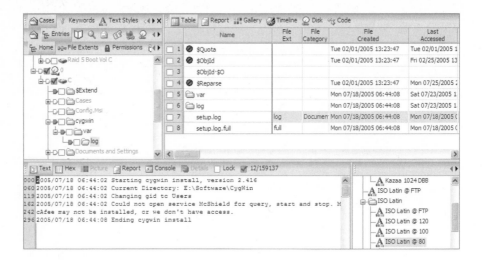

# Table Pane Navigation

Now that we've covered most of the Case Entries view features in the Tree pane, let's focus on the features of the Table pane. To simplify things for now, we have not covered the various tab views in the Tree pane. We'll come back to those later. The Table pane has several tabs, but the default tab is the table view in which the objects appear in a spreadsheet view with the various attributes or properties of the objects appearing in columns.

## Table View Tab

On the Table View tab, you can sort, hide, move, lock, and otherwise configure columns to streamline your examination. There are more columns than you can see at once unless you have multiple desktops configured to accommodate such a view. Except for those lucky enough to have dual monitor configurations, most of us need to arrange the columns so that meaningful and related information can be viewed.

One of the most useful features is the ability to lock a column, which is most often the Name column. When the Name column is locked, you can scroll through the columns and the object name remains visible throughout the process. To lock a column, place your cursor focus in that column, right-click, choose Column, and then choose Set Lock, as shown in Figure 6.14. A dark line appears on the right side of the locked column indicating the location of the "locked" column. As shown in Figure 6.15, when you scroll across the columns, the Name column remains visible.

**FIGURE 6.14**    To lock a column, right-click on that column, choose Column, and choose Set Lock.

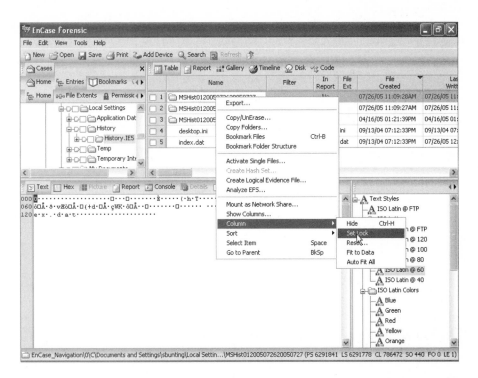

**FIGURE 6.15**    A dark line marks the right edge of the locked column. The column(s) to the left of the dark line will remain locked while those to the right of it will scroll by.

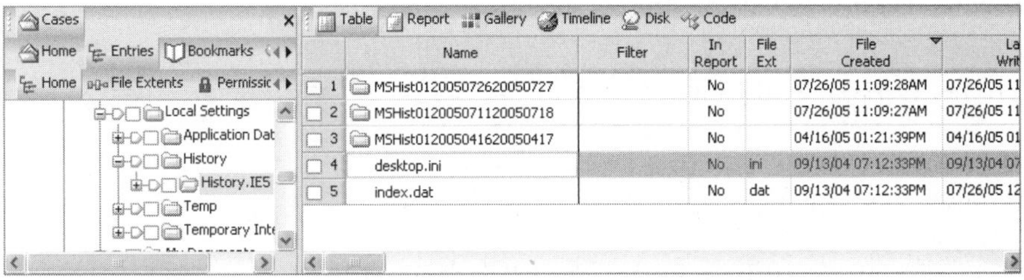

Sorting columns is an excellent analysis tool. With EnCase you can apply up to five sort levels, although three levels are the most you will typically ever require. To sort a column, you can right-click on it, choose Sort from the context menu, and pick your option from among those offered. Or you can simply double-click on the header of the column you want to sort and EnCase does it automatically. In Figure 6.16, the cursor is over the column header, and we've just applied a sort. The little red triangle indicates the direction of the sort. If you want to apply a second sort, simply hold down the Shift key and double-click on the column header. Figure 6.17 shows two triangles on the column, which indicates that a second sort was applied. You can also right-click on the column to be sorted and choose among the options under Sort.

**FIGURE 6.16** Double-click the column header to sort a column. Note the red triangle indicating the column sorted with the triangle representing the "direction" of the sort.

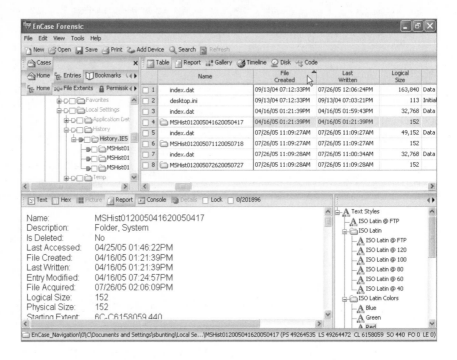

**FIGURE 6.17** To apply a second sort, hold down Shift while double-clicking the column header. Two triangles appear on the column.

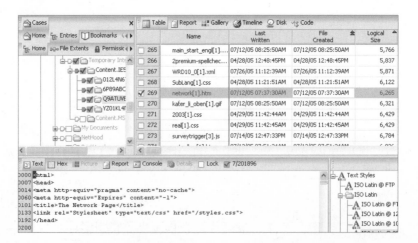

If you want to sort in the opposite direction, you need only hold down the Ctrl key while double-clicking the column header. If applying a second sort, hold down both Ctrl and Shift while double-clicking the column header. If you prefer using menus, right-clicking on a column provides a variety of sort options under the Sort submenu. To remove a sort, double-click on the column header. Without the Shift key, this action replaces the old sort with your new sort. You can also right-click anywhere in the table and choose Remove Sort under the Sort submenu. This returns all columns to their unsorted state.

EnCase features a very useful sort that is not obvious but that you'll find extremely useful. You can sort on the very first column (which has no name). When you have items "blue checked" and selected, a simple double-click to this column brings all your selected items to the top; the sort is between those selected and those not selected. Once you have your files selected and sorted on the "blue checkmark" column, you can add a second sort to put your selected files in chronological order. In Figure 6.18, several files of interest were selected from several hundred in the sample. Once selected with blue checkmarks, they were sorted by the unnamed column containing the blue checkmarks. They were subjected to a second sort based on time, creating a chronological listing of the files selected.

**FIGURE  6.18**     An undocumented but extremely useful sort occurs when you select files and sort on the unnamed column header above the blue checked boxes. EnCase sorts between those selected and those not selected.

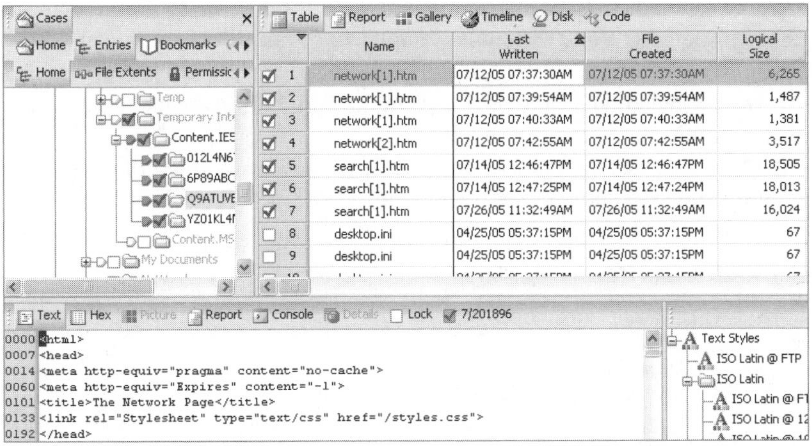

Columns can be hidden or displayed easily. This allows you to remove irrelevant data and focus on what's important to your case. The quick way to hide a column is to place your cursor on it and press Ctrl+H. Pressing Ctrl+H again does not act as a toggle, but rather will hide another column, which is the one your cursor moves to after you hide a column. There are two ways to show a hidden column. You can right-click in the Table pane and choose Show Columns, as shown in Figure 6.19. Any box that is hidden or deactivated will not have a blue check in its adjoining box. You can place blue checks in these boxes, click OK, and they are restored. With this feature, you can be precise in selecting which columns to display. Another option for restoring columns involves right-clicking in the Table pane, choosing Columns, and then selecting Reset. This restores the window to the default setting of displaying all columns.

**FIGURE 6.19** Right-clicking in the Table pane and choosing Show Columns gives you precise control over which columns are displayed.

Of all the things that can be done to columns, perhaps the most useful is the ability to pick them up and move them around. In this manner, relevant data can be compared within the context of other relevant data. It is handy to have that data next to the comparison data rather than somewhere off the screen where you can't see it. To move a column, place your cursor over the column header, press the left mouse button, and drag the column to where you want it moved. Release the mouse button and the column moves to its new location. You can even replace a locked column by dragging a new column onto the locked column. If you ever get your columns hopelessly rearranged, hidden, and otherwise not to your liking, use the Reset command (see the previous paragraph) to restore the default settings.

The various columns have names in their column header that describe the property or attribute of the objects. Those column names are listed in Table 6.2.

**TABLE 6.2** Column Names Explained

| Column Header Name | Description |
| --- | --- |
| Name | Identifies the object as a file, folder, or volume. It is sometimes preceded by an icon that indicates the object's status. |
| Filter | If a filter or condition is applied, this box will contain the name of the filter or condition. |
| In Report | This column indicates whether the object will appear in the Report tab. By default, objects do not. A blank here means null and indicates no, or false. A dot represents a yes, or true. If you want an object to appear in the Report tab view, you need to turn it on. |

**TABLE 6.2**    Column Names Explained    *(continued)*

| Column Header Name | Description |
| --- | --- |
| File Ext | This column displays the file's file extension if it has one. Windows uses file extensions to determine which application to use to open it while other OSs instead use header or other metadata information to do so. EnCase reports the actual extension used by the file. If it has been changed, the real extension remains an unknown until a file signature analysis is run. |
| File Type | File types will return information from the File Types view and table based on file extension. |
| File Category | The file category is likewise pulled from the File Types table and is a general category, such as documents or images. |
| Signature | This column is populated after a file signature analysis and returns the result of that process. The results could be "match", "! Bad Signature," etc. This area will be discussed in a Chapter 8. |
| Description | Briefly describes the object (file, folder, volume), some of its attributes, and what the icon means that sometimes accompanies the object name. |
| Is Deleted | True (Yes, or "dot") or False (No, or null) to indicate whether file has been deleted. |
| Last Accessed | Indicates date/time a file was last accessed. The file does not have to change but only be accessed. Programs vary in the way they touch this time stamp. It may or may not reflect user activity. Some hex editors allow data to be altered and no date/time stamps are changed. |
| File Created | Indicates date/time a file was created in that particular location. You can edit a file after it was originally written, giving it a last written date/time later than originally written (created). If you move it to a new location, the file will take on a new creation date/time for when and where it was moved, making it "appear" to have been created after it was last written. This concept confuses many, but the key is understanding that the creation date/time indicates when it was created *in its location* and that files are moved around after they were last written. |
| Last Written | Displays date/time that a file was opened, data was changed, and the file was saved. If the file is opened and the data isn't changed, there shouldn't be a change in the last written date/time. |
| Entry Modified | Displays date/time that a file size was changed. This pertains to NTFS and Linux file systems. If a file's data changed but not its size, this date/time doesn't change. |

**TABLE 6.2**    Column Names Explained    *(continued)*

| Column Header Name | Description |
| --- | --- |
| File Deleted | Reports the date/time of file deletion as reported in a Windows Recycle Bin INFO2 database. |
| File Acquired | Reports date/time the evidence file in which object resides was acquired. |
| Logical Size | Actual size of data in a file from first byte to last byte, reported in bytes. |
| Physical Size | Actual size of the file plus slack space. This figure reflects the amount of clusters occupied by the file in bytes. If a cluster is two sectors (2 x 512), that cluster is 1,024 bytes. If a file is 2 bytes and contained within one cluster, then that file has a logical size of 2 bytes and a physical size of 1,024 bytes. |
| Starting Extent | Starting cluster for a file in the format: Evidence File Number (order within the Case) \| Logical Drive Letter \| Starting Cluster Number; in the case of resident data in a master file table (MFT), the starting cluster will be followed by a comma and the byte offset from the beginning of the cluster to the beginning of the data. |
| File Extents | Lists the number of data runs or extents for a file. If a file has 1 extent, then the clusters are contiguous and it is not fragmented. If this number is 2 or more, the file is fragmented. Details of the extents are available two ways. One is from the File Extents subtab in the Tree pane for any file selected in the Table pane. A better way to see the detail is to place the cursor on the File Extents column in the row for a particular file. A Details subtab is then available in the View pane. |
| Permissions | Displays whether or not security settings have been applied to the object. If you see a "dot" or true indicator (Yes, etc.), then security settings apply and details are available in the same manner as file extents (the Permissions subtab in the Tree pane or the Details subtab in the View pane). Windows and Unix permissions are detailed in the resulting window. |
| References | Displays the number of times the highlighted file is referenced or bookmarked. If an integer value is in this column, the details are available in the same manner as file extents (the References subtab in the Tree pane or the Details subtab in the View pane). |
| Physical Location | The physical location is the number of bytes into the device that a file begins. In the case of Unallocated Clusters (UC), EnCase reads the UC as one virtual file based on reading the FAT (FAT System) or $Bitmap (NTFS). In the case of UC, the physical location will be the number of bytes into the device that UC begins, which is the byte offset to the first unallocated cluster on the device. |

**TABLE 6.2** Column Names Explained *(continued)*

| Column Header Name | Description |
| --- | --- |
| Physical Sector | The starting sector where a file starts. |
| Evidence File | Displays the evidence file in which object resides. |
| File Identifier | The file table index number. In NTFS, this is the record number in the MFT. For ext2/3 and Reiser (Linux) and UFS (Unix), this is the Inode Number; for HFS/HFS+ (Macintosh), this is the Catalog Number. |
| Hash Value | The MD5 hash value of each file is displayed after Compute Hash Value is run from the Search tool window. |
| Hash Set | Displays the hash set a file belongs to if it matches a known value in the hash library. If it doesn't match or no library has been defined, nothing appears in this column. |
| Hash Category | Displays the hash category a file belongs to if it matches a known value in the hash library (usually set up as Known and Notable, but can be defined by the user). If it doesn't match or no library has been defined, nothing appears in this column. |
| Full Path | Displays the full path to the file, including the evidence file name. |
| Short Name | Displays DOS 8.3 file name. A file named *LongFileName.txt* would appear here as *LONGFI~1.TXT*. |
| Unique Name | Displays the file name for files as they are mounted in Windows Explorer after EnCase Virtual File System is activated and the device is mounted. |
| Original Path | If the file is an allocated, nondeleted file, this column is blank. If the file is deleted and has been overwritten, this column will show which file has overwritten the original file. If the file is in the Recycle Bin, this column shows the original location of the file when it was deleted. |
| Symbolic Link | Unix and Linux systems as well as AIX use symbolic or soft links, which are files and are similar to the link files in Windows. They contain no data about the file that is pointed to; their value lies mostly in pointing to resources on other systems. |

## Report Tab

The Report tab is between the Table view and the Gallery view (see the next section). It displays information about the Table pane children of the object selected in the Tree pane. To include details of those children, you'll need to toggle on the In Report column in the Table view first. You can do this to a group by selecting a batch of files, right-clicking on the In Report column, and choosing Invert All Selected. When in the Case Entries view, the Report tab is good for generating quick reports about files. When in the Bookmarks view, the Report tab will be the main generation point for your final EnCase reports. Figure 6.20 shows a report generated in the Table pane while in the Case Entries view.

**FIGURE 6.20**    Report tab view while in Case Entries view. By going to the Table view and toggling on In Report for the RAID 5, a full detailed report is generated in the Report tab.

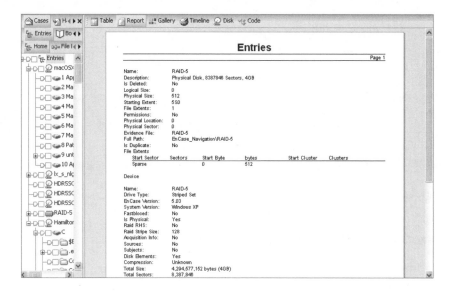

## Gallery Tab

The Gallery view is one of the tabs located in the Table pane. From this view, you can view images in the case at whatever level you choose, from one folder to the entire case. Using the Show All green button in the Tree pane, you can direct the content of the Table pane.

Until a file signature analysis has been done, EnCase displays images based on the file extension. After the file signature analysis has been completed, the files will display based on their file header information. Netscape renames its cached files and removes their extensions. Without a file signature analysis, the temporary Internet files stored by Netscape are not visible as images within EnCase. When KaZaA starts a download, the file name has a .dat extension. Many files exist as partial downloads that are images but won't display until a file signature analysis is completed. We'll discuss how it is done in a later chapter, but it is an important step if you want to see all images in the Gallery view.

While in the Gallery view, you can select image files, bookmark image files, or copy/unerase image files, individually or in groups. You can change the size of the image thumbnails by right-clicking in the Table pane and selecting Fewer Columns, More Columns, Fewer Rows, or More Rows, as shown in Figure 6.21.

**FIGURE 6.21**    You can change the size of the Gallery view thumbnails by right-clicking and choosing fewer/more columns or rows.

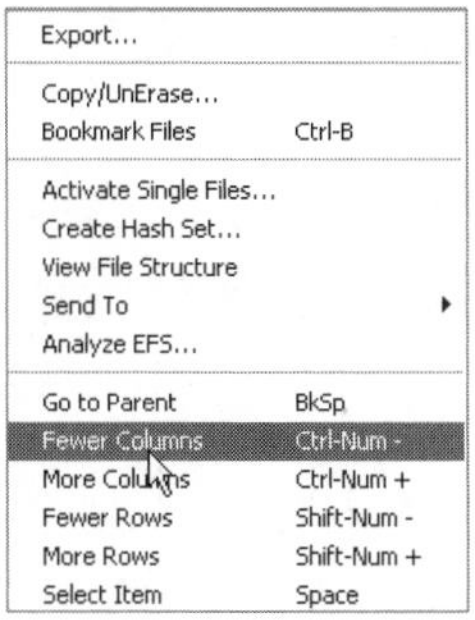

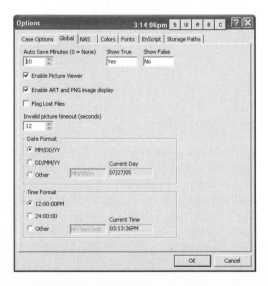

In the past, corrupted images have caused system crashes; however, EnCase now has built-in crash protection. When corrupted images are detected, they are cached and EnCase does not present them again. They are cached at the case level. If images are corrupted and cached, an option appears to clear this cache. If you want to clear this cache, right-click on the case in the Cases view and select Clear Invalid Image Cache. Under Tools ➢ Options ➢ Global, you may change the time that EnCase allows to read an invalid image before it times out and caches it. This setting defaults to 12 seconds but can be changed, as shown in Figure 6.22. Figure 6.23 shows the EnCase Gallery view.

**FIGURE 6.22**    Under Tools ➢ Options ➢ Global, you can change the timeout period EnCase waits before caching an invalid image.

**FIGURE 6.23** EnCase Gallery view showing all images in a folder

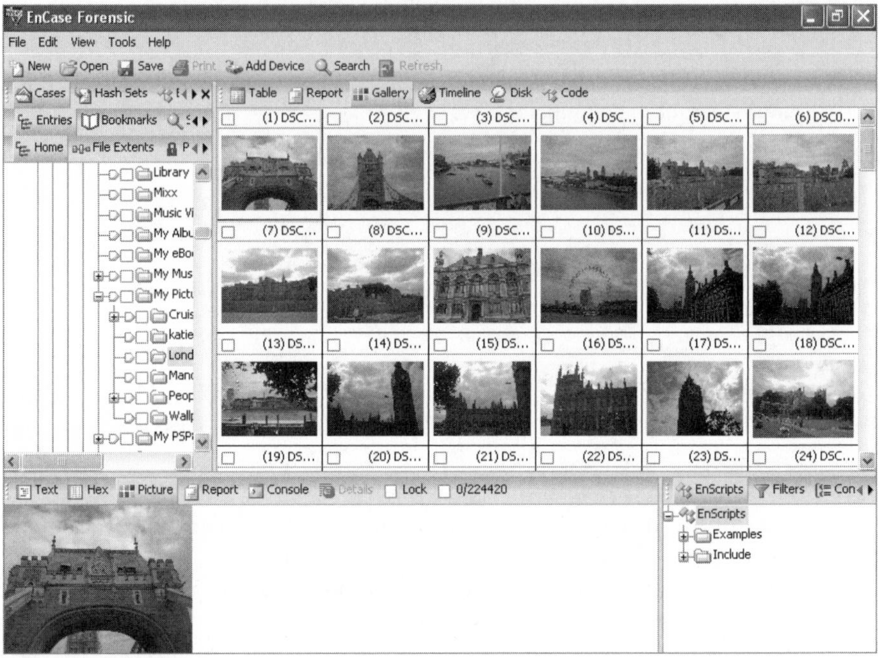

EnCase supports America Online (AOL) .art files (files with an .art file extension). AOL uses a proprietary form of compression known as Johnson–Grace compression, named after the company that developed it. As a bandwidth-saving measure, AOL converts other image types to .art files, which produces an extremely high compression rate.

Support for .art files comes with an AOL installation, but that isn't always desirable. Due to legal reasons, reportedly there was a period when Windows 2000 didn't ship with support for AOL .art files. Support later became available for Windows 2000 as a download option on the Microsoft site. Use Google to search "Microsoft.com" for "Johnson–Grace" to locate the download page. If you are still using Windows 2000, this "fix" will install a series of dynamic link library (.dll) files and doesn't require a restart. XP installs with .art file support, at least at press time.

## Disk Tab

Maybe I need a life, but I make frequent use of the Disk tab. Typically this is one of the first views I go to when I first preview a device. At a glance, the topography of the drive is at your fingertips. It is available as a Table pane view from the Entries tab of the Case view. By default, you see a series of colored square blocks, each representing one sector. They are color-coded as to their function, and a legend is available in the lower right that decodes the mystery of the various colors, as shown in Figure 6.24. Figure 6.25 shows a physical drive with an NTFS partition in the Disk view.

**FIGURE 6.24**    Color-coded legend for Disk view available in the Filter pane

**FIGURE 6.25**    Full Disk view of a physical drive with NTFS partition. The focus is on the MBR, which is the first sector of the drive and is color-coded primary red. Highlighted in the View pane are the 64 bytes constituting the partition table for this drive.

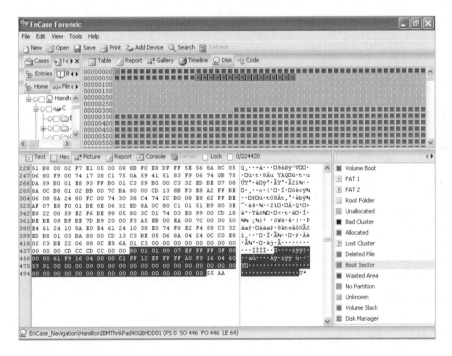

If you right-click in the disk area, you can "go to" a sector by typing in the sector number. Also available from the right-click menu is the ability to add or delete partitions, which is quite helpful if someone "fdisked" their drive. Finally, the right-click options include the ability to switch from a sector view to a cluster view, as shown in Figure 6.26.

**FIGURE 6.26** Right-click options from Disk view include adding or deleting partitions, "going to" a sector or cluster, or switching to a cluster view.

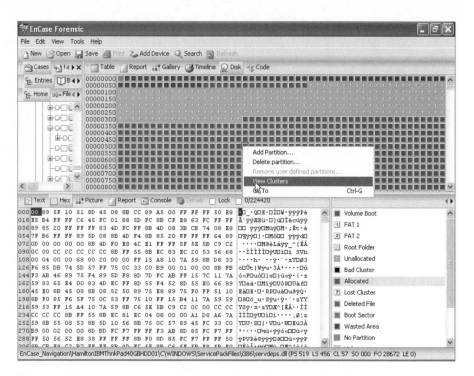

When you are in the Cluster view, remember that clusters are logical units that exist within a partition. When you are sitting on the first cluster, note in the GPS (see the section "Navigation Data (GPS)" later in this chapter) that it is physical sector 63. Sectors 0–62 are outside the partition. Figure 6.27 shows the same drive in a cluster view.

## Timeline Tab

The Timeline view enables the examiner to review chronological activity in a graphical view. By default, all dates and times are enabled and appear in the view. The checkmarks at the top of the view allow you to toggle the various time stamps on or off. In the Tree pane, using the green Set Included Folders trigger you can select the level of Table pane content, ranging from single folders to multiple folders, volumes, devices, or even the entire case.

A particularly interesting view is often simply that of looking at deleted files only. If a person knew on a given date they were the target of an investigation, such a view often reveals file-deletion activity shortly thereafter. In the Timeline view, it can be seen easily and visually. Figure 6.28 shows a Timeline view where the only dates and times are for file deletions.

**FIGURE 6.27**    Cluster view of the same drive shown in Figures 6.25 and 6.26. Note the first cluster is physical sector 63, as seen in the GPS in the bottom of the screen. The first track, sectors 0–62, aren't seen in the cluster view.

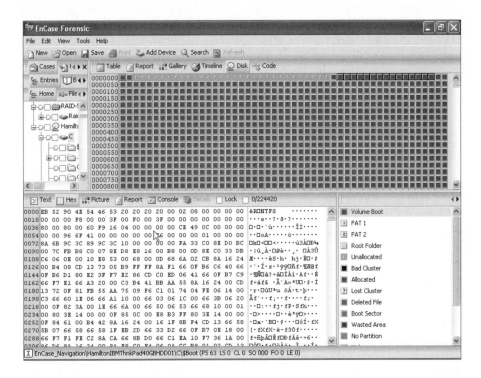

**FIGURE 6.28**    EnCase Timeline tab showing only dates and times for file deletions. Such a focused view can be quite revealing and depicted visually. The two boxes with numbers show the number of files deleted at those times.

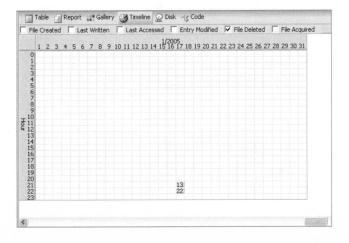

Sometimes you need to drill down and get more detail. You can double-click in numbered boxes and drill down or right-click and choose Higher Resolution (choose lower if you want to get less precise). Alternatively, you can use the plus and minus keys on the number pad and achieve the same result. Figure 6.29 shows drilling down to get more detail.

**FIGURE 6.29** Drilling down and achieving higher resolution in the timeline. The same files from Figure 6.28 are shown with higher resolution. Each tiny red square represents a file, and placing your cursor on it displays its contents in the view pane.

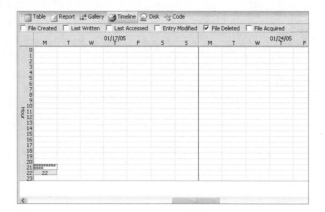

Each of the different date and time stamps is separately color-coded. Toggling each one on and off is a quick way to check which color is coming and going as you toggle. If you right-click in the timeline area, you are presented with the dialog box that you used to change the resolution, but there is an added choice: Options. Selecting Options provides you with the color codes, as shown in Figure 6.30, along with the ability to change them if you like. Another option is the ability to manually specify a range for the timeline, which is nice if you are looking at a precise period and want to exclude all other data.

**FIGURE 6.30** Color codes are available by right-clicking in the timeline and choosing Options. From this same dialog box, you can change the colors or manually specify a time range.

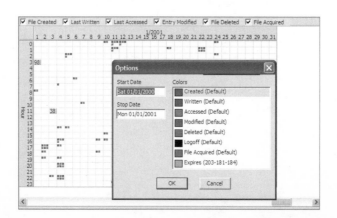

There is no reporting or printing feature for the timeline. The best way to use it is to take screen shots. Those images can be included in Microsoft PowerPoint presentations or placed as images in your final report, be it web based or as a printed document. These images can make a powerful addition as a link in a web-based report.

## Code Tab

There is one more tab in the Table pane in the Case Entries view, and it is used for editing EnScript code. If you open the Code tab, normally nothing is visible. You will need to select an EnScript (Tree pane view or Filter pane option) and place it in an edit mode for code to appear in this window.

# View Pane Navigation

The View pane is where the data is found. The functionality of the View pane is driven by the content of the Table pane. When you are in the Case Entries view, these options enable different ways to view data. The method you choose will depend on your preferences and the task you are performing. If your data is ASCII text, nothing beats the Text view for simplicity and formatting options.

## Text View

In the Text view, the content is driven by the object selected in the Table pane. The format of the output is determined by the current text style as specified in the Text Style view. With EnCase 5, the text style is now also available at your fingertips in the Filter pane in the lower-right corner. With this added feature, you can fine-tune your text style without changing your views. You can even add new styles or edit existing ones all from the Filter pane. Figure 6.31 shows the Text view with the text style options in the Filter pane.

While in the Text view, you can sweep data by clicking and dragging on it to select it. From there you can bookmark, export, or copy/paste data as needed.

## Hex View

Another way to view data is in the Hex view. As shown in Figure 6.32, in this view each byte is seen in hexadecimal notation on the left side and is also represented in a Text view in the inset to the right of the Hex view. Hex is the pure raw data (binary data expressed in hexadecimal notation), whereas the text displayed is interpreted or influenced by code pages. When you need to see raw data, use the Hex view.

**FIGURE 6.31** Text view of the boot.ini file. The text style is ISO Latin @ 80, which is easily changeable in the Filter pane.

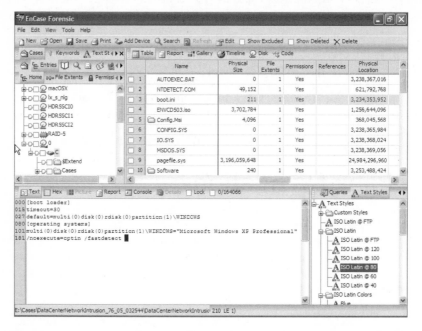

**FIGURE 6.32** The Hex view of the same file shown in Figure 6.31. Note the Text view inset to the right and the text style options at the far right.

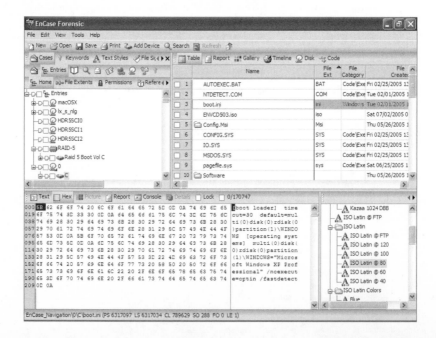

Like the Text view, the Hex view lets you select data and do many things with it, such as bookmarking, exporting, copying/pasting, and so forth. You will see in later chapters that you can bookmark this data and view it in many different ways. The data can be viewed as text, integer values, date/time stamps, partition tables, or DOS directory entries, just to name a few. You may pass this data to third-party decoding tools as well. When you get into advanced analysis or research and testing, you will spend considerable time in the Hex view.

## Picture View

If EnCase detects that the file selected in the Table pane is an image, it will attempt to view the image using the Picture view in the View pane. If the file is not detected as an image, the image box will be unavailable. EnCase determines file type based on extension until a file signature analysis has been completed, at which point the program determines file type based on the file's signature instead of its extension. File signature analysis will be covered in detail in Chapter 8.

Figure 6.33 shows a file as an image. This file is from Netscape/Mozilla's Internet cache. Its file name has been changed and its extension has been stripped. EnCase would not detect this file as an image until a file signature analysis was completed. In this case, the file signature analysis has been completed and this file has been detected as an image file and is shown as a picture.

**FIGURE 6.33**    A file signature analysis detected that this Netscape Internet cache file was an image, and it is shown as an image automatically in the View pane.

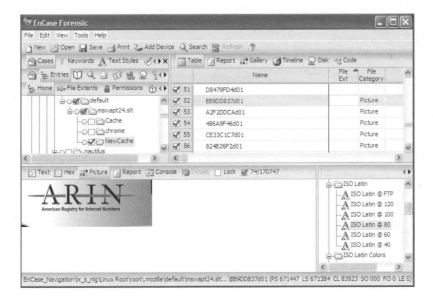

## Report View

The Report view is a detailed report of the properties of the object selected in the Table pane. You will see all the attributes and properties of the object in this view, and if file permissions are in effect, they will be detailed as well. It is a quick way to obtain focused information on an object. You can right-click on the report and export it as a web page or as a document. Sometimes you need lots of details about a couple of files. Here is the place to come to view that information and create a quick report.

## Console View

The Console view is typically blank. Its purpose is to receive output from EnScripts and other EnCase processing routines if you opt to direct the output to the console. Recall when we were hashing drives that the completed output could be directed to the console, as shown in Figure 6.34. If the box is checked, the output is sent to the console as shown in Figure 6.35. Once the data is in the console, it can be passed to another EnScript or copied and pasted for whatever reason you may have.

**FIGURE 6.34**    Output of this hashing routine may be sent to the console by checking the box.

**FIGURE 6.35**    The Console view after receiving data from a completed hashing routine

## Details View

This view is typically unavailable, unless you place your Table pane focus on a particular object's column for which details are available. Recall from earlier in this chapter that the columns File Extents, Permissions, and References produce details that are available under this tab.

## Lock

The user may "lock" a view type for the View pane. When the lock is on, EnCase will view data in the View pane that you have locked until you toggle the lock off. This is often useful when you want to see all data in hex, including pictures. EnCase, without the lock on hex, would view an image in the Picture view. The lock is a simple toggle on and off feature using a check in the box to the right of the Details view tab.

## Dixon Box

We covered the function and purpose of the Dixon box earlier in this chapter. It is located immediately to the right of the Lock feature. The Dixon box indicates the number of selected objects in the case and the total number of objects in the case. If no objects are selected, clicking in the box selects all objects in the case. If objects are selected, clicking in the box deselects all currently selected objects.

You should develop a habit of keeping a close watch on the Dixon box when selecting objects for an action. It can save you considerable time that can result from unintended copy/unerase or other actions. Suppose you select Unallocated Clusters for a search and then forget to clear the selection when you are done. Next, you locate a couple of files that you want to copy. You select those two files and choose to copy the selected files. If you glance at the Dixon box, you should see 3 selected instead of 2, which should prompt you to modify your selection before proceeding. If you didn't bother to check first, you better have lots of space and time—EnCase will do as you directed and copy the entire unallocated space, along with the two files you really wanted to copy.

If you start an action and it seems to be taking longer than it should, and you realize you have subjected more files than you intended to the operation, you can usually abort the process by double-clicking on the progress bar in the lower-right corner. You will be prompted to confirm your decision to cancel the process under way.

Depending on what you are doing, aborting in this way is not always an option. Sending a "search hit" in the unallocated clusters to a third-party viewer is one such example. Once that process starts, the only way to stop it is to stop EnCase. EnCase is a powerful tool and will caution you or prevent you from making poor or destructive choices. But as we mentioned earlier, it doesn't stop or caution you from making choices that are not particularly smart ones. EnCase is quite accustomed to carrying out laborious tasks that can take hours or days.

The Dixon box is a valuable indicator and tool that helps you make good decisions, and also allows you to select or deselect globally very quickly. You should utilize it to its fullest extent—it can save you considerable time as you process cases.

You will often select many files in varied locations for later action. Before proceeding with a desired action, check to see which files you have selected. The Dixon box can tell you how many, but not which ones. There are two quick methods of seeing all of your selected files together. First, you can apply the green "Set Included Folders" trigger at the case level and sort on the column containing the selection boxes. Double-click on the nameless column header (above the check boxes) that contains the blue checkmarks and all selected files will be at the top of your sort. Alternatively, you can apply the green "Set Included Folders" trigger at the case level and activate a condition in the Filter pane (lower-right box). Under General Conditions, there is an option called Selected Files Only. Double-click that option and you will see only the files you have selected in the case. Remember to turn off this option when you are done by toggling it off on the toolbar. There will be an icon clearly marking its presence with a plus sign. Toggle it off (click on the icon), and the plus sign becomes a minus sign. The condition is now off and all files are visible again.

**FIGURE 6.36**    Navigation Data (GPS) is displayed in the bottom of the screen as indicated by the arrow. This information indicates your precise position in the evidence file.

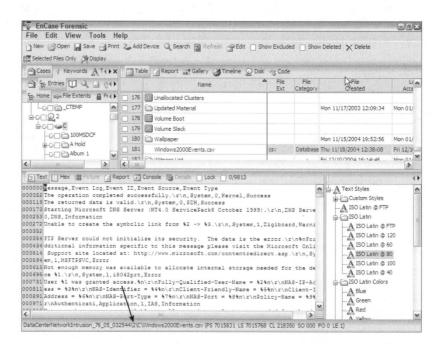

# Navigation Data (GPS)

EnCase 5 displays your precise location in the evidence file at the bottom of the screen, as indicated by the arrow in Figure 6.36. Prior versions displayed it in the bar separating the View pane from the Tree and Table panes. This is real-time information and is updated whenever you change the data being viewed. While its official title is Navigation Data, most examiners simply call it the GPS. GPS stands for Global Positioning Satellite, and this navigation system provides precise information on your exact position on the planet earth. The Navigation Data at the bottom of the screen tells you where you are in an evidence file with the same relative precision as GPS and hence the name GPS is widely used.

**TABLE 6.3** Navigation Data Explained

| Name | Indicator | Description |
| --- | --- | --- |
| Full Path Name | | Standard path-naming convention starting with the case file name, followed by the device name, followed by the complete path to the file currently being accessed. |
| Physical Sector Number | PS | Physical sector number of the data currently being accessed. Each device starts at sector 0 and ends with a number based on the number of sectors in that device, minus one (1,000 sectors are numbered 0 through 999). |
| Logical Sector Number | LS | The logical sector number relative to the partition you are in. Each partition is numbered with sectors starting at 0 and ending on a number based on the number of sectors in the partition minus one. |
| Cluster Number | CL | The cluster number for the data being accessed. Remember that clusters are logical constructs within a partition. If you are outside a partition, in the MBR for example, don't expect to see a cluster number! |
| Sector Offset | SO | The byte offset value within the sector where the data currently accessed resides. With 512 bytes per sector, expect these values to range from 0 to 511. |
| File Offset | FO | The byte offset value within the file currently being accessed. Values will range from 0 to the number of bytes in the file minus one. If you are sitting on the first byte in a file, the FO is 0. If you are sitting on the last byte of a 123-byte file, the FO is 122 (123 − 1 = 122). |
| Length | LE | The length of bytes currently highlighted/selected. It defaults to 1 until you select data by clicking and dragging to select data. This indicator is very useful when selecting ranges of data for analysis, bookmarking, or exporting. |

The information displayed is quite detailed. As seen in Figure 6.37, the information reads from left to right and in the format described in Table 6.3.

**FIGURE 6.37**   Navigation Data

DataCenterNetworkIntrusion_76_05_032544\2\C\Windows2000Events.csv (PS 7015831 LS 7015768 CL 218350 SO 000 FO 0 LE 1)

The GPS indicator is an extremely valuable tool. You should familiarize yourself with its format and make frequent reference to it. It is great tool for teaching and data research. With some research tasks, you can't function without it. Regardless of your purpose, using it and understanding this indicator will make you a better examiner.

# Find Feature

EnCase is, by far, one of the most user-driven products I have ever used. I can't recall ever sending a suggestion to Microsoft and later seeing it in one of its products. By contrast, I have seen several suggestions sent by users to Guidance Software appear later as features in EnCase.

The Find feature is an example of a user-suggested feature and one that is quite useful. It's not one that jumps out at you, but once you discover where it is and what it can do, you'll make frequent use of this feature.

When you are in the Text or Hex view, the Find feature is available to search the data in that view. It is also available in the Console and EnScript Code views for use in programming. You can right-click in the data area and choose Find. A shortcut key is defined also: Ctrl+F. You can also choose Find from the Edit menu. As the Edit menu is always context sensitive, your cursor focus must be in the data area of the View pane for this command to appear on the Edit menu.

The Find dialog box is very straightforward in appearance and function, as shown in Figure 6.38. Before activating the feature, you can select text or data from the data present in Text or Hex view and that data will auto-fill into the Expression text box, saving you time and preventing typing errors. Once the dialog box is open, you can choose regular text or GREP search options (we'll cover GREP in Chapter 7). You can search the entire document, from the cursor to the end of the file or document, or within the area of data that you have currently selected. After the first hit, you can scroll to the next hit by pressing the F3 function key.

**FIGURE 6.38**   The Find dialog box is accessed from the data area of the View pane. It has powerful search features and can save you time when you want to search for an expression in a file.

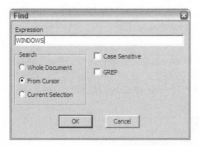

# Other Views

In the lower-right corner is the Filter pane, where Guidance Software programmers have neatly packaged a handy interface that places several powerful and frequently used tools at your fingertips. In previous versions, the filters and queries were in the View pane with the Text, Hex, Report, and Picture viewers. In EnCase 5, these functions have been separated into the View pane and Filter pane. The Filter pane interface is shown in Figure 6.39, and its features, from left to right, are briefly described in Table 6.4. We will cover these features in detail in later sections or chapters.

**TABLE 6.4**    Filter Pane Tabs Explained

| Tool | Description |
| --- | --- |
| EnScript | Also available by selecting View on the toolbar, this interface allows you to run, edit, or create EnScripts to help you process your case. |
| Filters | Filters are special EnScripts that allow you to include only files that meet your filter conditions. Many filters are included, and you can add more if you choose. You can filter for files associated with Hotmail, for example, or there are plenty more from which to choose. |
| Conditions | Conditions are new to EnCase 5. They differ slightly from filters in that conditions allow the user to specify parameters with a simple wizard-type interface, whereas with filters, the user has to work with code to achieve the same effect. Many conditions are already created and can assist you in analyzing data with considerable ease, power, and granularity, all within a flexible and easy-to-use interface. |
| Queries | Queries allow you to combine filters or conditions into a filter using Boolean logic. In simple terms, this means you can combine a condition for all "Movies" with a condition for "files created after $n$ date". The Boolean operator would be "AND" since you would want both conditions to be True for the query to find your files. Queries allow you to take very powerful tools and combine them into even more powerful and granular tools. The interface is simple. If you aren't using queries, you are missing out on a very useful examination tool. |
| Text Styles | Text styles are also available under the View menu on the toolbar. Included as a tool in the lower-right corner, this function is located right where it is most needed: immediately adjacent to the data it will format for viewing. In Chapter 2, "File Systems," we covered how to create a text style for viewing a 32-byte wide FAT directory entry. You can create new views, edit existing ones, or change between text styles. Because it is adjacent to the data, the effect is immediately apparent. You will save considerable time if you access the text style interface from this new location. |

**FIGURE  6.39**    The Filter pane user interface in the lower-right corner places EnScripts, filters, conditions, queries, and text styles at your fingertips for quick and easy access to these frequently used tools.

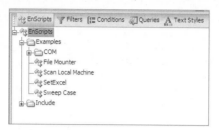

## Adjusting Panes

The various panes may be adjusted to suit your viewing preferences. Between the Tree and Table panes, between the two bottom panes and the two upper panes, and in the bottom between the View pane and the Filter pane in the bottom right, you will see vertical and horizontal separator bars. If you place your cursor over these bars, as shown in Figure 6.40, the cursor changes to a horizontal or vertical sizing indicator, allowing you to left-click and drag the bar to the desired location.

**FIGURE  6.40**    Placing your cursor on the horizontal or vertical separator bar causes the cursor to change to a sizing indicator, indicated by an arrow, that you can click and drag to adjust pane sizes.

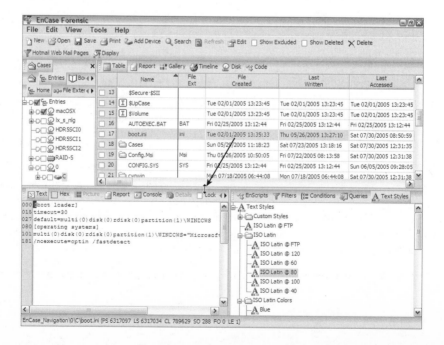

EnCase views can be greatly enhanced by working in a multiple-monitor environment. You can span your EnCase view over however many monitors your budget will support and greatly increase your viewing ease and efficiency. Giving EnCase plenty of screen real estate allows you to open the upper-left quadrant and have available all views, including their names, as shown in Figure 6.41. The Table view also benefits greatly from additional screen real estate.

**FIGURE 6.41**    The various views are concentrated in the upper-left interface. EnCase benefits greatly by having additional screen real estate for this interface.

---

**EXERCISE 6.1**

## Navigating EnCase

In this exercise, we'll create a new case, add an evidence file, and explore together the many features and interfaces of EnCase 5. Let's get started.

- Create a folder structure for a new case as described in the beginning of this chapter. Name your case folder name **Navigation**.

- On the CD, locate a folder named Navigation and copy its single evidence file into your case's Evidence folder.

- Start EnCase, create a new case, name it **Navigation**, and point the Temp and Export folders to the correct path under the folder structure you just created.

- Save your case, naming it **Navigation** and saving it in the root of the folder named Navigation.

- Click Add Devices. In the Tree pane, highlight Evidence Files, right-click, and choose New. Browse to your new case, specifically to the Evidence folder, and click OK. In the Tree pane, highlight your new evidence path. In the Table pane, select the evidence file FileSigAnalysis and click Next, Next, and Finish. We'll use this same evidence file for a later chapter for dealing with file signature analysis, so don't worry too much about the name. Just have fun navigating and exploring EnCase views and features.

- Before doing any work, save your case again now that you have added evidence.

- In the Tree pane of EnCase in the Cases ➤ Entries ➤ Home view, you should see your evidence file named FileSigAnalysis. Based on its icon, what kind of device is it? (Answer: Floppy)

- In the Tree pane, highlight the root level word Entries. In the Table pane you should now see the single floppy device. In the View pane, click the Report tab. Did your evidence file properly verify? What file system is on this device? (Answer: FAT12) How many sectors does it contain? (Answer: 2,880) On what date was it acquired? (Answer: 8/12/2003) How many sectors per cluster? (Answer: One)

- Back in the Tree pane, place your cursor on the floppy icon. In the Table pane, you see five objects, one of which is a folder named FileSignatureAnalysis. Place your cursor on that folder in the Table pane. In the View pane, open the Text tab. What color is the data? (Answer: Red) In this case, what does this color indicate? (Answer: Directory data)

- In the exercise in Chapter 2 you should have created a text style for viewing FAT directory entries. In the Filter pane in the bottom-right corner, use the navigation triangle to scroll over to the Text Styles feature. In the tree structure below it, locate your 32-byte wide FAT directory text style and select it. Your data should snap into place, revealing each 32-byte directory entry on a separate line. While you are there, try applying different text styles to the data and see how useful this added location is for the text style interface. You'll probably never go back to accessing it again from the View menu!

- In the Tree pane, place your cursor on the folder FileSignatureAnalysis. You should see ten files in the Tree pane. In the Table pane, place your cursor on the file jpeg image.jpg. In the View pane, you should see the image appear. In the View pane, switch to the Hex view by clicking on its tab. You are now seeing the hexadecimal notation for binary data. Note the first 4 bytes of the JPEG file, which are FF D8 FF E0. This is one of several JPEG headers. We'll get into that more in a later chapter, but you should get used to seeing it and recognizing right away.

- Go back to the Table pane, where ten files are listed, and click on the Gallery view tab. Only two images are showing. At this point, EnCase is looking to file extensions for file type since we have not yet run a file signature analysis (which we will do in a later chapter). Even though other images are present in this list, only two are legitimate JPEG images with .jpg extensions, and they are shown by EnCase.

- Go back to the Table view in the Table pane. Locate and highlight the file named jpeg image.jpg. The picture should resolve and appear in the View pane. If not, switch to the Picture view and the image will appear. In the View pane, place a check in the Lock box. This should lock the View pane in the Picture view.

- Go to the top of the list in the Table pane. Examine each of the ten files by highlighting them, forcing them to resolve as pictures in the View pane as you do. As you go through this examination, you will note that four of the files resolve as images. Recall there were only two images shown in the Gallery view. Even though a file signature analysis has not been done, if you force a file to be viewed as an image in this manner, if it is an image it will appear using this technique regardless of extension.

- As you locate files that are images, select them. You can do this by clicking in the square box to the left and adjacent to each file, or you can press the spacebar, which places a blue check and advances down the list by one. When done, you should have selected four files. Check the Dixon box, and it should confirm four out of 16 selected.

- At the top of the Table pane, double-click in the nameless column header above the blue check boxes. You have sorted those selected from those not selected, forcing all of your selections to the top of the list. You can only sort in one direction with this particular column. By default, it is a reverse sort and places the selected items at the top. While this is a short list, imagine the usefulness of doing this at the case level with thousands of files.

- Add a secondary sort to this sort. Go to the File Created column. Hold down the Shift key and double-click on the File Created header at the top of this column. You are now looking at your selected files in chronological order based on when they were created. They were all created on the same date, with just a few seconds separating each of them. Note that they all have last-written dates that predate their file creation, which makes it appear they were last written before they were even created. In fact, they were, as they were really created elsewhere, modified elsewhere, and moved to their present location. As you'll recall, the created date reflects when they were moved or created at their present location.

- In the Table pane, click on the Timeline tab. Uncheck all boxes except File Created Date. You should see the number 10 in the timeline area, indicating 10 files with file creation dates. In the Filter view, scroll over to Conditions. Go down the tree until you find General Conditions. Open the tree under General Conditions and double-click on Selected Files Only. The number in the timeline should change from 10 to 4. You are now seeing only your selected files in the timeline. Double-click on the number 4 until it resolves at a higher resolution, showing four distinct boxes for the four files selected. Place your cursor on each, and each of the image files should resolve in the bottom window. Click on the Table view. Click on the plus sign on the Selected Files Only icon on the toolbar. This toggles off the filter, and all 10 files should appear again in the Table view.

- In the Tree pane, click on the "Set Included Folders" trigger at the case level. If you click in the polygon-shaped box, it should turn green. When you do so, note that all objects in the case now appear in the Table pane. Even so, all selected files are still together at the top of the list since the previously defined sorts are applied to the new data brought into this view when you applied the "Set Included Folders" trigger. Turn off the "Set Included Folders" trigger by clicking on it again.

**EXERCISE 6.1** *(continued)*

- In the Tree pane, highlight the floppy device icon. In the Table pane, click on the Disk view. In the View pane, click on the Hex tab. In the lower-right corner, scroll over to the Legend tab and click on it. This reveals the legend for the Disk view. You are looking at a floppy. It is a volume device and does not have an MBR. What occupies its first sector, however, is a VBR. After the VBR you see FAT1 and FAT2. Following the FAT is the root directory, shown in green. Immediately following the root directory is the first cluster that can hold data for files. Place your cursor on the first blue square.

- Look at the GPS in the bottom of the screen. You should be on PS33 LS33 CL02. Recall that on FAT usable clusters start at 02 and that the first two FAT entries (00 and 01) hold other metadata. With a floppy, the volume starts with the first sector, and thus the physical sector and the logical sector offsets are the same, which is something you won't often see. Move your cursor one blue box to the right of your present location. You should be on PS34 LS34 CL03. Note that you have moved one box, and the cluster number and the sector numbers both advanced by one. With a floppy there is one sector per cluster, and therefore one sector equals one cluster. If you right-click in the disk area you will note that View Clusters is grayed out. Because you are looking at a floppy with one sector equaling one cluster, the Sector view and the Cluster view are one in the same.

- Right-click in the data area and choose Go To. Type **2879** and click OK. You are now sitting on sector 2879. As there are 2,880 sectors on this floppy (0–2879), you are sitting on the last sector of this device. Click the Table view to exit the Disk view.

- In the Tree pane, highlight the folder FileSignatureAnalysis. In the Table pane, highlight the file "no header in table and matches no other header MATCHES.txt". In the View pane, click the Text view tab. You should see some text in this file. The fifth word in this file is the word *file*. With your cursor, click and drag over this word to select it. Note in your GPS that the LE is 4, indicating the length in bytes of the selected data. With the word file selected, press Ctrl+F or right-click and choose Find. Accept the default, which is Whole Document. Click OK and the first search hit should be the text you selected. Press F3 to find the next search hit, and it should find the second and final search hit. You can press F3 until you hear the error beep, indicating there are no more matching search hits.

- Save your case and exit EnCase.

## Other Case-Level Views

For the most part, we have thus far concentrated on the views that emanate from the Case Entries tab in the Case view because we can access and see our data. As we start to process our cases, we will go to various other case-level tabs to perform various analytical functions. Some of the tabs we have referenced already as well as others will be covered in later chapters. The various tabs are shown in Figure 6.42, and those tabs and their subtabs are described briefly in Table 6.5.

**FIGURE 6.42**    The various case-level tabs

**TABLE 6.5**    Case-level Tabs

| Tab or View | Description | Subtabs |
|---|---|---|
| Entries | Displays devices and their objects (volumes, folders, data) | Home, File Extents, Permissions, and References |
| Bookmarks | Displays all bookmarks in case. From here bookmarks of all types can be organized and the final report generated. | Home, Log Records (if created), Registry (FIM and Enterprise), and Snapshot (FIM and Enterprise) |
| Search Hits | When keyword searches are conducted, the results are displayed in this tab. | |
| Email | Once the case is scanned for e-mail content, the results are displayed in this tab in a standard tree format. Attachments are displayed in the attachments subtab. To scan, right-click on the Email root and choose Email/Internet Search. You can choose all or pick from various options. | Home and Attachments |
| History | Once the case is scanned, Internet history from the popular browsers is parsed and displayed in this tab. | |
| Web Cache | Once the case is scanned, the temporary Internet files or cached files from the popular web browsers are parsed and rendered in this tab. | |
| Devices | Displays the various devices in the case. In the Table pane, you can reorder the devices by clicking and dragging. You may also manually configure RAIDS by right-clicking in the Table pane and choosing Edit Disk Configuration. | Home, Acquisition Info, Sources, Subjects, Read Errors, Disk Elements, CRC Errors |

**TABLE  6.5**    Case-level Tabs  *(continued)*

| Tab or View | Description | Subtabs |
|---|---|---|
| Secure Storage | EFS (Encrypted File System) encrypts data in system files and the Registry. This tab requires the EDS certificate to function. Right-clicking on the root Secure Storage and choosing Analyze EFS returns the results of this scan and decryption. The *EnCase Decryption Suite Manual* fully describes the use of this function. | |
| Keywords | This is the case-level keyword tab. Keywords created and stored here are stored in the case file. There is also a global Keywords tab. Those keywords are stored in the Keywords.ini file. Case-level keywords are only available at the case level. Global keywords are available to all cases. You can create organizational folders in the Tree pane. In the Table pane, you create keywords. Keywords will be covered in the next chapter. | |

# Global Views

Above the case level, EnCase has several views that affect the EnCase environment and are thus considered global. While they can be selectively applied to a case, features from the global tabs are available to all cases. We saw a unique situation in the previous section where there was both a global and a case-level Keywords tab. The tab you are working with will determine whether the keyword is global or case specific. Aside from the Keywords tab, all other global tabs exist only at the top or global level. Figure 6.43 shows the major global views or tabs after they have been opened and "placed" next to the Cases tab.

**FIGURE  6.43**    Global views are all opened and appear in a tab format adjacent to the Cases tab.

So far, we have referenced some of the global views, gone into great detail on others, and some we have as yet to cover. Table 6.6 lists the various global views and briefly describes their purpose.

**TABLE 6.6**   EnCase Global Views and Functions

| View or Tab | Description |
| --- | --- |
| Keywords | This is the global keyword tab. Keywords created and stored here are kept in the Keywords.ini file. There is a case-level Keywords tab described in the previous section. Those keywords are stored in the case file. Case-level keywords are only available at the case level. Global keywords are available to all cases. You can create organizational folders in the Tree pane. In the Table pane, you create keywords. Keywords will be covered in the next chapter. |
| Text Styles | Text styles are used to create or select different formats and code pages by which to view data. We have shown you how to create a custom text style in Chapter 3 when we created a 32-byte-wide text style by which to view DOS directory entries. When working with foreign languages, you'll need to create text styles for specific languages. While accessible from the View menu, text styles are most easily used from the interface in the lower-right corner. |
| File Signatures | Windows uses file extensions to determine a file's type and which application to use to open it. File extensions can be altered, deleted, or not used at all (many operating systems don't use file extensions). Many files have unique data headers or file signatures by which they can be identified regardless of file extension. EnCase uses file extensions initially to determine file type. After a file signature analysis is conducted, EnCase relies on this analysis to determine a file's true nature. The File Signatures tab accesses the database of file signatures used by EnCase. You can create new ones or edit existing ones. You can also copy headers from here to conduct searches. |
| Hash Sets | Files or streams of data can be subjected to a hashing algorithm known as MD5. The resultant value is a 128-bit number that is statistically unique to that file, thus creating an electronic fingerprint for that file. Sets of hash values are created for related groups of files. A collection of hash sets constitutes a hash library. This tab accesses the database of hash sets from which the user selects hash sets and creates a hash library to apply to the cases under current examination. This will be covered in detail in Chapter 8. |

**TABLE 6.6** EnCase Global Views and Functions *(continued)*

| View or Tab | Description |
| --- | --- |
| File Types | Files are identified in Windows by their file extensions. This tab accesses a database of file types based on extensions. As with other databases, this one can be modified by adding, deleting, or modifying entries. You determine which file viewer (EnCase, Windows, or the installed viewer) to use to view the various file types. |
| File Viewers | EnCase provides the ability to connect to third-party external viewers. Using this tab, you access the database of installed viewers and can add, delete, or modify them. Any viewer installed here will be available off the right-click Sent To option. Before sending a file to an installed viewer, as previously mentioned, EnCase must first copy the file out to the Temp directory before passing it to the installed viewer. |
| Security ID | When a security identifier can't be resolved to a user name, this table allows security ID (SID) numbers to be associated to a username. The SIDs are stored and available globally in all future cases. This situation arises when a SID number is present on a domain workstation. The SID can't be resolved to a user locally as that information is stored on the domain controller (server). When this information is retrieved from the server, this table permits the manual entry of this resolved SID/username pair. Once resolved in this table, EnCase reports the username with permissions associated with SID. |
| EnScripts | The interface from which EnScripts are run, created, modified, etc. EnScripts are powerful tools that automate case processing. They will be covered more in Chapter 10. They are also available from the interface in the lower-right corner. |
| EnScript Types | A table or listing of all the types and syntax for the EnScript programming interface. |

As you navigate to views other than Cases ➢ Entries ➢ Home, you may find yourself wondering where you are and how to navigate. Just remember the grand scheme that is in place, which manifests itself in the three hierarchical bars at the top of the Tree pane. From here, you get to almost anywhere. The top bar holds the global views and options, and is the "jumping off" point to enter the Case view. Only the Case view has any subtabs below it. The second bar contains the various case views, the default of which is the Entries view, which in turn defaults to its subtab named Home, from which you access the files in your case. The bottom bar of the three holds subtabs for the various case views, which change according to the tab above. These three bars are depicted in Figure 6.44.

At any point, your path is clearly outlined on the tabs. As you activate a tab, that tab is brought to the front in a three-dimensional appearance. You can easily see your path outlined in this way through the various levels, as shown in Figure 6.45.

**FIGURE 6.44** Navigation within EnCase is governed by the three hierarchically arranged bars at the top of the Tree pane. The contents of each level are driven by the tab selected in the level above it, except of course the top level.

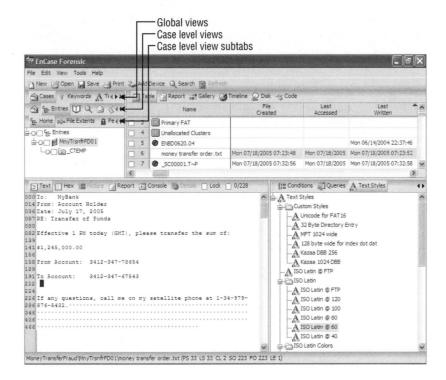

**FIGURE 6.45** Looking at the 3-D tabs that are brought to the front, you can see that you are in the Case view, working in the Entries case-level view, working in the File Extents subtab.

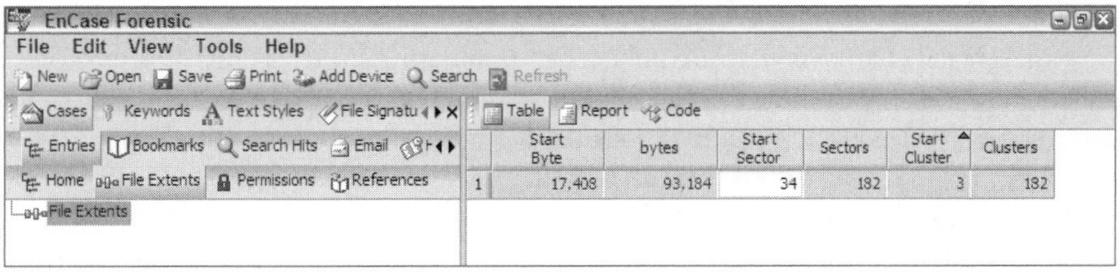

## EnCase Options

EnCase provides an interface that allows the user to change many of the EnCase environment properties. This interface is available under Tools ➢ Options.

When a case is open, the first tab will be a Case Options tab, which allows the user to change the case name, examiner name, and the paths to the Temp and Export folders. Whenever you change drive letters, it can affect the path that EnCase stores for the Temp and Export folders. When EnCase is called upon to send a file to one of these paths, and it doesn't exist because the drive letters have changed, EnCase returns the error shown in Figure 6.46. The error doesn't tell you the fix, only the problem—that it can't find the path to the folder. To fix this problem, you need to correct the paths for the Temp and Export folders, which you do from the Case Options interface.

**FIGURE 6.46**    The error message returned when the path to the Temp or Export folder is incorrect. Change the path under Tools ➢ Options ➢ Case Options to correct the problem.

The Global tab contains several options that affect EnCase globally. We have mentioned that EnCase, by default, uses a dot to indicate a Boolean true condition and null (nothing) to indicate a Boolean false condition. Many of the columns in the Table view contain dots or nulls to indicate the presence (or absence) of a condition or property. Figure 6.47 shows the default global values, including the dot and null under Show True and Show False, respectively. To change this to a more meaningful value, many examiners replace the dot with Yes and the null with No, as seen in Figure 6.48.

There are several other options presented on this tab that affect the EnCase environment. As needs arise, just remembering where they are accessed is usually sufficient. You can make a very useful change to the date format that will cause the day of the week to be displayed in all date/time values. This change is not documented in the manuals, but is a great timesaver when you need to know the day of the week, which is often quite important in analysis work. The default value for dates is *MM/DD/YY*, which returns, for example, *08/01/05*. By changing to Other and customizing the string to *ddd MM/dd/yy*, you ensure that it will return *Mon 08/01/05*. This is usually quite adequate for displaying the day of the week.

You can, however, be very elaborate with your customization. Changing the string to *dddd MM/dd/yy* will return *Monday, 08/01/05*, and changing it to *dddd MMM dd, yyyy* will return *Monday, Aug 01, 2005*.

**FIGURE 6.47** Global options showing the default values. Note that Show True is populated with a dot and Show False is populated with a null.

When you enter the custom string, it is case sensitive, so pay close attention to details. You may encounter a legacy EnScript that only works with the default date time format and usually involves prompts for the user to input date and time ranges. If you experience EnScript difficulties in that regard, and those are truly rare encounters, switch back to the default to run that EnScript. You can restore your customized string when you finish.

**FIGURE 6.48** Boolean Show True is replaced with Yes and Show False is replaced with No. These values are more meaningful when displayed in context. Shown also are changes to the date format that cause the day of the week to be displayed, which is a very useful tweak.

As you can see from the various tabs, there are many options you can change as needed. If you work with foreign languages, you'll need to work with the Fonts tab. Detailed instructions are available on the Guidance Software website. If you work in a networked lab and have one central source for your EnCase environment files (INI files), you can map those paths on the Storage Paths tab.

One final tab, the Colors tab, deserves our attention as examiners often find it necessary to modify slightly some of the default colors. You can radically change the EnCase color palette from this tab. We recommend you make small incremental changes. In this fashion, you change one feature's color palette and examine its impact throughout the EnCase environment before making additional changes.

Two colors often changed or tweaked are the Bookmark and Search Hit colors since the defaults are rather pale and don't show well in certain viewing and lighting conditions. If you double-click on the property Bookmark, for example, you are presented with a dialog box. Double-click on the background, and you are presented with the color palette. Initially, you should probably stick with the same basic color but choose a more saturated and visible one, as shown in Figure 6.49. The color palette options are endless, but you should proceed cautiously, making small incremental changes and evaluating before making more changes.

**FIGURE 6.49**    The color palette for the Bookmarks background is changed from the Tools ➢ Options ➢ Colors tab.

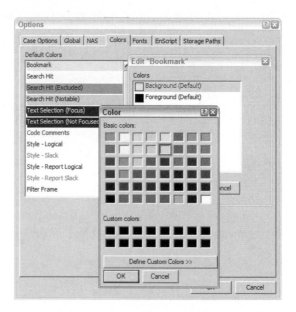

## Thinking Outside the Box

We have just spent an entire chapter dealing with the EnCase interface. Sometimes it is good to get out of that frame of reference for a while so we can truly think outside the box! With that in mind, let's digress by jumping into the Macintosh environment, which is more like culture shock than a digression.

This case has neither a happy nor a sad ending as it is very much still in progress. Accordingly, certain case details must remain purposefully vague.

The target of this investigation is a scientist who stands accused of manipulating research data to apply for and receive government research grants. This has been ongoing research spanning many years as well as previous employers, and it involves megabucks. It was the government research integrity office that initially discovered the altered data and initiated the investigation, which has since broadened.

I was tasked with seizing and imaging all the computer systems used by this scientist, which was a daunting task since there was no cooperation from the scientist and little information. My directive was simple, or so it seemed: Get it all! The systems covered the gamut and included Windows, Solaris, and Macintosh boxes, some of which were actively connected to scientific instrumentation.

At some point later in the process, months down the road, certain data files were identified as being relevant. They were on a Mac G4 system. These files were among hundreds of like files covering the research life of this scientist, with data ranging back to the early 1980s. Recall that some operating systems don't use extensions to identify and associate files to applications. Macintosh happens to be one such system. Examining these files in the EnCase environment provided no information as to which scientific application created the files, and cooperation was not forthcoming.

We typically think of FastBloc as a hardware write-blocking device that we use in Windows. We can use it with EnCase, or we can use it within Windows with the Explorer interface or with other third-party tools. What we often don't think of are the uses that are beyond the norm or the out-of-the-box applications of FastBloc.

In the case at hand, I used EnCase to restore the Mac image onto a drive of identical make, model, and geometry. I attached the restored drive to my FastBloc FE. I connected the FastBloc FE to my lab Mac G4 via a 1394 cable and booted the system. Upon boot, the questioned hard drive was mounted, read only, and sitting on my Mac desktop awaiting my perusal. My first thought was that this was far too easy. I was right!

My first task was to run an MD5 of the mounted physical drive using the Mac "terminal" interface. This interface provides a BSD Linux command-line environment. After about 90 minutes or so, the hash was completed and the value matched the acquisition hash reported by EnCase. This was great—I had established that the drive under examination was identical to the one acquired and nothing had changed when it was mounted in the Mac environment.

Based on my discoveries using EnCase, I knew the identity and exact location of the files in question. Using the Mac equivalent of Windows Explorer, which is called Finder, I navigated to the files in question. Mac stores information about files in metadata that is viewable via a Get Info command that is similar to the Properties command in Windows. There are at least three ways to access this command. If you select a file and press Command+I, you get it immediately.

A second way is via a right-click menu option called Get Info. Since Mac likes to hobble its users by only providing a one-button mouse, you have to hold down the Control key while clicking the one-button mouse to access the right-click options. If you wish to use a Mac to its fullest potential, buy a real mouse with two buttons, a USB connection, and you are an instant Mac power user!

The third way is under Finder. Select the file and from the File menu on the toolbar, choose Get Info.

The Get Info results for the files in question immediately revealed the identity of the scientific analysis program that created the files. Armed with that information, we were then in a position to read the data for the first time in this investigation.

Mac, unlike Windows, does not use a registry to store installation information for programs. When programs are installed on a Mac, the installation information is usually stored with the program files. What this means for the forensics examiner is that you can run just about any program that is on the read-only target drive and it will run flawlessly (see the note regarding licensing at the end of this sidebar). If you have any difficulties because of the read-only status, just drag the application over to your applications folder on your system drive and you are back in business.

When I attempted to run the relevant scientific application to read the data, I encountered yet another issue. This was a legacy program and wouldn't run under Mac OS X, requiring instead the Mac Classic environment. As it turns out, Mac ships Classic support with OS X. While not a clearly marked road to follow, it is on the install disk labeled Additional Software. Pop in the CD, follow the prompts, and five minutes later you have support for legacy programs running under Mac Classic.

After a seemingly long journey, I was able to run the scientific applications, read all the data, and export it in several formats readable by the investigators. When done, I ran another MD5 of the target drive. After all that activity, reading data and running programs directly from that drive, not one bit had changed and the MD5 hashes were all alike.

FastBloc FE is a truly versatile device, and it does block all writes regardless of the environment in which it is run. Don't be afraid to think out of the box and use it in nontraditional ways, documenting and testing along the way to assure the integrity of your processes and analyses.

Note: In this case, to avoid legal issues over licensing, I purchased a license for the latest version of the involved software. Even though licensed for the latest and greatest, I used the older version on the target drive as well so as to see the data using the same version of the software (as did the accused party).

# Summary

This chapter covered the EnCase environment and its features and functions. We covered how EnCase organizes its views into increasing granular content, starting with the Tree pane, moving to the Table pane, and ending with the View pane. What is displayed in any given pane depends on the object highlighted in the pane before it in the hierarchy.

Additionally, what is shown in the Tree pane, and subsequently in the Table and View panes, is governed by the tabs on the three hierarchical bars located at the top of the Tree pane. Those bars are arranged, from top to bottom, as global views, case-level views, and case-level subtab views. The top-level bar (global) drives the content of the bar below it (case level). The case-level bar drives the content of the case-level subtab bar. At any point, you can see your path outlined by the 3-D raised tabs.

We covered how to create a folder structure to contain the various case files. In addition, we described how to create a case within EnCase.

While in the Cases ➢ Entries ➢ Home view, the Table pane offers the Table, Report, Gallery, Timeline, Disk, and Code views. From the Table view, you can see all the case objects, folders, and files. Their properties are listed in columns. You can move, sort, or hide columns from view. The Report view provides a quick report format listing various object properties. The Gallery view shows all images based on file extension. If a file signature analysis has been run, the Gallery view will be based on the file signature data.

The Timeline view offers a chronological view of data in a graphical environment. The Disk view displays a device according to a color-coded legend. It defaults to Sector view, which can be changed to Cluster view. As each sector is highlighted, its data is shown in the View pane. The Code view is for running, creating, or editing EnScripts, which are short programs that can automate and customize case processing.

While in the Cases ➢ Entries ➢ Home view, the View pane offers the Text, Hex, Picture, Report, and Console views. Depending on the highlighted data in the Table pane, a Details tab may also be available. The Text view shows plain text while the Hex view shows both hexadecimal notation and text view. The Picture view shows images. The Report view shows case object properties in a ready-to-export format. The file can be exported in RTF or HTML format. The Console view accepts input from processing routines or EnScripts that can be passed to another EnScript or copied and pasted. Certain columns (Extents, Permissions, and References) provide additional details in the View pane. When those columns are highlighted, the Detail pane appears.

At the case level, EnCase offer several views or case-processing features. They can be accessed from the View menu, or much more conveniently on the case-level toolbar. Those views are called Bookmarks, Search Hits, Email, History, Web Cache, Devices, Secure Storage, and Keywords. The Bookmarks view holds all of your case bookmarks and is the point from which your final report is generated. You create or select keywords from the Keywords view. There is both a case-level and global-level Keywords tab. Case-level keywords are stored in the case file, and global keywords are stored in the keywords.ini file. After you search for a keyword, you can see the results in the Search Hits tab or view.

After conducting a system scan for e-mail and Internet artifacts, the e-mail artifacts are found in the Email tab. History and Web Cache artifacts are found in tabs by those same names. From the Devices tab you can look at device properties or generate a report. You can rearrange devices in a case from this view as well as manually rebuild a RAID configuration. The Secure Storage tab is for processing EFS artifacts and requires the EDS certificate and module.

At the global level, EnCase offers Case, Keyword, Text Styles, File Signatures, Hash Sets, File Types, File Viewers, Security IDs, EnScripts, and EnScripts Types views. The Case view is the jumping-off point to work with the case. The Keyword view is a database of keywords available to all cases. Text styles can be accessed more conveniently in the Filter pane in the lower-right corner interface. They create the format and code page combinations for viewing data. The file signatures view is a database of file header information used to determine file types.

The File Types view is a database of file types and extensions. From this view, file viewers for file types may be selected. File viewers is a database of user-installed third-party viewers. When installed, these viewers are available for default viewing via selection in the File Types view. They are also available under the right-click Sent To option. Hash sets are collections of hash values that can be selected and made into a hash library for hash analysis. In the Security IDs view, you can manually associate Unix and Windows security ID numbers with usernames when they aren't locally resolvable. The EnScripts view provides access to run, create, or edit EnScripts. Finally, EnScript types is a help feature for EnScript programmers, providing ready access to all EnScript types and their syntax.

# Exam Essentials

**Understand how EnCase organizes its workspace**    Know how the three bars function at the top of the Tree pane. Understand and be able to explain how the hierarchical bar, tab, and pane systems interact. Understand how content in one bar, tab, or pane drives content in its subordinate, or dependent, bars, tabs, or panes. Understand and explain the differences between global views, case-level views, and case-level subtab views.

**Understand how to navigate within EnCase.**    Understand the hierarchical tree structure displayed in the Tree pane. Know the function of the Show All trigger and the file selection functions. Understand and be able to explain how they differ. Know how to move, sort, hide, and lock columns in the Table view. Understand what information is provided in the Report view and how is can be used. Explain the Gallery view and what information will be displayed and under what conditions. Explain the function and importance of the Timeline view. Know the function and purpose of the Disk view and be able to explain the meaning of the various color-coded elements.

Understand and explain the differences between the Text and Hex views. Describe the purpose of and know how to create and select a text style. Also describe the purpose of the Report view in the View pane. Explain when the Details tab will be available as a View pane tab while in the Cases ➢ Entries ➢ Home view. Explain the purpose of the Console tab and describe where and how it receives its input.

Describe how the Pictures tab on the View pane functions. Explain the purpose and function of the Lock button. Understand and be able to explain the Dixon box and how it assists the examiner.

**Know which features are available in the Filter view.** Explain how to access the EnScript tab in the Filter view in the lower-right corner. Explain briefly the differences between filters, conditions, and queries. Understand how these three tools can assist with an examination. Describe how to toggle off a filter, condition, or query once activated. Explain how to access the Text Styles view in the lower-right corner. Understand how the lower-right corner options are context sensitive based on the Table pane view.

**Understand the relationship between the Edit menu and right-click menu.** Be able to describe the context-sensitive nature of the Edit menu on the toolbar. Describe how the right-click menu is a reflection of the options available on the context-sensitive Edit menu.

# Review Questions

1.  In the EnCase Windows environment, must an examiner first create a new case before adding a device to examine?

    **A.** Yes

    **B.** No

2.  Proper file management and organization require that which of the following should be created prior to acquiring evidence?

    **A.** Evidence, Export, and Temp folders

    **B.** Unique naming conventions for folders belonging to the same case

    **C.** All subfolders saved under one folder with the same unique name

    **D.** All of the above

3.  The EnCase methodology dictates that the lab drive used to store EnCase evidence files must have which of the following prior to acquiring an image?

    **A.** FAT 32 partition

    **B.** NTFS partition

    **C.** Clean format

    **D.** Previously wiped and sterile partition

4.  When creating a new case, the Case Options dialog box prompts for:

    **A.** Name or (case name)

    **B.** Examiner name

    **C.** Default export folder

    **D.** Temporary folder

    **E.** All of the above

5.  What determines the action that will result when a user double-clicks on a file within EnCase?

    **A.** The settings in the TextStyles.ini file

    **B.** The settings in the FileTypes.ini file

    **C.** The settings in the FileSignatures.ini file

    **D.** The settings in the Viewers.ini file

6.  In the EnCase environment, the term *external viewers* is best described as:

    **A.** Internal programs that are copied out of an evidence file

    **B.** External programs loaded in the evidence file to open specific file types

    **C.** External programs that are associated with EnCase to open specific file types

    **D.** External viewers used to open a file that has been copied out of an evidence file

7. Where is the list of external viewers kept within EnCase?

   **A.** The settings in the TextStyles.ini file

   **B.** The settings in the FileTypes.ini file

   **C.** The settings in the FileSignatures.ini file

   **D.** The settings in the Viewers.ini file

8. When the copy/unerase feature is used, EnCase saves the selected file(s) to which folder?

   **A.** Evidence

   **B.** Export

   **C.** Temp

   **D.** None of the above

9. Can the Export folder be moved once it is saved within a case?

   **A.** Yes

   **B.** No

10. Files that have been sent to external viewers are copied to which folder?

    **A.** Evidence

    **B.** Export

    **C.** Temp

    **D.** None of the above

11. The Temp folder of a case cannot be changed once the case has been saved.

    **A.** True

    **B.** False

12. Files stored in the Temp folder are removed once EnCase is properly closed.

    **A.** True

    **B.** False

13. How do you access the setting to adjust how often a backup file (.cbak) is saved?

    **A.** Select Tools ➤ Options ➤ Case Options

    **B.** Select View ➤ Options ➤ Case Options

    **C.** Select Tools ➤ Options ➤ Global

    **D.** Select View ➤ Options ➤ Global

14. What is the maximum number of columns that can be sorted simultaneously in the Table view tab?

    **A.** Two

    **B.** Three

    **C.** Five

    **D.** 28 (maximum number of tabs)

**15.** How would a user reverse-sort on a column in the Table view?

    **A.** Hold down the Ctrl key and double-click the selected column header.

    **B.** Right-click on the selected column, select Sort, and select either Sort Ascending or Sort Descending.

    **C.** Both A and B.

**16.** How can you hide a column in the Table view?

    **A.** Place the cursor on the selected column and press Ctrl+H.

    **B.** Right-click on the selected column, select Column, and select Hide.

    **C.** Right-click on the selected column, select Show Columns, and uncheck the desired fields to be hidden.

    **D.** All of the above.

**17.** What does the Gallery view tab use to determine graphics files?

    **A.** Header or file signature

    **B.** File extension

    **C.** File name

    **D.** File size

**18.** Will the EnCase Gallery view display a .jpeg file if its file extension was renamed to .txt?

    **A.** No, because EnCase will treat it as a text file.

    **B.** Yes, because the Gallery view looks at a file's header information and not the file extension.

    **C.** Yes, but only if a signature analysis is performed to correct the "File Category" to "Picture" based on its file header information.

    **D.** Yes, but only after a hash analysis is performed to determine the file's true identity.

**19.** How would a user change the default colors and text fonts within EnCase?

    **A.** The default colors and fonts settings cannot be changed by the user.

    **B.** The default colors and fonts settings can be changed by right-clicking the selected items and scrolling down to Change Colors and Fonts.

    **C.** The default colors and fonts settings can be changed by clicking the View tab on the menu bar and selecting the Colors tab or Fonts tab.

    **D.** The default colors and fonts settings can be changed by clicking the Tools tab on the menu bar, selecting Options, and selecting the Colors tab or Fonts tab.

**20.** An EnCase user will always know the exact location of the selected data in the evidence file by looking at the:

    **A.** Data bar

    **B.** Dixon box

    **C.** Disk view

    **D.** Hex view

# Answers to Review Questions

1.  A. In the Windows environment, you must first create a new case before the Add Device selection appears on the toolbar.

2.  D. Any folders created for a specific case should be created beforehand, and they should be grouped together under one folder with the same unique name as the case name and case file name.

3.  D. A hard drive used to store evidence files should be completely wiped of any data to prevent any chance of cross-contamination.

4.  E. The Case Options dialog box asks for all of the options listed when a new case is created.

5.  B. The FileTypes.ini file stores information on files such as types, extensions, and viewers used to access the file.

6.  C. External viewers are programs that EnCase uses to open specific file types.

7.  D. The Viewers.ini file stores information on external programs that EnCase uses to open specific file types.

8.  B. When EnCase copies selected items or undeletes files, they are saved externally to the Export folder.

9.  A. Yes. The Export folder can be moved by selecting Tools in the menu bar and selecting Options, and then changing the path of the Default Export Folder under the Case Options tab in the resulting dialog box.

10. C. When files are opened by external viewers, they are first copied to the Temp folder before the external viewers can access the files.

11. B. Once a case has been saved, the EnCase user can change the location of the Temp folder by selecting Tools ➢ Options and changing the path of that folder.

12. A. EnCase will empty the Temp folder once the program has properly shut down. However, files will still remain in the Temp folder if EnCase has shut down improperly.

13. C. To adjust the amount of minutes the backup file is saved can be found by selecting Tools in the menu bar and selecting Options, and then changing the time in the Auto Save Minutes box under the Global tab of the resulting dialog box.

14. C. EnCase allows the user to sort up to five columns in the Table view tab.

15. C. The user can use either method to reverse-sort on a column.

16. D. All three methods will hide selected columns from the Table view.

17. B. The Gallery view displays images based on the "File Category - Picture", which is determined by file extensions until such time that a file signature analysis is run.

**18.** C. When a signature analysis is performed, EnCase will update or correct the "File Category" to "Picture", in this particular case, based on the information contained in the file header.

**19.** D. A user can change the way colors and fonts appear by selecting the Tools tab and then clicking Options to change colors and fonts.

**20.** A. The Navigation Data bar displays the selected data's exact location, including the full path, physical sector, logical sector number, cluster number, sector offset, and file offset.

# Understanding, Searching for, and Bookmarking Data

**ENCE EXAM TOPICS COVERED IN THIS CHAPTER:**

- ✓ Understanding data
- ✓ Conducting basic searches
- ✓ Conducting advanced GREP searches
- ✓ Bookmarking your findings
- ✓ Organizing your bookmarks for reporting

We've heard it said and we'll hear it said again: "It's all about the 1s and the 0s." Computers store or transmit data as strings of 1s and 0s in the form of positive and negative states or pulses. From that we get characters and numbers, all of which make up the data we find on computer systems. In this chapter, we'll begin with a review of binary numbers and their hexadecimal representations. Once we have a firm grasp of how data is stored, we'll describe how to perform simple basic searches for that data. Then, we'll step into the more advanced searching techniques known as GREP. GREP is a very powerful search tool and one you need to master both for the examination and for everyday forensics.

Understanding data and locating it would not be very beneficial if there were not some way of marking those findings and rendering them into some organized format that would later be generated into a report. EnCase has a very powerful and, equally as important, flexible bookmarking and reporting utility.

The first thing that your client or the prosecutor will see of your work and talent is your report. It needs to present well and read well. It will form the first, and maybe the last, impression they will have of your work and your capabilities. You can be the world's sharpest and brightest forensics examiner, but if you can't render your findings into an organized report that is easy to navigate, read, and understand, you will not do well in this most aspects of this field.

More than a few times I've heard the comment that EnCase doesn't have a very good reporting feature. I'm always taken aback by that remark as it has, in my opinion, an excellent report-generating utility that exists at several levels. Furthermore, the bookmark view provides so many ways to organize and customize the resultant report, which is probably the most flexible and customizable in the industry. Finally, you are given the option, at all levels of reporting, of generating an RTF (Rich Text Format) or web document.

In all fairness to that criticism, I am convinced, based on many ensuing discussions that followed this criticism, that the remark has its roots in a lack of awareness and training in using EnCase's reporting utilities. It is time to close that knowledge gap. Because reporting your findings is a critical element to your success as a forensics examiner, Appendix A is devoted to that very topic. In addition, the CD that accompanies this book contains a sample report that you can use as a template or front-end for your EnCase-generated report. As we conclude this chapter with the basics of bookmark organization, Appendix A will pick it up from there and take you through the steps of creating a top-quality report.

# Understanding Data

In this section, we'll cover binary data first, which is how 1s and 0s are rendered into human-readable characters and numbers. Following that discussion, we cover the hexadecimal representation of binary data. As 1s and 0s aren't very readable or workable in their raw form, programmers have developed an overlay by which binary data can be viewed and worked with that's much easier. It's simply called "hex."

We wrap up our discussion of data with the ASCII table and how each character or decimal number therein is represented by a binary and hexadecimal value. As computing has become global, the limits of the ASCII table meant that not all the world's languages could be represented by 1 byte or 256 different characters. Accordingly, Unicode was born; 2 bytes are allotted for each character, making possible 65,536 different characters in a language. We conclude, therefore, with an overview of Unicode.

## Binary Numbers

Computers store, transmit, manipulate, and calculate data using the binary numbering system, which consists purely of 1s and 0s. As you may know, 1s and 0s are represented in many forms as positive or negative magnetic states or pulses. They can be lands or pits, light passing or not, pulses of light, pulses of electricity, electricity passing through a gate or not, and so forth. When you think about it, there are seemingly endless conditions where you can create a yes or no condition that can be in turn interpreted as a 1 or 0. Binary is absolute; it is a 1 or a 0. It is a yes or no condition with no maybes, although you can assemble a sufficient number of 1s and 0s arranged to spell "maybe!"

Binary numbers are arranged in organizational units. The smallest unit is a bit. A bit is a 1 or a 0 and is capable therefore of having only two possible outcomes. Two bits can have four possible outcomes, which are: 00, 01, 10, or 11. Three bits can have eight possible outcomes, while 4 bits can have 16. Four bits is also the next unit and is called a "nibble." Table 7.1 shows the possible number of outcomes, up to 4 bits.

**TABLE 7.1**     Number of Outcomes from 1 to 4 bits

| Number of bits | Number of Outcomes | Binary Number |
|---|---|---|
| 1 (bit) | 2 | 0 or 1 |
| 2 | 4 | 00 01 10 11 |
| 3 | 8 | 000 001 010 011<br>100 101 110 111 |
| 4 (nibble) | 16 | 0000 0001 0010 0011<br>0100 0101 0110 0111<br>1000 1001 1010 1011<br>1100 1101 1110 1111 |

If we continued this table, we'd quickly fill the rest of the book—for every bit we add, we double the possible number of outcomes over the previous number. Mathematically, we are working with exponents or powers of 2, which are written as: $2^0 = 1$, $2^1 = 2$, $2^2 = 4$, $2^3 = 8$, $2^4 = 16$, etc. The powers of 2, as previously noted, add up quickly, as seen in Table 7.2.

**TABLE 7.2** Base 2 Raised to Powers from 0 to 128

| Base Number | Power | Decimal Value |
|---|---|---|
| 2 | 0 | 1 |
| 2 | 1 | 2 |
| 2 | 2 | 4 |
| 2 | 3 | 8 |
| 2 | 4 | 16 |
| 2 | 5 | 32 |
| 2 | 6 | 64 |
| 2 | 7 | 128 |
| 2 | 8 | 256 (8 bits) |
| 2 | 9 | 512 |
| 2 | 10 | 1,024 (1 kilobyte) |
| 2 | 11 | 2,048 |
| 2 | 12 | 4,096 |
| 2 | 13 | 8,192 |
| 2 | 14 | 16,384 |
| 2 | 15 | 32,768 |
| 2 | 16 | 65,536 (16 bits) |
| 2 | 17 | 131,072 |

**TABLE 7.2**    Base 2 Raised to Powers from 0 to 128    *(continued)*

| Base Number | Power | Decimal Value |
|---|---|---|
| 2 | 18 | 262,144 |
| 2 | 19 | 524,288 |
| 2 | 20 | 1,048,576 (1 megabyte) |
| 2 | 21 | 2,097,152 |
| 2 | 22 | 4,194,304 |
| 2 | 23 | 8,388,608 |
| 2 | 24 | 16,777,216 |
| 2 | 25 | 33,554,432 |
| 2 | 26 | 67,108,864 |
| 2 | 27 | 134,217,728 |
| 2 | 28 | 268,435,456 |
| 2 | 29 | 536,870,912 |
| 2 | 30 | 1,073,741,824 (1 gigabyte) |
| 2 | 31 | 2,147,483,648 |
| 2 | 32 | 4,294,967,296<br>(32 bits) (Number of possible outcomes with CRC) |
| 2 | 40 | 1,099,511,627,776 (1 terabyte) |
| 2 | 50 | 1,125,899,906,842,620 (1 exabyte) |
| 2 | 64 | 18,446,744,073,709,600,000 (64 bits) |
| 2 | 128 | 340,282,366,920,938,000,000,000,000,000,000,000,000<br>(128 bits) (Number of possible outcomes with MD5) |

Did you ever wonder why a hard drive was rated by the manufacturer as 30GB and yet when you put it in your computer, it was only 27.9GB? Many people think they have been shorted 2.1GB and call tech support. It may also be raised as a question by opposing counsel wanting to know why EnCase didn't see all of the drive. The answer could rest with an HPA or DCO, as previously discussed in Chapter 4. If, however, you are seeing all the sectors on the drive, an HPA or DCO is not the answer. The answer is, in part, found in Table 7.2. Note that the terms *kilobytes*, *megabytes*, *gigabytes*, *terabytes*, and *exabytes* were inserted at their respective locations. If a drive contains 58,605,120 sectors, it contains 30,005,821,440 bytes (multiply the number of sectors times 512 bytes per sector). A manufacturer, as they wish to paint their drive in the best possible light, uses base-10 gigabytes (1,000,000,000). They simply move the decimal point over nine places and round it off, calling it a 30GB drive. Computers don't care about marketing at all and work with a binary system, whereas 1GB is 1,073,741,824 bytes ($2^{30}$). If you divide 30,005,821,440 by 1,073,741,824, you'll find the answer is 27.94 and some change. Thus your computer sees a drive with 30,005,821,440 bytes as having a capacity of 27.9GB. EnCase reports the drive as having 27.9GB as well. If opposing counsel asks where the missing 2.1GB went, you can now explain it!

So far, we've covered a bit and a nibble (4 bits). The next organizational unit or group of bits is called a *byte*, which consists of 8 bits and is the most well-known term as well. A byte also contains two 4-bit nibbles, called the left nibble and the right nibble. A byte can be combined with other bytes to create larger organizational units or groups of bits. Two bytes is called a word; 4 bytes is called a Dword (Double Word).

Dwords are used frequently throughout computing. The Windows Registry, which will be covered in a later chapter, is full of Dword values. As a Dword consists of 32 bits (4 bytes with each byte containing 8 bits), it is used frequently as a 32-bit integer. You'll see plenty of Dwords in this business.

Larger than a Dword is the Qword or Quad word, which, as you might have guessed, consists of four words. As a word is 2 bytes, four words consist of 8 bytes. As a byte consists of 8 bits, 8 bytes (Qword) contains 64 bits. You'll encounter more Dwords than Qwords, but Qwords are out there and you need to be at least familiar with the term and its meaning.

Table 7.3 shows these various bit groupings and their properties. These are terms you should understand well because they are part of the core competencies that an examiner should possess. Advanced computer forensics deals with data at the bit level. Before attending advanced training, it is a good idea to review these concepts so they don't hold you back and, better yet, so you can move forward with a firm grasp of the subject matter.

The byte is a basic data unit, and understanding how it is constructed and evaluated is an important concept. From our previous discussion, we know that it consists of 8 bits and that it has two 4-bit nibbles, which are named the left nibble and the right nibble. Figure 7.1 shows the basic byte, with a left and right nibble each consisting of 4 bits, for a total of 8 bits.

**TABLE 7.3**   Names of Bit Groupings and Their Properties

| Name | Bits | Binary |
|---|---|---|
| Bit | 1 | 0 |
| Nibble | 4 | 0000 |
| Byte | 8 | 0000-0000 (Left and right nibbles) |
| Word | 16 | 0000-0000 0000-0000 |
| Dword (Double Word) | 32 | 0000-0000 0000-0000<br>0000-0000 0000-0000 |
| Qword (Quad Word) | 64 | 0000-0000 0000-0000<br>0000-0000 0000-0000<br>0000-0000 0000-0000<br>0000-0000 0000-0000 |

**FIGURE 7.1**    A byte consists of 8 bits subdivided into two nibbles, each containing 4 bits; they are known as the left and right nibble.

| Left Nibble | | | | Right Nibble | | | |
|---|---|---|---|---|---|---|---|
| $2^7$ | $2^6$ | $2^5$ | $2^4$ | $2^3$ | $2^2$ | $2^1$ | $2^0$ |
| 128 | 64 | 32 | 16 | 8 | 4 | 2 | 1 |
| 0 | 0 | 0 | 0 | 0 | 0 | 0 | 0 |

Recall that there are 256 possible outcomes for 8 bits or 1 byte. Thus when a byte is being used to represent an integer, 1 byte can represent a range of decimal integers from 0 to 255, or 256 different outcomes or numbers.

If you look at Figure 7.1, you see that each of the eight positions (8 bits) has a value in powers of 2. Also shown is their decimal value. The least significant bit is at the far right and has a decimal value of 1. The most significant bit is at the far left and has a value of 128. If you add all the decimal numbers, you find they have a value of 255. By turning the bits on (1) or off (0) in each of these positions, the byte can be evaluated and rendered into a decimal integer value ranging from 0 to 255.

To demonstrate how this works, Figure 7.2 shows how this evaluation is carried out for the decimal integer 0. For the values represented by each bit position to equal 0, all must be 0 and all bits are set for 0. This is fairly simple to grasp and is, therefore, a good place to start.

**FIGURE 7.2**    All bits are set to 0. All decimal values are 0 and add up to 0.

| Left Nibble | | | | Right Nibble | | | | |
|---|---|---|---|---|---|---|---|---|
| $2^7$ | $2^6$ | $2^5$ | $2^4$ | $2^3$ | $2^2$ | $2^1$ | $2^0$ | <---- Power of 2 |
| 128 | 64 | 32 | 16 | 8 | 4 | 2 | 1 | <---- Decimal Equivalent |
| | | | | | | | | |
| 0 | 0 | 0 | 0 | 0 | 0 | 0 | 0 | <---- Binary Code |
| 0 | 0 | 0 | 0 | 0 | 0 | 0 | 0 | 0+0+0+0+0+0+0+0=0 |

At the other extreme is 255. When we added all the decimal numbers, their total was 255. Thus to represent the decimal integer 255, all bits must be on, or 1. Figure 7.3 shows a binary code for a byte with all bits on. When you add the numbers in each position where the bit is on, the total is 255.

**FIGURE 7.3**    All bits are on, or set to 1. Each bit position's decimal value is added and since all are on, the value is 255.

| Left Nibble | | | | Right Nibble | | | | |
|---|---|---|---|---|---|---|---|---|
| $2^7$ | $2^6$ | $2^5$ | $2^4$ | $2^3$ | $2^2$ | $2^1$ | $2^0$ | <---- Power of 2 |
| 128 | 64 | 32 | 16 | 8 | 4 | 2 | 1 | <---- Decimal Equivalent |
| | | | | | | | | |
| 1 | 1 | 1 | 1 | 1 | 1 | 1 | 1 | <---- Binary Code |
| 128 | 64 | 32 | 16 | 8 | 4 | 2 | 1 | 128+64+32+16+8+4+2+1=255 |

Since we've visited the two extremes, let's see what happens somewhere in between. If we evaluate the binary code 0110-0011, as shown in Figure 7.4, we see that the bits are on for bit positions representing 64, 32, 2, and 1. The others are off and return a 0 value. If we add these numbers in the positions where the bits are on, we find that this binary code represents the decimal integer 99.

**FIGURE 7.4**    Evaluating binary code 0110-0011, we find bits on for bit positions 64, 32, 2, and 1. Adding those numbers returns a decimal integer value of 99.

| Left Nibble | | | | Right Nibble | | | |
|---|---|---|---|---|---|---|---|
| $2^3$ | $2^2$ | $2^1$ | $2^0$ | $2^3$ | $2^2$ | $2^1$ | $2^0$ |
| 8 | 4 | 2 | 1 | 8 | 4 | 2 | 1 |
| | | | | | | | |
| 1 | 0 | 0 | 1 | 1 | 0 | 0 | 0 |
| 8 | 0 | 0 | 1 | 8 | 0 | 0 | 0 |
| | 8 + 0 + 0 + 1 = 9 | | | | 8 + 0 + 0 + 0 = 8 | | |
| | | | 9 | 8 | | | |

The system is fairly simple once you understand the concept and therefore demystify it. Using this analysis method, you can determine the decimal integer value for any byte value. Admittedly, a scientific calculator is much faster, but you will eventually encounter analysis work where you must work at the bit level, and understanding what is occurring in the background is essential for this work.

# Hexadecimal

Working with binary numbers is, with practice, fairly simple. You can see, however, that the numbers in the left nibble are a little large to easily add in your head. Back in the beginning of computing, programmers apparently felt the same way, and developed a shorthand method of representing and working with long binary numbers. This system is called hexadecimal; most people simply call it "hex." You've no doubt heard of or used "hex editors." EnCase has a hex view for viewing raw data, and as a competent examiner, you need to be well versed in hex.

A hexadecimal number is base-16 encoding scheme. The base-16 stems from the number of possible outcomes for a nibble, which is 16. Hex values will normally be written in pairs, with the left value representing the left nibble and right value representing the right nibble. Each nibble, evaluated independently, can have 16 possible outcomes and can therefore represent two separate numbers ranging from 0 to 15. To represent these decimal values with a one-character limit, the coding scheme shown in Table 7.4 was developed and standardized.

**TABLE 7.4**   Hexadecimal Values and Their Corresponding Decimal Values

| Decimal | Hexadecimal |
| --- | --- |
| 0 | 0 |
| 1 | 1 |
| 2 | 2 |
| 3 | 4 |
| 5 | 5 |
| 6 | 6 |
| 7 | 7 |
| 8 | 8 |
| 9 | 9 |
| 10 | A |
| 11 | B |
| 12 | C |
| 13 | D |
| 14 | E |
| 15 | F |

Using this system of encoding, we can express the decimal values from 0 to 15 (16 different numbers or outcomes) using only one character. As each nibble evaluated alone can have a maximum decimal value of 15, we have a system where we can have one character to represent the decimal value of each nibble. Figure 7.5 shows how this works when each nibble is evaluated independently using the hex encoding scheme. In the figure, a hex value of 98 means the left nibble has a decimal value of 9 and the right nibble has a decimal value of 8.

**FIGURE 7.5**   The hexadecimal encoding scheme at work. The left nibble has bits on for 8 and 1 and has a value of 9. The right nibble has bits on for 8 only and has a value of 8. Thus this binary coding (1001-1000) would be expressed in hexadecimal format as 98, or 98h.

| Left Nibble | | | | Right Nibble | | | |
|---|---|---|---|---|---|---|---|
| $2^3$ | $2^2$ | $2^1$ | $2^0$ | $2^3$ | $2^2$ | $2^1$ | $2^0$ |
| 8 | 4 | 2 | 1 | 8 | 4 | 2 | 1 |
| | | | | | | | |
| 1 | 0 | 0 | 1 | 1 | 0 | 0 | 0 |
| 8 | 0 | 0 | 1 | 8 | 0 | 0 | 0 |
| 8 + 0 + 0 + 1 = 9 | | | | 8 + 0 + 0 + 0 = 8 | | | |
| | | | 9 | 8 | | | |

Using this system, we have a shortcut method for expressing the binary code 1001-1000, which is hexadecimal 98. This is usually written as 98h to differentiate it from the decimal number 98. Using our previous method of evaluating the decimal value of this same byte, as shown in Figure 7.6, we determine that the bits are on for bit positions 128, 16, and 8. Adding these up, we find that the decimal value for this same binary coding is 152. Thus 98h, decimal 152, and binary 1001-1000 are all equal values, just expressed differently (base-16, base-10, and base-2).

You may also see hex denoted another way, which is with "0x" preceding it. For example "98h" could also be written as "0x98". This method finds its roots in some programming languages (C, C++, Java, and others) as leading "0" tells the parser to expect a number and the "x" defines the number that follows as hexadecimal. So as to keep things simple, we'll use the suffix "h" to denote hex, but you will see it in other publications using the other method.

**FIGURE 7.6**   The same binary coding shown in the previous figure evaluated as a decimal value. The bits are on for bit positions 128, 16, and 8, which total 152 for the decimal value.

| Left Nibble | | | | Right Nibble | | | | |
|---|---|---|---|---|---|---|---|---|
| $2^7$ | $2^6$ | $2^5$ | $2^4$ | $2^3$ | $2^2$ | $2^1$ | $2^0$ | <---- Power of 2 |
| 128 | 64 | 32 | 16 | 8 | 4 | 2 | 1 | <---- Decimal Equivalent |
| | | | | | | | | |
| 1 | 0 | 0 | 1 | 1 | 0 | 0 | 0 | <---- Binary Code |
| 128 | 0 | 0 | 16 | 8 | 0 | 0 | 0 | 128+0+0+16+8+0+0+0=152 |

To test our understanding of hexadecimal encoding, let's try a couple more examples using simple logic and not diagrams. At the very outset, we used the example, in Figure 7.3, of all bits being on, meaning we add all the bit position decimal values and arrive at a decimal value of 255. Without resorting to diagramming, we can easily convert this to a hexadecimal value just using some logic. With all 8 bits on (1), each nibble's 4 bits are likewise on when we evaluate them independently. When a nibble's bits are all on, all the nibble's bit positions are totaled and they equal 15. Thus each nibble's decimal value is 15. The hex encoding for decimal 15, according to Table 7.4, is F. Thus each nibble's hex value is F and, combined, they are FF.

Figure 7.7 shows an EnCase hex view in which FFh has been bookmarked and viewed as an 8-bit integer. Its binary coding (1111-1111) is shown as well as its decimal value of 255 and its hex value of ff. Not yet discussed is another interpretation of this data, which is as a signed integer and with a value of -1. Further this value has a character represented by it as well, which is a y with two dots over it. We will cover the ASCII table in the next section and the character issue will make better sense.

**FIGURE 7.7**    EnCase hex view of FF bookmarked and viewed as an 8-bit integer. Note the various interpretations of this data that are possible.

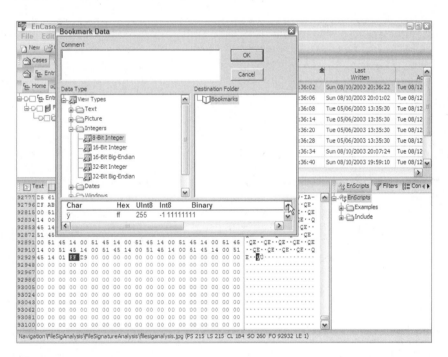

Let's take that logic one step further to arrive at a hex value for the decimal value 254. That is, in simple terms, 255 minus 1! If all bits are on for 255, to get 254 we need to turn off the bit for the bit position value of 1, which is in the rightmost position. Thus, 255 is binary 1111-1111 and 254 is 1111-1110. To convert this to hex, at a glance, we know the left nibble is still F as nothing changed there. The right nibble is 1 less than before and should be decimal 14 (8 + 4 + 2 + 0). From Table 7.4, we know the hexadecimal value of decimal 14 is E. Thus the hexadecimal value for decimal 254 is FEh.

## Characters

As we ended the preceding section, we mentioned that FFh, in addition to representing a decimal integer value of 255, could also represent a character, which in this case was a y with two dots over it. When data is stored or used by a program, the program defines the type of data it is. Without getting too involved in programming terminology, data can be text, integers, decimals, and so forth. Let's focus on when that data is text.

## ASCII

If the data is in a text format, the characters to be displayed are derived from a standard chart called the ASCII chart. This stands for the American Standard Code for Information Interchange and was created by Robert W. Bemer in 1965 to create a standard for interchange between the emerging data processing technologies.

In the simplest of terms, the chart maps characters and escape codes to binary or hexadecimal values. If everyone uses the same mapping scheme, then when the text letter A is needed, 41h is used and everyone with the same mapping system could read the letter A correctly since they were all using the same character mapping scheme.

Using this system, 7 of the 8 bits were used to create a table of 128 letters, numbers, punctuation, and special codes. Seven bits provides for 128 different outcomes or characters. This portion of the table (0–127) is called the ASCII table. It is sometimes called low or low-bit ASCII.

As much of this data was transmitted, the 8th bit was a parity bit and was used for error checking to determine whether an odd or even number of binary 1 bits were sent in the remaining 7 bits. The sending and receiving units had to "agree" or be in sync with the same odd or even parity scheme. When that was established, the sender sent a parity bit and the receiver used the sent parity bit to validate the received data. It is rarely used anymore as other more reliable and sophisticated error checking systems have evolved. Besides that, we needed to use that extra bit for more characters!

As computing evolved and encompassed more disciplines and languages, additional characters were needed. When the PC was born in the early 1980s, IBM introduced an extended ASCII character set in 1981. They did away with the parity bit and extended the code to 8 bits, which provided twice the number of characters previously allowed with the 7-bit system. The new character set, called the extended ASCII character set, provided 128 additional characters to the basic set. Most of these characters were mathematical, graphics, and foreign language characters. Another term you will hear applied to the new 128-character set is the high-bit ASCII set.

You will find the complete set of ASCII character codes (low-bit and high-bit) in on this books Website. If you will look over the entries, you will see them displayed in ascending decimal value order. Each line or item in this 256-character list has a decimal value, a hexadecimal value, and a character code. Since everything is stored in binary, as 1s and 0s, it also lists its binary coding as well.

Before we move away from the ASCII character codes, let's touch upon a couple of fine points that can help if well understood and possibly impede if not understood. The first point is that uppercase and lowercase letters are represented by entirely different code. An uppercase E is 45h while a lowercase e is 65h. As we get into searching for data, the concept of searching for data based on case sensitivity will emerge, whereas searching for 45h is different than searching for 65h. We'll get into that in detail soon enough. For now, just recognize that the two are different.

Understanding that upper- and lowercase letters are different is easy. What may be confusing are numbers. If I type the number 8 and it is stored as text, then 8 will be 38h. If the integer value of 8 is being stored for some math function, then it is likely stored as 08h since its data type is no longer text. Conversely, sometimes you will see what appear to be characters showing in the middle of gibberish when you are viewing binary data through the text view. In these cases, EnCase is looking at binary data through the ASCII character set and when hex values correspond with printable ASCII characters, they are rendered as such even though they really aren't stored or used within the context of being text.

If numbers aren't confusing enough, sometimes you will find numbers stored as ASCII characters, while those same numbers are stored elsewhere as integers. A good example of this would be IP addresses. Sometimes the program will store an IP as 128.175.24.251, which is pure human-readable ASCII text. Another program may store this IP in its integer form, which is the way the computer actually uses it. This same IP would read 80 AF 19 FB. In this method each of the four octets of an IP address are represented by a single byte or 8-bit integer. Using the above plain-text IP address, decimal 128 is 80h, decimal 175 is AFh, decimal 24 is 19h, and decimal 251 is FBh. If that isn't confusing enough, another program may store this same IP as FB 19 AF 80, which is the reverse order. KaZaA, iMesh, and Grokster store IP information in this manner.

To summarize, the hex string 54 45 58 54 could be interpreted in several ways, depending on the context in which it is used and stored on the computer. As a 32-bit integer, it would represent a value of 1,413,830,740. As four separate 8-bit integers (as an IP address could be stored) it would interpret as IP address 84.69.88.84. If KaZaA were storing this same IP, it would be reversed and interpreted as 84.88.69.84. Finally, if it were found in the middle of a string of text, it would be interpreted as TEXT, in all uppercase letters.

As you progress in the field, this will become second nature. Text will usually quite obviously be text when you see it. When you have to interpret integers, you'll usually be following an analysis guideline that describes where and how a certain piece of data is stored. You may, however, be conducting research in which you are reverse-engineering a data storage process. Under those conditions, you are flying blind, using trial and error to determine how data is stored and what it means forensically. For now, just remember that data can be interpreted in different ways, depending on the program and the context in which it is being used.

# Unicode

As computing became global and the limits imposed by a 256-character code set could not accommodate all the characters in some languages, a new standard had to emerge. Unicode was the answer to this challenge. Unicode is a worldwide standard for processing, displaying, and interchanging all types of language texts. This includes those previously encompassed by the ASCII set, which were primarily those using letters (mostly the Western European languages).

In addition, the Unicode characters allow for languages that use pictographs instead of letters, which are primarily the Eastern country languages, such as Chinese, Japanese, and Korean.

To encompass such a broad set of characters, Unicode uses 2 bytes per character instead of 1 byte per character. Unicode was introduced into EnCase with Version 4 and allows processing of any language for which there is an established code page or character set, which covers most of the world's written languages.

Although many languages don't require Unicode to render their character sets, many store text in Unicode. Sometimes they store the same text in ASCII and in Unicode simultaneously. The letter A in ASCII, we recall, is 41h. The letter A in Unicode is 4100h. Searching for 41h is different than searching for 4100h. As we begin our discussions on searching, you'll want to remember the differences between ASCII and Unicode in that regard. As considerable data is stored in Unicode, unless you have a good reason not to, you'll want to search for your data in both formats, ASCII and Unicode. Figure 7.8 is an EnCase view showing a string of text that is stored in a Unicode format.

**FIGURE 7.8**    Text string stored in Unicode. Note the 00h after each character.

# Searching for Data

Using EnCase's search tool, you can search for keywords anywhere on the physical drive. You can search the entire case (all devices in the case) at once or any subset of data within the case, down to a single file. There is even a new tool called the "Find" tool that allows you to search within a block of selected text. This tool was covered in the previous chapter, as you may recall, and is available as a right-click option (also available by pressing Ctrl-F) in the View pane while in the Text or Tex views.

In this section, we'll cover the creation and management of keywords at the global and case level. We'll discuss how to search and your options when conducting a search. We'll end this section with GREP, which means "Globally search for the Regular Expression and Print." This tool comes from the Unix domain and is a very powerful tool for constructing searches. It allows you to be extremely focused or very broad, as the situation warrants. In the section that follows, we'll get into working with the results of your searches soon enough when we cover viewing and bookmarking in detail. For now, let's focus on learning good search skills.

# Creating and Managing Keywords

You can't conduct a search without first creating a string of characters for the search engine to find. In EnCase, those search strings are called *keywords*.

Keywords, once created, are stored in a file for later use. Up through and including EnCase Version 3, keywords were stored in the case file and were case specific (unless exported out and transferred manually to another case). With EnCase Version 4, keywords became a global resource and were stored separately in a global keywords.ini file. With EnCase Version 5, the best of both worlds were combined and keywords can be either global (stored in the keywords.ini file) or case specific (stored in the case file).

Having it both ways is great, but as you'll soon come to realize, it adds another layer of complexity to the process. You must first give some thought as to whether you want the keyword to be global (available to all cases) or case specific (available only to the current case). Once that decision is made, you must then take care to create the keyword and save it in the correct location. If you need to modify or otherwise locate a keyword, you need to remember at which level you stored it. Finally, you must remember that you can have keywords selected simultaneously from both resources (the global and case levels).

Of course, having keywords selected and available from both resources is the way it is supposed to work, and it is a powerful feature. You must, however, be cognizant of this as you conduct subsequent searches: keywords stay selected until you turn them off, from both resources. When selecting keywords from both resources, you need to remember to turn them off in both resources as you complete your searches and begin new ones. You don't want to waste resources conducting searches that you don't intend. With those considerations in mind, let's create some keywords and start searching.

Keywords are created from the keyword view. As shown in Figure 7.9, there is a case-level keyword view and a global-level keyword view. As the 3-D tabs for Cases and Keywords are brought to the front, you can follow the path shown in the figure and tell we are working in the case-level keyword view. Where you place your keyword (global or case level) will determine its storage location. The interfaces are otherwise identical. The only difference between them is where they store the keyword data.

Thus, your first decision in this process is whether you wish this keyword to be available only to this case or if you wish it to be available globally to all cases from this point forward. There are many schools of thought on this topic, and we probably won't reach any consensus here.

First of all, you may have grown accustomed to having keywords at the case level from versions 1 through 3 and like working that way and don't want to change. If that is the case, stick with the case-level keywords and turn off the global view so as to not become confused.

You may have grown to like having keywords globally stored from version 4 and want to work that way exclusively. Within the global view, you can create a folder structure such that you have global keyword folders and case-specific keywords. In this manner you can have all keywords stored in one location and yet separate them using folders. If you are in a networked lab environment with your INI files in one location for all, there are advantages to such an approach.

**FIGURE 7.9**   EnCase v5 provides keyword views (storage) at the global or case level. The arrows show the locations of the two interfaces.

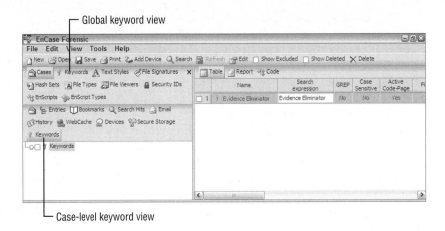

You may also like the idea of having it both ways: storing some keywords globally and some keywords locally with the case. If a keyword is clearly case specific, such as an individual's name or other identifying information, you may opt to store that keyword with the case. On the other hand, you may develop a really useful search string using GREP that you wish to use on all cases from this day forward. Such a keyword is a good candidate for global storage.

At the extremes, the global or case level decisions are easy. It's the middle area that sometimes gets a little murky. If you store it in one location and want to later move it, don't worry—they can be moved around. You can do this by exporting and importing keywords, which we'll cover later in this section.

To create a case-level keyword, you must navigate to the case-level keyword view. You may tab to it on the case-level tab bar, as shown Figure 7.9. While in the case view, you may also access the case-level keyword view from the view menu, under cases, as shown in Figure 7.10.

When you begin to create keywords, it is best to get organized from the beginning. Some examiners like to have a "flat file" for their keywords with no folder structure. Some like to store their keywords in folders to keep things organized. Figure 7.11 shows how folders can be used to organize keywords. At any level that you wish to create a folder, place your cursor on that level, right-click, and select New Folder. You can name the folder at the time of creation or rename it later by selecting it and pressing F2. Renaming a folder is also a right-click option.

**FIGURE 7.10**    When in any case-level view, other case-level views can be accessed from the View menu under cases. In this example, the case-level keyword view is being accessed.

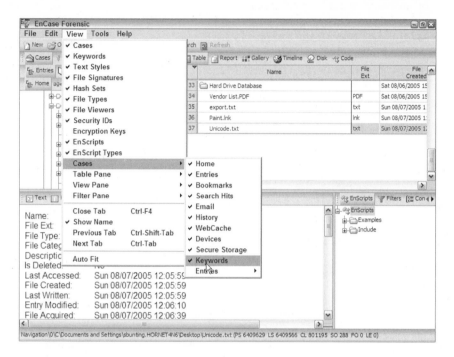

Additionally, you can delete a folder by selecting it and pressing the Delete key or right-clicking and choosing Delete. You can move a folder from one location to another by simply by dragging it and dropping it in the new location within the tree pane. You can rearrange the order of folders at a given level by highlighting their parent folder in the tree pane. The child folders will appear in the Table pane. The folders in the Table pane have "handles,"—the number box at the left side of the Table view for each row or folder. You can drag the folder up or down in the order by dragging and dropping the folder row by its handle.

If you use folders to organize keywords, you can view, add, or modify those keywords by selecting that folder in the Tree pane, as shown in Figure 7.12. The same Set Included Folders trigger used in the Case view also works here and in other views. By turning on the Set Included Folders trigger in the Tree pane, you can work with keywords from that level down in the Table pane, as shown in Figure 7.13.

Thus far, we've spent considerable time and effort locating and organizing our keywords. Now it's time to create a keyword and to select the various search options. In the Tree pane, choose the folder you want to hold the keyword by highlighting it. Once you do, there are several methods for launching the New Keyword dialog box. You can right-click in the Table pane and choose New. The same command is available from the Edit menu. You can press Insert on the keyboard, or you can right-click on the containing folder in the Tree pane and choose New. Regardless of the launch method, you are presented with the New Keyword dialog box shown in Figure 7.14.

**FIGURE 7.11** Keywords can be organized into folders at either the case or global level. Right-click at the desired folder level and choose New Folder. You can rename folders by pressing F2 or using a right-click option, as shown.

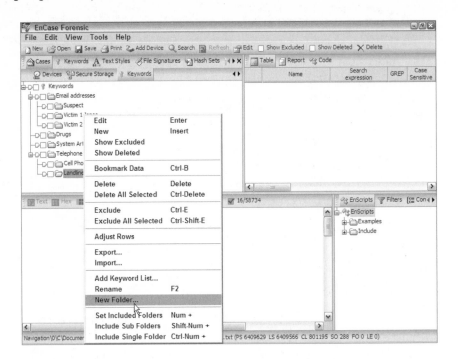

**FIGURE 7.12** If you highlight a keyword folder in the Tree pane, you can work with its contents in the Table pane.

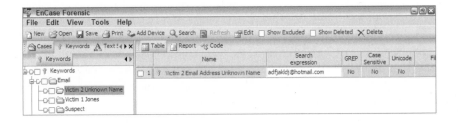

**FIGURE 7.13**    The Set Included Folders trigger works not only in the Case view, but in other views as well. Here the trigger is turned on at the top level, placing all keywords in all folders in the Table pane.

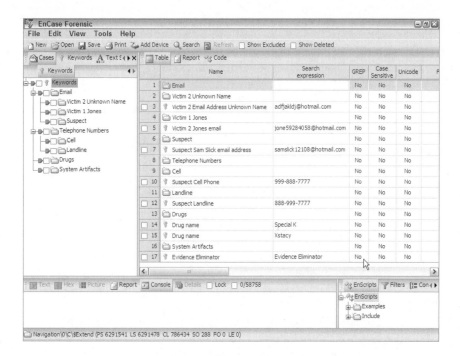

**FIGURE 7.14**    The New Keyword dialog box may be launched by several methods. Here, you create keywords and assign search options to go with it.

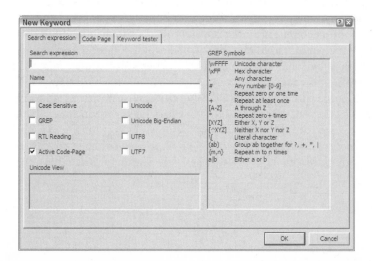

The dialog box provides numerous options or controls. We'll begin with the Search Expression box as it as the core component of your search. In this box, you enter your search string At this point, we are keeping our search simple. As we are working with the case from the previous chapter, we are going to search for two keywords associated with a message about a money pickup, or so we surmise. Enter the search expression *bank*, as shown in Figure 7.15.

**FIGURE 7.15** By default searches are not case-sensitive, meaning EnCase searches for upper- and lowercase hex values for your keyword, as seen in the Unicode View box and indicated by the pointers.

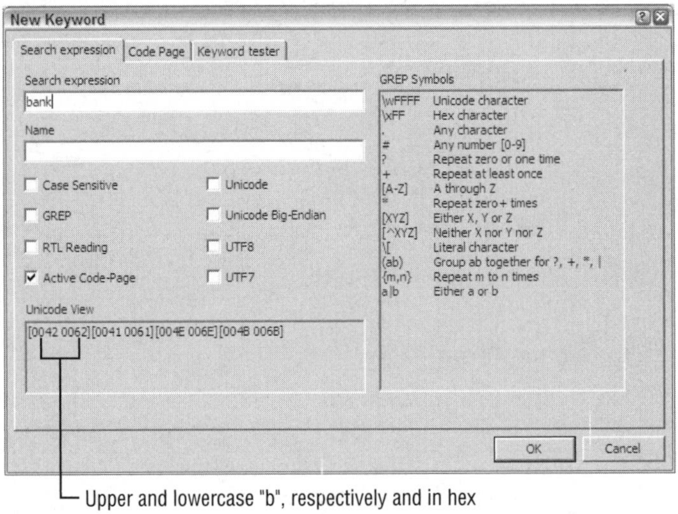

Upper and lowercase "b", respectively and in hex

If you look in the gray box labeled Unicode View in Figure 7.15, you see the hex values for the characters you entered in brackets in both their upper and lowercase values. By default, your search is not case-sensitive and the search will look for both the upper- and lowercase letters of the search expression you entered. Most times, you probably should accept this default setting to find your search string in its varied renditions of all caps, no caps, or mixed caps.

Searching for both upper- and lowercase increases your search time compared to a case-sensitive search. If you know your search term appears in a certain format, you can select a case-sensitive search to save time and reduce the number of false positives. When you do, only the hex values for the case you have entered for your search expression appear in the Unicode View, as shown in Figure 7.16. Remember from the previous section where we said that searching for an upper case letter was different than searching for the lower case of the same letter as they are both represented by different hex values in the ASCII table.

**FIGURE 7.16**    When making the search case sensitive, only the hex values for the keyword exactly as you typed it appear. Compare this to Figure 7.15, where the search was not case sensitive, and hex values for both upper- and lowercase were present.

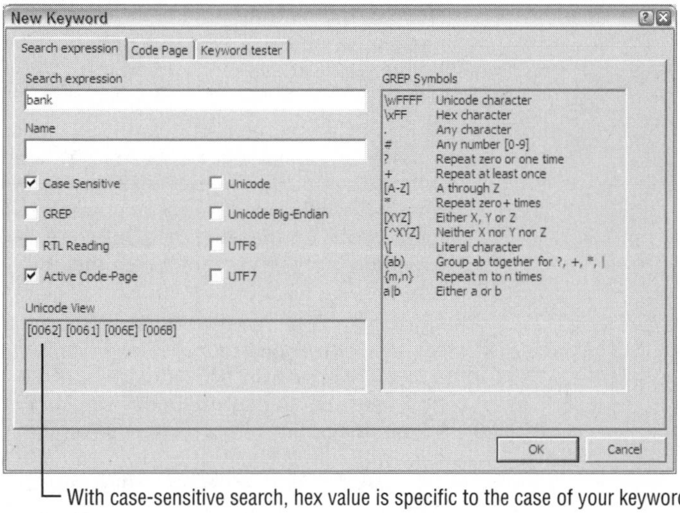

With case-sensitive search, hex value is specific to the case of your keyword

For purposes of our search, we won't use any other search options. You have, however, many other search options to choose from for a variety of searching needs. Those options are described in Table 7.5.

**TABLE 7.5**    Keyword Search Options

| Tab | Name | Description |
| --- | --- | --- |
| Search Expression | Name | Giving your keyword a descriptive name can be helpful as this "label" appears with it in the Search Hits view. Some keywords are obvious and may not need a name. When you have complex GREP expressions, account numbers, foreign language words, or the like, naming is very important. |
| Search Expression | Case Sensitive | While already covered in detail, this option turns on or off the case sensitivity of your search. With it on, the search will be done exactly according to the case you specified. |
| Search Expression | GREP | With this option, you can use the standard GREP input symbols and characters to create custom searches that can range from extremely focused to very broad, depending on your search needs. GREP is covered separately in the next section. |

**TABLE 7.5** Keyword Search Options *(continued)*

| Tab | Name | Description |
| --- | --- | --- |
| Search Expression | RTL Reading | RTL stands for "Right to Left" reading, meaning the search will be conducted in a right-to-left sequence for languages that use this convention. |
| Search Expression | Active Code Page | Since EnCase supports foreign languages, you need to employ language-specific code pages, and checking this option will often be necessary when working in that mode. If working in foreign languages, see specific instructions on the Guidance Software website or Chapter 20 of the Version 5 user manual. |
| Search Expression | Unicode | Unicode, as previously discussed, uses 2 bytes (16 bits) for each character compared to 7 bits for low ASCII and 8 bits for high ASCII. If this option is off, searches will not find your search expression if it appears in Unicode. When this option is on, searches will find your search expression in both ASCII and Unicode formats. Unless you specifically don't want to find your search term in Unicode, you should turn this option on if you wish to conduct a thorough search. |
| Search Expression | Big-Endian Unicode | PC-based Intel processors process data in a Little Endian format, meaning the least significant bits are read first. Non-Intel processors are used in Unix and Mac systems, and those processors work in the reverse order from the Intel. This is called Big Endian. The most significant bits are read first, which is the reverse of Little Endian. When searching for data stored in this format, select this option. When Mac switches over to Intel-based processors in 2006, it will be important to know from which system Mac OS X data originated. |
| Search Expression | UTF-8 | An encoding scheme defined by the Unicode standard in which each character is represented as a sequence up to 4 bytes. The first byte tells how many bytes follow in the multibyte sequence. It is commonly used in on the Internet and in web content. |
| Search Expression | UTF-7 | An older encoding scheme that is mostly obsolete. It uses octets with the high bit clear, which are the 7-bit ASCII values. It is used for mail encoding, but it is a legacy scheme. |
| Code Page | Code Page | Using the various code pages in this list, EnCase can display and search for foreign languages. Working with foreign languages is covered in Chapter 20 of the EnCase user manual. |

**TABLE 7.5** Keyword Search Options *(continued)*

| Tab | Name | Description |
|---|---|---|
| Keyword Tester | Keyword Tester | With this new feature, you can test keywords on sample data files before running them against your case. This can save you hours of runtime, particularly when you are testing new GREP expressions. When you switch over to the Keyword Tester tab, your keyword carries over. Browse to the file containing your test data and click Load. The results are displayed in the View pane in both hex and text. If you need to tweak your keyword, do so in the keyword box, and the results in the View pane are displayed in real time, making it very handy for fixing keywords. |

Before we actually conduct a search, we need to consider two other methods of bringing keywords into EnCase: importing or adding keyword lists. Before you can import, you must know how to export, because importing involves importing a previously exported keyword list from within EnCase.

To export a keyword list for import, with all search properties intact, the best way is to organize them into a folder if they don't already exist in that format. You can right-click keywords in the Table pane and drag them to a Tree pane folder. Upon releasing the mouse, you get an option to move or copy. Choose Copy. When you are done, you have the keywords you wish to export in one folder. Alternatively, you can export the entire list if you like by starting your export at the root level of the keyword list in the Tree pane. To export, in the Tree pane right-click on the folder level at which you wish to export and choose Export. Figure 7.17 shows the resulting dialog box. Simply browse to a suitable location for your export file and click OK to finish.

**FIGURE 7.17** The Export dialog box for exporting a keyword list for importing. Browse to a suitable location and click OK to finish.

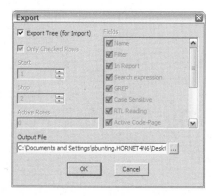

To import an exported keyword file, choose the level or folder in the Tree pane for your import location and right-click. Choose the import option and you will be prompted for the path to the import file. Once that file is located, click OK, and the entire folder structure is imported in the same exact tree structure as it existed when you exported it.

Another method of adding keywords is by adding keyword lists. Choose the location for your keyword list. You can select a folder in the Tree pane or add it to a folder's list of keywords in the Table pane. From either, right-click and choose Add Keyword List to open the dialog box shown in Figure 7.18.

**FIGURE 7.18**    The Add Keyword List dialog box. Keywords can be typed or pasted in from other lists.

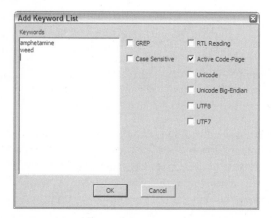

Keywords can be typed in to this dialog box or pasted in after being copied from other lists. The various search options selected apply to all keywords in the list. When you have finished adding to your list, click OK, and the new keywords are added at your selected location. If you don't want the same options for all keywords, you can change them after they have been added as a group.

## GREP Keywords

One of your keyword options in Table 7.5 was that of a GREP search. As we mentioned earlier, GREP is a very powerful search tool derived from the Unix domain, and it means "Globally search for the Regular Expression and Print." In Unix (or Linux), GREP is a command that recognizes a series of characters that are included in search strings, greatly adding to the versatility of string searches. EnCase embodies many of those GREP characters in its search engine, giving the examiner pretty much the same search utility in EnCase as a search done with GREP in Unix.

The sheer power and flexibility of using GREP expressions over a regular search strings is phenomenal. Clearly, GREP expressions are tools the competent examiner must know well. It is also a topic to which considerable attention is given in the certification examination. Tests aside, GREP expressions are fun to work with and can really save you time and allow you to search for information you couldn't find any other way.

Table 7.6 lists the various GREP characters supported by the EnCase search engine. As you go through the list and see the examples, you'll begin to appreciate their utility. Next, we'll work with some examples that will help you with practical applications of GREP expressions in real-world searches.

**TABLE 7.6**    Syntax for GREP Characters or Symbols

| GREP Symbol | Meaning |
| --- | --- |
| . | A period is a wildcard and matches any character. |
| \255 | A decimal character (period). |
| \x | A character represented by its hex value. For example, \x42 is the upper-case B. Rather than searching for *B*, we can search instead for \x42. |
| ? | A question mark after a character or set means that the character or set can be present one time or not at all. An example is *kills?*, which finds both *kill* and *kills*. |
| * | An asterisk after a character matches any number of occurrences of that character, including zero. This one is similar to a question mark, but instead of one time or not at all, it means one time, not at all, or many times. An example is *sam_*jones*, which finds *samjones*, *sam_jones*, or *sam___jones*. |
| + | A plus sign following a character matches any number of occurrences of that character, except for zero. Again, this one is similar to its cousins (? and *), except that the character preceding it must be there at least once. It can be present once or many times, but must be present to match. An example is *sam_+jones*, which finds *sam_jones* or *sam___jones*. It does NOT find *samjones* as the underscore must be present at least once since zero is not allowed. |
| # | A pound sign matches a numeric character, which is zero through nine (0–9). For example, *####* finds *1234*, *5678*, or *9999*, but does not find *a123* or *123b*, etc. |
| [ABC] | Any character in the brackets matches one character. For example "re[ea]d" will find "read" or "reed", but will not find "red". |
| [^ABC] | A circumflex preceding a string in brackets means those characters are not allowed to match one character. For example, *re[^a]d* finds *reed*, but does not find *read* since *a* is not allowed to match. |
| [A-C] | A dash within the brackets defines a range of characters or numbers. For example, *[0-5]* finds *5* but does not find *6*. |

**TABLE 7.6**   Syntax for GREP Characters or Symbols *(continued)*

| GREP Symbol | Meaning |
| --- | --- |
| \ | A backslash preceding a character means that character is a literal character and not a GREP symbol or character. For example, *##\+##*finds *34+89* or *56+57*, but does not find *566+57*. Preceding the + with a \ tells EnCase that the + is not to be treated as a GREP character, but merely as a plus sign. |
| {X,Y} | The character preceding may repeat x to y times. {2,4} would repeat two to four times. For example, *a{2,4}* finds *aa* or *aaa* or *aaaa*. It does not find *a*. |
| (ab) | Groups characters in () for use with + * \|. See the next symbol for an example. |
| a \| b | The pipe symbol acts as a logical OR, and *a\|b* finds *a* or *b*, but not *c, d,* etc. To combine the previous symbol with this one for a more meaningful example, *encase\.(com)\|(net)* finds *encase.com* and *encase.net*, but does not find *encase.org* or *encase.gov*. |
| \w1234 | Allows searching for Unicode code, where 1234 is four integers for Unicode code from Unicode chart. |

Now that we have the syntax for GREP, we can use a little creativity along with what we have learned thus far to create some very useful GREP expressions. While we are doing it, we'll see how GREP works and it will become second nature after a while. As an added bonus, you'll get to see EnCase's "Keyword Tester" in action, which will prompt you to use it quite often; it is a great way to test keywords and will save you loads of time.

We are often faced with finding numbers, but often don't know what the numbers are but only know the format in which they should appear. In a corporate environment, we may want to know whether employees are storing Social Security numbers in plain text on their workstations. Such a practice may violate company policy or worse (if employees are stealing the numbers). In a criminal investigation, we may want to search for Social Security numbers that a suspect may have stolen, but we don't know the numbers. In either setting, we are looking for unknown Social Security numbers and we want them all if they are present.

We know that Social Security numbers are nine digits, but we also know that sometimes those numbers are separated by spaces, such as 123 45 6789, or by dashes, such as 123-45-6789. Sometimes there are no spaces or dashes, such as 123456789. Thus, we want one GREP expression that will find nine digits stored in any of the three formats.

As our starting point, we need to find nine numeric characters, so we need #########. Next, we need to allow for separators consisting of a space or a hyphen, but we also need to allow for no separator at all. The GREP expression *[ \-]?* means we will allow character in the brackets to appear either one time or not at all. Within the brackets is a space or a literal hyphen. We will allow one to appear either once or not at all. If we inserted the *[ \-]?* between the third and fourth numeric characters and again between fifth and sixth numeric characters, we'd have the expression we need: *###[ \-]?##[ \-]?####*.

If we were to test this GREP expression, it would find each of our examples above and in all three formats. At first glance we might be satisfied with our expression, but the moment we tested it on a real case, we would be overwhelmed by the number of false positives returned. In Figure 7.19 we used Keyword Tester in EnCase to illustrate this point. Our GREP expression is inserted as our keyword and GREP is enabled. We created a text file with three different SSN formats along with a string of ten numbers. Using our Keyword Tester, we browsed to the test file and then clicked Load. The search engine looks for the keyword in the test data and returns the results.

**FIGURE 7.19**    The Keyword Tester is used to test a GREP expression against a small text file containing sample text to search.

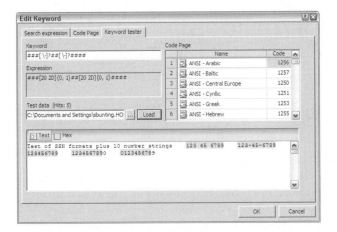

As we can see, this expression finds the occurrence of any nine numbers grouped together. The first three are SSN examples and it finds them, but it also finds the latter two, which are strings of ten numbers. We would want nine numbers and no more. The way we have this GREP string constructed, it will find nine numbers among 10, 11, 12, 13, 14, or more numbers. Arrays of more than nine numbers are quite common, and finding them all is clearly not in our best interest. We want nine and no more.

If we were to take our expression and apply some logic, and then some GREP characters, we could remedy the situation. Let's first apply the logic.

To find nine numbers standing alone instead of nine numbers in a string of more than nine numbers, we could apply a rule of sorts to our expression. We could say that the character preceding or following nine numbers can be anything except a number. Such a condition finds nine numbers standing alone, which is what we want. We now have our logic in place.

Next, we need to express our logic in a GREP expression. To create such a condition using a GREP expression, we use the brackets and the circumflex to specify what we do not want. Thus. the expression *[^#]* says that the character can't be a number. Anything else will match, but not a number. If we append this to the front and back of our string, it looks like *[^#]###[ \-]?##[ \-]?####[^#]*. Figure 7.20 shows this revised GREP string being tested against our test data file. It finds nine number strings in any of our SSN formats, but it does not find ten numbers. It works—and we are done.

**FIGURE 7.20**   We've used the EnCase Keyword Tester to test the revised GREP expression. By adding [^#] to the beginning and end, we found only nine digit SSN strings and not strings of ten or more digits..

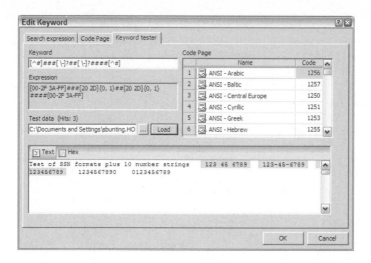

Sometimes we need to locate web mail addresses from one of the major ISPs that allow anonymous free accounts (such as Hotmail, Yahoo!, and Netscape). There are others for sure, but these three account for most that you encounter and are a good starting point for our example. You can modify your search as needs dictate. We could create three separate keywords (@hotmail.com, @yahoo.com, and @netscape.net) or we could use one GREP keyword to find all three.

There is usually more than one way to create a workable GREP expression, but typically one way is cleaner or easier to work with. To solve our problem, let's make use of the parentheses and pipe (logical OR) expressions. So that we find e-mail addresses and not URLs (Uniform Resource Locators, better known as web addresses), we begin with the @ symbol. Because any one of the three services can match, we place each within parentheses and separate them with an OR, or pipe symbol. Our expression thus starts as *@(hotmail)|(yahoo)|(netscape)*. This means that any string that begins with the @ symbol followed by hotmail OR yahoo OR netscape will match and be found.

From a practical sense, we could probably stop there and find what we are seeking, but since we want to learn more about GREP, let's complete our exercise. To find ".com" or ".net" on the end of this string, we need to add some more GREP characters. The period, or dot, is easy, but we need to make it a "literal period" because a period without the literal symbol is a wildcard character in GREP. We represent it as \. which means a literal period.

To find ".com" or ".net", we use the same method we used in the preceding paragraph to find the mail services: the string in parentheses separated by logical OR (pipe symbol). Our final GREP expression is *@(hotmail)|(yahoo)|(netscape)\.(com)|(net)*. When we test it, as shown in Figure 7.21, it finds the web mail services we are seeking and does not find the others, which was our intent.

**FIGURE 7.21** We've used the Keyword Tester again to test our expression, which finds e-mail addresses for any of the three web mail services we were seeking.

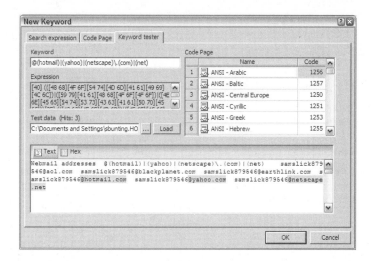

## Tracking Numbers and Drug Runners with Brown Shorts

A mailing service had been receiving regular packages from a young man for several months. Each time he declared the contents as videotapes. One day the young man dropped off a package and promptly left after paying the fee. On this occasion he had failed to package it properly. The clerk had to repackage the parcel when he left. Instead of a videotape, as declared, the package contained a large bottle of Percocet. The clerk promptly called the police, who began an investigation.

The intended recipient of the Percocet found it in her best interest to cooperate as she happened to be an employee of a law enforcement agency in another jurisdiction. As it turned out, the young man sold a variety of painkillers via e-mail, which was arranged by "referral" by a trusted third party. The sting was set up using the soon-to-be-former law enforcement employee, and the young man was arrested when he attempted to mail the next parcel at the mailing service counter. His pocket change at the time of his arrest was just under ten thousand dollars.

A search of his apartment revealed no details regarding his operation, and I was asked to examine the computers he used at his place of employment. It turns out he was a chemist and accessed several computers as he moved about his lab. The involved systems were imaged and the details started to unfold.

The defendant was a member of a website that offered six levels of password-protected forums for its members. The forum topic at all levels was strictly devoted to the use of drugs, with an occasional referral for sales. Our defendant had two identities, one as a user and one as a dealer. When folks wanted to know where the user obtained his painkillers, he'd refer them to himself under his other identity. The recommendation and referral was always with the highest regard, naturally.

The operation was simple. All sales were paid using Western Union money transfers. All amounts were sent in increments that were less than one thousand dollars so that no identification was required to send or receive funds. A challenge question and answer was all that was required, which was all sent in an e-mail. All used the various anonymous web mail services, especially "hushmail," to disguise their identities. All used abbreviated and altered code words for the drugs to avoid detection by company web or e-mail content filters. For example, "o*y" was used for oxycodone. There was quite a list and all users of this website used it religiously in their web posts and in their e-mail.

All shipments were sent via United Parcel Servcie (UPS) as they preferred to use couriers with "brown shorts" for whatever reason. As soon as the money was received, the drugs were sent via UPS and the defendant sent an e-mail to his customers along with the UPS tracking number. The defendant tracked the various shipments using the UPS web-tracking service to assure delivery.

While conducting the forensics examination, it became apparent to me that UPS tracking numbers were the common link as they appeared in cached web pages and e-mail correspondence between the defendant and his customers. If all UPS tracking numbers could be located, it would link together deliveries, e-mail addresses, quantities, payments, real names, real addresses, and dates and times.

I contacted UPS and they provided sufficient information about the numbers and letters in their 18-character tracking number sufficient to build a GREP expression that would find all UPS tracking numbers in their various formats. With that search term in place, all UPS tracking numbers were located.

Identical tracking numbers were grouped together, and all information relating to that number and its drug sale was linked together. Using this method, I identified all of his customers (over 20 scattered around the country) by their real names and physical addresses. With this information, it was easy to build a spreadsheet that accurately depicted his sales to each customer. It was easy to understand why he walked around with ten thousand in cash in his pocket.

In the final analysis, it was by dumb luck that he was caught originally, but it was computer forensics alone that revealed the depth and details of his operation. It was a GREP expression that located UPS tracking numbers that greatly facilitated the latter. When the details of his operation were fully delineated, a guilty plea swiftly followed.

For those who may wish to use this GREP expression in their investigations, it is included along with a few others in Table 7.7. The DVD contains a folder named "GREP_Expressions," which holds a file by the same name. The below GREP expressions are contained in this file so that you may copy them directly to avoid making typographical errors. One tiny error can make a huge difference in the outcome. These GREP expressions were working at press time, but any vendor or programmer can make a change that could alter the results in the future. You should test them periodically with "known data" to be sure they are current.

**TABLE 7.7**    Some useful GREP Expressions

| GREP Expression | Description |
|---|---|
| 1Z[ ]?[a-z0-9][a-z0-9][a-z0-9][ ]?[a-z0-9][a-z0-9][a-z0-9][ ]?[a-z0-9]#[ ]?####[ ]?###[ ]?# | UPS tracking numbers: As it is an 18-character string, which is very unique, to date no false positive has been found. Figure 7.22 shows this GREP expression being tested in the Keyword Tester. |
| [a-z][a-z]#########us | US Postal Service Express mail tracking number |
| value="###########"> | FedEx tracking number as it appears in a web form. Too many false positives occur with the raw number, so this one finds it in a web form. It doesn't eliminate false positives altogether, but it does reduce them tremendously. When a number is located in a web form, a second search for the specific number often locates it in other locations. |
| <title>(MSN )?Hotmail | Locates web page title used by both old and new Hotmail web pages. |
| \x2E\x20\x20\x20\x20\x20\x20\x20\x20\x20 ....................\x2E\x2E | Locates "dot" "double dot" signature for FAT directory entries. |
| (http)\|(ftp)\|(https)://[a-z#_\-]+\.[a-z#_\-\.]+ | Finds URL addresses starting with, of course, HTTP, FTP, or HTTPS. |
| <!\-\- ##:##:##\-[a-z0-9][a-z0-9][a-z0-9] [a-z0-9][a-z0-9] \-\-> | Locates header for AIM Plus history files. If AIM plus is installed, these files contain IM content. When they "roll off" or are deleted, this will find them in the unallocated clusters as well. |

**FIGURE 7.22** A GREP expression that locates UPS tracking numbers is tested against the known tracking number in EnCase's Keyword Tester.

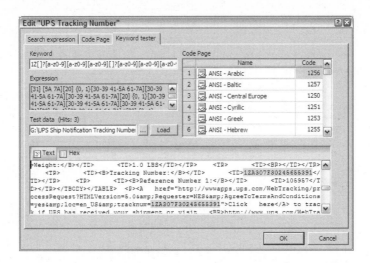

Creating GREP expressions is both challenging and fun. When you create useful ones that can be used in future cases, be sure to place them in your Global Keywords view. The Keyword Tester is a very handy utility to test GREP expressions. Without it, you pretty much have to test expressions against your case data, which is time consuming. GREP expressions will greatly assist you with your cases, and you should take the time necessary to become very adept at creating and using them.

## Starting a Search

Now that we have created keywords, it is time to use them to conduct searches. Before you start a search, you must first give some thought as to where you are going to search. If you are seeking very recent e-mails, you may wish to focus your search, initially at least, in the e-mail client data files. This is certainly faster than searching the entire case. Select the files you wish to search by clicking in the boxes thereby placing "blue checks" on them, but first make sure there are no other files checked. If there are, clicking once in the Dixon box will clear them. If you wish to search all files in the case, you can click in the Dixon box once to clear it and once again to select all files. As shown in Figure 7.23, it is a good idea to compare the number of files you know you wish to search with the number shown in the Dixon box.

In addition to selecting the files you wish to search, you must select the search strings or keywords by which to conduct your search. If you don't select any, the default and only option is to search for all keywords, which is something you rarely wish to do. You select keywords with blue checkmarks. If you are using both case-level keywords and global keywords, you will have to visit both views (case level and global) to turn off keywords from previous searches and turn on keywords for your next search.

**FIGURE 7.23**    The Dixon box shows one file selected out of 16 files in the case. This figure coincides with our intent to search one file—the unallocated clusters.

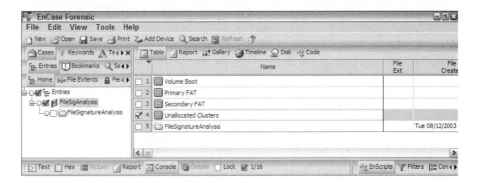

Once you have selected the files as well as the keywords for which you wish to search, begin your search by clicking Search on the toolbar or selecting Search from the Tools menu options. The Search dialog box, as shown in Figure 7.24, will appear, and you are faced with a series of decisions concerning various search options.

**FIGURE 7.24**    The Search dialog box contains various search options from which to choose.

For a simple search, it is often sufficient to choose Selected Files Only, Search Each File For Keywords, and Selected Keywords Only. I often refer to this as a "three corners search" as you are selecting only the options in the three corners of what appears to be somewhat of a triangular layout of the options. After making your selections, you can start a simple search by clicking Start. Table 7.8 describes in detail the various search options available from the Search dialog box.

**TABLE 7.8**    Options in the Search Dialog Box

| Option | Description |
| --- | --- |
| Selected Files Only | If you don't select this option, by default, EnCase will search every byte of every sector of all devices in the case. If you choose this option, EnCase searches only the files that are selected with "blue checkmarks". The Dixon Box box displays the number of files selected and that will be searched by this function. |
| Search Each File For Keywords | If you don't check this box, EnCase doesn't search any files for keywords. If you don't select this box, you must run a file signature analysis or a hash analysis, or both. |
| Verify File Signatures | If you choose this option, EnCase will run a file signature analysis on the selected files or, if none are selected, all files in the case. EnCase compares file header information in files with file header information in a database along with file extensions. The next chapter deals extensively with file signature analysis. |
| Compute Hash Value | If you choose this option, EnCase computes an MD5 value on the selected files or, if none are selected, all files in the case. The resultant hash value is also compared to hash values in the hash library, if the latter is defined. The next chapter deals extensively with file signature analysis. |
| Re-compute Hash Value | If you choose this option, EnCase will recompute the hash values for all files on the replaced live device. For a local acquisition, this is not necessary. For network acquisitions, this option is often used to recompute hash values on the live machine when they have been previously subjected to a hash analysis. |
| Search File Slack | If you choose this option, EnCase searches the space between the end of the logical file and the last byte of the last cluster allocated to the file. This option must be selected to find data located in FAT32 directory entries. |
| Undelete Files Before Searching | If you choose this option, EnCase will logically "undelete" files before searching the data. This will find keywords in those rare cases where a keyword spans the starting cluster and the next unallocated cluster. The next unallocated cluster may or may not belong to the file, but for purposes of this search, the assumption that it does belong is forced on the search criteria. |
| Search Only Slack Area Of Files In The Hash Library | To use this option, a previous hash analysis must have been done or one must be done in conjunction with this search. If a file exists in the hash library, regardless of category (notable or known), the logical file is not searched. The file slack area of files found in the hash library is, however, searched. This feature can save time with searches as known files are excluded from search while their slack areas are still searched. If this feature is turned off, a file selected for search will be completely searched (both logical file and slack) even if it exists in the hash library. |

**TABLE 7.8**    Options in the Search Dialog Box *(continued)*

| Option | Description |
| --- | --- |
| Selected Keywords Only | As previously mentioned, you need to preselect keywords to be searched. By selecting this feature, only searches for those keywords are conducted. When you select this feature, it returns the number of "selected keywords." If you do not select this feature, it returns the total number of keywords you have available for search, and this is the number of keywords for which EnCase will search unless you instruct otherwise. Rarely will you wish to search for all keywords, so take care to select your keywords, choose this option, and check the number to make sure it at least approximates the number of keywords you have selected. |

Once you have started a search, the progress bar in the bottom-right corner appears. It gives you the approximate time remaining to complete your search and reports the number of search hits thus far found. You may stop a search at any time by double-clicking on the progress bar and confirming your intent to terminate the search. As search hits are found, the Refresh button on the toolbar changes from a drab gray to green. If you click this button, search hits found thus far are sent to the Search Hits view. In this manner, you can start reviewing search hits as they are located, which is particularly useful when long searches are running and inquiring minds want answers.

## Viewing Search Hits and Bookmarking your Findings

As keywords are found and sent to the Search Hits view by either completion of the search or a click of the Refresh button, a folder is created for each keyword in the search. The folder takes on the name of the keyword itself unless you have given it a name. If the keyword has a name, the folder will be named after the name of the keyword rather than the keyword itself. This feature is another important reason for giving keywords a meaningful name. A folder named after numbers or the characters in a GREP expression is often not very descriptive, especially weeks or months later.

Much analysis work can be done directly from the Search Hits view. The Search Hits view is a case-level view, which can be accessed from the case-level tab bar or by going to the View menu if you are in any case-level view.

When viewing search hits, you have some viewing options available. While in the Search Hits view, you can click the View Search Hits button on the toolbar or choose the option from the right-click menu. As shown in Figure 7.25, the resulting dialog box allows you to group search hits in several ways.

**FIGURE 7.25** The View Search Hits dialog box allows you to view search hits in different views or groupings.

You can turn on or off the device or keyword groupings, and you can change the grouping sort order by dragging up or down. When viewing search hits in multiple devices, you may wish to view the search hits in each device separately, as shown in Figure 7.26. Conversely, you may wish all keyword hits grouped together and not segregated by device. The option is yours, and this feature controls those viewing options.

**FIGURE 7.26** Search hits are shown grouped first by device and second by keyword. This grouping keeps search hits segregated by device.

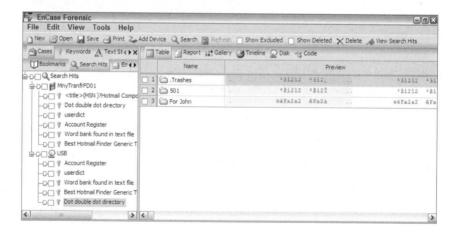

Regardless of how you choose to group and view your search hits, you have many tools and options available from the Table pane when accessing the right-click menu. These tools and options are shown in Figure 7.27 and fully described in Table 7.9.

**FIGURE 7.27**    Search hits tools and options menu available via the right-click while in the Table pane

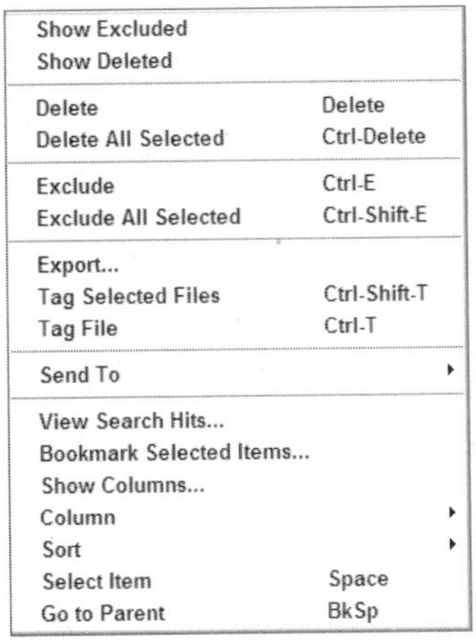

| | |
|---|---|
| Show Excluded | |
| Show Deleted | |
| Delete | Delete |
| Delete All Selected | Ctrl-Delete |
| Exclude | Ctrl-E |
| Exclude All Selected | Ctrl-Shift-E |
| Export... | |
| Tag Selected Files | Ctrl-Shift-T |
| Tag File | Ctrl-T |
| Send To | ▶ |
| View Search Hits... | |
| Bookmark Selected Items... | |
| Show Columns... | |
| Column | ▶ |
| Sort | ▶ |
| Select Item | Space |
| Go to Parent | BkSp |

**TABLE 7.9**    Right-Click Menu Options in Table pane of Search Hits View

| Menu Name | Description of Function |
|---|---|
| Show Excluded | If a search hit has been marked Exclude, it will be hidden from view, but not deleted. Toggling on Show Excluded brings excluded search hits back into view. When an excluded search hit is shown, it will appear in red. To "un-exclude" an excluded search hit, you exclude it a second time, as it acts as a toggle even though not labeled as such. Show Excluded is also available on the toolbar. |
| Show Deleted | If a search hit has been marked Delete, it will be hidden from view, but not deleted until you exit the case (soft delete). Until then, deleted items can be shown and undeleted. Toggling on Show Deleted brings deleted search hits back into view. When a deleted search hit is shown, it will appear with no highlighted color in contrast to other colors. To undelete a deleted search hit, you delete it a second time, as it acts as a toggle even though not labeled as such. Show Deleted is also available on the toolbar. |
| Delete | Deletes the highlighted search hit. It is a "soft delete" and can be undeleted until you exit the case. At that point, the deletion becomes permanent. Deleting a search hit again, while it is shown, undeletes it. |
| Delete All Selected | Acts in the same manner as the Delete option, except that it deletes all selected or blue checked files. |

**TABLE 7.9**   Right-Click Menu Options in Table pane of Search Hits View *(continued)*

| Menu Name | Description of Function |
|---|---|
| Exclude | Excludes the highlighted search hit. Excluding a search hit again, while shown, "un-excludes" it. |
| Exclude All Selected | Acts in the same manner as the Exclude option, except that it excludes all selected or blue checked files. |
| Export | An option to export a list of properties regarding the files containing the search hits. The properties are user selectable, and the output is a tab-delimited text file. If you assign it an .xls extension, it will automatically open in Excel with no intermediate steps. |
| Tag Selected File | Tags the files containing the selected search hits. The files are accessible in the Case view. By this method, the examiner can mark or select files for further analysis or processing. |
| Tag File | Functions the same as Tag Selected File except that it operates to tag only the file of the highlighted search hit. |
| Send to | Sends the file containing the search hit to any installed viewer. Once a viewer is installed, this is an option. |
| View Search Hits | Provides the menu by which search hits can be grouped and viewed. |
| Bookmark Selected Items | Launches the window by which search hits may be bookmarked. This will be covered in detail in the next section. |
| Show Columns | Same function as in Table pane of Case Entries view. You can turn on or off the view of selected columns |
| Column | Same function as in the Table pane of the Case Entries view. You can hide columns, lock columns, reset to the default view, or size columns to fit data. |
| Sort | Columns can be sorted as in the Table pane of the Case Entries view. They can be sorted from this menu or by clicking on the column headers. |
| Select Item | This option will select or blue-check a search hit. Using the mouse to click the blue-check box is easier. Easier yet, pressing the spacebar blue-checks or selects a search hit and advances one row to the next search hit. Selected search hits are saved when you save the case file. As such, they remain selected when you reopen the case. |
| Go To Parent | Any time you choose this option, you advance your selection or focus upward one level in the Tree pane. You are going to the parent container of the object in the Table pane on which you activate this option. |

# Bookmarking

Bookmarks are references to specific files or data. Also, they can be notes inserted into the book-mark structure to provide additional information. Bookmarks can be created nearly anywhere that data is located, including the Search Hits view. By having all bookmarks available in a single view, which is the Bookmarks view or subtab, the bookmarks can be organized into a hier-archical tree that is subsequently rendered as a report of your findings and analysis.

As previously emphasized, creating a well-written, meaningful report that also presents well is a critical skill for the competent examiner to develop. Because bookmarks are the foundation of your report, bookmarking is likewise a critical skill.

Some bookmarks are created by EnCase as background logging functions, such as the search summary and the case time settings, but most are created directly by the user. In this section, we'll cover the various types of bookmarks and how to create them. As we conclude this section, we'll show you the basics of arranging and organizing your bookmarks, which will pave the way for our report-writing session in Appendix A.

## Highlighted Data Bookmark

One of the most common bookmark types is the Highlighted Data bookmark. It is often called a sweeping bookmark or a text fragment bookmark. To create such a bookmark, you locate the data of interest in the View pane and select the text or data using a left-click and drag technique, with the starting point being the first byte in the data of interest. When the last byte is selected, release the left mouse button, and the text or data is selected and shaded or marked in a dark blue. Place the cursor in the highlighted or selected area, right-click, and choose Bookmark Data, as shown in Figure 7.28.

**FIGURE 7.28**    Highlighted data or a sweeping bookmark is created by selecting the text or data of interest, right-clicking in the highlighted area, and choosing Bookmark Data.

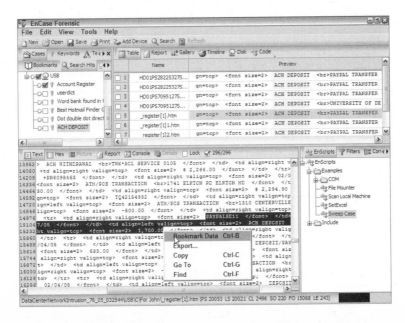

Once presented with the Bookmark Data menu, you may enter comments concerning the data, choose a location in the bookmark tree for your bookmark, or choose among various data types for viewing, as shown in Figure 7.29. Creating a comment is very straightforward. You can type a comment or paste one in if you prefer. The maximum length for a comment is 1,000 characters.

**FIGURE 7.29**   Bookmark Data options menu from which you may enter a comment, choose a folder from the bookmark folder tree, and select a data type by which to view your bookmarked data.

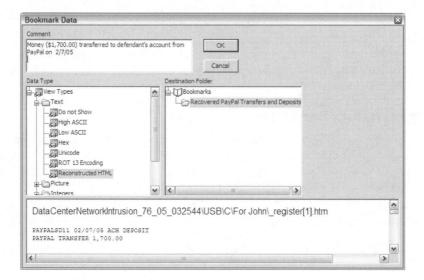

In the Destination Folder pane of the Bookmark Data window, you select the folder into which the bookmark will be placed. You can click and drag folders within this pane to rearrange the tree. You can right-click on any folder level and create a subfolder for that folder. You can highlight any folder and press F2 to rename it. Renaming is also a right-click menu option.

Creating folders with meaningful names and doing so in a logical outline or tree format is essential for generating good reports. The folder names act as headings and subheadings in your report outline. It is easier to add this structure as you go along when things are fresh in your mind and therefore easily and accurately labeled.

The data types from which to choose for viewing your data make this bookmark a most powerful feature. The types range from simple ASCII views to partition entries, dates, images, and various text styles for foreign languages and other special views. Table 7.10 lists the various data types along with a brief description of each type.

**TABLE 7.10**    Bookmark Data Types

| Group | Data Type | Description |
| --- | --- | --- |
| Text | High ASCII | High ASCII includes all characters in the full ASCII table (256 characters). |
| | Low ASCII | Low ASCII characters consist of the first 128 characters only, which are mostly the alphabetic and numeric characters along with the common punctuation marks. |
| | Hex | Displays the values in their hexadecimal representation, which is a base-16 numbering system that was discussed in the beginning of this chapter. |
| | Unicode | Displays Unicode text in a normal format instead of "A.B.C." as it would view in ASCII. Unicode uses two bytes per character instead of the one-byte ASCII system. |
| | ROT-13 | ROT-13 encoding is simple ASCII text rotated 13 characters so as to appear encrypted. ROT-13 makes text obscure, not secure, and is often used in newsgroups. Microsoft also uses it extensively throughout the Windows Registry. Letters and special characters do not change. Only the alphabetic characters rotate, which makes this encoding scheme easy to recognize. You will use this data type when we cover Windows OS artifacts in Chapter 9. |
| | Reconstructed HTML | Renders HTML code into a text view. HTML is the language of the Web. Thus, this view is extremely useful in bookmarking web page fragments. |
| Picture | Picture | EnCase's built-in viewer will view the following image types: JPG, GIF, EMF, TIFF, BMP, ART (AOL Johnson-Grace), and PSD (Adobe Photoshop). |
| | Base64 Encoded Picture | Base64 is a type of encoding used for e-mail attachments whereby high-bit ASCII characters are encoded using low-bit ASCII characters. To do so, file sizes actually grow by about 30%. |
| | UUE Encoded Picture | Another encoding scheme for e-mail transport. |
| Integers | 8-bit 16-bit 16-bit Big Endian 32-bit 32-bit Big Endian | Display data in an integer format in either 8, 16, or 32 bit arrays. If Big Endian, the most significant bit is stored and read first. |

**TABLE 7.10**     Bookmark Data Types  *(continued)*

| Group | Data Type | Description |
| --- | --- | --- |
| Dates | DOS | Packed 16-bit value used by DOS to store month, day, year, and time. |
| | DOS Date (GMT) | Displays data as a DOS date and converts to GMT. |
| | Unix Date | The number of seconds that have lapsed since "epoch," which is January 1, 1970, at 00:00 GMT (32-bit hexadecimal value). |
| | Unix Text Date | The same base reference as above, except that the number of seconds since epoch is a ten-digit number instead of a 32-bit hexadecimal value. |
| | HFS | Macintosh file system numeric value representing month, day, year, and time. |
| | HFS Plus Date | Macintosh file system numeric value representing month, day, year, and time. |
| | Windows Date/ Time | 64-bit hexadecimal value for Windows date/time. |
| | Lotus Date | Date value for Lotus Notes database file. |
| Windows | Partition Entry | Interprets 64-byte partition table values. |
| | DOS Directory Entry | Interprets 32-byte DOS directory entries. |
| | Windows 95 Info File Record | Interprets data from Windows 9*x* INFO files, which are the Recycle Bin database files. |
| | Windows 2000 Info File Record | Interprets data from Windows 2000, XP and 2003 INFO2 files, which are Recycle Bin database files. |
| Styles | Text Styles | This is often used for foreign language support, but there are other uses. Any custom text style you create will be available here after it is created. |

After you have entered your comment, selected a destination folder, and selected a data type, click OK. Your bookmark is sent to the Bookmark view available from the case-level tab. You may want to preview each bookmark as it is created to make sure that you created what you intended and that you placed it correctly in the intended location. Bookmarks are stored in the case file and also in the backup file. It is a good practice to save after each bookmark. It only takes a second or two to press Ctrl+S. The practice creates a good habit that can translate into saved data and work when bad things happen to good people, good software, and good computers.

## Notes Bookmark

A notes bookmark is very versatile and can hold notes, comments, or most anything in a text format that you can paste in that enhances or further explains information in your report. The limit is 1,000 characters, and there is a built-in formatting tool for changing font size, bolding, italicizing, and setting indentations.

To create a notes bookmark, right-click at the location where you wish to insert the bookmark and choose Add Note. Alternatively, pressing the Insert key gives the same result. You can add a note from the Tree pane or the Table pane. You can even add one directly from within the Bookmark Data window in the Destination Folder pane from the right-click menu.

Once you are viewing the Add Note Bookmark menu, as shown in Figure 7.30, you may type or paste in your text. The formatting options are straightforward. There is a check box labeled Show In Report, which is selected by default. This means that your notes bookmark will appear in the Report view, which is typically the result you desire. The note will append to the bottom of the bookmarks in the selected folder as somewhat of an "end note." If you prefer it at the front, or anywhere else, you can go to the Table View pane and click and drag it by its handle to the desired location.

**FIGURE 7.30**    Add Note Bookmark menu from which text can be typed or pasted in. Limited formatting options are also available.

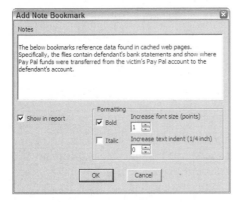

Figure 7.31 shows where the note created in Figure 7.30 was moved from its default position at the bottom to the top, serving as a description of the bookmarks that follow. Note that two note bookmarks were inserted between two bookmarks to act as spacers to give additional separation. Each of the two notes bookmarks used as spacers contain one blank space each. Figure 7.32 shows the Report view for the layout created in Figure 7.31.

**FIGURE 7.31**    Notes bookmark moved from bottom (default placement) to top. Two "blank" notes bookmarks are used to create separation between two highlighted data bookmarks.

| | | Bookmark Type | Preview | Comment | Page Break | Show Picture |
|---|---|---|---|---|---|---|
| ☐ | 1 | Note | | The below bookmarks reference data found | No | Yes |
| ☐ | 2 | Highlighted Data | \<font size=2\>    01/26/0 | January 26, 2005 Transfer of $1,940.00 via | No | Yes |
| ☐ | 3 | Note | | | No | Yes |
| ☐ | 4 | Note | | | No | Yes |
| ☐ | 5 | Highlighted Data | \<font size=2\>    01/20/0 | January 20, 2005 transfer of $1,750.00 via | No | Yes |

**FIGURE 7.32**    Report view of layout created in Figure 7.31

Folder Information Bookmark

A folder information bookmark is used when you wish to depict the folder structure in a bookmark. It may be also used to display information about devices or volumes. Depending on whether it is a device, volume, or folder, the information returned will vary. For acquired devices, acquisition information and geometry will be reported if the Include Device Information box is checked. If any number other than zero (1–3) is present, the folders for that device will be presented graphically in as many columns as the numbered entered. For this reason, zero columns will return nothing for the graphically folder display.

If the object bookmarked is a volume, the volume geometry and properties are displayed, again assuming the Include Device Information check box is selected. Any folders in the volume are graphically displayed based on the value in the columns box. If the object bookmarked is a folder, only folder information is graphically portrayed.

To create a folder information bookmark, right click on the object (device, volume, or folder) in the Cases view in any pane where you have access to it. Choose Bookmark Folder Structure, and you will see the menu presented in Figure 7.33. Here you will make selections that will determine the properties of the bookmark.

**FIGURE 7.33**    The Bookmark Folder Structure menu options

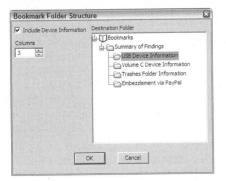

If you leave Include Device Information checked, you will receive detailed information about the device, including acquisition information and geometry, as you are bookmarking a device. The number of columns will determine the number of columns for the graphical portrayal of the folders in the device. You should also choose a destination folder. To assist in creating a nice-looking, organized report, it is helpful to place bookmarks in descriptive folders in a tree structure. In our example shown in Figure 7.33, we placed this bookmark in a folder named USB Device Information.

Figure 7.34 shows the report view for this device. Notice how the folder created to contain the bookmark imparts a nice heading in the report. Such practices or techniques are the building blocks of good reports. The report view begins with the acquisition and geometry information. At the end of the report you will note the folder structure graphically portrayed. The folder structure shown here is small and is visually acceptable.

**FIGURE 7.34**    Report view of a bookmark folder structure for a USB device

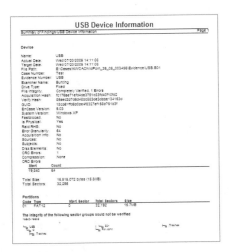

If a bookmark of this type is made of a hard drive with hundreds of folders, this diagram quickly becomes massive and confusing. Accordingly, it best to set the columns to zero and turn off this feature when bookmarking the folder structure of devices containing large numbers of folders. If certain folders are significant, you can bookmark only those folders and their subfolders using the same bookmark type. The result will be focused and much easier to view in the report.

## Notable File Bookmark

A notable file bookmark inserts a bookmark or reference to a file that contains information significant to your case. When you create a highlighted data bookmark, the data is shown in the bookmark and report. When you create a notable file bookmark, the data is not bookmarked. The bookmark contains the attributes or properties of the file. When you create your report, you'll have a choice of a document format or a web format. If you choose a web format, the notable file bookmark will have a link to the file, and the file will be exported with the report so it can be accessed via the hyperlink in the report.

To create a notable file bookmark, right-click on the file from the Table view of the Case Entries view. Choose the Bookmark Files option and you will be presented with the menu shown in Figure 7.35.

**FIGURE 7.35**    Bookmark Files menu options

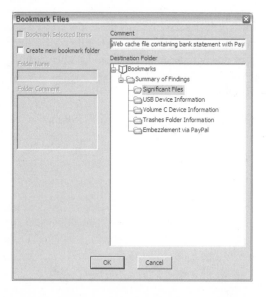

The choices are relatively simple. You choose a destination folder; once again, creating well-named folders is important. You can create a folder within the destination folder pane or use the Create New Folder check box and window to do so. You may add a comment specific to this bookmark if you like. The Report view created by this bookmark is shown in Figure 7.36. As it stands, by default, the information provided about the file is anemic at best. We will remedy that by changing the bookmark's properties.

**FIGURE 7.36**    Report view of notable file bookmark; by default, few properties are shown.

### Significant Files

| | |
|---|---|
| Summary of Findings\Significant Files | Page 1 |

1) Embezzlement\USB\C\For John\HD01PS7095127SO00LE17012.html
Web cache file containing bank statement with PayPal transactions

To change the properties of bookmarks so that additional properties are shown, you edit the properties of the containing folder and all subfolders below it receive the same properties. If you make these changes at the "right" level, you need only do it in one location, and all your bookmarks will appear uniformly formatted with property information. If there are certain folders that require something different, they can be edited by exception, and those changes will only apply to those folders and their subfolders. How you do this starts to take on the flavor or your personal preferences and style to some degree. With that in mind, you can start to see the power and flexibility available within the EnCase reporting function.

Figure 7.37 shows a folder structure that is evolving as we build our report. We have created a master container folder that is our report label: EnCase Computer Forensics Report. The root folder contains two subfolders—Device and Acquisition Information, which hold device and case information, and acquisition information, respectively. This folder and its bookmarks rarely need changes to the bookmark properties and appear adequately as they are.

**FIGURE 7.37**    A bookmark folder structure arranged in an organized tree with meaningful folder names

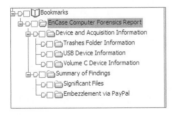

The second folder under the root folder—Summary of Findings—is the one containing notable files bookmarks and other bookmark types that benefit greatly from an enhancement of the bookmark properties. If the edits are done at the level of the Summary of Findings folder, all its subfolders receive the same bookmark properties and will look sharp when the report is produced.

To edit the properties of bookmarks, right-click on the parent folder at the level you wish to apply the changes and choose Edit. The menu you will see next is shown in Figure 7.38. In this menu, certain properties have been inserted in the left pane, which is called Format. When working with a system with permissions (NTFS, Linux, etc.), this is my "standard" format. If there are no permissions involved, such as with a FAT volume, I turn off the permissions. If a particular set of bookmarks needs something special, hash values and categories for example, I make those changes by exception. You can modify the format to suit your needs and preferences, or set them to your lab standard if one exists.

**FIGURE 7.38**     The Edit Bookmark Folder properties menu showing a typical report format

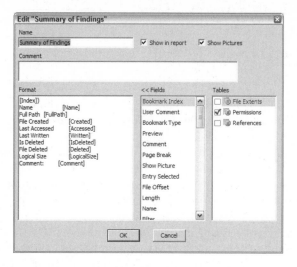

**FIGURE 7.39**     Report view after changing bookmark properties

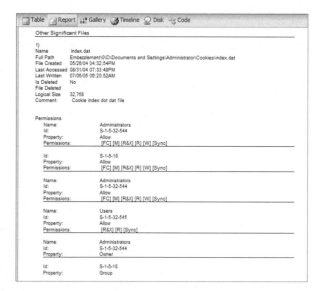

 Once you create and tweak a bookmark report format that you would like to use as a standard, copy the text in the Format pane and place it in a text file located in a convenient location. In subsequent cases, you need only copy and paste this text in the Format pane and the work is done very quickly and uniformly.

To add fields to your bookmark report format, choose them from the Fields pane by double-clicking them in the order you wish them to appear. Clearly selecting everything for inclusion would normally be too much information and would overload the reader and detract from the effectiveness of the report. You will have to find a level of detail that suits your purposes. To bring file permissions, extents, or bookmarks into the report, check them in the Tables pane. The Permissions option has been selected for inclusion, as shown earlier in Figure 7.38. The final result of the format shown in Figure 7.38 is depicted in the report view shown below in Figure 7.39.

## File Group Bookmark

A file group bookmark is much like a notable file bookmark; the major difference is that they are created by bookmarking files that have been blue-checked or selected. The icon created in the Table view is different for a notable file and a file group bookmark, which can be seen in the list of EnCase icons in Appendix B. With a notable file bookmark you can have comments that are unique to each file. When you create a file group bookmark there is one comment for the group that can be placed at the folder level. It is a good practice to have a folder for each group of related file group bookmarks so that the folder comment is applicable to the bookmarks it contains. You can always create a notes bookmark to further describe bookmarked findings.

To create a file group bookmark, first select the files you wish to include with blue checkmarks. Before you begin, however, get in the practice of checking the Dixon box to make sure it is clear. It wouldn't be the first time an examiner created thousands of file group bookmarks when they only intended to create a few! Once you have selected the group of files for bookmarking, right-click on one of the selected files and select Bookmark Files, or press Ctrl+B. Whenever you have files selected, you have the option available in the dialogue box to Bookmark Selected Items, as shown in Figure 7.40. If no files are selected, this option is grayed out.

Place a checkmark in the Bookmark Selected Items check box to create a file group bookmark. If you need to, select a destination folder for your group. I suggest that you place file group bookmarks in separate folders, with folders designated for each like grouping of files. You can create a new folder in the destination folder pane using the right-click menu, or you can do so by clicking the Create New Bookmark Folder check box and Folder Name features to the left of the destination folder pane. The latter provides the added option of a folder comment, which can be useful.

As with a notable file bookmark, the same bookmark folder edit options are available as covered in the previous section. If you have applied the bookmark folder formatting options at the proper top-level folder, they will apply to all subfolders automatically. As previously mentioned, you can override the top-level formatting options by inserting different formatting options at any subfolder level you choose. The Edit menu options are the same for all bookmark folders.

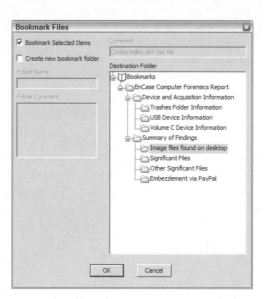

## Other Bookmarks

When running various analysis routines, threads, or EnScripts, the results are often displayed with option to bookmark the results. Figure 7.41 shows the result of a hashing routine in which the results are displayed with the option to bookmark them. The bookmark option becomes available by selecting the Note check box. The results are automatically pasted into a notes bookmark that is sent to the root of the Bookmark view. Notes bookmarks are very versatile. You can click and drag the resulting bookmark to a folder of your choice for inclusion in your report.

**FIGURE 7.41**   Hashing thread displays results can be sent to a bookmark by clicking the Note check box.

You may expect that the following threads or routines will provide the option to bookmark their results upon completion:

- Recover Folders
- Hashing Devices/Volumes
- Copy/Unerase
- Restore
- Searching
- File Signature Analysis
- Hashing Files
- Verify Single Evidence File
- Acquire

You will note in Figure 7.41 that you can also send the result to the console. From the console tab, you can access this information. The results in the console tab can be copied and pasted elsewhere, or the results can be used by an EnScript if so coded. Some EnScripts will write their results to the console as part of their output. You should be cautious of this approach because anything already in the console is usually overwritten.

## Organizing and Other Options

From the Table view pane and the Tree view pane, you have the ability to organize your findings. In the Tree view pane, you can add, delete, and move folders around. You can change the order of any folder's contents by selecting the container or parent folder in the Tree view pane, forcing its contents into the Table view pane. From the Table view pane, any item can be moved around in the order by clicking and dragging on its handle. You can drag an item in the Table view pane to another folder in the Tree view pane by the same click-and-drag method. Right-click and drag provides even more in the way of granular copy, move, or move selected item options.

As with the search hits in the Table view, bookmarks in the Table view have many of the same right-click menu options. Probably the most used of these is the Delete, Delete Selected, Show Deleted, Exclude, Exclude Selected, and Show Excluded options. The same rules apply in the Bookmarks view as in the Search Hits view with these functions. Deletes are soft deletes until you exit the case, at which time the deletes are permanent. Show Deletes and Show Excludes bring deleted or excluded items back into view. To undelete or "un-exclude," delete or exclude a second time, toggling the feature on or off.

EnCase creates some background bookmarks that default to the root of the bookmark tree structure. One such bookmark is the search summary, which is a cumulative summary of keyword searches, hit counts, and dates/times relating to those searches. Another such bookmark is the case time settings bookmark, which notes whether daylight savings time is being factored into dates/times and whether all dates/times are being converted to one time zone.

As most examiners create an elaborate tree structure for their bookmarks and subsequent reports, these background summary bookmarks are often overlooked and left in the root. If you'd like to include them in your report, create a folder for each with a descriptive name, move the folders to an appropriate location, and move the bookmarks into those folders.

At any time, you can switch to the Report tab view and view the finished report for any folder in the Tree pane. In the Tree pane, you can use the Set Included Folders option, better known as Show All, at various levels to expand your final report to the desired level. In this way, you can preview the final report and modify it before exporting it. When you are finished, use the Set Included Folders option to show your entire report in the Report view. As shown in Figure 7.42, if you right-click in the Report view area, you will be given the option to export your report in either a Document (Rich Text Format, a generic word processing format) or as a Web Page (HTML web format).

**FIGURE 7.42**   Right-click report export options from Report view tab. The Web Page option creates a robust paperless report.

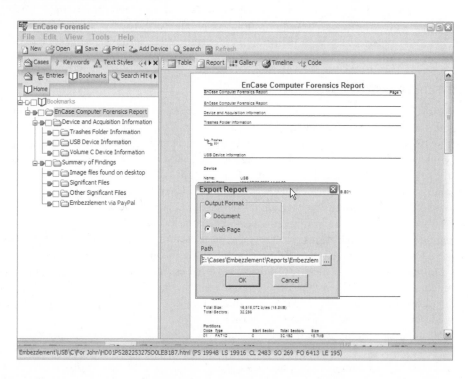

As you will come to see later, the Web Page format is where the true power and flexibility of EnCase's reporting function shines. The default output creates a Gallery view and a Report view. All files bookmarked as Notable File Bookmarks and File Group Bookmarks are exported out and hyperlinked in the report. All images in the case are exported and placed in a Gallery view. To launch the paperless report, double-click on the file Frame View.html in the root of the outputted files. The resultant report is shown in Figure 7.43. The default output can be a stand-alone paperless report or it can be wrapped with a template that includes your narrative and other information that contains hyperlinks to your EnCase report, which creates a paperless report that really snaps.

**FIGURE 7.43**    A paperless report is launched by double-clicking Frame View.html. Note that both a Report and a Gallery view are  available in the paperless report.

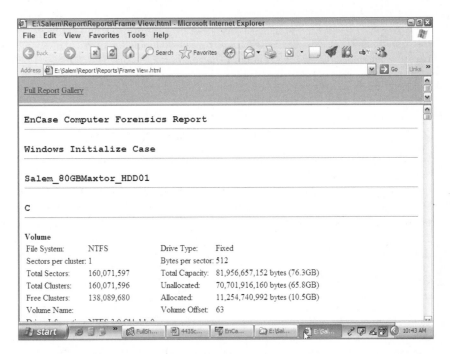

Bookmarks in EnCase are very powerful and very flexible. Examiners are encouraged to take the time to work with each of the features. In this manner, you can learn to quickly and easily create bookmarks that will be used to generate professional reports that convey your hard work and findings in a clear and meaningful way. In Appendix A, we will cover extensively how to work with your bookmarks to generate such reports.

**EXERCISE 7.1**

### Searching for Data and Bookmarking the Results

In this exercise, we'll import keywords and conduct a GREP keyword search of our case for data, matching our keyword. When found, we'll examine the search hits, bookmarking the results using various data views. To complete the process, we'll create a paperless report, showing the results of our work.  Let's get started.

- Create a folder structure for a new case according to our standard folder naming and structuring conventions. Name your case folder name **OnlineDrugSales**. Create a new case, pointing it to your newly created folders. Before you place any evidence in your case, save your case in the root of the folder OnlineDrugSales, which will also be the default name for your case. Locate an evidence file on the CD named ThumbDrive_Evidence_File\DefFrostyUSB16MB_TD01.E01. Place it in the evidence folder for your newly created case.

- Let's add an evidence file by clicking on Add Device. Create a path to the evidence folder on your new case. Locate the above evidence file in the right pane and bring it into your case. Now that your evidence file is in your case, click Save again.

- Go to your case-level Keyword view tab. In the Tree pane, right-click at the root of the tree and select Import. Browse to the CD and to a folder and file named Keywords_For_Import\Keywords_For_Import.txt. When you locate it, click OK to complete the import. You should have several GREP expressions, which are the ones mentioned earlier in this chapter. Browse to the keyword in the Tracking Numbers folder and blue-check the one for UPS Tracking Number. Browse to the Windows Artifacts folder and blue-check the one for the dot double dot directory. You should have selected two keywords for your search.

- Locate the Dixon box, and make sure it is clear. If not, click it once to set it to 0. Click it again to select all files in the case.

- On the toolbar, click Search. then click Selected Files Only, Search Each File For Keywords, Search File Slack, and Selected Keywords Only. Click Start and your search should complete very quickly. In the completion status report, click the Note option and then click OK. Click Save again.

- On the case-level tab bar, go to the Search Hits tab. In the Tree pane, select the UPS tracking number keyword. In the Table pane, note one search hit in which a UPS tracking number was located. In the View pane, switch to the Text view. Select all the readable text by placing your cursor on the first byte and clicking and dragging to the last byte of text. Right-click in the selected text and choose Bookmark Data. In the destination folder, right-click and create a folder named EnCase Computer Forensics Report and create a subfolder under it named Email Orders. Select Email Orders as the destination folder. Under data types, choose Text \ Low ASCII. Enter an appropriate comment and click OK. You should have a bookmark in the Bookmarks view tab.

- Click on the Dixon box to clear all selected files. In the Table view where the tracking number hit is located, right-click and choose Tag File. The Dixon box should now reflect one file as selected. Go to the Case Entries view and click the Set Included Folders trigger at the case or root level. All files in the case are now showing in the Table view. In the Filter pane (lower right), go to the Conditions tab. Go down the tree to General Conditions and double-click on the condition Selected Files Only. Your one selected file should now be the only file showing. This is especially useful when many files are selected in this manner. Note the location of the tagged file, which is in the My Documents\Email Orders\Customer SB folder. On the toolbar click the Selected Files Only filter icon, turning the + into a -, thereby turning the filter off. Navigate in the Tree pane to the My Documents\Email Orders\ Customer SB folder, and you'll see three files, including one selected file.

- Leave your file selected. In the Table view, highlight the file August 20 2005 order.txt. In the View pane, note its contents as contained in and therefore related to the file you already have selected. Blue-check this file. Look at the contents of the third file (Original Order with Address.txt). The contents appear strange. Let's leave it alone for now and bookmark the two files first.

- Right-click in the Table view pane and choose Bookmark Files. In the destination pane, create a folder File Group Bookmark under the folder Email Orders and select it as the destination folder. In a real report, you'd name this something more meaningful, but here we are getting you used to various techniques and this helps you see the results. Be sure to click Bookmark Selected Items. Click OK.

- In the Table view pane, highlight the file Original Order with Address.txt and view it in the View pane using the Text view tab. Note that numbers and special characters appear normally, but characters are abnormal. With time, you'll recognize this as ROT-13 (rotate characters 13 places) encoding. It is used frequently in newsgroups and in the Windows Registry. It is also used by some nefarious characters as a simple but effective technique to skirt around corporate e-mail and web content filters. In the View pane, select all the text (click and drag). In the highlighted area, right-click and choose to bookmark data. Under data types, select Text\ROT -13. In the bottom pane, the text should decode and make its contents readable. For a destination folder, create a folder under Email Orders, name it **ROT13**, and select it as the destination. Click OK to finish.

- In the Tree pane, navigate to the My Documents\My Pictures folder. Click on the Dixon box to clear selected files. Place a blue check (select) next to each of the two images files. The Dixon box should show two files selected. Right-click in the Table view pane and choose Bookmark Files. Make sure Bookmark Selected Items is checked. Create a destination folder named Images as a subfolder directly under EnCase Computer Forensics Report and select it as the destination folder. Click OK to finish.

- In the Tree pane, go to the folder My Documents\Dates and Times. There is a file by the same name within it. Highlight it in the Table pane. View it in the View pane as hex. In the Text view, place your cursor on the first character immediately following the > in the first appearance of → . In the hex section, sweep that byte and the following 3 bytes for total of 4 bytes. You should have highlighted the hex string E2 49 07 43 in hex and not in its ASCII version above it. You are looking at a 32-bit Unix date stamp. It is 4 bytes and is also known as a Dword. In hex, right-click and choose Bookmark Data. Under Data Type choose Dates\Unix Date and the date will decode. Create a destination folder under EnCase Computer Forensics Report, name it **Dates and Times**, select it as the destination, and click OK.

- With the same 4 bytes still selected, right-click and choose Bookmark Data once again. Under Data Type, choose Integers\32-bit Integer. The number should resolve to a ten-digit integer. This is the number of seconds since January 1, 1970, 00:00:00 GMT. This number is 1124551138 and is ten digits. You'll come to recognize it on sight as a Unix text or numeric date stamp. Not surprisingly, you see this same integer a little further down in the text and labeled as such. Sweep (select) that particular ten-digit number in the Text pane. Right-click, choose Bookmark Data, and choose as the data type Dates\Unix Text Date. The value should decode as the same value in the previous example. Place this bookmark in the destination folder Dates and Times. Go the bottom of this text document and locate an 8-byte hex string located between "→(8 byte hex string)←". This hex string should read 60 8D D7 95 9C A5 C5 01. Sweep that hex string, not the ASCII rendition created just for your viewing pleasure! Bookmark the data and choose as a data type Dates\Windows Date/Time. Place the 64-bit Windows date/time stamp in the destination folder, Dates and Times.

- Go the Bookmarks view tab. In the Tree pane, highlight the folder Email Orders. In the Table pane you should see two folders and one highlighted data bookmark. In the Tree pane, under Email Orders, right-click and create a new folder, naming it Highlighted data bookmark. In the Tree pane, highlight again Email Orders, forcing the highlighted data and now three folders in the Table view pane. In the Table view pane, drag, by its handle, the highlighted data bookmark to the folder in the tree pane named Highlighted data bookmark and drop it on that folder. You have moved a bookmark into a newly created folder.

- In the Tree pane of the Bookmark view, highlight the folder EnCase Computer Forensics Report, right-click, and choose Edit. Locate a folder and file on the CD named Format_Template\Format_Template.txt. Open the file, select the entire contents (Ctrl+A), and copy the entire contents to the Clipboard (Ctrl+C). Place your cursor in the format pane of the EnCase Edit window and paste in the contents of the Clipboard (Ctrl+V). Click OK. You have created a format for your report and placed it at the top level.

**EXERCISE 7.1** *(continued)*

- In the Tree pane, activate the Set Included Folders trigger at the EnCase Computer Forensics Level. All bookmarks should appear in the right pane in the Table view. In the Table view pane, switch to the Report tab and the final report should generate. Right-click on the Report view and choose Export. In the next menu, create a folder in your case folder structure and name it **Reports**. Choose the Report folder as the destination folder. Choose Web Page as the type. Give the name of the file as **report**. Click OK and the report will generate.

- Go to the folder in your case folder named Reports. Double-click on the file therein named Frame View.html. Your paperless report will launch. Visit the Gallery tab and the full report tab. Most likely, if using Microsoft Internet Explorer, you'll have to allow the blocked content to view first before you can use the gallery or see images in the full report. If there's anything you want to change in your report, change it in EnCase and export it again. If you want to see what this report looks like when finished, it is included on the CD in a folder titled Chap07_Exercise_Report. Double-click on the file Frame View.html.

- Save your case and exit EnCase.

When EnCase exports bookmarked files for the Web Page report format, it changes their filename to coincide with the bookmark index number. A file named mypic.jpg bookmarked as index 6) in the report will have 0006.jpg as its exported filename. If you need to move items around, it is best to do it in EnCase rather than in a web editing tool so as to keep the report index numbers in sync with their corresponding filenames.

# Summary

In this chapter, we covered data in its binary and hexadecimal formats. We learned that various storage devices have physical, optical, or electrical states of positive or negative, yes or no, on or off, etc. that are rendered into 1s and 0s. Binary (base-2) is a system based strictly on 1s and 0s and is the system used by computers to store and transmit data.

A bit is the smallest unit and can have two outcomes, 1 or 0. A byte consists of 8 bits and can have 256 possible outcomes. A byte is made up of 2 four-bit nibbles. Of those two nibbles there is a left nibble and a right nibble. Each nibble can have 16 possible outcomes.

Two bytes combined is called a "word," which is 16 bits. Four bytes combined is called a Dword, which is 32 bits. Larger still is a Qword, which is four words and 64 bits.

Hexadecimal is a programmer's shortcut for expressing binary numbers. Each nibble of the byte is evaluated separately. As each nibble can have 16 possible outcomes, those integer values are represented by a single character ranging from 0 to F (0, 1, 2, 3, 4, 5, 6, 7, 8, 9, A, B, C, D, E, F), which represents the integers 0–16, respectively. Each nibble is represented by a single character, and the two characters are combined to represent the entire byte.

ASCII was originally a 7-bit character set consisting of 128 of the common numbers, characters, and special characters. It is also called low-bit ASCII. To include some foreign languages, graphics, and math symbols, this character set was expanded to an extended 8-bit character chart. It consists of 256 characters and is often called high-bit ASCII.

As computing became global, the world's varied languages could not be expressed in a 256-character set. Unicode evolved to remedy this situation, allowing 2 bytes per character.

EnCase uses keywords as search stings by which to conduct searches. Keywords can be global (stored in the keywords.ini file) or case level (stored in the case file). Keywords can be created individually or in groups using keyword lists. Keywords can be imported from EnCase keywords that were exported for import.

When searching, you create and select keywords by which to search. You also select the data on which the search is to be conducted. You have various options when searching, such as case-sensitive searches, Unicode searches, and others. You can create specialized code pages for foreign language searches.

Another type of search option is a GREP search. GREP searches allow special characters to be used to construct search terms that can greatly enhance your searching capabilities.

Once a search has been conducted, the results are sent to the search hits view, which is a case-level tab. Search hits can be grouped and sorted in various ways by device and/or by keyword. Search hits can be sorted in the Table view pane. They can be deleted or excluded and viewed once deleted or excluded. By deleting or excluding a search hit a second time, they are undeleted or "un-excluded."

Files containing search hits can be tagged for further analysis in the Case view. Files containing search hits can be bookmarked from the Search Hits view.

There are several types of bookmarks. One of the most common and feature-rich bookmarks is the highlighted data bookmark. Using this bookmark, data can be viewed in vast array of different formats. The destination folder can be selected, created, or rearranged.

Files can be bookmarked individually as notable file bookmarks or in groups of files that have been selected, using the file group bookmark. Bookmarked files are exported and hyperlinked in the Web Page report feature.

Devices, volumes, and folders can be bookmarked using the folder information bookmark. The output of this bookmark varies according to the object bookmarked. Device information is included if that option is checked. The column setting determines the number of columns into which the folders are arranged in their graphic representation. A setting of 0 turns off the graphic folder representation.

Bookmarks have folder format properties that can be modified by editing a bookmark folder. There are many fields or properties from which to choose, including file permissions when those properties are present. When formatting options are set, they apply from that point down in the tree unless modified in any particular subfolder.

Bookmarks can be moved, deleted, or rearranged. Bookmarks are the foundation from which reports are generated. Creating a well-organized tree of bookmarks with meaningful folder names is essential to creating a good report. Examiners should take the time necessary to learn to create well-designed and well-organized bookmarks as they translate into well-designed and well-organized reports.

# Exam Essentials

**Understand binary data concepts.**    Understand and explain how binary data is stored and translated into human-readable text and numbers. Be able to interpret a binary byte into its hexadecimal format. Understand hexadecimal representation and be able to convert between binary, hexadecimal, and decimal formats. Be able to interpret a binary byte into its integer or ASCII value.

**Know and understand the ASCII and Unicode character sets.**    Explain what the 7-bit low-bit ASCII character set is. Explain what the 8-bit high-bit extended ASCII character set is and how it evolved. Explain how a given hex value could be a character in one context, but an integer in another context. Understand and explain the difference between 09h (decimal integer 9) and 39h (printed character 9).

Understand how Unicode evolved and how many bytes are used to represent one character. Know how many characters can be represented by Unicode.

**Understand keywords and their implementation into the search process.**    Explain how to create case-level and global keywords. Understand and be able to explain where keywords are stored and when they are saved. Be able to export and import keywords. Understand the importance of naming keywords.

**Understand GREP search expressions.**    Know and be able to explain what GREP means. Be able to create GREP expressions to search for specified search strings. Given a GREP expression, be able to determine which strings will match and which strings will not match. Know the purpose and function of the keyword tester.

**Know and understand how to conduct searches.**    Understand and be able to explain how to conduct a search in EnCase. Know what search options are available from the search menu and how they affect the search results. Know in which file(s) search hits are stored.

**Understand the Search Hits view.**    Understand and explain the features and functions available in the Search Hits view. Explain how files containing search hits are bookmarked or tagged. Explain how search hits are deleted or excluded, as well as how they are viewed and restored. Understand how search hits can be grouped and sorted using the view search hits options.

**Know and understand how to create bookmarks.**    Understand and be able to describe what a bookmark is and how to create each bookmark type. Understand how to view data in different formats by using a highlighted data bookmark. Explain how to select destination folders. Explain the importance of organizing folders into a meaningful hierarchical format with folder names that describe their contents. Explain how to move folders and bookmarks. Describe how a report is generated. Understand the two types of report formats that can be generated from the Report view. Explain the process of generating a paperless report.

# Review Questions

1. Computers use a numbering system with only two digits, 0 and 1. This system is referred to as:

   **A.** Hexadecimal

   **B.** ASCII

   **C.** Binary

   **D.** FAT

2. A bit can have a binary value of:

   **A.** 0 or 1

   **B.** 0–9

   **C.** 0–9 and A–F

   **D.** On or Off

3. A byte consists of ___ bits.

   **A.** 2

   **B.** 4

   **C.** 8

   **D.** 16

4. If 1 bit can have two unique possibilities, 2 bits can have four unique possibilities and 3 bits can have eight unique possibilities, this is known as the power of two. How many unique possibilities are there in 8 bits ($2^8$)?

   **A.** 16

   **B.** 64

   **C.** 128

   **D.** 256

5. When the letter "A" is represented as 41h, it is displayed in:

   **A.** Hexadecimal

   **B.** ASCII

   **C.** Binary

   **D.** Decimal

6. What is the decimal integer value for the binary code 0000-1001?

   **A.** 7

   **B.** 9

   **C.** 11

   **D.** 1001

7. Select all of the following that depict a Dword value:

   **A.** 0000 0001

   **B.** 0001

   **C.**  FF 00 10 AF

   **D.** 0000 0000 0000 0000 0000 0000 0000 0001

8. How many characters can be addressed by the 7-bit ASCII character table? 16-bit Unicode?

   **A.** 64 and 256

   **B.** 128 and 256

   **C.** 64 and 65,536

   **D.** 128 and 65,536

9. Where does EnCase (Version 5) store keywords?

   **A.** Within each specific case file (.case & .cbak)

   **B.** In the keywords.ini file

   **C.** Both A and B

   **D.** None of the above

10. When performing a keyword search in Windows, EnCase searches:

    **A.** The logical files

    **B.** The physical disk in unallocated clusters and other unused disk areas

    **C.** Both A and B

    **D.** None of the above

11. By default, search terms are case-sensitive.

    **A.** True

    **B.** False

12. By selecting the Unicode box, EnCase searches for both ASCII and Unicode formats.

    **A.** True

    **B.** False

13. With regard to a search using EnCase in the Windows environment, can EnCase find a word or phrase that is fragmented or spans in noncontiguous clusters?

    **A.** No, because the letters are located in noncontiguous clusters.

    **B.** No, EnCase performs a physical search only.

    **C.** No, unless the File Slack option is deselected in the dialog box before the search.

    **D.** Yes, EnCase performs both physical and logical searches.

14. Which of the following would be a search hit for this keyword (exclude the quotation marks): "His"

    **A.** this

    **B.** His

    **C.** history

    **D.** Bill_Chisholm@gmail.com

    **E.** All of the above

15. Which of the following would be a search hit for this GREP expression: [^a-z]Liz[^a-z]

    **A.** Elizabeth

    **B.** Lizzy

    **C.** Liz1

    **D.** None of the above

16. Which of the following would be a search hit for the following GREP expression: [\x00-\x07]\x00\x00\x00...

    **A.** 00 00 00 01 A0 EE F1

    **B.** 06 00 00 00 A0 EE F1

    **C.** 0A 00 00 00 A0 EE F1

    **D.** 08 00 00 00 A0 EE F1

17. Which of the following would be a search hit for the following GREP expression: Jan 1st, 2?0?06

    **A.** Jan 1st, 2006

    **B.** Jan 1st, 06

    **C.** Both A and B

    **D.** None of the above

18. Which of the following will *not* be a search hit for the following GREP expression: [^#]123[ \-]45[ \-]6789[^#]

    **A.** A1234567890.

    **B.** A123 45-6789.

    **C.** A123-45-6789.

    **D.** A123 45 6789.

19. A sweep or highlight of a specific range of text is referred to as:

    **A.** File group bookmark

    **B.** Folder information bookmark

    **C.** Highlighted data bookmark

    **D.** Notable file bookmark

    **E.** Notes bookmark

**20.** EnCase exports bookmark reports as what format?

   **A.** As a Word (.doc) document

   **B.** As a Rich Text Format (.rtf) document

   **C.** As a web (.html) page

   **D.** Both A and C

   **E.** Both B and C

# Answers to Review Questions

1.  C. Binary is a numbering system consisting of 0 and 1 used by computers to process information.

2.  A. *Bi* refers to two; therefore, a bit can only have two values, 0 or 1.

3.  C. A byte consists of 8 bits or two 4-bit nibbles, commonly referred to as the left nibble and right nibble.

4.  D. $2^8$ is 2×2 eight times, or 2×2×2×2×2×2×2×2=256.

5.  A. Values expressed with the letter "h" as a suffix are hexadecimal characters. EnCase can display the letter "A" in text or hexadecimal formats.

6.  B. Starting from the right, the bits are "on" for bit positions 1 and 8, which totals 9.

7.  C and D. A Dword is a 32-bit value. "A" is incorrect as it depicts 8 binary bits or one byte. "B" is incorrect as it depicts 4 binary bits or one nibble. "C" is correct as it represents four hexadecimal values with each being a 8 bits (4 × 8 = 32 bits). "D" is correct as it represents 32 binary bits.

8.  D. $2^7$ is 2×2 seven times or 2×2×2×2×2×2×2=128 while$2^{16}$ is 2×2 sixteen times = 65,536.

9.  C. In Version 5, keywords can be saved in specific case files (.case and .cbak) as well as globally in the keywords.ini file.

10. C. EnCase performs a search of not only logical files but of the entire disk to include unallocated clusters and unused disk areas outside the logical partition.

11. B. By default, the Case Sensitive option is not selected; therefore, search terms are not case-sensitive unless you select that option.

12. A. By selecting the Unicode box, EnCase will search for both ASCII and Unicode formats.

13. D. EnCase can perform both physical searches as well as logical searches for keyword(s) that span noncontiguous clusters.

14. E. Since the entry allows for characters to precede and follow the keyword and the default setting does not have the Case Sensitive option enabled, all the selections apply.

15. C. The GREP symbol ^ means to exclude the following characters. So the above GREP expression excludes the alpha characters (a through z) before and after the keyword but will find non-alpha characters such as numbers.

16. B. The GREP expression above permits a hexadecimal range from 00 through 07 followed by hexadecimal values 00 00 00 and any other characters.

17. C. The GREP expression ? calls for the preceding character to be repeated 0 or 1 time. The above GREP expression calls for 2 or not, then 0 or not, followed by 06.

**18.** A. The GREP expression [^#] means that it cannot be a number, meaning the first character and last character following the 9 can't be numbers. Therefore, selection A will not return as a search hit because the number 0 follows the number 9.

**19.** C. The highlighted data bookmark is a sweep or highlight of a specific text fragment.

**20.** E. EnCase can export bookmark reports as both documents (.rtf) and web pages (.html).

# File Signature Analysis and Hash Analysis

---

## ENCE EXAM TOPICS COVERED IN THIS CHAPTER:

- ✓ File signatures and extensions
- ✓ Adding file signatures to EnCase
- ✓ Conducting a file signature analysis and evaluating the results
- ✓ Understanding the MD5 hash
- ✓ Creating hash sets and libraries
- ✓ Importing hash sets
- ✓ Conducting a hash analysis and evaluating the results

In this chapter we will cover two data analysis techniques that are core skill sets for the competent examiner as they are used in most examinations. You should, therefore, strive to master these techniques and their associated concepts.

The first technique is the file signature analysis. Most files have a unique signature or header that can be used by the operating system or application program to identify a file. Often files have filename extensions to identify them as well, particularly in a Windows operating system. The file extensions and headers should, in most cases, match, although there are a variety of exceptions and circumstances where there is a mismatch, no match, unknown information, or anomalous results. A file signature analysis will compare files, their extensions, and their headers to a known database of file signatures and extensions and report the results.

The second technique is the hash analysis. We have used the MD5 hash to verify acquisitions of digital evidence, such as hard drives or removable media. We'll use that same MD5 hash to derive 128-bit hash values of individual files and compare them to known databases of hash values. In this manner we can identify known files by their MD5 hash. If they are known "safe" files, such as program files, they can be eliminated from further analysis. If they are known contraband files, they can be quickly identified and bookmarked.

Both techniques are important tools for the forensics examiner to use when analyzing data. We'll begin our discussion with the file signature analysis.

# File Signature Analysis

As you can imagine, the number of different file types that currently exist in the computing world is staggering—and climbing daily. Many, certainly not all, have been standardized and have unique file signatures or headers that precede their data. The two bodies that have undertaken this standardization are the International Standards Organization (ISO) and the International Telecommunications Union Telecommunications Standardization Sector (ITU-T). When standardized headers are present, programs can recognize files by their header data. Also, many standardized files have unique extensions that are associated with the file's unique header.

## Understanding Application Binding

The process by which an operating system knows how to open a particular file type with a given application is called application binding. There are many methods employed by various operating systems, and it is beyond the scope of this book to enter this realm too deeply, but we must at least give it some consideration so as to understand the topic at hand.

Windows, for example, uses file extensions to associate or bind specific file types with specific applications. File extensions are the letters that follow the last "dot" in a file name. Under this system, a file with the extension of .pdf will typically be opened by Adobe Reader. Windows cares only about the extension and nothing about the header. If you take a .jpg file and change its extension to .pdf, Windows will pass it along to Adobe Reader to open. Adobe Reader will report an error or problem with the file and it will fail to open.

> Windows stores its application binding information in the Registry. As this setting can vary between users, it is stored in the user's Registry file, which is ntuser.dat. The key where this information is found is \Software\Microsoft\Windows\CurrentVersion\Explorer\FileExts. Each registered extension will have its own key. Each of those keys has two subkeys: OpenWithList and OpenWithProgids. The information directing which program to open the extension is in these two subkeys.

This anomaly, if you will, gives rise to a data hiding technique in which the user changes the extension of the file to obscure its contents. If a file named MyContrabandImage.jpg was changed to lansys32.dll and moved to the system32 folder, the casual observer would probably never find it. Even a systems administrator would probably miss it. Even if noticed, an attempt to open it in Windows would fail. EnCase would not, however, miss its contents once a file signature analysis had been conducted, which we'll soon understand as we progress.

Other operating systems such as Linux and Unix use header information to bind file types to specific applications. Those systems are, therefore, not dependent on file extensions. You will find that many files on those operating systems do not have file extensions.

Mac operating systems use a combination of methods to bind files to applications. Macintosh uses the Hierarchical File System Plus (HFS+) on its current operating system, which is OS X. Macintosh legacy systems used an older version of this file system known as HFS. As part of the file system metadata, a Mac stores a 32-bit value called a *file type code* and another 32-bit value called a *creator code*. File type codes are 4-byte codes describing the various file types. Creator codes are 4-byte values assigned to various programs that create files. As of about 2003, there were well over 58,000 different file type and creator codes available in a third-party database for use in analyzing these codes. Legacy Mac operating systems use this metadata (file type code and creator code) to bind files with applications.

This system allows considerable flexibility, much to the delight of Mac users. One JPEG image can be opened by one program while another JPEG image can be opened by another program based on the application that created the file rather than on its extension.

The Internet is changing the way the Mac operates, as cross-platform file exchanges are a way of life. When OS X arrived on the scene, application developers were asked to add file extensions as files were created by programs. Mac users protested, but the protests fell on deaf ears as Mac still insists on extensions for new Mac applications.

Mac OS_X uses a list of seven rules of precedence for application binding. The first priority goes to "user defined," meaning that if a user chooses that a specific file will be opened by a specific application, this setting will override all other settings. The second priority goes to the "creator code," meaning that the application that created the file will open it as long as there is no overriding "user defined" setting. The third priority is that of file extension, which is new to the Mac world with the advent of OS_X. If there is no "user defined" setting and no creator code, Mac OS_X will use the file extension as the means to bind the file to an application. The last four rules of precedence are rather complex and go beyond the scope of our discussion. If the topic interests you, simply "Google" "Apple.com" for the phrase "application binding."

Currently with OS X (Tiger), if a Mac file lacks a "user defined" setting and lacks a "creator code," it looks next to the file extension to determine which application to use to open that file. If that file name extension has been renamed to hide the file's true nature, it hangs and doesn't open. Thus as file extension application binding finds its way into the Mac operating systems, it creates another method for obscuring data on those systems. You can expect to see more file name extensions in the future when you examine Mac systems as application developers, despite protests, are being instructed to use file name extensions when they create applications. Following that trend, you may expect the use of file extension changes to hide data on Mac systems to rise commensurately.

## Creating a New File Signature

When conducting a file signature analysis, EnCase compares a file's header, if one is present, with its extension, if one is present. This information is compared to a database of known file signatures and extensions that is maintained within EnCase and stored in the FileSignatures.ini file.

To better understand the information stored in the file signatures database, let's examine the information in this database and create a new file signature. First we must go to the File Signatures view, which is located on the Global tab bar (or under the View menu, choose File Signatures). The File Signatures view lists the container folders in the Tree pane and the list of file signatures in the Table pane. Placing the View pane in the Report tab view, you can see the data in a report format for each file signature type, which is the same data visible in the Table view in a tabular format. This view is shown in Figure 8.1.

To add a record, first select the category for the signature and select the folder by that name in the Tree pane. You can right-click on that folder in the Tree pane (or you can right-click in the Table pane) and select New. You can also press the Insert key. All these methods result in the New File Signature dialog box as shown in Figure 8.2.

Deleting a record is as simple as right-clicking on a particular record and choosing Delete. As with search hits and bookmarks, you have the same Delete, Exclude, Show Delete, and Show Excluded options. A delete is a "soft delete" until you exit EnCase, at which time it becomes permanent. To undelete or "un-exclude," delete or exclude a second time, toggle off the feature.

In our example, we added an **MP3 Music File** signature and placed it in the multimedia category. After entering the hex string, we chose the GREP option. For the extension, we entered **mp3**, as seen in Figure 8.3. When done, we clicked OK and the new signature was added to the database. This point is a good time to select Save All from the File menu.

**FIGURE 8.1** File Signature view provides an interface to a database of file signatures from which you can add, modify, or delete file signature records.

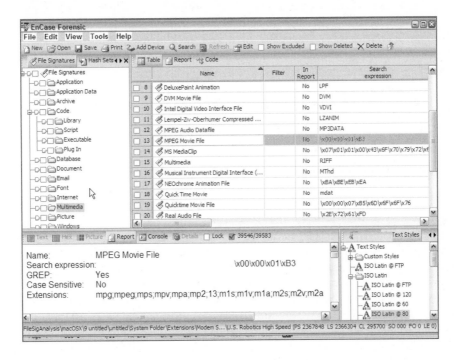

**FIGURE 8.2** The New File Signature dialog box lets you enter the header string (with any applicable search options) and the name of the signature. The file extensions are entered on the Extensions tab.

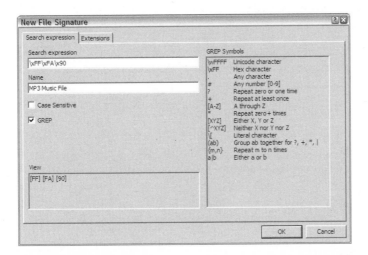

**FIGURE 8.3**    The extension for the file signature is entered on the Extensions tab.

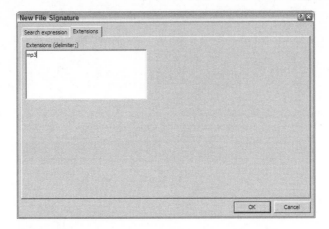

Let's modify a record. You can double-click on a file signature to open its properties, or you can right-click and choose Edit to open the same properties screen. In our example, we are choosing the email category or folder and the file signature named Outlook Express Email Storage File. From our analysis work, we have determined that this file signature is used not only by Outlook Express but also by MSN Mail for its local storage. The former has a file extension of .dbx and is already entered in the Extensions tab. There is no extension listed for the MSN Mail extension, which is .MailDB. We are going to modify the name to include MSN mail and add the MSN mail extension. Double-click on the file signature Outlook Express Email Storage File and you'll see the dialog box shown in Figure 8.4, which also reflects a name change for the file signature.

**FIGURE 8.4**    You can modify a file signature by changing its name.

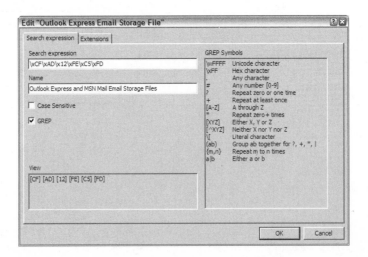

**FIGURE 8.5** Separate multiple extensions with a semicolon delimiter and no spaces.

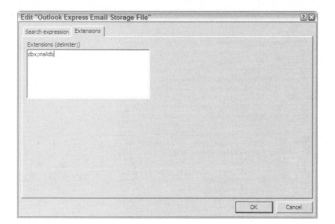

After changing the name to something that reflects its dual role, we next go to the Extensions tab. Multiple extensions are separated by a semicolon as a delimiter. No spaces are used, only the delimiter. In our case, we're adding the extension .maildb, as shown in Figure 8.5. When done, click OK to change the record. To save the database in the INI file, choose Save All from the File menu.

## Conducting a File Signature Analysis

Now that we have an understanding of the information in the database, let's use the information contained in the database to carry out a file signature analysis. From the File Signatures view, switch back to the Case Entries view. When running a file signature analysis, typically you want to run it over all the files in the case so that EnCase can rely on the true file type for all files in the case instead of their extensions. With that in mind, use the Dixon box to select all files in your case. Next, simply click on the search icon on the toolbar. It is from the Search dialog box, as shown in Figure 8.6, that you access the file signature analysis utility.

To run a file signature analysis, simply choose all selected files, click the Verify File Signatures check box, and click the Start button. EnCase examines every file selected and looks at its header to see if there's a matching header in the database. If it finds one, then the header is known. EnCase next looks at the file's extension and compares it with the extension listed in the database for that known header. If the header is known and the extension matches, EnCase reports a match. If there is no extension for a given header in the file signature table, EnCase will report a match for any extension as long as the file's extension doesn't match any other header listed in the file extension table.

If EnCase can't find the file's header in the file signature database and it also can't find the file's extension in the database, EnCase reports the status of this file as unknown.

If EnCase locates a file's header in the file signature database, the header is known. If the extension that should correspond with the file's header is missing or incorrect, the header information is presumed correct and prevails. In such cases, EnCase reports the alias for this file with the convention *FileType.

**FIGURE 8.6**    The file signature analysis tool is enabled from the Search dialog box. It can be run alone or along with a searching and hashing thread.

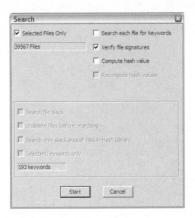

Figure 8.7 shows files in a Mac OS X system. In particular the files shown are images from which the user can select for their desktop. The highlighted file name is Mac OS Background. Note the file, like many on Mac systems, is missing a file extension. As no file signature analysis has yet occurred, EnCase relies on file extensions for file type. Because there is no extension, EnCase does not show this file as an image. If we look at the data in the Hex view, we note that its header is FF D8 FF E0, which with time we will immediately recognize as a JPEG image. Note that the Table view columns have been optimally arranged for file signature analysis and they are, from left to right, Name, File Ext, Signature, File Type, and File Category.

**FIGURE 8.7**    Image files on a Mac system that have no file extensions. Since no file signature has yet been run, EnCase relies on file extensions and does not yet recognize these files as images.

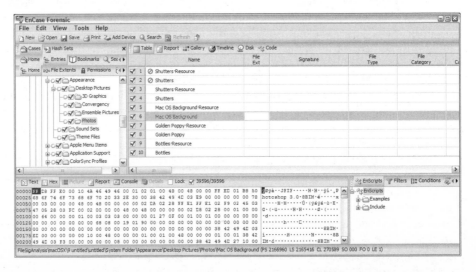

When a file signature analysis has been conducted and a file with a known header has a missing or incorrect extension, its "alias" is reported based on the file header information. Figure 8.8 shows the same image files after the file signature analysis has been run. Under the File Category column, EnCase now reports the file as a picture. Under Signature, EnCase reports the alias as *JPEG Image. Because EnCase now knows this file is a picture, the Picture view is enabled in the View pane and the file would default to the Picture view. Many of you no doubt recognize the image as one associated with the Mac operating system.

**FIGURE  8.8**     The same picture files after a file signature analysis has been conducted. Note the file category is Picture and the alias is reported as *JPEG Image.

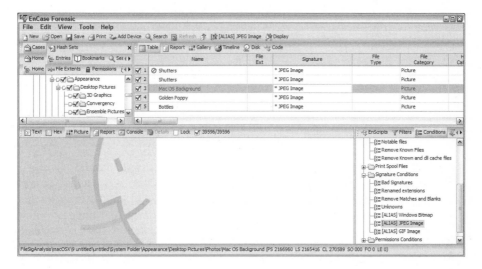

Another set of conditions often occurs during file signature analysis that is known as a *bad file signature*. When EnCase discovers a file that has a known extension and that extension has a known header, but the file's header does not match that header or any other header in the database, the file is reported as having a *!Bad Signature*. The file signature status types reported by EnCase are summarized in Table 8.1.

Although it is a rare occurrence, you can sometimes encounter an anomaly in which a file header matches a known header and the extension is in the table but has no header. In this case, EnCase believes the header information and reports the file with an alias for the header even though the file extension is correct. This sounds a bit confusing until you see an example, and then it makes perfect sense.

If EnCase were to encounter a text file during a file signature analysis and the first two letters of the text file were someone's initials, such as PK, we would encounter this anomaly. EnCase would see the initials as a header that was known in the table, which is the header for a zip file. A text file can start with anything, so it has no header. EnCase expects to see a .zip extension with a zip header. EnCase resolves conflicts using the header information, which means the file would be reported with an alias for a zip file even though it was a bona fide text file. These encounters are very rare, but should they occur, you will recognize them for what they are based on your understanding of the file signature process and the rules for evaluating and reporting the results.

**TABLE 8.1**   Summary of File Signature Analysis Status Report

| File Name | Header | Header in Table | Extension | Status |
|---|---|---|---|---|
| picture.jpg | FF D8 FF E0 | Known | Known and matches | Match |
| picture.dll | FF D8 FF E0 | Known | Known and incorrect | Alias *JPEG Image |
| anyfile.zza | FF D6 FE FF | Unknown | Unknown | Unknown |
| picture.jpg | D8 D8 FF E0 | Unknown | Known and doesn't match | !Bad Signature |

Some published documentation erroneously reports that the File Type column is updated after completion of a file signature analysis. This does not occur. File type is based on information stored in the FileTypes.ini database for the file's extension. If there is information on a file extension in this database, the information is returned. If there is no extension or if the extension is not in the database, nothing will be reported in this column. Should information change in this database about a file's extension, only then would this information change. An example of this would be editing a file extension record from within the File Types view tab. The entry in the file category would change after file signature analysis if the file was determined to be of a type that is a picture. EnCase changes its file category to a picture so that it may be viewed as such by EnCase. If the file type is not a picture, no change will be made to this column. The file signature column will always be updated after a file signature analysis is conducted for all logical files in the case that have not been overwritten.

File signatures are an important part of the examination process and should be done at the beginning of your processing so that both you and EnCase are seeing files for what they really are. Many examiners run a file signature analysis right after the evidence file is verified. Some run it routinely right after recovering folders. Some run it simultaneously with the first search. Whichever you prefer, you should run early in the case and make sure you do it for all cases. To make sure we understand this important tool, let's check our understanding of the file signature analysis tool with an exercise.

**EXERCISE 8.1**

## File Signature Analysis

In this exercise, we are going to run a file signature analysis on a very small evidence file that contains a very concise example of all the various file signature analysis results that you will typically encounter. The file names depict their file signature conditions and are intended to help you understand the results. It is a good exercise to do shortly before your examination to help solidify the file signature analysis concepts. Let's begin.

- Create a folder structure for a new case according to our standard folder naming and structuring conventions. Name your case folder name FileSigAnalysis. Create a new case, pointing it to your newly created folders. Before you place any evidence in your case, save your case in the root of the folder FileSigAnalysis, which will also be the default name for your case. Locate an evidence file on the CD named FileSigAnalysis\ FileSigAnalysis.E01. Place it in the evidence folder for your newly created case.

- On the toolbar, click Add Device. Create a path to your new evidence file if one does not exist. Locate your new evidence file in the right pane of the Add Device window and complete the steps to bring the evidence file into your new case. Once it has been added, click Save.

- In the Tree pane, select the root of your case tree, forcing the newly added device into the Table view pane. From the table view pane, select the device. In the View pane, select the Report tab and confirm that the evidence file verified.

- Return to the Tree view pane and select the newly added device. It should contain one folder, named FileSignatureAnalysis. Select that folder and the ten files in that folder should appear in the Table view pane. Arrange your columns to optimize them for file signature analysis. Arrange them, from left to right, as follows: Name, File Ext, Signature, File Type, and File Category.

- In the Table view pane, switch to the Gallery view. EnCase sees three files with extensions that indicate they are pictures and attempts to show all three, but only two are visible. Switch back to the Table view. Click the Dixon box to place a checkmark in it to select all files in your case.

- Click Search on the toolbar. Click the options Selected Files Only and Verify File Signatures. Click Start and the process should complete in seconds.

- In the Table view, sort the Signature column by double-clicking on the column head. Add a secondary sort on the File Ext column by holding down the Shift key and double-clicking on its column head.

- The first file in the list should be a JPEG file with a bad or corrupted header. If you look at the data in the Hex view, you'll see that the header does not match that of a JPEG header. Since it matches nothing else either, it is reported as "!Bad signature". The file name clearly spells out its contents.

- The second file in the list is a Thumbs.db file, which is created when a user opts for the thumbnail view in Windows Explorer.

- The third file in the list is a JPEG image file with its extension renamed to .dll. EnCase is now correctly reporting it in the "File Category" column as a picture along with its alias of *JPEG. The fourth and fifth files are much like the third file in that their extensions, or lack thereof, were causing them to be incorrectly reported and viewed. The file signature analysis remedied that situation and since it is now reported in the "File Category" column as a picture, EnCase will now display it as such in all views in which pictures are shown.

- The sixth file in the list is the anomaly we discussed where a text file (TXT), which has no header, contains a string where a header would be found that matches a known header. EnCase reports this file based on its header even though it is a valid text file. Note carefully the first two characters of the text file as they are PK, which is the header for a zip file.

- Files 7 through 10 are examples of various files that match.

- File 11 has both an unknown header and an unknown extension and is reported as unknown.

- Switch to the Gallery view in the Table view pane. EnCase reports six files now as pictures and attempts to display them. One fails to display as its header is corrupted. EnCase is now displaying images it did not display before the file signature analysis.

- Save your case and exit. You may use this evidence and case file at any time you need to quickly review the file signature analysis and reporting.

# Hash Analysis

When we discussed acquisitions and verifications in Chapter 4, we covered the concept of hashing using the MD5 algorithm. An MD5 hashing algorithm, like other hashing algorithms, can be applied to any stream of data. All that is needed is a starting point and an ending point. In the context of acquisitions, the hashes were of volume and physical devices. In this section, we take a more granular approach and conduct our hashing at the file level.

# MD5 Hash

As you recall, an MD5 hash is an algorithm that is calculated against a stream of data with the end result being a 128-bit value that is unique to that stream of data, be that stream a device, volume, file, or a stream of network data. The odds of any two dissimilar files having the same MD5 is one in $2^{128}$, which is 340 billion billion billion billion and some change. The resultant statistical value is such that you can infer that the only file that will produce the same hash value as that file is an exact duplicate of that file. Said another way, if two files have the same hash value, we can safely infer that the two files are identical in content. The inverse of this is also true, in that if two files produce different hash values, those files do not have the exact same content. A file's name can be the same or different, and it doesn't matter which because the hash calculation is conducted on the data contained in the file only and the file's name is stored elsewhere. These concepts form the basis of hash analysis.

# Hash Sets and Hash Libraries

When a file is hashed, the result is one hash value of one file. A hash set is a collection of one or more hash values that are grouped together because of common characteristics. The hash set may be a collection of hash values from a hacking tool such as SubSeven. In such a case, the hash values for that program are calculated and then gathered together into a group of values and given a label, for example, SubSeven. Hash set examples could be Windows XP program files, case "xyz contraband files," and the like.

EnCase has a feature that allows you to import hash sets from external sources. EnCase also lets you create custom hash sets at your discretion.

First, we'll create a custom hash set. The process is very simple. Before you can create a hash set, the files you wish to include in the set must first have an associated hash value. To generate a hash value for a file or group of files, select the files for hashing by placing a blue check in the box at the extreme left of the row in the Table view. Make sure you clear the Dixon box first. To select all the files in a case, you can use the Dixon box or the top level in the Tree pane view. To select files at folder or device levels, place a blue check in the Tree pane view at the desired level, and all files and folders from that level down will be selected.

Once you have selected your files for hashing, click Search on the toolbar. As with file signature analysis, file hashing is enabled through the Search dialog box. You can conduct searches, file signature analysis, and file hashing simultaneously by selecting all those options, or you can run them separately by selecting them separately. As shown in Figure 8.9, we are going to limit the task to computing hash values only by clicking Selected Files Only and Compute Hash Values, leaving all other options unchecked. We click Start to begin the task.

You may select Recompute Hash Values if you are making your acquisition over the network and there is a concern that the hash values may have changed since they were first computed.

**FIGURE 8.9** File hashing is enabled by checking Compute Hash Values in the Search dialog box.

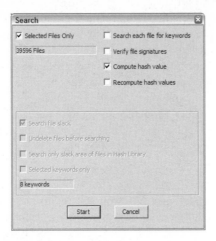

When the task or thread completes, a status report is displayed as shown in Figure 8.10. You can see the number of files processed and the start and end times. In this case, you can see that almost 40,000 files were hashed in less than 3 minutes. Combining the task of hashing with searching will slow down the job considerably. If you opt to, you can include the hashing summary in your bookmarks by selecting Note before clicking OK.

**FIGURE 8.10** Our status report provides information on the processed task along with the option to bookmark the report.

At this point, you have created a hash value for all selected files, and the column Hash Value is populated for all files that were selected for hashing. To create a hash set, first click on the Dixon box to clear all selections. Next, select only the files you wish to include in your hash set. Once you have selected the desired files for inclusion, right-click in the Table view pane and choose Create Hash Set. The hash set will be created from all selected files, so once again make sure you are including only the files you intend in this option. Your options are shown in Figure 8.11. You need simply supply a name for the hash set and assign a category.

**FIGURE  8.11**    In the Create Hash Set dialog box, supply a name for the hash set and assign it to a category, usually Known or Notable.

The name for the hash set should be brief and describe clearly the contents of the files represented by their hash values in this set. In our example, we named them **OSX_Desktop_Photo_Options**. Usually system files such as these are innocuous and are categorized as Known so they can be eliminated from processing or view. In this example, however, we were interested in determining if those files were copied and appear elsewhere in our case. For this reason, we will consider them as Notable and categorize them as such. When it comes to assigning a Known or Notable status, keep in mind that we are forcing hashes into one of two categories. Many of the filters or conditions will operate on these two strings ("Known" and "Notable"), and both spelling and case sensitivity are important. When you click OK, the hash set is created and placed in the root of the Hash Sets view.

Switch to the Hash Sets view by tabbing to it on the Global tab bar or by accessing it from the View menu. If you have a large number of hash sets, it may take a while to load them into the Hash Sets view. In the Tree pane of the Hash Sets view, most examiners typically have nothing more than the root, which is hash sets. In the Table view to the right is typically a flat file listing of all the hash sets. The hash sets are individual files with the extension .hash, and they are stored in the folder Program Files\EnCase5\Hash Sets. The file name is derived from the name you assigned when you created the hash set.

While a flat file arrangement obviously works, arranging hash sets in a folder structure provides a much better interface for managing and selecting hash sets from which to build hash libraries, which we cover very soon. By creating folders in the Tree pane and moving hash sets into them, you are simultaneously creating folders in the Windows environment and moving files between those Windows folders. This differs from most EnCase views in which the folders created are virtual folders within EnCase and have no corresponding Windows folders and files.

By creating a folder structure like the one shown in Figure 8.12, you ensure that hash sets are contained in organized folders and the folder's contents can be selected with one click. With a large flat file, the selection process requires more effort.

**FIGURE  8.12**    The Hash Sets view with organized folders created in the Tree pane to contain different categories of hashes. Note the one hash set we just created is in the root and not yet placed in a folder.

| | | Name | Filter | In Report | Category | Count |
|---|---|---|---|---|---|---|
| | 1 | Child Porn | | No | | |
| | 2 | Known | | No | | |
| | 3 | Other Notable | | No | | |
| | 4 | OSX_Desktop_Photo_Options | | No | Notable | 74 |

Our goal in visiting the Hash Sets view is to place the hash set we just created in an appropriate folder and to include it in the hash library. First, we click and drag it to the appropriate container folder, which in our example we are placing in the Other Notable folder. Next we select all files in the Hash Sets view by placing a blue check at the root level. Our final step is to build a hash library from all the selected hash sets.

A hash library is the total collection of hash sets that have been selected for inclusion in the hash library. The hash library, in turn, consists of the hash values that will be used for analysis and comparison with data loaded in the EnCase case. To build or rebuild this library, right-click in either the Table or Tree pane and select Rebuild Hash Library. The library automatically rebuilds and when it finishes, you are presented with a message box informing you of the completion and of the number of hash sets that were included in the hash library, as shown in Figure 8.13. Click OK to finish the task. The hash set we created is now included in the hash library.

**FIGURE 8.13** When the hash library has been rebuilt, a message box informs you the task is completed and provides a count of the number of hash sets in the hash library.

EnCase has a feature for importing National Software Reference Library (NSRL) hash sets. Simply download the set in a zip file. Extract the zip file into the folder Program Files\EnCase5\Hash Sets\. Launch EnCase and from the Hash Sets view, right-click and choose Import NSRL. You will browse to the folder containing the file NSRLFile.txt. Once you select that file and click Open, the import process will run. When it is completed, right-click on the root of hash sets and choose Update. When done, your NSRL hash sets will be available in a folder named NSRL. You may view them from this folder. You may need to edit categories to suit your circumstances and needs. EnCase also supports importing "Hashkeeper" hash sets. Instead of choosing "Import NSRL," choose instead "Import Hashkeeper" and you will be prompted to browse to the "Hashkeeper" files with the ".hke" extensions.

# Hash Analysis

Once you have calculated hash values for the files in your case and you have built or rebuilt your hash library, you are in a position to reap the benefits afforded by hash values. Recall that when conducting a search for keywords that one of the search options was to Search Only Slack Area Of Files In Hash Library, which is shown in Figure 8.14. With this option selected, files identified by their hash values as being in the hash library are not subjected to the search process.

By eliminating known files from the search, the searching process is much faster, yet the slack area of these files, which can harbor evidence from previous files, is thoroughly searched. For this option to work, you must have previously computed hash values for the selected files or you must select Compute Hash Values when you search using this option.

WARNING

When you select hash sets for inclusion in the hash library and you subsequently conduct an analysis using those hash values, you are locating files meeting criteria contained in those hash values. Thus, you are imposing a search on the files in the case by this process. When selecting hash sets for inclusion in your hash library, make certain you are within the scope of your search authority, whatever that may be in your particular case. Let's assume your search authority in a case was limited to evidence relating to an embezzlement. If you included known child pornography hash sets in your hash library and located child pornography using hash analysis, you have most likely exceeded the scope of your search authority in most jurisdictions. Make sure hash sets that are in your hash library are included or covered within the scope of your search authority!

**FIGURE  8.14**    Choosing Search Only Slack Area Of Files In Hash Library eliminates known files from the search based on their hash values, speeding up the search and yet still enabling the search of their slack areas.

There is more than one way to conduct an analysis using hash values. A simple method is to arrange the columns to optimize for hash analysis. To do so, rearrange them so they are, from left to right, Name, Hash Value, Hash Set, and Hash Category. Use the Set Included Folders option in the Tree pane at the case level, which forces all folders and files to show in the Table view. In the Table view, sort on the Hash Category column by double-clicking on its column head. Add a secondary sort to the Hash Set column by holding down the Shift key and double-clicking on its column head. Files are sorted first by their hash category and second by their hash set.

In the Table view pane, place your cursor on any row, but specifically in the column Hash Category, and press N on the keyboard. If there are any notable hash values, you are immediately looking at them, as shown in Figure 8.15.

**FIGURE 8.15** Columns have been sorted first by hash category and second by hash set. Place the cursor in the Hash Category column and press N. This scrolls you to the notable hash values, which are sorted and grouped together.

| | | Name | Hash Value | Hash Set | Hash Category |
|---|---|---|---|---|---|
| ☐ | 2003 | java.security | 247e22567c02a5ccbadf7d64897e0c5b | Z00246 Netscape 6-0 | Known |
| ☐ | 2004 | LINEAR_RGB.pf | a387b65159c9887265babdef9ca8dae5 | Z00246 Netscape 6-0 | Known |
| ☐ | 2005 | Mac OS Background | e615fa9f27b73bfe17829i8aed77a9a0 | OSX_Desktop_Photo_Options | Notable |
| ☑ | 2006 | 🗀 Desktop Pictures | 59971c53b69bc9314a0f080a2d0f4b59 | OSX_Desktop_Photo_Options | Notable |
| ☑ | 2007 | 🗀 3D Graphics | a05e5f6f2d36da892bbc806711ca95 | OSX_Desktop_Photo_Options | Notable |
| ☑ | 2008 | UFO 2·Resource | dd4dc04cab76610e988157275300d05a | OSX_Desktop_Photo_Options | Notable |
| ☑ | 2009 | UFO 2 | 243893b8e8f6ffefd5211e72d07de4d1 | OSX_Desktop_Photo_Options | Notable |
| ☑ | 2010 | UFO 1·Resource | cb54685dabdd24dcb8d8b56a75e6b3c2 | OSX_Desktop_Photo_Options | Notable |
| ☑ | 2011 | UFO 1 | 054a25a6fd18989c38a1b0b9ed11c740 | OSX_Desktop_Photo_Options | Notable |
| ☑ | 2012 | Tub·Resource | 8f3c413a11ae75bbc2b0af6efb461025 | OSX_Desktop_Photo_Options | Notable |
| ☑ | 2013 | Tub | 79a29a26cf22bccf89326a66f6502d8e | OSX_Desktop_Photo_Options | Notable |
| ☑ | 2014 | Capsule | d9afc8c13765c91123d6ac35a8095351 | OSX_Desktop_Photo_Options | Notable |
| ☑ | 2015 | Capsule·Resource | 015b9e673936c23a67f0815498f9015f | OSX_Desktop_Photo_Options | Notable |
| ☑ | 2016 | 🗀 Convergency | f0f3c7eecb36cb323c461e5b4bd9d277 | OSX_Desktop_Photo_Options | Notable |
| ☑ | 2017 | Convergence 4 | de0bc838be64f02e8aaa74de57c9254b | OSX_Desktop_Photo_Options | Notable |
| ☑ | 2018 | Convergence 4·Resource | 49cc41f387869b03db4ea02e27974902 | OSX_Desktop_Photo_Options | Notable |

Another method of analyzing files by their hash values is to use conditions, which are filters with a simple GUI for user input. Perhaps we wish to sort by some other criteria such as time and see what notable files are in the case. Using a date and time sort and a condition for notable files, we can display only notable files in chronological order.

To do so, rearrange your columns to bring your created, accessed, and last-written dates and times next to the name column. Next, you should sort on a date and time appropriate to the case. We'll sort on the file created date only. Next, tab to the Conditions view in the Filter pane. On the conditions tree, browse to the condition Hash Conditions | Notable Files and double-click it. The filter loads, parses through the case, and when done only files whose hash value is categorized as Notable are in view, presented in chronological order based on our sort.

As mentioned earlier, the default conditions that enable the hash sets filtering rely on the strings "Known" and "Notable." For these conditions to produce accurate results, be sure to exercise care with case and spelling when creating and importing hash sets. More than once, I've seen these categories incorrectly spelled while importing hash sets from examiners who are super folks and willing to share their work, but unfortunately there is no spell checker within most forensic tools.

Hash analysis can assist you by cutting down on searches by eliminating known files. It can also assist you in rapidly locating files that can be identified from databases of known contraband or inappropriate content files, such as child pornography, adult pornography, hacking tools, and the like. Keep your hash sets up to date and share them when you develop unique sets. You should conduct your hash analysis early on in your case so the benefits can be realized from that point forward in your examination.

## Hash Analysis

In this exercise, we'll take a hash set created by an examiner in another jurisdiction to determine if files found in one of their cases is also present in your case. In doing so, you will add a hash set, rebuild your hash library, and conduct a hash analysis. Don't be surprised, however, if you encounter some data hiding along the way and find the need to apply some other previously learned skills. Let's get started.

- An examiner has contacted you to assist in an investigation. This examiner has checked a machine belonging to a suspected terrorist and among his findings were numerous images of aerial reconnaissance and images of critical port and shipping facilities. You are about to examine a piece of media from a person who is believed to be another member of this same group. The other examiner is sending you a hash set that he created of the aerial images to see if the images he found are also present on the suspect's media that you are examining.

- Before starting EnCase, take the hash set file from the examiner (located on CD in the folder HashSet\AerialReconPhotosFromTerrGroupMember.Hash) and place the file in the folder Program Files\EnCase5\Hash Sets\. If you have a folder structure under Hash Sets, such as Notable or Other Notable, place this notable hash set in an appropriately named folder.

- Create a folder structure for a new case according to our standard folder naming and structuring conventions. Name your case folder name **SuspectedTerrorist**. Start EnCase and create a new case, pointing it to your newly created folders. Before you place any evidence in your case, save your case in the root of the folder SuspectedTerrorist, which will also be the default name for your case. Locate an evidence file on the CD named HashAnalysisExercise\SuspectedTerrorist.E01. Place it in the evidence folder for your newly created case.

- On the toolbar, click Add Device. Create a path to your new evidence file if one does not exist. Locate your new evidence file in the right pane of the Add Device window and complete the steps to bring the evidence file into your new case. Once it has been added, click Save.

- In the Tree pane, select the root of your case tree, forcing the newly added device into the Table view pane. From the Table view pane, select the device. In the View pane, select the Report tab and confirm that the evidence file verified.

- Return to the Tree view pane and select the newly added device. If you preview the files and folders on the device, you will see hundreds of deleted files with invalid clusters, with the extension .t~p. These are residual files left behind from a free-space wiping utility. (First hint!)

**EXERCISE 8.2** *(continued)*

- Let's start with our hash analysis. We have the hash set file from the other examiner in with our other hash sets. It is in EnCase's native hash set file format and no import is needed, but we do need to add it to our hash library. Go to the Hash Sets view and make sure you can see the hash set you added in the folder, which is AerialReconPhotosFromTerrGroup-Member. At the Tree pane root level, place a blue check at the root level to select all hash sets (including the one you just added). Right-click and choose Rebuild Hash Library. When done, click OK.

- Go back to the Case Entries view and let's next hash our files. Using the Dixon box, select all files in your case, which should be 759 files. Click Search on the toolbar. Select the options Selected Files Only and Compute Hash Value. Click Start. The status report should indicate that six hash values were generated, as nearly all the files in this case are residual file names with no associated data.

- Place your Set Included Folders trigger at the root of your case to show all files in the Table view pane. In the Filters pane (lower right), go to the Conditions tab and locate Hash Conditions | Notable Files. Double-click on the Notable Files condition and the Table view should reflect only files with notable hash values. In this case, there are none. Do we release our suspect or do we look a little deeper? Let's look deeper.

- In the images folder, we hashed a zip file and not its component files. We are looking for images, so perhaps that is a good place to dig deeper. Locate the file Images\Images.zip. In the Table view, right-click on Images.zip and select View File Structure. Click OK on the next screen and EnCase will mount the zip file, revealing the compressed files as individual files. Note that the Dixon box has changed and you have selected only 759 or 769 files, as mounting the zip file added files to the case. On the Dixon box, click once to clear the selections. In the Tree pane, place a blue check in the Zip Volume check box and 10 files should now be selected. You could look at the mounted files in the Gallery view, but you don't know for sure what the images are you are seeking. You know only their hash values.

- Let's hash those mounted files. Click Search on the toolbar. Select the options Selected Files Only and Compute Hash Value. Click Start. The status report should indicate that nine hash values were generated.

- Place your Set Included Folders trigger at Zip Volume to show all files in the mounted volume only in the Table view pane. In the Filters pane (lower right), go to the Conditions tab and locate Hash Conditions | Notable Files. Double-click on the Notable Files condition and the Table view should reflect only files with notable hash values. In this case, once again, there are none. Do we release our suspect or do we look a little deeper? Let's look deeper.

- We seemed to have forgotten the first part of this chapter, which was file signature analysis. Let's see what benefits can be derived from this tool. On the Dixon box, clear all files and select all files in the case. Click Search and choose Selected Files Only and Verify File Signatures. Click Start and when done click OK.

- In the Tree pane, place the Set Included Folders trigger at the root to show all files in the case in the Table view pane. In the Filters pane (lower right), go to the Conditions tab and locate Signature Conditions | Renamed Extensions. Double-click on the Renamed Extensions Files condition and the Table view should reflect only files whose extensions have been renamed. In this case, there is a file named HDCapCalc.dll with a renamed extension. EnCase is reporting to us that its alias is *ZIP Compressed file. Let's mount it and see what its contents are.

- Right-click on the file HDCapCalc.dll and choose View File Structure. Click OK and the file will mount, revealing its contents. Before we can see those contents, we must first turn off the condition by toggling off the condition on the toolbar. Place your Set Included Folders trigger on the HDCapCalc.dll Zip Volume and you will see a series of image files in the Table view pane. If you switch to the Gallery view, you can see that they appear to be aerial images of the sort described by the other examiner, but we need to know for sure they are exactly the same images. We make that determination by hashing those mounted files and comparing those values to the values provided by the other examiner in the hash set file.

- Clear the selected files in the case by clicking once on the Dixon box. In the Tree pane under the virtual folder named HDCapCalc.dll, place a blue check in the Zip Volume check box and seven files should now be selected.

- Let's hash those mounted and selected files. Click Search on the toolbar. Choose Selected Files Only and Compute Hash Value. Click Start. The status report should indicate that six hash values were generated.

- Place your Set Included Folders trigger at Zip Volume of HDCapCalc.dll to show all files in the mounted volume only in the Table view pane. In the Filters pane (lower right), go to the Conditions tab and locate Hash Conditions | Notable Files. Double-click on the Notable Niles condition, and the Table view should reflect only files with notable hash values; in this case there are four. If you switch to the Gallery view, you are now looking at four images that are identical to the files found by the other examiner.

- Save your case. It's also time to pick up the phone and call the other examiner with the results. It's a good thing you drilled a little deeper into the case!

If you'd like, you can copy out the program and documentation for the hard drive capacity calculator. It is free and calculates hard drive capacities based on CHS (legacy) or absolute sectors. Normal output is based on capacity; however, you can also force the output into MB, GB, or TB as needed. There is a comprehensive program guide that is in a Word document in the subfolder with the program.

# Summary

In this chapter, we covered file signature analysis and hash analysis. File signature analysis is a tool used within EnCase to identify a file by its header information, if it exists, rather than by the default method, which is file extension. File header and extension information is stored in a database in the file FileSignatures.ini. File signature information can be added, deleted, or modified in the File Signatures view, which is a global view.

Until a file signature analysis is run, EnCase relies on a file's extension to determine its file type, which will in turn determine the viewer used to display the data. A file signature analysis is initiated or run from the Search dialog box. Once a file signature analysis is run EnCase will view files based on file header information and not based on file extension. This is critical for viewing files whose extensions are missing or have been changed.

After a file signature analysis has been run, EnCase reports the results in the column named Signature. If a file's header and extension information are correct and match the information in the database, EnCase will report a match. If there is no matching header for a file and no matching extension, EnCase will report the file as Unknown. If a file's extension is in the database and the file's header does not match the header in the database for the file's extension and further does not match any other header in the database, EnCase will report the file as having a bad signature. Finally, if a file's header is in the database and the extension is missing or doesn't match for the header, the signature has precedence in determining file type and the file's alias is reported in the Signature column, preceded by an asterisk.

File hashing and analysis, within EnCase, are based on the MD5 hashing algorithm. When a file is hashed using the MD5, the result is a 128-bit value. The odds of any two dissimilar files having the same MD5 hash is one in $2^{128}$ or approximately one in 340 billion billion billion billion. Using this method one can safely statistically infer the file content will be the same for files that have identical hash values, and the file content will differ for files that do not have identical hash values.

The MD5 hash thus forms a unique electronic fingerprint by which files can be identified. Using this method files are hashed and collected in sets for files having similar characteristics. These groupings of hash values are called hash sets. Each set is given a name describing the group of files represented by the hash values. Furthermore each hash set is assigned to a hash category, usually Known or Notable.

Files are hashed from within the Search dialog box. Once files have been hashed and have hash values, you can create hash sets by selecting files, right-clicking, and choosing Create Hash Sets. Hash sets are stored as individual files, with the file name being the name of the hash set and the extension .hash. They are stored in the Hash Sets folder under the EnCase5 folder.

Hash sets are managed from the Hash Sets view. Hash sets can be organized into folders, added, deleted, or modified. Also from this view, hash sets can be imported from NSRL or Hashkeeper hash databases. From this view, selected hash sets are placed into the hash library, which is a collection of hash sets by which files currently viewed within EnCase will be compared and analyzed. Once hash sets are selected, the hash library is created from the right-click menu option Rebuild Hash Library.

Once files have been hashed, each file's hash value is listed. If during the comparison process the hash value matches any value in the hash library, its hash category and hash set are also reported. Using this method, you can identify known files of various types. Known system and program files can be eliminated from further examination and searching, thereby saving time. Files that are notable for various reasons (hacking tools, contraband files, etc.) can be identified and appropriate action taken.

Hash analysis and file signature analysis should both be carried out in the beginning of your examination so that their benefits may be utilized at the outset. Reporting or output from both tools can be analyzed by sorting on appropriate columns. In addition, various conditions are available to assist with both file signature analysis and hash analysis. Both tools provide information to EnCase internally and to the examiner that greatly assist in the speed and accuracy of the examination process.

# Exam Essentials

**Know and understand the file signature process.** Understand and explain what a file header is. Be able to explain what a file extension is and how it is used in a Windows environment. Understand how a file type and category is determined before and after the file signature analysis process. Understand how EnCase views files and the importance of the file signature analysis to the proper viewing of file types.

**Understand the purpose and function of the File Signature view.** Know where the file signature database is stored. Explain how a file signature is created, modified, or deleted. Be able to explain what information is stored in a file signature record.

**Understand and interpret the results of the file signature analysis.** Know and understand what constitutes a file signature match; a bad signature; an unknown signature; and a file signature "alias." Explain how to use EnCase's column sorting features or file signature conditions to analyze or view the results of the file signature analysis.

**Know and understand file hashing and analysis.** Understand and be able to explain the MD5 algorithm. Know the length of an MD5 hash and the approximate odds of any two dissimilar files having the same MD5 hash value. Explain the significance of files having the same or different hash values. Explain the concept of an MD5 hash being an "electronic fingerprint."

**Know and understand what constitutes a hash set.** Explain how to hash a file. Explain what a hash set is and how it is created. Understand and be able to describe the process of naming and categorizing hash sets. Know where hash sets are stored and be able to explain their file naming convention.

**Understand the purpose and function of the Hash Sets view.** Explain what tasks can be carried out in the Hash Sets view. Understand and be able to explain the difference between hash sets and hash libraries. Explain the purpose of the hash library and how one is created.

**Understand and interpret the results of the file signature analysis.** Describe the information provided in the hash category and hash set columns. Be able to explain what it means when a file has a hash value that returns a Notable value in the Hash Category column. Explain the importance of hash analysis in reducing search times. Understand and be able to explain how to use EnCase's column sorting features and hash conditions to analyze or view file hashing results.

# Review Questions

1. When running a signature analysis, EnCase will:

   **A.** Compare a file's header to its hash value.

   **B.** Compare a file's header to its file signature.

   **C.** Compare a file's hash value to its file extension.

   **D.** Compare a file's header to its file extension.

2. A file header is:

   **A.** A unique set of characters at the beginning of a file that identifies the file type

   **B.** A unique set of characters following the file name that identifies the file type

   **C.** A 128-bit value that is unique to a specific file based on its data

   **D.** Synonymous with file extension

3. The Windows operating system uses a file name's _____ to associate files with the proper applications.

   **A.** Signature

   **B.** MD5 hash value

   **C.** Extension

   **D.** Metadata

4. Linux/Unix operating systems use a file's _____ to associate file types to specific applications.

   **A.** Metadata

   **B.** Header

   **C.** Extension

   **D.** Hash value

5. The Mac OS X operating system uses which of the following file information to associate a file to a specific application?

   **A.** "User Defined" setting

   **B.** File name extension

   **C.** Metadata (Creator Code)

   **D.** All of the above

6. Information regarding a file's header information and extension is saved by EnCase in the _____ file.

   **A.** FileSignatures.ini

   **B.** FileExtensions.ini

   **C.** FileInformation.ini

   **D.** FileHeader.ini

**7.** When a file's signature is unknown and a valid file extension exists, EnCase will display the following result after a signature analysis is performed:

**A.** Alias (Signature Mismatch)

**B.** !Bad Signature

**C.** Unknown

**D.** Match

**8.** When a file's signature is known and the file extension does not match, EnCase will display the following result after a signature analysis is performed:

**A.** Alias (Signature Mismatch)

**B.** !Bad Signature

**C.** Unknown

**D.** Match

**9.** When a file's signature is known and the file extension matches, EnCase will display the following result after a signature analysis is performed:

**A.** Alias (Signature Mismatch)

**B.** !Bad Signature

**C.** Unknown

**D.** Match

**10.** When a file's signature and extension are not recognized, EnCase will display the following result after a signature analysis is performed:

**A.** Alias (Signature Mismatch)

**B.** !Bad Signature

**C.** Unknown

**D.** Match

**11.** Can a file with a unique header share multiple file extensions?

**A.** Yes

**B.** No

**12.** A user can manually add new file headers and extensions by:

**A.** Manually inputting the data in the FileSignatures.ini file

**B.** Right-clicking the file and choosing Add File Signature

**C.** Choosing File Signatures view, right-clicking, and selecting New under the appropriate folder

**D.** Adding a new file header and extension and then choosing Create Hash Set

**13.** Select the correct answer that completes the following question: An MD5 hash…

**A.** …is a 128-bit value.

**B.** …has odds of one in $2^{128}$ that two dissimilar files will share the same value.

**C.** …is not determined by the file name.

**D.** …all of the above.

**14.** EnCase can create a hash value for the following:

   **A.** Physical devices

   **B.** Logical volumes

   **C.** Files or groups of files

   **D.** All of the above

**15.** What portion of an evidence file does EnCase analyze during the verification process to yield an MD5 hash value?

   **A.** Data area

   **B.** Entire evidence file

   **C.** Case information

   **D.** None of the above

**16.** Will changing a file's name affect the file's MD5 hash value?

   **A.** Yes

   **B.** No

**17.** Normally a hash value found in a hash set named "Windows XP Home Edition" would be reported in the Hash Category column as:

   **A.** Known

   **B.** Notable

   **C.** Evidentiary

   **D.** Nonevidentiary

**18.** With regard to hash categories, evidentiary files or files of interest are categorized as:

   **A.** Known

   **B.** Notable

   **C.** Evidentiary

   **D.** Nonevidentiary

**19.** An MD5 hash of a specific media generated by EnCase will yield the exact same hash value as an independent third-party MD5 hashing utility.

   **A.** Yes

   **B.** No

**20.** A hash _____ is comprised of hash _____, which is comprised of hash _____.

   **A.** set(s), library(ies), value(s)

   **B.** value(s), sets(s), library(ies)

   **C.** library(ies), set(s), value(s)

   **D.** set(s), values(s), library(ies)

# Answers to Review Questions

1. D. A signature analysis will compare a file's header or signature to its file extension.

2. A. A file header identifies the type of file and is located in the beginning of the file's data area.

3. C. The Windows operating system uses a file's extension to associate the file with the proper application.

4. B. Linux/Unix operating systems uses a file's header information to associate file types to specific applications.

5. D. When determining which application to use to open a file, Mac OS X gives first precedence to "user defined" settings, second precedence to "creator code" metadata, and third precedence to "file name extension." If none of these are present, other rules come into play.

6. A. Information about a file's header and extension is saved in the FileSignatures.ini file.

7. B. When a file's signature is unknown and a valid extension is present, EnCase will display the status as being "!Bad Signature."

8. A. When a file's signature is known and an inaccurate file extension is present, EnCase reports the Alias in the File Signature Column and may update the File Category column.

9. D. When a file's signature is known and an accurate file extension is present, EnCase will display the result as a match.

10. C. When a file's signature and extension are not recognized, EnCase will display the result as unknown.

11. A. A unique file header can share multiple file extensions. An example of such as case is a .JPEG or .JPG file which share the same file header \xFF\xD8\xFF[\xFE\xE0\xE1].

12. C. A user can manually add new file headers and extensions by accessing the File Signatures views and creating a new header and extension under the appropriate folder.

13. D. An MD5 hash is a 128-bit hash value and the odds of two different files having the same value is one in $2^{128}$. A file's MD5 hash value is based on the file's data area, not its file name, which resides outside the data area.

14. D. EnCase can calculate hash values for any of the above.

15. A. EnCase will only analyze the data area of an evidence file during the verification process.

16. B. Merely changing a file's name will not affect its MD5 hash value because the hash value is based on the file's data, not its file name.

**17.** A. These hash sets have been produced from known safe sources and are categorized as "Known." In most cases they are non-evidentiary and can be ignored when conducting searches and other analyses.

**18.** B. Evidentiary files or files of interest are categorized as Notable.

**19.** A. Regardless of the MD5 hashing utility, the hash value generated will have the same result, as the MD5 hash is an industry standard algorithm.

**20.** C. A hash library is comprised of hash sets, which are comprised of hash values.

# Chapter

# 9

# Windows Operating System Artifacts

---

**ENCE EXAM TOPICS COVERED IN THIS CHAPTER:**

- ✓ Windows dates and times
- ✓ Adjusting for time zone offsets
- ✓ Recycle Bin and INFO records
- ✓ Link files
- ✓ Windows 2000 and XP folders
- ✓ Recent folder
- ✓ Desktop folder
- ✓ My Documents folder
- ✓ Send To Folder
- ✓ Temp folders
- ✓ Favorites folder
- ✓ Cookies folder
- ✓ History folder
- ✓ Temporary Internet files
- ✓ Swap file
- ✓ Hibernation file
- ✓ Printing artifacts

Just a few years ago when Microsoft was announcing the release of Windows XP, many examiners were proclaiming the end of computer forensics. They claimed that the new security features of Windows XP were going to virtually eliminate all forms of *artifacts* and other evidence. Of the folks making these dire warnings, some were among the "who's who" of computer forensics. Windows XP arrived, and just like its predecessor (Windows 2000), it offered more operating system artifacts than did any release of Windows to date. In fact, artifacts are still being discovered as of press time, and no doubt more will be forthcoming.

As operating systems grew more complex, they simply stored more data. As operating systems evolved and became more complex, paradoxically their user interface had to simplify so that computers could be used easily by the below-average user. To facilitate this interface and its ease of use, the operating system had to store even more information about the user, their actions, preferences, and credentials. The result of such data storage is an environment that is loaded with logs, files, lists, passwords, caches, history, recently used lists, and other data. Some is in plain text, some is obscured, and some is encrypted (albeit weak encryption for the most part). As a general category or label, we refer to this type of data or information as *operating system artifacts*. Most important, this data can be used to as evidence to identify users and their computing activities.

The subject of Windows operating system artifacts could well fill several books. Clearly such an endeavor is well beyond the intent and purpose of this guide. In this chapter, our focus is on developing a solid understanding of the more common operating system artifacts rather than trying to cover them all.

# Dates and Times

It is difficult to approach any Windows operating system artifact without some prior appreciation for how Windows stores and uses dates and times. Dates and times are ubiquitous on any modern operating system. Their uses are countless and their storage formats vary. Sometimes they are stored in local time and sometimes in Greenwich Mean Time (GMT, also known as Universal Time or Zulu Time). Sometimes, usually involving Internet-related data, the times are local to the time zone where they were generated and not necessarily local to the host computer. If there was ever a topic that will cause you to pause and scratch your head in this business, the time issue is at or near the top of the list.

One need only look at the forensic list servers and message boards to see the questions related to date and time stamps. While it is great to pose questions and have them answered by other examiners, there is no substitute for research and testing by the individual examiner. Once you have tested and validated your findings, only then will you have a true understanding and first-hand knowledge as, until then, it is only hearsay!

# Time Zones

Before attempting to understand how time is stored and interpreted, we must first understand the context in which it is being interpreted. By *context*, we are referring to the time zone reference in which the time was stored. Because the world is divided into time zones and computers must keep track of time relative to those time zones, the various operating systems must implement methods to account for time zone differences. In order that you may accurately interpret date and time stamps, you must understand how operating systems and EnCase resolve these differences. While each operating system has its own method, we are going to limit our discussion to the Windows operating systems.

For Windows file attribute dates and times (modified, accessed, and created, which are often called MAC, or media access control, times), the file system in use determines whether the date and time is stored in local time or in GMT.

When date and time stamps are recorded in a FAT file system, they are stored in the 32-byte DOS directory entry and are stored in local time, which is the time for the time zone in which the computer exists and is configured. This system was developed when computing was more local and less global.

As computing became more global and the Internet evolved, Microsoft developed the NTFS file system and with it implemented a more elaborate and yet more logical time storage scheme. Dates and times stored for file creation, last written, last accessed, and last entry modified are stored in GMT using a 64-bit Windows date and time stamp. The operating system displays dates and times to the user based on the local time zone offset, which is normally set when the system is first configured, but can be adjusted at any time.

Just because a computer was seized in a particular time zone does not mean it is configured for that time zone. Figure 9.1 shows the Windows dialog box in which the time zone is set. As computers can be moved from one zone to another, incorrectly configured, or deliberately altered, the time and time zone offset may not be accurate. To resolve these issues, you need to know the machine's BIOS time and the time zone offset for which it is configured so that you may apply the correct time zone offset to your case.

**FIGURE 9.1**   Windows Date and Time Properties dialog box showing the Time Zone tab from which the user sets the local time zone

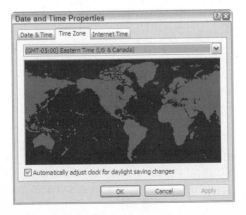

Prior to EnCase 4, you had to change the time zone offset of your examination machine using the dialog box shown in Figure 9.1 to match the time zone of your evidence. Both EnCase 4 and EnCase 5 provide an interface by which the examiner may set a time zone offset at the case or device level so that all devices in a case are in proper time zone synchronization.

Aside from MAC times, as a general rule, you will find that current versions of Windows (2000 and XP), regardless of the file system in use, store most other dates and times in GMT, but there are exceptions. By other dates and times, we are referring to dates and times stored in the Registry, Internet history databases, and other operating system artifacts. Generally you'll be looking to a published source to make such determinations. At other times, you'll be on your own to test and validate the data to make the determination.

## Windows 64-Bit Time Stamp

Before we get into determining time zones and actually making adjustments, let's first examine the Windows 64-bit date and time stamp. This time stamp is one that you'll learn to spot at a glance as you gain experience. Figure 9.2 shows a 64-bit Windows time stamp. It is an 8-byte string (64 bits), and its most significant value is 01h, which is located at the far right of the string as it is stored in little endian. As you'll recall, little endian values are calculated from right to left; thus the most significant byte is on the right and first entered and calculated.

**FIGURE 9.2**    The Windows 64-bit time stamp with the most significant bit (01h) stored to the far right of the 8-byte string

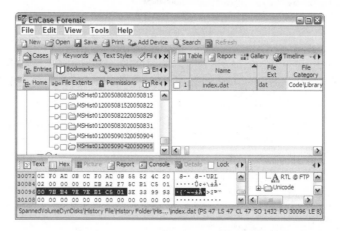

Now that we understand what the time stamp looks like, let's discuss how it tracks time. Let's start with a concept we've already covered. If you'll recall, a Unix time stamp is a 32-bit integer value that represents the number of seconds that have lapsed since epoch, which is January 1, 1970 00:00:00 GMT. It's an incredibly simple concept and with a little math, you can figure that the most number of seconds that can be represented by this value is $2^{32}$, which is the integer value "4,294,967,296."

On Monday, December 2, 2030, at 19:42:58 GMT 4,294,967,296 seconds will have lapsed since epoch and the Unix time stamp will no longer be able to track time as it currently exists. No doubt a new time scheme will replace it, but with everything in computing, legacy issues seem to always persist and cause problems in unanticipated ways. As that time draws near, approximately 25 years from now, we can probably expect another event similar to Y2K.

 Just because the Unix time stamp uses the label "Unix," do not think this date format is limited to Unix machines. The Unix time stamp is used on many platforms and is used heavily on the Internet. You should expect to find the Unix time stamp used frequently on Windows-based machines.

With that understanding of the Unix time stamp, let's look next at the Windows 64-bit time stamp. Instead of a 32-bit integer used by Unix, Windows uses a 64-bit integer. Rather than tracking seconds like Unix, Windows tracks the number of 100-nanosecond intervals (10- millionth of a second intervals). And finally, instead of starting on January 1, 1970 00:00:00 GMT like Unix, Windows starts on January 1, 1601, at 00:00:00 GMT.

Some basic math tells us that $2^{64}$ (64-bit value) can represent a maximum integer value of 18,446,744,073,709,500,000. If you divide this number by the number of 100-nanosecond intervals that tick by in a year, which is a paltry figure at 315,576,000,000,000, you find that this time stamp can address a date range of 58,000 plus years starting at 1601. It is clear that Microsoft was looking to the future when they created this one!

To show this at work, let's look at two Windows 64-bit date stamps that are shown in Figure 9.3. In this figure you can see two time stamps. The first one is selected and the second one, which follows immediately, is bookmarked. These are time stamps appearing in an index.dat file for the daily Internet history. In this particular file the two time stamps are identical except that the first date is stored in local time and the second date is stored in GMT. This is one of those cases where Windows deviates from the norm and stores a time in local time. As the local time offset for this host computer is Eastern Time (GMT -0500) and daylight savings time is in effect (making it GMT -0400), we would expect the times to differ by exactly four hours.

In Figure 9.3, the EnCase bookmark feature is used on the selected data (right-click and choose Bookmark Data). When the data is viewed as a Windows date and time, specifically using the Local Time option, the 64-bit value is resolved to the date and time, Sunday, September 4, 2005, 14:28:49. Users of prior versions will note that EnCase 5 now provides for a Windows date and time Local time option that was not available in previous versions. The Local time option resolves time exactly as it is stored and does not apply the offset from GMT thus rendering accurately any time stored as local.

In Figure 9.4, the second date is selected, bookmarked, and viewed as a regular Windows date and time. As this value is stored in GMT, we do not use the Local time view. This value correctly resolves to the exact same date and time as the first date. EnCase applies the local time offset (GMT -0400) to the GMT time that is stored and both time stamps can be resolved accurately.

**FIGURE 9.3**   Two Windows 64-bit time stamps, one stored in local time and the other stored in GMT. As local time is EDT (GMT -0400), the difference between these two time stamps should be exactly four hours.

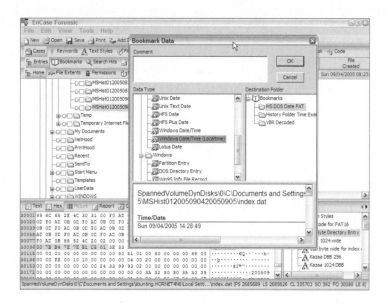

**FIGURE 9.4**   Windows 64-bit time stamp bookmarked and viewed with local offset from GMT applied

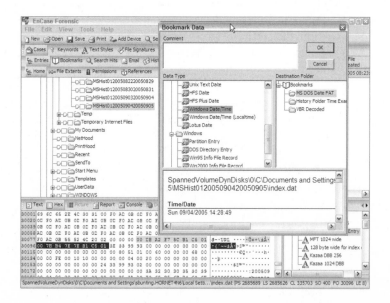

Let's carry this one step further and look at the exact values that are stored. The first date is the hex string "00 DB A2 F7 5C B1 C5 01". Because EnCase doesn't provide a viewer for 64-bit integers, you have to enter this into a scientific calculator. This value is stored in little endian, so you must enter the string in the reverse order, or "01 C5 B1 5C F7 A2 DB 00", as shown in Figure 9.5. After the string is entered in the hex mode, clicking the radio button for the decimal view or mode converts the hex string to an integer value, which is "127,703,177,299,680,000". If we apply the same methodology to the second date hex string "00 7B B4 7E 7E B1 C5 01", we find that it resolves to an integer value of "127,703,321,299,680,000". These two integer values represent the number of 100-nanosecond intervals since January 1, 1601, 00:00:00 GMT.

**FIGURE 9.5**    The Windows 64-bit time stamp is entered in a scientific calculator in reverse order because it is stored in little endian format.

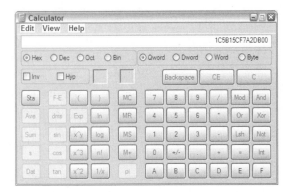

Rather than calculate these two dates from the year 1601, let's look at the difference between the two time stamps, which still examines the underlying principles and does so with somewhat smaller numbers. If we subtract one integer from the other, we find the difference is "144,000,000,000". As we know the difference between these two values is four hours, the difference between the two integers should be the number of 100-nanosecond intervals that occur in four hours. Let's see if that is true.

We know that there are 60 seconds in a minute and 60 minutes in an hour. Therefore there are 3,600 seconds in one hour. In four hours, there are 14,400 seconds. As a 100-nanosecond interval is one 10-millionth of a second, we multiply 14,400 seconds by 10,000,000 to convert seconds to 10-millionth seconds. The result is 144,000,000,000 and matches the difference between the two integers that we know are separated by four hours. We also know that EnCase is properly interpreting the time stamps and offsets, thus validating our tool.

Manually calculating Windows 64-bit time stamps is not something the examiner wishes to do with any degree of frequency, if at all. Fortunately EnCase provides tools to convert these values for you. There is merit, however, in understanding how such dates are generated and stored. You may be asked some day in court, or you may need to engage in research and validation of data or tools. In either event, you'll be better prepared.

# Adjusting for Time Zone Offsets

By now we have an understanding of how Windows stores time stamps, and we also understand the importance of time zone offsets in determining accurate times. It is now time to determine the time zone offset for a system and how to adjust the EnCase environment so it will display properly.

With Windows, the time zone offset is stored in the Registry. The Registry is a large database of system configuration settings. It is stored in several files and is viewed and manipulated with a Registry editor such as regedit, which is a built-in Windows utility. In Chapter 10, we'll cover the Registry in more detail. If you are comfortable mounting and navigating the Registry, or you wish to jump ahead to Chapter 10, the time zone offset can be manually ascertained in the following manner:

1. Determine which control set is the current control set. Mount the system Registry file as you would other compound files by right-clicking and choosing View File Structure, and navigate to System\NTRegistry\Select\Current. View this value as a 32-bit integer value. The value stored here (n) determines which control set is current. In Windows NT/2000, the system Registry key can be found by default in C:\Winnt\System32\Config. For Windows XP/2003, the system Registry key can be found by default in C:\Windows\System32\Config.

2. In the system key, based on the value found above, navigate to the control set matching that number (n), which is the current control set. Under that control set, navigate to System\NTRegistry\ControlSet00n\Control\TimeZoneInformation. Under that key, there are several values that are used to establish the local time zone offset. Table 9.1 lists those values and how they are used to determine the time zone offset.

**TABLE 9.1** TimeZoneInformation Key Values and Their Meaning

| Value Name | Data Type | Description |
|---|---|---|
| ActiveTimeBias | 32-bit integer | The number of minutes offset from GMT for the current system time. |
| Bias | 32-bit integer | Based on the time zone setting, the number of minutes offset from GMT for that time zone. |
| DaylightBias | 32-bit integer | Based on the time zone setting, the number of minutes offset from GMT for that time zone when daylight savings time is in effect. |
| DaylightName | Unicode Text String | The name of the time zone for daylight savings time setting. |

**TABLE 9.1** TimeZoneInformation Key Values and Their Meaning *(continued)*

| Value Name | Data Type | Description |
|---|---|---|
| DaylightStart | Binary (4 two-byte sets; ignore last 8 bytes) | Date and time daylight savings time starts in the format: Day \| Month \| Week \| Hour. Day: first two bytes or 16 bits. Evaluate as 16-bit integer. 7 days of week are numbered 0–6, starting with Sunday (0). Month: second two bytes. Evaluate as 16-bit integer with months numbered 1–12, with January being 1. Week: third two bytes. Evaluate as 16-bit integer with weeks numbered starting with 1. Hour: fourth two bytes. Evaluate as 16-bit integer with hour of the day being when the time will change, based on a 24-hour clock. Example shown in StandardStart. |
| StandardBias | 32-bit integer | Based on the time zone setting, the number of minutes offset from GMT for that time zone when standard time is in effect. |
| StandardName | Unicode Text String | The name of the time zone for standard time setting. |
| StandardStart | Binary (4 two-byte sets; ignore last 8 bytes) | Date and time standard time starts in the format: Day \| Month \| Week \| Hour. All values evaluated as in DaylightStart value. A typical StandardStart value would appear as: 00 00 \| 0A 00 \| 05 00 \| 02 00 Day = 00 00 = 0 = Sunday Month = 0A 00 = 10 = October Week = 05 00 = 5 = 5th week Hour = 02 00 = 2 = 0200 hrs |

The ActiveTimeBias indicates, in minutes, the current offset from GMT. If you are in a time zone that uses daylight savings time and ActiveTimeBias equals the StandardBias, the computer is set for standard time. If the ActiveTimeBias equals the DaylightBias, the computer is set for daylight savings time. The StandardName will indicate the time zone setting for the host computer under examination.

An easier way to derive this information is through the use of the Initialize Case EnScript, in which you can choose to have this information summarized in a concise and informative bookmark. In Chapter 10, we'll cover EnScripts in more detail. For now, you can easily launch the Sweep Case EnScript from the Filter pane and use it for the limited purpose of determining the time zone information. The Initialize Case EnScript is a module of the Sweep Case EnScript. When you open the Initialize Case EnScript menu by double-clicking on Initialize Case, as shown in Figure 9.6, you may select the Timezone option as the output.

**FIGURE 9.6** The Windows Initialize Case dialog box lets you extract and summarize time zone information in a bookmark.

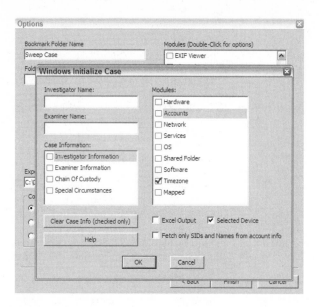

Once you have selected the Timezone option, click OK to close the configuration window for the Initialize Case module. Then click Finish and the EnScript runs. It takes some time to run as it must mount the system Registry hive, extract the information to a "note" bookmark, and then close the mounted Registry. When done, the time zone information is summarized in a bookmark, as shown in Figure 9.7. In the example shown, the time zone offset is Eastern Time, which is GMT -0500 hours.

**FIGURE 9.7** Time zone information summarized in a bookmark. Information was generated by the Sweep Case ➤Initialize Case ➤Timezone EnScript.

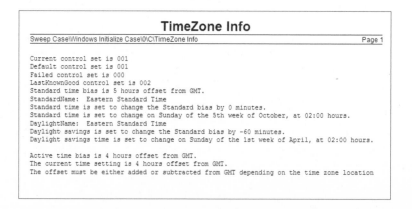

We now have two methods by which to determine the time zone offset for which the host computer is configured. Once that offset is known, the next step is to apply that offset to the case or individual devices if they have differing offsets. When done, all devices will be in sync with regard to time zone and you can examine dates and times accurately.

As this step is critical to an accurate examination when dates and times are at issue, this is a step that should be done at the very outset of your examination. Accordingly, you should include this step in your case processing checklist and place it at the beginning as a standard mandatory step in the process.

To adjust for the time zone offset, go the Tree pane and select the appropriate device, or select the case if all devices in the case have the same time zone offset. Right-click on the case or the device and choose Modify Time Zone Settings, as shown in Figure 9.8.

**FIGURE 9.8**    To adjust for time zone offset, right-click on the case or device and choose Modify Time Zone Settings.

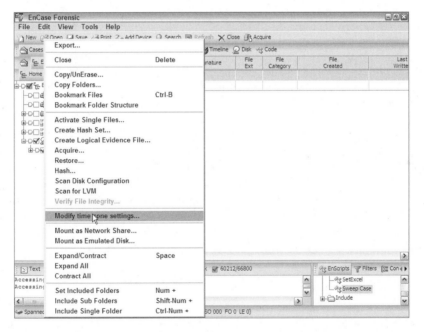

Choosing Modify Time Zone Settings will open the Time Properties dialog box, as shown in Figure 9.9. This dialog box lets you enter the time zone information from your Registry examination or the output of the Timezone EnScript. The dialog box will default to adjusting for daylight savings time unless you opt to turn it off. Unless you have a compelling reason to do otherwise, it is recommended that you adjust for daylight savings time when it is in effect. Once you have entered your settings, click OK and the proper time zone offset will be applied at the case or device level you chose at the outset.

**FIGURE 9.9**    The Time Properties dialog box lets you enter the time zone offset for the selected device or case.

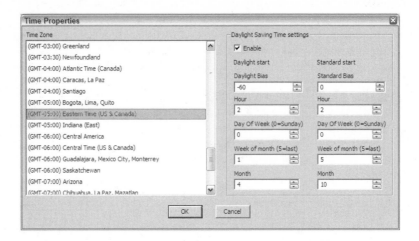

At this point, your device or case will display the time stored in GMT to the accurate local time zone offset. So that we understand how all this ties together, let's examine how the entire process works by looking at a date and time stamp from its point of origin to its interpretation by EnCase.

In our hypothetical example, a suspect is using a computer in Oregon that is running Windows XP and formatted using the NTFS file system. The time zone offset is configured for the Pacific Time Zone (GMT -0800) and is configured to automatically adjust for daylight savings time. The date and time is Sunday, October 12, 2003 16:01:22 PDT. Daylight savings time is in effect and thus our current offset is "GMT -0700". At this point in time, our suspect causes a file to be written to his system that ultimately becomes a file of interest in our case. Here is what happens from time it is written until we view it in EnCase:

- The precise time the file was written, in local time, was Sunday, October 12, 2003 16:01:22 PDT

- As this system is NTFS, the operating system converts the local time to GMT before storing it. To do so, the OS adds seven hours (current offset) to the time, making it Sunday, October 12, 2003 23:01:22 PDT.

- The OS stores this date in the following 64-bit hex string: "2A 42 17 C1 14 91 C3 01". We know this can be converted to a little endian 64-bit integer that would represent the number of 100-nanosecond intervals from January 1, 1601 00:00:00 GMT.

- The following day, the suspect's computer is seized for later forensic examination.

- The date and time is now Monday, September 5, 2005, at 11:44:00 EDT and the forensic examination is occurring in the Eastern time zone.

- As our examination machine is configured for Eastern time (GMT -0500) and daylight savings time is in effect, our current offset is Eastern Daylight Savings Time (GMT -0400), EnCase will default to the local offset for viewing time stamps unless told otherwise.

- EnCase first determines that the NTFS file system is in place and decodes the time stamp in GMT as "Sunday, October 12, 2003 23:01:22". Next EnCase looks to the offset applied and if daylight savings is to be applied if in effect.

- If we did not account for the offset in the evidence file, EnCase would subtract the default local offset and apply daylight savings (GMT -0400) from the time stored in GMT and show the file as "Sunday, October 12, 2003 19:01:22".

- As we follow past practices, we determine the time zone offset in the evidence file and find that it is PST (GMT -0800) and that daylight savings was in effect (GMT -0700). When we apply this time zone setting to our device, when EnCase reads the time stamp, it converts the date to PDT (GMT -0700) by subtracting seven hours from the time stamp as stored in GMT. It therefore correctly displays the time stamp as "Sunday, October 12, 2003 16:01:22", which matches the date and time the file was written in its local time zone.

It is important to note that had this same scenario involved a FAT system, no adjustments would have been required as the time would have been stored in local time. Of course, the MS-DOS time stamp used in FAT systems, while simple, is also limiting.

The MS-DOS time stamp lacks seconds for last accessed times as the 2 bytes that would record that information are used in FAT 32-file systems to describe starting clusters when they exceed 65,536 clusters. Also, the MS-DOS time stamp only allows 5 bits to describe seconds. Because $2^5$ (5 bits) only provides 32 outcomes, this falls short of the 60 seconds in a minute. Thus the stored seconds only go as high as 30 (actually 0–29) and are multiplied by 2 to achieve a time in seconds. One times two shows as 2 seconds. Two times two shows as 4 seconds, and so forth. You won't see an MS-DOS time that is odd. You will only see even numbers for seconds for MAC times in FAT file systems.

The Windows 64-bit time stamp used to track MAC times in NTFS is, by contrast, a much more robust and accurate means of tracking time than the MS-DOS time stamp used for the same purpose in FAT. With complexity, however, comes the need for deeper understanding of the underlying principles and more sophisticated analysis tools.

Now that we understand times and time zones, let's now apply this knowledge as we examine other operating system artifacts, as time stamps are found throughout them.

# Recycle Bin

By default when a user deletes a file in Windows, the file is placed in the Recycle Bin. To bypass the Recycle Bin, the user must hold down the Shift key while pressing Delete. As few users are aware of this option, most deleted files pass through the Recycle Bin on most systems.

When a file is in the Recycle Bin, the user has the option to restore the file to its original location. A user may select a file or files and delete them from the Recycle Bin. The final option in the Recycle Bin is to empty it, which deletes all the files in the Recycle Bin.

With that, we have described the basic operation of the Recycle Bin as the user sees it. To enable this functionality, much is taking place under the hood. As examiners, we need to understand the fine details of the Recycle Bin process so we may competently examine and later explain the evidence found therein. With that in mind, let's examine underlying activity for each of the Recycle Bin's basic functions.

When a file is deleted and sent to the Recycle Bin, the directory or MFT entry for the file is deleted. Simultaneously, a directory entry or MFT entry is made for the file in the Recycle Bin. The new file name bears no resemblance to the original file name, however, as there is a specific naming convention applied to files placed in the Recycle Bin. The naming convention follows this format:

[D] (for deleted) [*original drive letter of file*] [*index number*] . [*original file extension*]

If, for example, the file C:\My Files\letter.doc were deleted and sent to the Recycle Bin, its new file name in the Recycle Bin would be "DC1.doc" if it was the first file sent to the Recycle Bin.

For earlier versions of Windows, the index numbers start at 0 for the first file sent to the Recycle Bin and sequence by 1 for each file added. Currently, however, Windows XP starts its index numbers at 1 instead of 0. If the index number for whatever reason becomes an issue, it is also a good practice to test and verify the results on a test box using the same version and service pack of Windows that is in question.

When you view a file in the Recycle Bin, you see the file's original name and path along with other information. As the deleted file no longer bears its original file name, the displayed information must be stored somewhere, and that storage location is a hidden file named INFO2. Thus when a deleted file receives a new name in the Recycle Bin, an entry is also made in the INFO2 file for the deleted file.

The INFO2 file is a database file containing information about the files in the Recycle Bin. When you look at files in the Recycle Bin, you are actually viewing the contents of the INFO2 file. Thus when a file is sent to the Recycle Bin, the following information is placed in the Recycle Bin: the file's original file name and path (entered twice, once in ASCII and again in Unicode), the date and time of deletion, and the index number. The index number is the link between the new file name and the INFO2 record as it is common to both.

In Figure 9.10 the file "DualMonitorStation.JPG" has been deleted. Because the data did not move and a new file name was created for this data in the Recycle Bin, the icon for DualMonitorStation.JPG has a red "X" indicating the file is overwritten as the starting cluster is in use by another file.

**FIGURE 9.10**    A file is deleted and sent to the Recycle Bin. EnCase reports the file as overwritten because the starting cluster is in use by the new file name created in the Recycle Bin.

When we go to the Recycle Bin, we find that the file has a new name, De3.JPG, as shown in Figure 9.11. The letter D is for deleted. The letter e indicates from which drive letter the file was deleted. The number 3 is the index number that links this file to its record in the INFO2 file. The file extension remains unchanged.

**FIGURE  9.11**     When file is sent to the Recycle Bin, it is renamed and an entry is made in the INFO2 database.

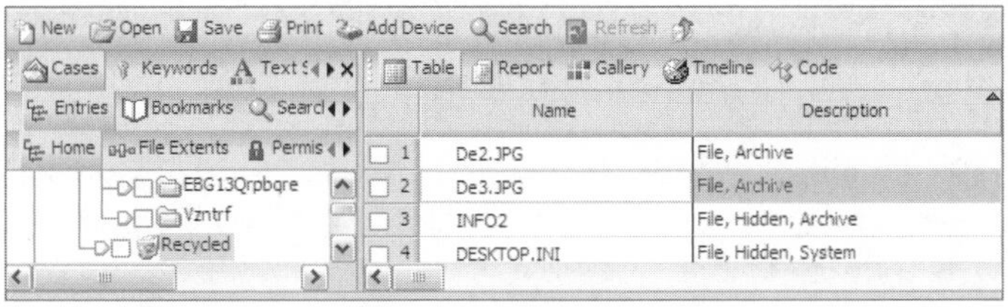

Each record in an INF02 database has a fixed length that varies according to the Windows version that created it. Table 9.2 shows the various operating systems and the length of their INF02 database records. Interestingly, the name of the Recycle Bin varies also with the Windows version, and those names are likewise listed in the table.

**TABLE  9.2**     Comparison of Recycle Bins by Windows Version

| Operating System | Recycle Bin Folder Name | INFO2 Record Length |
| --- | --- | --- |
| Windows 9x/Me | Recycled | 280 bytes |
| Windows NT | Recycler | 800 bytes |
| Windows 2000 | Recycler | 800 bytes |
| Windows XP/2003 | Recycler | 800 bytes |

The length of each record is important because EnCase provides a bookmark viewing tool that decodes the fields in the INFO2 records, allowing you to include this information in a sweeping data bookmark. In order to use this bookmarking tool, you must know both the starting point and the record length. If we create a text style for the correct record length, the starting point is easy to identify, and it also greatly facilitates accurate sweeping or highlighting of the data. We covered how to create custom text styles earlier, so we'll simply show the correct settings for an "NT" INFO2 record in Figure 9.12.

**FIGURE 9.12** Text style settings for "NT" INFO2 record. Remember to go to the Code Page tab and deselect the Unicode option; in its place select Latin 9 (ISO) for the code page.

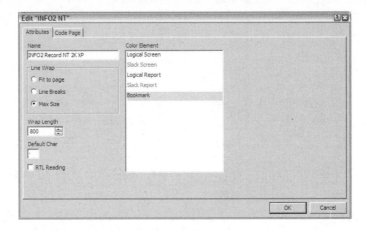

Once you have highlighted the INFO2 record in the Table view, its data is viewable in the View pane. Choose the Text view and apply your newly created text style as shown in Figure 9.13. Note that the data has been selected starting with the drive letter, which is the first character or byte of each record in the database. Remember this byte as it will have significant importance later on. The selection will end on the row following the record one space short of where the drive letter of the following record starts (or would have started on that row were there another record). For clarity, we have selected three of the four records. Note also the length of our selection in the extreme lower-right corner, which is 2,400 bytes. We have highlighted three records that are each 800 bytes, so the length of selected data is correct.

**FIGURE 9.13** Three of four INFO2 records are selected. At 800 bytes for each record, a total of 2,400 bytes have been selected.

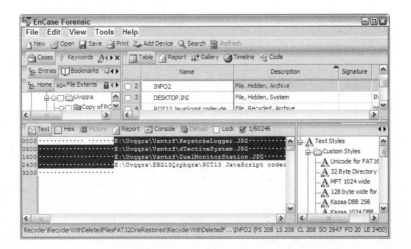

To complete the bookmark, you right-click in the selected data and choose to bookmark the data. To properly decode and view the data, you must select the proper view type, which is Windows ➢ Win2000 Info File Record. When you choose this view type, the data is decoded and displayed in the bottom pane, as shown in Figure 9.14. Choose a destination folder and click OK to complete the bookmark.

**FIGURE 9.14** INFO2 record data decoded in a bookmark using view type Windows | Win200 Info File Record

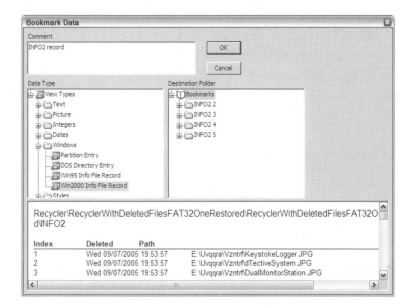

With Windows NT/2K/XP/2003, an added artifact appears in the Recycle Bin. When a user first deletes a file, a folder bearing the user's security ID (SID) number appears. Each user on the host system is assigned a SID, which is a globally unique identification number (GUID). Anything the user deletes goes into that uniquely named folder. From a forensic point of view, this is the real-world equivalent of throwing away trash with your name and social security number stamped all over it. Deleted files may be traced back to their owner through the SID.

The process of manually resolving the SID involves mounting the Security Accounts Manager (SAM) Registry file and reconstructing the SID from the data therein and linking it to a username. EnCase spares you that agony by scanning the SAM hive when loading your evidence files, thereby resolving SID numbers to locally authenticated users on the fly.

There are several ways to determine the user associated with a SID. In the case of the Recycle Bin, simply highlight the Recycle Bin in the Tree pane. In the Table view pane, place your focus on the folder bearing the name of the SID that is the focus of your inquiry. For that folder, go to the Permissions column and place your cursor in the column. When you do so, the Details tab becomes available in the View pane. Go to the Details tab and scroll down to the owner to determine the user associated with that SID. This process is shown in Figure 9.15.

**FIGURE 9.15**    NT Recycle Bin with folders bearing SID numbers for names. The SID owner can be found in the Details tab when highlighting the Permissions column in the Table view pane.

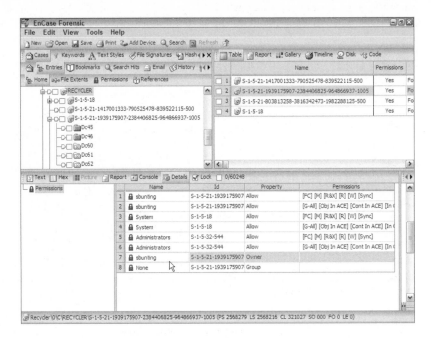

This process works for local logon accounts where the host computer's SAM stores the SID and other credentials. When the user logs onto a Windows domain, the SID information is not stored on the local host, but rather on the domain controller (server). EnCase can't scan the SAM hive on the local machine to obtain the SID numbers (they aren't there), and thus usernames will not be resolvable under these conditions. Therefore, when domain logons are occurring, you will need to obtain the username for the SID in question and manually enter the SID and username in the Security ID's view. After that, EnCase will remember that SID and username combination and resolve it for you.

When the user empties the entire Recycle Bin, directory or MFT entries for all files in the Recycle Bin are marked as deleted. The INFO2 database is adjusted to its default or empty size of 20 bytes (Windows XP/2003), thereby removing any INFO2 records from the active Recycle Bin database. If, however, you examine the file slack that immediately follows the 20-byte empty bin header, you'll see many of the INFO2 records that were in the Recycle Bin before it was emptied.

There is another circumstance you may encounter, and that is when a user restores a file from the Recycle Bin. There is little in the way of documentation on this condition, and the results from it may confuse you when you view an INFO2 record in which this has occurred. When a file is restored, a record is created in the directory or MFT for the folder where the file was originally located when it was deleted. The entry for the file in the directory or MFT of the Recycle Bin is marked as deleted. So far, this is fairly logical and straightforward.

What happens next, however, is a little less than intuitive. The entry in the INFO2 record is not deleted. Rather, the very first character of that record, which would normally be the drive letter from which the file was deleted, is changed to 00h, as shown in Figure 9.16. This process is analogous to the process of deleting a file or folder in a FAT volume where the first byte of the 32-byte entry is changed to E5h. Just as Windows Explorer ignores any entry beginning with E5h, the Recycle Bin interface ignores any record beginning with 00h.

**FIGURE 9.16**    When a file in the Recycle Bin is restored to its original path, the first character of its INFO2 record is changed to 00h.

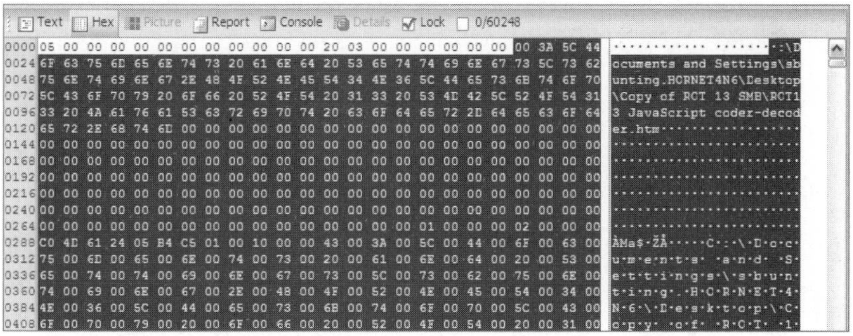

Although it isn't commonly done, instead of emptying the entire Recycle Bin, a user can delete individual files from the Recycle Bin. From within the Recycle Bin, you can delete a selected individual file or selected groups of files by pressing the Delete button, right-clicking and choosing Delete, or choosing Delete from the File menu. When this occurs, the file or files being deleted have their directory or MFT entries marked as deleted. Instead of deleting INFO2 records, moving them around, and adjusting the size of the INFO2 record, Windows handles INF02 records for files deleted from the Recycle Bin the same as files restored from the Recycle Bin. If individual files are deleted from the Recycle Bin, the first character of their INFO2 record is changed to 00h.

If files from the Recycle Bin have been restored or deleted from the Recycle Bin, we know that the first character of their INFO2 record will be 00h. This indicates the status of the record as null (restored or deleted) and tells the Recycle Bin not to display those records. The index numbers in these "null" records will be reused. If another file is subsequently deleted and placed in the Recycle Bin, you may expect that those index numbers will be used again.

When the INFO2 database is processed by EnCase, the records for files restored or deleted from the Recycle Bin and those subsequently added to the Recycle Bin (deleted and placed in Recycle Bin) are parsed and will display with the same index number, as shown in Figure 9.17. EnCase does not make any distinction between active Recycle Bin records and null Recycle Bin records. It processes and reports both types of records. The information displayed is accurate, but may not be the complete story if files were restored or deleted from the Recycle Bin.

**FIGURE 9.17** The first record has been restored and has the same index number (1) as the fifth record, which has been subsequently deleted and added to the Recycle Bin.

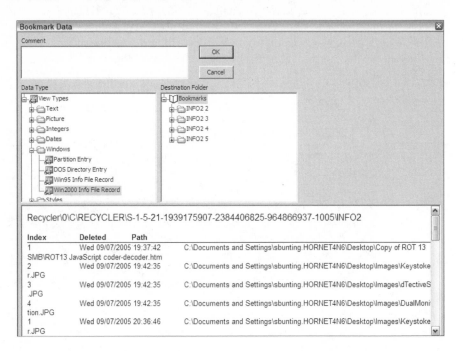

If artifacts in the Recycle Bin are critical elements in your case and you need to determine if files have been restored or deleted from the Recycle Bin, search the INFO2 records for the hex string "00 3A 5C". This string looks for ":\" preceded by 00h and would indicate records in the INFO2 database for files that were restored or deleted from the Recycle Bin. With that information, you can further examine original paths for restorations and examine directory or MFT entries for file names, starting clusters, and so forth. From that information, you may be able to determine what actually occurred to a file after it "left" the Recycle Bin.

While understanding the function of the Recycle Bin is critical and the ability to manually process it is a necessary skill, automated processing has its place in order that we may process our backlog of cases. To that end, an EnScript is available under the Sweep Case EnScript that processes INFO2 records that are intact as well as fragments that may be found anywhere on the device.

To use this EnScript, double-click on the Sweep Case EnScript in the Filter pane. Select the Recycle Bin INFO Record Finder and double-click it to access its Options dialog box, as shown in Figure 9.18. You can select the entire device, all INFO2 records, or just selected files. Click OK, provide a destination folder name for your bookmark, and click Finish. The EnScript will run and present you with a nice report in your bookmarks.

**FIGURE 9.18**     You access the Recycle Bin INFO Record Finder script by double-clicking it in the right pane of the Sweep Case EnScript Options dialog box.

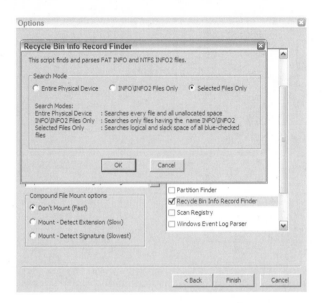

One could not complete a discussion of the Recycle Bin without covering what happens when the Recycle Bin is configured to be bypassed altogether. The obvious consequence is that files are deleted from their original locations and are not sent to the Recycle Bin at all, making processing the INFO2 records a moot point.

Fortunately for forensics examiners, such a configuration is not the default configuration and making the changes is anything but obvious or intuitive. In fact, most users are not aware that it is an option. Nevertheless, security-conscious individuals or those wishing to cover their tracks may configure their systems to bypass the Recycle Bin when deleting files.

To configure your system to bypass the Recycle Bin, you must change the properties of the Recycle Bin. From either the Desktop or Explorer Recycle Bin icon, right-click on it and select Properties. Your choices are displayed in the Recycle Bin properties dialog box shown in Figure 9.19. If you have more than one hard drive, you have the choice of creating the options globally or setting the options on a "per drive" basis. In Figure 9.19 the option Do Not Move Files To The Recycle Bin. Remove Files Immediately When Deleted has been selected. This option is being applied on the Global tab, thereby negating or overriding any individual drive options. With this setting selected, any file deleted will be deleted directly and not sent to the Recycle Bin.

This setting, when applied, is implemented by means of values stored in the Registry. This feature is represented by the NukeOnDelete Registry value set to 01h, which is found in the full Registry path: HKEY_LOCAL_MACHINE\SOFTWARE\Microsoft\Windows\CurrentVersion\Explorer\BitBucket. This setting is shown in the regedit interface in Figure 9.20. If this same setting were not globally applied but rather applied to a specific drive, the same value would appear in a subkey of this Registry key named after the drive letter to which it applied. These two subkeys ("c" and "e") of the BitBucket key can also be seen in Figure 9.20.

**FIGURE 9.19** The Recycle Bin Properties dialog box provides the option to bypass the Recycle Bin globally to both hard drives on this system.

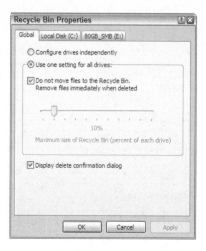

**FIGURE 9.20** Registry settings for bypassing the Recycle Bin globally for all attached drives

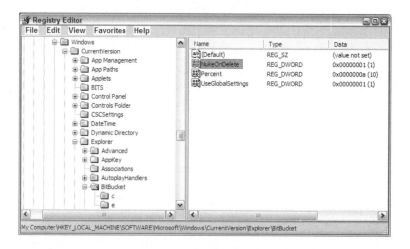

Applying this setting does not remove the Recycle Bin folder once it has been created, nor does it remove whatever contents that may be in the Recycle Bin when the setting is applied. Once this setting is applied, whenever a file is deleted the option of sending it to the Recycle Bin is no longer available.

If you are processing a case and you see a lot of user files that have been deleted, yet you find little or nothing in the of INFO2 record artifacts, you should suspect that the Recycle Bin has been bypassed. To confirm this suspicion, you could mount the Registry and examine this Registry value.

The Registry will be covered in detail in Chapter 10, after which you may wish to revisit this section. This text is also quite modularized, so you may wish to jump ahead now.

# Link Files

Link files are shortcut files and have the file extension .lnk. Link files refer to or link to target files. These target files can be applications, directories, documents, or data files. They can also be non–file system objects such as printers or various management consoles. Clicking on a shortcut causes the target file to run. If is an application, the application is launched. If it is a document, the registered application runs and opens the document.

Link files are ubiquitous through Windows. Later in this chapter we'll cover the Recent, Start, Desktop, and Send To folders, which consist, for the most part, of link or shortcut files. As you will come to appreciate, they are one of the fundamental pieces of the GUI point-and-click environment.

Shortcuts have associated icons (little pictures) that display in the Explorer interface or on the desktop if a shortcut is present there. These icons are predefined, but can be changed by the user. To change a shortcut's icon, right-click on the shortcut and choose the Properties command. Choose the Shortcut tab as shown in Figure 9.21.

**FIGURE 9.21**    Shortcut tab of the Properties dialog box for a shortcut or link file

In addition to being able to change the icon, you can change other properties of the shortcut, including its target file from this interface. To change its icon, click on the Change Icon button to open the dialog box shown in Figure 9.22. Other icons are usually available with the default one. The user can browse and use other "canned" ones. There are tools that let you create your own.

**FIGURE 9.22** The Change Icon dialog box allows the user to change a link or shortcut file's icon.

The forensic importance of link files lies in their properties, their contents, and the specifics surrounding their creation. Let's examine these various aspects so that we may better understand their function and hence their forensic importance. Let's first look at how they are created.

Links files are ubiquitous. There are few places you can't find them. They are created by the operating system upon installation and by applications with which they are installed. They are created by user activity without the user's knowledge. Finally, they can be created quite deliberately by the user. Each category of link file creation has its own significance.

The operating system creates many link files by default when you install a particular version and service pack of Windows. The desktop is one very obvious place where you will immediately see some of the default installation icons. The Recycle Bin link file is a typical default desktop link file. There are others, and they are in other locations that we'll cover as we address specific locations.

When applications are installed, link files are placed in various locations, some optionally and some automatically. These link files provide the user the ability to launch the newly installed application. By default, a link file is almost always created in the appropriate program folder that appears on the Start menu. Usually as an option, link files can be created on the desktop or on the quick launch taskbar.

Certain actions by the user create link files without their knowledge. As the user is creating virtual "tracks in the snow," such files are of particular forensic interest. Specifically, when a user opens a document, a link file is created in the Recent folder, which appears in the root of the user folder named after the user's logon name. The link files in this folder serve as a record of the documents opened by the user.

Users can create link files or move them or copy them to other locations. When a user wishes frequent access to a program, file, folder, network resource, or other non–file system resource (printer, etc.), they can create a shortcut (link file) in an easy-to-access location, most often the desktop. To create a desktop shortcut, the user right-clicks on the desktop and chooses New ➢ Shortcut. The Create Shortcut wizard appears, as shown in Figure 9.23, and guides the user through the process of selecting a target and giving the shortcut a name. A shortcut or link file to a folder named My Hacking Tools, Second Set of Books, Underage Cuties, or SSNs for Sale would have obvious evidentiary value.

**FIGURE 9.23**    The Create Shortcut wizard allows the user to create shortcuts, which are actually link files.

Link files, like any other file, have MAC time stamps that can be significant. If a program was installed on one date and a link file was created later, it can reveal that the user was not only aware that the program existed, but went out of their way to create easy access to launch it. Each time a link file is "used," knowingly or unknowingly, information about the target file is updated in the contents of the link file; thus the link file itself is modified each time it is used if the target contents have changed, which they nearly always do. When you understand the contents of the link file, why this occurs will become clear. To that end, let's examine the contents of a link file.

The data contained inside a link file describes the various attributes of the target file. It should be obvious that the complete path to the target file would be contained therein, and it is. In addition, various other attributes of the target file are recorded. The volume serial number on which the target file or folder exists is recorded. This can be useful for connecting a file to a unique volume. The file's size in bytes is recorded, which can be of use to the examiner. While other information is recorded, of most interest are the MAC time stamps of the target file. This information provides a second set of MAC times for the target file and can prove quite valuable in an examination.

The MAC times are listed in the following order: Created, Last Accessed, and Last Written. They are located in the link file at byte offsets 28, 36, and 44, respectively. Byte offsets start at 0 and can be identified easily on the GPS under FO, which stands for *file offset*. Figure 9.24 shows the cursor on byte offset 28, which can be verified by looking at the file offset in the GPS.

**FIGURE 9.24** The cursor is on byte offset 28 of a link file. Starting at this byte and for the next 23 bytes (24 total), three 64-bit Windows time stamps show the created, last written, and last accessed times for the target file.

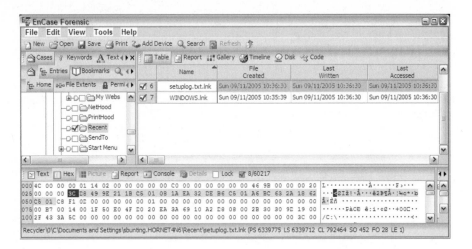

 We often use the simple acronym CAW, as in the call of a crow, to help examiners remember the order these time stamps appear. "C" is for created, "A" is for last accessed, and "W" is for last written.

If you start at byte offset 28 and sweep a total of 24 bytes (the LE indicator in GPS shows length or number of selected bytes), you have selected the three Windows 64-bit time stamps for created, last written, and last accessed times for the target file. Once the data containing the time stamps is selected, right-click in the selected data and choose to bookmark data. Under view types, choosing Dates ➢ Windows Data/Time displays all three dates in their respective order (create, last written, and last accessed), as shown in Figure 9.25.

Link files, like many files, have a unique file header. The hex string "\x4C\x00\x00\x00\x01\x14\x02" is used to verify file signatures. This string may also be used for finding link files anywhere they may exist.

Link files have a very complex structure, and decoding each field or piece of data within link files is beyond the scope of this text. As for many tedious tasks facing the examiner, EnCase provides an automated method for decoding these files using an EnScript. The EnScript for parsing link file data is a subset of the Sweep Case EnScript. When you launch the Sweep Case EnScript, you eventually arrive at the Options dialog box, from which you select (click in a box to insert a blue check) the Link File Parser EnScript, as shown in Figure 9.26.

**FIGURE 9.25**    Created, last written, and last accessed times for a target file in a link file are bookmarked.

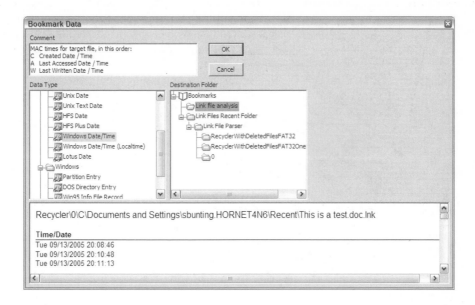

**FIGURE 9.26**    The Link File Parser EnScript is a subset of the Sweep Case EnScript and is selected in the Options dialog box.

If you double click on the Link File Parser EnScript, you may choose from various options for running the EnScript, as shown in Figure 9.27. You may select which link file properties you wish to include in your report. The default is to include everything. You may choose to apply the EnScript to selected files only or to the unallocated clusters. The EnScript uses the file header to find the data in the unallocated spaces. The default setting is to apply time zone offsets, but you may disable that if circumstances warrant. When you are done applying options, click OK.

**FIGURE 9.27**    The Link File Parser dialog box options

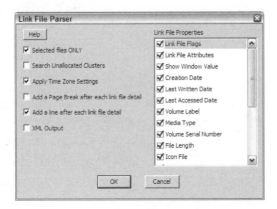

Once you have returned to the options screen for the Sweep Case EnScript, you need to specify a destination folder for your bookmark. Click Finish to run the EnScript. The results can be found in the Bookmarks view, as shown in Figure 9.28. The output is neatly arranged and is quite detailed for each link file.

**FIGURE 9.28**    The Report view of a bookmark created by the Link File Parser EnScript

```
Link Files Recent Folder\Link File Parser\0                                        Page 1

Link File:              0\C\Documents and Settings\sbunting.HORNET4N6\Recent\SchedLgU.Tx
                        t.lnk
Link File Offset:              0
Link File Size:         529
File Flags:             HASITEMID | ISFILEORFOLDER | HASRELATIVEPATH | HASWORKINGDIRECTO
                        RY
File Attributes:        ARCHIVE
ShowWindow Value:              SW NORMAL
Created Date:           Fri 02/25/2005 13:15:24
Last Written Date:      Sun 09/11/2005 09:53:53
Last Accessed Date:     Sun 09/11/2005 10:35:39
Volume Label:           C
Media Type:             Fixed
Volume Serial:          60 2B 51 8B
File Length:            24952
Base Path:              C:\WINDOWS\SchedLgU.Txt
Working Directory:      C:\WINDOWS
--------------------------------------------------------------------------------
```

Note that link file data can be found almost anywhere. As link files are processed, they are stored in RAM memory, which is volatile data. As often happens, the operating system writes this volatile data that is currently not in use to the swap file (pagefile.sys) to temporarily hold it there while it makes room in volatile RAM for a current task. The swap file, by default, is configured to adjust in size as determined by Windows. As this adjustment occurs, clusters that were formerly allocated to the swap file find themselves in unallocated space, thereby placing link files in the unallocated space along with other data.

With Windows XP, if the system is placed into hibernation, the contents of RAM are written to the hiberfil.sys file. As the result of this process, link files, not to mention other data, may be found in this file.

As we have seen, link files provide significant information to the examiner. We'll cover several folders in detail in which link files are found, as their significance varies based on where they are found. Before delving into those specific folders, let's examine the general directory structure created on current versions of Windows (2000 and XP) as the directory structure itself is forensically significant in the information it offers.

# Windows 2000 and XP Folders

Each version of Windows has its own unique directory structure and file and folder naming conventions that differentiate that version from the other versions. With experience, the examiner can usually have a good idea which version of Windows is installed by looking at the directory structure and certain telltale file and folder names. Despite how convincing these naming and structure conventions may appear, these normal conventions are not cast in granite. The final determination of what operating system is installed is derived from the Registry, which we'll cover in Chapter 10.

Nevertheless, the examiner should be familiar with the directory structures and file and folder naming conventions that are normally used by the various versions of Windows. With that knowledge and familiarity, navigating and locating operating system artifacts is greatly facilitated along with an understanding of their significance as they relate to a particular version of Windows.

The folder name that contains the Windows system files has varied with Windows versions. With Windows 9*x* versions, the system files were contained in the Windows folder. System files were stored in the folder WINNT with Windows NT and 2000. Just when we thought there was some discernable logic in their naming conventions, Windows XP came out and reverted back to storing the system files in the folder Windows. That seems straightforward enough, but things can deviate from this convention if an upgrade from one version of Windows to another occurred or if the user engaged in customization. Table 9.3 shows the system folder naming conventions and user profile folders for various versions of Windows. The naming conventions are for default new installations and do not apply to upgrades.

All versions of Windows NT (NT, 2000 XP, and 2003) create a unique artifact when the user first logs onto the system. A folder is created under Documents and Settings (2000, XP, and 2003) or under Profiles (NT) that bears the name of the logged-on user. This folder, called the root user folder, is created regardless of whether the user logs on locally or through a domain. Thus the directory naming convention itself bears forensic value in identifying the user by their logon name. Figure 9.29 shows the various root user folders created under Documents and Settings.

**TABLE 9.3**    Default New Installation System Folder Names and User Profile Folder Names for Various Versions of Windows

| Operating System | User Profile Folders | Default System Folder |
|---|---|---|
| Windows 9x/Me | No Documents and Settings Folder | C:\Windows |
| Windows NT | No Documents and Settings Folder<br>C:\WINNT\Profiles | C:\WINNT |
| Windows 2000 | C:\Documents and Settings | C:\WINNT |
| Windows XP/2003 | C:\Documents and Settings | C:\Windows |

**FIGURE 9.29**    Root user folders created under the folder Documents and Settings

Windows, for the most part, segregates or compartmentalizes that user's configuration, environment, and document files into subfolders under the root user folder. Further, by applying security credentials and permissions to each user's folders, one user is generally precluded from accessing another user's data, unless a user is granted administrator or system privileges. Forensically, this is most convenient as potential evidence for each user is neatly labeled and compartmentalized. Figure 9.30 shows the various subfolders created under the root user folder that are designed to contain the user's documents along with their configuration and user environment data.

At the same time that the root user folder and its subfolders are created at first logon, another significant file is created, which is the NTUSER.DAT file. This file is selected in the Table view pane in Figure 9.30. As we'll come to better appreciate in Chapter 10, this file is comprises the user's Registry hive.

The Registry is a very large database of system settings and configurations. The contents of the NTUSER.DAT file are settings specific and unique to that user only. In Chapter 10, we cover some of the contents of this file. For now, you should understand that the file creation date for this file would normally indicate when the user first logged onto the computer under examination. This file is modified just as the user is logging off, so the last written date of this file would normally indicate when the user last used the computer under that username.

**FIGURE 9.30**    Folders containing the user's documents along with their configuration and environment data are created as subfolders under the root user folder.

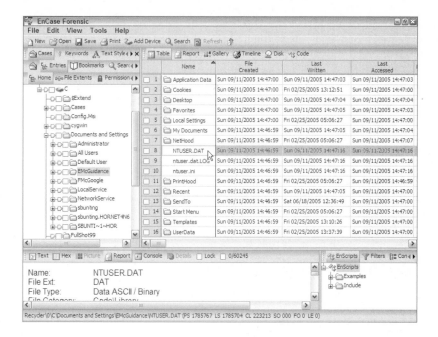

 Another file is created in the root user folder at first logon that is of interest to those working in domain environments where roaming profiles are in use. Roaming profiles allow users to log onto various domain computers and have their user profiles follow them around. For the most part, this roaming profile consists of all of the files and subfolders under the root user folder. There are exceptions, however, and they are defined in this file created at first logon, which is the ntuser.ini file. Any folders listed after ExclusionList= in this file will not be included in the user's roaming profile. By default, those folders excluded in the roaming profile are the following folders found in the Local Settings folder: History, Temp, and Temporary Internet Files. In a domain setting where roaming profiles are used, files found in these three folders were created locally on that machine as they don't "follow" the user around in the domain. This file can be modified on an individual basis or by group policy.

The operating system artifacts covered by the remainder of this chapter are found in the subfolders under the root user folder. Our approach as we conclude this chapter will be that of examining the artifacts found in the folders that are generally the most significant ones for the examiner to analyze.

# Recent Folder

When we discussed link files, we described that whenever a user opens a document, a link file is created in the Recent folder located under the root user folder. The user is unaware that this file is being created or modified. If the same document in the same location is later reopened, the link file is updated with the target file's updated information.

The purpose of the Recent folder is to provide a user interface that is a listing of documents the user has recently created or modified. You can access this interface by clicking the Start button and then selecting My Recent Documents, as shown in Figure 9.31. By default, Windows displays the last 15 documents opened by the user.

**FIGURE 9.31**    The Recent folder contains link files that are used to populate the My Recent Documents menu with the last 15 files the user opened.

The Recent folder contains only link files. Windows looks to the MAC times of the link files to determine the most recent "link" file and looks to the content of the link file to display the information. If you select the properties of any file listed under My Recent Documents, the information displayed will be the properties of the file contained in the link file and not necessarily those of the file itself.

Although Windows displays only the last 15 documents, the number of link files contained in the recent folder can easily be in the hundreds and span months or years. For any one file in a specific path, there will be only one link file in the recent folder for it. Each time it is accessed, the link file content is updated. The file naming convention for link files in the Recent folder is to use the complete file name plus the extension .lnk. For example, a file named MyFile.doc would be given a file name of Myfile.doc.lnk in the Recent folder.

Link files in the Recent folder, probably as much as any other link file, are likely to be in RAM and from there be swapped out to the pagefile.sys file. Once in the swap file, an adjustment to the size of the swap file places them into the unallocated space. If a drive is formatted, these link files will lose their directory pointers, but the data is still there unless overwritten. The Link File Parser EnScript can be run and much of this data can be recovered from the unallocated clusters regardless of how the data was placed there.

Link files can reveal a wealth of information. Take the time to understand them, perform your own testing and research regarding their behavior, and then use that knowledge when conducting examinations.

One of the first places I examine in a case is the Recent folder. I quickly sort the files chronologically by last written time. It serves as a quick litmus test and timeline to see what kind of files the user has been accessing and, better yet, where those files are located on their system. This approach can quickly point the way to the user's favored or hidden storage locations, saving you lots of time and quickly focusing your resources in the right direction.

# Desktop Folder

The files of any type located on your desktop are stored, in part, in the Desktop folder located in the root user folder. These files can be any type, but are typically shortcuts (link files), applications, or documents. When a user first logs on and their root user folder is created, their Desktop folder has very little in it. Currently Windows XP Service Pack 2 deposits a shortcut file to the Window Media Player in the Desktop folder of all new users.

Just because there is only one shortcut file in the user's Desktop folder does not mean that the user has only one file or icon on their desktop. Interestingly, the files on your desktop have more than one source of origin. Any file that appears in the Desktop folder of the root user folder named All Users appears on the desktop of every user on that local host computer.

Other desktop objects are defined in the Registry, such as the Recycle Bin. In addition to the Recycle Bin, the user may opt to have other desktop objects such as My Computer, My Network Places, Internet Explorer, or My Documents. You access the option to place these objects on the desktop by right-clicking on the desktop and selecting Properties. In the resulting dialog box, you navigate to the General tab and click the Customize Desktop button. From there, as shown in Figure 9.32, it's a simple matter of checking the items you wish to appear on your desktop. These settings are also stored in the Registry.

Thus the contents that are displayed on the typical Windows 2000 or XP desktop are derived from three sources, which are the Registry, the All Users desktop folder, and the user's Desktop folder. If the host computer is in a domain environment and the user authenticates to a domain, the desktop can have yet another source. Group policy settings can direct that individual users or groups of users have a specified desktop, thereby providing a uniform fixed desktop to domain users.

**FIGURE 9.32** This dialog box gives users the opportunity to select several items to be displayed on their desktop.

Shortly after looking at the Recent folder, I examine the user's Desktop folder, which contains the files or shortcuts that user placed there or caused to be placed there. Often people place items they frequently access on their desktops, making it another good indicator of the user's activities and preferences.

# My Documents

Under each root user folder there will be, by default, a folder named My Documents. By default it will contain a subfolder named My Pictures and most likely My Music and my eBooks, depending on the Windows version and service pack installed.

The purpose of this folder is a secure and segregated location for each user's file and folders. Most programs will default to saving files in My Documents. The My Pictures folder will typically contain four sample pictures named *blue hills*, *Sunset*, *Water lilies*, and *Winter*, all of which are JPEG files. Beyond the default content, other files and folders in this folder are there as the result of user activity.

# Send To Folder

The purpose of the Send To folder is to contain the objects or links that will appear in the Explorer interface under the right-click option Sent To. Several items appear here by default upon installation, and other items are created when various programs are installed. While the user can add items here manually, this doesn't often happen. It is a good place to examine to locate attached media such as zip drives and the like.

# Temp Folder

The Temp folder is a subfolder of the Local Settings folder. As the name implies, the purpose of the Temp folder is to temporarily store files. There seems to be no end to the type of files you can find here. This is a good place to look after running a file signature analysis as often programs create working copies of open documents in this area, changing their extensions. Some programs delete them when done, and others simply leave behind their garbage. I once found three files that were over 2GB each in this area. They apparently were created during a major system malfunction and were rich with evidence.

This area is normally hidden from the user and is certainly an area you wish to examine carefully. In addition to having hidden or backup copies of files here, programs often write their temporary install files and folders in this area as well, as you can see in Figure 9.33.

**FIGURE 9.33**     The Temp folder can contain temporary files from program installation that are often overlooked when removing programs.

Often a user will remove a program from an area they can access, such as Program Files, but will fail to remove files and folders in this area as it is very much out of the way and normally hidden. You may, therefore, find evidence here that refutes a claim that the user never had a given application installed on their system. You may find other Temp folders in other areas of the file system, but the important thing to remember is that this Temp folder (located under the Local Settings folder of the root user folder) is specific to the user.

# Favorites Folder

The Favorites folder contains Internet shortcut files for Microsoft Internet Explorer. Internet shortcut files function in a similar way to link files in that they contain information about their target and the user accesses the target by clicking on the shortcut file. In this case, the files have an extension of .url, which stands for Uniform Resource Locator. The target of an Internet shortcut is a URL, which is typically a web address but could just as easily be to a file on the local host or on a network resource.

A URL file has a unique header—[InternetShortcut]—and can be seen in Figure 9.34. Immediately following the header is the path to the URL target. The header can be used to search for deleted shortcuts.

**FIGURE 9.34**     The data area of a URL file. This one is a default favorite that takes you to Hotmail. Note the file header [InternetShortcut].

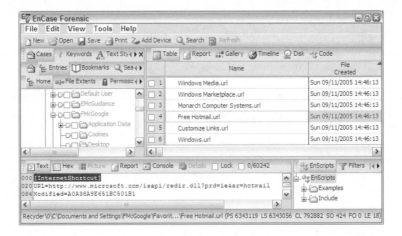

It is important to understand that some Internet shortcut files are loaded during installation. These "default" favorites can vary slightly depending on the Windows version and service pack. Additionally, some computer manufacturers use a customized original equipment manufacturer (OEM) version of Windows that may contain favorites to their company website or to those of their close affiliates. Figure 9.35 shows a default set of favorites for an OEM installation of Windows XP.

**FIGURE 9.35**     Default favorites from an OEM version of Windows XP

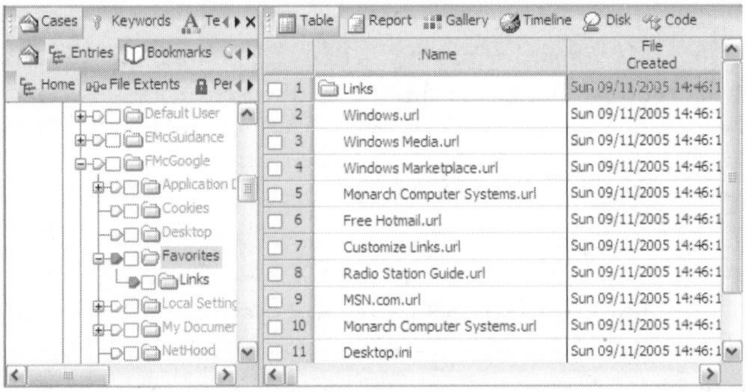

We now understand the purpose of the Favorites folder and the structure and purpose of URL files. We also understand that we can expect, by default, that there will be some favorites preinstalled in this area. Some programs, when they are installed, may place a URL to their company site in this area. Some may ask first and others may not. Beyond those favorites, for the most part, what is placed in this area is done or at least caused by the user. Some websites may provide a mechanism by which they can be added to the user's favorites, with the user's permission.

Some malicious code may add favorites without the user's knowledge if their machine is vulnerable to such an action. Often a telltale signature of such an act is that the creation date for multiple favorites is within the same one- or two-second time period, making it clear that it was "automated" and not a manual act by the user.

When you examine this area, you will often find a very elaborate tree of well-organized folders. When you compare this to the default, it is clear that such acts are carried out by the user. You will find that the Favorites folder is a valuable area to examine and that the evidence found here corroborates other findings. If a user claims that their visits to inappropriate websites were accidental, such can be easily refuted if the user has established an elaborate folder structure of favorites containing those same inappropriate websites.

# Cookies Folder

The Cookies folder is located under the root user folder. Cookies are pieces of code created by websites and placed on the user's local computer. The code is supposed to be for the purpose of enhancing the user's browsing experience, in theory, but can be used for nefarious purposes. The data in a cookie is created by the website and its true content or purpose is often unknown. Because of this, cookies are a serious security concern.

Cookies take the form of *user name@domain name.txt*. Each cookie is contained in one file, as shown in Figure 9.36. The total collection of cookie files is under the management of an index.dat file, which contains data about each cookie and pointers to the cookie file and to the originating web domain name. The index.dat file contains dates, and the cookie itself contains internal dates. The internal dates of a cookie describe when it was last modified by the website and its date of expiration.

Some analytical examiners have been successful at using a cookie with a known expiration period and have used that time period in conjunction with the cookie's expiry date to prove or disprove the accuracy of the system time when the cookie was last modified. Thus there is certainly value in understanding cookie internals.

Several cookie decoders are available, but probably the best and easiest to use is CookieView, written by Craig Wilson. It is made to work in conjunction with EnCase as a viewer. When it is installed as a viewer, you can right-click on a cookie in EnCase and use the Send To feature to pass the cookie file to CookieView, which will open externally and decode the values in the cookie, as shown in Figure 9.37. You can download CookieView from `www.digital-detective.co.uk`.

**FIGURE 9.36**     Cookie files in the Cookies folder. The cookie data is visible in the View pane.

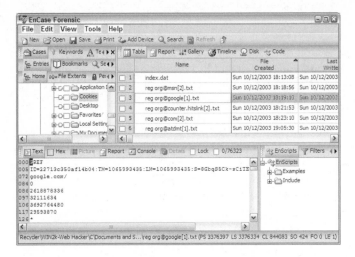

**FIGURE 9.37**     Cookie data decoded by CookieView, which can be installed as a viewer in EnCase. The data decoded here is the same raw data shown in Figure 9.36.

# History Folder

The History folder is located under the Local Settings folder, which is in turn under the root user folder. The History folder, as the name implies, contains the history of the user's Internet browsing history. It enables you to go back and find websites they have recently visited. When you click the History button on the Internet Explorer toolbar, the History window opens, usually on the left side of the browser window, as shown in Figure 9.38.

**FIGURE 9.38**　The Internet history feature shows the Internet history listing.

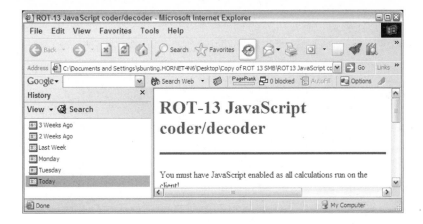

There is a top level or main index.dat database file that sits at the root level in the History.IE5 folder. All the history for the period covered is contained in this file. The default period is 20 days. Under the History.IE5 folder are folders that have unique folder names. These folder names correspond with periods of time conforming to the convention *MSHist01DateRange*. The date range is in the format *YEARMODAYEARMODA*. These periods of time are in sync with the time periods you see in the history window of your browser. Figure 9.39 depicts a typical History folder with the folders named after date ranges.

**FIGURE 9.39**　Folders named after Internet history date ranges have been located under the History.IE5 folder

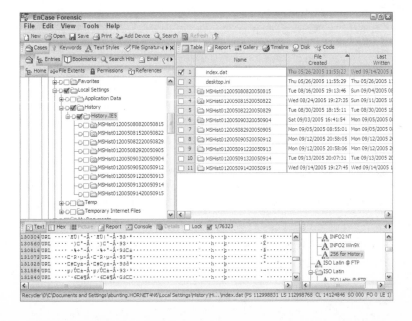

Table 9.4 maps the folder names in Figure 9.39 to their Internet history interface counterparts shown in Figure 9.40. It further describes which type of index.dat file is stored within that folder.

**TABLE 9.4**    History Folder Names Are Translated and Linked to Their Browser History Folder

| History Folder Name | Date Range | Browser History Folder |
|---|---|---|
| MSHist012005091420050915 (Index.dat File Type: Daily) | Sept 14, 2005 to Sept 15, 2005 | Today |
| MSHist012005091320050914 (Index.dat File Type: Daily) | Sept 13, 2005 to Sept 14, 2005 | Tuesday |
| MSHist012005091220050913 (Index.dat File Type: Daily) | Sept 12, 2005 to Sept 13, 2005 | Monday |
| MSHist012005090520050912 (Index.dat File Type: Weekly) | Sept 05, 2005 to Sept 12, 2005 | Last week |
| MSHist012005082920050905 (Index.dat File Type: Weekly) | Aug 29, 2005 to Sept 05, 2005 | 2 weeks ago |
| MSHist012005082220050829 (Index.dat File Type: Weekly) | Aug 22, 2005 to Aug 29, 2005 | 3 weeks ago |

There is an index.dat Internet history database file located in each of the folders named after date ranges. The various history index.dat files (main history, daily history, and weekly history) are all slightly different in their internal structures. Fortunately, EnCase 5 will decode the history for you and present it in a separate view that lets you analyze that information and bookmark it for inclusion in your report.

For EnCase to parse the history files and decode them for viewing, you must first direct EnCase to search for the various Internet artifacts; history is but one that EnCase will decode by this process. Go to one of these tabs: Email, History, or Web Cache. In the Tree pane, right-click and choose Email/Internet Search, as shown in Figure 9.40.

Once the Email/Internet Search dialog box appears, deselect all options except for Internet Explorer. When this option is run, EnCase will parse and decode both the Internet Explorer history and web cache. We'll cover the web cache in the next section. Figure 9.41 shows this dialog box and the selection of Internet Explorer only. Click OK when ready, and the thread runs with the progress bar indicating the approximate time remaining.

**FIGURE 9.40**    Email/Internet Search is launched with a right-click in the Email, History, or Web Cache tab view.

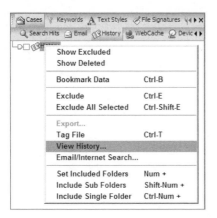

**FIGURE 9.41**    The Email/Internet Search dialog box lets you search for and decode mail, history, and web cache.

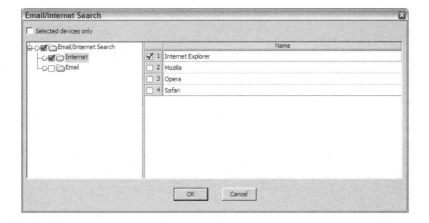

When the process completes, go to the History tab to see the results. From this view, you can sort by any of the columns. You can sort by date so as to view the history in a timeline. Using the conditions, you can filter and view by host, user, name, or URL. You may prefer to select and bookmark individual entries, or select them all and bookmark them all at once. When bookmarked, the entries are sent to the Bookmarks view for later inclusion in your report. Figure 9.42 shows a bookmarked Internet history report.

**FIGURE 9.42**   Two Internet history entries are bookmarked and appear in Bookmarks view as they would appear in your final report.

| Internet History |
|---|

| Internet History | Page 1 |
|---|---|

| Name: | 0 |
|---|---|
| Name: | Internet Explorer |
| Name: | Weekly |
| URL: | file:///C:/Program%20Files/Paragon%20Software/Partition%20Manager/BM/WINBM.HLP |
| User: | sbunting |
| Visit Count: | 1 |
| First Date: | Tue 09/06/2005 20:22:52 |
| Second Date: | Mon 09/12/2005 20:58:05 |
| Expiration Date: | Mon 10/03/2005 00:22:54 |
| History Path: | 0\C\Documents and Settings\sbunting.HORNET4N6\Local Settings\History\History.IE5\MSHist01200090520050912\index.dat |
| Name: | Weekly |
| URL: | file:///E:/Software/Mount%20Everything/Download%20Link%20for%20Paragon%20Mount%20Everg%203.x%20Professional%20Version%20(element%205%20Ref%20%23%2012272645).txt |
| User: | sbunting |
| Visit Count: | 1 |
| First Date: | Tue 09/06/2005 20:04:27 |
| Second Date: | Mon 09/12/2005 20:58:05 |
| Expiration Date: | Sun 10/02/2005 23:57:20 |
| History Path: | 0\C\Documents and Settings\sbunting.HORNET4N6\Local Settings\History\History.IE5\MSHist01200090520050912\index.dat |

**NOTE** A little-known or understood fact is illustrated in Figure 9.42. Whenever a file on the host computer is opened or saved and that file is a registered file type, an entry is made in the history database (main, daily, and eventually weekly). The file is local and it is not cached, so don't expect to find it in the cache. Instead of the record beginning with URL, as would be the case with a web address, the record begins with *file:///*, followed by the full path and file name. Many believe the file must be opened in Internet Explorer for an entry to be here, but such is not the case. If you click on a file and open it with its application, it will appear here. Expect to see Microsoft Office documents of all sorts as well as other file types.

# Temporary Internet Files

The Temporary Internet Files (TIF) folder is located under the Local Settings folder. The purpose of the folders contained under the TIF folder is to contain the files downloaded and cached from the Internet. By storing or caching these files, when a user returns to a site they visit often, the browser checks to see if the files in cache are current. If so, there is no need to clog the Internet downloading files that are locally cached and current. In that case, the file in cache is used and not downloaded. In this manner, traffic on the Web is lessened and the user sees their web page more quickly.

Naturally there must be a method to store and manage these files. By now you shouldn't be surprised to find that yet another index.dat file is used for this purpose. While named the same as the other index.dat files we have thus far discussed, this one also differs somewhat in its structure and purpose from the others. The web cache index.dat file sits in the root of the Content.IE5 folder. Under the Content.IE5 folder are at least four folders whose names consist of eight random alphanumeric characters each. As more cached files are created, a commensurate number of these folders are created to hold them. On systems where considerable browsing activity occurs, the presence of 15 or 20 of these folders is very typical.

A typical web page consists of many files, typically a dozen or more. As those files are downloaded from the source website, they are written to the cache files. When they are written, the name of the cached file is usually modified slightly from its original name. A file that is downloaded and that has an original file name of menuicon.jpg will be stored in cache as menuicon[1].jpg unless a file by that name (menuicon[1].jpg) already exists, in which case it would be incremented by 1 and named menuicon[2].jpg.

The index.dat file keeps track of these file name changes, among other things. Each file in cache has an entry in the index.dat. That record records its original file name in its complete URL and stores its cached file name so they can be linked back together. Each record tracks the folder number in which the cached file name is stored, along with several time stamps and other metadata. The cache folders are numbered starting at 0, and they are listed at the beginning of the index.dat file in the order of that numbered sequence. The first one listed is 01h, the second one listed is 02h, and so forth until they are all listed and numbered. They are easy to spot at a glance.

As mentioned in the previous section when we discussed Internet history files, EnCase 5 will read the TIF index.dat and reconstruct the web cache views for you. The various columns in the Table view describe the various attributes of each cached file, based on a combination of the cached file's attributes and the data from the index.dat.

In the previous section, we already described the process of having EnCase 5 carry out the Email/Internet Search, selecting only the Internet Explorer option. Using this option, the Cookies, History, and TIF folders are processed and the results are shown in the History and WebCache tab views.

If you go to the WebCache view tab, after running the Email/Internet Search, the Table view will list all of the files in the cache folders. If you select any file, you can see it in the View pane in any one of the normal views. The Report view will show the file in web format as the user saw it. If the file is a web page consisting of other files, EnCase 5 will insert those files if they are in cache. If the file is one of the component files, such as a picture file, it will only show the picture in a stand-alone view. Figure 9.43 shows a Hotmail message that was read and stored in cache. If a user opened a web mail attachment, the attachment will be in the cache as well.

Cached items or files can be bookmarked just as any search hit or history entry. Select the cached files you wish to bookmark, right-click, and bookmark the data. After you choose your destination folder in your bookmarks, click OK and your cached file will appear in your Bookmarks view, ready for inclusion in your final report.

Cached files will show the Internet web page very close to how the user saw it. Obviously some minor formatting changes are done to make things fit in the EnCase viewing environment. While the format may change slightly, the content is otherwise present.

**FIGURE 9.43**    This web cache view shows the front end of a Hotmail message that was read and stored in cache. The message content is further down and off the screen.

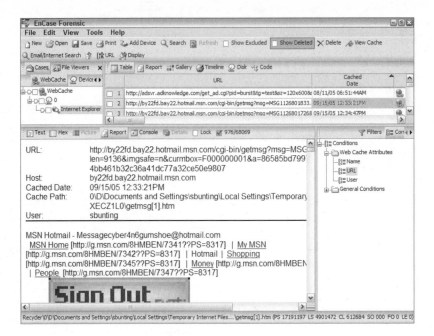

The Temporary Internet Files (TIF) folder is not just used by Internet Explorer. On the same folder level as Content.IE5, if you see a folder that begins with *OLK* followed by some random characters, you are looking at the folder in which Outlook opens its attachments. Don't confuse Outlook with Outlook Express. Outlook opens its attachments in this folder and does purge them at times, but certainly not always. The user will often attempt to save an attachment and the default location, believe it or not, turns out to be this OLK folder. Users don't pay attention and save it where it is, thinking it is in My Documents like almost every other save they have done in Windows. After they save it, they can't find it as the OLK folder is hidden and Explorer doesn't allow you to navigate to it. Expect lots of attachments to be in here! There is a PowerPoint presentation on the CD that covers these in detail. Look for OLK Folders Explained.ppt. You will also find that Outlook Express opens attachments directly in the cache folders under TIF as do popular web mail services. The exercise at the end of this chapter is one you will definitely want to do. You should follow along carefully as it will show you how Hotmail opens and stores attachments in ways that may surprise you.

## Artifact Recoveries After Formatting

A well-established publisher recently received a return-mail bundle from his local post office. As it turned out, the bundle of returned magazines did not belong to the publisher, but belonged instead to a brand-new competitor who had copied his publication so closely that the post office thought it belonged to their long-established postal patron and understandably mistakenly delivered the magazines being returned due to undeliverable addresses.

Upon closer inspection, the new magazine's editorial page revealed the new publisher as a recently departed employee of the publisher. Upon an even closer inspection of the mailing address labels, the incorrect addresses being returned matched those in his customer database in both form and content, including a couple of misspellings.

As theft of intellectual property was patently obvious, the publisher contacted counsel. Counsel in turn asked that I examine the former employee's hard drive to locate, to the extent possible, any evidence that would support their case.

Unfortunately, the hard drive had been used by the former employee's replacement for several weeks and problems occurred. To remedy the problem, the outsourced system administrator formatted the drive and reinstalled the OS after which it was again used by the former employee's replacement. Did I mention that they had also removed the former employee's files from the server? All this had transpired despite the fact that they had prior knowledge that the former employee was leaving to start a business of his own!

There wasn't an intact file left belonging to the former employee. Nevertheless, all link files, FAT32 directory entries, and URLs were extracted from the unallocated clusters and slack spaces. That information was pulled together and the events were reconstructed.

The link file content (file path and name, MAC times, and logical size) revealed that the former employee had accessed the customer database on the server at all times until he began his plans to start a competing business. His intent to start his own business was marked and time stamped by a sudden and extensive set of URL strings and web content for everything pertaining to starting one's business, from legal issues to supplies. It was at that critical juncture that the customer database was copied onto the employee's workstation. The database on the server was reduced to one-third its original size when he trashed thousands of entries. The target file sizes in the link files clearly showed this activity occurring within a 20-minute time period! From that point forward, the former employee never accessed the database on the server, or at least no evidence of such was found.

When the database was moved to the employee's workstation, the link file content from scores of recovered link files showed the file size of this database steadily increasing as he spent his last three months conducting searches, developing the customer database, and setting up his competing business on his former employer's time.

He created a competing website using some of his employer's images so much so they appeared almost as mirror site. The web mail traffic with his web developer was also recovered.

To top it off, there was even a link file that showed the customer database on a CD on his last day of his employment. The customer database, as he transferred it to CD, was 25 percent larger than it was when he started while his employer's customer database was slashed by nearly two thirds its original size. All this information was derived from recovered link file content, corroborated by URL entries.

When confronted with a substantial quantity of incriminating evidence, the former employee, through counsel, entered into an agreement with his former employer to avoid civil damages that would have bankrupted him. In the agreement, he admitted to the wrongdoing, agreed to shut down the website and cease his publication in it current format, permitted imaging of his company's computers to establish a baseline, and agreed to future imaging and examination of his data under certain agreed-upon conditions.

The agreement was far more restrictive upon his business than any judge would likely have ordered, but to avoid the expense and possible treble damages from an adverse ruling, he agreed to those conditions.

Most of the evidence that forced his hand resulted from recovered link file content along with other supporting data. All of it, without exception, was found in the unallocated clusters or in slack space. When the link file information was placed in a spreadsheet and accompanied by graphs and a timeline, the customer database story unfolded. When accompanied by other evidence relating to him starting up his business while on his former employer's time clock, the icing was on the cake.

# Swap File

Windows and other operating systems have a limited supply of RAM with which to function. When they run out of RAM, they write some of the data that is in RAM to a file whose dedicated purpose is to cache RAM memory. This file is generically called a swap file, but more correctly called a *page* file. It is located in the root of the system drive, and its name is pagefile.sys on current versions of Windows.

When examining systems, you should always check this file. You may often find evidence that was written in RAM that was never in file format on the hard drive. You may find unencrypted text fragment in this file that are encrypted in their file format. If it was ever in RAM, it could be in the swap file. It is best to always search this file with the Unicode option enabled as files that appear normally in regular text can appear in Unicode when they are in RAM.

# Hibernation File

With Windows 2000 and XP, allowing the computer to "hibernate" became an option. For a machine to power off and go to sleep and yet come back to life at the precise point where it went to sleep, the contents of RAM must be written to a file. Hence, we have the hibernation file, named hiberfil.sys, which is located in the root of the system drive.

As the total contents of RAM are written to this file, this file will be the size of your system's RAM memory. If the computer has never been in a hibernation mode, the file will exist at the size of your system RAM, but will be filled with 00h. Once it has been in the hibernation mode, the contents will reflect the last time the machine was in hibernation mode. The same processing guidelines apply to this file as with the swap file because they both contain the contents of RAM at various points and for different reasons.

Figure 9.44 shows the location of the pagefile.sys swap file and the hiberfil.sys hibernation file on a Windows XP system. Note that because the system from which it came had 1GB of RAM memory, the swap file in this case is over 3GB and the hibernation file is 1GB.

**FIGURE 9.44**    The swap file (pagefile.sys) and the hibernation file (hiberfil.sys) are both located in the root of the system drive.

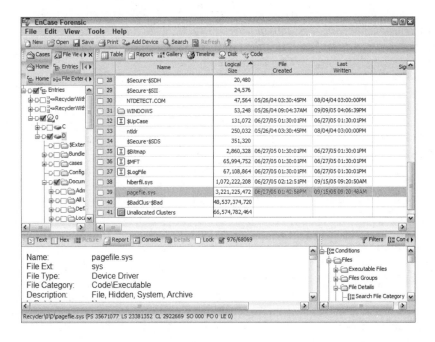

# Print Spooling

When computers print files in a Windows environment, a print spooling process occurs. Spooling involves writing the print job to a couple of files so that the print job can run in the background while the user continues working with their applications. The print job is placed in a queue and prints as the printer is available to do the job. When the print job is done, the spooling files are deleted by the operating system.

When you set up your printer definition, you have the option of choosing either RAW or EMF mode. The RAW mode is a straight graphic dump of the print job. With the EMF mode, the graphics are converted to the EMF (Microsoft Enhanced Metafile) image format, and each printed page is represented by individual EMF files. These EMF files are not stand-alone files, but rather they are embedded within another file.

For each print job, two files are created. On Windows NT and 2000, these files will be located in Winnt\system32\spool\printers. On Windows XP\2003 these files will be located in Windows\system32\spool\printers. The location is configurable by the user in the Registry key HKEY_LOCAL_MACHINE\SOFTWARE\Microsoft\Windows NT\CurrentVersion\Print\Printers\DefaultSpoolDirectory. To that extent, it could exist anywhere.

If the workstation is connected to a network, spool files will also be sent to the server. Normally these temporary files are deleted at all locations after the print job is completed, and finding these files as allocated files is rare, unless the printer were offline and the spool files were in queue awaiting the printer to come back online—at which point the job would complete and the files would be deleted. I have seen hundreds of these spooled files on a Windows 2000 domain controller that were allocated files. For whatever reason, the server refused to delete these files when the print job was done. Bugs and poor configurations often leave added artifacts beyond your normal expectations.

Of the two temporary files created for each print job, one is called a shadow file, with the extension .SHD, and the second is called the spool file, with the extension .SPL. The file name will consist of five digits, and there will be a matching pair of files for each print job, differing only by their extension. For example, a print job may create the following two files: 00003.SHD and 00003.SPL. On some configurations you may find the five digits preceded by letters, such as FP00002.SHD and FP00002.SPL. The shadow file (SHD) is analogous to a job ticket. It contains information about the print job that includes the username, the printer, the name of the file being sent to print, and the print mode (RAW or EMF).

The spool file (SPL) contains the same kind of print job information, although formatted differently, and it contains the actual print job graphical data. When the mode is RAW, the graphic content is just that—a raw output of the graphical stream needed by the printer to output the job. Figure 9.45 shows two spool files created by a print job. The printer was offline and the files are allocated files awaiting the printer to come back online. The spool file contains considerable information about the print job. This particular print job was done in the RAW mode, which is not commonly encountered as it is not the default mode.

**FIGURE 9.45**     Print job shadow and spool files on Windows XP. This print job was done in the RAW mode, which is not the default mode and is thus less common.

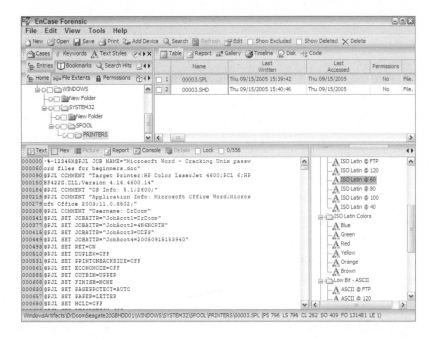

By default, printing is done using the EMF mode. Usually special circumstances or issues are present to warrant a change to the RAW mode, and it must be configured manually. Thus most of the print jobs you will recover will be in the EMF mode, which are easily recovered.

Each page of printed material will be represented by an EMF file embedded within the spool file in the order that they will be printed. Figure 9.46 shows shadow and spool files for an EMF print job. This was the same document printed in the RAW mode and shown in Figure 9.45.

An EMF file has a unique header, which also varies with the operating system. Note that the EMF header is highlighted in Figure 9.46. Table 9.5 lists the EMF header for the various operating systems in which they appear. Thus, when attempting to recover print jobs, you should use the search string that applies to the operating system in use. Even then there are some variants with these EMF headers even within the same version of Windows. If you fail to find any EMF headers, you may shorten your search string to the portion that is common to all, which is \x01\x00\x00\x00. Doing so will obviously result in a significant number of false positives, and there are some better approaches to try first.

**TABLE 9.5**   EMF Header Search Strings for Different Versions of Windows

| Operating System | EMF Header (GREP Search Strings) |
|---|---|
| Windows XP | \x01\x00\x00\x00\x5C\x01<br>\x01\x00\x00\x00\x84\x00 |
| Windows 2000 | \x01\x00\x00\x00\xD8\x17<br>\x01\x00\x00\x00\x58\x6E |
| Windows NT & 2000 | \x01\x00\x00\x00\x18\x17 |
| Windows 9x<br>(Win 9x handles print jobs differently and the process is not described here) | \x01\x00\x00\x00\x58\x00 |
| Universal Search String (some false positives likely and can miss undocumented variants) | \x01\x00\x00\x00[\x5C\x84\xD8\x58\x18][\x01\x17\x6E\x00] |
| Windows 2000 & XP (very precise!) | \x01\x00\x00\x00..\x00.{34,34}EMF |
| Windows 9x only | \x01\x00\x00\x00\x58\x00\x00\x00 |

**FIGURE 9.46**   Print job shadow and spool files on Windows XP. This print job was done in the EMF mode, which is the default mode.

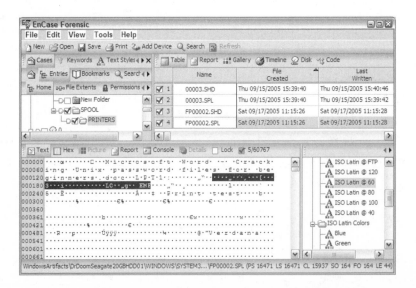

WindowsArtifacts\DrDoomSeagate20GBHDD01\WINDOWS\SYSTEM3...\FP00002.SPL (PS 16471 LS 16471 CL 15937 SO 164 FO 164 LE 44)

If your search involves Windows 2000 or XP, the search string listed in Table 9.5 for that purpose is very precise and you will rarely encounter a false positive. If your box involved a Windows XP upgrade over Windows 9x, you'll be looking for both, and you'll want to also use the one for Windows 9x only.

You may search for EMF print jobs in spool files, but remember that you will rarely encounter them as allocated files. Mostly you can expect to find them in slack space, unallocated clusters, paging files, and hibernation files. When you find a valid EMF embedded file or fragment, select the first few bytes of the search hit, bookmark the data, and view it as a picture. Figure 9.47 shows a recovered EMF print job as it is being viewed as a bookmark. The document contained in this print job consists of multiple pages, and there is an EMF header for each page as there is an EMF file for each page embedded in the spool file. When you do the exercise at the end of this chapter, you'll get to process this same spool file and see each page represented by separate EMF files.

**FIGURE  9.47**    EMF print file located, bookmarked, and viewed as a picture

To automate this process, the Sweep Case EnScript has a file finder feature. If you double-click on File Finder, you can choose EMF as a file type. In this manner, EnCase can recover print jobs for you with automated processing.

# Legacy Operating System Artifacts

Thus far, the artifacts mentioned have been for the current operating systems, namely Windows 2000/XP/2003. Windows 9x systems, while rapidly disappearing from the scene, are still encountered. Table 9.6 lists several artifacts that we have already covered, but shows where they can be found on Windows 9x systems. Other than being located in a different place or named differently, they are functionally the same.

**TABLE 9.6**   Windows 9x artifacts and their paths

| Description | File Name and Path |
| --- | --- |
| Swap File | C:\WIN386.SWP |
| Recent folder whose contents show on Windows 9x Start ➢ Documents menu | C:\Recent |
| Desktop items | C:\Desktop |
| My Documents | C:\My Documents |
| Internet cache and index.dat | C:\Windows\Temporary Internet Files\Content.IE5 |
| Cookies files | C:\Windows\Cookies |
| Internet History files | C:\Windows\History |
| In the event that "profiles" are configured, each user will have their own set of the above files contained in the following directory: | C:\Windows\Profiles\<user name>\ |

**EXERCISE 9.1**

## Windows Artifacts Recovery

In this exercise, we will examine most of the Windows artifacts addressed in this chapter, plus we'll explore some little-known web cache behaviors regarding e-mail attachments.

- Create a folder structure for a new case according to our standard folder naming and structuring conventions. Name your case folder name **Windows Artifacts**. Create a new case, pointing it to your newly created folders. Before you place any evidence in your case, save your case in the root of the folder WindowsArtifacts, which will also be the default name for your case. Locate an evidence file on the CD named WindowsArtifacts\DrDoomSeagate20GBHDD01.E01. Place it in the evidence folder for your newly created case.

- On the toolbar, click Add Device. Create a path to your new evidence file if one does not exist. Locate your new evidence file in the right pane of the Add Device window and complete the steps to bring the evidence file into your new case. Once it has been added, click Save.

- In the Tree pane, select the root of your case tree, forcing the newly added device into the Table view pane. From the Table view pane, select the device. In the View pane, select the Report tab and confirm that the evidence file verified.

- Return to the Tree view pane and navigate to the folder Documents and Settings\DrDoom\Recent. In the Table view pane, take a quick look at the kind of activity the user has been engaged in. Place a checkmark in the recent folder, selecting all of the link files within, and deselect the desktop.ini file. The Dixon box should show *6/557*. Launch the Sweep Case bookmark, select the Link File Parser only, and double-click it to access its options. Leave the default settings, but place a check next to Selected files ONLY. Click OK, name your bookmark folder **Recent**, and click Finish. Go to your Bookmark tab and examine the results.

- Return to the Case Entries view and in the Tree pane, navigate to Documents and Settings\DrDoom\Desktop. Examine its contents. What appears to have been added by the user? Open the folder Hacking Documents. Bookmark the folder structure of the desktop folder. Clear the Dixon box and select the three files in the Hacking Documents folder. Create a bookmark for them, placing them in a bookmark folder named Desktop Contents.

- Return to the Case Entries view and in the Tree pane, navigate to the Recycler. There are two folders named after SIDs, but you don't have the SAM by which to resolve them. The folder ending in *1008* has contents. In the Table view pane, place your cursor or focus on the INFO2 file. In the View pane, switch to the Text view. Create a text style for INFO2 records that is Max Size and with a wrap length of 800 bytes (remember to set code page to Other and Latin 9). Apply that text style and they should line up. You should note that something seems odd about the first and last record as they start with 00h instead of the drive letter. This is because one file was restored and the other was deleted from the Recycle Bin. Place you cursor on byte offset 20 (see GPS for FO 20). Sweep a total of 2,400 bytes (see GPS for LE of 2400). Right-click in the selected text and choose to bookmark the data. For View type, choose Windows ➢ Win2000 Info File Record. Select a proper destination folder, such as Processed INFO2 Record. Before clicking OK, you might add a comment that record 1 and 3 had beginning byte values of 00h, indicating they were restored or deleted from the Recycle Bin. Click OK.

- Go the Bookmarks view and to the INF02 record bookmark you just created. Take note of the paths for records 1 and 3. Go to the Case Entries view and navigate to the original paths of those two entries. Can you determine if either one or both were restored? If so, bookmark the file and make a note that the file was in the Recycle Bin, but was restored to its former location.

- Go the History view tab. In the Table view pane, right-click and choose Email/Internet Search. Select only the Internet Explorer option and click OK. Go to the History tab and in the First Date column, double-click on the column header to view the history in chronological order. In the left pane, place a check on Internet Explorer. In the Table view pane, right-click and choose to bookmark data. Create a destination folder named Inet History. Make sure Bookmark Selected Items is checked and click OK. You now have a bookmark showing the entire history. If you go to the Bookmarks view and place your cursor on the Inet History folder in the Tree pane, a History tab appears next to your Home tab. You can see the history if you switch to this tab. If you choose this Inet History folder to be in your report, the contents of the History tab will be with it.

- Go the Web Cache tab. In the filter pane, navigate to Conditions ➢ Web Cache Attributes ➢ URL. Double-click on URL. We understand that a file was sent to our suspect in a Hotmail and it was named aerial01.jpg, and we want to see if he opened it in cache. In the Edit Conditions menu under URL Find, type **aerial**. This will find any URL in which the word *aerial* appears. Click OK and we find two instances. Bookmark both of them, with appropriate comments, and place them in a folder named Opened Image Attachments.

- You should take careful note here of what you just found. The file that was sent as an attachment and opened on this computer in Hotmail web mail and was named: aerial01.jpg. When it was stored in cache, it was renamed aerial01[2].jpg. There will be an entry in the web cache index.dat for this new file name as it is cached. There will be no reference to this newly named cache file in any of the history files, but there will be references in the history files in URLs when the original file name (aerial01.jpg) was requested. Those references are obscure, and the best way to find them is to search the history index.dat files for the original file name minus its extension (aerial01) and to do so with the Unicode search option enabled because it appears in plain text and in Unicode.

- You should take careful note of something else that has occurred. When you set a condition that the URL string had to contain *aerial*, two entries were returned. We've discussed the first, which was the original file name, but with its name changed slightly for cache storage. The other entry returned was another JPEG, named CALOMP9Z.JPG. If you look, you'll see that the image appears identical. If you hash the cached files, you will find that the original file and this file that appears to be an identical image have the same hash values and are, in fact, identical except for their file names. This file name (CALOMP9Z.JPG) will only be tracked or referenced in the web cache or TIF index.dat file and will not have an entry in any of the history files. Note also that this file is not stored with brackets with a number ([1], [2], etc.) appended to the file name. It is a shadow copy of the original attachment file but with a different name, created and stored for whatever reason Microsoft felt necessary. You will find it a characteristic of e-mail file attachments stored in TIF to be lacking the typical brackets with a number. They are randomly generated 8-byte alphanumeric strings, so the developers apparently felt they would not likely be replicated and didn't bother with the bracketed numbers standard for inbound file names. Outlook Express will also use this area to open attachments, and those attachments will have a file name lacking the brackets and numbers as well. It should be obvious by now that when you are looking for e-mail attachments in web cache, you should start with those without the bracketed numbers. If you find web mail attachments, examine their URLs for something unique to their attachments. Use that string in a URL condition to quickly find those attachments. Let's see how that works with Hotmail, and you can learn from that to apply it to other services.

- While still in the Web Cache tab, let's apply another condition. This condition will allow us to find URLs associated with Hotmail attachments, which is a useful condition to apply in the field, given the frequency of Hotmail attachments in typical forensics examinations. In the previous example, we were looking for a specific attachment. If you carefully looked at the URL, you'll see a string that relates to Hotmail attachments: mimepart=. In the Filter pane, under Conditions, double-click the condition named URL. This time, enter **mimepart=** as the expression (not GREP!) and click OK. What you will see are all attachments and the page from which they were requested. This returns both cached file names for the original file name as modified for cache plus the shadow copy created with an entirely different file name with the bracketed numbers in the file name.

**EXERCISE 9.1** *(continued)*

- Let's recover a print job. Return to the Case Entries view and in the Tree pane, navigate to the WINDOWS\systems32\spool\PRINTERS folder. Note the presence of two sets of spool files. Clear the Dixon box and then select the two sets of spool files (.SPL extensions). Go to your Global Keyword tab. Create a GREP keyword with this string: \x01\x00\x00\x00..\x00 .{34,34}EMF. Name it EMF files. Make sure you select this keyword and deselect all other keywords in both the global- and case-level keyword views. Conduct a search for this keyword in the two sets spool files you selected (Dixon box should show *4*). When done, go to the Search Hits view. You should first note that there were no search hits in the shadow files as they contain only job ticket information. You should also note that of the two spool files, only one contained search hits. One spool file was from a RAW print job (not often encountered) and contains no EMF data files. The search hits were only in the spool file from the EMF print job. Sweep the first few bytes of your first search hit. Right-click and choose to bookmark your data. View your bookmarked data as a picture and the print job should display. Create a destination folder (Recovered Print Jobs) and complete your bookmark. Repeat this for each of the search hits in this spool file until you have recovered all the pages of the print job. The print job you just recovered was an EMF print job (FP00002.SHD & FP0002.SPL). The same exact file was printed on a different printer and by a different user (User is DrDoom) in the RAW mode (00003.SHD & 00003.SPL). You can see that the job ticket information is formatted differently in the two different printing modes.

- Save your case and exit. You may use this evidence and case file at any time you need to quickly review the file signature analysis and reporting.

# Summary

In this chapter, we covered a wide array of artifacts produced by the Windows operating system. Before we could examine specific artifacts, we had to consider one artifact that was common to most artifacts: time. The NTFS file system stores its MAC times in GMT, whereas FAT file systems store their MAC times in local time. FAT uses and MS-DOS time stamp for MAC times; NTFS uses the Windows 64-bit time stamp for MAC times. The Windows 64-bit time stamp measures the number of 10 millionth-of-a-second intervals since January 1, 1601, at 00:00:00 GMT.

When displaying time to the user, NTFS file systems convert the GMT time to local time using the local time offset stored in the Registry. EnCase 4 and 5 use the default offset based on the offset for the examiner's machine. If the offset on your evidence under examination differs from this offset, it can be modified. The Registry can be manually examined for this information or the Sweep Case/Initialize Case/Time Zone EnScript will return the same information with much less effort.

The Recycle Bin is the default location where Windows sends files that have been deleted. The directory entry from the file's original location is marked as deleted and a new entry is created in the Recycle Bin folder. The new name will begin with D for deleted. It will be followed by the letter of the volume from which the file was deleted. It will be followed next by the index number of the file in the INFO2 record. The file will retain its original extension.

All files in the Recycle Bin are tracked and displayed to the user using the INFO2 database. It consists of 800-byte records (280 bytes if Windows 9x) for each file in the Recycle Bin. The record contains the index number, the original file name and path, and the date/time the file was deleted. If the Recycle Bin is on an NT system, the Recycle Bin will have folders for each user's deleted files, and the folders will be named after the user's SID number.

Link files are shortcut files. They are created by Windows, by programs, by user activity without their specific knowledge, or by deliberate intent of the user. The link file contains data about its target file. Among other information, this internal data contains: the name and path of the target file; the volume serial number; the logical size of the target file; and the created, accessed, and written times (CAW) at byte offsets 28, 36, and 44, respectively.

Windows NT, 2000, XP, and 2003 create a series of files that are unique to each user. Windows NT stores them under Profiles while Windows 2000,XP, and 2003 store them under Documents and Settings. The first time a user logs onto one of these systems, a root user folder is created bearing the user's logon name. Nearly all data unique to that user is segregated and secured in these folders. Under the root user folder are several folders created by default, many of which are of forensic interest.

The Recent folder is one of the folders created under the root user folder. The Recent folder contains link files of files and documents opened by the user. Windows displays the most recent 15 of these link files in the My Recent Documents view.

The Desktop folder is another folder created under the root user folder. While the user's actual desktop that they see has content from several possible sources, the contents of this folder, aside from the default content, is placed there by the user and is unique to that user's desktop.

The My Documents folder is another folder created under the root user folder. It contains, by default, at least a My Pictures subfolder and sometimes My eBooks and My Music subfolders, depending on the Windows version and service pack that created them. The purpose of My Documents is to create a unique and secure location for each user's documents. Generally, that which is under My Documents, aside from default folders and files, is attributable to the user the folder belongs to.

The Send To folder is another folder created under the root user folder. Its contents appear in the Windows Explorer right-click menu as Send To options. The user can (but doesn't typically) manually add items to this folder. It is most often populated by application installations and by Windows itself. It is a good place to look for external storage devices, such as zip drives and the like.

The Temp folder is another folder created under the root user folder. It is a vast dumping ground for temporary files. Looking at this area after a file signature analysis can prove quite beneficial. Files located here are specific to and attributable to the user.

The Favorites folder contains special link files for use with the Internet Explorer web browser. These special link files are called Internet Shortcut files and have the extension .url.

The target file for these special shortcut files is a URL address. Some favorites are created by default, some are created by applications or websites, and some are created by the user. Very elaborate folder configurations are a telltale sign that the structure and contents were created by the user.

The Cookies folder contains individual files that contain pieces of code stored by websites to enhance the user's browsing experience, in theory. This code can likewise be misused or exploited. Each cookie is a file using the format username, followed by the @ symbol, followed by the website name. Each has a .txt extension. The cookies are managed by a database file named index.dat, which is located in the Cookies folder.

The History folder contains a series of index.dat files located in folders named after date ranges. The History.IE5 folder contains the main history index.dat file. Each of the subfolders under the History.IE5 folder contains an index.dat file for the time period referenced in the containing folder's date-range name. These files are parsed and displayed in the History tab after running the Email/Internet Search feature in EnCase 5 using the Internet Explorer option.

The Temporary Internet Files (TIF) folder is used to store files that are downloaded from the Web and viewed in Internet Explorer. Other applications are known to use this area for file storage. Outlook Express and Hotmail both open attachments in the cache folders. Outlook creates a separate folder for opening its attachments and is located under TIF; the folder is named beginning with OLK. The Content.IE5 folder contains an index.dat file that tracks the files cached by Internet Explorer (not other applications). This file tracks, among other information, the original URL and file name, the file name as stored in cache, and the cache folder in which the file is stored. This database is parsed and the contents of the cache are displayed in the WebCache view of EnCase 5 after running the Email/Internet Search feature using the Internet Explorer option.

The swap or paging file is used to temporarily store RAM memory when RAM space runs short for its current needs. This file is currently named pagefile.sys on current versions of Windows and is located in the root of the system drive. The hibernation file, named hiberfil.sys, is used by Windows 2000 and XP to go into a hibernation mode to conserve power. The contents of RAM are written to this file so that when the system wakes up, RAM can be restored from this file. It is also located in the root of the system drive. Both these files should be routinely examined as they contain valuable data that can be found in no other location.

When Windows prints data, it caches the print job into two spool files per print job (Windows 2000 and XP). This process allows the print job to function behind the scenes, enabling the user to continue working. Print jobs are placed in queue, and it is essentially a first in, first out (FIFO) operation unless you are working in a networked environment in which certain users or machines have priority status with regard to printing. On a stand-alone workstation, the files are stored in system32\spool\printers. This path is a subfolder of the system root, which is either WINNT or WINDOWS. If the workstation under examination is in a domain environment, you will likely find the spool files on the server as well. When the print job completes, the two spool files are deleted.

The spool files have extensions of .shd and .spl. The former is called the shadow file and the latter is called the spool file. The shadow file contains printer job information only. The spool file contains printer job information and the actual print job data itself. If the printer is configured for the RAW mode, the print job data will be one continuous stream of graphical output data. If the printer is configured for the EMF mode (the default and therefore most common), each printed page of output is represented by an EMF file embedded within the spool file. They appear sequentially arranged in the order that the pages will print.

EMF files have unique headers, but many variants of the header exist even within the same version of Windows. Headers can be located and print jobs can be recovered. As spool files are deleted after the print job, rarely will you find them as allocated files. Most times, you will find them in unallocated clusters, in the swap file, in the hibernation file, or in file slack, but you should search everywhere to be thorough.

# Exam Essentials

**Know and understand time stamps.**   Understand and explain how NTFS differs from FAT in the method by which it stores MAC times. Be able to explain GMT and local time. Know how to determine the time zone offset for an evidence file. Explain how to modify the time zone offset for a device. Explain the 64-bit Windows date and time stamp as compared to the DOS and the Unix time stamp.

**Understand the purpose and function of the Recycle Bin.**   Explain how Windows normally deletes files. Describe what happens to file names (directory or MFT record entries) when a file is deleted from its original location and moved to the Recycle Bin. Explain the naming convention of a file name when it is located in the Recycle Bin. Describe what information is contained in the INFO2 file. Explain the purpose and function of the INFO2 file. Explain what happens to the INFO2 record entry for a single file that is either deleted or restored from the Recycle Bin. Understand what happens to the INFO2 file when the entire Recycle Bin is emptied. Know the INFO2 record lengths for various versions of Windows. Be able to create a text style for an INFO2 record and bookmark the data in the INFO2 record.

**Understand the purpose and function of link files.**   Understand how, where, and why links files are created. Know what link files are created by the operating system, applications, and by the user, both knowingly and unknowing. Describe how to create a desktop shortcut. Be able to explain, in detail, the contents or data portion of a link file. Know which time stamps are stored inside the link file, particularly the specific time stamps names (MAC), the correct order of their appearance, the byte offsets at which they are located, and the time stamp format. Explain the concept of a target file in the context of a link file.

**Know and understand the root user folder and its default subfolders.**   Understand and explain what a root user folder is and when it is created. Describe the folders created under the root user folder. Understand and explain the purpose and function of the Recent folder, specifically what kind of files it contains, how they are created, what purpose these files serve for the user, and the forensic significance of the files found in this folder.

Explain the purpose and function of the My Documents, Send To, Temp, and Favorites folders. Explain why the contents contained in the root user folder and its subfolders are usually attributable to the logged-in root user or owner of these folders and files.

**Know and understand the contents, purpose, and function of the Cookies, History, and Temporary Internet Files folders and their contents.**   Know and understand what a cookie is and the file naming convention in which they are stored. Explain the purpose of the index.dat file found in the Cookies folder.

Explain the purpose of the History folder. Know the purpose of the main history index.dat file located in History.IE5 folder. Explain the naming convention of the subfolders located under History.IE5. Describe the purpose of each index.dat file located in each of these subfolders as it relates to the user interface in Internet Explorer. Aside from containing Internet history, explain what other local file information may be found here and how it is created.

Explain the purpose of the Temporary Internet Files (TIF) folder. Explain the purpose of the index.dat file located in the Content.IE5 folder. Know the contents of the subfolders under Content.IE5 folder. Explain how and why files are cached in these folders. Describe how and why a file name is changed or modified when stored in cache. Know which file stores both the cached file name and the original file name (in the URL).

Explain how EnCase 5 parses and displays the contents of the Cookies, History, and Temporary Internet Files. Describe what other files, aside from cached web page content, found in the TIF subfolders.

**Understand the Windows printing process.**   Understand and be able to explain how Windows prints data and which files are created in the process. Explain the concept of spooling. Explain the contents of a shadow file and know what extension this file will have. Explain the contents of a spool file and know what extension this file will have. Describe the default location for printer spool files and understand that it can be modified by the user. Be able to explain the differences between RAW and EMF modes. Explain which mode is the default and most commonly encountered mode. Explain what files are produced in the EMF mode and in which file they are stored. Explain how multiple-page printed documents are handled in the EMF mode. Explain the manual process by which EMF print jobs can be recovered.

# Review Questions

1. An operating system artifact can be defined as:

   **A.** Information specific to a user's preference

   **B.** Information about the computer's general settings

   **C.** Information stored about a user's activities on the computer

   **D.** Information used to simplify a user's experience

   **E.** All of the above

2. A FAT file system stores date and time stamps in _____ whereas the NTFS file system stores date and time stamps in _____.

   **A.** DOS directory and local time

   **B.** Zulu time and GMT

   **C.** Local time and GMT

   **D.** SYSTEM.DAT and NTUSER.DAT

3. Where does Windows store the time zone offset?

   **A.** BIOS

   **B.** Registry

   **C.** INFO2 file

   **D.** DOS directory or MFT

4. The date and time of when a file was sent to the Recycle Bin can be found in:

   **A.** INFO2 file

   **B.** Original file name's last access date

   **C.** DOS directory or MFT

   **D.** index.dat file

5. When a text file is sent to the Recycle Bin, Windows changes the short file name of the deleted file to DC0.txt in the Recycle Bin. Select the best choice that explains the deleted filename.

   **A.** D=DOS, C=character, 0=index number, file extension remains the same

   **B.** D=DOS, C=drive letter, 0= index number, file extension remains the same

   **C.** D=deleted, C=character, 0= index number, file extension remains the same

   **D.** D=deleted, C=drive letter, 0= index number, file extension remains the same

6. When a document is opened, a link file bearing the document's file name is created in the _____ folder.

   **A.** Shortcut

   **B.** Recent

   **C.** Temp

   **D.** History

7. Link files are shortcuts or pointers to actual items. These actual items can be:

   **A.** Programs

   **B.** Documents

   **C.** Folders

   **D.** Devices

   **E.** All of the above

8. In NTFS, information unique to a specific user is stored in the _____ file.

   **A.** USER.DAT

   **B.** NTUSER.DAT

   **C.** SYSTEM.DAT

   **D.** None of the above

9. In Windows XP, by default, how many recently opened documents are displayed in the My Recent Documents folder?

   **A.** 4

   **B.** 12

   **C.** 15

   **D.** Unlimited

10. Most of a user's desktop items on a Windows XP operating system would be located in the _____ directory.

    **A.** C:\WINDOWS\Desktop

    **B.** C:\WinNT\Desktop

    **C.** C:\WINDOWS\system32\config\Desktop

    **D.** C:\Documents and Settings\(*user name\Desktop*

11. As this file will hold the contents of RAM when the machine is powered off, the _____ file will be the size of the system RAM and will be in the root directory.

    **A.** hyberfil.sys

    **B.** WIN386.SWP

    **C.** PAGEFILE.SYS

    **D.** NTUSER.DAT

**12.** Where can you find evidence of web-based e-mail such as from MSN Hotmail or Google's GMAIL on a Windows XP system?

   **A.** In Temporary Internet Files under Local Settings in the user's profile

   **B.** In Unallocated Clusters

   **C.** In the pagefile.sys folder

   **D.** In the hiberfil.sys folder

   **E.** All of the above

**13.** File names with the .url extension that direct web browsers to a specific website are located in which folder?

   **A.** Favorites folder

   **B.** Cookies folder

   **C.** Send To folder

   **D.** History folder

**14.** Data about Internet cookies such as URL names, date and time stamps, and pointers to the actual location of the cookie is stored in:

   **A.** INFO2 file

   **B.** index.dat file

   **C.** EMF file

   **D.** pagefile.sys file

**15.** On a Windows 98 machine, which folder is the swap or page file contained in?

   **A.** WIN386.SWP

   **B.** pagefile.sys

   **C.** swapfile.sys

   **D.** page.swp

**16.** When you are examining evidence that has been sent to a printer, which file contains an image of the actual print job?

   **A.** The Enhanced Metafile (EMF)

   **B.** The shadow file

   **C.** The spool file

   **D.** The RAW file

**17.** The two modes for printing in Windows are _____ and _____.

   **A.** Spooled and Shadowed

   **B.** Spooled and Direct

   **C.** Spooled and EM

   **D.** EMF and Raw

18. Although the Windows operating system removed the EMF file upon a successful print job, the examiner may still recover the file as a result of a search on its unique header information in areas such as Unallocated Clusters or swap file.

    **A.** True

    **B.** False

19. The index.dat files are system files that store information about other files. They track date and time stamps, file locations, and name changes. Select the folder that does *not* contain an index.dat file.

    **A.** Cookies

    **B.** History

    **C.** Recycle Bin

    **D.** Temporary Internet Files

20. The Temporary Internet Files directory contains:

    **A.** Web page files that are cached or saved for possible later reuse

    **B.** An index.dat file that serves as a database for the management of the cached files

    **C.** Web mail artifacts

    **D.** All of the above

# Answers to Review Questions

1. E. Operating system artifacts serves as information used by the computer to fulfill certain user- and system-specific requirements and needs.

2. C. A FAT file system stores date and time stamps in local time while the NTFS file system stores date and time stamps in GMT.

3. B. Windows stores the time zone offset in the Registry.

4. A. When a file is sent to the Recycle Bin, the date and time of when the file was deleted is saved in the INFO2 file.

5. D. When a file is sent to the Recycle Bin, Windows changes the short filename to D for Deleted, followed by the drive letter and the index number. The file extension for the deleted file remains the same.

6. B. When a user opens a document, a link file bearing the document's filename is created in the Recent folder.

7. E. Link files are shortcuts to a variety of items such as programs, documents, folders, and devices such as removable media.

8. B. In NTFS, information unique to a specific user is stored in the NTUSER.DAT file.

9. C. By default, the My Recent Documents folder displays 15 recently opened documents; however, the actual folder may contain hundreds more.

10. D. A specific user's Desktop items are located in the path C:\Documents and Settings\(*user name\Desktop* in a Windows XP operating system.

11. A. When the system goes into hibernation, the contents of RAM are written to the file "hiberfil.sys", which is the exact size of RAM and located in the root of the system drive.

12. E. Evidence of web-based e-mail is commonly viewed but not saved. Therefore, its contents may be found in the Temporary Internet Files folder, Unallocated Clusters, or the pagefile.sys and hiberfil.sys folders.

13. A. The Favorites folder contains files links that directs the browser to certain websites. These link files usually have a name that describes the website followed with the .url extension.

14. B. Information about an Internet cookie such as the URL name, date and time stamps, and pointers to the actual cookie are stored in the index.dat file.

15. A. The swap file is saved as WIN386.SWP in a Windows 98 machine while Windows XP saves it as pagefile.sys.

16. C. The .spl or spool file contains an image of what is sent to the printer to be printed.

17. D. The two printing modes in Windows are raw and EMF.

**18.** A. Even though Windows deletes the EMF file after a print job has been completed, EnCase may still be able to recover the file by doing a search of its unique header information.

**19.** C. The Recycle Bin does not contain an index.dat file; it contains the INFO2 file.

**20.** D. The Temporary Internet Files directory contains all of the above-mentioned items.

# Chapter

# 10

# Advanced EnCase

Our final chapter is a collection of advanced analysis concepts and tools. We begin with working with deleted partitions. We'll rely heavily on concepts covered in Chapter 2 as we examine the MBR, VBR, and recovered deleted partitions.

There are a large number of complex files that can be "mounted" within EnCase for further examination and analysis. We describe the various ones supported, how they are mounted, and what to expect when they are mounted.

Among the files that EnCase can mount are the system Registry files. A number of files comprise the system Registry of the most current versions of Windows. We'll discuss how the files are mounted and the various Registry keys that are derived from those files. As understanding the Registry is an important forensic skill, we'll explore some Registry research techniques with the live Windows Registry on a little-understood Registry key. From that research, we'll better understand that particular key and develop valuable Registry research skills in the process.

Throughout the text we have made reference to and used some basic EnScripts. In this chapter, we cover how to use the current EnScript feature set and its options.

E-mail seems to be a consistent factor in nearly every forensic examination. E-mail clients abound and EnCase 5 provides support for most of the mainstream clients, with more under development. We'll cover which clients are currently covered and how EnCase 5 mounts and displays various e-mail databases.

While we are on the topic of e-mail, we will explore base64 encoding, which is the most commonly encountered method for encoding e-mail attachments. We cover how EnCase handles it automatically as well as how to manually extract it from the unallocated clusters.

EnCase versions 4 and 5 have three optional modules that you can purchase. The EnCase Decryption Suite (EDS) decrypts data and files encrypted with the Windows Encrypted File System (EFS). We'll cover the basic features of this module.

Two other modules are available: the Virtual File System (VFS) and the Physical Disk Emulator (PDE). VFS mounts the evidence file device as a file system so that it is available as a mounted volume in Windows. With this mounting, all data, including deleted folders and files, can be analyzed in Windows with third-party tools or Windows system tools. PDE is similar, but mounts the evidence file device as a physical device in Windows. We'll discuss the similarities and differences between the two modules and how they can be used to further your examinations.

Sometimes you need to export an application to run a file in its native environment, so we'll cover that technique. Occasionally you may need to restore an entire drive to boot and run the system as the suspect used it. That technique is called *restoration*, and we'll cover that as well.

# Locating and Mounting Partitions

As we go through this section, we'll make frequent references to concepts covered in detail in Chapter 2. If you aren't comfortable with MBRs, partition tables, VBRs, partition types, physical and logical sector addresses, CHS, and tracks, you may want to reread that chapter or at least refer to it frequently to refresh your understanding.

You should recall that the MBR is located at the very first physical sector of a hard drive. Although it contains important boot code, it also contains the partition table that can describe up to four partitions on that hard drive. The partition table consists of 64 bytes and starts in physical sector 0 at byte offsets 446 through 509. Each of four possible partitions is described by a 16-byte string.

Figure 10.1 shows the partition table in sector 0, byte offsets 446 through 509, selected and bookmarked. You should note that we are working in the Disk view in the Table pane. When the data is viewed in the bookmark as a Windows partition entry, the data relating to the defined partitions is parsed and displayed. In this case, the partition type is 07h, which is NTFS. Its status is 80h, which means that the partition is the active, bootable partition. Using the legacy CHS system, the start point for the partition is 0:1:1 and the stop point is 1023:254:63. The more meaningful information follows the CHS addressing, which is the starting sector and the size in sectors. The size of the partition is 145,211,474 sectors, relative to sector 63, which is the starting sector. If we add 63 to 145,211,474 and subtract 1, we arrive at 145,211,534, which is the sector number of the last sector in the partition.

**FIGURE 10.1**    64-byte partition table selected, bookmarked, and viewed as a Windows partition entry

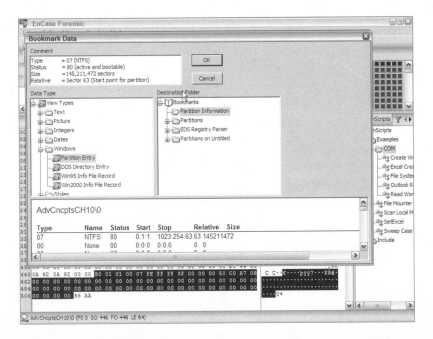

Since we know the starting sector of the partition from the partition table, we can easily go to that sector to view the first sector of the partition, which we have learned is the VBR. In our example, the first sector of the partition is at sector 63. If we go to that sector, we will be at the VBR. Figure 10.2 shows the data found at sector 63, which is the VBR. The position indicator (GPS) confirms we are at physical sector (PS) 63. VBRs have headers or signatures that will eventually allow us to find them if the partition table entries are deleted. One of these signatures or headers is selected (first 7 bytes) in Figure 10.2. If you'll recall from Chapter 2, the first 3 bytes are the jump instructions and the string that follows describes the operating system that did the formatting.

**FIGURE 10.2**    This partition starts at sector 63, which contains the VBR.

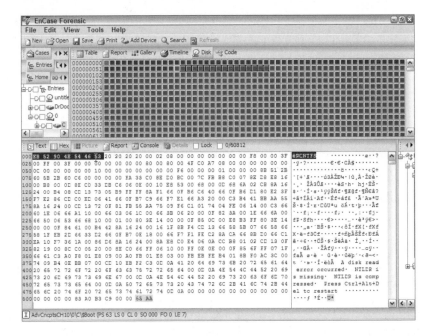

If a partition utility such as fdisk is used to remove a partition, the 16 bytes for that partition in the partition table are changed to all zeros. Figure 10.3 shows a partition table after fdisk was used to remove all partitions. The partition itself, however, and all of its data are untouched by the process. It is similar to the process of deleting a file whereby only the pointers to the data are removed or altered while the data remains unchanged. With that in mind, it should be apparent that a partition can be easily recovered under these circumstances.

To recover deleted partitions, you must locate the beginning of the partition by locating the VBR. As VBRs have telltale signatures, they are relatively easy to locate. While looking for VBRs, you will encounter a few search hits that are not partitions. Each NTFS partition keeps a backup copy of the VBR in the last sector of that partition. Of course, knowing where a partition ends is also useful information. The recommended method of recovering partitions is to start with the partition found nearest the beginning of the drive and work from that direction, restoring partitions as you go. When you do, you'll find that many of your "hits" will be within allocated files or within the restored partition, as in the case of the backup VBR.

**FIGURE 10.3**    The partition table contains all zeros after fdisk was used to remove all partitions. There is no directory structure and all squares in the Disk view indicate "no partition."

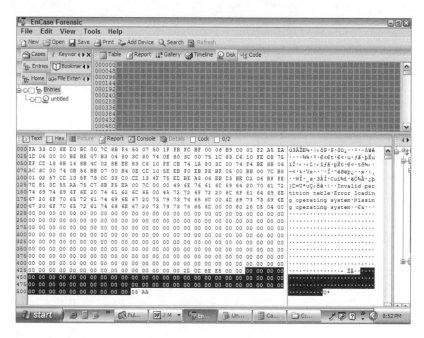

We know that the MBR is in the first sector of the drive, which is sector 0. As most drives currently have 63 sectors per track and the remainder of the first track is unused, we can expect sectors 1 through sector 62 to be all zeros. Some tracking utilities write data in this space, but most of the time it will contains zeros. Sector 63 is the first sector of the second track and where you will normally find the beginning of the first partition. On older drives, where there were 39 sectors per track, look at sector 39 for the beginning of the first partition.

Most certainly we could have crafted a search term to locate this VBR, but because we know where to look, it is often quicker to go to that sector first. The drive in our example is an older one with 39 sectors per track. If we take a shortcut and go immediately to sector 39, we see a VBR at that location. While in the Disk view and with your cursor on the sector containing the VBR (beginning of the partition), right-click and choose to add a partition. You will see the Add Partition dialog box, as shown in Figure 10.4. EnCase will parse the data in the VBR and use that information to populate the fields in the dialog box, which will be used to correctly rebuild the partition. Click OK and EnCase will restore the partition and the directory structure will be visible in the Tree pane view.

**FIGURE 10.4**    The Add Partition dialog box contains information parsed from the VBR by EnCase and is subsequently used to restore the partition when you click OK.

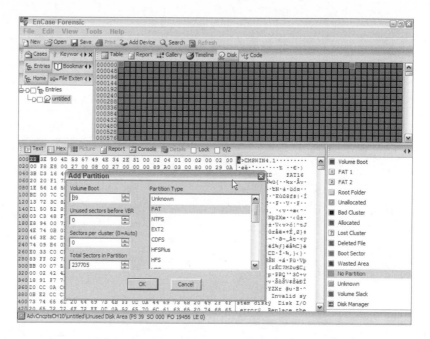

It is important to note that the evidence file is not changed by this process. Even after you have restored the partition, if you go back and check, you will find that the partition table still contains all zeros. EnCase restores the partition virtually with pointers contained within the case file. Figure 10.5 shows the correct directory structure after the partition was restored.

If you need to remove a partition, go to the sector where you created the partition, right-click, and choose to delete the partition. Alternatively, you could right-click anywhere in the Disk view and choose to delete all user-defined partitions.

If you have more than one partition to restore, it then becomes advantageous to search for partitions. You could create a series of search strings and search for them manually; however, EnCase has a well-designed EnScript to do that work for you. Like most EnScripts, it is an option or module within the Sweep Case EnScript. Once you run the Sweep Case EnScript, you will see the Options dialog box. Select the Partition Finder. If you double-click the Partition Finder, you will find there are no options, but you'll see a nice description of what to expect, as shown in Figure 10.6. Click OK to close the Partition Finder dialog box, create a destination folder for your bookmark, and click Finish to run the EnScript.

**FIGURE 10.5** After the partition is recovered, the directory structure is restored to normal.

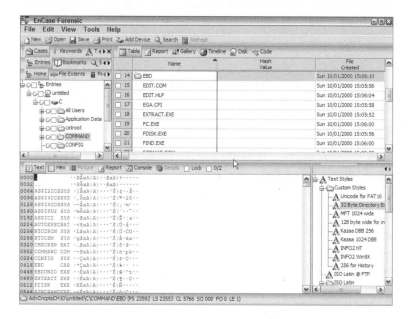

**FIGURE 10.6** The Partition Finder EnScript will locate partitions and note them in a bookmark.

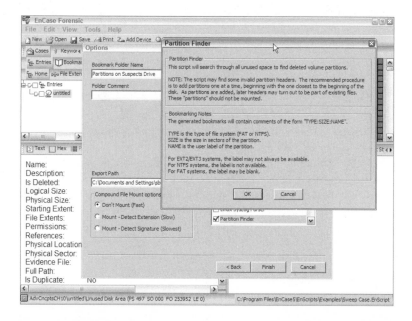

If you go to the Bookmarks tab, you'll typically find the partitions located by the EnScript along with some false positives. The bookmark will contain a comment for each hit that describes the partition parameters in the format of *Partition Type : Size in Sectors : Name*. Figure 10.7 shows the results of the Partition Finder. You will note that two hits were reported and the comment section shows the information about the partition. Note that the columns have been arranged in an optimal manner for this task. The data is seen in the Preview column, followed by partition information in the Comment column, and followed finally by the sector in which the bookmark occurs in the Bookmark Sector column.

**FIGURE 10.7**   The Bookmark view shows the results of the Partition Finder. Note the columns and their arrangement.

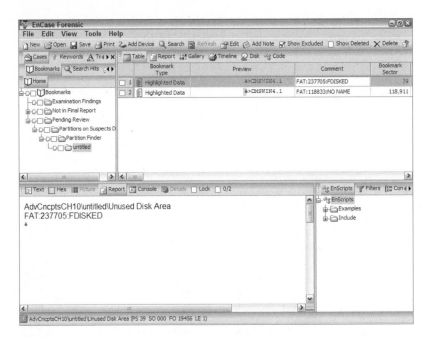

By arranging these particular columns as shown in Figure 10.7, you can see at a glance which bookmarks are most likely partitions and which are most likely not. It is also helpful if you sort them on the Bookmark Sector column; this will arrange them in the order they appear on the device.

Now it is time to logically examine the results. While not in the current view, we examined our device before we started this process and determined it contained 237,744 total sectors. The first bookmarked item starts at sector 39. As the device has 39 sectors per track, sectors 0–38 (39 sectors) appear on the first track. Sector 39 marks the beginning of the second track and the normal location for the first partition. It makes sense, therefore, that this search hit is describing a valid partition. If we look at its size, which is 237,705 sectors, we find that it covers nearly the entire drive except for 39 sectors. Because there are 39 sectors in the first track that are outside the partition, we have accounted for the entire drive with this partition restored.

If we examine the other search hit, located at sector 118,911, we can conclude that it is contained within the recovered partition. We might therefore conclude that it is a false hit, a backup VBR, or data within a file. With that conclusion, we could dismiss it and move on—or we could consider one more possibility. Suppose there were, at one time, two partitions on this drive and that the user removed them and partitioned the device as one large partition. The first partition starting at sector 39 would have been overwritten immediately, but the partition starting somewhere out there in the middle of the drive might still exist and be recoverable.

Let's place our cursor or focus on that second bookmark starting at sector 118,911. If we switch to the Disk view tab, we find that we are immediately placed on sector 118,911. If we switch to the Hex view in the View pane, we see data that appears to be a VBR. If we right-click on that sector in the Disk view and choose to add a partition, EnCase reads the data in the VBR and populates the Add Partition dialog box. EnCase doesn't know what preceded the partition, and so it assumes there are 63 unused sectors (1 track at 63 sectors per track) preceding the VBR. To avoid including these 63 additional sectors on the front of our restored partition, change that value from 63 to 0, as shown in Figure 10.8, and click OK to restore the partition.

**FIGURE 10.8**   Sector 118,911 contains what appears to be a VBR. Right-click on that sector, add a partition, and change the unused sectors before VBR to zero.

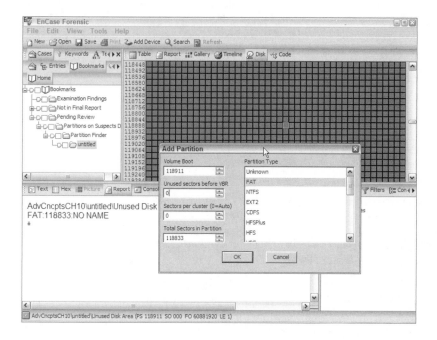

When the partition is virtually restored, you can go to the Tree pane and check the resulting directory structure to see if it appears to be correct. When it's right, it's obviously right and when it's wrong, it's obviously wrong. In our case, the bookmark indicated a valid partition that had been removed and the drive had been partitioned to one large partition. We can now analyze the restored partition, running searches and bookmarking our findings.

Figure 10.9 shows the directory structure for the restored partition. Note that the volume name has been changed to "Recovered Partition" to better describe that partition and to prevent confusion. EnCase 5 permits this volume name change as a right-click option when the volume is selected. As you can see in the Disk view, this partition occurs in the middle of the drive.

**FIGURE 10.9** The old partition recovered from the middle of the drive. Note that the volume name was changed virtually, in EnCase, to "Recovered Partition."

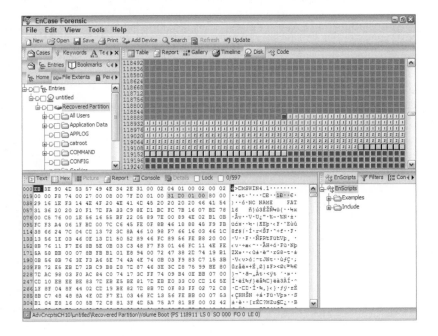

EnCase provides a Recover Folders feature. It is available at the volume level by right-clicking and choosing Recover Folders. EnCase will scan the volume for both FAT and NTFS directory structure metadata and will restore what it can. You should run this feature very early in your case as a routine task. This same feature can be used to recover folders from formatted volumes as the recovery process is the same.

**EXERCISE 10.1**

## Partition Recovery

In this exercise, we will examine a drive on which the partitions have been deleted using fdisk. We'll locate and recover those partitions.

- Create a folder structure for a new case according to our standard folder naming and structuring conventions. Name your case folder name **PartitionRecovery**. Create a new case, pointing it to your newly created folders. Before you place any evidence in your case, save your case in the root of the folder PartitionRecovery, which will also be the default name for your case. Locate an evidence file on the CD named Advanced\ FDiskedDrive2GB.E01. Place it in the evidence folder for your newly created case.

- On the toolbar, click Add Device. Create a path to your new evidence file if one does not exist. Locate your new evidence file in the right pane of the Add Device window and complete the steps to bring the evidence file into your new case. Once it has been added, click Save.

- In the Tree pane, select the root of your case tree, forcing the newly added device into the Table view pane. From the Table pane, select the device. In the View pane, select the Report tab and confirm that the evidence file verified.

- Go back to the Tree pane and look at the physical device. There should be no volume or directory structure present. If you place your cursor on the physical device in the Tree pane, the Table pane should show one entry for "unused disk space." When you see this condition, you should be thinking of a few causes. One is that you forgot to plug in your dongle; were this the case, you'd see "EnCase Acquisition Version" in place of "EnCase Forensic" or "EnCase Enterprise". Once you eliminate that possibility, then it is time to consider that the drive has been wiped or that the partition has been deleted.

- Switch to the Disk view in the Table pane. All sector boxes should be gray, indicating unpartitioned space. Go to physical sector 0. You should see data in the View pane, indicating this drive has not been wiped. In sector 0, sweep 64 bytes starting at byte offset 446 and ending at byte offset 509. Bookmark the data and view it as a Windows partition table. As the data was all zeros, we see nothing for a partition table entry, meaning the partition was removed.

- We know this drive has 63 sectors per track, based on our reading of the drive label. Based on our knowledge of disks, we would expect the VBR of the first partition to be at the beginning of the second track, which would be physical sector 63. Navigate to physical sector 63. We immediately see what we now recognize as a VBR and most likely NTFS.

- Right-click on physical sector 63 and choose Add Partition, accept the defaults, and click OK. Go to the Tree pane and use the Set Included Folders trigger to refresh the device tree. When you do, you should see a volume and directory structure. Navigate through it and make sure it appears to be a correct and valid recovery. It should appear correct immediately; if it weren't, it would stand out as very wrong! We are done, right? Perhaps, perhaps not. Next, let's survey the sector layout.

- If we look at the Report view for our device, we can quickly see that our device is approximately 2GB and that our recovered partition is approximately 1GB. Perhaps we are not yet finished!

- We can run the Partition Finder EnScript and locate possible partitions, or we can manually look around in the vicinity of physical sector 2,056,319 and see what we can find. It is easier to run the EnScript. When you are done, you'll see three entries in the Bookmarks view. If you sort them on the column Bookmark Start, you'll have them arranged in the order they appear on the drive.

- If you highlight the first one and switch to the Disk view, you land at that sector. If you do this for each of the three, you'll see that the first one is the backup VBR for the first partition that we already recovered; we should ignore that one. If you look at the second and third one, you'll see that they are a matched set. The second bookmark begins in the sector immediately following the backup VBR for the first partition (first bookmark), and it also precedes the sector for the third bookmark by six sectors. A FAT32 has a backup VBR six sectors after the VBR, so it's logical to conclude that the second bookmark at physical sector 2,056,320 marks the VBR for the second deleted partition.

- Place your cursor on physical sector 2,056,320 in the Disk view. Right-click and choose Add Partition. Instead of accepting the default of 63 unused sectors before the VBR, change this to **0** and then click OK.

- Go to the Tree pane. Refresh your Tree pane by clicking the Set Included Folders button off and then back on. You should now see the second partition restored. With that, you have recovered two deleted partitions.

- Click Save All and exit EnCase.

# Mounting Files

Many files are compound in nature. A compound file contains data that may be hierarchical, compressed, encrypted, or a combination of these methods. Its raw data is often illogical, difficult, or even impossible to view in its native state. EnCase can decode and mount these files so they are displayed in a logical or hierarchical format. In this manner, the examiner can see the data in the file in a more meaningful and logical format. The process is the same for mounting any compound file. You simply right-click on the file, select the View File Structure option, and then click OK in the resulting dialog box. Figure 10.10 shows the right-click menu with the option View File Structure selected.

**FIGURE  10.10**    To mount a compound file, right-click on it and choose View File Structure.

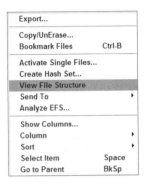

EnCase mounts the compound file and you can navigate its structure from within the Tree pane beginning at the special icon denoting the root of the mounted compound file, which is shown in Figure 10.11. To unmount a mounted file, right-click on the special icon in the Tree pane view and choose Close, and the mounted file will be unmounted.

**FIGURE  10.11**    This special icon denotes a mounted compound file. Note the hierarchical file structure mounted below the special icon.

Often there are temp files that are compound files. Running a file signature analysis reveals these file as having an alias of " * Compound Document File" in the file signature column. These files are good candidates to mount and examine.

The list of files that can be mounted seems to grow with each release of EnCase. There is a condition on the CD that you can import into your conditions. This condition filters for most of the files that are known to be mountable. If you edit the condition after importing it in, you'll see that it seeks files by certain extensions, others by name, and others by a file signature condition. You can add or delete from this list of conditions as you wish.

To import this condition, go to the Filter pane and select the Conditions tab. Place your cursor on the File Groups folder, right-click, and choose to import. Browse to the file on the CD in a folder named Conditions and select the file named compound file condition.txt. Click OK, and the condition will import into your list of available conditions.

Table 10.1 shows a list of the most common files that can be mounted within the EnCase environment. There is a brief description of the file and what data can be seen upon mounting.

**TABLE 10.1** Listing of Common Compound Files That Can Be mounted in EnCase

| File | Type | Description |
|------|------|-------------|
| .dbx extension | Outlook Express E-mail | Mounting places e-mails in a hierarchical structure instead of viewing in a flat file. |
| .mbx extension | Outlook Express E-mail (earlier versions) | Mounting places e-mails in a hierarchical structure instead of viewing in a flat file. |
| .doc extension | Microsoft Word Document | Mounting places various objects in a folder structure so that you can view the various document properties such as the data, document summary information, etc. |
| .xls extension | Microsoft Excel Spreadsheet | Mounting places various objects in a folder structure so that you can view the various document properties such as the data, document summary information, etc. |
| .ppt extension | Microsoft PowerPoint Document | Mounting places various objects in a folder structure so that you can view the various document properties such as the data, document summary information, etc. |
| .zip extension | WinZip compressed file | Mounting decompresses the archives, presenting the individual files for examination. |
| .pst extension | Outlook E-mail | Mounting places e-mails in a hierarchical structure instead of viewing in a flat file. Outlook's structure is very detailed. |
| .MailDB extension | MSN Mail (has dbx header and structure) | Mounting places e-mails in a hierarchical structure instead of viewing in a flat file. |
| .msi extension | Microsoft Installer | Mounting shows some of the properties of this installer package. |
| Thumbs.db | Hidden system file created when using Explorer in the thumbnails view | Mounted file shows thumbnails of images in folder on the last occasion the user viewed thumbnails. Can show thumbnail images of files that were deleted. It also shows that user saw images and was aware of contents, which is very useful in cases where inappropriate or unlawful images are at issue. |

**TABLE 10.1**  Listing of Common Compound Files That Can Be mounted in EnCase

| File | Type | Description |
|------|------|-------------|
| System.dat<br>User.dat<br>System<br>Security<br>Software<br>SAM<br>Default<br>NTUSER.DAT | Registry files for Windows 9*x* and NT systems | Mounting these files parses the specific Registry hive and allows the examiner to navigate that branch of the Registry in a hierarchical view. The Registry will be covered in detail in the next section. |
| .tar extension | tar compressed file | Mounting decompresses the archives, presenting the individual files for examination. |

Some compound files can be searched without mounting them; others require mounting before they can be searched. For the most part, the determining factor is whether the data is compressed, encrypted, or both. For example, ZIP or TAR files are compressed and a normal search using the active code page won't find data within them. If, you mount them, however, the compressed text is uncompressed during mounting and they can then be searched.

An Outlook PST file, for example, stores its data using Outlook compressible encryption. Thus, it is compressed and encrypted. If you search this file using the active code page, don't expect to find any meaningful data. If you mount this file, the data is uncompressed, decrypted, and displayed in a hierarchical structure. In this format, it may be easily searched.

When you run the Email/Internet Search feature, EnCase mounts the various files you have selected (Outlook causes the PST file to be mounted, Outlook Express cause the DBX and MBX files to be mounted, etc.). Once you have them mounted, you can effectively search them.

Microsoft Office documents can be searched without mounting. Mounting Office documents doesn't decrypt or uncompress data; it simply places data in a hierarchical format for organized or logical viewing.

Thus, it is important to understand which files can be searched without mounting and which files can't be searched until they are mounted. Also, it is important to understand that certain files are mounted as part of other processing, such as the Email/Internet Search, in which the files for the selected options are mounted.

EnCase provides a file mounting EnScript that will mount files for you, based on options that you select when you run the EnScript. It is a stand-alone EnScript and not a module of the Sweep Case EnScript; thus you will find it at the same level as the Sweep Case EnScript under EnScript\Examples. As shown in Figure 10.12, when you double-click the File Mounter EnScript, you will have the option to mount the following compound file types: DBX, GZIP, PST, TAR, Thumbs.db, or ZIP. As further options, the process can be based on file extension, file signature, or both and can also be limited to selected files. In this manner, you can mount files using an automated tool and subsequently search their contents.

---

## Searching for Outlook PST Data in the Unallocated Clusters

Outlook leaves fragments of its data throughout the hard drive in slack space, in unallocated space, in the swap file, and in the hibernation file. This space can't be mounted as a PST file and searched, but it can be effectively searched for Outlook data. The first step is to create a keyword to search. When you create the keyword, you need to select a Unicode search and turn off the active code page. Next, go to the Code page tab. Go down the list of available code pages until you reach the Outlook Compressible Encryption code page, which is code number "65003" and is often number 48 on the list, but that could vary as the list will include all code pages installed on the Windows version on your examiner workstation. Place a checkmark next to this code page. Click OK to create your keyword. Search your case using this keyword. Go to the Search Hits view. Your search hits that appear as gibberish are Outlook-compressible encryption that has been found but that you can't yet view until you create a text style for Outlook-compressible encryption. In the Filter pane, go to the Text Style tab and create a new text style. Name it **Outlook Compressible Encryption**. On the Text Style Code page tab, deselect the Unicode button and select Other. Go down the list until you find Outlook Compressible Encryption, which is code number "65003." Highlight it and click OK to create the text style. Select your new text style and the gibberish should change to viewable text. Bookmark any text in your search hits and while in the Bookmark data view, under View Types, your newly created text style will appear as an option. When you select Outlook Compressible Encryption as the view type, your bookmark will be viewable in plain text. Select a destination folder, click OK, and you are done.

---

**FIGURE 10.12**     File Mounter EnScript options

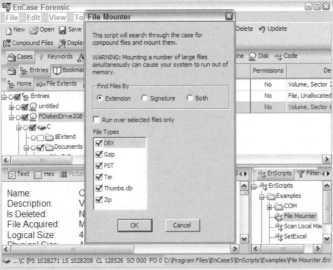

# Registry

The Windows Registry is a central repository or database of the configuration data for the operating system and most of its programs. While it creates a convenient central location for this data, it also creates the potential for a single point of failure that can bring the system to a halt. Due to that vulnerability, the operating system uses safeguards to enable recovery to safe configurations through the use of "last known good configuration" and restore points in Windows XP.

**WARNING**    To understand the Registry as seen in EnCase, you need to understand the live Registry as seen in Windows. As we go through this chapter, we will explore and in some cases make changes to your system Registry. No discussion of Registry changes would be complete without the customary warning: Changing your system Registry could harm your operating system. Consequently, if you aren't comfortable with doing so, don't. If you wish to make changes, back up your Registry first or create a restore point before proceeding.

With the warnings behind us, let's proceed. To be certain, the Registry is a gold mine of forensic evidence. Since Microsoft discourages users, administrators included, from accessing or modifying the Registry, they are doing their part in helping us preserve evidence, for which we are most grateful. As an examiner, you need to be very comfortable navigating within and working with the data in the Registry. Comfort comes with knowledge, understanding, and experience, which are the precise goals of this section.

In this section, we provide a background of the Registry, including its history and its current structure. We'll introduce you to the terminology associated with the Registry, such as hives, keys, subkeys, and values.

Once we describe the terminology and structure, we'll cover research techniques that will enable you to look under the hood and truly understand the internal workings of the Registry. We'll target a very obscure and little understood Registry key for this research. When we are done, you will join a relatively elite group of examiners who understand and properly interpret the function and values contained in this key. Its forensic usefulness will unfold before your eyes!

If you are going to testify as to what a particular value in the Registry means, you need to be able to demonstrate and explain those values. After completing this section, you should have the tools and techniques to do so.

## Registry History

If you trace Windows back to its roots, its predecessor was MS-DOS. MS-DOS was a command-line interface whose configuration settings, by today's standards, were, at most, anemic. MS-DOS received its configuration settings from two modest little files: config.sys and autoexec.bat. The config.sys file primarily loaded device drivers, and autoexec.bat was for setting environment variables, running programs, and the like.

The first Windows GUI was Microsoft Windows 3.0. This first version of Windows introduced INI files as containers for configuration files. These were flat text files with no hierarchical structure, and related configuration data was sectionalized. Text files made it difficult to store binary data, and they were numerous and lacking in organization.

Windows 3.1 followed shortly after Windows 3.0, and with it came the rudiments of the system Registry as a repository for system configuration settings. Windows 95 and NT 3.5 expanded the Registry to the structure and interface that we recognize today in Windows XP, although it was fraction of the size and complexity of today's Registry. The files in which the Registry values are stored have gone from two with Windows 9*x* to six or more with Windows 2000/XP/2003.

## Registry Organization and Terminology

The Windows Registry is stored in files called *hives* at a physical level. The interface for the user and applications takes on a logical scheme or format that resembles the directory structure used by Windows Explorer to store data in files and folders. Instead of using folders, the Registry uses keys. Instead of using files, the Registry uses values. If you think of it using that analogy, you are well along your way to understanding the hierarchy and terminology.

The interface by which the user primarily views or modifies the Registry is with the Registry editor tool. With Windows 2000, you had to choose between two Registry editors (regedit.exe or regedt32.exe) depending on the task at hand. Either would allow you to view and navigate the Registry, but each had capabilities and limitations that the other did not have, forcing a choice at times. Fortunately, Microsoft resolved that problem with the release of Windows XP/2003 and combined all features into one Registry editor known simply as regedit.

Microsoft does not provide a shortcut to the Registry editor on any known dialog box. In fact, Microsoft keeps the Registry well below the radar screen, making only brief mention of the Registry in the Windows help feature. At every stage Microsoft recommends against editing the Registry, even to the point of recommending that administrators edit the Registry as a last resort. That being said, you'll find regedit.exe in the root of Windows and usually access it from the Run command. To open the Run command, hold down the Windows key and press R (for run). In the resulting window, type **regedit** and press Enter. Figure 10.13 shows the Registry editor when you open it. The left pane is known as the key pane, and the right pane is known as the value pane.

**FIGURE 10.13** The Windows XP Registry editor

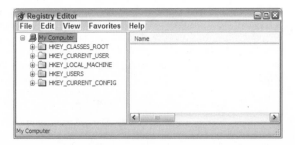

The Windows Registry consists of five root-level keys, shown in Figure 10.13. Those root keys, along with a brief description of their purpose, are listed in Table 10.2. Of those five root keys, only two are master keys, while the remaining three are derived keys that are linked to keys within the two master keys.

**TABLE 10.2**    Five Root Keys of the Registry

| Root Key Name | Description |
| --- | --- |
| HKEY_CLASSES_ROOT | Used to associate file types with programs that open them and also used to register classes for Component Object Model (COM) objects. It is the largest of the root keys in terms of the Registry space it occupies. This key is derived from a linked merger of two keys, which are HKLM\Software\Classes and HKCU\Software\Classes. This merger effectively blends default settings with per-user settings. |
| HKEY_CURRENT_USER | Used to configure the environment for the console user. It is a per-user setting (specific only to this user) and is derived from a link to HKU\SID, where the SID is the user's security identifier. |
| HKEY_CURRENT_CONFIG | Used to establish the current hardware configuration profile. This key is derived from a link to HKLM\SYSTEM\CurrentControlSet\Hardware Profiles\Current. Current is derived from a link to HKLM\SYSTEM\CurrentControlSet\Hardware Profiles\####, where #### is a number that increments starting at 0000. HKLM\SYSTEM\CurrentControlSet, in turn, is a link to HKLM\SYSTEM\ControlSet###, where ### is a number that increments starting at 000. Which Control Set is current and used to create this key and subsequent link is determined by the value located in HKLM\SYSTEM\Select\Current. |
| HKEY_LOCAL_MACHINE | Used to establish the per-computer settings. Settings found in this key apply to the machine and all of its users, covering all facets of the computer's function. This key is a master key and is not, therefore, derived from any link as are the previous three keys. |
| HKEY_USERS | Used to contain the user environment settings for the console user as well as other users who have logged onto the system. There will be at least three subkeys—.DEFAULT, SID, and SID_Classes, where the SID is that of the console user. You may also find SIDs S-1-5-18, S-1-5-19, and S-1-5-20, which are for the LocalSystem, LocalService, and NetworkService accounts, respectively. Any other SIDs found here will belong to other users who have logged on to the machine. This key is a master key and is not, therefore, derived from any link. |

At a physical level, each of the logical master keys has its source data stored a file that is called a hive. In each of the two master keys (HKLM and HKU), there are subkeys named for each of the hive files. Table 10.3 shows the hive keys and their associated hive files from which they originate. These hive files are located in the folder %SYSTEMROOT%\System32\config.

**TABLE 10.3**    HKLM Hive Keys and Their Corresponding Hive Files

| Hive Key | Hive File |
| --- | --- |
| HKLM\SAM | %SYSTEMROOT%\System32\config\SAM |
| HKLM\SECURITY | %SYSTEMROOT%\System32\config\SECURITY |
| HKLM\SOFTWARE | %SYSTEMROOT%\System32\config\software |
| HKLM\SYSTEM | %SYSTEMROOT%\System32\config\system |

If you look at the live Registry under the master key HKLM, you see the above four hive keys, plus you will see one more that is named HARDWARE. Interestingly, HARDWARE is a dynamic key with no source hive file at the physical level. It is created as a dynamic key in RAM when Windows XP boots. When the system shuts down, the data in this key is gone.

Thus far, we've covered the hive keys and files located in HKLM. The master key HKU has its share of hive files as well. In fact, each subkey under HKU is a hive key with a corresponding hive file. The hive files for HKU are found in several locations. Table 10.4 shows the various hive keys in HKU and their source hive files. When SID is referenced, it is the SID of the console user or other past logged-on user. When UserName is referenced, it is the user name that corresponds to the SID.

**TABLE 10.4**    HKU Hive Keys and Their Corresponding Hive Files

| Hive Key | Hive File |
| --- | --- |
| HKU\.DEFAULT | %SYSTEMROOT%\System32\config\default |
| HKU\S-1-5-19 | Documents and Settings\LocalService ntuser.dat |
| HKU\S-1-5-19_Classes | Documents and Settings\LocalService\Local Settings\Application Data\Microsoft\Windows\UsrClass.dat |
| HKU\S-1-5-20 | Documents and Settings\NetworkService ntuser.dat |
| HKU\S-1-5-20_Classes | Documents and Settings\NetworkService\Local Settings\Application Data\Microsoft\Windows\UsrClass.dat |

**TABLE 10.4**    HKU Hive Keys and Their Corresponding Hive Files *(continued)*

| Hive Key | Hive File |
| --- | --- |
| HKU\SID | Documents and Settings\UserName\ntuser.dat |
| HKU\SID_Classes | Documents and Settings\UserName\Local Settings\Application Data\Microsoft\Windows\UsrClass.dat |

When the system loads these hives into the Registry, there is one key that lists or maps the loaded hive files with their corresponding Registry hive keys. This key is an excellent place to visit as it shows the relationships between hive files and hive keys that are loaded on the system, which is shown in Figure 10.14. This key may be found at HKEY_LOCAL_MACHINE\ SYSTEM\CurrentControlSet\Control\hivelist but only in the live Registry. When the system is shut down, none of the hives are loaded.

**FIGURE 10.14**    Key "hivelist" shows currently loaded hive files and their mapping to Registry hive keys

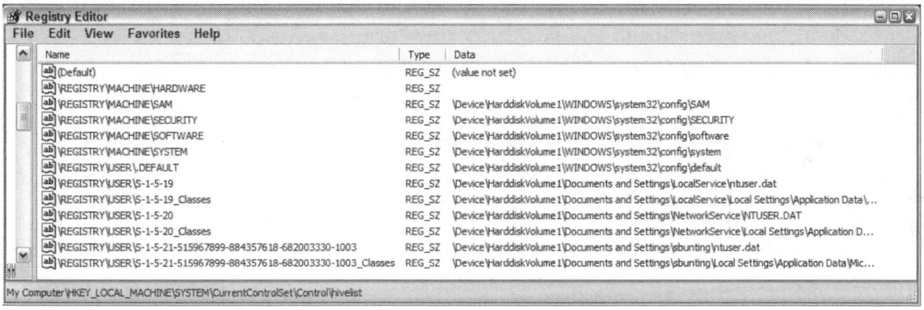

As we mentioned earlier, the Registry keys are displayed in the left, or key, pane of the Registry editor. It is from this pane that you may navigate among the various Registry keys. The right, or value, pane is the pane in which you view or access the Registry values. A value has three components: its name, its data type, and its data. Figure 10.15 shows the Registry editor in which a series of values are shown in the right, or value, pane. In the value pane there is a column for each of the three value attributes (name, type, and data).

All values have names; there can't be a null name. A value's name is analogous to a file's name. A value name can be up to 512 ANSI characters in length (256 Unicode characters), except for the special characters question mark (?), backslash (\), and asterisk (*). Furthermore, Windows XP reserves all value names that begin with a period (.). Just as no folder can contain two files with exactly the same name, no key can contain two values with exactly the same name.

**FIGURE 10.15**   Registry editor showing Registry values in the right, or value, pane

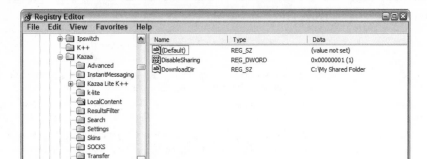

Each value contains data of a specified data type. That type is specified by number that is interpreted by the Registry API so that the user sees the data type in plain text. Table 10.5 shows each of the data types, their corresponding number, and a brief description of what the data type means. When you see a Registry value in EnCase versions that precede version 5, only the data type number will be shown, not the plain-text version rendered by the Registry API. EnCase 5 interprets the numeric value and returns the plain text data type as shown in Table 10.5. In all versions, the data type appears in the file type column.

**TABLE 10.5**   Listing of Registry Value Data Types

| Data Type | Number | Description |
| --- | --- | --- |
| REG_NONE | 0 | Data type is not defined. |
| REG_SZ | 1 | Fixed-length text string expressed in user-friendly format, which is often used to describe components. |
| REG_EXPAND_SZ | 2 | Variable or expandable length data string. |
| REG_BINARY | 3 | Binary data that is displayed in editor as hex. |
| REG_DWORD | 4 | 32-bit double word values and the most common data type found in the Registry. |
| REG_DWORD_ LITTLE_ENDIAN | 4 | 32-bit double word values with bytes in reverse order. As Intel already stores data in this format, this term is synonymous with REG_DWORD and they have the same numeric value. |

**TABLE 10.5**    Listing of Registry Value Data Types *(continued)*

| Data Type | Number | Description |
| --- | --- | --- |
| REG_DWORD_BIG_ ENDIAN | 5 | 32-bit double word value with bytes in normal order, with the highest bit appearing first. |
| REG_LINK | 6 | An internal-use only data type for Unicode symbolic link. |
| REG_MULTI_SZ | 7 | Multiple-string field in which each string is separated by a null (00h) and with two nulls (00 00) marking the end of the list of strings. |
| REG_RESOURCE_ LIST | 8 | Listing of resource lists for devices or device drivers (REG_FULL_RESOURCE_DESCRIPTOR). You can view but not edit these lists. |

# Using EnCase to Mount and View the Registry

We've now covered the basics of the live Registry as seen by the user in a Registry editor. It is the logical interface by which the Registry hive files are addressed, viewed, and edited. The live Registry, as thus far depicted, and the Registry as seen in EnCase will have noticeable differences.

When you view the Registry in EnCase, you are looking at only the hive files, and the view will differ from a live Registry view in many ways. For example, you will not see the Hardware key that exists in the live Registry under HKLM. This key is a dynamic key, created at boot, and exists only in RAM while the system is loaded and running. There is no Hardware hive file for this dynamic key.

You have seen that certain keys exist virtually as links to keys on the master keys. You should not therefore expect to see the virtually created keys, but you can certainly view their data by going to the key to which they are linked. For example, don't expect to see HKEY_CURRENT_USER in the EnCase Registry. However, we know that this key is derived from the SID key under HKEY_USERS and that the SID key is actually a hive key whose source file is NTUSER.DAT, which is located in the root of the SID user's folder (root user folder). By mounting and viewing a particular user's NTUSER.DAT, you are looking at what was their HKEY_CURRENT_USER key and its content (user environment/profile) when they were last logged on.

In the previous section (when we discussed mounting files), we referenced the Registry files as being *mountable* files within EnCase. Just like any other mountable file, to mount a Registry hive file you need only right-click on one of the hive files and choose to view its file structure. Before you mount the file, however, you must first locate it. EnCase makes this task very easy by using the Conditions feature. Go to the Filters pane, navigate to the Conditions tab, and double-click on the Registry files condition, which is located in the File Groups folder. With this condition set, activate the Set Included Folders trigger at the device level and the Registry files will appear in the Table view pane, as shown in Figure 10.16.

**FIGURE  10.16**    The Registry files condition is set with the Set Included Folders button activated at the device level. All Registry hive files are then displayed in the Table view pane.

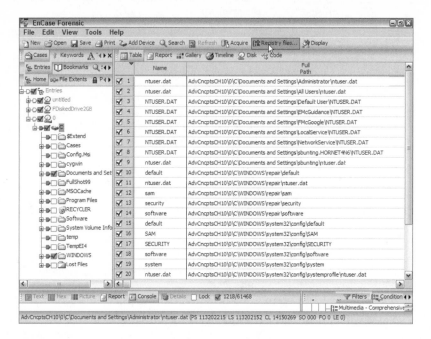

If you look at the five hive files (SAM, SECURITY, software, system, and default) located in the %SystemRoot%\system32\config folder, you will note that they have a counterpart by the same name located in the %SystemRoot%\repair folder. The ones in the repair folder are there for repair purposes (basic configuration) if things go wrong. We want the active Registry hive files in the config folder. Don't confuse the two!

To mount any of the hive files, simply right-click on the desired file and choose to view its file structure. As some of these files are very large and complex, mounting them may take some time, but usually less than a minute. When the file mounts, you can navigate through the various keys as you would any hierarchical file structure. If you used the Registry files condition to locate the hive files, before you can navigate and see values in the Table pane, you'll need to turn off that condition by clicking on it on the toolbar. When a value is displayed in the Table view pane, you will see its name in the Name column, its data type in the File Type column, and its data in the View pane in either the Text or Hex view.

Figure 10.17 shows the system hive file mounted. The Select key contains four values. While the others are important, we wish to know which Control Set is current, and the value named Current contains the data that makes that determination. In this case, the data for the value named Current is a DWORD data type and the data reads 01 00 00 00. This value translates into, simply, one, and the current control set is one. Forensically, we look to the values contained in ControlSet001 to be that of the CurrentControlSet.

**FIGURE 10.17**     The system hive file is mounted. The Select key contains a value named Current whose data determines the CurrentControlSet.

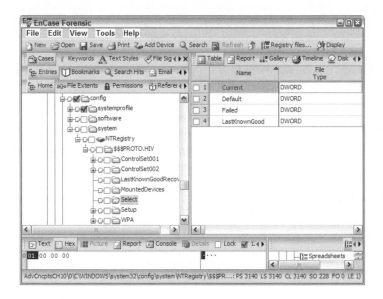

When you use the Registry files condition to locate Registry hive files, you may find several copies of Registry hive file backups in various locations. Hackers are very good at backing up their Registries before experimenting with hacking tools. They have learned the hard way that it pays to back up their Registry, particularly when working with Trojans and other nefarious utilities. You may find considerable evidence of their activities in these backup copies, so don't overlook them.

# Registry Research Techniques

You should, by now, have a good understanding of the Registry and how it is logically organized. You should be familiar with the Registry editor and navigating the Registry keys. You should be able to determine a value's name, data type, and data. You should also grasp the differences between the live Registry in Windows and the offline Registry as viewed in EnCase.

While a basic understanding is good, this section is intended to go well beyond the basics. We are going to use a third-party tool to monitor writes to the Registry while we hack it. We will target the UserAssist key with our research. When we are done, you will truly appreciate the Registry and tools used to examine it. What's more, you'll discover a new source of evidence that has been hidden and lacking in proper documentation for too long.

If you are hesitant to modify your Registry, just read along and keep your fingers off the keyboard. If you choose to follow along with the research on a live system, I suggest backing up your Registry and doing it on a test box rather than a production system. Everything we will describe here I have done on a least a dozen systems and caused them no harm. The first one, however, was a test box. Just remember that even monkeys fall out of trees on occasion, so play it safe as you proceed.

When you click the Start button in the bottom left of Windows, you are presented with a list immediately above it. On the bottom left is the word Programs with a green arrow pointing to the right. Immediately above the word Programs is a list of programs that you can launch by clicking on them. As you can see, this listing of programs is actually broken down into two sections. The bottom section of programs is set off by two horizontal lines, one at the bottom and one at the top, forming somewhat of a subtle container or box. The top section of programs is called the pinned area, whereby the user can add or delete items by dragging and dropping, hence the word pinned.

We are going to focus our attention on the lower section, the one shown in Figure 10.18 that is set off by the two horizontal lines marking its upper and lower boundaries. You have probably noticed that the content of this area changes while the upper section remains fixed unless you change it manually or add a program that places its program in this section. This lower section derives its content from a Registry key called the UserAssist key, and the contents are based on some Microsoft magic formula involving frequency and recency. This key clearly tracks both attributes.

You will find nothing from Microsoft that documents the relationship between this feature and the UserAssist Registry key. Accordingly you will find nothing from them that suggests or supports the next step, which will be to remove a subkey from the UserAssist key that will cause this feature to display nothing, thereby establishing its source in the Registry. You needn't worry; the moment you reboot, Windows will regenerate the key just like a lizard grows a new tail when the old one is pulled off. Don't expect, however, that Windows will replace any key that you remove as this simply doesn't normally occur.

Before we remove the subkeys, we are going to look at their content and then do some other things first. Let's first look at the data in this key. Hold down the Windows key and press R. In the Run window, type **regedit** and press Enter. In the key pane, navigate to HKCU\Software\Microsoft\Windows\CurrentVersion\Explorer\UserAssist. Under this key you will see two subkeys: {5E6AB780-7743-11CF-A12B-00AA004AE837} and {75048700-EF1F-11D0-9888-006097DEACF9}. Despite their uninteresting names, the latter key holds some extremely interesting and valuable contents. Under the latter key, navigate to its subfolder, named Count. The values contained in the value pane for the Count key are shown in Figure 10.19.

If the latter key had an ugly and uninteresting name, the contents of the Count subkey at first seem just as meaningless. What you are looking at is ROT-13 encoding. It dates back to the days of the Romans, and it decodes by rotating the character set 13 places. Using this scheme, *a* equals *n*, *b* equals *o*, *c* equals *p*, and so forth. For whatever reason, someone at Microsoft likes this encoding scheme as it is used frequently in the Registry to obscure content. Case sensitivity conveys in the encoding and numbers and special characters remain unchanged. Because of these characteristics, you know it at a glance when you encounter it. Now that we know what it is, let's have some fun with it and develop some knowledge and understanding along the way.

**FIGURE  10.18**    The Windows Start menu divides programs. The content in this area is dynamic and is generated by data stored in the UserAssist key.

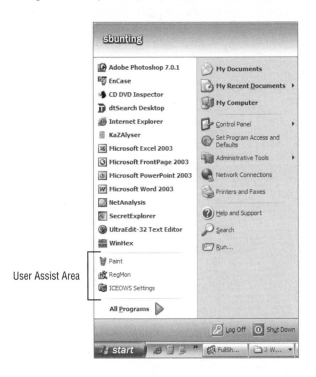

**FIGURE  10.19**    Values contained in the Count key appear meaningless but they aren't.

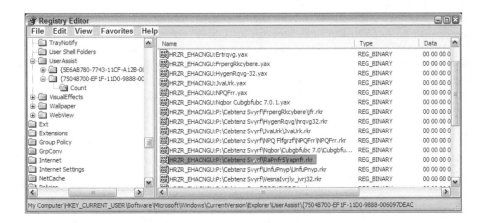

In Figure 10.19, one value is highlighted: HRZR_EHACNGU:P:\Cebtenz Svyrf\RaPnfr5\ rapnfr.rkr. If you double-click a value, it will open an editor allowing you to view or edit the value's data. Figure 10.20 shows the editor open for this value. This value appears as a 16-byte or 128-bit value and, because of its length, it too appears obscure and meaningless at first glance. As everything has a meaning or purpose, let's take things one step at a time and decipher this value, beginning with its name.

**FIGURE 10.20**     Double-click any value and an editor opens allowing you to view or edit the data.

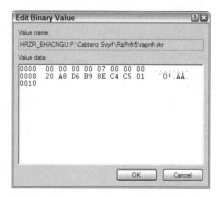

Starting with EnCase 5, you can bookmark data and have, as a view type option, the ability to decode ROT-13. This will serve us well when it comes time to decode ROT-13 within EnCase, but for now, we'll use an external encoder and decoder. This will help us quickly understand the encoding scheme and further allow us to generate ROT-13 search terms.

Go the folder on the CD labeled ROT13 and double-click on the single web document in this folder. This is a ROT-13 encoder/decoder that is based on JavaScript that has been released into the public domain. You must have JavaScript enabled to run it, and you'll have to get past the browser prompts that temporarily block the code pending your approval. Once you have passed those hurdles, you have two windows: one for input and another for output. Since the code rotates 13 characters, which is one-half the alphabet, the input window can accept either encoded or decoded text, as one is a mirror of the other.

If you paste the string HRZR_EHACNGU:P:\Cebtenz Svyrf\RaPnfr5\rapnfr.rkr into the decoder, you'll immediately see the decoded string in the bottom output window, which is UEME_RUNPATH:C:\Program Files\EnCase5\encase.exe. Link files and executable files will be preceded by UEME_RUNPATH. When a program is run, its path is encoded and recorded as the value name. Because this key is tracking the frequency and recency of programs and other accesses, it stands to reason that we should find that information in the data portion of this value.

If you recall, the data was 16 bytes. This data actually breaks down into three distinct pieces of data. The last 8 bytes is a 64-bit Windows timestamp, and it represents the last time the program was opened. It is stored in GMT and displayed in the local time zone offset. When you see

8 bytes of data ending with 01h, there's a good chance that you are looking at a Windows time-stamp. With the timestamp, we have resolved the recency piece of the puzzle.

Immediately preceding the 8 bytes comprising the timestamp, there is a Dword (4 bytes or 32 bits). This Dword is a 32-bit integer that is a counter for the number of times that the program, link file, or other object has been opened. The very first time a program or link file is recorded, it is assigned a counter value of 06h, which is decimal six. From that point forward, it will increment one for each time that particular program, link file, or object is opened. It seems to give each program 5 bonus points the first time it is opened. I would venture a guess that this is part of some weighted averaging scheme that figures into their calculation, along with some pixie dust from Microsoft.

If the data for the counter for a particular program were to display 6E 00 00 00, we'd find this to be decimal 110. To accurately state the number of times this program had been opened, we'd have to subtract 5 from this value, making it 105 times that the program had been opened.

The first 4 bytes or Dword still remains an unknown. It clearly is tracking some value and may perhaps be some combined index of frequency and recency, but that is pure conjecture. If you can figure this part out, I'd appreciate hearing from you.

Forensically we have some pretty good information. We can tell that a particularly program or tool has been opened a certain number of times, and we can track the date and time it was last opened. If we encountered a string that read HRZR_EHACNGU:P:\Qbphzragf naq Frg-gvatf\fohagvat.UBEARG4A6\Qrfxgbc\FhoFrira\rqvgfreire.rkr and we decoded it, we'd find it to be UEME_RUNPATH:C:\Documents and Settings\sbunting.HORNET4N6\Desktop\Sub-Seven\editserver.exe. That piece of information is already most significant as it shows that the user is building a SubSeven Trojan with this tool.

If we decoded the last 8 bytes of this value's data (40 F1 C8 61 58 C5 C5 01), we'd find this program was last opened on Thursday, 29 September 2005 20:46:23 -0400. If we further decoded the counter, which is 0E 00 00 00, we'd find it was decimal 14. We would subtract 5 from that number and we could state that the SubSeven Trojan editor program had been opened nine times, with the last time being on Thursday, 29 September 2005 20:46:23 -0400. Clearly, this is significant evidence!

So far, this has been an imaginary venture, with you relying on me telling you how this key works. All that is about to change as we begin our research and validation of this information. So far, you have only been navigating the Registry. The next phase will involve deleting keys and adding keys. If this is your first time working with the Registry, do this only on a test box. If you are comfortable working with the Registry, you may still wish to do this only on a test box. I consider this a safe exercise and have done it many times on many boxes, but your mileage could vary. With the warnings out of the way, let's have some fun.

For the first part of our research, go the SysInternals website at http://www.sysinter-nals.com. Locate and download their free utility regmon for Windows NT/2000/XP. Double-click on the regmon.exe executable, and this utility will launch in its default mode. This program has the capability to monitor every read or write to the Registry. In its default mode, that is exactly what it is doing. You'll be faced with an information overload as the screen fills and scrolls with Registry activity. The program tracks the time, the process making the read or write, the Registry path, and the value. Figure 10.21 shows regmon in its default mode as it reports on all Registry activity.

**FIGURE  10.21**    regmon in default mode

To make things a little more manageable, regmon has the ability to filter its output. Click Options and choose Filter/Highlight. By default, you will see all of the check boxes in the bottom selected, which means that regmon is reporting everything. Deselect the check boxes except Log Writes and Log Successes. In this mode, you are only logging successful writes, but even that alone can result in a huge volume of activity. We want to report only on successful writes to the UserAssist key, so in the Include entry box, type **UserAssist***. When you are done, the Regmon Filter dialog box should look like Figure 10.22. Click OK when you are done. Then select Edit ➢ Clear Display to clear the screen and start with a fresh slate.

**FIGURE  10.22**    regmon filter settings

To test that regmon is set up and working properly, open any program and watch the regmon interface. You should see values being written to the UserAssist key only, and the key value names will be in ROT-13. For now, let's leave regmon running so we can watch writes to the UserAssist key. At any point you wish to clear the screen, just select Edit ➢ Clear Display.

Next we are going to do several steps. We are going to create a Registry key, remove two Registry keys, stop and restart Explorer, and then watch the result of our work. The Registry key that we are going to create is a one that tells Windows not to encode in ROT-13. By creating this setting, we ensure that all writes to the UserAssist key will be in plain text, allowing us to observe all activity very clearly. By removing the two keys with big ugly names, we'll clear the contents of all ROT-13 entries. By stopping and restarting Explorer, we effectively achieve a soft reboot that resets the Registry. This causes our new setting to take effect, and it also causes the two deleted keys to regenerate. With those steps in place, we can watch and analyze the activity taking place in this key. Let's get to work.

First, click your Windows Start button and observe which programs are in the dynamic User-Assist area. Make a note somewhere so you can refer to it later if you would like.

If you are not comfortable creating a Registry key, go to the folder on the CD named User-AssistSettings and double-click on the file named UserAssistSettings.reg. Click Yes so that the proper key and values are written to your Registry.

If you'd prefer to have the experience, or you don't trust others writing to your Registry, you can do it manually. Open regedit and navigate to the following key: HKEY_CURRENT_USER\Software\Microsoft\Windows\CurrentVersion\Explorer\UserAssist. In the left, or key, pane, right-click on the UserAssist key and choose New ➢ Key. Name the new key **Settings**, adhering to the case sensitivity as given. When done, you should have a new subkey under User-Assist named Settings.

Next you need to add a value to the Settings key. Place your cursor on the Settings key, right-click on it, and choose New ➢ DWORD Value. Name the value **NoEncrypt**, adhering to the case sensitivity as given. The default value of the data is 0, so we need to change it. Double-click on the value NoEncrypt and you are presented with a dialog box that lets you edit the DWORD value. Change the value data from hex zero to hex one. Click OK and your setting is complete.

Figure 10.23 shows the addition of the Settings key and the NoEncrypt value set to hex one. If you used the file on the CD, the setting included another value, which is nothing more than a RegistryChangeNote string comment that I place in the Registry whenever I make an edit. It helps document changes and provides a way to quickly search for my user edits.

**FIGURE 10.23**    The UserAssist key after adding the Settings key and NoEncrypt value

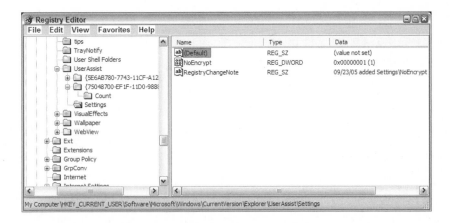

Our next step will be to remove the two UserAssist keys that have long, uninteresting names: {5E6AB780-7743-11CF-A12B-00AA004AE837} and {75048700-EF1F-11D0-9888-006097DEACF9}. Right-click on either key and choose Delete. You will see a prompt asking if you wish to delete this key and its subkeys; click Yes. With regedit, there is no undelete function or Recycle Bin. Delete means delete! Repeat the deletion process for the other key, so that your finished result matches Figure 10.24. Keep both regedit and regmon open and running during the next step.

**FIGURE 10.24**    The UserAssist key after the removal of two keys with long, uninteresting names

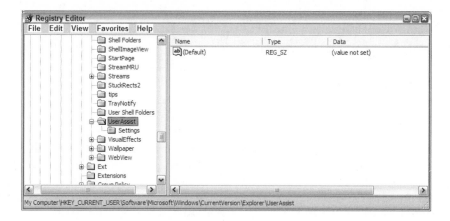

Next, we are going to stop and restart explorer.exe to refresh Explorer and the Registry. It's also a good troubleshooting technique for those times when Explorer hangs or misbehaves. Press Ctrl-Alt-Del to bring up the Task Manager and click the Processes tab. Locate and highlight explorer.exe in the list of running processes, as shown in Figure 10.25. Click End Process and click through the warning dialog box that appears next to stop Explorer. Your desktop depends on Explorer, so it will temporarily disappear. Don't worry; we'll bring it back in a minute.

**FIGURE 10.25**    Using Task Manager to stop explorer.exe

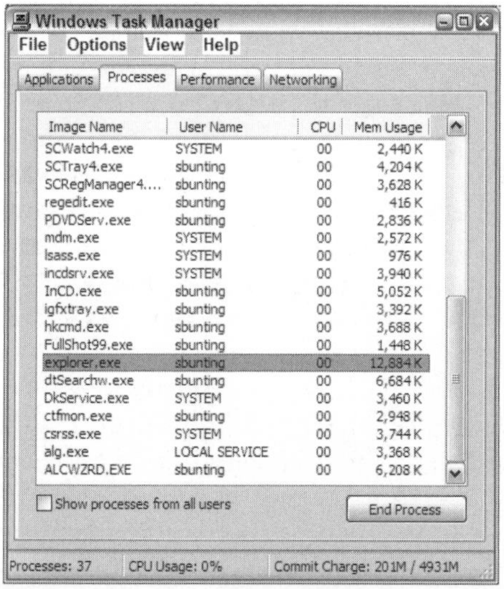

Now that you have stopped Explorer, it is time to restart it. While still in the Task Manager, go to the Applications tab and click New Task. Navigate to %SystemRoot%\explorer.exe, as shown in Figure 10.26, and click OK to restart Explorer. Everything should return to normal and you can now close your Task Manager. As part of stopping and restarting Explorer our Registry settings were refreshed. If you don't touch anything else and go directly to the Windows Start button, nothing should be in the dynamic UserAssist area. Your Registry is refreshed, and there is no data in the UserAssist keys with which to populate this area, clearly establishing the relationship of this Windows feature with the UserAssist key.

**FIGURE 10.26**    Using Task Manager's New Task function to restart Explorer

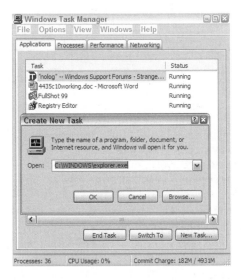

The regmon and regedit utilities should still be open as we did not close them. If you closed them, opening them now will reflect in the UserAssist key. Make regedit the active window and press F5 to refresh its contents. You should note that Windows regenerated the two keys that you deleted. Go to the Count subkey under the key {75048700-EF1F-11D0-9888-006097DEACF9} and note its contents. The value names should be minimal and no longer encoded in ROT-13. They should appear in plain text.

Make regmon the active window and clear its screen. We are now prepared to watch the User-Assist key in action and appreciate its forensic value. Select Start ➢ Programs ➢ Accessories ➢ Paint. Go to regmon and look at the entries. Some of the information is of little forensic value while other information is most significant. If you process the last 8 bytes of the data as a 64-bit Windows timestamp, the date and time will reflect the instant you opened the program. The counter for the Microsoft Paint link and the Paint executable appear for the first time as 06 00 00 00. If you close Paint and reopen it, both the link and executable will sequence to 07 00 00 00. As you will recall, to determine how many times a program was opened, convert the 32-bit value in the counter to decimal and subtract 5. Table 10.6 shows the attributes of the typical values found in this key and how they are interpreted.

**TABLE 10.6**    UserAssist Key Value Attributes Decoded

| Decoded Value Name (normally ROT-13) | Description | Unk Data | Counter (Dword) | 64-bit Windows Timestamp |
|---|---|---|---|---|
| UEME_RUNPATH:C:\Documents and Settings\sbunting.HORNET4N6\Desktop\SubSeven\SubSeven.exe | Path to executable | 00 00 00 00 | 08 00 00 00 Decimal 8 minus 5 = 3 times actually run | 10 85 CF 65 BB C6 C5 01 Sat, 01 October 2005 15:07:41 -0400 Time is the instant that program was last run and is stored in GMT and converted to local offset |

There are two values that appear in the list by default, aside from the default value; they are UEME_CTLCUACount:ctor and UEME_CTLSESSION. The former has a 16-byte data value, but the timestamp bytes typically appear as all zeros. The latter has an 8-byte value with no timestamp present. These would appear to serve as some kind of control or master counters. They seem to have no forensic value and you can ignore them in your analysis.

If you go back to regedit, you can see the final result of the various writes. First you need to press F5 to refresh the view. Depending on how many times you opened Paint, you will see that reflected in the counter value and the date and time will reflect the last time it was opened.

You might not be excited over how many times the user opened Paint, but certainly if the user accessed other more interesting programs, the values in this key can provide significant evidence. Let's see what other information we can garner from our analysis of this key.

Often forensics examiners post questions to message boards asking if there's any way to tell whether the user has altered the time on a system. Although there several indicators to be considered, the UserAssist key provides some significant information. The most common user interface for modifying the date and time is the date and time applet available from the icon in the System Tray or in the Control Panel. You'll be pleased to know that the UserAssist key tracks this access. You can even tell whether it was accessed from the System Tray or the Control Panel, in addition to how many times it was accessed and the date and time of last access.

Make regmon the active window and then double-click on the date/time icon in the System Tray. The resultant entry in the UserAssist key is UEME_RUNCPL:timedate.cpl, which is the Control Panel program to set the date and time (%SystemRoot%\system32\timedate.cpl). Since this is the first time we've run the timedate Control Panel since we dumped the old data and started fresh, the counter should return a value of 06 00 00 00 or decimal 6. If we subtract 5, we get the actual count, which is one time. If we look at the last 8 bytes to resolve the date and time, we'll find that it reflects the date and time of the instant that we opened the date and time Control Panel. You should now start to understand how this key works.

Let's suppose that while we have this timedate Control Panel open, we are going to change the year to 2003 so that we can engage in some nefarious activity and push the timestamps back to confuse later investigative efforts. Once done, we click OK to change the year and off we go. After we have engaged in our nefarious acts, whatever they may have been, those acts will bear the timestamp of today's date, but in the year 2003. Now it is time to change our time back to make it accurate again. We open the timedate Control Panel and change the year back to the current one. We click OK and the time is accurate again.

If we look at regmon we will see that we caused two writes to the UserAssist key value: UEME_RUNCPL:timedate.cpl, one for each time we accessed the timedate Control Panel. These two writes are recorded by regmon and are shown in Figure 10.27. As last write wins, we would expect the actual Registry to bear the data reflecting the last write. This means the counter will reflect 07 00 00 00 or decimal 7, which will actual be 2 after we subtract 5 from 7.

**FIGURE  10.27**    regmon captures the writes when the timedate Control Panel is accessed.

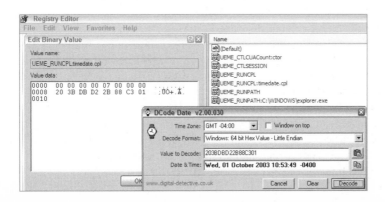

The date timestamp for the UserAssist key value, UEME_RUNCPL:timedate.cpl, however, is the interesting part; the date and time the instant the Control Panel was opened was in 2003, and this is the timestamp that will appear in the above value. Figure 10.28 shows the data portion of the value UEME_RUNCPL:timedate.cpl, which resolves to the date and time we changed to in order to confuse the investigation. Naturally such a finding can shed some light on what was taking place and pinpoint a precise date and time on which to closely examine files bearing those timestamps.

**FIGURE  10.28**    The date and time associated with value UEME_RUNCPL:timedate.cpl reflects the time the instant it was last opened, which can help establish that dates and times were altered.

We mentioned that accessing the timedate Control Panel left a different signature if it was accessed via the Control Panel instead of the icon in the System Tray. We have seen it accessed from the System Tray thus far. If we access it from the Control Panel, it will leave a value of UEME_RUNCPL:"C:\WINDOWS\system32\timedate.cpl",Date and Time. You can easily verify this by accessing it with regmon running. What is important is that the common denominator in both instances is the string timedate.cpl.

We have modified our UserAssist key so that is does not encode to ROT-13, and we have cleared out past data to see how this key functions. Using this technique, we can test a variety of user activities and observe their tracings in this key. Armed with that knowledge, we can examine the suspect's UserAssist key and properly interpret the data therein.

In this business it's often best to focus our efforts. Thus, if we suspect that the user tampered with timestamps, we can take the string timedate.cpl and convert it to ROT-13, which would be gvzrqngr.pcy. We can create a keyword with this ROT-13 string and search the Registry for it. If we find it, we can resolve the data portion of that value and see what information it provides.

Taking the techniques we have learned, we can test any user activity, observe the plain text string on our modified test platform, create a ROT-13 version, and search for it in a like manner. There are times, however, when we don't necessarily know what we are looking for and processing all of the values in this key might reveal activities that have thus far remained hidden. Doing this one at a time can be time consuming. The Sweep Case EnScript can help.

From the Sweep Case EnScript, open the Scan Registry module by double-clicking on it. Under the Scan Registry options, navigate to and select User Activity ➢ HKCU - UserAssist. Even though not labeled as such (as of v5.04a), this option process both the {5E6AB780-7743-11CF-A12B-00AA004AE837} and {75048700-EF1F-11D0-9888-006097DEACF9} values and their respective Count subkeys.

Currently this option processes the raw output contained in this value and does not convert the ROT-13 to plain text. It outputs the data as a string of 16 hex values. When this EnScript is run, you can go to the bookmark, view it in the Table view, and export the data in the Name, Type, and Value columns, as shown in Figure 10.29. You should note that the data is available in a tab named Registry Values that is located next to the Bookmark Home tab. It becomes visible when you place your focus on the output folder for this EnScript. If you provide the export file name with an .xls extension, it will immediately open in Excel and be formatted and ready to view.

When the output is viewed in Excel, it's a simple matter to select the entire column containing the value names, copy it to the Clipboard, go to the ROT-13 decoder, paste the Clipboard contents into the input window, copy the contents of the output window to the Clipboard, and paste it back into the Value Name column. You can now view the decoded content in a spreadsheet.

If something piques your interest, you can go to that value in the mounted Registry and bookmark your significant finding, decoding the individual data values (counter and 64-bit Windows timestamp). As you can't currently view the value name in ROT-13 within EnCase, you'll need to decode it externally and paste it in so that you have the decoded text in your bookmark. In the live Registry, we found this key under HKey_Current_User. In EnCase, this key will be found in the NTUSER.DAT hive file for the user in question; you would need to mount the file first. Perhaps as the value of the data contained in this key becomes better known, this EnScript will be improved to process the data into more meaningful output.

**FIGURE  10.29**    Results of the User Activity / User Assist option in the Scan Registry module. The value name, type, and data are being exported to a file with an .xls extension.

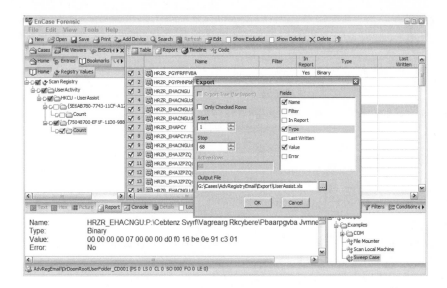

For those who would prefer that the UserAssist key not record data at all (for speed or privacy reasons), there is a value that you can add to the Settings key to accomplish this. Under the Settings key, create a DWORD value, name it **NoLog** (adhering to case sensitivity), and edit the value to 1 to turn it on. Restart or perform a soft reboot, and the UserAssist key should not record any more data. This value setting is rarely encountered; documentation for this setting is sparse at best and not supported by Microsoft.

# EnScript and Filters

EnScript is a proprietary programming language and application programming interface (API) that exists within the EnCase program environment, which means that EnCase must be running to run EnScripts. EnScript adheres to the ANSI C++ and Java standards for expression evaluation and operator meanings, making for an easy transition for those accustomed to programming in those languages. Even though EnScript adheres to those standards, only a small subset of C++ features is incorporated. In short, EnScript uses C++ operators and general syntax, but uses different classes and functions.

EnScripts are scripts or small pieces of code that automate various forensic processing tasks. Examiners can use the EnScripts provided by Guidance Software, Inc., or they can create their own or share them among other examiners. For those interested in creating their own EnScripts, some programming background, particularly in object-oriented programming (OOP), is most helpful. Guidance Software offers a four-day class in EnScript programming for those seeking training in this area.

We have used several EnScripts throughout the course of this text. As you'll recall, they can be accessed from the View menu, but probably more conveniently from the Filter pane in the lower-right corner.

## EnScript Navigation and Paths

When you access the EnScript view or tab, the available EnScripts are visible in the Tree pane, as shown in Figure 10.30. Under the root EnScripts, you will find a folder named Examples. Under Examples you will find several EnScripts that ship with EnCase, among them Sweep Case. The COM folder contains several examples of EnScript functionality. If you are running EnCase Enterprise or FIM, you will have a folder named EE, which contains EnScripts that are specific to Enterprise and FIM.

**FIGURE 10.30**    The EnScript Tree pane view of available EnScripts

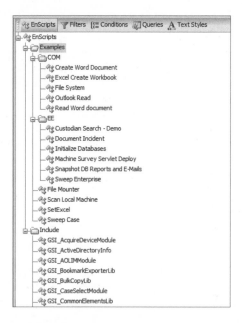

At the bottom of the EnScript root tree, at the same level as Examples, you will find the Include folder. Many EnScripts share common code. Rather than write and store the code multiple times, the shared pieces of code are stored in the Include folder and are called by the EnScript when needed. These EnScripts can't be run alone, and the contents of this folder are best left alone unless you understand and can write EnScript code.

The EnScript folder structure is not a virtual structure, but rather reflects an actual set of folders and files in Windows. To properly access and display these folders and files within EnCase, naturally EnCase must know their path in the Windows environment. By default EnCase stores these folders and files in the path C:\Program Files\EnCase5\EnScripts\.

If you are a lab environment that shares various EnCase resources, you can share EnScripts from one location. To change the path for your EnScripts, go to the EnScript view or tab and right-click on the any folder or EnScript in the Table pane and choose Change Root Path, as shown in Figure 10.31. At that point you need to simply browse to the path where you wish to store and use your EnScripts. The Include folder can be moved, but is tracked relative to the EnScript root path. If you decide to change it from that relative path, select Tools ➢ Options dialog box and click the EnScript tab in the Options dialog box.

**FIGURE 10.31**    Change Root Path is a right-click option from within the EnScript Tree pane that enables the user to change the location for storing and accessing EnScripts.

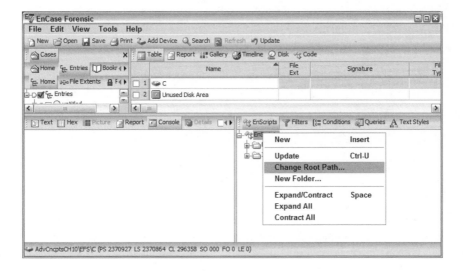

## Editing, Copying, Moving, and Deleting EnScripts

For those of you who wish to edit EnScripts, you need only right-click on the desired EnScript and choose Edit Source. After you have completed your edits, run Compile (located on the toolbar) to check for errors. This option runs the code, checking for errors, but does not execute the EnScript. While you are editing, you are doing so under the Code tab. You can have several EnScript codes open simultaneously and move between tabs to copy and paste code as you wish. To close any code's tab, select that tab and click the X to the right, right-click and choose Close, or press Ctrl-F4.

You can copy, delete, or move EnScripts as you can most objects in EnCase by simply dragging and dropping or by accessing the right-click menu for more options. You can create folders within EnCase to organize and contain EnScripts. When you do, folders by the same name and relative path are created within Windows.

## Running EnScripts

Running an EnScript, as we have seen, is as simple as double-clicking on the EnScript name in the EnScript Tree pane. As we have also seen, many EnScripts have several modules and each of the modules may have additional options. You will find the Windows Initialize Case module (see Figure 10.32) of the Sweep Case EnScript particularly useful. By running it with each case, you can put an attractive and informative front-end on your report. There is a Linux version included as well.

**FIGURE 10.32**     The Windows Initialize Case EnScript is a module of the Sweep Case EnScript.

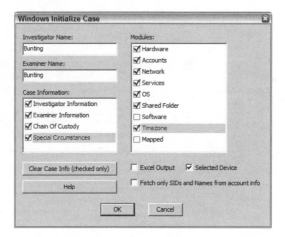

Many modules and options are available within the Sweep Case EnScript, with improvements and additions constantly in the works. You should take the time to try them all on small test sets of data so that you understand how they work and how they can help you process more evidence in less time.

Some EnScripts will write to the console in addition to their normal output. Some EnScripts may only write to the console. The Console tab is located in the View pane at the far right of the available tabs, between the Report and Details tabs. When an EnScript writes to the console, that output is also appended to the console.txt file that is located in the root of the EnCase program files.

## Filters, Conditions, and Queries

Filters are specialized EnScripts that allow you to filter your case based on a set of parameters. For example, you could filter for all files with the .xls extensions to only view spreadsheets.

Several filters are included in EnCase when you install it. Filters are available, quite appropriately, from the Filter pane, immediately to the right of the EnScript tab. Filters, like EnScripts, need only be double-clicked to be applied.

If you wish to create a filter, you'll have to do so using code. Conditions are new with EnCase 5 and allow you to create filters, but to do so using preset parameters available through dialog box choices. Conditions are available from the Conditions tab, which is between the Filters tab and the Queries tab, all of which are located in the Filter pane. You can build very powerful and useful conditions in addition to the ones that have been provided. Probably the easiest way to get started creating new conditions is to edit a condition (right-click and choose Edit) that approximates what you are trying to create. Once you visit the various filter conditions in the Edit mode, the road map becomes very clear for creating your own conditions.

Queries can be created from a combination of filters or conditions. Queries are available from the Queries tab. You can create a query by right-clicking and choosing New. At that point, you can select which filters or conditions to include. You can also change the associate Boolean logic. If conditions are powerful, queries can be even more so.

When you run a filter, condition, or query, it appears on the toolbar as an icon with a + sign in it to indicate the filter, condition, or query is active. Figure 10.33 shows the JPG Extension condition on the toolbar with a plus sign. When you apply a filter, it remains on until you turn it off. You turn them off by simply clicking on the plus sign on the toolbar. When the plus sign turns into a minus sign, the filter, condition, or query is turned off. It is easy to forget that a filter is on, so when you aren't seeing things the way you expect to see them, check the toolbar first for a filter, condition, or query.

**FIGURE 10.33** The JPG Extension condition has been applied and its icon appears on the toolbar with a "+" sign indicating its "active" status.

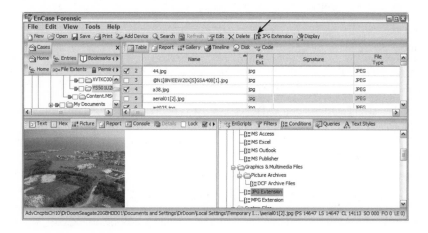

For those seeking more information on the syntax for EnScripts or filters, visit the Guidance Software website at http://www.guidancesoftware.com. The information is contained in the section "EnScript Language Reference." Also, the various EnScript classes and functions are available within EnCase by choosing the View command and then selecting the EnScript Types tab.

# E-mail

In the previous chapter, we discussed recovering Microsoft Internet Explorer history and cache using the Email/Internet Search feature. When we launched this feature to search for cache and history, we asked you to first disable the e-mail search. Therefore, you have at least seen where the feature is located. During this section, we'll use that feature as we explore how EnCase 5 parses e-mail artifacts and presents them to you in a logical format in an easy-to-use interface.

EnCase provides a utility to search for supported e-mail types and to parse and mount them. The Email tab (which is a subtab under the Cases tab) will be the location for viewing them in a logical format. The e-mail messages will displayed in a typical e-mail format such as From, To, Subject, Created Date, Sent Date, Received Date, Header, and Attachments; this information exists within any given e-mail database. Currently, EnCase 5 supports the following e-mail types:

- Outlook (PST)
- Outlook Express (DBX/MBX)
- AOL 6, 7, 8, 9
- Hotmail
- Yahoo!
- Netscape webmail
- mbox (a common flat file format)

Often it is best to get an idea of what kind of mail clients and files are on your system before proceeding. There's little use in running an Email/Internet Search process on your system if you are faced with an unsupported e-mail client. When you know what e-mail client(s) you have, you know what to expect.

The easiest way to survey your system is by combining a few filters and conditions into a master e-mail finder query. If you go to the Queries tab, right-click, and choose New, you have the basic screen from which to start your creation. Simply right-click in the bottom section and add as many conditions or filters as you like. When done, change the default Boolean logic of AND to OR so that any file matching any of the filters or conditions will be returned. Figure 10.34 shows a query after it is built. Running such a query tells you what kind of e-mail activity is on your system and does so in seconds once you've created it.

The Email tab does not get populated without user action. There are two actions that will populate this tab. The user can mount any compound e-mail file while in the Entries tab from the Table view, and this will result in both mounting the file and populating the Email tab. If you located an Outlook PST file, right-clicked on it, and selected View File Structure, you would see its mounted structure in both the Tree pane view and the Table view. If, after mounting it, you went to the Email tab, you would also find its contents, but in a much more logical and viewable format.

The other method of populating the Email tab is by running an Email/Internet Search. We've already done this in the previous chapter. It can be activated from the Email, History, or Web Cache tabs by right-clicking on the root folder in the Tree pane of any of those tabs. When you initiate the Email/Internet Search process, you are presented with an options window from which to choose from the various supported types. When we previewed our system with the e-mail finder query, we discovered a wide variety of e-mail types, ranging from mbox (Mozilla Thunderbird) to Yahoo! and Hotmail webmail. By knowing what e-mail types are present, we can limit our Email/Internet Search to those types, saving some processing time. Figure 10.35 shows the settings in the Email/Internet Search options window for our limited search.

**FIGURE 10.34**　This query combines several e-mail filters and conditions into a master e-mail finder.

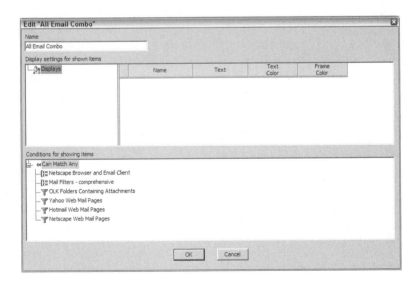

**FIGURE 10.35** Email/Internet Search limits the search to those e-mail types found during our query.

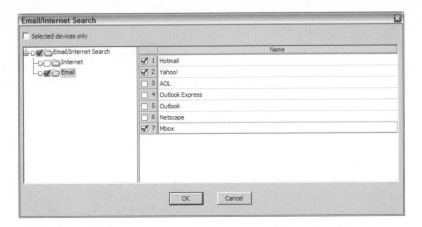

If you choose any webmail types, the Internet history and cache will be processed automatically without you having to select it. If any compound e-mail files are found, they are mounted so that the Email tab can be populated. When the web cache is processed, compressed files found in it are mounted. Many web services are sending e-mail and other web forms in a compressed format for better speed over the Internet; in addition, it adds an element of security through obscurity, at least to the extent that obscuring data secures that data. Before searching the web cache, it is a good idea to process it first so that the compressed files can be searched after they are mounted. Also, many of these compressed files do not have file extensions after they are mounted, which is all the more reason to process the cache to mount them before searching and conducting a file signature analysis.

Figure 10.36 shows a series of mounted GZIP files found in the web cache. In this particular case, these files are from Hotmail, Yahoo!, and Gmail. Not all files related to webmail will be populated on the Email tab. Invariably new services come out and existing ones change frequently, making it difficult to keep code current that is contained in EnScripts, filters, and conditions. It is best, if you want to leave no stone unturned, to sort and peruse through the web cache and see what you can find. There are conditions or filters you can apply to zoom in on the cache. With a little trial and error, you will soon be able to process the cache quickly and effectively with the help of filters and conditions.

Once the Email/Internet Search is complete, you can see the results in the Email tab. The Tree pane will display the e-mail in its hierarchical structure with regard to source and folders. The Table view pane will list the individual e-mails with the Name column containing the e-mail subject name. The View pane, when switched to the Report view, displays the e-mail with a brief header, along with the message and the attachment if any. Figure 10.37 shows this organization and display of an e-mail message found in the inbox of an mbox e-mail type (Mozilla Thunderbird).

Immediately to the right of the Email/Home tab is the Attachments tab. If an e-mail that you have selected has an attachment, you can view that attachment by going to the Attachments tab.

**FIGURE 10.36** GZIP files in cache have been mounted. These came from Hotmail, Yahoo!, and Gmail.

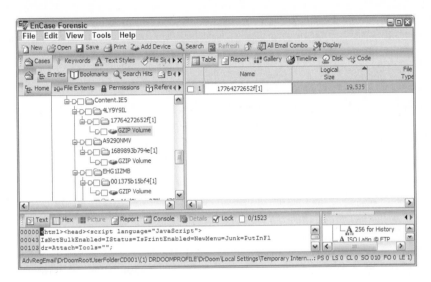

**FIGURE 10.37** Email tab viewafter processing

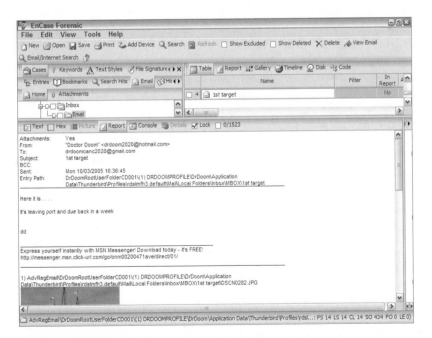

You may easily right-click and bookmark any e-mail from the Table view. As with other EnCase views, you may select multiple e-mails and bookmark them. Once bookmarked and placed in a destination folder, the bookmarked e-mails are viewable from the Bookmark view.

Each of the columns in the Table view displays the various attributes of each e-mail message to the extent such information is present. Table 10.7 lists those column headings and a brief description of their meaning.

**TABLE 10.7**    Email Tab Column Headings Explained

| Column Heading | Description |
|---|---|
| Name | Subject line of the e-mail message—can vary depending on e-mail client. |
| Filter | Name of filter applied—helps focus or narrow down the entries you have to view. |
| In Report | The Boolean indicator that determines whether or not the entry is included in the Report tab. |
| From | Sender line of the e-mail message—drafts may not have a sender, depending on e-mail client. |
| To | The intended recipient of the e-mail—again, drafts may not yet have had a recipient designated. |
| Subject | Subject line of the e-mail message. Not a required line and could be blank. |
| CC | Party to whom e-mail was copied—may or may not be present. |
| BCC | Party to whom e-mail was blind copied—may or may not be present. |
| Created | Date the e-mail message was created; expressed in local time format. |
| Sent | Date the e-mail message was sent; expressed in local time format. |
| Received | Date the e-mail message was received; expressed in local time format. |
| Header | Internet routing information contained in standard e-mail headers. Some internal e-mail (AOL to AOL) may not have headers. |
| Folder | The location of the entry from within the mounted compound file. This information will vary between the various e-mail clients. |
| Entry Path | The location within the mounted volume where the e-mail artifact resides. |
| Attachments | The number of attachments contained in the e-mail message. |

## E-mail and Registry Examinations

In this exercise, we will examine e-mail artifacts using the Email/Internet Search feature in EnCase 5. In addition, we will mount a Registry hive file and examine its contents.

- Create a folder structure for a new case according to our standard folder naming and structuring conventions. Name your case folder **EmailRegistry**. Create a new case, pointing it to your newly created folders. Before you place any evidence in your case, save your case in the root of the folder EmailRegistry, which will also be the default name for your case. Locate an evidence file on the CD named Advanced\DrDoomRootUserFolder_CD001.E01. Place it in the evidence folder for your newly created case.

- On the toolbar, click Add Device. Create a path to your new evidence file if one does not exist. Locate your new evidence file in the right pane of the Add Device window and complete the steps to bring the evidence file into your new case. Once it has been added, click Save.

- In the Tree pane/Entries tab, select the root of your case tree, forcing the newly added device into the Table view pane. From the Table pane, select the device. In the View pane, select the Report tab and confirm that the evidence file verified.

- From the Tree pane/Entries tab, go to the Filters tab and select the Queries tab. Right-click on the root of the query and select New. In the bottom pane where it starts "and can match any" right-click and change the logic to OR. Right-click again and select New. Start with filters; add Hotmail Web Pages and click OK. Right-click and select New, add Yahoo Web Pages, and click OK. Repeat the process, adding the filters Netscape Web Pages and OLK Folders containing attachments, and then adding the condition Mail Filters – comprehensive. Name this query **Master Mail Finder** and click OK. Double-click your new query to run it, clicking OK at the prompt, and you should see it appear on your toolbar as applied. Trigger the Set Included Folders button at the case level and you should see the e-mail involved in your case. You can see webmail, mbox mail (Mozilla Thunderbird), and Outlook Express mail.

- Go to the Email tab, right-click on the root of Email, and choose Email/Internet Search. You could fine-tune the options, but since this is a small evidence file, there's no problem running all options. Click OK to run.

- Visit each of the following: Email tab, History tab, and Web Cache tab. As you examine the Email tab, you'll see Thunderbird configured to accept POP mail from Google's new Gmail. Locate an e-mail containing an attachment. Sort the web cache view by Cached Date, and you'll be seeing the web cache in chronological order.

- In the Tree pane/Entries tab, navigate to the Temporary Internet Files. Under each of the cache folders, note that there are mounted GZIP files. These files were mounted during the Email/Internet Search process and can be viewed, searched, or subjected to other processing. Note that mounted GZIP files lack file extensions and that a file signature analysis would be in order if you wished to examine this area in more detail.

- Navigate to the root of the root user folder for user DrDoom. Locate the NTUSER.DAT Registry hive file in the Table pane. Right-click on the NTUSER.DAT file and choose View File Structure.

- Locate the mounted NTUSER.DAT hive file in the Tree pane and navigate to NTRegistry\ $$$PROTO.HIV\Software\Microsoft\Windows\CurrentVersion\Explorer\UserAssist\ {75048700-EF1F-11D0-9888-006097DEACF9}\Count\.

- The Table pane contains the values for this key. You have been told that the suspect was making Trojans with SubSeven and you located the folder SubSeven in one of the subfolders of My Documents. You know that the editserver.exe file is used to customize the Trojan, and you want to know if the user has been using this program to create custom Trojans. Open the ROT13 encoder/decoder and type **editserver.exe** to see what text string appears when encoded, which is rqvgfreire.rkr. Look at the list of values and see if you see that string.

- As there are relatively few entries, you can quickly locate it. Place your focus on the value in the Table pane, forcing its associated data into the view pane. In the View pane, switch to the hex value and you will see a 16-byte hex string. The last 8 bytes of this string make up the Windows 64-bit timestamp for when this program was last opened. Sweep those last 8 bytes, bookmark that data, and view it as a Windows 64-bit date/time. You should see the date and time the user last opened this program as Mon Oct 03, 2005 03:00:49PM (EDT). Although you can't tell it from the available data, the time zone offset for this evidence file was Eastern Daylight Time (GMT-0400). Place this bookmark in an appropriately named destination folder.

- Immediately to the left of the 8-byte timestamp is the counter, which is a DWord value (32 bits or 4 bytes). Sweep those 4 bytes, bookmark them, and view them as a 32-bit integer. The result will be decimal 9. If we subtract decimal 5 from 9, we can say that the user opened this program (SubSeven's editserver.exe four times, with the last time being: Mon Oct 03, 2005 03:00:49PM (EDT).

- Save your case and exit EnCase.

## E-mail Is Great, But...

E-mail is a rich source of evidence. Usually its content is less formal than normal business communications and often captures facts, opinions, comments, actions, and so forth that would never be found in any other evidence.

Sometimes, however, some nefarious individuals are e-mail wary and their e-mail often appears quite sterile and uninteresting. In a recent examination, still under investigation, such was the case. Two public officials exchanged e-mail that was quite boring, yet the investigators knew something was going on, but they lacked the evidence to prove their case after five months of investigating.

I was asked to do a computer forensics examination of the involved computer systems. While looking at their corporate webmail in the temporary Internet files, yawning from the boredom, something jumped out at me. There were hundreds of files that were either wwwpage[#].htm or wwwtwoway[#].htm. Upon opening them, the evidence displayed was incredible. The two officials were communicating using text messaging from computer to computer and from computer to pagers to communicate below the radar screen. The text messages and the pager numbers were completely cached in the temporary Internet files. There were several hundred of them going back nearly three years.

As boring as the e-mail was, the text messages were just the opposite. The content was raw, uninhibited, and quite incriminating. Needless to say, the investigators were ecstatic and the investigation was rapidly moving forward at press time.

There are thousands of ways to communicate and most have web interfaces, which means there's probably something cached. Sometimes if you don't know what you are looking for, there is no substitution for sifting through the web cache and looking for patterns, significant visits to a particular site, and so forth. It's slow and tedious, but sometimes the reward is worth the effort. Once you figure out how they are communicating, you then know what to look for and the rest is easy.

# Base64 Encoding

While we are on the topic of e-mail, it is a good time to discuss e-mail attachments. If you'll recall from our discussion of the ASCII table, all of the printable characters are contained within the first 128 bytes of the 256-byte table. These first 128 bytes are also called *low-bit ASCII* as all 128 characters can be represented using 7 bits.

When the first protocols were developed for communicating between computers, the characters transmitted were low-bit ASCII (7 bits), and the eighth bit of each byte was used for parity or error checking to make sure the 7 bits arrived accurately. All was well for a while until programs or other files containing binary data needed to be sent. Such a data transfer involved sending characters above number 128; this meant using the eighth bit, which was needed for parity.

Thus the need to transmit binary data led to the development of various encoding schemes to facilitate this transfer. By encoding data, 8-bit data (binary) can travel through data paths that only support 7-bit data (text). The first encoding method, historically, was uuencoding. This simple method used spaces in the encoding scheme. As a space could occur at the end of a line and some gateways strip spaces at the end of lines, the method resulted in corrupted data at unacceptable levels.

A second encoding method, called xxencoding, was developed. Although it fixed some of the problems with uuencoding, it never became popular and is rarely used.

The third encoding method is the most popular and widely used: base64 encoding. Base64 was introduced with the Multipurpose Internet Mail Extensions Standard, better known as the MIME standard. Because the MIME standard provides many other benefits and base64 avoids the pitfalls of the previous methods, base64 has become the most widely used encoding method and is also the most secure method.

There is a fourth method of encoding that you may encounter known as BinHex. It is used primarily for transferring files among Macintosh systems. The Macintosh file system uses a data fork and a resource fork, and BinHex creates a third part called a header. The three parts (data fork, resource fork, and header) are combined into a single data stream that is slightly compressed and encoded. Using this encoding scheme, Macintosh files, complete with metadata, can be transmitted to other Macintosh machines.

Since base64 is the most commonly encountered approach, we'll focus on that particular encoding scheme. In the previous section covering e-mail, we saw how EnCase automatically decoded e-mail attachments, placing them on a separate tab. Figure 10.38 shows an e-mail attachment on the Attachment tab that is already decoded and displays as an image. This automated processing saves considerable time and the results are easily bookmarked for your report.

**FIGURE 10.38**   Base64 e-mail image attachment automatically processed and displayed on the Attachment tab

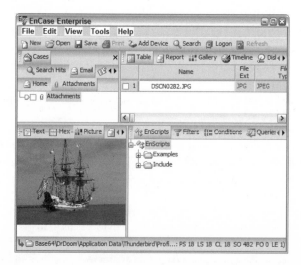

Often examiners encounter non-image base64 attachments, such as documents, spreadsheets, zip files, and the like. EnCase automatically processes them as well. They are decoded and displayed as they were attached by the sender. Figure 10.39 shows a zip file in the form of an e-mail attachment. If you wanted to see its contents, you could double-click on the zip file. EnCase would pass the file to the application registered by Windows to open zip files, and you could view the contents of the zip file in the Windows environment. Alternatively, you could go to the Entries view, locate the zip file, mount it (right-click and choose View File Structure), and view its contents within EnCase.

**FIGURE 10.39** Base64 e-mail zip file attachment automatically processed and displayed on the Attachment tab

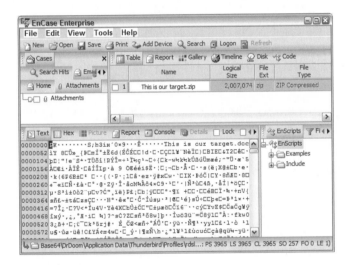

When base64 attachments appear in the unallocated clusters, they usually require manual processing to extract them. Before you can extract them, you must find them. Base64 encoding has header information, some of which is unique and consistent, and it has a footer or marker to establish its endpoint. Figure 10.40 shows the header information that precedes base64 data. By searching for strings associated with these headers and footers, we can locate base64-encoded data in the unallocated clusters or wherever it may occur. These strings are **base64** and **_NextPart_** (these strings are case-sensitive).

If the base64 attachment is an image, finding the header information is usually sufficient as EnCase's internal viewer can view the encoded data by simply bookmarking the first byte of the encoded data. In Figure 10.41, we have placed our cursor on the first byte of the base64 encoded data of a JPEG image, bookmarked it, and viewed it as a base64 image.

**FIGURE 10.40**    Base64 header information that precedes base64 data, noting the search hits on the above strings

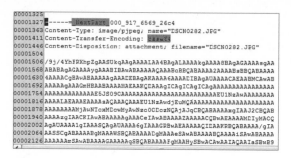

**FIGURE 10.41**    Placing the cursor on the first byte of base64 image data, bookmarking it, and viewing it as a Base64 Encoded Picture

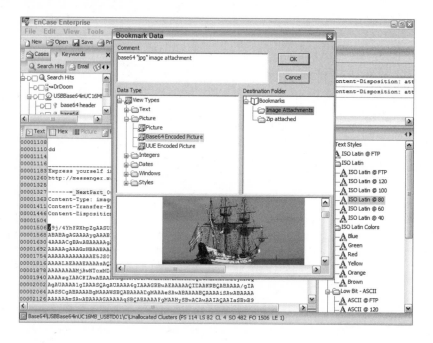

Just as you can search for JPEG headers by searching for the string
**\xFF\xD8\xFF[\xFE\xE0\xE1]**, you can search for a JPEG image encoded in
base64 by using its unique header. The string for this search is **/9j/4Yh**. This is
not a GREP search and should be run with case sensitivity enabled to make
your search both fast and precise.

If the base64 attachment found in the unallocated cluster is a non-image file, you will need to
identify its beginning and end, export the data out of EnCase, and use a third-party tool to convert
the encoded file to its original format. To locate the beginning and end of the base64 encoded
data, search for the string **_NextPart_** (case sensitive). This string appears at the beginning and end
of base64-encoded data. After you have searched the unallocated clusters for the start and end
markers, sort the search hits by the Bookmark Start column. This places your search hits in the
order you wish them to appear.

Locate the beginning of the data you wish to extract, as shown in Figure 10.42. Note that the
_NextPart_ is followed by three Content lines. The third content line in our example contains
the file name, which is "This is our target.zip". The actual beginning of our encoded file starts
with the first hyphen in the string of hyphens that precedes _NextPart_. If you look carefully at
Figure 10.42, you will see that the cursor is sitting on that beginning byte, which is a hyphen.
The file offset (FO) for that byte indicated in the GPS is 2021929.

**FIGURE 10.42**   The beginning of base64 file with the cursor sitting on the first byte of
data to be exported

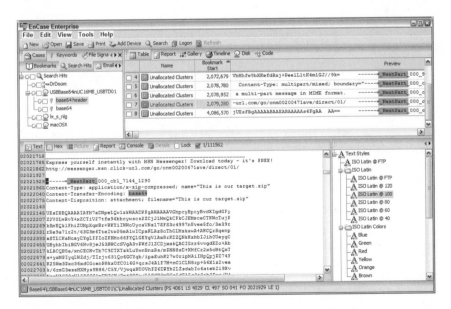

Next we need to locate the end of the file. You can simply click on the first byte, hold the left button down, and drag until you reach the end, which may take considerable patience, or you can do it the smart way, which we'll describe next. In our example, we have a search hit marking the start and end of our target base64-encoded file. If we advance to the next search hit, we land on the end, or at least within a few bytes of the end. Figure 10.43 shows the search hit _NextPart_ as the end marker. Actually the true end of the encoded file is located on the last hyphen to the right of _NextPart_. If you look carefully at Figure 10.43, you'll see the cursor sitting on that byte, which is a hyphen. The file offset (FO) for that byte is 4029254.

**FIGURE 10.43**     The end of the base64 file with the cursor sitting on the last byte of data to be exported

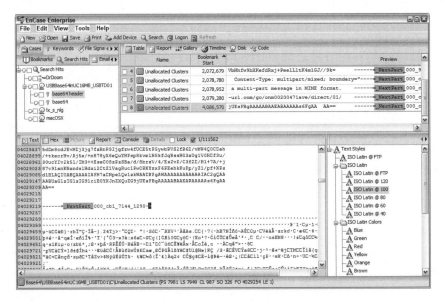

Before exporting the data, you need to know how much data to capture. If you open your calculator and subtract the difference between the file offsets (start and end) and add one to that figure, you'll arrive at the correct number. In our example, the difference is 2,007,325, to which we add one, thus making the figure 2,007,326.

Now that we know the start and end and how much data to export, go back to the beginning of the data by returning to the preceding search hit. Place your cursor on the beginning of the base64-encoded file as shown in Figure 10.42. With your cursor precisely located on the first byte, right-click and choose Export. You will see the Selection dialog box, as shown in Figure 10.44. The Custom Range selection is the default option and the one you want. The start location is the file offset where your cursor currently resides. The length is the figure that we just calculated. So we enter **2,007,326** in this box. You should next enter a path, and since this is data with no file name, you need to give it one. In our example, the file was named "base64data.b64". If you accept the other defaults and click OK, the base64-encoded file will be exported from within EnCase to a file in Windows.

**FIGURE 10.44**    The Selection dialog box for exporting data from within EnCase

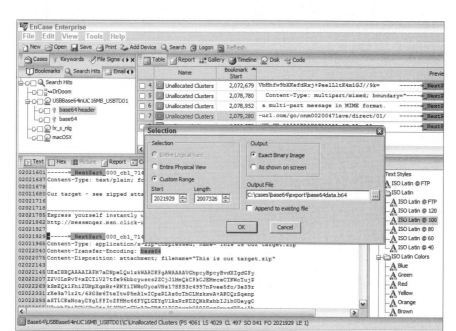

The hard part is now behind you; all that remains is to decode the data with a third-party tool. There are several free utilities you can use. Sometimes simple is best, and the Funduc shell decoder meets this criterion. Go to http://www.funduc.com/decext.htm and download their Decode Shell Extension tool. Once installed, this tool will appear as a right-click option in the Windows Explorer interface. With the Decode Shell Extension tool installed, locate the base64 file that you just exported, right-click on the file, and choose the option Decode. You will see the Decode Shell Extension dialog box shown in Figure 10.45, which displays the file name of the file to decode. Click Yes and the file will be decoded. You will be asked next if you'd like to open the decoded file, which you most certainly will want to do.

**FIGURE 10.45**    The Decode Shell Extension dialog box shows the name of the file to be decoded.

If you compare the base64-encoded file size with its decoded file size, you will see that the encoded file size is larger. Since you have to send 8 bits through a 7-bit data pathway, the encoding scheme has to use more that one byte to represent a byte. Typically file sizes will grow by approximately 30 percent when encoded with base64. Figure 10.46 shows the encoded file size at 1,961K and the decoded file size at 1,423K. In this case the encoded file increased in size by 30.9 percent.

**FIGURE 10.46** Explorer view showing the file "this is our target.zip" after decoding. Note that the encoded file is approximately 30 percent larger than its decoded version.

# EnCase Decryption Suite (EDS)

EDS provides the EnCase examiner with the ability to decrypt files and folders encrypted with the Microsoft Encrypting File System (EFS). This will function for local or domain authenticated users. EFS is key-based, meaning the user who encrypted the files with the key will be the only one able to view the encrypted data, unless, of course, the user's password used to create the key is known. Naturally, encrypted text that can't be read also can't be searched and forensic efforts will be thwarted by EFS.

EDS has overcome those obstacles and provided tools, some automated, for circumventing EFS issues. This decryption process is automatic for locally authenticated users who did not manually protect their operating system Syskey, which is the more common scenario. When the Syskey has been protected or the logon was through a domain, problems are more complicated, but by no means insurmountable.

The EDS module will support EFS in Windows 2000 Professional and Server as well as Windows XP Professional and Windows 2003 Server. There are some variations in the decryption capabilities based on operating system version and the user logon configurations that are in place.

Windows 2000 EFS can be decrypted automatically without input or password cracking, since EDS can gather all the information locally needed for automatic decryption if the accounts are not protected by the Syskey. Windows XP and 2003 Server are, however, a different matter. There is a higher level of security with these two products requiring EnCase to have the password to complete the decryption process. If the password is not available, there are several different routes for obtaining the password, ranging from dictionary cracking to exporting local user accounts to NT password cracking software.

In the event that one is careless enough to allow the auto-login feature to be configured, EDS can automatically recover the password from all versions supported versions of Windows (2000 Professional and Server, XP Professional and 2003 Server). Auto-login is the feature by which the computer starts and automatically completes the logon using a password that is stored and encrypted.

In addition, EDS provides support for obtaining passwords from password-protected Outlook PST files. EDS can also decrypt and bypass the password protection on the Lexar Jump-Drive Secure (Version 1.0 security architecture using 128-AES encryption).

EDS is an add-on module that must be purchased. The examiner is provided with a file containing the license certificate that is specific to a dongle. This certificate must be placed in the path Program Files\EnCase5\Certs\. Once the certificate is in place, start EnCase, and select Help ➢ About EnCase. If the certificate is recognized, it will be listed under Modules as EnCase Decryption Suite, as shown in Figure 10.47.

**FIGURE   10.47**    About EnCase lists installed modules.

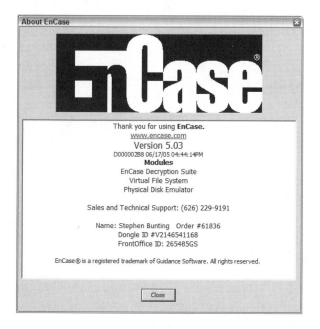

EFS may not be an issue that you encounter often, and hence you may not see the immediate value of EDS in your routine examinations. However, there are few cases in which valuable information from the protected storage area of the Registry can't be obtained. Windows offers to remember passwords for users and similarly offers the auto-fill feature. Many users accept these offers of assistance and their sensitive information is stored in the protected storage area of the Registry. However, this information is not encrypted well and EDS automatically decrypts it when you mount the Registry. Although you can navigate to this data, it is easier to have the EDS Registry Parser (a module within Sweep Case) process it for you. The results are neatly bookmarked, as shown in Figure 10.48.

**FIGURE 10.48** Usernames and passwords recovered from the protected storage area of the Registry by the EDS Registry Parser

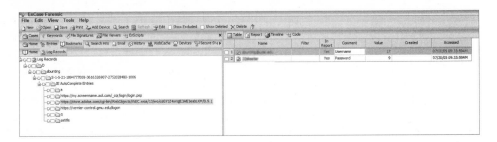

Guidance Software publishes a manual for all EnCase modules, including documentation of the EDS module. EFS processing can become rather involved, and this manual covers the topic in depth. It is updated periodically as new releases of EnCase become available. You can locate it easily on Guidance Software's website under Downloads in the Support section.

# Virtual File System (VFS)

VFS enables the examiner to mount the evidence as a read-only, off-line network drive. As such, the mounted volume is available in Windows and can be browsed with the Explorer interface or examined by third-party tools.

EnCase treats the unallocated clusters as though it were a logical file, and when the evidence volume is mounted, the unallocated clusters are addressable within Windows as a logical file. As an added bonus, all deleted files and folders are available as well. Figure 10.49 shows an EnCase evidence image that has been mounted using VFS and is then available as a network drive in Windows. The unallocated clusters are showing as one 23GB file; you also have access to the Lost Files folder and all files and folders in it.

If EnCase supports the image file type for use within EnCase, VFS will mount it. This includes: EnCase Evidence Files, dd images, SafeBack (V2) images, and VMWare images. In addition, live computer forensic devices can be mounted with VFS and include a local machine preview of removable media; a local machine preview using FastBloc Classic, FE, and LE hardware write-blocking devices; crossover or parallel cable connection previews; local Palm Pilot previews; and EnCase Enterprise or FIM live network previews.

**FIGURE 10.49**    An EnCase evidence file mounted with VFS and appearing as a network drive in Windows

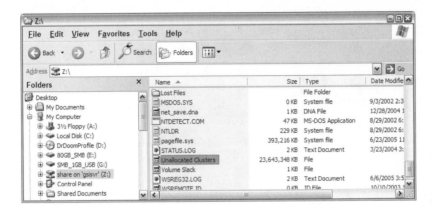

Interestingly, all file systems that EnCase supports can be mounted with VFS in Windows Explorer. Currently that list of supported file systems includes the following:

- Windows file systems (FAT 12, 16, and 32 and NTFS)

- Linux file systems (Reiser, EXT2, EXT3)

- Unix file systems (Solaris UFS)

- Macintosh (HFS, HFS+)

- BSD (FFS)

- AIX (JFS and JFS2)

- TiVo 1 and 2

- CD/DVD (Joliet, ISO 9660, UDF, DVD, HFS)

- Palm (Palm OS)

VFS installs in the same manner as EDS. VFS is a separate module that is purchased. Upon purchase, the licensed user is provided with a certificate that is keyed to the user's dongle. The certificate must be placed in the path Program Files\EnCase5\Certs\. Once installed, the installed modules can be viewed from the Help ➤ About EnCase screen, as shown in Figure 10.50.

VFS can mount only one mount point at a time, but it can mount at four different levels: the case level, the disk/device level, the volume level, or the folder level. Whichever level you choose, before you can change to another level you must first dismount the current mount, as you can only have one mount point at any time.

To perform a VFS mount, choose the level for your mount by placing your cursor on it. Right-click on the chosen level and choose Mount As Network Share, as shown in Figure 10.51.

**FIGURE 10.50** Installed modules are listed on the About EnCase screen available on the Help menu.

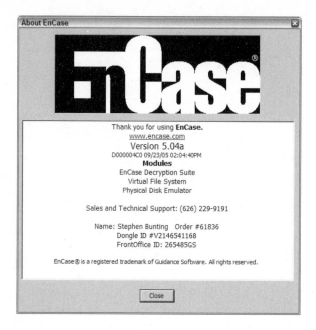

**FIGURE 10.51** Choose Mount As Network Share to perform a VFS mount at the case level.

You will be prompted next with a Mount As Network Share dialog box, where you will click OK, accepting all defaults. Figure 10.52 shows this dialog box.

**FIGURE  10.52**    The Mount As Network Share dialog box

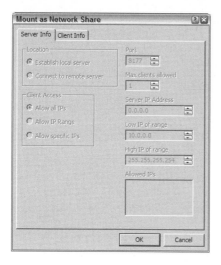

When you are done, the various devices in your case will be available under one network share drive letter in Windows. In Figure 10.53, you will see that we have mounted all devices in this case, which are two Windows file systems (FAT 32 and NTFS), a Macintosh OS X file system (HFS+), and two Linux file systems (EXT2). Amazingly enough, all these file systems are now available in a Windows interface through the VFS module. VFS can also mount EnCase Logical Evidence Files, and it is the primary integration point for processing collected and preserved data for electronic evidence discovery (eDiscovery) in civil litigation.

Once mounted, the possibilities for third-party examinations are seemingly endless. At the very least a thorough examination should include a virus scan and a spyware/Trojan scan with at least two different products to be thorough. VFS simplifies this task greatly, saving much time and money compared to other methods of achieving the same task.

To dismount or end VFS, the user must double-click in the lower right of the EnCase screen where the Virtual File System is constantly blinking while VFS is running. When you double-click this blinking object, as shown in Figure 10.54, you will receive a prompt asking if you wish to cancel the VFS process, which you confirm by clicking Yes.

As with the EDS, Guidance Software documents the VFS module in the EnCase Modules Manual, which is available on their website. Advanced features and techniques are described in this publication.

**FIGURE 10.53**   Windows, Macintosh, and Linux file systems are all available simultaneously in a Windows interface through one VFS mount point.

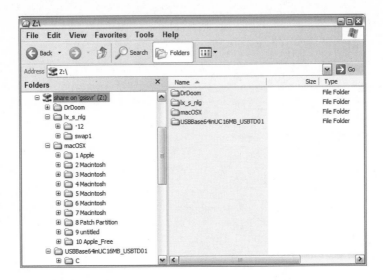

**FIGURE 10.54**   To stop VFS, double-click on the blinking Virtual File System in the lower-right corner.

# Exporting Applications

As some applications create proprietary file formats, viewing them in their native environments is necessary as part of the examination process. Viewing a file in its native environment often means running the application that created it. One of the reasons for using VFS to mount the suspect drive is to run the applications on that drive, but despite our best efforts, sometimes that method fails to yield satisfactory results. In plain English, the application often crashes when you attempt to run it from other than its installed drive and path.

As with most forensic tasks, there is usually more than one way to achieve a desired result. With EnCase, you can easily copy an application's folder and all its subfolders and files onto the local drive. If you place everything in the path required by the application, you can often have success running an application, even though some features may not be available since the program is not fully installed. Many programs are good candidates for this technique. Photoshop (version 7 and earlier), Password Vault, and Lotus Notes are examples of programs that can be successfully exported and run.

To demonstrate this technique, we will export the application Lotus Notes. Lotus Notes is an e-mail client and personal information database used in the corporate world. Lotus Notes does not depend on Registry settings for its environment settings. Rather, it relies heavily on the file notes.ini to configure its environment. If you attempt to export and run Lotus Notes anywhere other than its installed and defined path, it will not run. Therefore, note the location of the folder Lotus when you export it from within EnCase; you'll need to relocate it in that exact path on your examination machine drive.

 Lotus Notes, when installed in a corporate setting, will almost always be password protected. It is beyond the scope of this book to explain the details of how this encryption is applied and circumvented. Often, a system administrator can assist you with the password. If you encounter Lotus Notes, this is an issue you will need to address right away.

In the Tree pane of the Entries view, locate the folder you wish to export. In this case, we are going to export the folder Lotus and all of its files and subfolders. Place your cursor on the folder you want to export (Lotus in our example). Right-click on the folder and choose Copy Folders. Browse to the precise location where you wish to export the application. In our case, we want to export the folder Lotus to the root of the C: drive since that is where it is located on the suspect's drive. Figure 10.55 shows the Copy Folders dialog box, which defines the export path as C:\. If you click OK, the application will be exported or copied to the specified path.

**FIGURE 10.55**    The Copy Folders dialog box lets you define the destination for the application export.

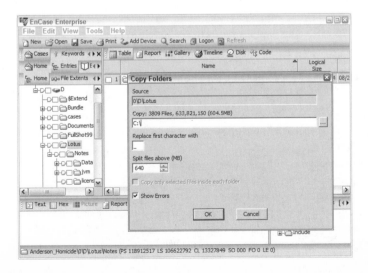

Once you've copied or exported the application, you'll need to browse to its location in Windows Explorer. The next step is to locate the program executable, which in our case is notes.exe. Figure 10.56 shows the executable in Windows Explorer.

**FIGURE 10.56** The next step is to locate the program's executable.

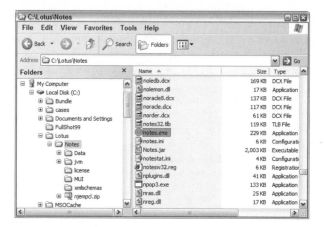

Once you have located the program's executable, double-click on it to launch the program. In the case of a password-protected configuration of Lotus Notes, you will next be prompted for the password. Figure 10.57 shows the Lotus Notes splash screen and password prompt. In this instance, the system administrator has joined the suspect's "group" and changed the password in order that we may examine the e-mail client. The system administrator provided us with the changed password. This was done on the suspect's machine using a restored copy of the drive.

**FIGURE 10.57** The Lotus Notes executable is launched and a password prompt appears.

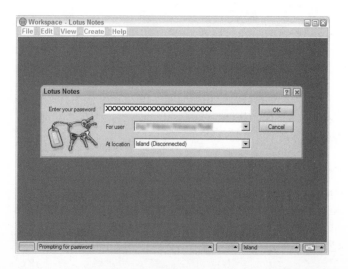

Once you have entered the password, you'll have full access to the Lotus Notes e-mail client as the user last used it. Any items stored locally are fully available in this interface. You can capture screenshots or export items in a plain-text format using the Lotus Notes export utility. Figure 10.58 shows the Lotus Notes welcome screen; here you can navigate to the various areas of the Lotus Notes client.

**FIGURE 10.58**    The Lotus Notes welcome screen and interface

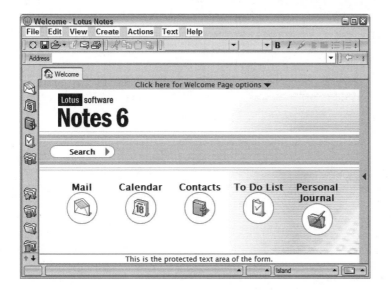

# Restoration

Another method of running applications on the suspect's drive is to restore the evidence file to another drive. In this manner, you can mount the restored drive and examine it or boot your system using the restored drive. Using the latter method, you can see the system very much as the suspect did.

EnCase provides the option to restore either the logical or the physical drive. If your original evidence is a physical device, restoring the logical device only does not allow for verification as an exact copy. Usually the physical drive is the best method for restoration, especially if your intent is to boot the suspect drive after restoration.

When restoring, EnCase copies everything at the level selected (logical or physical), sector by sector, to the target media. The drive you're restoring to must be of equal or larger size. When the restoration is complete, EnCase will verify the restoration and provide hash values of the restored drive. If the target drive is larger, as it often will be, the excess sectors are not included in the verification hash as the hash value represents only the number of sectors restored. The examiner should understand this, and a separate MD5 hash of the restored drive must be conducted only on the restored sectors for the values to match.

One 80GB hard drive model will most likely not have the same number of sectors as another model rated at 80GB. When you select a drive to restore to, compare the number of sectors to determine if the target drive is of equal or larger capacity.

You may optionally wipe the target drive before restoring to it, but this is not necessary as EnCase provides the option to wipe any remaining or unused portion of the drive after all the sectors have been restored. Once you have selected an appropriate target device, mount it in Windows.

To restore an image, at either the logical or physical level, begin in the Tree pane of the Case view. Select either the logical or physical device icon, right-click on it, and choose Restore. As shown in Figure 10.59, EnCase displays the Restore Drive dialog box. Here you specify the local device for restoration. Choose Local Drives and click Next.

**FIGURE 10.59**  The Restore dialog box

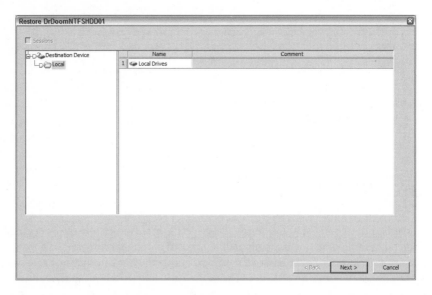

EnCase next displays the local logical and physical drives that are available for restoration. These drives appear in the Choose Devices dialog box, as shown in Figure 10.60. As a safety measure, EnCase will not display the drive on which Windows is running. Choose the appropriate target device for your restoration and click Next.

**FIGURE 10.60**    The Choose Devices dialog box lets you select the target drive for restoration.

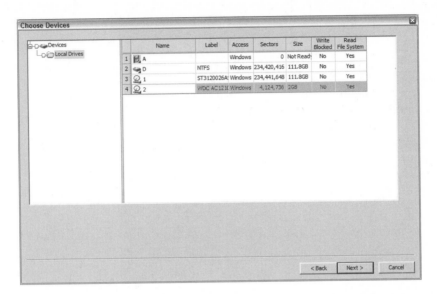

After you choose the target drive for the restoration, EnCase provides some final options before the restoration begins. Those final options are displayed in the Drives dialog box, as shown in Figure 10.61. The first option is Wipe Remaining Sectors On Target, which, when selected, causes any remaining sectors on the drive to be wiped. The second option is Verify Wiped Sectors. This option name does not accurately describe its function. Its actual purpose is to cause EnCase to verify the restored sectors, comparing the acquisition hash value with the hash value of the restored sectors. The final option is to choose the characters used for wiping the remaining sectors. The default value is 00h but can be any hex value you specify. When you are ready, click Finish. EnCase will prompt you asking you if you wish to proceed. Type **Yes** and click OK to confirm and start the restoration.

When the restoration is complete, EnCase will display a verification report, as shown in Figure 10.62. The acquisition hash from the evidence file will be displayed as the Input Hash while the Output Hash will be the verification hash of the restored sectors. To verify, these values must be identical.

As a final note, if the restoration is to be made of a logical device, your preparation will be somewhat different. A logical volume must be restored to a volume of the same type and of equal or greater size. If the evidence file volume to be restored is NTFS and 500MB in size, the target volume must be formatted to NTFS and must be 500MB or larger in size. To determine the size and properties (partition type) of the evidence file volume, refer to the Report view for the volume. When you restore the logical volume, make sure you select the logical drive letter of the target drive.

**FIGURE 10.61** Final restoration options are displayed in the Drive dialog box.

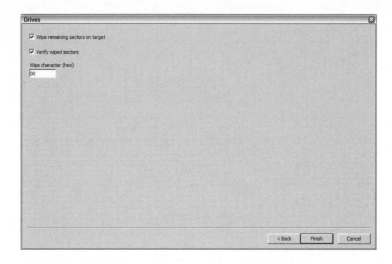

**FIGURE 10.62** The verification report shows that the input and output hashes match.

Guidance Software has published a white paper on restoration issues. It is available on their website in the "white papers" section. I recommend that all examiners read this publication; it covers many important considerations relating to restoration and proper handling of the target device after the restoration.

# Physical Disk Emulator (PDE)

The PDE module is similar to the VFS in many ways, but there are some clear and distinct differences. PDE can only mount a physical disk or volume. When PDE mounts either of these devices, they are not presented as a network share, but rather as a physical disk or volume to Windows for mounting. When this occurs, the mounted physical disk or volume will appear in the Windows Logical Disk Manager, which is a service that starts when there is a need to configure hard disk drives and volumes and stops when that process is done. Figure 10.63 shows the Windows Logical Disk Manager after a 1.8GB physical drive has been mounted within EnCase using PDE. This mounted drive shows as physical disk 3 and is further mounted as drive letter F.

**FIGURE 10.63**    The Logical Disk Manager shows the physical disk mounted in Windows by the EnCase PDE module.

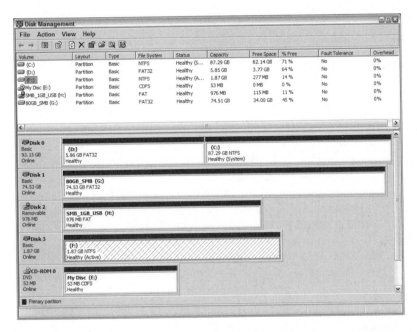

The process of mounting a physical device or volume with PDE is very similar to that of mounting with VFS. First, select the physical or logical device to mount by placing your cursor on it, right-click, and choose Mount As Emulated Disk. You will see the Mount As Emulated Disk dialog box, which should default to the Server Info tab, as shown in Figure 10.64. A local port is assigned to the mount and the number will appear in the window, which can be changed if you like. Once the port is in use, it remains assigned for all future mounts. To release this port and assign another port, you need to restart Windows. This issue or process is really rather academic as I've never seen a reason to change the default port or change it after it was assigned. But if you encounter that need, you now know the rules.

**FIGURE 10.64** The Mount As Emulated Disk dialog box showing the Server Info tab

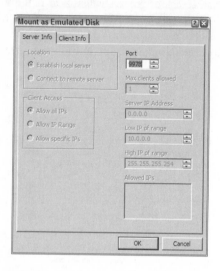

A second tab is available in the Mount As Emulated Disk dialog box. The Client Info tab, as shown in Figure 10.65, provides certain advanced options. If a CD is mounted, you can choose which sessions of a multisession CD you wish to have mounted. If you are using VMWare (discussed in a later paragraph), you need to enable caching per the set of instructions for setting up VMWare. Caching allows files to be added, modified, or deleted as needed and to have these changes cached to a file for use by VMWare. In addition, these cached files can be saved and reused in future sessions. You stop or end PDE in the same way you would VFS, which is by double-clicking on the blinking Physical Disk Emulator in the lower-right corner.

**FIGURE 10.65** The Client Info tab of the Mount As Emulated Disk dialog box

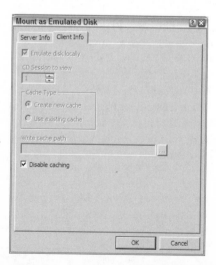

PDE supports the same evidence file formats and live computer forensics evidence as does VFS. When PDE mounts in Windows, however, only file systems recognized by Windows will be supported and mounted, which means only NTFS and FAT. If neither the NTFS nor FAT file system is present, no file system will mount, but the physical device will be available. As you'll recall, by contrast, VFS will mount in Windows any file system supported by EnCase.

**WARNING**   Don't use PDE to mount EnCase images or previews of a local hard drive. If Windows, especially XP, detects a multiple instance of the same drive on the local box, you will likely experience the proverbial BSOD (Blue Screen of Death).

Another subtle difference between PDE and VFS is that PDE presents the physical disk or volume as is to Windows whereas VFS presents the file system as EnCase sees it. What does this really mean? Windows can't see unallocated clusters, and when PDE presents a physical disk to Windows to mount, you won't see unallocated clusters in the Explorer interface. Quite by contrast, when you mount using VFS, EnCase treats the unallocated clusters as one contiguous logical file, and that logical construct is passed to Windows when VFS mounts. With VFS, unallocated clusters are viewable in the Explorer interface.

The same rule or logic applies to deleted files. As EnCase undeletes deleted files and displays them, VFS presents this logical reconstruction of deleted files to Windows when VFS mounts; thus, deleted files will be viewable in the Explorer interface with VFS. With PDE, don't expect to see deleted files.

These differences are subtle, but the difference is truly magnified in the case of a recovered partition. If you recover a partition with EnCase and mount the physical drive with PDE, Windows sees only the physical disk and can't mount the recovered partition since it is not there. By extreme contrast, if you mount the same physical drive with the recovered partition using VFS, the recovered partition as EnCase sees it is passed along to Windows and you can see the entire partition in the Explorer interface.

It is important to understand the similarities and the differences between the two modules; clearly some tasks are module specific while some tasks can be carried out in either. For example, if your intent is to process the unallocated clusters, you need to use VFS. If your intent is to scan for viruses or malware, either module will suffice.

One of the most popular capabilities of PDE is that of using it in conjunction with VMWare. When you have the physical disk or volume mounted in Windows as a physical disk, VMWare can take that physical disk and mount it as a virtual machine. This means you can often virtually boot and run your suspect's drive totally within the EnCase and VMWare combined environments. This can save considerable time and expense compared with the traditional method of restoring the image to a drive and booting it in the suspect's box.

The entire process of using VMWare with PDE as well as the advanced features of the PDE module are well documented in the PDE manual provided by Guidance Software. As with EDS and VFS, PDE is an optional module and must be purchased separately from the basic EnCase software. It installs in the same manner, via a license certificate keyed to your dongle, and must be stored in the Certs folder. About EnCase, as with EDS and VFS, lists all installed modules and is the place to check to be sure that EnCase is seeing your certificate and matching it properly to your dongle.

Often the question arises as to which module should be used for which task. Table 10.8 lists various tasks and the proper module (VFS or PDE) for the job, along with a brief description of the reason.

**TABLE 10.8**     Forensic Tasks and the Proper Module (VFS or PDE) for the Job

| Task | Module | Rationale |
|---|---|---|
| VMWare | PDE | VMWare needs access to physical disk. |
| Virus or Malware Scan | PDE<br>VFS | If not interested in deleted files.<br>If interested in deleted files. |
| Extracting Internet history from unallocated clusters | VFS | PDE does not provide access to unallocated clusters. Only VFS provides this access. |
| Using Windows Explorer to peruse Linux or Macintosh | VFS | PDE only allows mounting of file systems supported by Windows. VFS mounts any file system supported within EnCase. |
| Using any third-party tool in Windows to examine a partition recovered in EnCase | VFS | PDE presents the device as is and Windows won't see the recovered partition. VFS presents the file system as EnCase has restored it. |

# Putting It All Together

Together we have covered the gamut of the major features of EnCase 5. The order in which we have proceeded was largely determined by the most logical learning progression, which has no connection to the order in which you might conduct a forensic examination. So what is the best order in which to conduct a forensic examination? Clearly there are a few basic steps that progress in a certain sequence, but beyond that the order is most often determined by the examiner based on the nature and urgency of the case.

Over the years, many examiners have asked for a list of suggested steps for an examination. Over time, with input and suggestions from many colleagues, I have assembled such a list. It should never be regarded as mandatory or as a standard. Rather, consider it a suggested approach that is dynamic, flexible, and rarely if ever all inclusive. Every case is different, and both the tools and the computing environment are in a constant state of change. Also please keep in mind that any search (hash analysis included) must be conducted within the scope of your search authority. With those caveats and conditions stated, the list of suggested steps follows:

- Log your case information into your lab case management database or case book.

- Examine and document the computer systems under examination, taking care to conduct both an internal and external inspections and carefully recording your findings in photos, notes, or forms created for that purpose.

- Determine the method of acquisition, preview (if applicable), and acquire the image of the media.

- Make certain that all sectors on the drive have been identified and actually acquired (determine if HPA or DCO is present).

- Make a backup copy of all images, store the original in a secure location, and conduct your examination on copies.

- Obtain the system times from all machines under examination and simultaneously record the known time from an accepted time standard.

- Once images are acquired and brought into the case, make certain that the file integrity is verified.

- Preview the images acquired. Determine the total sectors on the various devices; reconcile those sectors with sectors in partitions to make certain all partitions are mounted and accounted for. Recover and mount any deleted partitions.

- Run Recover Folders on all volumes.

- Run the Case Initialization EnScript to include time zone settings. Adjust time zone offsets if necessary so that times will be accurately displayed. Also obtain owner information, operating system version, etc.

- Use conditions to determine if EFS encryption is applied. If so, take what steps are needed to decrypt so that analysis work can proceed on encrypted data.

- Run file signature and hash analysis (make certain the hash library is within the scope of your search authority). Analyze results of both analyses.

- Use conditions or queries to ascertain which types of e-mail are present on the system. If unsupported types are found, process with other tools as needed.

- Conduct the Email/Internet Search so that compound files are mounted for subsequent searches and that compressed files in the web cache are likewise mounted and available for searching.

- Use conditions to locate compressed files (zips, etc.). Mount them so that the compressed data can be available for searching and processing.

- Examine the directory and file structure to get an overview of the device, users on the system, and programs that appear to be installed.

- Use VFS or PDE to mount devices in Windows to conduct virus and malware scans. This should occur early in your processing; if the machine is hacked and someone else is in control, such a finding is best known early as that significantly alters the case.

- Examine briefly the root user folders under Documents and Settings, specifically surveying the Recent, Desktop, Send To, History, Temp, Temporary Internet Files, Cookies, My Documents, and Recycle Bin folders to get a profile of users and their activities.

- With the Email/Internet Search completed, examine the contents of the Email, History, and Web Cache tabs.

- Examine the contents of the Program Files folder to see if any significant programs are installed (encryption, evidence removal tools, hacking, etc.).

- Process the UserAssist key and export the value name and data to a spreadsheet. Copy the value name data (entire column) to the Clipboard, paste it into a ROT13 decoder, copy the results to the Clipboard, and paste the decoded values into the spreadsheet. Examine the results to see if significant programs have been run that aren't showing up elsewhere. Combine the information in this key with the information in the Recent folder to get a good idea as to user activity, and conduct further inquiries as indicated.

- Structure keywords and conduct searches. Evaluate the search hits. Refine keywords and add more as needed. Run additional searches and evaluate results.

- Run the File finder EnScript to recover images or other files of interest to the case.

- Run the Link File Analysis EnScript.

- Look for evidence of data on removable drives, network or remote storage, and so forth.

- Run the INF02 Recycle Bin Recovery EnScript.

- Run the EDS Registry parser to extract passwords and auto-fill information.

- Run the Scan Registry EnScript to pull out extensive artifact information from the Registry.

- Search for and process artifacts of past print jobs from deleted spool files.

- Analyze the web cache for significant patterns and examine individual pages as needed.

- Locate instant messaging clients and process any artifacts or messages that may be logged.

- Locate any peer-to-peer file sharing software. Process the associated artifacts.

- Locate financial software and process any associated databases in their native environment.

- Examine Photoshop files in their native environment to check for images or text data that may be hidden in layers.

- Run third-party tools on mounted devices using VFS or PDE as may be indicated.

- Examine log files (event logs, web server logs, FTP logs, error logs, AOL logs, etc.).

- Conduct any other specialized inquiries as may be dictated by the specifics of the case.

- Use PDE to mount physical device and run VMWare to boot the suspect's drive to see it as the suspect saw it. Alternatively, restore the image out to a drive and use the restored drive to boot the suspect's computer, again viewing their system as the suspect saw it.

- Run a file Verify File Integrity check and bookmark your findings.

- Bookmark all significant findings, organize bookmarks, and create your final report.

- Archive all data onto archival media, verifying copies of evidence files.

This is, again, a suggested list and one that you can customize and modify as circumstances warrant. Lists are helpful, but you should avoid getting into a checklist trap, where you methodically process according to a standardized checklist. Such an approach becomes habitual and can inhibit creativity and examinations that are beyond the list or out of the box.

Computer forensics is an extremely dynamic field, one in which the playing field is constantly changing. New technologies are evolving daily. As examiners, we should be reactive to trends and able to adapt rapidly to changes.

Five years ago, computer forensics examiners were generalists. Today, things have changed. Computing in general has become far more complex than it was five years ago. One can no longer be an expert in all areas; the field has become too vast. Specialty areas are emerging. Not only must you be a generalist, but you must also develop specialties based on the type of work in which you are emerged. The age of computer forensic specialty areas is here, and there's only one direction it can go: up.

If you think about the development over the past 5 years and try to imagine what computing will be like in 5, 10, or 15 years, it is simply too much to even comprehend. We will be facing technologies that we cannot even begin to imagine today. As always, training and education will be the keys to meeting these new challenges.

Although training and education are important, they aren't the complete solution. We can't possibly begin to be an expert in all areas, so we must develop strong informational networks among computer forensics examiners. Information-sharing networks allow us to share knowledge and techniques and foster problem solving in real time regardless of your geographical location.

With those parting thoughts in mind, if we are to meet the challenges of the future of computer forensics, we all need to embrace a couple of very simple goals. First, we must put aside our differences and all work together to form and nurture informational networks. Finally, each of us must make a commitment to excellence and seek out all possible education and training opportunities. We now live in an information age and the more information we have, the better off we'll be in facing the challenges of the future.

In the field of computer forensics, excellence is not an option; it is an operational necessity. Excellence, on the individual level, is a combination of integrity, perseverance, a commitment to the highest standards of the profession, and a never-ending thirst for knowledge through research and education.

My best wishes and regards to you on your EnCE certification testing and in your career.

# Summary

In this chapter, we covered a wide array of advanced techniques and concepts. We began with a review of our previous discussions of partitions as a predecessor to recovering them when deleted. The partition table is located in the MBR at byte offsets 446–509. In those 64 bytes, up to four partitions can be described in 16-byte strings. When one or more partitions are deleted, their corresponding entries in this table are removed and replaced with zeros. This is often described as fdisking.

Even though the entry in the table may be zeroed out, the VBR marking the beginning and containing the parameters of the partition often remains untouched, depending on where it is and what subsequent actions have taken place.

When the first partition is missing, we can usually look to the first sector of the second track to find the VBR. With that located, we can restore the partition by right-clicking on that sector in the Disk view and choosing Add Partition. Usually we accept the default values and the partition is restored by clicking OK.

When the partition is missing elsewhere on the drive, using the Partition Finder EnScript to locate VBRs works well. It is best to work in one direction, starting from the beginning of the drive, and restore partitions as they are found.

Many files are compound in nature. They can be flat files that contain objects (Office documents), they may be flat files that have a hierarchical structure (Registry hive files), they may be files that are compressed (zip files), or they may be files that are compressed and encrypted (Outlook PST files). EnCase supports and mounts many different types of compound files. To mount a compound file, right-click on it and choose View File Structure. The resultant mounted structure may be browsed from the Tree pane/Entries tab.

The Windows Registry is an enormous database containing configuration information for your hardware and software environment. The data is contained, at a physical level, in a series of hive files. The hive files are addressed by the user and programs by a logical addressing scheme that is hierarchical and similar to the files and folders used in the Explorer interface.

Instead of Explorer, the interface by which to view or edit the Registry is called regedit. Instead of folders, the Registry uses the term *keys*. The term *subkey* is used when it is showing a subordinate relationship between keys. Instead of files, the Registry uses *values*. Values have three components: the value name, the data type, and the data. In regedit, the left pane is called the key pane, and only keys are viewed in this pane. The right pane is called the value pane, and only values are viewed in this pane.

The live Registry is made up of five root keys: HKEY_CLASSES_ROOT, HKEY_CURRENT_USER, HKEY_CURRENT_CONFIG, HKEY_LOCAL_MACHINE, and HKEY_USERS. Of these five, only the last two are master keys. The first three are derived keys that exist as links to keys within the master keys. The two master keys are the logical representation of the various physical hive files.

The hive files (SAM, SECURITY, software, and system) form the hive keys under HKEY_LOCAL_MACHINE by the same names. These hive files are located in the folder %SYSTEMROOT%\System32\config. There is no hardware hive file because the HKLM\HARDWARE key is dynamic, created at boot, supports the booted hardware configuration, and is gone when the system shuts down.

The HKEY_USERS key is made up of many hive files representing the SID numbers of the various users who have logged onto the system. Usually, there are at least three: .DEFAULT, SID, and SID_Classes, where the SID is that of the console user. The hive file for the .DEFAULT key is at %SYSTEMROOT%\System32\config\default. The hive file for the SID key is the file NTUSER.DAT, located in the root of the root user folder for the username corresponding to the SID. The hive file for the SID_Classes key is the file UsrClass.dat, located in Documents and Settings\UserName\Local Settings\Application Data\Microsoft\Windows\, where the UserName corresponds to the SID.

The live Registry as seen in Windows differs from the offline Registry as viewed in EnCase. Volatile keys such as the HARDWARE key under HKLM will be nonexistent. Three of the five root keys are derived keys and won't be seen as such; however, the subkeys within the master keys from which they are derived from links can be viewed. To view the Registry in EnCase, simply mount any of the hive keys by right-clicking and choosing View File Structure.

EnScripts are short pieces of code that automate forensic processing or tasks. EnScripts can be used as shipped with EnCase by simply double-clicking on the desired EnScript and following any prompts to configure options. For those with the proper skills, EnScripts can be created or edited within the EnCase environment. EnScripts are accessible from the View menu under EnScripts or by accessing them from the EnScripts tab of the Filter pane.

In addition to EnScripts, the Filter pane contains filters, conditions, and queries. Filters are simply specialized EnScripts that allow you to filter the case for various attributes, such as extension or file type. To create a filter, you must enter code. Conditions are filters, but the interface by which they are created is a set of dialog box options that build the code in the background for you. Filters and conditions are powerful tools. There are many that ship with EnCase, and conditions are easy to create. Queries allow the user to create combinations of filters and conditions using Boolean logic operators.

EnCase 5 (as of 5.04a) supports the following e-mail types: Outlook (PST), Outlook Express (DBX / MBX), AOL (6, 7, 8, 9), Hotmail, Yahoo!, Netscape, and mbox. The Email tab displays these e-mail formats when they are presented in a logical view. To populate the Email tab with one of these e-mail types, you can mount its corresponding compound file (if applicable) in the Entries tab. The other method of populating the Email tab is by going to the Email, History, or Web Cache tab and right-clicking in it root and selecting Email/Internet Search. Whenever a webmail type is selected, the web cache and history are processed whether or not they are selected. E-mail can be bookmarked individually or in selected groups. The results can be viewed in the Bookmark view and included in your final report.

EnCase has three optional modules that are purchased separately from the main software product. The EFS module is used to decrypt data encrypted with Microsoft Encrypting File System. In some cases the decryption is automatic and in other cases the password must be obtained through various cracking methods. In addition to decrypting EFS, the EFS module automatically decrypts data stored in the protected storage area of the Registry. This data consists of passwords that Windows remembered for the user, and it consists of data stored for use with the auto-fill feature.

The VFS module mounts any file system supported by EnCase as an offline, read-only network drive. In this manner the user can access all logical files, all deleted files that EnCase can recover, and the unallocated clusters within the Windows environment. In this way, third-party tools can be used against those logical file system objects as seen by EnCase.

The PDE module mounts the physical device or volume as a physical disk in Windows. Only file systems supported by Windows can be mounted, meaning that only NFTS and FAT will be available. All other file systems will be available at a physical level only. PDE can work in conjunction with VMWare to mount the suspect's drive as a virtual machine, boot it, and see it as the suspects saw it, saving considerable time and money, plus providing another valuable examination tool.

# Exam Essentials

**Understand partitions, partition tables, MBRs, and VBRs.** Know the location of the main partition table on a hard drive. Describe what the partition table does and what information it contains. Explain what happens when a partition is removed, particularly what is affected and what is not. Understand how to locate deleted partitions and restore them using EnCase.

**Understand compound files and how they are mounted.** Describe different types of compound files and be able to provide examples. Know which compound files can be mounted in EnCase 5. Be able to describe the process of mounting files within EnCase. Explain the importance of mounting files.

**Understand the purpose and function of the Windows Registry.** Explain the purpose of the Windows Registry. List the five root keys of the Windows Registry. Know which of the five keys are master keys and which are derived keys. Explain a hive file. Know the names and locations of the hive files. Understand and explain the logical structure of the Registry. Explain the difference between keys and values. Know the three attributes of a value. Describe the Registry interface tool and how it is launched. Explain the difference between the live Registry in Windows and the offline Registry in EnCase. Explain how to mount the Registry in EnCase. Explain which hive files correspond with which logical keys in the live Registry.

**Understand EnScripts, filters, conditions, and queries.** Explain the function of EnScripts. Know how to navigate to and run a typical EnScript. Describe how to change the root path of the EnScript folder. Explain the purpose of filters and conditions. Describe the differences between filters and conditions. Describe the process of creating a condition. Explain how to navigate to and run a filter or condition. Understand how to create a query and how to change the Boolean logic.

**Understand and know how to conduct e-mail examinations.** Explain the various types of e-mail clients, applications, and services. Explain the difference between an e-mail client and web mail. Describe which e-mail types are supported currently within EnCase. Explain two methods by which the Email tab is populated. Describe under which conditions the History and Web Cache tabs are populated even when no browser is selected. Explain how webmail works and where to look for artifacts.

**Understand the purpose and function of the EFS module.** Explain what EFS means. Describe the system used by Windows to encrypt data. Explain under which conditions password recovery will be automatic. Know the purpose of the protected storage area, specifically which data is stored there. Describe how EFS processes the protected storage area.

**Understand the purpose and function of the VFS and PDE modules.** Understand the function of the VFS module. Know which file systems will be displayed in Windows when using the VFS module. Explain the type of mount that VFS will present to Windows. Describe the various levels at which VFS can mount. Understand the function of the PDE module. Explain which file systems will be displayed in Windows when using the PDE module. Describe the primary differences between the VFS and PDE modules. Explain which module mounts deleted files and unallocated clusters in Windows.

# Review Questions

1.  How many sector(s) on a hard drive are reserved for the master boot record (MBR)?

    **A.** 1

    **B.** 4

    **C.** 16

    **D.** 62

    **E.** 63

2.  The very first sector of a formatted hard drive that contains an operating system is referred to as:

    **A.** Absolute sector 0

    **B.** Boot sector

    **C.** Containing the master boot record (MBR)

    **D.** All of the above

3.  How many logical partitions does the partition table in the master boot record allow for a physical drive?

    **A.** 1

    **B.** 2

    **C.** 4

    **D.** 24

4.  The very first sector of a partition is referred to as:

    **A.** Master boot record

    **B.** Physical sector 0

    **C.** Active primary partition

    **D.** Volume boot record

5.  If a hard drive has been fdisked, EnCase can still recover the deleted partition(s), if you point to the _____, right-click, and select Add Partition.

    **A.** Master boot record

    **B.** Volume boot record

    **C.** Partition table

    **D.** Unallocated space

6.  In an NTFS partition, where is the backup copy of the volume boot record (VBR) stored?

    **A.** In the partition table

    **B.** Immediately after the VBR

    **C.** The very last sector of the partition

    **D.** An NTFS partition does not store a backup of the VBR.

**7.** EnCase can mount a compound file, which can then be viewed in a hierarchical format. Select an example of a compound file.

**A.** Registry file (i.e., .dat)

**B.** E-mail file (i.e., .dbx)

**C.** Compressed file (i.e., .zip)

**D.** Thumbs.db

**E.** All of the above

**8.** Windows XP contains two master keys in its Registry. They are HKEY_LOCAL_MACHINE and:

**A.** HKEY_USERS

**B.** HKEY_CLASSES_ROOT

**C.** HKEY_CURRENT_USER

**D.** HKEY_CURRENT_CONFIG

**9.** In Windows 2000/XP, information about a specific user's preference is stored in the NTUSER.DAT file. This compound file can be found in:

**A.** C:\

**B.** C:\WINDOWS\

**C.** C:\Documents and Settings\username

**D.** C:\Documents and Settings\All Users\Application Data

**10.** In an NTFS file system, the date and time stamps recorded in the Registry are stored in:

**A.** Local time based on the BIOS settings

**B.** GMT and converted based on the system's time zone settings

**11.** EnScript is a proprietary programming language and application programming interface (API) developed by Guidance Software, Inc., designed to function properly only within the EnCase environment.

**A.** True

**B.** False

**12.** Since EnScript is a proprietary programming language developed by Guidance Software, EnScripts can only be created by and obtained from Guidance Software.

**A.** True

**B.** False

**13.** Filters are a type of EnScript that "filters" a case of certain file categories based on a set of parameters such as file types, dates, and hash categories. Like EnScripts, filters can also be changed or created by a user.

**A.** True

**B.** False

**14.** Select the type of e-mail that EnCase 5 is *not* capable of recovering.

   **A.** Microsoft Outlook and Outlook Express

   **B.** AOL

   **C.** MSN Hotmail and Yahoo!

   **D.** Netscape

   **E.** None of the above

**15.** Which method is used to view the contents of a compound file that contains e-mails such as a PST file in EnCase 5?

   **A.** Right-click and select View File Structure.

   **B.** Run the Email/Internet Search feature and select the types of e-mail to recover.

   **C.** Both A and B

   **D.** None of the above

**16.** EnCase 5 cannot process web-based e-mail such as MSN Hotmail or Yahoo! because the information can only be found on the mail servers.

   **A.** True

   **B.** False

**17.** The EnCase Decryption Suite (EDS) will *not* decrypt Microsoft's Encrypting File System (EFS) on the _____ operating system.

   **A.** A.Windows 2000 Professional and Server

   **B.** Windows XP Professional

   **C.** Windows 2003 Server

   **D.** Windows XP Home Edition

**18.** At which levels can the VFS module mount objects in the Windows environment?

   **A.** The case level

   **B.** The disk or device level

   **C.** The volume level

   **D.** The folder level

   **E.** All of the above

**19.** The Physical Disk Emulator (PDE) module is very similar to the Virtual File System (VFS); the module can mount a piece of media that is accessible in the Windows environment. Select the type(s) of media that the Physical Disk Emulator *cannot* mount.

   **A.** Cases

   **B.** Folders

   **C.** Volumes

   **D.** Physical disks

   **E.** Both A and B

**20.** The Virtual File System (VFS) module mounts data as _____ while the Physical Disk Emulator (PDE) module mounts data as _____.

   **A.** Network share and emulated disk

   **B.** Emulated disk and network share

   **C.** Virtual drive and physical drive

   **D.** Virtual file and physical disk

# Answers to Review Questions

1. E. The first 63 sectors of a hard drive are reserved for the MBR even though its contents are contained in the very first sector.

2. D. The very first sector of a formatted hard drive with an operating system is referred to as a boot sector, which contains the MBR and is located at absolute sector 0.

3. C. The partition table allows for four logical partitions.

4. D. The very first sector of a partition contains the volume boot record.

5. B. EnCase can still recover deleted partitions if you point to the very first sector of the partition, which is the volume boot record, right-click, and select the Add Partition command.

6. C. When a hard drive is formatted with an NTFS partition, a backup of the VBR is stored in the last sector of the partition.

7. E. The above listed file types are all examples of compound files that EnCase is able to display their contents in a hierarchical format.

8. A. The other master key is HKEY_USERS. The other choices are derived keys that are linked to keys within the two master keys.

9. C. Each time a profile or username is created, the NTUSER.DAT file is also created for the specific profile. This compound file is stored locally within the username under C:\Documents and Settings unless the system was upgraded from NT 4.0, at which time it is stored in *%systemroot%\profiles\username*.

10. B. In an NTFS file system, the date and time stamps recorded in the Registry are recorded in GMT, which is then displayed in local time based on the system's time zone settings.

11. A. True. Since EnScript is a proprietary programming language, it is designed to function properly only in the EnCase environment.

12. B. False. Although EnScript was developed by Guidance Software, anyone with computer programming skills and knowledge of the programming language can develop his or her own EnScripts.

13. A. True. Since filters are in essence EnScripts, any user can modify an existing filter or create his or her own.

14. E. EnCase 5 can recognize and recover all the above listed types of e-mails.

15. C. EnCase 5 allows the user to view the contents of compound files containing e-mails by either right-clicking the file and selecting View File Structure or by running the Email/Internet Search feature.

**16.** B. False. Contents of web-based e-mails may reside in areas such as Temporary Internet History, cache (pagefile.sys), hiberfil.sys, and unallocated clusters. While executing the Email/Internet Search feature to recover web-based e-mails, EnCase will look for such e-mails in Internet history and cache files.

**17.** D. Microsoft Windows XP Home Edition does not include the EFS feature.

**18.** E. The VFS module can also mount data at the case, disk or device, volume, and folder levels.

**19.** E. The Physical Disk Emulator can mount volumes and physical disks in the Windows environment; however, it does not mount cases or folders.

**20.** A. When a user selects the VFS module, EnCase will prompt the user with a Mount As Network Share dialog box. When a user selects the PDE module, EnCase will prompt the user with a Mount As Emulated Disk dialog box.

# Appendix A

# Creating Paperless Reports

In the not too distant past, computer forensics reports were typically printed documents. As the volume and complexity of computing in general has grown, computer forensics reports have likewise grown and evolved. The current trend is toward paperless web-page style reports that are contained on CDs or DVDs.

EnCase's web page reports provide a powerful tool to convey your findings. They are extremely flexible; you create the hierarchy and structure when you create your bookmarks. The more organized and articulate you are as you create folder structures and names, the better your reports will appear in either format, but especially in the web page version.

While content is always important, presentation is probably even more important. It is the first thing seen by everyone and it is the medium by which your content is delivered. You may be the sharpest examiner around and every examination you do may be the epitome of computer forensics examinations, but if your report is ugly and technically intimidating, case agents and prosecutors will shy away. Your challenge is to package your technical findings into a report that looks good, that is easy to read, and that tells a story with links to technical findings.

If you are to be a successful examiner, at some point you will have to convey your findings to a third party who has very little understanding of computers. These third parties are typically case investigators, attorneys, judges, hearing boards, juries, and the like. You will have to explain, verbally and in written reports, very technical concepts in terms that the layperson can understand. It takes time, practice, skill, experience, and creativity. Most of all, it requires that you be willing to take the extra effort to make it happen. When you create reports that your readers can easily read and understand, the results you see will speak for themselves.

It is beyond the scope of this book to transform you into a brilliant technical writer, but we can provide you with a presentation-grade template that you can adapt that will greatly improve the appearance and readability of your reports. We'll also give you some ideas and suggestions that can help you with your reports. The template we will adapt is one that has its roots in a template developed by Roy Rector a few years ago. Roy is a police officer in Austin, Texas, and part-time instructor with Guidance Software, Inc. In the latter capacity, he shared this template with the many classes he taught.

I have made many changes to the original template, but the most significant change was that of making it easily adaptable for other users to employ. To make it work for you, you need only rename your agency seal file name to agency.jpg, insert your signature in place of mine, change the agency name and address information on the headers, and insert your biographical information in place of mine. Assuming your bio is relatively current, the entire change can be done in minutes.

When done, this template gives you an organized and attractive shell in which to write your narrative and create links to the EnCase report. In this manner the reader can read a narrative in which you explain what you did and what you found. As you describe significant findings, you will create hyperlinks to the EnCase report where the actual evidence exists. The reader can follow the link, view the evidence, and return to reading your narrative. It makes reading and navigating your report a pleasure.

In addition, the shell or template has separate pages on which to describe your hardware analysis, which can be accessed by hyperlinks. If terminology is an issue, there is a glossary page that can be accessed via hyperlinks. There is also a page on which you may place your bio so that it is readily viewable.

At the center of these pages is your EnCase report, which will have links to it from many different sources. You can add third-party reports and provide links to them as you wish. It is almost limitless what you can do when you create your reports in this manner. When we conclude, we'll show you how to arrange your files for placement on a CD or DVD, including a couple of files needed to automatically run your media when placed in the drive. Once you've created and submitted one paperless report, both you and your readers will insist on them in the future.

# Exporting the Web Page Report

If you aren't comfortable working with bookmarks, it might be a good time to review that section in Chapter 7, perhaps even reviewing the exercise. You need to be very adept at creating folders and giving them meaningful names as well as moving them around to create organization and structure. I often start out creating a very linear folder structure until the case starts to materialize as evidence is found. Once the case evidence materializes, it is time for you to organize your folder structure accordingly.

I typically create a master or root folder named EnCase Computer Forensics Report, which in turn becomes the title of the report. Under that root folder I create two subfolders: Acquisition and Device Information and Examination Findings. I arrange the Acquisition and Device Information first, followed by the other one. Figure A.1 shows this folder structure.

**FIGURE A.1**    Bookmark folder structure

For the Acquisition and Device Information folder, I place nothing in the Format window, accepting the defaults. For the Examination Findings folder, I apply a standard template of format settings that I store in a text file and paste in. We discussed format settings in Chapter 7 and how a template can be stored on a file. This setting applies to all child objects unless they need to be customized.

When your bookmarks are completed and you are satisfied with their structure and appearance, it is time to export your report. Apply the Set Included Folders trigger at the root level of your report, typically at the folder EnCase Computer Forensics Report. If you will look again at Figure A.1, you will see the Set Included Folder trigger activated at this level. In the Table pane, switch to the Report view or tab. If your report is long, as many are, the report could take some time to generate. When done, your report will appear in the Table pane as one long linear report. You should scroll through it and check for problems before you continue.

When you are ready to export your report, right-click anywhere on the report in the Table pane and choose the Export option. Next you will see the Export Report dialog box listing your options. Choose the Web Page option.

At this point, you will need to choose a path for the web page report. There are several pre-built links to the EnCase Report and Gallery views that expect the path to be in the Reports folder. If you wish to have a seamless migration to the template, you should put your report in a folder named Reports and place it in the root of your case name folder at the same level as the Temp and Export folders. If you follow this standard, the template links should always work without modification. You will also need to give your report a name. In order to create a standard, use the case name for the report name. Figure A.2 shows the Export Report dialog box, with the settings we have discussed. Click OK to generate your report.

**FIGURE A.2**    The Export Report dialog box with settings for a web page report

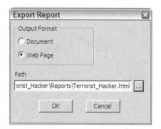

Once your report is generated, you should go to your Reports folder and see that the output is as expected. EnCase will create several standard files. The Frame View.html file is an HTML frame page that sets up frames to hold the report web page content. The toc.html file is the table of contents file that appears at the top of the page and allows you to switch between the Full Report and the Gallery views. The toc.html file is placed in a frame at the top of the frame page where it remains regardless of the content in the lower frame, which switches between the Gallery and Full Report views.

The gallery.html file contains, as the name implies, the gallery view of all images in the case. When selected from the table of contents, it appears in the lower frame. The case name.html file

(Terrorist_Hacker.html file in this case) contains the full report and displays by default in the lower frame when Frame View.html is opened. Frame View.html is the file that will open when launching an EnCase report. Thus any hyperlink that is designed to open the EnCase report should be pointed at this file. Figure A.3 shows the files created by the EnCase web page report.

**FIGURE A.3**    Files created by the EnCase web page report

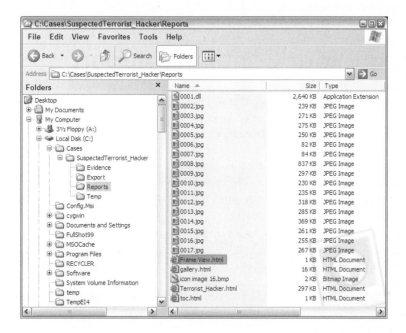

When you look at the files created, you will some other files created as well. If you have bookmarked a folder structure and have opted to show the folders in a hierarchical format, the file icon image 16.bmp is created and allows the folder icon to be used repeatedly to show this structure. The other files shown in Figure A.3 are mostly JPEG, or image, files. They are mostly from bookmarked files. A bookmarked file will be exported with the report and the report will have a hyperlink to the file. The file's name is changed to match the bookmark index number, and its file name extension remains the same.

In our example case, we had some hacking tools. We did not bookmark those files, as they would have been exported with the report, causing our antivirus software to work overtime. If we turned it off to allow the export, then the reader would be potentially jeopardized by a hyperlink to known malware. To document them, we bookmarked their folder structure and exported a list of file names and attributes that will be available via a hyperlink.

Now that we understand the files created by an EnCase web page report, we are ready to create a report around them. Before going further, it is always a good idea to launch the EnCase report by double-clicking the Frame View.html file and reviewing the contents in your browser. Make sure everything is the way you want it to appear before going further. If there are problems, fix them in EnCase now and export the file again.

If your Full Report file is excessively large, it may take a long time to load in your browser. If the load time is long on your forensics machine with robust resources, you need to consider what the load time is going to be on your reader's machine, which usually has minimal resources. If that is a concern, now is the time to go back into EnCase and export your report in as many sections as it takes to make it manageable in a browser. Place the first section in the folder Reports, the second in folder Reports2, and so forth. You can tie them together later with hyperlinks in an index.

# Creating Your Container Report

Now that you have created and exported your EnCase report, it is time to place it within your container report. This container report is the polished gateway or front-end to your EnCase report. It contains the splash screen, summary, data analysis report, hardware analysis report, general procedures, a glossary, and the examiner's bio. Each of these reports, pages, or tabs, or whatever you prefer to call them, has a standard format and a standard set of navigation menus. Table A.1 lists each report, page, or tab by file name, along with its description and a listing of standard and suggested or optional hyperlinks found within it.

**TABLE A.1** Individual Reports Found in the Container Report

| Name | File Name | Description | Hyperlinks |
|------|-----------|-------------|------------|
| Initial Splash Screen | index.htm | This is the home screen and is the initial screen that is first seen upon auto-run. Edit, for each, case the case name, number, and case officer information. | Standard Links: Home About the Examiner Summary Data Analysis Hardware Analysis General Procedures Glossary |
| About the Examiner | about.htm | Examiner's bio that is updated periodically as needed. Including it in the report makes it available to all readers at the outset. | Standard Links: Home About the Examiner Summary Data Analysis Hardware Analysis General Procedures Glossary |

**TABLE A.1**    Individual Reports Found in the Container Report *(continued)*

| Name | File Name | Description | Hyperlinks |
|------|-----------|-------------|------------|
| Summary | summary.htm | Summary containing brief background about case along with links to the EnCase report and significant case findings. | Standard Links: Home About the Examiner Summary Data Analysis Hardware Analysis General Procedures Glossary EnCase Report EnCase Gallery Links to the more significant findings in the case |
| Data Analysis | data_ analysis.htm | This contains the detailed narrative of your examination, from acquisition to final conclusions. As findings are described, hyperlinks are inserted linking the reader to the specific index in the EnCase report. | Standard Links: Home About the Examiner Summary Data Analysis Hardware Analysis General Procedures Glossary EnCase Report EnCase Gallery Links to all findings as they are described Links to reports created by third-party software Links to exported files |
| Hardware Analysis | hardware_ analysis.htm | Page that describes all hardware in the case, including a report of system time compared to known time standard. | Standard Links: Home About the Examiner Summary Data Analysis Hardware Analysis General Procedures Glossary Links to photographs of computer equipment associated with the case |

**TABLE A.1**    Individual Reports Found in the Container Report *(continued)*

| Name | File Name | Description | Hyperlinks |
|------|-----------|-------------|------------|
| General Procedures | general_ procedures.htm | Lists the general procedures typically employed in a case. This doesn't usually require editing unless you introduce significant changes to your processing routine. | Standard Links: Home About the Examiner Summary Data Analysis Hardware Analysis General Procedures Glossary |
| Glossary | glossary.htm | A glossary of terms typically encountered in a computer forensics report. | Standard Links: Home About the Examiner Summary Data Analysis Hardware Analysis General Procedures Glossary |

Before going further, it is important to understand that you will be editing web pages that contain hypertext markup language (HTML) as its source code. This is the language of the Web. It is not necessary to edit raw code, nor is it particularly desirable to do so even if you have the requisite skills, as coding is slow and tedious. Rather, you should use a full-featured HTML editor so that you can quickly get the job done. There are many such editors out there, some of which are free. Microsoft Word can be used as an HTML editor, but it is not a very good one for this task. I recommend you use Microsoft FrontPage, which is the tool we'll use in this appendix as we edit our reports.

 Examiners should be aware that FrontPage uses a Temp folder under the Local Settings of the user account on the examination machine. This can be an issue if working with contraband or sensitive files, and may require cleanup. Some examiners use a clean restoration of their examination machine for each case to mitigate such concerns.

Before you start editing, you need to get all your folders and files in place so that the paths you create with your hyperlinks will remain intact. On the book DVD, locate the CD Container Report. The files and folders contained in that folder are shown in Figure A.4. You should create a folder, name it with your case name, and copy these files and folders into that folder.

Once you have created a folder dedicated to your report and have copied the container report files and folders into it, you should locate the folder named Reports in your EnCase case folder. The Reports folder contains the EnCase web report that you exported. There is a folder by the same name (Reports) in the container report files and folders. Your final step in organizing and setting up your files and folders is to copy all files and folders in the EnCase web report folder named Reports into the folder by the same name (Reports) located in the folder you named to contain your paperless report.

**FIGURE A.4**   Files and folders needed for paperless report

| Name ▲ | Size | Type |
|---|---|---|
| _vti_cnf | | File Folder |
| _vti_pvt | | File Folder |
| images | | File Folder |
| Reports | | File Folder |
| VideoLan | | File Folder |
| about.htm | 25 KB | HTML Document |
| autorun.exe | 28 KB | Application |
| autorun.inf | 1 KB | Setup Information |
| data_analysis.htm | 10 KB | HTML Document |
| general_procedures.htm | 11 KB | HTML Document |
| glossary.htm | 24 KB | HTML Document |
| hardware_analysis.htm | 6 KB | HTML Document |
| index.htm | 9 KB | HTML Document |
| summary.htm | 8 KB | HTML Document |

**NOTE**   On the book DVD, this Reports folder already contains the files and folders from the EnCase Reports folder to show you the finished product. Normally you should keep this folder empty after you create your working template to avoid the possibility of mixing report files from old cases.

Once you have folder created and it contains the files and folders shown in Figure A.4, and the Reports folder contains the files and folders from the EnCase web report folder (also named Reports), you are ready to edit and prepare your paperless report.

If this is the first time you've set up your paperless report, take a couple of minutes to customize this report for you and your agency. You will need to do the following:

- Obtain your agency seal in a JPEG format. Name it agency.jpg and place it in the images folder of the paperless report, overwriting the one there by the same name. The present agency seal is 188 pixels wide and 133 pixels high. If you keep your agency seal size within these parameters, it should fit nicely with little or no adjustment.

- Scan your signature and save it as a GIF file with the name of signature.gif, placing it in the images folder, again overwriting the one there by the same name. The present signature is 559 pixels wide and 259 pixels high. If you keep your signature size within these parameters, it should fit nicely with little or no adjustment.

- Using FrontPage, open the file index.htm. Edit the top-right section, entering your agency, name, address, and contact information in place of the generic information. Copy this block to your Clipboard. Save your changes to index.htm. Make the same changes (pasting from the Clipboard) to the following files: about.htm, summary.htm, data_analysis.htm, general_procedures.htm, hardware_analysis.htm, and glossary.htm. As you make the changes, save each file and close it.

- Using FrontPage, open the file about.htm. Place your bio information on this page, overwriting the current bio information. Save this file when complete.

- Using FrontPage, open the file data_analysis.htm. Place your name and information under the signature on this page, overwriting the current information. Save this file when complete.

- You have now completed customizing the container report for your paperless report. Create a folder on your desktop and name it Paperless Report Template. Copy the files and folders in Figure A.4 into this template folder. Open these files: index.htm, summary.htm, data_analysis.htm, and hardware_analysis.htm. Remove information that is specific to the example case, leaving behind all the generic information that you wish to remain in your template. Save your changes as you go. Delete the folders and files in the Reports folder in order to leave it empty and clean for your subsequent case reports.

With little effort, you have customized the current paperless report for you and your agency. Further, by copying your work into a separate folder, you have created a template to use for future reports that is ready to be copied and used as is.

For each report that you create, as a matter of routine, you will place case-specific information in each of the following files: index.htm, summary.htm, data_analysis.htm, and hardware_analysis.htm. You will, from time to time, update your bio (about.htm). You probably won't change the general procedures or glossary files very often.

Let's turn our attention back to the paperless report that we are creating. For the most part, you are ready to use FrontPage to create your narrative in the data analysis report that describes your examination process and findings. It is beyond the scope of this book to delve into technical writing or style issues. For ideas on content or style, look to the example on the DVD. To help you complete your report, we need to address two issues: creating bookmarks and hyperlinks, and burning our final report to a CD that will run automatically.

## Bookmarks and Hyperlinks

Let's turn our attention now to creating bookmarks and hyperlinks, which are the features that truly make paperless reports appealing. A bookmark in an HTML document is different from a bookmark created in EnCase. A *bookmark* is a Microsoft term for the HTML code or tag that is called an anchor. An anchor, or bookmark, simply creates a specific point in a document to which you can direct a hyperlink. Instead of saying "See EnCase report for details," we'll create a significant number of bookmarks within the EnCase report pointing the various pieces of evidence contained within it. As we write our report narrative, we'll create hyperlinks pointing to these bookmarks that will allow the reader to click the hyperlink and be immediately taken to the section of the EnCase report that provides the evidence described in the narrative.

Let's create a bookmark. Using FrontPage, open the file Terrorist_Hacker.html, which is located in the Reports folder and contains the main body of the EnCase report. We want to take our reader directly to the files that were found to match the hash values from another system under examination in a possible terrorism case. With experience, you'll quickly determine where to place bookmarks. It is both an art and a technical skill.

In our case, we have decided to create a bookmark on the title leading to these images. Select the text where you wish to create your bookmark and choose Insert ➤ Bookmark (press Ctrl+G when you're using FrontPage 2003). Figure A.5 shows the selected text and the dialog box that opens when you insert a bookmark. You should note that the bookmark name is, by default, the selected text with underscores inserted where spaces existed. If your HTML editor doesn't insert underscores for spaces, it is a good practice to insert them. Click OK to create your bookmark. For you to be able to create a hyperlink to this newly created bookmark, you must save the file in FrontPage first by choosing File ➤ Save or pressing Ctrl+S.

**FIGURE A.5**

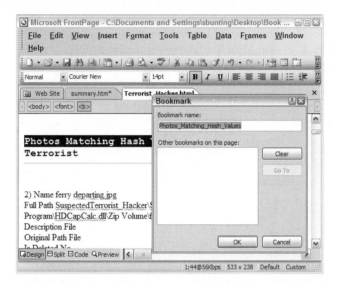

Now that we have created a bookmark or anchor, let's create a hyperlink to it. In our sample case, finding image files that match image files on another possible terrorist's computer is a significant finding and one we decide is worthy of placement on our summary page. Using FrontPage, open the file summary.htm, which is our summary page. We'll use this summary page to provide a background paragraph and an abbreviated statement of findings. It is a place for the reader to go to quickly look at the more significant findings in a case. After creating the paragraphs for the summary page, we have decided that we want to create a hyperlink in the sentence where we described having found images matching the hash values in another case. In this manner, the reader can read about our findings and follow a link to see the images right away.

Generally it is not considered good style to hyperlink entire sentences within a body of text. Rather, you should select brief phrases or strings of words within a sentence for your hyperlink. These words should readily describe what could be found at the hyperlink. You can start to see that you need to carefully compose your sentences to accommodate your hyperlinks. You will develop this style and technique with practice.

Let's create a hyperlink using the two words *four images*. As shown in Figure A.6, select those two words and then choose Insert ≻ Hyperlink, or press Ctrl+K to open the Insert Hyperlink dialog box. Our bookmark is contained in the file Reports\ Terrorist_Hacker.html, so navigate to and highlight that file, as shown in Figure A.6.

At this stage, if you clicked OK, you would create a hyperlink to the file. A hyperlink to a file will take you to the beginning of a file. Since we want to take our reader to a specific point in a very large file, we must point the hyperlink to a bookmark or anchor contained within the file. To do so, highlight the file containing the bookmark, and click the Bookmark button on the right side of the Insert Hyperlink dialog box. Figure A.7 shows the Select Place In Document dialog box that results from clicking the Bookmark button. Select the name of the bookmark, click OK to close this dialog box, and then click OK again to close the Insert Hyperlink dialog box.

**FIGURE A.6**    The Insert Hyperlink dialog box in Microsoft FrontPage 2003

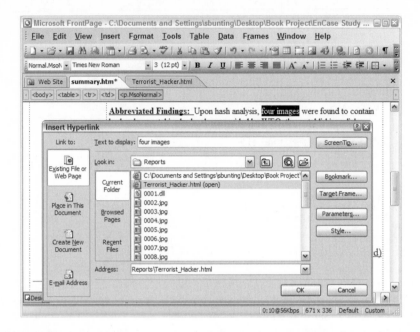

**FIGURE A.7**    The Select Place In Document dialog box enables you to create a hyperlink to a bookmark within a file.

We have created our hyperlink, and as you can see, the two words *four images* appear in blue and are underscored, indicating a hyperlink. If we place our cursor over the hyperlink, we can see the path for the hyperlink in the lower left of the FrontPage window, as shown in Figure A.8. In our example, the path is: *Reports*/Terrorist_Hacker.html#Photos_Matching_Hash_Values, where *Reports* is the folder name containing the file named Terrorist_Hacker.html. The # sign denotes an anchor or bookmark, which in our example is named Photos_Matching_Hash_Values.

**FIGURE A.8**

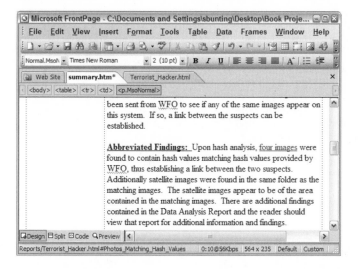

If we want to test our hyperlink, we can save our file in FrontPage and then open the file summary.htm with our browser. If we click our new hyperlink, it will take us directly the bookmark we created in our EnCase web report.

Our next step is to complete our various reports, using a combination of bookmarks and hyperlinks to allow readers to quickly view exhibits and evidence and then use their browser's Back button to continue reading. Once your report is done, you are ready to burn your paperless report to a CD or DVD.

# Burning the Report to CD or DVD

The final step is the easiest part. The more difficult task is making sure that your report is complete and accurate, and that all of the hyperlinks work, before committing it to a CD or DVD. It is good practice to have another examiner in your office walk through the report when you are finished. When you are ready, you simply need to start your favorite CD or DVD burning software and create a data CD or DVD. The files and folders that you need to place on your CD or DVD are all those files and folders in the folder you created to contain your paperless report. Figure A.9 shows the files and folders in Nero Express as they are about to be burned to a CD.

Most of the files and folders have been thoroughly discussed thus far. The HTML documents are simply the various reports we have been editing and are described in Table A.1. The Reports folder contains the EnCase web-based report. The images folder contains the various images needed to display the container report. The _vti_cnf and _vti_pvt folders contain metadata used by FrontPage. You need them, but they are best left alone. There are two files in the root of the CD needed for the CD to auto-run when inserted: autorun.exe and autorun.inf. You need not do anything with them other than make sure they are present. They work in unison to open your CD, launching the file index.htm when the CD auto-runs.

**FIGURE A.9**   Files and folders needed on the CD for a paperless report

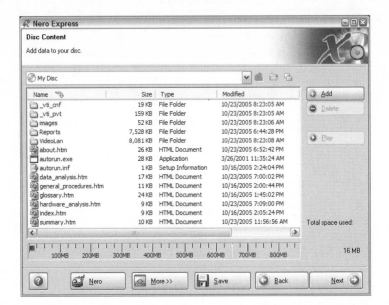

There is one folder present that has not yet been mentioned: VideoLan. The purpose of this folder and its contents are described near the end of the Data Analysis report. Videos often present challenges when playing them. They may be incomplete or partially corrupted. VLC Media Player is an open source, cross-platform multimedia player that can handle almost anything, including streaming video protocols and partial KaZaA downloads. When Windows Media Player won't play a video, VLC Media Player often will. It also operates with low overhead without all the bells and whistles of its commercial counterparts. I include it for those times when readers call about a video that won't play. By including it, the problem is more often than not easily remedied by installing VLC Media Player.

At this point, once you finish burning your CD or DVD, your paperless report is complete. It is advisable to burn one CD or DVD and test it thoroughly before continuing. When you are satisfied, burn as many copies as are needed. If your reader's machine is configured to allow CDs or DVDs to auto-run, they need only insert the media and start following links. For those whose auto-run capability has been disabled, they will need to know on which file to click to run your report. For those readers, I simply affix a label to the CD case advising to click the file index.htm to begin the report if it doesn't auto-run.

The entire set of files and folders shown in Figure A.9, which are about to be burned to a CD by Nero Express, are included on the CD in the folder CD Container Report. If you burn those folders to a CD, you will have the paperless report we just created in this appendix. You can read it, see how it works, and get ideas for your own paperless reports. Best of all, you can use it as a template with just a few minor adjustments. Once you start submitting paperless reports of this caliber, your readers will prefer them, as will you.

# Glossary

# A

**absolute sectors**   Using absolute sectors is a logical method for addressing sectors on a drive. It is also called Logical Block Addressing (LBA). This addressing scheme evolved when the older addressing scheme using cylinder, head, and sectors encountered limitations at the 528MB level. LBA or absolute sectors begin at sector 0 and continue upward to $N$-1, with $N$ being the number of addressable sectors on the drive. To determine the capacity of a drive in bytes that uses LBA, simple multiply the total LBA sectors $\times$ 512.

# B

**BIOS**   BIOS stands for Basic Input Output System, and is a combination of low-level software and drivers that function as the interface, intermediary, or layer between a computer's hardware and its operating system. They load into RAM from three possible sources: 1) from the motherboard ROM (ROM BIOS), 2) from the adapter card ROM (examples: video card, SCSI card), and 3) from a disk in the form of device drivers. The terms *BIOS* and *CMOS* (RTC/NVRAM) are often confused and erroneously used interchangeably. They are separate systems, although they are closely interrelated and interdependent. The user interface for the settings that are stored in RTC/NVRAM memory are accessed through a setup program contained within the BIOS. The settings stored in RTC/NVRAM are read by the BIOS during boot to apply settings for your system configuration.

# C

**cluster**   A cluster is a group of sectors in a logical volume that is used to store folders and files. It is the fundamental storage unit within a volume and is also called an allocation unit. The number of sectors in a cluster or allocation unit is determined by the operating system or utility used to format the drive. The number of sectors per cluster will always be a power of 2 (2, 4, 8, 16, 32, 64, etc.).

**CMOS**   The process by which the RTC/NVRAM chip is produced (Complementary Metal-Oxide Semiconductor). CMOS is often used in lieu of RTC/NVRAM (the official term) and may be used in the context of the CMOS settings, which includes the system date/time (RTC) and the basic configuration data.

# D

**Daubert Test**   The Daubert Test is a legal test to determine the validity of scientific evidence and its relevance to the case at issue. The test arose from a U.S. Supreme Court decision in the case of *Daubert v. Merrell Dow Pharmaceuticals, Inc.* The test is a four-prong test comprised of the following:

1. Whether a "theory or technique . . . can be (and has been) tested;"
2. Whether it "has been subjected to peer review and publication;"
3. Whether, in respect to a particular technique, there is a high "known or potential rate of error;" and
4. Whether the theory or technique enjoys "general acceptance" within the "relevant scientific community."

From: *Daubert, supra, 509 U.S. at 592-594, 113 S.Ct 2786.*

**DCO (dynamic configuration overlay)**    DCO was introduced with ATA-6 and was initially intended as a means of limiting the apparent capacity of a drive. DCO space will appear at the end of the drive and is not seen by the BIOS.

# F

**FAT (file allocation table)**    Normally there are two file allocation tables (FAT1 and FAT2), and they are located at the beginning of a FAT volume, immediately following the volume boot record. The file allocation tables track the allocation status of all clusters and also track fragmentation.

**FAT12, 16, 32**    FAT12, FAT16, and FAT32 describe different versions of the FAT file system, all of which were introduced by Microsoft. FAT file systems use the file allocation table to track cluster allocation and fragmentation. FAT file systems use a series of 32-byte directory entries to track all other file attributes. A FAT12 can support $2^{12}$ clusters; FAT16 can support $2^{16}$ clusters; and FAT32 can support $2^{32}$ clusters. The cluster numbers are theoretical maximums; however, in actuality they support 4,084; 65,524; and 67,092,481 clusters, respectively, due to a number of reserved numbers and MBR-imposed limitations.

**FireWire or IEEE 1394**    Known as FireWire (the name licensed by Apple) or iLink (Sony), IEEE 1394 is yet another high-speed serial I/O standard. Its plug-and-play capabilities are on a parallel with USB. IEEE 1394 comes in two flavors, or speeds: 1394a is the original version, moving data at 400Mb/s, and 1394b is the latest version, moving data at 800Mb/s, with gigabit speeds planned soon. IEEE 1394 allows "daisy chaining" of devices, with a maximum of 63 nodes.

# H

**hard disk size**    Hard disk drive manufacturers and hardware engineers report drive capacities in units that are the same powers of 10 as other decimal units, i.e., 1 gigabyte = 1,000,000,000 bytes (10 to the power of 9). Expressing the drive size in this manner allows manufacturers to express their drive sizes using a higher number, thus "marketing" their product in the best possible light.

Computer operating systems and software generally use units derived from binary powers, i.e., 1 gigabyte = 1,073,741,824 bytes (2 to the power of 30).

Modern forensic software will examine a hard disk at sector level, which is usually made up of 512 bytes. This enables the forensic software to read all the data present on the disk, regardless of the reported capacities of the hard drive.

Example: Toshiba markets its MK2016GAP hard drive as being 20GB in size. EnCase forensic software reported a total of 39,070,080 sectors, which, multiplied by 512, would give a capacity of 20,003,880,960 bytes (20GB), which is consistent with Toshiba's figure. EnCase, however, reported the 39,070,080 sectors as having a capacity of 18.6GB. At first this seems at least inconsistent, perhaps even erroneous to the uninformed. The difference is resolved by simply dividing the total capacity of the hard drive in bytes (20,003,880,960) by a "software gigabyte," which is 1,073,741,824. Recall that this software gigabyte is 2 to the 30th power (see above). When this division is made, the capacity of the drive, as reported by EnCase and as used by the computer's software, is 18.63006591796875, or rounded off and expressed simply, 18.6GB, which is consistent with the figure reported by EnCase. The difference thus lies in the arithmetic base used between the two, with the manufacturers reporting in base 10 and the software reporting and using it in base 2.

**HPA (host protected area)**   HPA was introduced with the ATA-4 standard. Its purpose is to create a place at the end of the drive for vendors to store information (recovery, security, registration, etc.) that will not be seen by the BIOS and hence protected from user access or erasure (format, etc.).

# I

**IDE controller (Integrated Drive Electronics)**   IDE is a generic term for any drive with its own integrated drive controller. Originally there were three types, but only one survived, and it is known as ATA or (Advanced Technology Attachment). Officially, the IDE interface today is called ATA, and the two terms will often be used interchangeably. Two IDE connectors are found on the motherboard, one labeled primary IDE and the other secondary IDE. Each is capable of handling two IDE devices (hard drive, CD, DVD), for a maximum of four IDE devices. Of the two devices on same IDE ribbon cable, one is the "pinned" master and the other is pinned the "slave." Typically the boot hard drive will be attached to the primary controller and is the master if two devices are present on that IDE channel. Alternatively, you could use the CS or "cable select" method of pinning; in this approach the assignment of master/slave is done "automatically," provided you use a cable that properly supports CSEL Signaling. On an 80-conductor IDE/ATA cable using CS, the drive at the end of the cable will be assigned as master and the drive assigned to the middle connector will be the slave.

# L

**logical file size**   Most operating systems, including DOS and Windows, keep track of the exact size of a file in bytes. This is the logical size of the file and is the number that you see in the directory listing for a file. This number is different from the physical file size.

# M

**MBR (master boot record)**   An MBR appears on hard disks and is a one-sector-long record containing the master boot program and the master partition table. The MBR is always located at the first physical sector of a disk. The master boot program reads the partition table to determine which partition is the active bootable partition. Once the active bootable partition is located, the master boot program loads the first sector of that partition, which is the VBR (volume boot record). The master boot program tests that sector for the presence of its signature (hex 55AA). If it is present, the master boot program passes program execution to the VBR, which contains the code to load the operating system designated within that VBR.

# N

**NTFS (New Technology File System)**   The NTFS file system was first introduced by Microsoft in August 1993 with the release of Windows NT. NTFS 5 arrived on the scene with Windows 2000 and persists today with Windows XP/2003. NTFS is a much more robust file system than its FAT predecessor, offering greater security and recoverability. NTFS uses a simple bitmap and a file extents table to track cluster allocation. Cluster fragmentation and all other file attributes are tracked using an MFT (master file table). Each record in an MFT is 1,024 bytes in length, compared to the 32 bytes used by a FAT directory entry.

# P

**partition table**   The master partition table is located at byte offsets 446–509 of the master boot record. The table is 64 bytes in length and describes up to four partitions on the drive with up to four 16-byte records. The MBR's master boot program reads this record at boot time to determine which partition is active and bootable.

**physical file size**   The physical size of a file is the amount of space that the file occupies on the disk. A file or directory always occupies a whole number of clusters, even if it does not completely fill the cluster. A file always takes at least one cluster, even if there is no data in it (zero file size). Therefore, even if a file has a logical size of only one byte, its physical size is one cluster. You can readily see that when the cluster sizes become large (a large number of sectors in a cluster), there can be considerable wasted space on a drive. EnCase reports the logical and the physical size for every file and folder.

**POST (Power On Self-Test)**   The POST is a series of tests initiated by the computer when the power button is pressed and power first energizes the CPU. The tests make certain that the various circuits are properly functioning before the boot process can begin. When a computer passes POST, you typically hear one beep from the system speaker.

# R

**RAID (Redundant Array of Inexpensive Disks)**   A RAID is an array of two or more disks combined in such a way as to increase performance or increase fault tolerance. In a RAID 0, data is striped over two or more disks, which increases performance by reducing read and write times. However, if any disk fails in a RAID 0, all data is lost. In a RAID 1, data is mirrored over the drives in the array. A RAID 1 does not increase performance, but it does create redundant data, thereby increasing fault tolerance. In a RAID 5 configuration, typically data is stored on three drives, although other configurations can be created. Data is striped over two drives, and a parity stripe is created on the third. Should any one drive fail, it can be "rebuilt" from the data of the other two. RAID 5 achieves fault tolerance and increased performance. RAID 0 + 1 is a relatively new type of RAID. It is typically configured with four drives; one pair is used for striping data, and the other pair is a mirror of the striped pair. With this configuration, you again achieve high performance and fault tolerance.

**RAM (random access memory)**   A computer's main memory is its temporary workspace for storing data, code, settings, and so forth. Known as RAM, it exists as a bank of memory chips that can be randomly accessed. Before chips, tape was the primary media and accessing tape was and still is a slow, linear or sequential process. With the advent of chips and media on drives (floppy and hard drives), data could be accessed randomly and directly, and therefore with much greater speed. Hence, "random access memory" was the name initially given to this type of memory to differentiate from its tape predecessor. Today, most memory can be accessed randomly, and the term's original functional meaning, differentiating it from tape, has been lost to history. What distinguishes RAM from ROM, among other properties, is the property known as volatility. RAM is usually volatile memory, meaning that upon losing power, the data stored in memory is lost. ROM, by contrast, is nonvolatile memory, meaning that the data remains when the power is off. It is important to note that there are nonvolatile forms of RAM memory known as NVRAM (Non-Volatile Random Access Memory) and thus you should not be quick to assume that all RAM is nonvolatile.

**ROM (Read-Only Memory)**   ROM is a form of memory that can hold data permanently, or nearly so, by virtue of its property of being impossible or difficult to change or write. Another important property of ROM memory is its nonvolatility, meaning the data remains when the system is powered off. Having these properties (read only and nonvolatile) makes ROM memory ideal for files containing start-up configuration settings and code needed to boot the computer (ROM BIOS).

# S

**SATA Controller (Serial Advanced Technology Attachment)**   IDE (ATA) hard drives have been around for a long time, but the electronic circuitry by which the data was sent had reached its upper limit (133MB/s), as it moved in parallel. In August 2001 a new standard, known as SATA 1.0, was finalized and approved. SATA uses serial circuitry and data can be sent, initially, at 150MB/s, with

300 or more on the near horizon as SATA II standards (released in October 2002) find their way into the market. SATA drives require no "pinning" as do IDE drives. SATA ports can be found on most modern motherboards and often have RAID support available to them.

**SCSI (Small Computer Systems Interface)**    SCSI is an electronic interface that originated with Apple Computer systems and migrated over to other systems. It is a high-speed, high-performance interface, used on devices requiring high input/output such as scanners, hard drives, and so forth. The SCSI BIOS is an intelligent BIOS queuing read/write requests in a manner that improves performance, making it the popular choice for high-end systems.

**sector**    A sector is a contiguous group of bytes within a track and is the smallest number of bytes that can be addressed or written to on a drive. While it can vary, the number of bytes per sector is nearly always 512. By contrast, a CD-ROM will have 2,048 bytes per sector.

# U

**USB controller**    Universal serial bus (USB) is a relatively new external peripheral bus standard capable of high-speed serial input/output (USB 1.1 = 1.5Mb/s and USB 2 = 480Mb/s). It was developed to facilitate Plug-and-Play for external devices without the need for expansion cards and configuration issues.

# V

**VBR (volume boot record)**    The volume boot sector, also called the volume boot record (VBR) and often abbreviated "boot sector," is located at the first sector of the logical volume. It is the first sector of the "reserved" area; in the case of FAT12/16, it is often the only sector in the reserved area. The boot sector contains four distinct segments: the jump instruction to the boot code, the BIOS parameter block (BPB), the boot code and error messages, and the signature (0x55AA).

**voir dire**    In a judicial setting, this is an examination by opposing counsel to ascertain one's competency to testify.

# Index

**Note to the reader:** Throughout this index **boldfaced** page numbers indicate primary discussions of a topic. *Italicized* page numbers indicate illustrations. See also the appendices.

# The Only Official EnCE Study Guide Book/DVD Package on the Market!

*Get ready for both phases of the EnCase® Certified Examiner (EnCE) exam with the most comprehensive and challenging sample tests anywhere! The DVD includes:*

- Chapter-by-chapter exam coverage of all the review questions from the book

- Challenging questions representative of those you'll find on the real exams

- Two Bonus Exams available only on the CD

- Guidance Software™ products and evidence files to help prepare you for the challenging Phase II of the EnCE exam

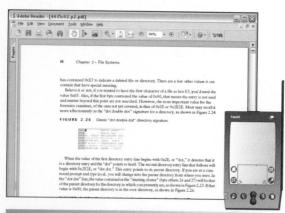

## Use the Electronic Flashcards for PCs or Palm devices to jog your memory and prep last-minute for the exam!

- Reinforce your understanding of key concepts with these hardcore flashcard-style questions.

- Download the Flashcards to your Palm device, and go on the road. Now you can study anywhere, any time.

## Search through the complete book in PDF!

- Access the entire *EnCase® Computer Forensics—The Official EnCE: EnCase® Certified Examiner Study Guide* complete with figures and tables, in electronic format.

- Search the *EnCase® Computer Forensics— The Official EnCE: EnCase® Certified Examiner Study Guide* chapters to find information on any topic in seconds.

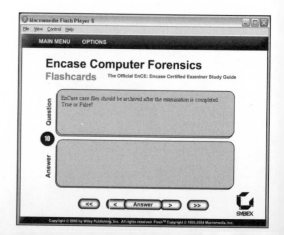